D1563342

Number One: Texas A&M Southwestern Studies

ROBERT A. CALVERT *and* LARRY D. HILL,
General Editors

HOOD, BONNET, AND LITTLE BROWN JUG

Hood, Bonnet,

and

Little Brown Jug

Texas Politics, 1921–1928

BY

Norman D. Brown

TEXAS A&M UNIVERSITY PRESS

College Station

Library of Congress Cataloging in Publication Data

Brown, Norman D.
    Hood, bonnet, and little brown jug.

    (Texas A&M southwestern studies; no. 1)
    Bibliography: p.
    Includes index.
    1. Texas—Politics and government—1865–1950.
2. Texas—Race relations.   I. Title.   II. Series.
F391.B847   1983   976.4'061   83-45099
ISBN 0-89096-157-3

Manufactured in the United States of America
FIRST EDITION

To the memory of Elfrieda Koehler,
"Aunt Sis"

Contents

List of Illustrations

Acknowledgments

MANY people helped me in the preparation of this study. I owe special thanks to Chester V. Kielman, former librarian-archivist of the Barker Texas History Center, University of Texas at Austin, and to the center's current director, Don E. Carleton; to Kent Keeth, archivist-librarian, Texas Collection, Baylor University; Mary M. Orgain, assistant director of libraries, University of Houston; Virginia Leddy Gambrell, director, Dallas Historical Society; Harry Middleton, director, Lyndon Baines Johnson Presidential Library; Charles R. Schultz, university archivist, Texas A&M University; and Ronald E. Marcello, coordinator of the Oral History Collection, North Texas State University. I would also like to express my appreciation to their staff members, especially Frances E. Rodgers and Ralph L. Elder, assistant archivists, Barker Texas History Center, and Kathleen Dillon, assistant curator, University Libraries, University of Houston.

My thanks are also due to the staff members of the Texas State Archives; Austin–Travis County Collection of the Austin Public Library; Capitol Legislative Reference Library, Austin; Photography Collection, Humanities Research Center Library, University of Texas at Austin; Southwest Collection, Texas Tech University; Alabama State Department of Archives and History; Southern Historical Collection, University of North Carolina at Chapel Hill; Manuscripts Division of the Library of Congress; New York State Library; Sam Rayburn Library; Manuscript and Archives Division, Yale University Library; Herbert Hoover Presidential Library; and Franklin D. Roosevelt Presidential Library.

Nora Crane and Carrie Crane Kearney, the daughters of Texas lieutenant governor and attorney general Martin M. Crane, and Mrs. Clare Kearney Galbraith, Crane's granddaughter, offered me the gracious hospitality of their home in Dallas and permitted me to copy excerpts from General Crane's papers. These papers have since been donated to the University of Texas Archives. Mrs. Dan Moody, Sr., of

Austin, talked with me in her home and generously allowed me to borrow her scrapbook of Governor Moody's political career. The Moody family also gave me permission to use the typescript of Mrs. Moody's diary of her four years in the Executive Mansion in North Texas State University's Oral History Collection. Dave Allred likewise authorized me to use Governor James V. Allred's papers in the University of Houston Library. Roy C. Coffey, E. L. Covey, and Frank M. Locke, among others, shared their reminiscences of the 1920s with me by letter.

The late Richard Fleming, curator of the University Writings Collection, University of Texas at Austin, made available to me a copy of Ghent Sanderford's unpublished manuscript, "The Ferguson Era, 1914–1944." Tuffly Ellis, director of the Texas State Historical Association, lent me a copy of David G. McComb's July 20, 1968, interview with Fleming.

I must thank Egla Washburn, who typed the final draft of the manuscript under severe time pressure. The University Research Institute of the University of Texas at Austin provided a Faculty Research Assignment grant for the fall of 1977 and a generous grant to have the manuscript typed. The Dora Bonham Fund of the University of Texas Department of History provided travel grants.

I wish to express my appreciation to Robert A. Calvert and Larry D. Hill for recommending that this study be the first number of a new series, Texas A&M Southwestern Studies, of which they are the general editors.

My wife Betty and children, David and Tracy, suffered with good grace my long absorption in Texas politics of the 1920s. My heartfelt gratitude to them. During much of the time I was writing the book, the family dog and cat, Woody and Puffin, kept me company in my study. Woody died in November, 1981, but as I write this Puffin still keeps his drowsy vigil.

HOOD, BONNET, AND LITTLE BROWN JUG

Introduction

WHILE the Progressive Era in the South has attracted the attention of a growing number of historians, Dewey W. Grantham has noted in a review essay that "there are still only a few books and dissertations on politics and social reform in individual Southern states during the Wilson years, and even fewer for the 1920s." For the 1920s he listed David D. Lee's *Tennessee in Turmoil: Politics in the Volunteer State, 1920–1932* (1979); a Vanderbilt University dissertation of 1969 on Governor Austin Peay's administrations in Tennessee from 1923 to 1927; and a University of South Carolina dissertation in progress on South Carolina in the 1920s.[1] *Hood, Bonnet, and Little Brown Jug: Texas Politics, 1921–1928*, is the first volume of a proposed two-volume study of Lone Star State politics from 1921 to 1938, the years of Republican ascendancy on the national scene, the Great Crash of 1929 and the subsequent Depression, and Franklin Delano Roosevelt's New Deal. It is based on the personal papers of state and national figures; Texas newspapers, especially the *Dallas Morning News*, which under George B. Dealey was virtually a paper of record; and a wide variety of other sources.

Until the New Deal, Lyndon B. Johnson remarked to members of the President's Council on Aging on February 16, 1965, most Texas elections were decided by whether you were prohibitionist or anti-prohibitionist, Klan or anti-Klan, for or against the local bridge. "I went through all those as a boy," he said. "I never heard of social security until I was 21 years old. All I heard was whether you were wet or dry, whether for the courthouse group or against them."[2] Johnson's teen years from twelve to twenty were those covered by this volume, and his analysis was accurate so far as it went. The book's somewhat enigmatic title refers to the three main issues in Texas politics from 1921 to 1928—the Ku Klux Klan, "Fergusonism," and Prohibition.

In 1924, Mrs. Miriam A. Ferguson, a housewife and mother, made a successful race for governor of Texas as a proxy for her husband, former Governor James E. Ferguson, who was barred from holding state office by his impeachment conviction of 1917 on ten charges of misusing state funds and other irregularities. Mrs. Ferguson faced a Klan-backed candidate in the Democratic runoff primary, and Texas voters were offered the choice of "a bonnet or a hood." For anti-Klan, anti-Ferguson Democrats the election represented the evil of two lessers, but a majority chose the old gray bonnet.

The use of "Little Brown Jug" to symbolize the Prohibition issue was suggested by Joseph Eastburn Winner's popular song of 1869, with its bluntly stated, respectability-be-damned challenge to temperance:

> My wife and I live all alone,
> In a little hut we call our own,
> She loves gin and I love rum,
> Tell you what it is, don't we have fun?
>
> Ha, ha, ha! 'Tis you and me,
> Little Brown jug, don't I love thee?
> Ha, ha, ha! 'Tis you and me,
> Little Brown jug, don't I love thee?[3]

Because Texas was a one-party state, personalities frequently played as large a role as issues in elections. The charismatic "Farmer Jim" Ferguson, as he was known, an orator of the old school, was the most important figure in Texas politics from 1914 to 1934; during that twenty-year period he or his wife was a candidate for state or federal office in every election year except 1928, and Mrs. Ferguson made a final, losing race for governor against W. Lee ("Pass-the-Biscuits Pappy") O'Daniel in 1940. Between them "Ma" and "Pa" Ferguson occupied the executive mansion for at least part of four terms, 1915 to 1917, 1925 to 1927, and 1933 to 1935. Despite his fall from political grace early in his second term, Ferguson kept a vest-pocket vote of thousands of tenant farmers, owners of small farms, and day laborers— the "boys at the forks of the creek." Political scientist V. O. Key, Jr., noted in his classic *Southern Politics in State and Nation* (1949): "The Ferguson personality, dominating Texas political life for over two decades, distracted the voter's attention from other matters and caused him to think of politics in terms of his like or dislike for 'Farmer Jim.' 'Ferguson men' swore by Old Jim."[4] But the progressive-prohibitionist wing of the Texas Democratic party detested him because he had defeated a dry, Colonel Tom Ball, in the election for governor in 1914 and had accepted money from Texas brewery interests.

Texas progressives felt especially close to President Woodrow Wilson. In the Democratic National Convention of 1912 the steadfast support of Wilson's "Immortal Forty" Texas delegates was of immense importance in overcoming the almost insurmountable odds against his nomination. After his election he named Albert Sidney Burleson of Austin United States postmaster general and appointed David Houston, a former president of the University of Texas and of Texas A&M College (later University), secretary of agriculture. They were joined by a third Texan in the summer of 1914, when Thomas Watt Gregory of Austin was appointed attorney general. Colonel Edward M. House of Texas became President Wilson's closest adviser and his roving ambassador to Europe. Texas congressmen cast vital votes for Wilson's "New Freedom" legislation, and Senator Morris Sheppard of Texas sponsored the Prohibition amendment to the Constitution.[5]

In *Progressives and Prohibitionists: Texas Democrats in the Wilson Era* (1973) Lewis L. Gould showed that statewide Prohibition became a major goal of progressive Wilson Democrats in the ten years after 1911 because it spoke directly to most of the perceived social problems of the state; it was also "the major divisive element" separating progressives and conservatives. The presence of substantial German and Mexican-American minorities in the state fueled ethnocultural conflict, of which the crusade against John Barleycorn became the chief symbol. Not until the United States entered World War I did the drys win control of the state government from the wets, who were strong in South and Southwest Texas. Identifying Prohibition with 100 percent Americanism and the need to protect soldiers from the temptations of vice and alcohol, and aided by the ouster of Governor Ferguson, who had vowed to lay the Prohibition issue to rest by ignoring it, the drys secured a sympathetic governor in William P. Hobby and won control of the legislature, which ratified the Eighteenth (Prohibition) Amendment to the Federal Constitution in March, 1918. A state constitutional amendment that would mandate statewide prohibition until national prohibition took effect was approved in an election held in May, 1919. A stringent enforcement statute, popularly named for its author, Senator W. Luther Dean of Huntsville, which went into effect in October, 1919, made it illegal to manufacture or market intoxicating liquors in Texas except for medicinal, sacramental, and industrial purposes and prescribed enforcement procedures and penalties.

In 1920, the election of "bone-dry" Pat M. Neff as governor over former United States Senator Joseph W. Bailey, an old-style conservative and antiprohibitionist, was hailed as a final victory, in the words of a Texas journalist, "for the achievements of the Wilson administration, prohibition and equal suffrage, the rule of right in this land of ours and for honest and progressive government conducted by honest and progressive men."[6]

Although it seemed for a season that progressivism had departed the national scene with the disintegration of the Wilson coalition and the Republican triumph in 1920, the decade of the twenties was not bereft of progressive reform. Nor did progressivism disappear from the South in the 1920s. Instead, as George B. Tindall has shown, it was "transformed through an emphasis upon certain of its tendencies and the distortion of others."[7] One of southern progressivism's surviving strains expressed itself in Prohibition enforcement, the antievolution crusade, and the efforts of the revived Ku Klux Klan to protect traditional moral standards and cultural values. "The Ku Klux Klan in Texas is made up almost wholly of misled and misguided good people who are on the moral side of moral questions and on the progressive side of economic questions," Wilsonian leader Thomas B. Love of Dallas explained to columnist Mark Sullivan in 1922:

They are almost wholly of the class of people who carried Texas for Woodrow Wilson in 1912. They have been organized in a large number of counties on the anti-Catholic issue. There is little prejudice against the Jews, and the negro question has had little or nothing to do with it. My opinion is that it is the sort of thing that "dances only one set." I think it will pass away within the next two years.[8]

As a post–World War I crime wave hit Texas, the Klan, which appeared in the state in late 1920, stood for "law and order" (as it understood the term) and against corrupt officialdom. It undertook a campaign of intimidation and violence—whipping, tar-and-feathering, and sometimes branding—aimed mostly at bootleggers, gamblers, adulterers, wife beaters, and other offenders against morality. City dwellers with rural backgrounds found themselves living in a rapidly changing environment and turned to the Klan because it promised to preserve traditional standards of personal conduct. As a result the hooded order achieved its greatest strength in Texas's booming cities. From 1922 to

1924 the Klan was the paramount issue in Texas politics when the organization elected city and county office-holders and legislators, and in 1922 it won one of the most important Klan victories in the nation—the election of Earle B. Mayfield, an admitted klansman, to the United States Senate.

Another strain of southern progressivism in the 1920s was what Tindall termed "business progressivism." This neo-Bourbon political philosophy emphasized the old progressive themes of public service and efficiency. It was broad enough to include administrative reorganization, tax reforms, good roads, better schools, and expanded health services, but it did not embrace any comprehensive challenge to conservative ideas in the area of capital-labor relations, and the South lagged in supporting broad social programs, such as state protection for women and children in industry and workmen's compensation laws.[9]

Among the business-progressive governors discussed by Tindall, Pat M. Neff and Dan Moody in Texas and Lamartine G. Hardman in Georgia were briefly noted as having failed to win the support of state legislatures.[10] This book describes the progressive reforms advocated by Neff during his two terms and Moody during his first term (the second term will be covered in volume 2), and discusses why the lawmakers and people of Texas rejected many of their proposals. Miriam Ferguson's administration, from 1925 to 1927, offered a "plebeian" contrast to the business-progressive administrations of Neff and Moody. "The Fergusons were elected by rustics," wrote V. O. Key. "As has often been true of southern governors with vivid personal appeal, they produced little in the way of governmental action to justify the support."[11] The 1925 legislature passed almost no bills of outstanding public interest. Mrs. Ferguson's administration was marked by behind-the-scenes domination by her husband; favoritism in the granting of highway contracts to firms that had advertised in Ferguson's political paper, the *Ferguson Forum*; the influence Jim Ferguson exerted on the State Textbook Commission; and pardons for thousands of state prisoners. In the murky world of statute books, there may well have been no illegality, but the Fergusons were guilty of a flagrant abuse of the ethical standards of public office.

Business progressivism in Texas had little to offer the Negro or the Mexican American. A law passed during the Neff administration barring blacks from Democratic party primaries was declared unconstitutional by the United States Supreme Court in *Nixon* v. *Herndon*

(1927). The Fortieth Legislature responded by giving political parties authority to determine their own membership, provided no one was excluded because of former political-party affiliations or views. There was some criticism of the corrupt South Texas machines, such as the Archie Parr organization in Duval County, but no serious effort was made to break up the power that rested on economic and political manipulation of the poorly educated Mexican Americans.[12]

In close sequence to Prohibition, the national cause of woman suffrage achieved its ultimate triumph with the ratification of the Nineteenth Amendment in 1920. Women had been able to vote, by state law, in Texas primaries since 1918, and Texas was the first southern state to ratify the federal suffrage amendment. The list of suffrage leaders in Texas included Minnie Fisher Cunningham, Jane Y. McCallum, Jesse Daniel Ames, and Annie Webb Blanton. With the vote secured, they set an example for other women by working hard in politics. The Joint Legislative Council, or "Petticoat Lobby," of the 1920s, a coalition of women's groups, became one of the most successful public-interest lobbying groups in Texas history. The organization backed legislation dealing with education, prison reform, Prohibition enforcement, maternal and child health, the abolition of child labor, and other social reforms.[13]

On the national scene in the 1920s, Texas was a pivotal state in the transitional struggle between the prohibitionist, native-stock, Protestant southern and western wing of the Democratic party and its urban, wet, new-immigrant northeastern faction. "Romantic in history, powerful in Democratic politics, Texas provides more interest for those watching political developments than almost any other State in the South," editorialized the *New York Times* in April, 1928. "Ever since 'the Immortal Forty,' under the unit rule, stood by Woodrow Wilson at Baltimore until the nomination was won, an importance attaches to the Texas delegation out of proportion to the size of its vote or the State's geographical and industrial significance."[14]

Thomas B. Love was the manager of the Woodrow Wilson movement in Texas in 1911–12 and helped direct dry progressives in the reform battles of the next decade. From 1917 to 1920 he served as assistant secretary of the treasury under Wilson's son-in-law, William Gibbs McAdoo. One of McAdoo's staunchest backers for president, Love, aided by other old Wilsonians like Marshall Hicks and Cato Sells, twice secured Texas's forty convention votes for him. These men and their followers regarded McAdoo as the heir of the Wilson legacy. When the Klan entered Texas politics, Love accepted its support for McAdoo. In the May, 1924, presidential primary, the Klan helped the McAdoo forces defeat both Senator Oscar W. Underwood of Alabama, who had the backing of most of Texas's wet leaders, and Governor Neff, who wanted to send to the national convention an uninstructed delegation favorable to himself. McAdoo's victory in Texas stimulated his flagging campaign and gave it the impetus to drive on to New York City, only to be halted by the 103-ballot debacle in Madison Square Garden. Love was preparing to carry Texas for McAdoo in 1928 when the Californian withdrew from the race on September 17, 1927.

Meanwhile, the control that Love and his lieutenants exercised over the state Democratic party was challenged by a group of young self-styled "liberal" Democrats, antiprohibitionist in sentiment, who wanted to end what they saw as an era of fanaticism that had held Texas in political thralldom. They had first come together under Dan Moody's "throw-the-rascals-out" banner in the 1926 campaign against the Fergusons. Although a strong dry, Moody was persuaded to join the revolt against the bossism of the "Dry Moses," as they called Love, and Love was kept off the Texas delegation, which supported favorite son Jesse H. Jones of Houston at the national convention in 1928.

The Democratic party stretched the South's loyalty to the breaking point by nominating Governor Al Smith of New York for president in 1928. Rural, Protestant, prohibitionist southerners were asked to support an urban, Catholic wet with ties to New York City's Tammany Hall. Cone Johnson, a dry Texas delegate, complained: "I sat by the central aisle while the parade passed following Smith's nomination and the faces I saw in that mile-long procession were not American faces. I wondered where were the Americans."[15] Bone-dry Democrats headed by Tom Love organized as the "Anti–Al Smith Democrats of Texas" and arranged a fusion electoral ticket with the Republicans for the Republican nominee, Herbert Hoover. The combination put Texas into the Republican column for the first time in a presidential election. This result set up a bitter contest between the "Hoovercrats," now calling themselves the "Anti-Tammany Democrats of Texas," and party regulars (dubbed "brass-collar Democrats" by the bolters) for control of the state party.

In addition to the presidential sweepstakes, Texas witnessed a heated contest for the United States Senate. By 1928 the Texas Klan was only a shadow of its former self. It made a halfhearted rally around Earle Mayfield, and his defeat in the runoff by Congressman Tom Conally was the final nail driven into its coffin. Connally's impressive victory was interpreted as marking a new era in Texas politics; it was proof that the Klan was becoming as impotent in the Lone Star State as it was elsewhere. Moreover, Jim Ferguson had backed three losers in 1928: Louis Wardlaw for governor against Dan Moody, Alvin Owsley for the United States Senate in the first primary, and Mayfield in the runoff. Political analysts saw this as evidence that he could not deliver his following to any candidate other than himself or his wife. The era ended with the Klan virtually extinct in Texas, Ferguson's political fortunes at their lowest point in eight years, and the stage set for a bruising intraparty fight in the "House of the Fathers."

CHAPTER 1

Pat M. Neff—
Apostle of Law Enforcement

"SHRIEKING of whistles, clanging of bells, racing of automobiles, and the flaring of fireworks ushered in the new year and attended the funeral of 1920 in Austin," the *Austin Statesman* reported on January 1, 1921. Congress Avenue, the city's main thoroughfare, was crowded with hundreds of people coming out of the downtown theaters and was lined its entire length on both sides with spectators watching the celebrators. As early as 9:00 P.M. the avenue had become lively as rockets, roman candles, and other fireworks were set off. "Shortly before midnight autoists forgot everything they knew about speed ordinances here and for a few minutes Congress Avenue resembled a crowded speedway. With automobiles going thirty to forty miles per hour, it is a miracle that no one was run over and killed," said the *Statesman*.

The only accident of the night occurred when an Overland automobile sped down Congress Avenue, hit an iron traffic marker at the corner of Ninth Street, and turned over. A crowd rushed to the scene. When the car was lifted to an upright position, three badly frightened but uninjured young men scrambled to their feet and fled, leaving the car where it lay for the curiosity of hundreds of midnight spectators.[1]

This was Austin's first New Year's Eve since national Prohibition had gone into effect at midnight, January 16, 1920. Although the *Statesman* made no mention of drinking among the merrymakers, bootleg spirits undoubtedly contributed to the evening's good cheer. Illicit stills were already in operation all over Texas. As a case in point, in the previous year a still with a capacity of 130 gallons a day had been found operating five miles north of Austin on a farm owned by United States Senator Morris Sheppard, the author of the Eighteenth Amendment. Dallas in the 1920s was the home of chock beer ("old molasses, old yeast, old corn pone, old shoe laces and old anything"), which was about 22 percent alcohol and was sold for twenty-five cents a bottle by a hundred or more bootleggers scattered all over town. Nonetheless, under the headline "Dan Cupid Has Busy Year; Booze Brigade Shrinks," the *Statesman* carried an Associated Press story that, while "Dan Cupid, well known archer," had set a new record in Manhattan and Brooklyn marriage licenses during 1920, "John Barleycorn" had had the worst year in his career, sending fewer people to the workhouse for intoxication than ever before.[2]

On January 18, 1921, many of these same New Year's Eve celebrators, joined by thousands from every section of Texas, hundreds of visitors from neighboring states, and a high-ranking delegation from Mexico, witnessed the dignified inaugural ceremonies for Governor Pat M. Neff. Hundreds of spectators crowded the Hall of Representatives in the big granite state capitol to see him take the oath of office and deliver his inaugural address. As the governor-elect approached the speaker's stand, he passed his ninety-year-old mother, Mrs. Isabella Neff, who was sitting in a rolling chair. "With the reverence of a devoted son, the man soon to be governor bent over the frail form of his mother and kissed her." After taking the oath, Neff kissed the "ancient and well-worn Bible" that had been used in inauguration ceremonies from General Sam Houston's time and then waved a kiss to his mother, who, overcome by her emotions, sat quietly sobbing with a handkerchief to her face. When he left the speaker's stand, Neff gave his mother a loving embrace. "It was a great day for her," said the *Dallas Morning News*," "greater than for anyone else in the great throng which was present, not excepting her son himself."[3]

Neff's inaugural address, instead of setting forth his policies, as was customary, "was meant to be the exordium, the preface to those deliverances which are to express his judgment of the State's legislative needs."[4] He stressed that Texas would always have big problems to solve:

No sooner do we dispose of one question than another arises to test our moral and mental fibre. Not until all the people become angelic will the fight for liberty and learning and law and freedom and civic righteousness be finished.

The people should understand, however, that the government was not the panacea for all the evils that warped and dwarfed the human race:

It has no quack nostrums for a distempered world. The people must not look to the government alone, but to themselves for relief. If the people in private life will practice and proclaim the old-time, homely virtues of honesty, industry and economy, they will not then find such fault with the government for the fallacies of social life, for the failures of the financial world, and for the mistakes that mark the pathways of men.

Neff then struck a confident note:

Texas furnishes an inviting field for constructive legislation. Nowhere could you find a land more conducive to the building of a high and enduring civilization than here where falls the light of the Lone Star. Not only is Texas a land of opportunity, but ours is a day of opportunity. Let no one throw himself across the track to block the train of progress. Obstructionists never win battles. It is the progressive, dynamic leader that counts. You, gentlemen of the Legislature, are privileged to be the spokesmen of a progressive and a forward-looking people.[5]

Under the influence of his Baptist upbringing, Neff broke with tradition and did not hold an inaugural ball. Neff and his wife did not approve of dancing. The governor-elect had written to the inaugural committee in Austin: "My suggestion is that the inaugural ball be omitted and in lieu thereof an informal reception be held, where everyone, regardless of social relations, church affiliations, may come and extend the warm handclasp of welcome and good wishes." Several letters were exchanged between Neff and the committee. He contended that the Texas capitol should not be turned into a dance hall to which only people who could afford high-priced tickets would be admitted. It should be open to all Texans for the inaugural ceremonies. His decision not to hold the ball won widespread approval.[6]

The new governor's parents had left Virginia for Texas in 1854 and built a small log house about twenty-five miles west of the frontier town of Waco. Neff's father (who died in 1882) served part time as a Texas Ranger, protecting settlers from Indian raids. Pat Morris Neff was born on November 26, 1871, the youngest of nine children. He obtained his first education between crops in a country school at Eagle Springs, in Coryell County, graduated from McGregor High School and, in 1894, from Baylor University. "It cannot be said that he was like other boys," his Baylor roommate, Samuel P. Brooks, commented later. "Strange to say, though a Texan born and a rustic, to this day he has never shot a gun, baited a fish hook, used tobacco in any form, nor drunk anything stronger than Brazos water. He does not know one card from another and cannot play any kind of a social game." Brooks added, however, that Neff was not a "molly-coddle. He enjoys a good joke and can tell one. He will go a long way round in order to avoid a fight, but if a fight must be, he goes the nearest way to his antagonist."

After teaching school for two years in Arkansas, Neff obtained a law degree from the University of Texas in 1897 and a master's degree from Baylor in 1898. On May 31, 1899, he married Myrtle Mainer, a former Baylor classmate; they had a son and a daughter. Neff practiced law in Waco from 1897 until 1921. Quickly becoming interested in politics, he served two terms in the Texas House of Representatives (1901–1905), and was elected speaker in 1903—the youngest man ever elected to that office. He was prosecuting attorney of McLennan County from 1906 to 1912 and during that time was twice invited to become assistant attorney general of Texas. An outspoken prohibitionist, Neff led a successful fight to vote the saloon out of McLennan County. He was active in religious and fraternal organizations, serving as clerk of the First Baptist Church of Waco, president of the Board of Trustees of Baylor University, and president of the Conference for Education in Texas; in addition, he was a Master Mason, a Grand Lodge officer of the Knights of Pythias, and a member of Woodmen of the World and Modern Woodmen of America.[7]

The austere, dignified Neff had a striking physical appearance and a reputation as an orator, though his high-pitched voice was sharp and cold. A contemporary said that "he looked like a statesman of the ancient picture type and in the books written by men with their fanciful portraits of the early fathers." Another observer wrote that he had "the stern visage; yea, he even looked the part of a parson who might have ridden with Hood's Texas Brigade." Frank M. Locke of Waco heard Neff debate at Lorena with Tom Dillworth, his opponent in the race for county attorney in 1906:

I remember Pat Neff well as he appeared that night, handsome and somber in appearance; his dress, dignified, precise and exact, in a dark blue or black suit, black belt and shoes, white shirt, detachable white linen collar turned down at the corners, a black four-way string tie dangled below the collar, contrasting with the white shirt. His black hair, neat and combed in the front, was cut full and rounded in the back and extended down to and somewhat over his coat collar. The left lapel of that coat was adorned with a white flower, completing the black and white theme. His platform manner was in keeping with his dress. He appeared completely at ease, sure-footed and at times a bit lofty; his voice was good, clear and resonant, and even in debate he spoke with the flair of an old-time orator.[8]

Neff attributed his ability to talk for hours in all kinds of situations without any voice trouble to the fact that he never acquired the smoking habit.[9]

In his own account of his race for governor in 1920, Neff said that no one asked him to run, that he did not ask anyone's permission, that "as a free-born American, and as a native son of Texas, without a conference with or advice from anyone, I announced my candidacy." He had no political alignments, no self-appointed or publicly recognized politician had an interest in or strings on him, and no business interests had any concern in, or took any notice of, his candidacy. "I knew of no wires to pull or buttons to touch that would elect me Governor," he said. "I did not hunt for any. To take my candidacy in person directly to the individual voter was my only chance, as I saw it and as I desired it." Without a campaign manager or political headquarters, Neff planned his speaking dates and mapped out his itinerary. He campaigned first on the outskirts of towns and in sparsely settled regions, generally speaking three to seven times a day. He spoke in thirty-seven counties never before visited by a candidate for governor. The friend who introduced him in Laredo remarked that the two-hundred-year-old town had never seen a candidate for governor. The old Confederate veteran who introduced Neff at his first speaking date in Leon County reminded the audience that no candidate for governor had spoken in the county since Sam Houston had appeared there more than sixty-five years before.

During his campaign Neff used every means of transportation from mule to airplane. He drove his Model T Ford about six thousand miles, patching his own blowouts and pumping up his own tires, and spoke approximately 850 times from January 1, 1920, to the last Saturday in August of that year. He recalled:

I stopped at all blacksmith shops and cross-road stores to exchange greetings with those thereabout. At these places one meets real folks; people who think straight and vote right. When I campaigned in a small town without a speaking date, as I frequently did, I made it a practice to shake hands with every person I could find, never skipping the man handling bacon in the back of the store, or the carpenter building a shack in the alley.[10]

Neff's platform proposed equal educational opportunities for all Texas children by making rural schoolhouses "informational and inspirational centers" and paying higher salaries to teachers. He also favored soil conservation; a proper system of marketing farm products; reduction in the tax rate by equalizing the burden of government; law enforcement; a reduction in the number of state employees; "purity of the ballot box"; reforestation of cutover land; construction of storage reservoirs to conserve water for irrigation; construction of water power plants for mills and factories along Texas streams ("Factories," the candidate said, "should be encouraged to operate in small towns where they can be easily kept Americanized"); the building of good roads; and the planting of trees along the roads wherever practicable. Neff said that Texas should not permit a few individuals to hold unused agricultural land for speculative purposes while more than 500,000 families in Texas owned no land: "I am not only in favor of opening up our agricultural lands for sale to small land owners but I am also in favor of the state extending her credit under proper regulations to her worthy and industrious citizens, enabling them to buy land with a small payment down and on long time, at a low rate of interest."[11]

Neff's major opponents in the primary were former United States Senator Joseph Weldon Bailey, a handsome, strapping man whose golden voice had held two generations of Texans spellbound; Robert Ewin Thomason, speaker of the Texas House of Representatives; and former Attorney General Benjamin F. Looney. The primary election was held on July 25, and Bailey led the field by a slight plurality over Neff. Thomason, who had lost thirty campaigning days when Governor William P. Hobby called the legislature into special session, finished third, and Looney fourth. Both of the losing candidates announced that they would support Neff, and the state witnessed a heated and often bitter runoff campaign during the next four weeks.

Bailey, the champion of a fiercely idolatrous following of old-style Texas conservatives, denounced Prohibition, woman suffrage, labor unions, the League of Nations, the Woodrow Wilson administration, socialism, monopoly, class legislation, and class domination. He asserted that only he could lead Texas back into the straight-and-narrow path of the time-honored principles of the old "Bailey Democracy." The Bailey forces dubbed Neff "the wild man from Waco." Neff, who promised to "make Texas the best place in the world to live," had the support of the prohibitionist leaders, most of the recently enfranchised women, and most of the Wilson progressives. He said of Bailey:

He praises the dead alone. He is the only living statesman; all others are dead. He walks with his face to the past and his back to the future. He is satisfied with everything except the League of Nations, the national administration, the State administration, the Democratic party, the President of the United States, Congress, the two Texas senators, the eighteen Texas congressmen, the State Legislature, prohibition, woman's suffrage, and the enforcement of the prohibition laws. However, Joe is highly pleased with himself.

Neff's defeat of Bailey by more than 79,000 votes marked the end of the former senator's influence in state affairs. Neff went on to win an easy victory over his Republican and American party opponents in the November general election.[12]

The Thirty-seventh Texas Legislature had been in session for a week before Neff's inauguration. Of a total of 142 members in the House of Representatives, 80 were freshmen, an unusually large number, and of 31 senators, 14 were new, the most since 1903. The House membership was temporarily reduced by one on February 10, 1921, when the body voted 114 to 13 to expel H. J. Neinast of Washington County for obstructing the draft during the war. Neinast had been elected on the American party ticket. There was comparatively little interest in the House speakership contest, and Charles G. Thomas of Denton County was unanimously elected following the withdrawal of A. B. Curtis of Tarrant.[13]

One of the young freshmen representatives, H. Grady Perry of Erath County, interviewed in 1968, recalled that the House was "predominantly composed of men past sixty years old, and a young fellow didn't have a chance to make a valedictory address to the House." Perry said that he could count on both hands, and perhaps on one hand, the number of young men serving in the House at the time. In 1976, calling attention to the fact that "the Texas legislature of today is made up mostly of lawyers," E. L. Covey, who had been a representative from Knox County in the Thirty-eighth and Thirty-ninth legislatures, recalled that in the 1920s

we had more of cross cut of the population of Texas. We had school teachers, several news paper publishers, doctors, farmers and cattlemen, bankers, pharmacists, merchants, and some of the finest lawyers that I have ever known. I believe that the Texas Legislature at that time tried to legislate for all the people rather than for certain groups.[14]

In his speech introducing Speaker Thomas to the House, Secretary of State C. D. Mims made a somewhat unusual plea for fair treatment of corporations at the hands of the legislature. "If you try to regulate every corporation in every way possible, you will drive them out of the State and our great resources will remain undeveloped," he warned. "It is not true that corporations have no conscience. They are composed of men who have as great and as much conscience as you or I." According to the *Dallas Morning News*, Mims's speech "caused some of the old-time legislators who remember the anti-corporation political sentiment of more than a decade ago to marvel at the change which the years have wrought." The *News* thought that the selection of Thomas, a businessman, for speaker instead of a lawyer also showed the trend of political affairs in the state.[15]

The Senate's presiding officer after January 18 was Lieutenant Governor Lynch Davidson, a wealthy Houston lumberman. Elected to the House from Harris County in 1919, he had filled a Senate vacancy in that session and was elected lieutenant governor in 1920. A ruddy-faced, red-haired, vigorous individual, plainspoken and brimming with energy, Davidson said that he had sought the state's second-highest elective office "with the thought in mind that it is time for the business men of this country to try to take some active part in the management of the State's affairs, and to use their business experience in doing so."[16]

Retiring Governor Hobby's last general message to the legislature presented no recommendations for new laws but was devoted to a recital of the laws enacted during his nearly four years in office. There was much speculation about what Neff's first message would contain, the general impression being that it would be confined to a presentation of the main policy of his administration, with possibly a few recommendations on what he considered the more important issues. So far as the members of the legislature were concerned, there was every outward appearance that relations between them and the new governor would be harmonious. Speaker Thomas said that both houses would work in perfect harmony with Neff and that as a result of this good feeling the legislature's work might be greatly expedited.[17]

Neff's first message to the Legislature on January 20, 1921, was notable for its brevity. He did not ask for any specific legislation but called upon the lawmakers to redeem the pledges made in the Democratic party platform adopted at Fort Worth on September 8, 1920, a copy of which he submitted as "our confession of political faith." "All party platforms should be carefully considered and faithfully followed," the governor asserted, adding that, as Democrats, "we are under bonds to observe the spirit and carry out the demands of the platform on which we were elected." Neff had astonished the politicians by allowing the Democratic State Convention, traditionally the "Governor's Convention," a free hand in drafting a platform and in selecting the State Executive Committee. In his message he spoke of his open-convention approach:

For the first time, perhaps, in more than a quarter of a century, the platform was not dictated by the nominee for Governor. The nominee in the recent election declined to take any part in the drafting of the party platform. It was drawn by and represents the crystallized thought of the representatives fresh from the people.

The translation of its planks into law should have priority over other legislative matters, he added. In conclusion, Neff promised within the next few days, and from time to time thereafter, special and specific messages in regard to important legislation.[18]

Although legislators had been streaming into Neff's office during the past week to make his acquaintance and learn more about him, William Greene Sterett, the veteran capitol reporter for the *Dallas Morning News*, had been unable to find a single man who was willing or able to say definitely what he thought about the governor. None could guess what he would be like in office. "I have never in my life met with such a case of a prominent and universally known man being so absolutely unknown," Sterett said. Neff was "remarkably calm on all subjects and besides, remarkably reticent for a Governor." What he seemed to be saying in his message and private interviews was: "The Democratic party framed a platform on which I made the race for the position to which I was elected. You made it. I did not. It was the Democratic consensus of opinion and hence you must legislate along the lines of its suggestion. I am with you in it and you can read and follow. I will do so, as well as yourself." Neff, said Sterett, "like the man who could not remember the Lord's Prayer, hung it at the foot of his bed and pointed at it when he retired, just pointed to the Democratic platform which most of the members of the House and Senate drew and then retired into reticence."[19]

Since 1917 administrative reorganization of the state had had the attention of both the executive and the legislative branches, and the state Democratic party had endorsed the idea in its 1918 and 1920 platforms. However, the only tangible result to date had been an act of 1919 establishing a Board of Control as a purchasing, auditing, and budgetary agency for various state institutions.[20] On January 27, Neff addressed himself to this question in the first of his promised messages on specific legislation. He recommended to his "Dear Co-Laborers" the elimination of duplication and waste in state administration. "It is to the everlasting shame of governments, municipal, county, State and national," he declared, "that they had never adopted the business methods of efficiency and economy that makes successful private corporations. Our government is a big financial business institution and should be operated in a business-like manner." The state had grown top-heavy in its governmental affairs, burdened with overhead expenses and too much machinery. It needed less legislation and more cooperation. Politics and business should be divorced. "At the earliest hour possible, there should be abolished every board and bureau, every office and commission, except just enough to administer the government in a simple, economical manner. This is the only way to take up the slack and give to the people a maximum service at a minimum cost." The governor recommended a number of consolidations that would, he said, save the state at least $100,000 a year and set a higher standard of efficiency.[21]

On February 7, Neff recommended passage of a law that would bring all state departments under legislative control for budgetary purposes and take from their control the power to use state funds or fees in determining the number of departmental employees and fixing their salaries. He specifically named the Fish, Game, and Oyster Commission, the Highway Department, and the Pure Food Department of the Agricultural and Mechanical College as needing correction. It was not a wise policy, he said, to permit any officer of any state department to collect fees and appropriate such fees to the running expenses of his department. Not only should all public funds be turned into the State Treasury, but they should be paid out by direct and specific legislation. Such a policy would curb extravagance, equalize salaries for like service, minimize leaks, and improve efficiency.[22]

Five days later Neff asked the legislature to authorize either the Penitentiary Commission or a committee of three businessmen to discontinue the operation of the Texas State Railroad and either lease or sell the road and all its equipment. Established by the state in 1896 to haul wood and ore to the foundries operated by the prison system near Rusk, the road was later extended to Palestine and Rusk to connect with other lines as a common carrier, increasing the total mileage to 32.7. The road continued to operate after the foundries closed in 1909,

and by 1921 the deficit amounted to $366,000. "Every time a wheel
has turned since the construction of this railroad, thirteen years ago, it
has thrown the State deeper in debt," Neff complained. "The rolling
stock of this road is now practically worthless, its roadbed is wornout,
and the entire system is depleted."[23]

At this point Lieutenant Governor Davidson stepped in and said
that the railroad should not be shut down but should be transformed
into a valuable property. Senator I. D. Fairchild of Angelina County
challenged Davidson to show what he as a businessman could do with
it, and both houses voted unanimously to set up a board to oversee the
railroad with Davidson the chairman. Davidson worked out a lease
with the Texas and New Orleans Railroad, which restored train service;
secured war-surplus rails to replace the "old streaks of rust"; bought
hand-hewn ties from farmers along the road; and used prison labor to
rebuild the line. When Davidson retired from office in 1923, the legislature asked him to remain as chairman of the state Railroad Board.[24]

The initial reaction to Neff's message of January 27 was generally
favorable. Sterett wrote humorously that the governor had appeared
"with a hacked butcher knife in his hand" and "engaged in wholesale
murder" of state agencies. "And from what I hear, he has not sheathed
his knife, but has stopped only for a moment to whet it on his boot."
After the initial surprise had passed away, however, it became evident
that public opinion, insofar as visitors, newspapermen, and lawmakers
represented it, was that the governor had done something for which
the people would loudly applaud him. Politicians with whom Sterett
talked said that if Neff had any further political ambitions he could
have done nothing better to advance them than recommend the abolition or consolidation of state offices. The *Dallas Morning News* reported that his propositions had met with only minimum resistance
from government clerks and their friends and that "it appears that
most, if not all of them, will have easier sailing than was believed possible." There was, however, a growing fear that Neff was not going to
stop his economy policy with consolidating boards and departments.
Some of his friends were saying, "Just wait until he gets the appropriation bills of $25,000,000 and he will show the state something about
economy." They predicted "that the blue pencil will leave a trail on
most of the pages."[25]

Neff was an enthusiastic supporter of law enforcement and his
message to the legislature on February 1 dealt with that subject. To

cope with what he saw as "a wave of crime" sweeping over Texas, he asked the lawmakers to repeal the suspended-sentence law enacted in 1911 and amended in 1913: "This law is the convenient vehicle in which a great number of criminals, both old and young, escape punishment for the gravest of crimes. It is the incubator of professional criminals." Likewise he urged the legislature to provide for removing local officials such as sheriffs and prosecuting attorneys who corruptly stood in the way of law enforcement. Legal proceedings for removal should be instituted beyond the local jurisdiction, "which may be contaminated by the same disregard for the law." He asked too for amendment of the Dean prohibition law to allow the liquor buyer to testify against the seller. Finally, it was Neff's opinion that prosecuting attorneys should not be permitted to allow a defendant charged with a number of law violations to plead guilty to all of them and serve all his sentences concurrently while the prosecuting attorney collected fees in each of the cases.[26]

The governor's strong emphasis on law enforcement, particularly of the Prohibition law, pleased the "ultramoral element" in Texas. "Information over the grapevine telegraph system is that you are making a 100% Governor," Samuel P. Brooks, president of Baylor University, wrote Neff. Atticus Webb, head of the Anti-Saloon League in Texas, informed the governor that for months he had been vigorously agitating the law-enforcement question and had been planning a series of conferences on the subject, first in the cities and then in the county seats of the more populous counties. "The purpose of these law enforcement conferences is to rally the mass of the people to strong moral support of efforts at law enforcement being made on the part of the local officials and at the same time to prod up any officials that are negligent of their duty in this line," he explained. If Neff would give "a good strong endorsement" to this plan, it would materially help in rallying the people, and in turn "it will react in accord with your program." A "law and order" mass meeting in Dallas at the end of February greeted a telegram from Neff with "deafening" applause and authorized the formation of the Dallas Law Enforcement League with a local attorney, Preston P. Reynolds, as chairman.[27]

Neff appeared before a joint session of the legislature on February 14 to make a personal appeal for enactment of his economy and law-enforcement programs. After telling the lawmakers that he did not intend at any time during his administration to have a spokesman on the

floor of the House and Senate but would expect every legislator to be
his representative and further all measures pertaining to the best welfare of the people of Texas, the governor briefly repeated his previous
arguments for reorganizing the state administration and vowed, "If I
had the power I would before the sun goes down tonight, abolish one-
third of the boards, commissions and bureaus now in operation that
are now in employ of the state." At this juncture the members gave
him an ovation lasting several minutes. Neff then declared that what
Texas needed most was a tightening up in law enforcement and the
creation of respect for the law. Although the governor had the constitutional authority to enforce the laws, his hands were "hog-tied" and
"barrel-staved" in attempting to carry out this power. He added that
fully one thousand Rangers could be used not only to suppress lawlessness but to protect officers who were trying to enforce the law and
preserve peace. He endorsed a bill introduced by Representative
A. S. Johnson of Ellis County allowing the governor to direct the attorney general to bring quo warranto proceedings against local officials
who willfully and corruptly refused to enforce state laws and stated that
if the bill was passed that day he was ready to proceed against such
officers. Neff also repeated his recommendation for amendment of the
Dean prohibition law to allow the liquor buyer to testify in court
against the seller.

The governor briefly touched on some other legislature measures.
He was favorable to education "from the little red-schoolhouse on the
roadside to my Alma Mater on yonder hill" (referring to the University
of Texas) and desired that every child in Texas might have every opportunity to equip himself to fight the battles of life. He also favored the
establishment of an efficient marketing system "to bring the fields of
the producer closer to the tables of the consumer." Texas needed more
factories to turn raw materials into finished products, and he hoped to
see the state's valleys dotted with factory chimneys. Texas should also
conserve its floodwaters and preserve the overflow of Texas streams.
Finally, he admonished the younger legislators not to be guided in
their views by persons who approached them on the capitol walk and
other outsiders—an oblique reference to lobbyists, who were sometimes called the legislature's "third house."[28]

Neff followed up his appearance before the legislature with a public exhortation "To the People of Texas" for law and order, in which
he besought the lawmakers to enact the Johnson bill and repeal the

suspended-sentence law. "The good name of Texas is at stake," he warned:

Her proud escutcheon is being hourly defiled by criminal law-breakers. From every part of the State, and from every point of the compass, there comes to me daily the discouraging tidings that crime is rampant, that vice in its most baleful and pernicious form is flaunting itself in the face of the people. The robber, the holdup man, the thief, the burglar, the gambler, the bootlegger and the murderer are all busy today with their respective professions, laughing to scorn the law and debauching some of the sworn officers of the State. Lawlessness seems atmospheric.

Neff, as governor, was ready to accept "crime's brazen challenge," and he called on the people to arm in behalf of a righteous cause: "The public conscience should be quickened and an aroused public sentiment in behalf of the law should see its reflected glory in the votes of the representatives of the people in legislative halls." He proposed to "every preacher who preaches, every speaker who speaks, and every writer who writes, regardless of race, or class, or caste, or politics or religion, that on Sunday, Feb. 20, a sermon be preached, a speech be made and an editorial be written that will help to create a respect for and an obedience to the laws of Texas." Neff subscribed himself "Yours for that righteousness that exalteth a nation."[29]

Despite this emotional appeal the legislature roughly handled Neff's law-enforcement program. On February 11 the House Judiciary Committee gave the Johnson officer-removal bill an unfavorable report, and on February 22 the House narrowly killed (61–59) a bill by Grover C. Morris of Medina County amending the Dean law to allow a violator to be convicted on the unsupported evidence of an accomplice or participant. "Defeat of this bill is the greatest victory for the bootlegger and the lawless element they have won in this State for many years," Neff declared in a statement given to the press with the notation "Not to be used if not printed in full." "The action of the House by its vote practically wiped off the books and made ineffective the prohibition law. The bootlegger is in high clover now." He added for good measure:

If the people of Texas are opposed to the enforcement of the prohibition law, then their Representatives have certainly carried out their wishes, because the bootlegger, the worst enemy civilization has, can now sell his liquor and he can not be convicted unless a third person will come to court and testify that he had no interest in the purchase of the whisky and that as an innocent bystander he saw the sale made. Not very often is a third person called into conference to witness a transaction of this kind. Lawlessness seems to have the right of way these days in Texas.[30]

Neff's remarks caused a near-open break with the House of Representatives. Representative Sid Crumpton of Texarkana, one of the sixty-one representatives who had voted to kill the Morris bill, expressed his resentment in a personal-privilege speech that was received with applause and cheers. "I didn't stand here the other day to defend the bootlegger!" Crumpton shouted. "I did not vote to sell out Texas to the bootlegger or destroy the Dean law, and I shall resent this unjust criticism." "It is easy enough for the press to publish that the Legislature has gone anti-prohibition," he continued. "But I voted to sustain the fundamental law of the land. I have always been a prohibitionist and always voted for prohibition. But the bill of rights specifies what constitutes the rights of a citizen." The House voted 81 to 30 to print Crumpton's remarks in the *House Journal*. The governor's statement was also ordered printed by a vote of 110 to 8.[31]

Neff refused to back down. A prominent member of the House saw him on February 25, expressed regret at the turn of events, and suggested that a break was imminent. The governor replied that he would be well able to take care of himself in that event. "I stand squarely on my statement made to the press and have no apologies to make to anyone," Neff told reporters. Reactions among prohibitionists were mixed. "I want to let you know that I endorse every word you say about the Boot Leggers Aid Society," Felix D. Robertson of Dallas wrote Neff. "For the life of me I dont see how any honest prohibitionist could vote against the amendment. But I have discovered that there are prohibitionists and *prohibitionists*. The people are with you. Don't doubt that and I am sure the knowledge gives you strength." However, a Nacogdoches dry was afraid that Neff's newspaper interviews "will inevitably lead to a breach between the Governor and the Legislative branch, and as soon as this is brought about, then the whole business will be clogged."[32]

Neff prodded Speaker Thomas to bring the Johnson bill up for consideration at the "very earliest hour." Fearful that the bill would be endangered by the estrangement between the governor and legislature, its supporters announced that a determined effort would be made to obtain a fair consideration of an amended version on its own merits.

Since Neff had stated that he favored the original bill, they argued that
the amended version could hardly be considered a purely administration measure. The House, however, also killed the amended bill.[33]

In the Senate too Neff had his problems. The senators voted 27 to
4 to override his veto of a bill sponsored by Senator H. L. Darwin of
Lamar County repealing the 50 percent occupation tax on pistol sales.
In his veto message Neff had declared that the bill would tend to increase crime rather than reduce it and that the best defender of the
home was "a shotgun loaded with buckshot." Senator R. M. Dudley
asked facetiously: "Do you think that a man who never shot a gun or
baited a hook is able to tell the difference between a shotgun and a
pistol for burgler or home protection purposes?" No one volunteered
to answer after the titters died down. It was the first time in many
years that a branch of the state legislature had passed a bill over a governor's veto. When the Senate notified the House that it had voted to
override the veto, the representatives broke into applause but then
sustained the veto, 71 to 43.[34]

"Neff did his part to keep prisoners in the penitentiary after they
had been sent there," noted one state historian. Texas was one of the
few states that placed almost total pardoning power in the governor's
hands. In 1893, to help the governor exercise the clemency power, the
legislature had created the Board of Pardon Advisers, composed of two
qualified voters appointed by the governor. In the ensuing years many
Texans had come to believe that the clemency power was a political
football. In his two terms Governor Thomas M. Campbell issued 783
pardons, and in four years Governor Oscar B. Colquitt issued 1,575
pardons. Under Governor James E. Ferguson the number soared to
2,253 between 1915 and 1917, while his successor, W. P. Hobby, pardoned 1,518 prisoners and paroled about 200 more in three and one-
half years.[35]

When Neff took office, he announced that for the past six years
pardons and paroles had been granted at the rate of more than three a
day and that "the too freely granting of pardons weakens the law and
makes of its enforcement a farce." Desiring to place himself "in opposition to this rapidly increasing disrespect for the courts and the law of
the land," he abolished the Board of Pardon Advisers and announced
that until further notice no pardon application would be considered except upon the written recommendation of the judge of the district
court from which the applicant had been sent to the penitentiary. Neff

would make his own investigation of the merits of the application. In his two terms the governor issued only 92 pardons and 107 conditional pardons. In 1924 he granted only 2 pardons, the smallest number granted during any one year in the history of the penitentiary system.[36]

For many years the penitentiary system had been under a cloud, with persistent rumors of brutality, drunkenness, and immoral conduct by employees, graft, and other irregularities. Almost daily after taking office Neff received charges against the penitentiary management. To learn the truth, on February 3 he asked the legislature to authorize the lieutenant governor and the Speaker of the House to appoint a committee, "consisting of not less than three nor more than five intelligent, honest, courageous citizens of the State, not holding public office," to conduct an investigation. He signed himself "Yours for a hundred per cent penitentiary system."[37]

Neff's message surprised the legislature, for that morning the House had adopted a Senate concurrent resolution calling for such an investigation by a nine-member joint Senate-House committee. According to Senator Harry Hertzberg of San Antonio, who, along with Lieutenant Governor Davidson and Senator Guinn Williams, had conferred a few days earlier on the matter with Neff, the governor had said, "Gentlemen, I have not been in the Legislature in seventeen years and I am not familiar with the subject, therefore, there is nothing I have to suggest." Hertzberg had walked to the capitol with Neff that morning, and he had given no hint of the message. What upset the lawmakers was Neff's inference that they were not qualified to serve on the investigating committee. Hertzberg remarked that he thought "intelligent, honest, courageous men could be gotten from the membership of the Legislature." Neff's tactlessness no doubt contributed to the irritation with him that came to the surface later in the session. The House and Senate ignored the governor's message and went ahead with the appointment of a committee made up entirely of legislators.[38]

Neff also ran into difficulties with the legislature on money matters. Under the Constitution of 1876 each lawmaker was paid five dollars a day for the first sixty days of the regular session and two dollars a day thereafter. The payment schedule was intended to discourage long sessions. The governor was authorized to call special sessions "upon extraordinary occasions," limited to thirty days and to such subjects as he might submit. During these special, or "called," sessions members received five dollars a day. The legislators disliked the two-dollar days, but it was not until 1901 that a way was accidentally found to escape them. Up to that time the close of the appropriation year was the last day of August. This compelled the legislature to address itself first to appropriations in the regular session; otherwise the state would run out of money. In 1901, however, acting on the governor's recommendation, the Twenty-seventh Legislature amended the laws to synchronize the appropriation and fiscal years—both were to end on August 31. The lawmakers soon awoke to the fact that they were no longer obligated to pass appropriation bills in the regular session and that by withholding action on them and on other measures recommended by the governor they could force him to call special sessions, during which the pay was five dollars a day. Wrote reporter Tom Finty, Jr., in 1923: "Since 1907, the appropriations have not been made in the regular sessions, and only two or three days of service at the $2 rate are rendered, these by the way of lagniappe. . . . Three or four special sessions in a biennium have become common." Nevertheless, the people had seven times rejected proposed amendments giving the legislators higher pay. The sixty-day regular session left many bad or hastily drawn bills in the governor's hands; he disposed of them with post-adjournment vetoes.[39]

The Thirty-seventh Legislature ran true to form. On February 25 the House voted to adjourn at noon on March 12, which would bring the regular session to an end one day after the expiration of the sixty-day period. The vote of 75 to 44 was in the face of urgent pleas by Speaker Thomas and Lee Satterwhite, chairman of the House Appropriation Committee, that the representatives remain until the general appropriation bills had been passed. "The only excuse that we can offer for not continuing in session is that our $5 per diem expires at the end of the sixty days," Satterwhite declared. "The only other reason I can think of is that you expect a call for a special session the next day in order to get the $5 a day and in that event you put the Legislature in the hands of the Governor entirely." J. Lewis Thompson of Harris County answered that the legislators wanted to go home and "make a little money there."[40]

On February 28 the Senate voted 20 to 6 to concur in the House's action. Lieutenant Governor Davidson urged Neff to postpone the call for the special session for thirty to sixty days to allow members to go home and straighten out their business affairs; otherwise there might not be a quorum during the first week of the session. Moreover, three major appropriation bills were not ready. It was his idea to have the House and Senate appropriation committees meet in Austin ten days before the special session began, finish the appropriation bills, and have them printed for immediate consideration. Neff was noncommittal at first but finally yielded. In a farewell message to the legislature on March 12, he told the members that a special session would be called at a later date and that he would again submit his plans for law enforcement and efficient and economic administration of state government. He said that he was calling their attention to this before adjournment so that they could think over his program, discuss it with the people at home, and be prepared when they came back to Austin to work in harmony for the good of the state.[41]

It was evident that the legislature had not been in sympathy with the high moral tone of Neff's administration or with his law-enforcement and reorganization recommendations. Virtually the only one of his proposals adopted was the consolidation of the Pure Food and Drug Department with the Health Department; also, the suspended-sentence law was amended to exclude from its benefits those convicted of automobile theft. Although the lawmakers' resentment toward Neff because of his harsh comments on their performance could explain the failure of his program, it could not explain why the legislature had rejected a larger percentage of bills than had any of its predecessors in recent years. Of slightly over one thousand bills introduced during the session less than two hundred were passed, and half of these were of a local character. "This is a murderous Legislature," one well-known member remarked early in the session. Commented the *Dallas Morning News*:

The blight of Governor Neff's advocacy fell on only a small number of the proposals which appealed in vain for the Legislature's favor. Most of them fell under a much wider and heavier prejudice, under the popular prejudice against the multiplication of statutes and against the passion of Governments of all kinds and degrees for meddling in the affairs and lives of individuals. Public opinion is in revolt against that ideal, of German conception, which makes a god of the State and children of its sovereign citizens.[42]

Lieutenant Governor Davidson echoed the *News*, saying that the session was noted more for the bills it did not pass than for those it did and that members realized that the state was now "law-ridden" and had endeavored not to burder further the people and the statute books. Perhaps, too, Neff's emphasis on law enforcement had diverted the legislature's attention from other matters. There was no redistrict-ing of any kind; the House passed both representative and senatorial reapportionment bills, but the Senate allowed them to die in com-mittee. Death also came to former Governor Hobby's constitutional amendment on home ownership, a medical-practice amendment, two blue-sky laws, a tick-eradication measure, a public-utilities bill, and a resolution calling for a constitutional convention. Nothing was accom-plished in the direction of tax reform. "There Was a Killing Frost Down Austin Way" was the caption of a John Knott cartoon in the *Dallas Morning News*, showing Neff as a farmer surveying a field of bills that did not come up.[43]

The legislature repealed the minimum-wage law for women and minors enacted in 1919. This bill, which established the Industrial Welfare Commission to investigate working conditions and set wages, had aroused the hostility of employers because it had some teeth. At the same time a new minimum-wage law was passed. On March 30, Neff signed the repeal bill and vetoed the new law, thus leaving the state without any minimum-wage legislation. According to the gover-nor, the existing law was unworkable and impractical, and the commis-sion had nothing to show for the more than $20,000 expended during the two years of its existence. His veto message characterized the new minimum-wage bill as unconstitutional, inconsistent with its real in-tent, and more defective and unworkable than the original law. The exception of nine classes of workers from the bill, and the manner in which these exceptions were written, constituted class legislation, he said, and took out of the scope of the bill the very people whom it was intended to benefit. Although Neff said that his veto should not be interpreted as implying that a just, workable, and constitutional minimum-wage bill was impossible, the subject was not revived in the antiunion climate of the early 1920s.[44]

The legislature did provide for the organization of cooperative marketing associations, granted towns of fewer than 5,000 inhabitants the right to establish the commission form of government, authorized incorporated cities to employ county tax collectors and assessors, and approved the creation of water and irrigation districts. In the area of public health authorization was given for the licensing and supervision of maternity homes, the establishment of city hospitals, and the cre-ation of a Board of Optometry for regulating the licensing of optome-trists. Reflecting concern over Japanese immigration to Texas, an act fostered by the American Legion and known as the "Jap bill" was passed restricting Japanese aliens from owning land in Texas and requiring the registration of alien-owned lands. The measure passed the Senate 22 to 0 and was passed by the House on second reading 93 to 27 and on a third reading without a recorded vote. Neff signed the bill.[45]

Among the appropriations passed were $3,000,000 to supplement the available school fund and aid in keeping the per capita school apportionment at $14.50; $4,000,000 for rural schools for the next biennium and a minor appropriation to meet the state's obligation under the Smith-Hughes Vocational Training Act; $1,350,000 to buy 135 acres of land adjacent to the University of Texas campus for the expansion of the institution; $1,500,000 for a tuberculosis sanitarium at Kerrville for veterans of World War I; and $50,000 to purchase a site for the West Texas Agricultural and Mechanical College.[46]

The appropriation for the expansion of the University of Texas was the outcome of a heated controversy over a proposal to abandon the original "Forty Acres" in favor of a new campus on a five-hundred-acre tract along the Colorado River near the Austin dam, which had been deeded to the university by George Washington Brackenridge of San Antonio. Robert E. Vinson, president of the university; the Board of Regents; and many faculty members, students, and former students strongly favored the move because of the cramped facilities the institution would soon face on the Forty Acres. Both Austin newspapers, the *American* and the *Statesman*, wrote editorials in favor of removal. Churches, store owners, boardinghouse keepers, and other property owners around the campus opposed the plan, however, and Regent H. A. Wroe of Austin, one of the three executors of Major George Washington Littlefield's estate, announced that Littlefield's bequests to the university totaling $800,000 would be voided if the university moved from its present site.

On January 5, 1921, the regents adopted a memorandum to Governor Hobby, Governor-elect Neff, and the House and Senate recommending removal of the university to the Brackenridge tract; Hobby submitted the memorandum to the legislature on January 12, along with his own recommendation for approval. Removal bills were introduced in both houses on January 25, and skirmishing began. On February 7, twenty-eight representatives led by R. A. Baldwin of Lubbock introduced a resolution calling for a statewide election to determine a permanent location for the university in either Austin or some other city or town. Senator J. C. McNealus of Dallas wanted to relocate the university at a point midway between Dallas and Fort Worth. He said that the two cities would raise at least $10 million and secure 500 to 1,000 acres of land, which they would gladly donate to the university. He declared, "It seems to me that it would be to the best interests of the University to remove it entirely away from Austin to keep it from exerting its influence over the Texas Legislature and to keep politics from figuring in its affairs." President Vinson called his idea "bunk." One House member made a short but very effective speech against the removal bill: "Mr. Speaker, just what sort of an institution is this for which we are asked to provide a campus? Is it a university or a goat ranch?"

Lee Satterwhite of Panhandle, who led the fight for the Bracken-ridge tract in the House, finally went to Vinson and reported that he thought the removal bill would be defeated but said that if Vinson would mark on a map of Austin the boundaries of an adequate campus around the Forty Acres he would introduce it at the proper time and that he thought that he could secure its adoption. "So the map was marked and the thing was done in that way," Vinson recalled. "It was a compromise, made with regret, the sacrifice of a golden dream, but there it is."[47]

Neff seemed reluctant to sign the bill, and Vinson and Austin citizens sent telegrams paid for by the Austin Chamber of Commerce to several hundred former students of the university, asking them to urge the governor to support the measure. Neff insisted that the chamber secure assurances from the Austin banks that if more than one-half of the appropriation was required within the first fiscal year they would advance the money without interest. This was done, the banks gave the required assurance, and Neff signed the bill on April 1, "applauded by Vinson, Folts, Perry, and Wroe." As he signed, the governor said, "The purchase of this land will fix forever the habitat of this seat of learning." Later Neff told Regent Frank C. Jones: "You need fear no uneasiness in reference to my relations to the University. I am for building her foundations and lifting her walls."[48]

Neff made liberal use of his veto power in dealing with the appropriations authorized by the regular session. He vetoed the $4,000,000 appropriation for rural schools and the $50,000 to establish the West Texas Agricultural and Mechanical College. He said that, while his judgment and heart applauded the college, hard times in the state plus the failure of the Democrats to endorse the proposal at their state convention in Fort Worth in 1920 made him feel duty-bound to withhold his approval. West Texans were furious, not only at the governor's vetoes but also at the legislature's failure to redistrict the state according to population. The explosion came on April 2 at Sweetwater, in Nolan County, where at a mass meeting citizens adopted resolutions stating that unless the legislature met West Texas's demands they would "call for the creation of a new State under which we hope to have equal rights and equal representation." "Governor Neff's veto of the small appropriation for the purchase of a site for the West Texas A&M College is full notice to the people of the West that they are living under a State Government which denies to them the chance to realize their hopes and aspirations," declared Representative R. M. Chitwood of Sweetwater.

That was the beginning of what became known as the "Sweetwater Secession Movement." Another mass meeting was held on April 6 under the auspices of the Young Men's Business Club of Sweetwater, at which a number of speeches were made and resolutions were unanimously adopted denouncing as "unjust and unexplained" Neff's veto of the A&M bill, deploring his veto of the rural-school-aid bill, and condemning as "subversive to the economy of a representative government the unwarranted refusal of the legislature of Texas to enact a senatorial re-districting bill at the passed session of the legislature, as demanded by the constitution." The meeting demanded that Neff hold the legislature in session until it organized the legislative branch on a constitutional basis. No specific mention was made of the threat in the resolution of April 2 to establish a new state, and in later years a West Texas Chamber of Commerce spokesman suggested that only a handful of hotheads ever seriously supported the secession movement and that the chamber had moved quickly to cool things off.[49]

Whether or not secession was ever seriously considered, it made good newspaper copy. The *Fort Worth Star-Telegram* ran a cartoon depicting West Texas as a hefty man in boots and Stetson reading about the Boston Tea Party in a history book. Another *Star-Telegram* cartoon showed Mother Texas surrounded by departing children. The *Dallas Morning News* ran a cartoon of a big bear labeled West Texas, with a tiny Pat Neff hanging precariously onto its tail.[50]

In a statement to the press on April 4, Neff made it plain that he was going to submit redistricting to the special session and that talk of

forming a new state in West Texas did not "in any way change his purpose as Governor." He declared that such talk was not seriously considered by the sober-thinking citizenship, even in West Texas, "beyond the effervescent oratory of the hour." Veteran Democratic leader
Marshall Hicks of San Antonio wrote the governor that, in his opinion,
the outbreak in West Texas was temporary: "It may be possible that in
the future a time may come when Texas should be divided, but the
cause of the division will be based upon a larger question than the location of a small branch of the A.&M. College. The opposition to you
growing out of this matter, is, in my judgment, purely local and will
not be enduring." "The breeze stirred up in West Texas over my veto
of the West Texas A & M College bill has not disturbed me much," Neff
told former Governor Thomas Campbell. "My mind has been so clear
that the bill should be vetoed that their resolutions of censure have not
really disturbed me." [51]

Still, West Texans came to believe that the publicity given to the
Sweetwater movement had opened the eyes of Neff and the rest of
Texas to the fact that their section was no longer content to be a step-
child. Judge Royston C. Crane, one of the leaders of the movement,
said later, "That [April 6] meeting and movement is the thing which
convinced Govr. Neff, the people of Texas and of the world that West
Texas *had arrived, knew what it wanted and intended to keep after it
until it got it.*" [52]

The end of the regular session found Neff visibly harassed by his
duties and problems. He ran the executive office with a staff of seven—
a secretary, two assistant secretaries, three stenographers, and a porter. A perfectionist, Neff made little use of his aides, preferring to handle as much detail as possible himself. [53] The abolition of the Board of
Pardon Advisers added greatly to his work load, for he personally investigated pardon applications. His secretary, R. B. Walthall, announced that the governor would read and study carefully every one of
the 189 bills awaiting his disposition. "You cannot imagine how busy it
is to be Governor," Neff wrote a relative during the session. "It is
worse than a roundup. At a roundup you do bed the cattle at times, but
it is a stampede here by day and by night. Just about the time you
think you have things well rounded up something breaks loose at a new
place." On April 28 he apologized to his son for not writing and explained: "I have been pressed every minute. I am in my office almost
every night until the lights go out at eleven. There is no end to work. It

gets worse all the time. Just about the time it looks like we are getting out of the brushy, something new breaks loose." During his first two years in office Neff never left the state. Perhaps he should have taken former Governor Hobby's advice to work occasionally just half a day: "You will make only half as many mistakes as when you work all day."[54]

The death of his elderly mother in the executive mansion on May 18, 1921, was a heavy blow to Neff. "She left to me a wonderful heritage, and it is my purpose to continue to abide by the principles she instilled into my life when a child," he wrote. "She was always to me my greatest inspiration, and all who knew her appreciated her many beautiful qualities of mind and character." Mrs. Neff left a 10-acre tract in Coryell County to the state for religious, educational, fraternal, and political purposes. Mother Neff State Park was the first official state park in Texas. In 1934 Pat Neff deeded to the state the balance of the park's total 259 acres. Adjacent to the Leon River, the park is now used primarily for camping, fishing, picnicking, bird watching, and nature study.[55]

On June 2, Neff left Austin to make a personal inspection of the penitentiary system, beginning with some of the prison farms. His visit followed an outbreak at the penitentiary at Huntsville, in which forty men had escaped after wounding two guards and shooting several dogs; the burning of the furniture factory at Huntsville; and the burning of the barns at the Shaw penal farm. During the first six months of 1921 290 prisoners escaped from the penitentiary and the farms— more than the number during the whole of 1920, though most were recaptured. During this period Neff had refused to use his clemency power. On May 28 he wrote to the prison commissioners to express dissatisfaction about the large number of escapes and declared, "When respect for law is established in Texas and the crime wave subsides, I expect to grant some pardons to meritorious convicts, but I do not intend to extend clemency to even one who has broken a trust or assaulted guards in an effort to escape."[56]

After inspecting seven of the farms, Neff returned to Austin on June 5. He told reporters that he had spoken, either in public or private, with approximately one thousand prisoners; had inspected their sleeping quarters, kitchens, and food; and had inquired about their general treatment, especially the manner of punishment. "The sleeping and eating were clean and sanitary, the food was wholesome and plentiful, and it was admitted by all the prisoners that the treatment

had been for some months entirely satisfactory," the governor declared. He had been given an exhibition of bloodhounds trailing a
black and pronounced it marvelous; the dogs had treed their quarry.[57]

Still the escapes continued; thirty-three convicts ran away from
the Clements prison farm on June 5, and a month later thirteen men
escaped from the Blue Ridge farm. When the press intimated that
the escapes could be attributed to Neff's no-pardon policy, Captain
J. A. Herring, chairman of the Board of Prison Commissioners (also
referred to as the Prison Commission), replied that "almost uniformly
the men responsible for these jail breaks are long-time, desperate criminals, who have not now and could not have had at any time any possible hope of pardon or parole." Privately he complained to Neff that the
publicity surrounding the legislative investigating committee was responsible for the unrest among the convicts and the many escapes and
attempted escapes. There was a "sickly, maudlin sentiment throughout
the country from a lot of people who know nothing about the convict
business, and who think they know all about it, who are attempting to
advise the convicts and their advice is usually of such a nature that it
causes the convicts to think they are being badly treated." Neff replied, "I share with you your views in regard to this matter."[58]

During the legislative session the press reported that before the
special session Neff would "go on the stump" to advocate his policies.
The *Dallas Morning News* warned him that such a campaign would be
likely to excite resentment among the legislators without arousing the
people and that he should try diplomacy: "That would promise him
larger results than he could expect to derive from warfare." A Waco
friend informed Neff that "the people seem to be almost unanimous in
opposition to the boot-legger bill suggested by you and also the bill
authorizing the removal of cases against officers to Austin for a trial,"
and he earnestly urged the governor not to present them to the special session.[59]

Ignoring this advice, Neff journeyed to McAllen in the Rio Grande
Valley to make an address on law enforcement to the annual convention of the Texas Press Association. He told his audience that, if
the legislators and the people would cooperate with him in putting
through his program, within a few months "Texas will be so dry that a
man will have to prime himself before he can spit." There were counties, he said, where saloons and gambling houses were running wide-
open and no indictments were being returned. He could name them,

he said, but did not think that that would be advisable. "I want to fix
the law so that we can convict on the testimony of the purchaser,"
thundered Neff. "There are persons in this State who are going about
declaring that the amendment of the law in this matter would shake
the foundations of the Republic. Well, I say that if such a thing as this
will shake the foundations of the Republic, let 'em shake." Just fifty-
eight persons had been sent to the "pen" in 1920 for violations of the
Prohibition laws. "Why more than that should have been sent from my
town alone and from yours, too."[60]

On June 17, Neff issued a call for a special session on July 18, a
week later than originally suggested. The legislature was asked to
make appropriations "within the available revenues" for the support of
state government; to provide additional funds for the public schools; to
repeal the suspended-sentence law and amend the Dean law; to provide "an effective law for the removal of officers who willfully and corruptly refuse to perform their official duties in the enforcement of the
law"; and to redistrict the state.[61] Neff followed this up with a series of
economy and law-enforcement speeches at Wharton, Palacios, Georgetown, Austin, Mexia, and Corsicana and at Mother Neff Park, in Coryell County. When Neff asked the members of his audience in Mexia to
raise their hands if they wanted the suspended-sentence law repealed,
practically every hand went up. Clapping his hands together enthusiastically, the governor said, "Hot dog, I wish you were members of the
Legislature." After pausing for a moment, he declared: "I don't think
the Legislature will pass a single one of these bills. During the last session of the Legislature I could not even get them up for discussion. No,
sir, I did not even have enough friends to get them on the floor. . . . I
don't think the special session will pass them, but I want to put those
Legislators on record once more." Wiping the perspiration from his
forehead, he added, "They can't do anything more than remove me
from office."[62]

At Mexia and Corsicana, Neff made charges of graft against certain
state employees who had padded their expense accounts or who had
received checks when "they never did a lick of work for the State." In
some counties as much as $25,000 in state funds had been grafted in
one year by use of padded school rolls. He did not name any individual, though he said that he could call names. "Well, you ask, what am I
going to do about it?" he said to his Corsicana audience, and answered
his own question:

Nothing. What's that, you say; this is a funny kind of a Governor we have—all this crookedness going on and he isn't going to do anything to stop it! But I can't. I am powerless. There is not an officer in Texas that I can discharge except my own private secretary. Why, the janitor could steal the State Capitol and take it off with him, and I couldn't do a thing. Not a thing—except to look happy and say, "too bad." [63]

When the lawmakers assembled in Austin on July 18, both Lieutenant Governor Davidson and Speaker Thomas called for peace and harmony but served notice that in view of the present tense feeling growing out of the governor's recent speeches any further attacks would mean war. "It will not require but one criticism to start the fight, now smouldering," was one observer's prediction. Davidson took the position that the wisest thing the legislature could do was pass the appropriation bills and go home. "I am not one of those who believe the State of Texas is going to the bow-wows," Thomas told the House. "If those who go about criticizing and condemning the Legislature would spend one-third as much time in the committee room . . . endeavoring to solve the financial problems of the day, as they have in making political speeches, when no campaign is on, they would be in better position to criticize." "The person" making charges about graft and extravagance was invited to furnish the legislature with information that would allow it to investigate properly "instead of so much outside talk." [64]

The Senate State Affairs Committee favorably reported a resolution introduced by Senator Joe Burkett of Eastland calling on Neff to substantiate his charges of graft in state departments and to name names. The full Senate refused to adopt the resolution, but Senator Archie Parr of Duval County confronted the governor and asked for the evidence, saying that the Senate was either playing politics or was a coward, to which Neff sourly replied, "Maybe a little of both." "The House has adopted a resolution calling for the information and I feel it my first duty to supply it," the governor continued. "When the House has finished, if the Senate want it, I will be glad to give it to that body." Neff actually beat the House to the punch by sending in a special message submitting the reasons for his graft charges before the representatives had acted upon the resolution. The House received the message "in grim silence." Then a storm of oratory broke out. When Newt B. Williams of McLennan County attacked Neff for reflecting on the legislature's integrity, another McLennan representative, J. L. Quicksall, leaped to the governor's defense and attacked Williams's legislative record, charging that he had voted against "moral" bills. The House quickly adjourned. Now that the storm had broken, members were eager for a test of strength, wanting to know which side was in the ascendancy.[65]

The next day about thirty-five supporters of Neff's economy and law-enforcement programs organized a "People's Club" in the House and elected as chairman A. B. Curtis of Tarrant County. Quicksall said that, to judge from the names on the roster and those known to be in sympathy with Neff's program, a majority of the House stood for his bills in whole or slightly modified. The governor's partisans in the House discussed among themselves whether they would press a resolution endorsing the governor, but Neff asked them to withdraw it in the interest of harmony, and that was done. Neff told one West Texas member of the opposition that he was not creating a fight with the legislature, wanted none with it, and therefore expected unbiased consideration of his recommendations. A joint legislative committee was appointed on July 26 to investigate the governor's charges of graft. It reported on August 11 that, while some minor irregularities had occurred, there had been no financial loss to the state and that in each instance the money would be recovered.[66]

The legislature in its regular session had submitted five constitutional amendments to the voters at a special election on July 23. These amendments proposed (1) to increase the salaries of the governor and other constitutional officials, (2) to increase the Confederate pension tax on property from $.05 to $.07 per $100.00 of assessed valuation, (3) to increase the length of the regular legislative session from 60 to 120 days, increase the legislators' compensation to $10.00 a day, and reduce their mileage allowance to $.10 a mile; (4) to abolish the Board of Prison Commissioners and allow the legislature to reorganize the prison system; and (5) to change the suffrage laws by restricting suffrage to citizens (aliens had long been allowed to vote), allowing a husband or wife to pay the other's poll tax, and authorizing the legislature to provide for absentee voting. In a very light vote all the amendments were defeated except the suffrage amendment, which passed 57,622 to 53,910.[67]

On July 26, Neff renewed the recommendations that he had made in the regular session for consolidation of the State Warehouse and Marketing Department with the Department of Agriculture, transfer of the duties of the State Tax Board and tax commissioner to the state comptroller and the Texas Railroad Commission, abolition of the Agricultural Experiment Sub-Station Board and transfer of its duties to the Board of Directors of Texas A&M College, and transfer of the work of the Mining Board and the mine inspector to the Department of Labor. In the governor's judgment there were too many clerks, stenographers, and employees generally and too many traveling representatives— "superfluous perambulating agents of the State," he called them. The state government had been put "on wheels," a practice resulting in reckless waste. Neff recommended absolute economy and specific itemization of all appropriations. He told the lawmakers:

The eyes of five million people are looking to this Legislature to raise high the banner of economy and simplicity in the administration of their government. Graft and extravagance from the highest to the lowest amount is a problem that should be squarely faced and honestly solved. It should be remembered that little leaks break the dam. If we detect a little graft let us not belittle it, but expose it in order that all may know it and shun it.[68]

The joint committee of the House and Senate appointed to investigate the penitentiary system made its report on July 30. It found that the law and prison rules governing the punishment of convicts had been and were "grossly violated" and that many convicts had been brutally mistreated; sanitary conditions at the main penitentiary were "extremely bad, unhealthy, and obnoxious"; the law regarding quantity and quality of food for prisoners was disregarded; prisoners were not classified and segregated according to age, prison, and criminal record as required by law; laws regarding the educational and spiritual welfare of prisoners were ignored; the prisoners were given inefficient medical care, particularly the tuberculars; and the business management and supervision of the system by the Prison Commission was poor and ineffective. The system had operated at a "considerable loss" in 1920, and something more than just bad management was suspected. The committee believed that Commissioner W. G. Pryor had been "guilty of indifference and willful failure in the discharge of the duties of his office and of such gross negligence as amounts to malfeasance."

Noting that the use of chains to hang convicts from their wrists with their toes barely touching the ground was the principal form of punishment employed by farm managers, the committee recommended that the legislature prohibit chains and limit the use of the bat or strap and ensure that the laws governing prisoner welfare were strictly enforced and suggested a larger aid fund for discharged convicts and pardons for exemplary conduct. It recommended amendment of the law relating to the removal of prison commissioners to avoid impeachment proceedings. Regarding prison management, the committee recommended establishment of an advisory board consisting of three persons appointed by the governor, one of whom would be a woman, to serve without pay for two years. The board would visit the penitentiary at least once every three months and report quarterly to the governor and the Prison Commission. Finally, it recommended the sale of all the prison farms, the abandonment of Huntsville Penitentiary, and the erection of a modern prison within fifty miles of Austin, with sufficient adjoining farmlands and factories operated by prison labor.[69]

The joint legislative committee called on Neff on August 4 to try to persuade him to submit its report for action either to the special session or to a second special session. Neff refused to commit himself but left the impression that he was opposed to adopting a new penitentiary policy until the present system had been given another trial. Taking matters into its own hands, the legislature took up the report without waiting for Neff's decision and passed four bills carrying out its major recommendations. Pressure to secure the governor's approval began at once. Senator Harry Hertzberg, a member of the prison committee, wired Mrs. H. F. Ring of Houston, a prominent clubwoman and prison reformer, about the bill creating a supervisory board and abolishing the use of chains and excessive whipping:

Call upon the women of Texas to use their influence with the governor to approve these measures. It is reported that the governor may not approve both bills. . . .I expect the women of Texas to stand squarely behind this matter. It is a great chance to change the horrible conditions existing in the system. Continue to boomerang the governor for next ten days until he approves bill.

Neff allowed the prison-relocation bill to become law without his signature, vetoed the law relating to punishment of prisoners on the ground that existing laws and regulations covered the situation, and signed the other measures. On August 29 he announced that chains would not be used in the penitentiary system during his administration.[70]

Neff had been trying since May to get rid of the prison commissioner, W. G. Pryor, whom he believed to be guilty of mismanagement and graft, but Pryor refused to resign, alleging that the governor wanted him removed for political reasons. The attorney general had ruled that Neff could not remove Pryor or any other member of the commission. The legislature now passed a law allowing the attorney general, at the governor's request, to institute ouster proceedings against a prison commissioner. Neff asked the attorney general to bring suit against Pryor in the Twenty-sixth District Court of Travis County, and after a hard, bitter fight he was ousted on December 15, 1921. Neff appointed Walker Sayles of Eastland to fill the vacancy. The governor also appointed a committee to inquire into charges of irregularities and abuses at the training school for boys in Gatesville. "Nothing will be left undone to correct this whole situation and every effort will be made to fix the responsibility for existing conditions," he assured one inquirer. As a result of the investigation some of the higher officials in the institution were removed.

In September, Neff and the Prison Commission visited Huntsville Penitentiary with a view to assessing its value, so that the land could be sold and the prison moved to a site within seventy-five miles of Austin. A few days later the relocation committee visited a proposed site near Marble Falls, but nothing came of the plan because the legislature had failed to provide funds to finance it. Neff was opposed to selling all of the prison property, advocating instead the construction of a new system centering on the farms in Brazoria and Fort Bend counties. The legislature had appropriated only $175,000 of the $879,518 requested by the governor to operate the system until the 1922 crops were sold, and, rather than call a third special session, Neff borrowed $700,000 at 7 percent interest from the Brown-Crummer Company of Wichita, Kansas.[71]

On November 21, 1921, Neff and the advisory board began a week-long visit to Huntsville and the prison farms in South Texas. In an address to the prisoners he told them that no pardon could be secured through outside influence, that the true test of whether a convict was ready for his freedom was his conduct in prison, and that only men whose records were commended by prison officials would receive pardons. Up to that time Neff had granted ten pardons, but on Thanksgiving Day he granted pardons to thirty-five prisoners, including three women. "Permit me to say at this time that I am pleased with the fact that you have seen fit to pardon quite a few prisoners and that you hold out the hope of pardon to more," Senator Hertzberg wrote Neff. "In saying this, I am not actuated by any motive of sympathy for the prisoners at all, but I believe that this hope of pardon in the hearts of prisoners makes for better discipline in the penitentiary."[72]

In his message to the legislature on the first day of the special session, Neff had called for absolute economy in government expenditures "in the face of tightening credit, moneyless markets, and industrial depression" and had justified his vetoes of appropriations passed by the regular session. "It is a time to retrench rather than enlarge," he declared. The judiciary bill, composed largely of statutory positions and salaries, passed without much difficulty early in the session; however, a battle erupted over the education-appropriation bill carrying funds for the university and colleges. Over two weeks were spent in debate on the latter bill as the "retrencher," or People's Club, party in the House, led by Walter E. Pope of Nueces County, A. S. Curtis of Tarrant County, and H. S. Bonham of Bee County, sought to slash faculty salaries. On July 28 the House voted 81 to 37 to eliminate all the raises granted to University of Texas faculty members in 1920 and restore salaries to the level of 1919. The appropriation for the university was cut from $925,275 to $547,102 for each year of the biennium. The salaries of the faculty members of the Galveston Medical School were "cut to the quick," as the institution's annual appropriation was reduced from $139,525 to $92,065. Senators friendly to the University of Texas were indignant; Senator Hart Willis of Dallas said that, rather than accept heavy cuts that would make it a fifth-class school, he would favor closing its doors. "Not since the day James E. Ferguson vetoed the entire University appropriation has the future of the school looked darker, say its friends in the Legislature," reported the *Dallas Morning News*.[73]

With reduced impetus, but with a workable majority, the House economizers sliced salaries at Texas A&M College in the same way. The vote was 76 to 50. The steamroller, however, ran up and stopped against the walls of the College of Industrial Arts for Women, at Denton; an attempt to reduce faculty salaries there to the 1919 level was defeated 68 to 56.

The House insisted on passing the so-called "Pope Amendment," which specified that no salary should be raised in excess of the amount named in the itemized budget and that if a subject for which an appropriation was made was not taught the money would remain in the state treasury. A compromise proposed by a joint conference committee cutting faculty salaries at the University of Texas and A&M College by 20 percent on amounts in excess of $2,400 was rejected by the House 66 to 58 on the last night of the session. The legislature adjourned on August 16, without passing an appropriation bill for education. The departmental and eleemosynary appropriation bills were passed with many reductions. A disgusted representative, Barry Miller of Dallas, tried but failed to have the following poem printed in the *House Journal*:

> Here lies a called session, gone into the past,
> In cold dead hands, withered flowers enclasped
> Constituents neglected, a great state defaced,
> Thirty days wasted, a record defaced.
>
> It robbed a few teachers, deprived them of hope;
> And fed the dear people, "Amendments by Pope,"
> While Curtis of Tarrant and Bonham of Bee
> Ran the steam-roller and chortled in glee.
>
> The warehouse department—Nacogdoches too
> Were victims of Veatch's economy crew,
> It saved a plugged penny, and squandered a pound,
> It lacked much in brains, but it made up in sound.
>
> It strove hard to hinder, all higher education,
> And loved the poor farmer to verge of prostration,
> Till one night in August, it passed out, alas!
> It died as it lived, in a great puff of gas.[74]

Neff called a second special session to meet on August 17. In his message he expressed the hope that in the interest of Texas the two houses would "speedily reconcile and compromise your differences" and make the necessary appropriations. At the same time he told them to keep appropriations within the $19 million available to the state since under present financial conditions the tax burden should not be increased. He also advised the lawmakers that the senatorial redistricting bill passed during the session did not fulfill either the letter or the spirit of the Constitution or the Democratic party platform and that he was submitting the redistricting question to them for the third time.[75]

Insofar as his economy and law enforcement programs were concerned, the governor had had no better luck with the first special session than he had had with the regular session. All but one of the bills for the consolidation of overlapping departments were laid on the table. The Governing Board of the Agricultural Experiment Sub-Stations was abolished, and its duties were transferred to the Board of Directors of A&M College, which had control of the main experimental station. Amendments were made to the Dean prohibition law, making it easier to enforce, but the Johnson officer-removal bill and the repeal of the suspended-sentence law were killed. Neff abandoned the fight, telling reporters that he would not hold the lawmakers' noses to the grindstone by resubmitting his proposals to the second called session.[76]

The "retrencher party" in the House tried to stop action on the education appropriation bill by preventing a quorum. On August 19 the House issued orders to bring in nine missing members. After an all-night hunt, the sergeant-at-arms and the Travis County sheriff appeared with the missing men, and a quorum was achieved. Two of them had been summoned from their beds, while several others had been found in a camp at Deep Eddy bathing beach near Lake Austin. A conference committee reached agreement on a bill containing salary cuts that were less drastic than the House majority wanted but concurring in a House amendment limiting the University of Texas available fund to permanent improvements only and in that part of the Pope amendment specifying that no salary should be raised in excess of the amount specified in the budget. The Senate accepted the report 20 to 4, but in the House it was vigorously opposed by Pope, Curtis, Bonham, and other leaders of the People's Club. As had been the case from the beginning, the fight centered around the University of Texas; the other institutions were hardly mentioned. "I do not believe there has been a University of the first class in this State," Curtis asserted, "and I do not believe that we ought to support a University of the first class but that our taxes should be spent in maintaining an institution whose purpose is to train undergraduates." However, enough retrenchers parted company with their leaders to pass the conference report 76 to 47. Their work completed at last, the weary legislators adjourned on August 25. After careful study Neff approved the eleemosynary bill with reductions totaling $623,760, approved the departmental bill with minor reductions, and allowed the educational bill to become law without his signature.[77]

All faculty salaries at the state's institutions of higher education were cut 20 percent on the excess over $2,000. President Vinson of the University of Texas and President William Bennett Bizzell of the A&M colleges had their salaries reduced from $7,500 to $7,000. The heads of the other institutions received cuts ranging from $250 to $500. "Governor Neff is the first graduate of the University, I believe, to become Governor; naturally we all hoped big things from him," wrote a despondent Will Hogg, an alumnus of the University of Texas Law School. "I can't believe he realizes the harm that has been done by the bills that were passed by the legislature. I believe when he realizes it he will have the guts to try to undertake to rectify the mistakes." Hogg thought that the retaliatory efforts of Neff's enemies in the legislature had forced him to "compromise himself and his administration by standing for a lot of puny legislation aimed at some economies in the administration of the two biggest educational institutions in the State" and had given "at least two of the worst left-overs of the Ferguson regime a chance to prize in on the situation and force the Governor into a very weak position."[78]

The legislature had passed senatorial and representative reapportionment bills in the second called session, and Neff allowed them to become law without his signature. According to a student of reapportionment, "The Governor had apparently decided that while he could not afford to veto the bills and delay reapportionment still longer, he could by withholding his signature from them, show his extreme displeasure with what he considered to be an unfair apportionment." Most of the press criticism was directed at the senatorial bill, which postponed redistricting until 1924 to protect incumbent senators. The legislature was also reproached for creating districts of grossly unequal size. Neff believed that West Texas had not been fairly apportioned, telling one visitor frankly that he thought the people of that section "had a right to be indignant."[79]

Although Neff's relations with the legislature had apparently improved somewhat during the first called session—the governor was courteously received during a visit to the House chamber on August 10—his critics declared that he was austere and cold, that he never accepted the advice of party leaders, and that he was secretive about his future plans. "What does he do when members of this body go to him for information? He dodges the question," asserted one irate representative. "He has assumed an air of patronizing superiority, and is playing to the political galleries of Texas." When the first called session adjourned without passing the education bill, Neff accused members of forcing him into calling another session in order to collect their mileage and per diem allowances. On August 23 the governor was openly flouted upon the floor of the House when the representatives voted 82 to 32 to appoint a five-member committee to report on the feasibility of a state park in the Davis Mountains. The sponsor of the resolution, W. W. Stewart of Reeves County, charged that Neff had told him that he had vetoed an earlier concurrent resolution providing for a Senate-House committee because "the personnel of the committee did not suit him." The speaker then appointed the five men on the original committee to the new one. Neff, who was present at the rear of the chamber during the debate, later denied any such motive, saying that Stewart's remarks "were all wrong," but Stewart repeated his charges in a personal-privilege speech to the House on August 25. Still, Neff had his defenders. "I glory in the Governors Spunk and I am with him and there are many more now with him than there was when he became Governor," a district attorney wrote Neff's secretary. "The common people of this country are with him stronger than they ever were, and it is a common expression, 'why dont the Legislature do or offer to do something besides cuss the Gov.'"[80]

Neff had found the road to economy in state administration and better law enforcement strewn, in his words, with "piercing thorns"; he had little to show for all his efforts except the consolidation of a few overlapping departments and an amendment to the Dean law prohibiting the manufacture of intoxicating liquors in Texas for any purpose. The only action on his officer-removal proposal was a bill permitting a district judge to remove a county official for certain causes, but not for intoxication if it resulted from drinking liquor prescribed by a licensed physician.[81] Even his reputation as an "apostle of law enforcement" had not gone unchallenged. On July 20 the *Dallas Morning News* had taken him to task for failing in his denunciation of lawlessness to refer "to the most notable type of lawlessness prevalent in the State." "The series of assaults being carried on by masked men acting either officially or spuriously in the name of a secret organization purporting to sanction that character of violence is a development which cannot have escaped the notice of the Governor," declared the *News*. "It is a development that has outrun in Texas its progress elsewhere to the point where it really shames the State more than the existence of the crime wave at a time when every State had its own crime wave."[82] The unnamed "secret organization" to which Neff was accused of turning a blind eye was the Invisible Empire, the Knights of the Ku Klux Klan, which was rapidly becoming the most important and controversial issue in Texas politics.

CHAPTER 2

The Ku Klux Klan in Texas

THE second Ku Klux Klan, a revival of the post–Civil War organization, was founded on Stone Mountain, near Atlanta, Georgia, on Thanksgiving Night in 1915, by William Joseph Simmons of Atlanta, a former Methodist preacher and professional fraternalist. It was chartered by the state of Georgia as a "patriotic, secret, social, benevolent order under the name of and style of 'Knights of the Ku Klux Klan.'" After this brief, inconspicuous appearance in public, Simmons and his followers retired into relative obscurity and the "Imperial Wizard" himself into poverty. In the spring of 1920 the Klan enlisted no more than four to five thousand members in Georgia and Alabama.

Then, on June 7, 1920, Simmons formed a business partnership with a shrewd publicity expert, Edward Young Clarke, to "sell" the Klan to Americans in exchange for a sizable cut from the ten-dollar initiation fee called the "klectoken." In his role as head of the Propagation Department of the Klan, Clarke relied heavily on his business associate, Mrs. Elizabeth Tyler, though she never held an official post in the order. The Klan's ideology was a mixture of patriotism, 100 percent Americanism, anti-Catholicism, white supremacy, purity of womanhood, law and order, anti-Semitism, antiradicalism, and opposition to foreign immigration. Field organizers for the Klan, called "kleagles," would begin their membership drive by contacting the leading citizens of each community, thus giving the nascent Klan prestige. Next, the organizers would solicit the middle class, out of which came the bulk of Klan membership. Finally, the kleagles, who received four dollars out of each initiation fee, were not above approaching society's dregs. Thus each chapter or "klavern" was made up of a cross-section of the community, the only prerequisites for membership being that the applicant be white, Protestant, and native-born and have ten dollars. Feeding on disturbed postwar conditions, the Klan began a phenomenal growth that brought its membership to 100,000 by September, 1921, and to 700,000 by December, 1922.[1] "In its heyday I have ridden past the 'nightshirt factory' at Buckhead, in the outskirts at Atlanta, and seen the plant blazing with its lights," wrote newspaperman Thomas L. Stokes in 1940. "Twenty-four hours a day they were turning out the sheets and the hoods."[2] The money poured in. "I remember seeing drawers full of greenbacks out there at headquarters," said an Atlanta man who had known Simmons. "God alone knows how much they took in those years. They thought it would go on forever."[3]

To understand the Klan's remarkable expansion, it is necessary to try to enter sympathetically into the life of the ordinary people of the time, to understand the appeal of its mystery to imaginations starved by a narrow environment, and to try to feel as they felt the dramatic interest aroused by weird costumes, the spectacular secret initiations in meadow or creek bottom beneath the glare of the fiery crosses, the passwords and special passports, and the night parades through streets lined with awed spectators. "On the night the parade was expected to take place, the sidewalks around the courthouse were packed," wrote an eyewitness of a Klan parade in Eastland County, Texas:

Far away the trill of a bugle was heard and, as those on the nearest corner peered, they saw two ghostly figures on foot, one bearing an American flag and the other a fiery cross. Behind them came the Klansmen, four abreast. No sound was heard but the shuffling of many feet on the pavement, and for half an hour, row after row, they marched. At last the final rank completed the circuit of the square and melted into the darkness.[4]

A close observer of the Klan in Texas made the following suggestive remark to sociologist John Mecklin: "There is a great 'inferiority complex' on the part of the Klan membership—due in part to lack of education—Dallas and Fort Worth (where the Klan is especially strong) being largely populated by men and women reared in obscure town and country places where public schools are short-termed and scarce." Concerning Klan psychology, Mecklin, writing in 1924, described the average man of native-born American stock who filled the Klan's ranks:

He is tossed about in the hurly-burly of our industrial and so called democratic society. Under the stress and strain of social competition he is made to realize his essential mediocrity. Yet according to traditional democratic doctrine he is born free and the equal of the fellow who is out-distancing him in the race. Here is a large and powerful organization offering to solace his sense of defeat by dubbing him a knight of the Invisible Empire for the small sum of ten dollars. Surely knighthood was never offered at such a bargain![5]

The Klan came to Texas in the early fall of 1920. One of the order's top kleagles, Z. R. Upchurch, arrived in Houston in late September to represent the Klan at the annual reunion of the United Confederate Veterans, to be held in the city October 6 to 9, and to survey prospects for adding Texas to the Invisible Empire. Taking advantage of the sentiment for a heroic past rekindled by the presence of the elderly Confederate veterans in the city, Upchurch recruited about one hundred Houston citizens, the number usually required for a Klan chapter, and wired Clarke that the reunion might be an ideal occasion for installing the first Texas chapter. Imperial Wizard Simmons and Clarke, along with Nathan Bedford Forrest III, grandson of the imperial wizard of the original Klan, put in a prereunion appearance to fraternize with leading citizens. "Recruiting went forward discriminately—only men of notable standing taken in," noted Max Bentley, managing editor of the *Houston Chronicle* in an article on the Klan published in *McClure's Magazine* in 1924. He wrote: "The initial roster represented literally a glossary of Houston's *who's who*. The charter members were silk-stocking men from the banks, business houses and professions; and, although organized labor now dominates the Houston, Dallas, and Fort Worth klans, there was no labor element in the beginning."[6]

The Houston race riot of 1917 in which black soldiers of the Twenty-fourth Infantry, provoked by police brutality, mutinied and killed or mortally wounded sixteen whites, including five police officers, contributed to the support the Klan gained among the city's "best citizens." According to Mecklin, "The Klan organizer played upon the fear born of this unpleasant experience to induce many of the leading citizens of Houston to join the Klan as a means of protecting the whites against possible outbreaks by the returned Negro soldiery."[7]

Simmons's first act was to invite reporters to call. He told them that he was reorganizing the old Klan into a patriotic, fraternal, ritualistic society. According to a reporter for the *Houston Chronicle*, he did not mention Catholic "encroachments" or the Jews. "He pictured the klan in the rosy light of an organization of true Americans whose motive was to teach and inspire Americanism as we came to know it during the war. He pictured the klan as being a bulwark of loyalty to the flag and nation." On October 8 a line of marchers and horsemen in Klan garb was a feature of the Confederate Veterans' grand parade through downtown Houston. The robes worn in the parade had been made in a Houston overall factory for $1.50 each. That evening a Klan initiation ceremony was held in a field lighted with flaming crosses near Bellaire, a Houston suburb, and afterward the new klansmen chose "Sam Houston Klan No. 1" as the name of their chapter.[8]

Before leaving Houston, Upchurch appointed George B. Kimbro, part-owner of an ice-cream factory, king kleagle for Texas with full authority to organize the state. Kimbro rented an office in Houston and with a staff of about twenty kleagles began recruiting in a random fashion over the state. The second Klan to be chartered was in Humble, a small oil town north of Houston; Goose Creek had Klan No. 4; Beaumont, No. 7; Wharton County, No. 8; San Antonio, No. 31; Galveston, No. 35; Dallas, No. 66; Wichita Falls, No. 78; Austin, No. 81; El Paso, No. 100; and Fort Worth, No. 101. Only Southwest Texas, with its large Catholic Mexican-American population was relatively immune to the Klan, although there were Klan chapters in Brownsville, Mercedes, Edinburg, McAllen, and other towns along the Rio Grande. Members came in as fast as they could pay their initiation fee and be "naturalized" into the order. By January, 1922, membership had reached between 75,000 and 90,000, and the realm of Texas was organized under its first grand dragon, A. D. Ellis, an Episcopal priest from Beaumont, and divided into five provinces of districts headed by "great titans" with headquarters in Fort Worth, Dallas, Waco, Houston, and San Antonio. Brown Harwood of Fort Worth soon replaced Ellis. The great titan of Province No. 2 was a cheery, outgoing dentist, Hiram Wesley Evans, who had been "exalted cyclops" of the state's largest klavern, Dallas No. 66. Unofficial klanswomen organizations were formed in Dallas and Fort Worth in July, 1922, and the Women of the Invisible Empire of America obtained a Texas corporation charter in September, 1922, though the official Klan did not begin organizing women until 1923. In June, 1923, approximately 1,500 masked and robed klanswomen rode and walked in Fort Worth in the first official parade of its kind in the country.[9]

The Klan's first recruits in a community generally included many of the prominent citizens. "Everywhere I hear, as I heard in my first Texas town, that 'the best people' are among the klansmen," one traveler reported. A student of the Klan in Jefferson County concluded that "the Klan could not have reached the stature it did without the support of the county's political and civic leaders. Without them the organization would have had no real base of power from which to expand." A Dallas klansman explained that one reason why the Klan grew so rapidly in that city was that "Dallas is a strong Masonic city and the Klan grew rapidly among Masons and Shriners." So many Masons joined the Klan that in some communities the Masonic lodge became simply an adjunct of the local Klan chapter. "It's the fun-making, social side of the Masons," an Austin newspaperman was told, "just like the Forty and Eight in the Legion."[10]

Klansmen were expected to practice "Vocational Klanishness"— to trade with Klan businessmen in preference to nonklansmen—and many merchants and professional men joined the organization either out of fear of boycotts or in hopes of increasing their clientele. Politicians who were about to be defeated for reelection or who had never been able to get far in political preferment hoped to push themselves by means of the Klan's strength. They usually tried to build up a personal following among the klansmen. Duncan Aikman of the *El Paso Times* described the "Klan's corps d'élite" in the West Texas city as including the "motor-car magnates, the insurance go-getters, the realtorian archdukes, the slap-on-the-back bankers, the high powered selling dervishes, the dynamic contractors . . . all this massed and gullible Babbittry, which . . . joined the Klan for the greater glory of Protestantism and Better Business." A Dallas newspaperman recalled:

The Klan was quite a threatening organization—people were afraid to belong to it and afraid not to. One of the main reasons for its growth was fear of the boycott on the part of little businesses. And large firms encouraged their employees to join—they also feared the boycott. When an employee of some department store joined, they would introduce him at the next Klan meeting and announce that he was an employee of a particular store. The large stores were run by Jews, but they hedged in that respect.[11]

The white sheets covered some strange bedfellows. In Houston and Fort Worth the Klan enlisted labor support for a time, or at least the support of labor politicians. "According to the tale of the street, the Klan is made up, in the cities at least, mostly of men whose impulse in politics is radical," editorialized the *Dallas Morning News* in August, 1922. "The platform adopted by the Dallas County Democratic convention does not belie that report, while the platform adopted by the Harris County Democratic convention gives it a good deal of corroboration." The Klan-controlled Harris County convention wanted federal judges elected for four-year terms, regarded the open-port law as a "statutory monstrosity" that the legislature should slay, and demanded that unimproved land should "be taxed on the same basis as similar land that has been improved." "Klannishness, city klannishness at least, seems to have political propensities that no one would call staid," the *News* commented.[12]

Other critics of the knights, however, charged that the organization was dominated by big business. "Dallas, the city most thoroughly dominated by the utility interests, is the Klan stronghold," wrote Socialist George Clifton Edwards, a Dallas attorney, in the *Nation*:

At the great Dallas Ku Klux parade the electric company kindly cut off all the downtown lights and let the masked men march in their desired darkness. . . . The campaign manager of the Klan in Dallas was the law partner of the ex-mayor of Dallas who is the president of the Dallas street railway company. This union of fanaticism and finance has swept Dallas and the State.

Robert Duffus, writing in *World's Work*, reported that the Waco Klan had promised employers assistance in the campaign against labor unions, that the Dallas Klan had been organized by the head of the power and transit corporations, and that in Fort Worth, the man who was said to dominate the Texas Klan was a member of a law firm that represented national oil, packing, and power interests and had formerly represented the brewery interests. The *Ferguson Forum*, Jim Ferguson's paper, which was politically anti-Klan, charged that almost all of the men on the Klan steering committee in Dallas were "*representatives of practically every public service corporation in Dallas. On it are representatives of banking and other big financial powers. The same is true in Fort Worth. . . . The Klan administration in Fort Worth has been notoriously under the domination of the utilities and the big corporations.*"[13]

Many Protestant clergymen in Texas welcomed the Klan, seeing it as an agency of moral censorship and a unifying force against the Roman Catholic "menace," and either joined or at least gave it their tacit support. A minister was frequently made either exalted cyclops or kludd (chaplain) of a Klan chapter, and Methodist clergymen J. T. Renfro of Dallas and Alonzo Monk of Arlington left their pulpits to become itinerant Klan lecturers. The Klan did a bit of proselyting here and there, interrupting church services, marching down the aisle in full regalia, and handing the minister gifts of money, "usually trifling amounts," according to one observer. A funeral service in an Eastland church was interrupted by robed and masked figures who entered, placed a cross of red roses on the casket, and marched out. These church visitations served to publicize the order's religiosity. Generally the Protestant church press and conventions in Texas hedged or remained silent on the Klan issue, though some individual clergymen condemned its intolerance and lawless activities. "Never, until the advent of the Ku Klux Klan, did the Baptists persecute anybody," wrote Baptist leader J. B. Cranfill. He continued:

Some of them now are joining in their persecution of the negroes, the Jews, the Catholics and the foreigners because they have to keep step with their Klan companions. By so much, however, as any Baptist anywhere joins hands with any movement and sows the seeds of race prejudice and intolerance that uses subterranean methods of procedure, by that much he loses his grip on the age-long principles of the Baptist people.[14]

Sinners as well as saints joined the Klan, hoping to find haven, if its critics were to be believed. "In many cases the man who lays the lash across the bootlegger's back is not improbably a bootlegger himself," wrote Duffus. "In Dallas 90 per cent of the bootleggers were said to have joined." In his anti-Klan pamphlet *Liberty Dethroned*, Major A. V. Dalrymple of Fort Worth wrote angrily of a class of "Klancrats . . . composed of bootleggers, thugs, skunks and scoundrels, who pole-vaulted into the Klan at the very first opportunity to avoid their quota of tar and feathers." Mrs. Ida M. Darden, secretary of the Southern Tariff Association, confessed tongue in cheek that the Klan pledge to protect womanhood had held some appeal for her until, upon discovering

the names of some of those who were to be custodians of womanly virtue, I received the crowning shock of my life and my confidence broke under the strain. Among those who were to be trusted with this holy mission were men whose record of achievement along this line didn't qualify them for the job. On the other hand, I found on reliable authority that when womanhood was in their presence, it had all it could do to protect itself.

That the Klan's official lecturers were chosen more for oratorical ability than for truthfulness was exemplified by Joe G. Camp of Atlanta, who traveled in that capacity throughout Texas. In a speech at Fort Worth on April 22, 1922, Camp attacked the Klan opposition and then stated that "Attorney General Daugherty is a Klansman and, if the President of the United States is not an obligated Klansman, his sympathies are with the Klan."[15]

While present, anti-Catholicism, anti-Semitism, and antiradicalism were not as significant in the growth of Ku Kluxism in Texas as they were in the industrial states of the northeast, with their large immigrant populations from southern and eastern Europe. According to historian Charles Alexander, writing in 1965, the "distinctive quality" of the Ku Klux Klan in the Southwest was "its motivation, which lay not so much in racism and nativism as a moral authoritarianism." In Texas, Louisiana, Arkansas, and Oklahoma "the Klan was, more than anything else, an instrument for restoring law and order and Victorian morality to the communities, towns and cities of the region. Its coercive activity and its later preoccupation with political contests makes vigilantism and politics the main characteristics of Klan history in the Southwest."[16]

Anti-black prejudice seems to have given little impetus to the Klan's growth in most parts of Texas, although Klansmen committed acts of violence against blacks who crossed the color line and were intimate with white women. A journalist who traveled through the state in 1922 wrote that "the Ku Klux movement hereabouts is not conspicuously anti-Negro." He was told by a half-dozen faculty members of a normal school that, while the Klan did represent a strong determination to prevent "cohabitation and promiscuous intimacy between whites and blacks," its main purpose was "to inculcate a wholesome respect for law and order, including the laws against 'bootlegging' and gambling." The few blacks with whom he had an opportunity to talk were not, he said, greatly disturbed by it as far as the security of their own people were concerned. They said, as others did, that it was mainly an antibootlegging and anti–home-breaking organization, as far as they could see. The Knight's campaign of systematic terror—warnings, whippings, tarring and feathering—was aimed mostly at bootleggers, gamblers, pimps, child molesters, abortionists, wayward husbands and wives, wife beaters, and other offenders against morals. At meetings of the Dallas klavern, members would rise and say they knew a man who was running around with another man's wife or that another acquaintance was not doing right and should be taken care of. "Give his name to the kligrapp (secretary)," the cyclops would say. A former Dallas klansman declared that "most of the cases where the Klan took the law in their own hands were with moral degenerates." "The advantage of the protection afforded by the K.K.K. over the law is that it can rid the community of undesirables before they commit some serious offense," James T. Stacey explained in a letter to the *Dallas Morning*

News. "The law must wait until the offense has been committed. Another advantage is a doubt does not have to be so 'serious' before a conviction can be had."[17]

Texas newspapers recorded something like eighty whippings in the state in one year. Among the victims from February to July, 1921, were a Houston lawyer accused of fraternizing with blacks, a Houston merchant who annoyed high-school girls, a Webster stockman, a Brenham marshal, a Beaumont doctor accused of performing abortions, a Sour Lake justice of the peace, a Brenham man charged with disloyalty during the war and speaking German, a Houston attorney charged with annoying young girls, a Dallas service-station operator, two Goose Creek oil-field workers said to be undesirable citizens, a Goose Creek jitney driver, a Bay City banker charged with domestic troubles and infidelity, and a Timson man who had recently left his wife. A black bellboy in Dallas, accused of pandering for white women, was whipped, and the letters KKK were burned on his forehead with acid. Masked men castrated a Houston black dentist for alleged association with a white woman. A one-sided race war almost resulted when it was rumored that the blacks were threatening to retaliate, and whites armed themselves. The Klan suddenly emerged from anonymity and patrolled the streets. A Klan official appeared at the police station wearing a deputy sheriff's badge and arbitrarily took charge. A brigadier general of the National Guard had to be called in, "and for a time the city was perilously close to martial law."[18]

Texas's wave of violence crested in May, 1922, when nine blacks were burned, shot, or hanged by unmasked bands of white men. No member of the various mobs was arrested. On May 24, Governor Neff issued a statement deploring the mob spirit. "The growing tendency of mob law is indeed a sad commentary on our civilization," he said. The governor suggested that the legislature pass a law providing that a person accused of mob violence would be tried in a county other than the county in which the violence occurred. Two days later, in Waco, Neff's hometown, a young black accused of murdering a white man and attacking his woman companion was shot and killed by the girl's father after she exclaimed, "That's the man, Papa!" A mob took the body from the undertaker's, dragged it behind a truck to the public square, and burned it in the presence of five thousand spectators, many of them women. In early June thousands of armed white men in motorcars from almost every town in Limestone, Freestone, and Navarro counties scoured the hills and valleys in a fruitless all-night search for a band of blacks who had fought a gun battle with a posse. Panic-stricken blacks living between Kirvin and Simsboro left their cabins and hid in the timbered bottomlands. ". . . it is believed that they are too badly demoralized to again become aggressive," reported the *Dallas Morning News.*

The Klan almost always denied that it was involved in acts of terrorism, saying that anyone with a grudge could put on a mask and go prowling or send a threatening note signed with Klan symbols or initials to "make it stick." Still, Charles Alexander believed that "responsibility for a large majority of the vigilante forays in the Southwest rested heavily—and justly—on the secret fraternity." After reading accounts of about two hundred acts of masked violence in the region in the years 1921 to 1924, Alexander concluded that "most of these deeds involved a few Klansmen acting independently of their leaders." [19]

The Klan obtained immunity from punishment or even investigation through the simple strategy of taking into the membership district and county judges, district and county attorneys, justices of the peace, sheriffs and deputy sheriffs, United States marshals, constables, deputy constables, police commissioners, chiefs of police, policemen, mayors, newspaper editors, and reporters. In the summer of 1921 a king kleagle told a newly recruited kleagle that Sam Houston Klan No. 1 had engaged in some terroristic activity but felt secure from interference by the law because it "ran things its own way, and it had the mayor, the police force and practically all of the politicians." Fort Worth Klan No. 101 tarred and feathered a local gambler, paraded openly in the business district, and established firm control of the city government. At Waco police officers arrested three hooded men with their tarred-and-feathered victim; the McLennan County Grand Jury voted "no bill." The sheriff of Collin County was asked to join. He replied that he was unwilling to do so because his oath as a klansman might conflict with his oath of office. He was told that if the Klan contemplated any illegal action his brother members would safeguard his conscience by carrying it out without his knowledge. [20]

In Dallas, a Klan stronghold, it was reported that at least sixty-eight men had been whipped in the spring of 1922, most of them at a special Klan whipping meadow along the Trinity River bottom. No arrests were made. "The Police Commissioner in Dallas we believe to be a klansman," General Martin M. Crane, an anti-Klan leader, informed

Governor Neff. He also reported that "the Chief of Police is a klansman, as we understand, and nearly all of the police officers are klansmen. We understand that the Sheriff is a klansman—nobody denies it.
The Deputy Sheriff, we believe to be a klansman." Crane asked: "If the
Police Commissioner in Austin will refused to enforce the law against
klansmen, have we any right to expect results in Dallas? And as the Ku
Klux Klan was the obstruction to an enforcement of the law in Austin,
are you not normally certain that it is likewise the obstruction to an
enforcement of the law in Dallas?" A Dallas newspaperman recalled
that "the Klan's control of the police force was the main influence in
the city because it scared the people. It was pretty well talked around
that no Klansman would be fined in Police Court; not that it was true,
but the people believed it, so it might as well have been." [21]

The Klan dominated the Austin Police Department and the Travis
County Sheriff's Office, as the following incident demonstrated. Jeddie
Jeans, an Austin gambler, was seized on a downtown street; driven to a
clump of bushes east of the city; whipped, tarred, and feathered; and
then spilled out of a car in an alley on East Fifth Street with his own
pistol dangling from a cord around his neck. The city detective who
interviewed him, the chief of police, the police commissioner, and the
deputy sheriff who was sent to investigate the matter but did not
bother to question the victim refused to tell the Travis County Grand
Jury whether they had joined the Klan, while the county sheriff admitted paying his entrance fee of $16.50 to a kleagle at the Driskill Hotel.
The grand jury reported:

So, Jeans, if punished by the Klan, was operated on by plain clothes men of the
order, and when he returned to Austin his case was investigated by the uni-
formed crew who wore the badges of constituted law enforcement officers and
whose membership in the Klan is to be presumed by their refusal to testify
because "it might tend to incriminate them," when asked if they had joined the
order. The poor little cowed gambler was merely transferred from the brutal
operation in the brush to the sham performance in the city! [22]

In March, 1922, District Judge James Hamilton had to threaten to
jail Austin Police Commissioner J. B. Copeland and F. G. Reynolds,
secretary of the Austin lodge of the Woodmen of the World, before
they agreed to testify to the grand jury in the Peeler Clayton case.
Clayton had been shot to death on December 16, 1921, by a group of
men stationed in front of a downtown building known as Ku Klux Klan
Hall, where Austin Klan No. 81 was holding an initiation. [23]

Until the summer of 1921 resistance to the Klan had been passive. Men were watching it with growing fear, Catholics and Jews were restive and resentful, and a few black newspapers had protested, but nothing like organized resistance had been attempted. Citizens who opposed the Klan because it bred social discord expressed their feelings cautiously from prudent motives. It was apparent that no effective step could be taken except under the leadership of the very men who were eligible for Klan membership: American-born white Protestants. And so it came about. Resistance crystallized as suddenly as the Klan itself had arrived. Klansmen touched it off in Tenaha when they kidnapped from a hotel a young woman whom they thought to be a bigamist, stripped her to the waist, beat her with a wet rope, and applied tar and feathers. This act attracted nationwide attention, aroused public opinion, and afforded a tangible starting place for the first concerted assault upon the Invisible Empire.[24]

Some of the anti-Klan resistance was in the tradition of frontier individualism and vigilantism. An anti-Klan organization in South Texas announced that it would use "hot lead" in warring on the Klan. Former District Judge Erwin J. Clark of Waco found a note slipped through the mail slot in his office door: "Judge Clark: You are one of the leaders of the K.K.K. in Texas. You must leave the State in thirty days or we will plant you. (Signed) Anti-Ku Klux Klan of Texas." A West Texas man was warned anonymously that he "had better stop talking against the Klan." He replied by issuing handbills offering five hundred dollars to any klansman who would repeat the warning in person, and although he spent several hours walking up and down the main street of his hometown, Winchester in hand and revolver in belt, no one stepped forward to collect the reward. Lea Beatty of Lockhart, a former member of the legislature, warned that "if the Ku Klux order was not soon destroyed, there would be a number of first-class funerals in Lockhart and other parts of the State." "I am 75 years old," Beatty announced, "but I stand ready to take up my shotgun and go out in defense of civilized and lawful government. The time has come for us to speak out as to whether we favor a visible government or an invisible government."[25]

With only four opposing votes, delegates to the annual convention of the Texas Chamber of Commerce, meeting in Dallas, adopted a resolution condemning the Klan and petitioning Governor Neff to use all the means at his command to enforce the law against the organization, "or any other body of masked men, in the protection of the lives, liberty and property of citizens." A Fort Worth man opposed, saying that some of the very best men of his city were members and that the Klan existed because there had not been proper enforcement of the law. The resolution was introduced by the president of the chamber, Joseph Stephen Cullinan, a wealthy Houston oilman. Cullinan's parents were natives of County Clare, Ireland, and on March 17, Saint Patrick's Day, the Irish national flag always flew at Shadyside, the Cullinans' Houston home. In 1922 Cullinan began the yearly tradition of flying a black skull-and-crossbones flag atop the Petroleum Building, his headquarters in downtown Houston. When amused and puzzled citizens asked why, Cullinan always gave the same reply: "The display of the Jolly Roger is intended as a warning to privilege and oppression within and without the law—the latter including witch-burners, fanatics, and the like who fail to realize or ignore the fact that liberty is a right and not a privilege."[26]

The American Legion in some places denounced the Klan and in other places refused to do so. The Masons officially outlawed it and Andrew L. Randell, the grand master of Masonry in Texas, went over the state "giving the lie to the kleagles who had recruited heavily among young Masons." The Texas Bar Association denounced the Klan, and in San Antonio a young lawyer named Maury Maverick fought it, headed off a Klan-sponsored movement to prevent violinist Fritz Kreisler from playing in the city, and tried to liberalize the local bar association. As its president he edited a little paper, the *Whereas*, for which he wrote an article entitled "Koo Klucks Kondemned." Maverick, as the self-appointed "Imperious Gizzard," had held a "called meeting" attended only by himself, at which the "Koo Klucks" had been judged as wearers of nightgowns who were "fully as mentally developed as an ape."[27]

A few sheriffs and mayors announced that no masked Klan parades would be allowed in their towns. In September, 1921, Mayor Stanton Allen of Bartlett, about ten miles north of Austin, heard that the local Klan intended to parade. He hurriedly issued a proclamation forbidding it and ordered the city marshal to arrest any hooded and robed individuals who appeared on the streets. The Klan called off its parade. That same month El Paso klansmen informed police officers that they would stage a downtown parade. Chief of Police Peyton Edwards merely said no. Sheriff Seth Orndorff warned that he would round up all Klan members who took part in a masked parade. A reporter reminded him that a Klan parade in Houston had ended at the Harris County Courthouse and had last been seen disappearing into the section of the building housing the sheriff's office and asked him what he would do under such circumstances. "If they came into the court house they would stay in the jail department of that building," the *El Paso Times* quoted the sheriff as replying. The parade was not held.[28]

On October 1, 1921, Sheriff Bob Buchanan of McLennan County and two deputies tried to stop a fifty-member Klan parade in Lorena, fourteen miles south of Waco. Buchanan's attempt to tear the mask from the man carrying the American flag at the front of the parade precipitated a wild melee in which ten people were wounded, one mortally. For his pains Buchanan was shot through the right lung and right leg and was sweepingly rebuked by the McLennan County Grand Jury. A few months later county and town law officers in Laredo, on the Rio Grande, armed about one hundred special deputies and set up a machine gun to prevent a Klan parade. Sheriff John W. Saye of Young County told citizens: "I do not consider any organization or association that wears masks, operates in the night, and carries guns to perpetuate their purpose and to prevent their identification law-abiding citizens. So far as I know no deputy on my force is a member of the Ku Klux Klan, and should I find that there is such a member, he will find himself outside of the force." Two years later, however, Saye was defeated for reelection by a vote ratio of 4 to 1, suggesting that support for the Klan was still strong.[29]

Although one journalist estimated that "probably ninety per cent of the newspapers were represented in the Klan, usually through their advertising departments," several large Texas papers went after the hooded order. "Boys, you'd better disband," admonished the *Houston Chronicle*. "You'd better have one more meeting and adjourn *sine die*. You'd better take off your sheets, your banners, your masks, your regalia, and make one fine bonfire." The *El Paso Times*, under the leadership of editor James S. Black, aided by the "pungent pen" of editorial writer Duncan Aikman, conducted a vigorous fight against the Klan. On September 15, 1921, in an editorial entitled "The Ku Klux," Black reviewed some of the Klan's activities in other parts of the nation. "Apparently the Ku Klux with his ghostly trappings has not considered El Paso a safe place for night riding with masked face, but the general opinion elsewhere seems to be that it essays to set up a sort of super-government," he wrote. "And that is not Americanism." Black tried to collect the names of Klan members. He had some reporters steal into meetings. Others took down license-plate numbers of cars at the meetings. A reporter was hired to become an undercover klansman. Black's list turned up the names of several policemen, who had to sign affidavits that they were not Klan members. In September, 1922, District Attorney C. L. Vowell called Klan organizer C. L. Sirmans before a court of inquiry with Justice of the Peace Clark Wright presiding. Vowell forced Sirman to produce a roll of Klan members. Four police officers were fired.[30]

Two Dallas newspapers, the *Morning News* and the *Dispatch*, fought the Klan. The *News* made its stand clear after the Klan's first parade in Dallas on the evening of May 21, 1921:

The spectacle of eight hundred masked and white-gowned men parading the streets under banners proclaiming them Knights of the Ku Klux Klan and self-appointed guardians of the community's political, social and moral welfare . . . was a slander on Dallas, because the only conditions which could be given to excuse the organization of such a body do not exist. White supremacy is not imperiled. Vice is not rampant. The constituted agencies of government are still regnant. And if freedom is endangered, it is by the redivivus of the mob spirit in the disguising garb of the Ku Klux Klan.[31]

The *News* systematically reported every known instance of mob action, ran the *New York World*'s syndicated serial exposé of the Klan, and called for a law "making it at least prima facie evidence of unlawfulness to be abroad in a mask and disguised." A Knott cartoon in the October 8, 1921, issue of the *News* showed the familiar figure of "Father Texas" hit in the eye with tar and feathers with the caption "Don't the Boys Realize They're Giving the Old Man a Black Eye?" Noting that there had been six lynchings in Texas in 1921, four during a two-week period in December, the *News* asserted that all the lynchings had taken place following the appearance in Texas of

organized, systematic, oath-bound, masked mob action on a scale never before known. These mob appearances have been repeatedly attended by murder, breakings of jail, brutal assaults upon bound victims, and other forms of lawlessness calculated to appeal to the sort of the cowardice that seeks safety in numbers in disguise of face and person . . . The mockery of pretending to employ terrorism in the enforcement of law was never shown more blatantly than it has been shown in Texas during these last months.[32]

The *Dallas Dispatch*'s campaign was conducted by Glenn Pricer of its editorial staff. A fellow journalist wrote that Pricer had the good sense to realize, when Dallas was captured lock, stock and barrel by the Ku Klux Klan, that every man who joined wasn't an idiot or a fanatic simply because he had wandered into a silly organization. Pricer conducted a campaign that addressed itself to the horsesense of the ordinary man. He probably struck the most telling blows delivered against the Ku Klux Klan anywhere in this country.

At first Dallas klansmen operated in secret, but one night Pricer and some of his reporters went out to their meeting place in Fair Park and took down the license numbers of all the cars, checked the county office for the names of the owners, and then published about one hundred names in the *Dispatch*. "That certainly made some people mad," Pricer said later, adding that when friends came to his house "they often carried guns because they were afraid harm might come to them or to me."[33]

The Dallas Klan struck back at the papers with threats, subscription cancellations, and boycotts of stores that advertised in them. It was rumored that the *News* was controlled by Catholics. Joe G. Camp of Atlanta, an official Klan lecturer, characterized the paper in a Fort Worth speech as "a dirty, slimy, Catholic-owned sheet." Each of the hundreds of inquiries and accusations was answered with a personal letter by George Bannerman Dealey, president of the A. H. Belo Corporation, or by one of the staff. "The *News* is neither owned nor controlled by members of the Catholic Church," the letters explained, giving the church affiliation of each editor and principal stockholder and adding, "but the *News* does believe in religious tolerance for all sects." In the meantime, advertising fell off appreciably, and circulation had dropped by 3,000 at the end of 1922. When its mother paper, the *Galveston Daily News*, was sold to W. L. Moody, Jr., on March 22, 1923, the Klan crowed that the *News* had its back to the wall and that it too would soon be sold or bankrupt.[34]

District judges began charging their grand juries to investigate masked violence. "The American flag has no place at the head of a procession of men who hide their faces behind a mask," said Judge E. B. Muse of Dallas. On May 23, 1921, Judge W. H. Davidson vigorously denounced Klan activities in Beaumont and urged the grand jury to bring indictments against fifteen masked men who had whipped, tarred, and feathered Dr. J. S. Paul (accused by the Klan of performing two abortions) and had given him forty-eight hours to leave town. He said:

Get the names and return indictments in this court. Indict every one of them. I don't care how big they are, indict them. I have heard it said that it might not be popular for a Judge to condemn this affair, but I pass by these fool insinuations. I think our Judges should not be concerned in the administration of the law as to whether it is popular or not. As far as I am concerned, I don't care whether anybody likes it or not.

Judge E. A. McDowell of the Sixtieth District Court in Beaumont also denounced Klan violence and later in the year emerged "as the number one Klan foe in Jefferson County." [35]

Judge James R. Hamilton of the Criminal District Court of Travis County empaneled a grand jury for its June term with general instructions on criminal offenses. At that time the Klan had not made its presence known in Austin; there had been no threats or warnings, no floggings or boycotts. Hamilton recessed the grand jury and ordered the members back to attend to some unfinished business on Monday, June 27, 1921. On the Saturday night preceding the jury's reconvening, the Klan posted placards with captions in flaming red letters on telegraph poles, in the public parks, and even on a post in front of the county courthouse:

WARNING!

The vagabond must go.
The idler must go.
The rounder must go.
The pimp must go.
The bootlegger must go.
The gambler must go.
The agitator must go.
The lewd woman must go.
The houses of ill fame must go.
The innocent law abiding citizen need have no fear.
One hundred per cent Americanism must prevail.

THE KU KLUX KLAN

"We have an order here now that will do away with your courts and juries," Judge Hamilton was told, as he was about to go into the grand jury. His answer was to instruct its members "to make a thorough investigation of this unlawful, clandestine organization and of the peace officers of this city and county." Instructions were also given "to take such action as the weight of reason dictates and the law directs, under the advice of the County and District Attorneys." [36]

Hamilton's charge was widely publicized and brought him com-
mendations from anti-Klan citizens. A Marlin attorney wrote the
judge:

Read your charge to the Grand Jury in the morning paper on the Ku Klux. I
want to congratulate you on your courage and your respect for the Constitution
and Laws of Texas. If all of [the] judges in Texas had the courage to denounce
this masked lawlessness as you have done, these night-riding organizations
would soon be crushed under the weight of public opinion.

On October 3, 1921, Hamilton renewed his war on the Klan, again instructing the Travis County Grand Jury to investigate the organization.
"You cannot stop crime in this country by working at night with a
bucket of tar and a sack of feathers," he asserted. "Civilization and
good government begin and end at the polls and in the jury box." On
that October 3 seven other district judges, in their grand-jury charges,
denounced the Klan and called for a return to observance of law and
respect for constituted authority. The Klan was so feared, however,
and its oath was so binding on members that no indictments were returned until 1923.[37]

On July 25, 1921, during the first special session of the Thirty-
seventh Legislature, Wright Patman of Cass County introduced a resolution in the House condemning the operation of masked men in Texas
and instructing the imperial wizard to keep his representatives out of
the state. Patman declared that where laws were not adequate it was
the duty of the people to petition the legislature for redress. "Don't
put on robes and masks," he pleaded, "and subject a man or woman to
such outrages as have been committed in Texas recently." He vigorously attacked Simmons: "That man is a party to every act these
masked men have performed in Texas. . . . Who is this self-constituted
authority to request peace officers to report lax enforcement of the law
to him?" He warned that if the legislature by its silence encouraged
the Klan "we, also, are parties to the crimes." Patman was cheered
when he added, "Any state official who has taken the oath of office and
then taken the oath of allegiance to the Ku Klux Klan should resign his
office and go home." "There was never but one perfect man," he concluded, "and that man was crucified by the Ku Klux Klan."[38]

Patman and forty-eight other representatives petitioned Neff to
submit the Klan issue for legislation because the penalty for its acts was
not severe enough. Patman believed that the governor would do so if

the House went on record as favoring it. "The present Ku Klux Klan is tearing down the very thing the original organization was formed to safeguard—the privilege of a community to elect its own officers," he declared. "I want to tell the citizens of Texas we would pass such a law if the Governor will submit it." Although the jittery House tabled Patman's resolution 69 to 54, Neff, to Patman's surprise, submitted to the legislature "in order that they may be strengthened and made more enforcible, all the criminal laws of the State, together with the code of criminal procedure, for whatever legislation you may deem wise." Patman then prepared three bills, the principal one making it an offense punishable by fine or imprisonment for two or more persons to conspire together to injure, oppress, threaten, or intimidate any person or go in disguise upon the highway or on the premises of another with such intent. His other bills provided penalties for "carnal intercourse" between whites and blacks and for wife desertion and nonsupport of children. Patman said that through these bills he was seeking to remove the causes for the formation of secret organizations like the Klan.[39]

Patman's anti-Klan bill was given an unfavorable report by the House Committee on Criminal Jurisprudence, and although the other two measures were reported favorably, all three died on the House calendar when the first called session ended on August 16. Patman won a victory, however, on August 10, when the House voted 63 to 54 to table a resolution offered by John Davis of Dallas and sixteen other members allowing Caleb A. Ridley, pastor of the Central Baptist Church of Atlanta, to deliver an address on the Klan that evening in the House chamber. Making the motion to table, Patman said that he was opposed to "lending that much encouragement to the Ku Klux Klan. If a representative of the Ku Klux Klan wants to speak in Austin, let him go somewhere else than the Texas State Capitol." Patman, who shared a desk with Sam E. Johnson, Jr. (the father of Lyndon B. Johnson), recalled in an interview in 1972: "Sam Johnson took my side too. We had a few talks around and members came to our desk and we organized a little opposition to it there and beat it. He was up ready to speak. That's when the Ku Klux issue started in the legislature of Texas."[40]

The anti-Klan forces in Texas wanted Governor Neff to help their cause by denouncing the Klan by name for taking the law into its own hands. On June 17, addressing the Texas National Guard at Camp Mabry, near Austin, Neff declared that the "National Guard stands for law and order and is against lawlessness whether lawlessness wears a mask and marches through the streets of our cities at midnight, or whether lawlessness unshields its sword of anarchy in broad, open daylight." Although he failed to mention the Klan by name, Neff's statement seemed to condemn its methods and satisfied most opponents of the Klan for the time being. After his speech to the guard, however, Neff made no further comment about the Klan, and as the wave of masked violence continued, criticism of his silence mounted. "Texas waits . . . upon the word of the Governor," editorialized the *Dallas Morning News* on October 7, 1921:

Mr. Neff owes it to his office, to himself and to his State to come out plainly and voice the sentiments of outraged justice, trampled upon statutes and cruelly stricken down fidelity to duty. The friends of the Governor wonder at his silence. The friends of orderly administration of the law grieve at it. The time has come for outspoken fearlessness in Texas.

A few days later, however, Neff tendered the "entire civil and military power of the State" to McLennan County officials investigating the Lorena riot, along with a statement that "the law can and should be enforced only through the duly constituted authorities of the Government. No individual and no organization, however large, should be above the law." The *News* commended his remarks and told its readers: "The Governor of Texas has sounded a call for obedience to and support of the law. All good citizens will get the cobwebs out of their brains and heed it." In answer to a request from Neff, Attorney General W. A. Keeling ruled on October 15 that "all efforts of persons under any name they may have assumed to better the moral conditions of the country through the medium of threats, fear, intimidation and personal violence, is a violation of the spirit and letter of the Constitution and laws of Texas" and that every illegal act performed by them "would involve the guilt of all parties having knowledge or a general purpose to do illegal acts, or the actual knowledge of an illegal act." This ruling also applied to masked parades, "where such parade is a part of and in furtherance of a purpose to do some act which would be in violation of law." [41]

Marcellus E. Foster, president of the Houston Chronicle Publishing Company, wrote Neff that, while the governor's statements in regard to law and order had been "very helpful recently," he was inclined to believe that two or three leading Texas newspapers had done even more to suppress masked lawlessness. He chided the governor for his inactivity:

I believe that you could have been of very great help early in the year and could have perhaps prevented many lawless acts and probably some tragedies if you had come forward in a ringing message, calling the Klu [sic] Klux by name and denouncing that order or any other order which went out under cover of darkness and behind masks to take the law in its own hands.

To this rebuke Neff replied mildly: "You and I are working to the same end. We may travel, at times, very different roads, but the goal, I am sure, is the same."[42]

In January, 1922, Neff acted against lawlessness in the oil boom-town Mexia, in Freestone County, about seventy miles southeast of Dallas. Local authorities were either unwilling or unable to deal with the bootlegging, gambling, prostitution, and robbery. On January 12 the governor declared martial law in and around Mexia and directed a National Guard unit under Brigadier General Jacob Wolters and Texas Rangers headed by Captain Frank Hamer to take charge. In a state-ment defending his action, Neff said: "I was unwilling for the law to bow at the foot of the bootlegger, the gambler, the thug, and the crook. I was unwilling for crime to find a protecting shelter in the very center of Texas civilization." He added that "martial law will remain in force until every vestige of lawlessness is swept clean from every square foot of the Mexia community." According to Neff, more than three thou-sand persons left Mexia the first day after martial law was declared. "These three thousand were a part of the outlaws who were operating there, and they wanted to get away while getting away was good."[43]

Martial law was maintained for forty-seven days, and the area cov-ered was extended from time to time until it included all of Freestone County and a large part of Limestone County. It was lifted on March 1, 1922, when local citizens accepted a law-and-order plan suggested by General Wolters and pledged to assist local officers in enforcing the law. That day the Mexia Ku Klux Klan, No. 47, at a meeting held "somewhere in Mexia," endorsed Neff's action in establishing martial law and deplored the conditions that had made it necessary; approved and endorsed Wolters's plan, "whereby we hope to regain our former position as a law-abiding people in the eyes of the world"; and pledged their united efforts as an organization—"and our numbers are legion"— in upholding the dignity of the law. "We hereby serve notice on the

lawless element of our population because of the withdrawal of the
state constabulary force, we will not countenance any of the acts of lawlessness and violence that was so prevalent in our midst sixty days
ago," the Mexia Klan warned. "If your acts are such as merit court action we will see that you are carried to court. If the courts cannot handle your case or will not do so, we will handle it ourselves in our
own way." [44]

Following his declaration of martial law in Mexia, Neff made another appeal "To the People of Texas" for a vigorous campaign in behalf
of law and order, to which document he subscribed himself "Yours for
the law." In an address to the state convention of the Anti-Saloon
League of Texas in Fort Worth on January 17, he charged that "Crime—
cold, cruel, calculating crime—has been organized and commercialized
in Texas" and "it is now one of the established industries of the State. It is
bold and insolent. It is struggling for social and political recognition and
is challenging the forces of righteousness and making claims to respec-
tability in this state." Neff cited nonenforcement of the Prohibition laws
as the major cause of increased crime, with the suspended-sentence
law and a weakening of the criminal code as contributing factors. "The
law no longer has terror for evildoers," he charged. "We have minimized punishment for crime until it has stripped the law of its power.
A traditional and parasitic growth of technicalities has sucked the life
blood out of the penal code of Texas. Therefore lawlessness is rampant.
The wonder is not that so many guilty men escape, but that in our
present system any guilty man is ever convicted." Neff pledged to continue his cleanup campaign to the limit of his powers and to seek new
laws to further law enforcement. "While I am Governor," he said, in
speaking of Mexia, "no band of criminals will ever take charge of a community as long as a Texas ranger can pull a trigger." [45]

Neff, however, still refused to discuss the Klan or to condemn the
organization by name. When asked on March 23 for an expression of
his attitude toward its activities and mob lawlessness, he replied: "I
can add nothing to my Fort Worth law and order speech. In that
speech I used vigorous language in denouncing acts of lawlessness of all
kinds, whether by mobs or individuals, and I can not make my position
any clearer at this time. I stand for the strict enforcement of all the
laws of the land and this is all there is to it." In a *Dallas Morning News*
interview Senator H. L. Darwin of Lamar County said that, although
a governor of Texas was "mighty hard to beat for a second term," nevertheless a candidate who would get out against Neff on an anti-Klan

platform would give him "an awful tussle." "The people are tired of floggings and mob violence," Darwin said. "They are thoroughly aroused and they can not understand why their Governor has never taken a positive stand in the matter." Following publication of the interview in the March 24 issue of the *News*, Darwin, who was staying at the Adolphus Hotel in Dallas, received more than one hundred phone calls before noon, both local and long distance, urging him to run against Neff on an anti-Klan platform.[46]

Neff's silence was contrasted unfavorably with Louisiana Governor John Parker's recent statement calling on his state's officers to "suppress with an iron hand the evil of ku kluxism where it raises its head" and promising to seek an antimask law at the approaching legislative session. Said former Texas Governor Oscar B. Colquitt: "Governor Parker of Louisiana has spoken in no uncertain terms in regard of the K.K.K. Texas would appreciate to have her Governor speak no less decisively." Some Texans interpreted Neff's refusal to condemn the Klan by name as evidence that he himself was a member, but the governor told a reporter for the *Dallas News* that he did not belong to the Klan, did not intend to become a member, and had never been approached about joining. In one of his strongest statements to date Neff declared: "There is no occasion for any kind of masked organization in this country in connection with the enforcement of the law. All our laws should be enforced through the properly organized channels of the courts." He indicated that the whole executive force of the state, including the Texas National Guard if necessary, was at the command of law-enforcement officials in Dallas or elsewhere to put down floggings or to apprehend men who meted out punishment from behind masks. "I do not think that I need say any more," was his only response to other questions regarding the Klan.[47]

The most serious threat to the political activity of the Klan in the Dallas area was the Dallas County Citizens' League, formed on April 4, 1922, at a meeting of five thousand citizens in the Municipal Auditorium. The organization adopted resolutions deploring the existence of a secret order that engaged in terrorism. Said a league pamphlet: "Its opposition is based on the broad ground that the Klan is unlawful in that it cannot exist and function without violating the Constitution and certain statutes of the State, and that it is un-American because it can not exist and function without destroying that political and religious freedom that is the glory of our institutions."[48]

All candidates for office in Dallas County and some candidates for

Congress received from the league copies of an extensive question-naire. The first three questions were "Are you now a member of the organization known as the Ku Klux Klan? Is it your purpose or inten-tion to affiliate hereafter in any way with the Ku Klux Klan? Are you in sympathy with the purposes, practices, and objectives of the Ku Klux Klan?" "The difference between the Ku Klux Klan and the Citizens' League is fundamental," a league official declared. "There is no place to compromise. We want to know whether the officers that we elect believe that they have a right to take an oath to the Ku Klux Klan which will prevent their answering questions propounded by a court either State or Federal which are necessary to the ends of justice." The league asked Dallas Sheriff Dan Harston to provide the names of depu-ties who were klansmen. "We want this information so that we can make it public. We think all of the people are entitled to it. The mem-bers of the Ku Klux Klan, of course, have this information. Those who are not members are equally entitled to it."[49]

General Martin M. Crane, attorney general of Texas during Gov-ernor Charles Culberson's administration, was chairman of the league. He sought Neff's endorsement of the organization's course: "We do not wish a general statement as to the enforcement of the law, but what we do want is a statement from you condemning this oath-bound organiza-tion that puts its klan obligations above the law of the land. . . . I will thank you for an immediate response to the end that we may have the benefit of your official influence and power." When Neff remained si-lent on this and later requests, Crane ended the correspondence on June 21, informing the governor:

Our entire committee has been very much disappointed that no . . . word has ever yet come from you. I might add this further statement that so far as I was advised, every member of the Executive Committee, including Governor Col-quitt, were really anxious to support you for Governor. If their enthusiasm has been chilled in any way (and with some of them it has very much) it is because they believed that you were dodging the issue of the Ku Klux Klan, when you ought to have spoken out. This is frankly the situation. With me the incident is closed.[50]

On April 6, Mayor Sawnie Aldredge of Dallas issued a public statement saying that the Klan "has brought discord into this—a peaceful city; has set neighbor against neighbor, and has fanned the flames of prejudice" and urging the Dallas Klan to disband. He asked city employees who were members of the Klan to resign from the orga-

nization at once. He also asked the Dallas Citizens' League to disband
in the interest of harmony, but the league, while commending the
mayor's course, wanted indubitable proof that the Dallas Klan had disbanded before ceasing its activities. After a Klan meeting on April 8
members announced that the local organization saw no reason to disband. The Klan, however, said that it was willing to discontinue
masked parades, upheld constituted government, was against all forms
of law violations, was 100 percent American, and was willing to have a
local committee of nonklansmen attend a meeting and observe all of its
secret work (the Klan offered suggestions for the personnel of the committee). The Klan hotly denied any responsibility for recent outrages
in the Dallas area. It referred to its charitable work, notably a $40,000
contribution to Hope College, a Dallas institution for unfortunate
children.[51]

The Dallas Citizens' League endorsed a slate of candidates who
publicly opposed the Klan in the upcoming county elections. The Klan
then held a rally for candidates who had not been endorsed by the
league. "We are beating them here, as I am advised, very badly,"
Crane wrote on June 5. "I am advised that the better element, who
went into it on the impulse, are dropping out. They are now recruiting
with members not near so desirable as formerly—but even with all of
these our organization is much stronger than theirs. This is the information that I get from various sources." Crane's sources were mistaken. In the Democratic primary on July 22 all but one of the Klan-
supported candidates won, including Shelby Cox, who ran for district
attorney against the incumbent Maury Hughes, who had launched an
investigation of flogging. That night the victorious klansmen paraded
triumphantly through downtown Dallas. Marching at the front of the
unmasked parade were Cox, Sheriff Dan Harston, and Jack Thornton,
a prominent knight. The *Dallas Morning News* said that the election
was "probably the most decisive victory every achieved by any party or
political or quasi-political organization in the history of Dallas County."
The following year anti-Klan Mayor Aldredge and the rest of his ticket
were defeated for reelection by a margin of almost 3 to 1. "For the next
two years [1922–24] we lived in a community where every city and
county office was held by a member of the Klan or by a man who had
made peace with it," wrote John William Rogers in his history of
Dallas.[52]

A wave of Klan violence in Jefferson County in February and

March, 1922, led to the formation of a Citizens' Executive Committee in Beaumont to combat the Klan. On March 25, 1922, one hundred business and professional men signed a petition condemning mob violence and announced that a mass meeting would be held at the American Legion Hall on March 28. About sixteen hundred citizens attended and appointed a committee to "take steps to crush mob activity in Beaumont." Acting under the direction of Mayor B. A. Steinhagen, City Manager George Roark announced that all city employees would be required to sign an affidavit stating whether they were or had been members of the Klan. Anyone refusing to answer would be immediately dismissed, though employees who had resigned from the Klan and could prove it would be given consideration. "It is inimical to the public interest for any employee of the city to be a member of the Ku Klux Klan, and no member of such organization shall remain in the employ of the city," said the mayor in a public statement. A few days later, after almost all of the two hundred employees had been questioned, none admitted membership in the Klan.[53]

The Citizens' Committee sent a questionnaire to every state, county, and city official in Beaumont asking, "Are you a member of the Ku Klux Klan?" The officials were also asked whether they were connected or affiliated in any way with the Klan or with any organization that was in any way connected or affiliated with the Klan. "Your answers to these questions will be published," the committee warned. "If your answers are not received by the 6th day of April, 1922, that fact will be published." All but four public officials answered the questions in the negative. A few days later the grand jury called upon the Klan to disband, explaining that "even assuming that those responsible for its original construction, organized it with the purest motives, it is evident that a 'Frankesten [sic] Monster' has been created, which is no longer under control." On April 26 the Citizens' Committee filed a petition in district court asking for the removal of Sheriff Tom Garner from office on the grounds that he had become a member of the Klan in the spring of 1921 and that his oath to the Invisible Empire contravened his oath of public office.[54]

The Citizens' Executive Committee evolved into the Citizens' Central Committee to defeat the Klan through the ballot box in the Democratic primary on July 22. Its purpose was "to work against the attempt of the Ku Klux Klan to dominate politics in Jefferson County."

The group relied on essay-style newspaper advertising to get its anti-Klan message across to the citizens. On election eve and day the committee published a complete list of anti-Klan candidates. "The lines are pretty closely drawn and most every one have fully made up their minds as to how they will vote Saturday," State Representative B. E. Quinn wrote Neff. "The situation here has simmered down to a Klan and anti-Klan issue." Offered a clear-cut choice between Klan and anti-Klan tickets, the voters gave the Klan a sweeping triumph. A *Beaumont Journal* headline read: "Jefferson County/Ku Klux Ticket is swept into office, Take All Offices by Wide Margin in Landslide."

Reelected with Klan support were Sheriff Garner; D. P. Wheat, judge of the county court; W. A. Coward, county clerk; and Marvin Scurlock, county attorney. The Klan won the judgeship of the Fifty-eighth District, defeating a staunch foe of the order, Judge W. S. Davidson, by a 2-to-1 majority; won the county judgeship, defeating another anti-Klansman, J. B. Peak; elected the tax collector; and swept the three state-representative seats. In 1924, J. A. Barnes, a young attorney, defeated the Klan's great enemy, Mayor Steinhagen, for reelection. Barnes, though not a member of the local Klan, had its full endorsement in the campaign.[35]

In addition to its victories in Dallas and Jefferson counties, the Klan nominated a large majority of endorsed candidates in Harris (county seat, Houston), McLennan (Waco), Tarrant (Fort Worth), Wichita (Wichita Falls), and many less populous counties. The Klan's decision to enter politics had been made in the spring of 1922, when Hiram Wesley Evans, the great titan of Province No. 2 in Texas, moved to Atlanta as "imperial kligrapp" (national secretary). Evans, who described himself as "the most average man in America," immediately began working to turn the Klan into what he called "a great militant political organization." Working within the two major parties, the Klan would control nominations and elections over the nation. As Evans saw it, this would require eliminating Simmons and Clarke as powers in the Klan, setting its finances in order, and converting it into a "movement" rather than a terrorist organization or a lodge. Simmons resigned, undoubtedly under pressure from the Evans crowd, and on November 24, 1922, Evans was elected imperial wizard by the imperial klonvocation. "Texas was the star Klan state and we came to the meeting all ready to go ahead and do something," one of them told

Stanley Frost. "But when we got there we found the Klan was not going anywhere or aiming to do anything, so we got busy, and Simmons done saw the need of a change."[56]

Soon after he moved to Atlanta, Evans met in Houston with Judge Erwin J. Clark of Waco, a leading Klansman, and H. C. McCall, great titan of the Houston province of the Klan. McCall began joking with Evans about his flogging parties in Dallas. Evans stated that he was going to Dallas to discharge his secretary and see that the Klan got rid of his kleagle—that he was not going to stand for outrages of that kind. Clark later testified: "McCall spoke up with a laugh,—I cannot recall his words, but the substance of it was that Evans ought to quit his hypocrisy; that he knew of certain parties that were pulled in Dallas under Evans' supervision. He referred to one party particularly, where a negro was taken from a hotel there and branded across the forehead with the words 'K.K.K.'" Still, newspapers were soon reporting that there had been a "marked revision" in the rules governing the Klan's operations and that whippings would no longer be sanctioned.[57]

Once the decision had been reached to make a bid for political power, the Klan stepped up its membership drives, laying aside what few reservations it had previously had about admitting "aliens" to the organization. "They just throwed the doors open, and every man that had the money, they took him in to get his vote," recalled a former member of Corsicana Klan No. 55, "and they went further than that along about June, and if he did not have any money, they took his note payable in the fall, and the thing then was to get his vote." Klan leaders were adept in organizing the rank and file for political action. A former member of Dallas Klan No. 66 explained the methods used to obtain political control in that city:

The Klan had a system where the men who wanted to run for office would announce their intentions to the Klan. About six weeks before the deadline for filing for the regular election, the Klan would hold a primary. The men getting the most votes for each office would then become the Klan candidates and file on the regular ticket. All Klansmen supported the nominees of their own primary. So far as I know the Klan never supported non-Klansmen for office. The Klan candidates never came out openly as Klansmen. The campaigns were always secret but they did have mass meetings where only the Klan candidates spoke, leaving out the opposition.[58]

In Dallas the Klan set up precinct organizations with a chairman and an executive committee outside the regular Democratic party ma-

chinery, "virtually decreed" whom the county chairman would appoint
to such positions as election judges, and conducted fund-raising drives
for local Klan candidates. In Fort Worth, following the example of the
Dallas County Citizens' League, the Citizens' League of Liberty was
formed to oppose the Klan in the county elections. "There is no doubt
in my mind that the Klan is on the run here and last Friday night the
Kluxers 'hollered' for help," a leader of the organization wrote General
Crane. "Bill Hanger, Brown Harwood and Marvin Brown complained
that the Klux Kandidates were not getting the Noble Support they
should get from the Noble Klansmen and about 125 volunteered to go
forth and do all the hand clapping that the human strength could afford." "Little Bill Hanger" was acting like a baby that needed the attention of his parents—"some of his garments are very *damp* and [he]
is just 'yelling' his head off. He is dealing in personalities and is not
getting to first base with it." As in Dallas, this prediction of an anti-
Klan victory was premature. The Fort Worth Klan made its members
pledge to vote the Klan ticket, suspended two knights who refused to
support the entire slate, and swept to victory in the Democratic primary on July 22.[59]

The Klan was an issue in the gubernatorial election of 1922,
largely because Governor Neff was not openly hostile to the organization. Traditionally, Texas governors were reelected for a second two-
year term without much opposition. As early as the fall of 1921, however, opponents of the Neff administration began looking for a likely
candidate to challenge him in the Democratic primary of 1922. They
held nearly one hundred conferences over the state but found few candidates. Alvin M. Owsley of Denton, who had gained the rank of lieutenant colonel in the army in World War I, was "seriously considering"
making the race against Neff. Early in 1921, Owsley had been appointed head of the Americanization Commission of the American
Legion, and the following year he was elected national commander.
Houston businessman Will C. Hogg, however, told Owsley that he did
not believe that it was "opportune for you or anyone else to make a
campaign to defeat Governor Neff for re-election. I do not believe his
record is such as would enable you to defeat him." Although he was the
anti-Neff group's first choice, Owsley wisely decided to wait for a more
favorable opportunity to make a statewide race.[60]

District Judge E. W. Napier of Wichita Falls announced his candidacy on April 27, 1922, severely criticizing the Klan, calling it "a chal-

lenge to every principle for which Americans have stood for 150 years,"
and promising, if elected, to "drive such organization out of the State of
Texas." The judge had recently sentenced three Wichita Falls citizens to
jail for refusing to tell a grand jury whether they were members of the
Klan. Napier made a few speeches but withdrew from the race when his
five-year-old son underwent an operation for appendicitis.[61]

When Napier withdrew, Harry Warner, editor of the *Paris Morning News*, announced that he would file, though he would be able to
make only a very limited canvass. He said that he would devote himself
principally to the plight of the city and rural schools and criticized Neff
for failing to call a special session of the legislature to find a remedy.
Warner thought that Neff had fallen far short in many other matters
and that "he is lacking in the moral courage which should be possessed
by the executive of Texas." In a speech at Brownwood, Warner attacked the governor for his ideas about prison reform, the condition of
the rural schools, and the expense of government administration.
When Neff failed to mention the Klan in his opening campaign address, Warner accused him of being "lockjawed upon that vital issue."
"The klan aims at control of the State Government of Texas as well as
that of the county and city and it has grown to threatening proportions
during Neff's administration," Warner declared. "Neither by word nor
act has he sought to curb or condemn it. Neff's attitude has been most
complaisant and favorable to the ambitions of the klan." Warner promised, if elected, "to do everything within the broad powers of the executive to prevent Texans becoming serfs of an invisible empire governed
by secret conspirators whose faces are hidden and who are the execu-
tioners of their own decrees."[62]

Neff's other major opponent was Fred S. Rogers of Bonham. In
April, 1922, the Texas Non-Partisan Political Conference, representing
the Texas branch of the national Non-Partisan League, the Farm Labor
Union, the Texas State Federation of Labor, and the four railroad
brotherhoods, endorsed Rogers for governor and Joe Edmondson of
Grapeland for lieutenant governor. Former Governor James E. Ferguson, a candidate for the United States Senate, declared openly that he
was for Rogers and against Neff. Rogers had campaigned for Joe Bailey
in 1920, and the Neff people believed that the former senator was the
guiding hand behind his candidacy. "We understand that Fred Rogers
had Joe Bailey's consent to run for Governor," wrote Commissioner of
Labor Joseph Myers, "and was in close touch with him the day the

nomination was tendered by a few labor leaders, and that, in fact, Bailey wrote his entire platform." Luther Nickels, Bailey's law partner and his campaign manager in 1920, and C. E. Wilcoxson of Gainesville, one of the senator's right-hand men in the campaign, attended a strategy session of the Texas Non-Partisan Political Conference in Dallas on June 8 and announced that the Bailey organization would be "actively" behind Rogers. Although both Nickels and Wilcoxson insisted that Bailey had taken no part in the present campaign, the senator later asked James B. Wells, his old friend and political ally in South Texas, to help Rogers. "I have known him for years, and I know that he is our kind of a Democrat. If you will pass that word among our friends in your section you will do me a great favor and at the same time you will do our State a good service." No doubt similar letters went to other Bailey men.[63]

There was some opposition to Rogers among union men because Bailey had advocated the open shop in 1920. "Some of the oral pyrotechnics he [Rogers] performed during his eruption in the interest of Joseph Weldon [Bailey] during the late unpleasantness in his discussions of organized labor are now proving a grass burr under his own saddle blanket," a Neff partisan gleefully reported. "He is going to feel as seldom as an old maid at a Mother's Congress when the votes are counted. I heard a union plumber of Celtic lineage say yesterday in speaking of him 'That guy Square? Yis he's ez square a guy as iver poured powder in a safe.'"[64]

In his speeches Rogers criticized the extravagance and inefficiency of the Neff administration but said that the paramount issue of the campaign would be that the public school should not perish. He assailed Neff for not calling a special session to make provisions to maintain the rural schools, despite the petitions the governor was receiving from all parts of the state. He also bore down heavily on Neff's management of the penitentiary system. Claiming that it had cost the state something like a million dollars to operate the prisons for one year, Rogers declared, "It would not have been more expensive had all the prisoners been housed in the finest hotel in Dallas, each with private bath, and fed the best of food." He also criticized Neff for borrowing $750,000 to operate the prison system and failing to tell the people how much it had cost to secure the loan. Rogers promised to place farmers instead of politicians in charge of the prison farms to make them pay and to restore the pardon board abolished by Neff. As for

Prohibition, Rogers said that he was a lifelong dry but that "prohibition is a dead issue and I'm not going to dig up a corpse and hold it up before the people."

As in 1920, Neff was assailed for his failure to register for the wartime draft and for his aversion to such manly sports as hunting and fishing. "Pat Neff is a great orator," Rogers told his audiences, after relating his own experiences in France. "He may beat me talking, but I can sure beat him shooting a gun. I like to fish, too. Why, they pulled off a big hunt for him not long ago and the only request he made was that no man be allowed to shoot a gun." Wilford B. ("Pitchfork") Smith of Dallas, the fiery editor of a weekly newspaper called the *Pitchfork*, informed his readers that Rogers "stood on the front line with the heroic living, with the dead, and with the dying. While Pat Neff was scratching his head trying to remember his age, Fred Rogers was on the front line in France scratching cooties." [65]

Neff did not announce his candidacy for reelection until June 3, and he did not conduct an intensive campaign. He delivered his first speech in Plainview on June 24, less than a month before the Democratic primary. The *Dallas Morning News* commented on his first day of real campaigning: "Governor Neff swung back into the stride today that made campaign history in the race for the governor's nomination in 1920. He got out of a dust covered auto and shaved, and started shaking hands. He spoke twice today to 4,000 and shook hands with nearly 2,000." [66]

Although Neff did not publish a formal platform, he defended his administration in his speeches and outlined future goals. He explained that the depression was largely responsible for the plight of the schools, and he blamed a Gulf storm that had damaged the crops on the prison farms for the system's indebtedness. Neff said that the prison system had never paid expenses but that he was trying by every means possible to make it do so, calling on the state's best businessmen for advice. He also pointed out that all barbarous punishment had been discontinued in the state. He defended his law-enforcement record, believing that the people wanted him to carry out his oath of office. While martial law should be used cautiously, he said, he would not hesitate to use the strong arm of state government whenever and wherever it was needed. He declared that the prohibition laws should be made "pig-tight and bear-strong and then enforced by officers possessing the courageous spirit of dauntless crusaders."

Aware that Rogers was appealing for labor support, Neff said that labor had a right to organize and deal collectively with the employer. He added, however, that while he was governor he would not permit strikes to interfere with transportation or any other line of business. "It is the truth that civilization begins and ends with the plow," he told the state's farmers, mentioning the pink-bollworm bill passed in 1921, his fight against cattle diseases, and other assistance to Texas agriculture. Looking to the future, Neff called for tax reform, the building of good roads, the conservation of floodwaters, and the preservation of overflow lands. "Not one bucket of water," he asserted, "should ever reach the Gulf of Mexico through Texas streams." He also advocated a state-park system: "The people should have the breathing spots where they can enjoy nature in stream and tree, in rock and rill. We should have wayside parks and stopping places along our highways."[67]

Neff appeared to be indifferent to his opponents and never mentioned them by name. Noted one historian: "Some of his speeches can hardly be classed as campaign speeches, but deserve to be recorded as lectures on government." The governor and his managers kept their fingers on the public pulse, however. Neff was told that there was some criticism of his veto of the rural-school appropriation, his alleged sympathy with the Klan, his labor record, his refusal to pardon prisoners with meritorious applications, the management of the prison system, and his failure to apprehend those who had perpetrated the recent lynchings in the state. There were also complaints about the increase in the cost of state administration. Tabs were kept on Rogers's campaign. A Brenham attorney warned Neff that the Bailey people were organizing all over the state for "a still hunt campaign" and were "going to gather in all the dissatisfied element that they can to vote against you. I do not believe that they intend to let the people know what they are doing until perhaps, a few days before the election." Neff was told that the organizers of the Farm Labor Union in East Texas were taking promissory notes from the farmers for their initiation fees payable in the fall, to get them to support Rogers.[68]

The anti-Klan element in Texas felt that Neff, in the words of the *Dallas Morning News*, "owes to those whose suffrage he seeks a full and frank statement of whatever opinion he has formed on that subject [the Klan]." When a Dallas supporter threatened to withdraw his promise of support because of Neff's silence, the governor replied at length, reiterating that "I am not a member of the Ku Klux Klan, have never been a member, never made application for membership, and it is not my intention at any time to become a member. I am for the enforcement of the law through the organized channels of the court and in no other way." He continued:

Of course, I do not feel called upon as Governor to either declare myself for every good thing in the country or declare myself against the bad things of the country. The law defines the duty of a governor, and he must hold himself in position at all times to discharge as best he can the duties imposed upon him by the constitution and laws of the country.

I am trying to serve all the people of the State as Governor, and I find that I can best do that merely by doing the things defined by the laws to be my duties. If you cannot fully appreciate the thought I am trying to express, you would realize it in a very short time if you were to come down and occupy the Governor's office for a while.[69]

The Klan regarded Neff as a friendly neutral, and one of the governor's supporters wrote him, "I have a report from the K.K.K. that a letter was read at their last Dallas meeting from the state headquarters, endorsing your candidacy." A Beaumont klansman told Neff that he would get the "solid Klan vote and probably twenty-five per cent of the anti-Klan vote" in Jefferson County. In some counties both sides of the Klan question issued election tickets to their followers before the Democratic primary. On one of the tickets Neff was named for governor with klansman Billie Mayfield for lieutenant governor, and on the other Harry Warner was named for governor, with T. W. Davidson for lieutenant governor. "I am sure you didn't want Billie for your running mate any more than I did," Davidson wrote Neff after the primary. The secret fraternity often affixed its seal of approval to candidates when it was not solicited, and that seems to have been the case with Neff. His political position was secure enough, though he respected the Klan's influence enough not to challenge it head on, and the Klan delighted in picking a sure winner and in convincing others that its influence had been preponderant.[70]

Three weeks before the Democratic primary 400,000 members of the Federated Railroad Shopmen's Union, including several thousand members in Texas, went on strike across the United States. Violence flared in Denison, Houston, and other cities when the railroads began hiring workmen to replace the strikers. The companies appealed to Neff for protection of their property and the enforcement of the so-called open-port law. Passed during the Hobby administration to deal with a longshoremen's strike in Galveston that began in March, 1920, the measure made it unlawful for a person or persons "by or through the use of any physical violence, or by threatening the use of any physical violence, or by intimidation" to interfere with any person working at "loading or unloading or transporting any commerce within this state." Governor Hobby had proclaimed martial law in Galveston and sent in the National Guard. After several months the troops were removed, but several Texas Rangers remained to help local authorities maintain order. The strike was settled in December, 1920.[71]

Union leaders regarded the open-port law as an antistrike law, while its defenders argued that it left workers free to strike but not to use lawless methods to compel others to strike against their will or to disrupt commerce. Editorialized the *Dallas Morning News*, "It would be a logical retort to say that, in denouncing this law, organized labor is demanding exemption from the criminal code as a means of enabling it to prosecute strikes successfully.[72]

When the strike began, Neff sent several Texas Rangers to Denison to preserve order, but the situation got out of hand as strikers began seizing and flogging strikebreakers and then ordering them to Oklahoma with a warning not to return. On the night of July 11 twenty-four railroad employees were seized at the MK&T depot by about a thousand strikers and taken by car to the Red River Bridge. There they were whipped and sent across the state line into Oklahoma. Neff was in something of a political squeeze, for declaring martial law and sending in the National Guard would alienate a large segment of the labor vote in the upcoming Democratic primary on July 22. "Well, I don't know what I will do finally," he said on July 12, in a telephone conversation with the managing editor of the *Dallas Morning News*, "but I am carefully considering the situation from all angles and trying to do the right thing. I haven't ordered the troops out. As to whether I will I can not say at this time." Former Governor Hobby increased the pressure on Neff by asserting that enforcement of the open-port law would solve the strike problem in Texas: "There are plenty of men who will work if given the protection the law of the state provides, and why should the law not be enforced. . . . This act does not compel any one to work, but protects those who do work. The public policy and the duty of the state is plain under the law."[73]

Neff stalled for time. On July 14 he sent Adjutant General Thomas D. Barton to Denison to review the situation. Barton found the town in a state of "lawlessness." Strikers and railroad guards clashed on the

fifteenth. The following day Neff met with Barton and Captain Tom
Hickman of the Texas Rangers at Greenville. Arriving later that day in
Dallas, the governor told reporters that "at this time it is not necessary
to order out troops to either sustain commerce, protect life or property
in Denison. Things are in such a condition, however, that it is impossible to tell what a new day will bring forth." On July 19, Neff canceled
his speaking engagements and went to Denison to make a personal investigation, meeting with fourteen hundred strikers, the city commissioners, and a committee of citizens. In disguise he made the rounds of
the city at night and talked with those on picket duty. "My purpose was
to find duty's path and then walk therein," he wrote later. "The State
was my ward and the people were my clients. Therefore I did not permit myself to become sympathethically biased for or against the
strikers or the railroads." Neff decided that the serious situation at
Denison "demanded a positive stand for law and order" but that the
Rangers could handle it.[74]

In the Democratic primary on July 22, Neff had a majority of approximately 50,000 votes over his five opponents and thus avoided a
runoff. He received 318,000 votes to 195,941 for Fred Rogers, 57,617
for Harry Warner, and 18,368 for W. W. King. Commented the *Dallas
Morning News*:

No one expected that Governor Neff would be denied renomination. The term
of the governorship is made four years by the law of habit, and Governor Neff
enjoyed the additional safeguard of the preference of the klan. His victory is,
for these reasons, significant of nothing much. But it may have a smallness that
might be read by some as an evidence that Texas would have its Governor
more frank and courageous than he has shown himself to be.

George Clifton Edwards thought that there was hope in Rogers's showing, even though he and the farmer-labor platform had both evaded
the Ku Klux Klan issue and the use of troops and Rangers against the
railroad strikers. "What political progressive activity there is in Texas
has its origins among the farmers," Edwards claimed, "for the union
men are befooled by the daily papers and hoodwinked by the Gompers
type of labor leader."[75]

Neff's friends were surprised at the size of the anti-Neff vote, especially the vote for Rogers, and blamed it on the labor unions, the
"intolerant Bailey forces," and the "poison venom" that the Farm Labor Union had handed the "poor ignorant people." They ruefully ad-

mitted that they had been caught napping. "We were, as it appears, too confident, and permitted the labor organizations to 'put one over us,'" confessed a Wise County man. "The farmers were caught by the demogogery [*sic*] of Rogers just as they were in the days of the candidacy of Jim Ferguson for governor." Jacob F. Wolters told Neff that he had lost thousands of votes in Harris County because his name had appeared on what was presumed to be the Klan-endorsed ticket and said that "those Protestants who would have ordinarily voted for you, but who were opposed to the Klan, scratched your name."[76]

Neff admitted that it was "an uncertain year in political affairs. There were so many counter-currents and under-currents that it was difficult to know at times in what directions we were going." Still he had hoped for the largest majority ever given a candidate in Texas so as to increase "my influence for good," and he was disappointed in the result. "Thanks a thousand times for your splendid services during the recent campaign," he wrote to R. G. Storey, who had campaigned for him in East Texas. "No one in Texas took a more active part than you. Had my other friends done as you did the results would have been indeed different."[77]

Nevertheless, with his reelection assured, Neff could at last act in the railroad strike without worrying about the political consequences. The day after the primary he was closeted in the adjutant general's office for several hours with the state's military heads; although nothing was given out for publication, Neff decided to "mobilize practically the entire Ranger force at Denison." Then, on the evening of July 24, Colonel Charles S. Lincoln, assistant chief of staff of the Eighth Army Corps, stationed at Fort Sam Houston in San Antonio, called on the governor in his office in full military uniform and told him that he had orders from the federal government to remain there until he got a yes-or-no answer about Neff's intention in regard to placing the National Guard at Denison. Lincoln had visited Denison at the request of the War Department and had found the mood of the town "ugly." On the basis of his report, Secretary of War John W. Weeks felt that the national guard should be ordered out. "I have arranged to handle the Denison situation with State Rangers," Neff answered. Lincoln said:

"I have not been delegated to discuss the merits of the case with you, but to get a 'yes' or 'no' answer as the placing of State troops at that point. You take what time you need to make a definite answer but my orders are to remain in your office until a 'yes' or 'no' answer is received. If your answer is 'yes' the Federal Government will leave it to the State to handle; but, if your answer is 'no,' a thousand Federal soldiers out of San Antonio will be on their way to Denison in about thirty minutes after your 'no' answer is received by me."

Faced with this ultimatum, Neff spent three hours with the officer and made some long-distance telephone calls, "talked seriously to myself," and finally concluded that he was "unwilling for Federal troops to march on Texas soil for the purpose of enforcing Texas laws." He told Lincoln that Denison would be under martial law by daylight the next day and that five hundred guardsmen would be on their way to the city. "I took my stand for the supremacy and for the sovereignty of the State," Neff said, in defending his decision.[78]

On July 25 a zone in Denison including the railroad shops and two blocks of the downtown business district was placed under martial law, and units of the 142d Infantry National Guard moved into the city. After a gunfight erupted between some of the guardsmen and three unknown men in which fifty shots were exchanged, martial law was extended over the entire city. Neff placed sixteen other railroad centers under the open-port law, and Rangers were sent to preserve order. Martial law was lifted at Denton on October 21, 1922, and the open-port law was invoked, to be enforced by Captain Hickman's Rangers. On December 29, Neff lifted the open-port law at Sherman, Denison, Childress, Marshall, Tyler, and Palestine, effective at midnight January 1, 1923. After that date no Texas city remained under the law. Several years later the United States Court of Criminal Appeals nullified the open-port law, terming it "class legislation without pretense that the classification is other than arbitrary, capricious and unreasonable" and thus in violation of the Fourteenth Amendment.[79]

On the eve of the Democratic primary Neff had received a telegram from George E. Butcher, secretary of Dallas Klan No. 66: "Congratulations on your assured success. Mr. Z. E. Marvin and I have done everything we could for you. Any time we can serve you call upon us." A story in the *New York Times* called Neff "the darling of the Ku Klux Klan and law-abidding [sic] Texas." After the election Butcher and Marvin—the latter Hiram Wesley Evans's successor as great titan of the Dallas province—wired Neff congratulations, as did national kligrapp Evans: "Heartily congratulate you for your success in Saturday's election." Neff acknowledged these messages with the form letter he sent to all his other well-wishers. Actually, the Klan leaders had been more interested in the outcome of another statewide race, that for the Democratic nomination for United States senator. The outcome of that contest would give the Klan one of the best-known and most spectacular of its many victories in the 1920s.[80]

CHAPTER 3

Farmer Jim v. Prince Earle

IN 1922, Charles Allen Culberson, senior United States senator from Texas, was nearing the end of his fourth term. By virtue of his long service he was one of the four veterans of the Senate. The son of a popular East Texas congressman, David B. Culberson, Charles studied law at the University of Virginia. After serving as county attorney of Marion County, he served two terms as attorney general of Texas under Governor James S. Hogg before winning the governorship in 1894 in a campaign ably managed by Colonel Edward M. House. After the customary two terms, during which he secured a law banning prizefighting from the state and earned the title the "Young Christian Governor," Culberson, again with House's help, moved on to the United States Senate in 1899.

Lewis L. Gould has written that Culberson's "terse letters give few clues to his real thoughts. Discreet to the point of opacity, Culberson shunned controversy about his conservative views on economic questions and his staunch opposition to prohibition." His chief service in the United States Senate was as a member of the Committee on the Judiciary, which he chaired from 1913 to 1919. Culberson was Democratic minority leader from 1907 to 1910, but his health broke and forced him to resign the post. Thereafter alcoholism and physical ailments, including Bright's disease, made him an invalid—"the sick man of the Senate." Representative James Luther Slayden of San Antonio remarked in July, 1916, that Texas was "almost unrepresented in the Senate, poor Culberson so pitifully ill and Morris Sheppard so obsessed with prohibition and Wilson."[1]

Despite his ill health, Culberson sought a third term in 1916. He was opposed by former Governors Thomas Campbell and Oscar B. Colquitt; Samuel P. Brooks, president of Baylor University; and Congressman Robert Lee Henry of Waco. The senator was too ill to return to Texas to campaign but entrusted his interests to Judge Barry Miller of Dallas, his staunchest advocate and one of the state's outstanding

orators (in 1898, when Culberson was a candidate before the legislature for the United States Senate, Miller had won a seat in the state
Senate for the sole purpose of aiding his cause). Although Culberson
trailed Colquitt by 33,000 votes in the Democratic primary on July 22,
1916, his image as the pro-Wilson candidate gave him a decisive victory in the runoff. Colquitt's criticism of Wilson's foreign policy and
courting of the German vote in Texas enabled Culberson's backers to
portray Colquitt as "the arch enemy of the President" and to link him
to the German kaiser.[2]

Culberson's muscular affliction made speech-making difficult, but
the senator tried to compensate by sitting immaculately dressed in the
Senate chamber for a larger number of hours, answering a larger number of roll calls, and casting his vote on more measures than did any
other sitting senator. "He sits in his Senate seat, he hears all that is
said, and he votes on every roll call," wrote columnist Mark Sullivan.
"Occasionally, when you feel 'fed up' with the loquacity of some others, you find yourself disposed to look on Senator Culberson as an ideal
senator." "As is well known, I have not enjoyed robust health for some
time, but notwithstanding this, I have been a daily attendant upon the
sessions of the Senate," Culberson wrote, in an appeal to his constituents. "The sessions of the Congress, during my present term, cover
1,217 days, and I have not missed a day." It was left unsaid that the
senator had not been back to his native state for ten years.[3]

In the fall of 1921, Culberson's friends began asking him whether
he intended to seek a fifth term the following year. The senator sought
advice from his closest advisers, and some of them, including Thomas
B. Love and Colonel House, told him frankly that he could not win
because of his physical condition and should retire. Others, however,
offered strong encouragement. Will Hogg and journalist Irving S.
Cobb were in Hogg's office when Culberson's inquiry arrived and discussed the matter. "I concur in his [Cobb's] view that you ought to run
for re-election," Hogg advised the senator. "For Texas's sake, we hope
you will run and be re-elected, because Senator Culberson is a bigger
man singly than the great gross of these small fry who would like to
succeed you." After Culberson decided to run, his secretary and Washington, D.C., manager, Chesley W. Jurney, confided to Colonel House
the "real reason" for his candidacy:

I can say to you privately, that it is a question of life or death with the Senator.
If he wins, Dr. Ruffin says he is good for another six years, but if he gives up

this last interest in life, either voluntarily, or because of defeat, Dr. Ruffin feels it will be difficult to keep him on his feet for many months afterwards. . . . His life depends on keeping this last interest alive, his work in the Senate, and when that is taken from him, whether it be voluntary or by compulsion, he will, I am sorry to say, be beyond further encouragement.[4]

Culberson's friends realized that his poor health was the chief obstacle to a fifth term, since southern voters customarily reelected incumbent senators until death or voluntary retirement removed them from the political stage. The willingness of Texas voters to reelect Culberson in absentia in 1916 over five healthy challengers illustrated the strength of the seniority tradition in a one-party state. There were conflicting reports in Texas about the senator's condition, and voters wanted to know whether he was in full possession of his faculties and still capable of representing them. James B. Wells of Brownsville, who had carried the border counties for his old friend in 1916, wired Congressman John Nance Garner on April 2: "If you feel at liberty to say, what is your confidential, personal opinion of Senator Culberson's mental and physical ability to serve us for another term in the United States Senate?" Garner showed this wire to Jurney, and the two men secured Wells's consent to release the congressman's reply to the press.

Garner assured Wells (and Texas voters) that, while Culberson was "not as strong physically as he once was, he is strong enough to be there [in the Senate] all the time, and, of course, he is as capable mentally as he ever was." Garner reminded the voters that Culberson retained his important assignments on the appropriations and judiciary committees and assured them that "as long as he lives Charles A. Culberson will have a tremendous influence in the Senate." "With his present health, which has every prospect of being maintained, his office will be filled to the satisfaction of the people of Texas," Garner declared, adding, ". . . my personal relations with and admiration for Senator Culberson are such that I would support him against any one who might run against him."[5] Jurney sent copies of Garner's letter to nine hundred Texas newspapers for release on April 25 and gave a copy to every correspondent for a Texas newspaper in Washington.

Also made public early in April was a letter from Culberson to Major H. V. Fisher of Houston, in which the senator expressed his unqualified opposition to the Klan: "If not cured, it will usurp the functions of the State and be destructive of government itself. It will indeed overthrow our Anglo-Saxon civilization in its relation to our government. Steps should be taken, therefore at once to arrest its progress and finally to destroy it." If existing state law was inadequate for the purpose, he said, then the legislature should be called into extra session to supply the deficiency.[6]

Copies of a recent photograph of Culberson, together with a statement by him regarding his physical condition and a résumé of his work in the Senate during the past ten years, were mailed to his supporters in Texas. State headquarters were opened in the Oriental Hotel in Dallas, and meetings were held in some of the larger cities. As in 1916, Culberson remained in Washington, while Barry Miller campaigned for him at home. "While my name will be submitted to you in the forthcoming primary, yet candor impels me to say that I am not strong enough to make a canvass of the State," Culberson wrote his constituents. "My candidacy must therefore be left largely to the Democrats generally, men and women, who approve my views upon public questions and for whose support and friendship I will be profoundly grateful." Miller was soon on the stump, assuring the voters that, while the Senator's "step may be slightly feeble from his long service to you, his eyes and mind are bright" and that they "could not elect a man who can obtain in a dozen years what the senior Senator can right now" and reminding them that southerners had always shown gratitude to public servants who grew old in their country's service by keeping them in office.[7]

A number of prominent Texans considered entering the contest against Culberson but for one reason or another changed their minds. Samuel P. Brooks, who had challenged Culberson in 1916, meant to run again until the Klan issue arose but was unwilling to enter into "a scrabble under such conditions as then existed. I was not a Klansman and would have been slaughtered in every probability." Former Governor Thomas Campbell said privately that he was not a candidate and would not be unless the people or his party needed him. General Martin M. Crane of Dallas, who had served as attorney general and lieutenant governor of Texas in the 1890s, was "sorely tempted" but could not overcome his reluctance to campaign. "I enjoy so much better not holding any public office, that it would really be embarrassing for me to run," he confided. "I might begin to hedge and 'pussy-foot' like the others are doing now."[8]

It was rumored that Congressman Tom Connally might run, but he wrote in April, 1922, that "in view of all the conditions and the late-

ness of the date I have thought it best not to become a candidate." A
"great many" of Congressman John Nance Garner's friends throughout
Texas wrote him in the summer of 1921 "touching the Senatorial race,"
but he maintained that he could be of more service to his district and to
the state as minority leader in the House. "Speaking confidentially," he
wrote James B. Wells, "I believe that if the Democrats carry the House
next year and I am reelected to Congress, I will be elected Speaker."
His colleague Sam Rayburn briefly thought of seeking Culberson's
seat. "A race every two years gets pretty irksome," he told his sister.
After weighing various factors, however, Rayburn decided not to try
for the Senate. His real ambition was to "rise in the House," and now,
as chairman of the Democratic caucus, he believed that he was on his
way. Moreover, in a statewide contest, he would be handicapped by his
identification with former Senator Joe Bailey. Bailey's insensitivity to
public opinion in his business affiliations, notably with the Waters-
Pierce Oil Company, a branch of Standard Oil, in 1900, and his unsuccessful race for governor in 1920 made his chances of ever winning any
office again, in Rayburn's words, "as dead as hell." It was his curse,
Rayburn noted, that of "all the men in Texas who followed his [Bailey's]
flag in his black hour that I am the only one who today holds an office. I
am truly the last of the Mohicans."[9]

Thomas B. Love of Dallas, the national Democratic committeeman from Texas and one of the original Wilson men in the state, was
"strongly inclined" to be a candidate. As early as September, 1920,
while helping in the national Democratic campaign, he wanted some
talk started in Texas immediately "to the effect that I am likely to be a
candidate, or that I am going to be a candidate, so as to get my name
into consideration before my friends become otherwise committed."
He did not want it to appear that this was being done on his initiative,
however. As late as July, 1921, Love still believed that it was "my duty
to make this race," but when his friend Culberson decided to run,
Love loyally backed him, though he felt that Culberson would lose. "I
supported Culberson as I could not do otherwise in view of his uniform
and steadfast support of all the men and measures (except prohibition)
I have been interested in for a quarter of a century," Love explained.
In any event, Love's candidacy would have aroused strong opposition
among the state's wet leaders. "The only thing I have decided on is
that Tom Love . . . shall not go to the senate," wrote former Governor

James E. Ferguson, "and I here and now order him to tuck his tail and git."[10]

The *San Antonio Express* reported that Joe Bailey was urging former Governor Oscar B. Colquitt to run for the Senate. This bit of information created much comment, for it was generally thought that Bailey would favor Clarence Ousley of Fort Worth, a veteran editor of the *Fort Worth Record* and assistant secretary of agriculture in the Wilson administration, who had been Bailey's admirer and friend for twenty years. In July, 1921, Colquitt announced that he would make the race on a platform of states' rights, reduction of the tax rate, opposition to centralized government, and payment of a bonus to World War I veterans. He had second thoughts, however, because of his oil business, and in January, 1922, he offered to withdraw if Cone Johnson of Tyler would enter the race. Although Johnson's answer is not in the Colquitt Papers, the veteran East Texas Democrat did not become a candidate.

In February, Colquitt, in reply to an inquiry from J. A. Leaks of Navasota about his views on the Klan, said that he could see "no earthly use or justification for the KKK." On March 2 he wrote a long letter to Leake, which was intended for publication, strongly condemning the Klan. Somewhat later he added a memorandum on this letter: "The attached was the tentative platform on which I intended to run for the senate in 1922." At the time he wrote the letter, Colquitt announced that if the Klan tried to name the United States senator then he would make the race, but he did not in fact run. Despite Colquitt's withdrawal, there was no rush of Bailey men to Ousley, who also opposed the Klan.[11]

The early front-runner against Culberson was Cullen F. Thomas of Dallas. One of the recognized Prohibition leaders in Texas, Thomas had entered politics in Waco, serving in the Texas House from 1895 to 1897 and then as county attorney of McLennan County for three terms. In 1902 he made a heated but unsuccessful race for Congress against Congressman Robert L. Henry. A bitter political enemy of Senator Bailey, Thomas was on the anti-Bailey ticket as a candidate for delegate at large to the 1908 national Democratic convention. The Bailey men were victorious. The following year Thomas moved to Dallas to practice law. In 1912 he was permanent chairman of the State Democratic Convention and a Wilson supporter. For twenty years or

more Thomas had campaigned across Texas for other progressives, but
in all that time he had never been a candidate for a statewide office,
though he was frequently "mentioned" and "groomed." Campaigning
for fellow Baptist Pat Neff against Bailey, Thomas had labeled the senator's supporters as "Baileyachers" and expressed his "hearty contempt
for the Anheuser-Busch whacker whether he has a party or not." Bailey
in turn despised Thomas. Like Neff, Thomas had the confidence and
support of the "moral element," especially the numerically strong
Baptists.[12]

The *Houston Chronicle* hoisted the Thomas flag in January, 1921,
following a "strong indication" during a recent visit to the city that
he would be a candidate. "It goes without saying that Mr. Thomas, if
he desires to be senator, should be elected," the paper editorialized.
"Cullen Thomas stands for the best, and only the best, ideals in our
body politic. In every great political question confronting this state he
has never failed to be on the side of justice and truth." Enclosing a
copy of this editorial in a February letter to Robert Lee Bobbitt of
Laredo, Thomas noted that he had received so many voluntary offers of
support that he felt much encouraged. "A number of weekly papers
have declared for me. Many strong men throughout the State seem to
believe my chances are the very best." Some observers felt, however,
that Thomas would be fatally handicapped because he was married to
Senator Morris Sheppard's sister, and Texas voters would not want two
members of the same family in the Senate. Bailey's friend James B.
Wells called Thomas a "cheap demagogue . . . whose only motive in
running is to secure the place for himself by the side of his brother-in-
law, Morris Shepperd [*sic*]."[13]

In August, 1921, Thomas announced his candidacy in a "Heart-to-
Heart Appeal" to the people:

I want to go to the Senate not to peddle patronage; not to be a department
factotum; not to promote some pet project, but to devote my riper years to
those problems that mean so much for human advancement. I want to go to the
Senate to give battle for the weak against the strong; for human need against
organized greed; for the rights of men against arrogant privilege—not as a beg-
gar for special favors for selfish interests, but as a voice for the hard-pressed
every-day men and women of Texas.

"Many newspapers and the candidates themselves are saying that I
am, at this time, in the lead," Thomas confided to Will Hogg. Jim Fer-

guson conceded that Thomas was the "smartest one in the lot" and advised the readers of his *Ferguson Forum* that Thomas would be in the runoff. "The leaders have already anointed him for the nominee."[14]

In early April, 1922, Thomas issued a carefully worded statement on the Ku Klux Klan. He stated that, while he had never been a member of the organization and would not seek to become one in the future, he would cast no aspersion against its membership, which included "many of the best types of Texas citizenship." He praised the many generous charitable deeds done in its name and announced that he would not war on its published code of principles. Without directly condemning the Klan, Thomas did say, however:

The lash and tar bucket must go. No set of men can become so strong that they can rise above the law. . . . There is no room in this Republic for any sort of government, visible or invisible, inside or outside that government whose breath is the bill of rights. . . . Terrorism, organized or unorganized, must be stamped out. Mobocracy, whether masked or unmasked, must go.

The Klan was on trial for its life, the candidate declared. However worthy its purposes, the order must abandon its ironclad secrecy. "If the klan refuses to reform itself then the klan will be destroyed."[15]

The most colorful and controversial candidate in the race was former Governor James Edward Ferguson of Temple. Born near Salado, Bell County, on August 31, 1871, Ferguson was the son of a circuit-riding Methodist minister and farmer, who died when Jim was four years old. "We were as poor as Job's turkey," Ferguson recalled. "However, we weren't the only poor people. The country was full of them." He attended the Salado public schools "between the crops," read the books in his father's library, and spent two years in Salado College—until he was expelled for refusing to bring a teacher some firewood. In his words he "was as well educated as any country boy of that day."

In 1887, at the age of sixteen, Ferguson left home for the Pacific Coast, where for two years he worked as a grape picker; a teamster on a grain ranch; a roustabout in a San Francisco barbed-wire factory; a lumberjack in Washington Territory; a mine laborer in California, Nevada, and Colorado; and finally a bellhop in the Windsor Hotel in Denver, where he served Governor Horace Tabor, the "silver king." He then returned to Texas and after working on construction and railroad gangs went back to the family farm in Bell County in 1895. He farmed in the daytime and studied law at night. Admitted to the bar in 1897, he opened an office in Belton, the county seat. On December 31, 1899, he married Miriam Amanda Wallace, the daughter of a well-to-do Bell County farmer.

A few years after their marriage the Fergusons moved to Temple, where Jim founded the Temple State Bank in 1907 and joined all the local fraternal lodges. He also became a successful farmer and stock raiser. He took an interest in politics, shifting back and forth between progressive and conservative candidates. In 1902 he supported Robert L. Henry, a Bailey man, for the United States Congress but opposed Bailey's control of the Texas delegation in 1908. He supported a progressive, Attorney General Robert V. Davidson, for governor against Oscar B. Colquitt in 1910 but two years later switched to Colquitt and backed Champ Clark against Woodrow Wilson. In local-option elections Ferguson consistently opposed Prohibition, though he did not drink liquor.[16]

Ferguson jumped into the governor's race in 1914 on his own initiative. He adopted a style of speaking that mixed bad grammar, folksy stories, sarcasm, and slander in about equal proportions and appealed to the unsophisticated rural voter. "He swayed them like the storm sways the slender pines, and voted them in droves and platoons," an admirer wrote. "He spoke the language of the corn rows and the vernacular of the country stores." Edmund Travis, a onetime Austin newspaper editor, said in 1964 that Ferguson "purposely played ignorant to win the rural vote." "Farmer Jim," as he now labeled himself, earned the votes and loyalty of the white tenant farmers, "the boys at the forks of the creek," by promising to secure passage of a law to limit the landlord's share of the crops to one-fourth of the cotton and one-third of the grain when the tenant provided everything but the land. His opponent, Colonel Thomas H. Ball, was a seasoned Prohibition leader, but Ferguson made Ball's membership in the Houston Club a major issue, demanding to know why Ball, if he neither drank nor gambled as he claimed, did not resign from the club, where liquor was served and card games were played for money. Ferguson promised, if elected, to veto any bill that had anything to do with the liquor question no matter from what source it came. He beat the "durned high toned" Ball by 45,504 votes and buried his obscure Republican opponent in the November election.[17]

Once in office, Ferguson persuaded the legislature to pass a law regulating rents; the law was never enforced and was declared uncon-

stitutional by a state court in 1921. Still, he retained the support of the
dirt farmers and easily won reelection in 1916. Meanwhile, he had become involved in a controversy with the University of Texas. In June,
1917, he vetoed virtually its entire appropriation because the Board of
Regents had ignored his suggestions regarding the selection of a new
president and had refused to dismiss faculty members whom the governor found objectionable. "It does seem that a lot of people have gone
hog-wild on the subject of higher education," he remarked. His veto
forged a powerful coalition of former students of the university, prohibitionists, and woman suffragists seeking his removal. In August,
1917, the Texas House of Representatives voted twenty-one articles of
impeachment, and the Senate convicted him on ten. Five related to
unlawful use of state funds; two involved loans he received, one from
his bank in excess of the legal 30 percent limit and one in the amount of
$156,500 from parties later identified as Texas brewers; and three con-
cerned his relations with the University of Texas Board of Regents. The
Senate verdict removed Ferguson from office and made him ineligible
"to hold any office of honor, trust or profit under the State of Texas."
But his chief counsel, William Hanger, predicted, "Fergusonism will
be an issue in the politics of Texas every year there is an election held
until Jim Ferguson dies." And so it proved.[18]

Ferguson immediately began a campaign for "vindication." In November, 1917, he started a Temple-based weekly, the *Ferguson Forum*,
with himself as editor. The prohibitionists called it the "Ferguson for
Rum," but Jim liked to refer to it as "My Little Christian Weekly." It
was the main and almost his only means of communication with his
rural flock. "Why, those old fellows out there know but two things,"
Barry Miller remarked, after a swing through East Texas in 1918. "The
first is that Levi Garrett & Sons make the best snuff in the world, and
the second is that Friday is Forum day, the day the mails bring Ferguson's paper."[19]

With his friends still in control of the Texas Democratic Executive
Committee, Ferguson was allowed to run for governor in 1918 against
William P. Hobby, who as lieutenant governor had succeeded him in
1917. Ferguson was crushed in the primary, 461,479 to 217,012. Still
his enemies marveled at the 217,012 faithful. In keeping with his
family motto, "Never say 'die,' say 'damn!'" Ferguson kept his name
before the voters in 1920 by bolting the Democratic party and running
for president on his own American party ticket. His good friend State

Senator Temple H. McGregor of Austin was the party's candidate for governor against Pat Neff. In an effort to swell his vote, Ferguson asked Will Hays, chairman of the Republican National Committee, to use his influence to have Texas Republicans vote for the American party electors, who were pledged against the Democratic nominee, James Cox of Ohio, thereby ensuring a Democratic defeat in Texas. He sent a copy of this letter to the Republican presidential candidate, Senator Warren G. Harding of Ohio, in the hope that "you may find time to give the matters referred to, consideration, for the purpose of bringing about that which has heretofore been considered impossible, to-wit: taking Texas out of the Democratic column." All Ferguson got for his pains was a polite acknowledgment of his letter from Harding, and he had to be content with 50,000 votes—about 9.9 percent of the total. Even so, he kept the Ferguson movement alive and the hard core of his vest-pocket vote intact.[20]

According to his daughter Ouida, the senatorial election "shed a light of great political hope on Jim Ferguson. . . . He had been barred only from holding State office, and as this was a federal office, his enemies could not keep his name off the Democratic ticket." His wife, Miriam, protested that for many reasons, including the high cost of living and the cold winter weather, she did not want to go to Washington, and Jim agreed that, as a "true Texas horned frog," he did not relish the idea of facing the capital's winter climate but that, since that seemed to be the only avenue of vindication open to him at present, he felt that he could not pass it up. "Always eager to help her Jim, Mamma was easily convinced that this was the thing to do," said Ouida.[21]

On January 28, 1922, the American party's executive committee met in Temple with Ferguson and McGregor and resolved that "the American party as such be, and the same is hereby dissolved, and the members thereof are absolved from further allegiance thereto, and free to make such political alignment as to each individual may appear to the best interest of the state and preservation of free government among men." Ferguson announced his candidacy for the United States Senate in the *Ferguson Forum* of February 2, 1922. "This being a national office I am in no way disqualified to hold it. The American Party having been dissolved, my announcement is made subject to the Democratic primaries." The Texas Senate had voted to hang Ferguson's picture among the pictures of other Texas governors, and he said, "As

they forgave me, I gladly forgive them and now return to the house of
my fathers." The prodigal son had returned, but none except his faithful "boys at the forks of the creek" slew a fatted calf to welcome him.[22]

In an editorial in the *Forum* on April 6, 1922, Ferguson rapped the
Ku Klux Klan, advising the "many good men" who had joined the order to get out just as soon as they could. "Your arrogated mission to
save the American republic with an invisible empire is so plainly the
idea of a foolish fanatic, that sometimes I don't blame you for wearing a
mask," he chided. "Some of you I know would be ashamed to let anybody know what kind of a snipe hunt you had been on." Like Thomas,
however, Ferguson did not want the Klan question paramount in the
contest. "Any candidate for the high office of United States senator who
pitches his campaign on the ground that he is either for or against the
Ku Klux is not big enough to be a deacon in a colored church, let alone
be United States senator," he declared. "I am not going to Washington
as a Ku Klux senator. But I am going to Washington as a democratic
senator."[23]

Three klansmen entered the senate race—attorney Sterling P.
Strong of Dallas; former Congressman Robert L. Henry of Waco, who
became a member of the Klan in February, 1922; and Earle B. Mayfield, an attorney, former state senator, and member of the Texas Railroad Commission, who joined the Klan in Austin but stopped paying dues in February, 1922. The three men were competing for the
100,000 or more Klan votes in Texas, and this division threatened to
deny any of them victory in the Democratic primary on July 22.

In March, 1922, four of the Klan's great titans of the Realm of
Texas, Hiram Wesley Evans of Dallas, H. C. McCall of Houston,
Brown Harwood of Fort Worth, and Erwin J. Clark of Waco, met at the
Raleigh Hotel in Waco to decide which of the three klansmen in the
senatorial contest would receive the united support of the Texas Klan.
Ralph Cameron, the great titan of the San Antonio province, was not
present. When Clark entered the lobby at the Raleigh, he met Mayfield, who said that he was just passing through and waiting on the next
train and had come up to the hotel to see some friends. "I thought it
was rather coincidental at least that he was there at that time," Clark
said later. At one point in the discussion Evans slapped Clark on the
knee and said: "Erwin, I have a dead one in Dallas [Strong] and you
have a dead one here in Waco [Henry]. Mayfield is the man. Now, they

are all three Klansmen, and Strong and Henry are both good fellows, and we do not want to hurt their feelings. Let them ride for awhile and at the proper time we will ditch them and concentrate on Mayfield."

Clark replied somewhat indignantly that he did not propose to have his friend Henry treated that way; he was the strongest man of the three in the race, and Evans would become convinced of this if he would give Henry a little time. After considerable discussion an understanding that came to be known as the "Waco agreement" was reached. It was, in Clark's words, "that we take all the bars down, that all three Klansmen candidates run their race without let or hindrance from any of the State officers, and that the strongest man would win. It was further agreed that in the event there were two Klansmen in the run-off, the Klansman receiving the less number of votes would withdraw immediately after the first primary." Clark prepared a circular letter, dated April 17, 1922, to the exalted cyclopses in Texas, explaining the agreement. In the meantime, he advised Henry of the understanding and personally assured him that the other state officers would stand by it. Henry met with Harwood, now grand dragon of the Realm of Texas, at the Texas Hotel in Fort Worth in April and also received his "solemn promise and pledge" that no elimination contest among the senatorial candidates was contemplated and that he could make his arrangements for the campaign.[24]

On April 5, Henry went to Clark and asked permission to declare himself openly a klansman, because of the serious attacks being made against the Klan by the *Dallas Morning News*, Senator Culberson, and Cullen Thomas, which he as a klansman felt ought to be met. "That will not do at all," Clark replied. "Earle Mayfield is a klansman, and no one knows it. It is kept under cover. If you come out in the open you will be shot from both sides. An antiklan faction certainly will not support you, and I consider it inadvisable, Mr. Henry." Henry persisted and asked Clark to secure permission from the imperial wizard to uncover as a klansman and defend the organization and its principles. Clark placed a call to the "Imperial Palace" in Atlanta, but was told that both acting wizard E. Y. Clarke and Evans, now imperial kligrapp (secretary), were out of town. He explained the situation and was told that Clarke and Evans would be informed and would get in touch with him as soon as possible. The next morning Clark received a telegram from Little Rock, Arkansas, signed "E. Y. Clarke and H. W. Evans":

"Your request regarding Henry granted. Good luck and best wishes to you."[25]

In an address in Fort Worth on April 8, Henry displayed the telegram and defended the Klan in what the *New York Evening Post* called "ecstatic language":

We hurl defiance at destroying threats of the distinguished United States Senator, the distinguished candidate from Dallas, the Hon. Cullen F. Thomas. We challenge the Dallas News. Call on the battle. We are ready from this day on. Let the Citizens' League of Dallas rally. These gentlemen and that great journal tell you that the klan must be destroyed. I tell you that the Ku Klux Klan must and will survive.

General Martin M. Crane, chairman of the Dallas County Citizens' League, severely criticized Henry for his speech. "It seems that Mr. Henry had to apply to Imperial Wizard Simmons or some other high authority in the Klan for permission to tell us, his would be constituents, that he was a klansman."[26]

The morning after his Fort Worth speech Henry met Mayfield in the dining room of the Texas Hotel. The latter said that he had noticed that Henry had produced the telegram and remarked, "I think you made a mistake in stating it was from the Imperial Palace, because the people of Texas do not like the word 'Imperial,' and I think you might have just left that out." Mayfield himself avoided discussing the Klan issue, simply stating that it was "a matter over which the United States has no jurisdiction." He also declined to answer the Dallas Citizens' League questionnaire on whether he was a klansman: "The recent agitation about the Ku Klux Klan is confined largely to the city of Dallas and is nothing more nor less than a political fracas raised by Dallas politicians for the purpose of boosting the candidacy of a certain candidate [Thomas] for the United States Senate. I refuse to walk into their trap."[27]

Hiram Wesley Evans was determined to unite the Texas Klan behind Mayfield, despite the Waco agreement. "Mr. Henry is not the man we want," he told Clark in a meeting in Atlanta in May. "Earle Mayfield is in a position to get in touch with the big business of the country. Earle Mayfield is on the railroad commission. He is in line with the railroad interests of this country. He can even get in touch with—he can even approach—Standard Oil."[28]

On May 21, Evans met with Henry and Mayfield in Dallas. Grand

Dragon Harwood; Z. E. Marvin, acting exalted cyclops of Dallas Klan No. 66; George Butcher, secretary of the Dallas chapter; and Dudley M. Kent, exalted cyclops of Fort Worth Klan No. 101, were also present. Evans told the men that he had helped build up the Klan as a great militant political organization in Texas and elsewhere but that if Henry and Mayfield continued in the race it was inevitable that both of them would be defeated and he wanted to see whether the two would come to an agreement. When Henry showed the kligrapp the Little Rock telegram, Evans replied that "the understanding of the officials was that we needed a stalking horse, and we would make a stalking horse of you by giving you permission to come out in the open and defend the Klan; and that is the reason we gave you the authority, although Mr. Mayfield has been intended as our candidate all the time." When Henry still refused to yield, standing squarely on the Waco agreement, Evans threatened him: "If one of you is not out of this contest within 10 days, I am going back to Atlanta, Ga., and issue sealed orders to all local klans in Texas from the imperial palace there that you be eliminated, and that the klan support Mr. Mayfield." Henry then left the meeting.[29]

On June 10, Clark met with Mayfield, Harwood, McCall, Marvin, Butcher, Ralph Cameron, Sterling Strong's son True, and several other klansmen in the Driskill Hotel in Austin. Evans was not present. Mayfield insisted that Henry either withdraw or agree to an immediate elimination election. When Clark produced a recent letter from Evans stating that he "was not going to take any further action or interest in Texas politics this year" but was going to keep the Waco agreement, Marvin replied that he had later instructions. He, Mayfield, and Harwood made repeated demands for an elimination until Clark finally agreed to get in touch by phone with Henry, who was campaigning in West Texas. Henry revealed that he had information that would make it very unwise for him to agree to an elimination, and he was not going to do so. When Clark relayed this message to the others, they began abusing him and Henry. Finally Marvin jumped up from his chair and told Clark, "I am going back home tonight to Dallas, and I propose to call a meeting of the klan as soon as I get there, and it will be a dead shot for Earle Mayfield."[30]

Upon returning to Dallas, Marvin sent a circular letter to Klan chapters over the state advising them of the forthcoming elimination election in Dallas and asking them to hold elections and forward the results to him. When Clark learned of this letter, he protested to Harwood that any elimination would prove disastrous to the Klan, for factional lines had already been drawn, and it was too late now to change individual preferences without causing desertions and probably an open break in the ranks. On June 13, Harwood assured Clark over the phone that Marvin's action was unauthorized, that the Waco agreement would be honored and the Klans so informed, and that he would do everything in his power to prevent the elimination election in Dallas. The next day, however, Harwood told Henry that there would be an elimination by the Texas chapters and that a letter to that effect would be sent out later in the week. Henry relayed this unwelcome news to Clark, who again protested to the grand dragon, warning that the organization would not survive "a political hegira within its ranks."[31]

Despite Clark's protest, about 2,500 members of the Dallas Klan held a secret-ballot elimination election, probably on Friday, June 16. Mayfield received about 1,400 votes to 700 for Henry and 400 for Strong. Fort Worth Klan No. 101 conducted a similar poll, and again Mayfield received a majority of the votes. Harwood then sent word of these two large chapters' actions to the other Klans in the state, and within a short time nearly every active klansman in Texas, including the members of Henry's own Waco chapter, had accepted Mayfield as the "official" Klan candidate. After protesting to Evans in vain about Marvin's arbitrary actions, a disgusted Clark resigned his Klan offices on July 17, effective August 1, though he remained in the Klan until December, 1922.[32]

Sterling Strong withdrew from the Senate race in June in favor of Henry, who stubbornly refused to yield to Mayfield. Henry revealed details of the Waco agreement and subsequent developments to fellow klansmen in letters that were for them only and, he cautioned, "must not fall into Alien hands." He wrote: "*Just say to my friends everywhere that my strength is not going to be whispered away by an unfair and tricky whispering campaign of elimination. I put them on guard now.* I am gaining strength rapidly everywhere. Victory seems a certainty, *if we can meet and suppress unfair means.*" On July 14, Henry went public with the charge that "an insidious 'whispered propaganda'" was coming from the Mayfield camp that he would retire in Mayfield's favor; he vowed to stay in the race until every vote had been counted. He demanded that his opponent tell the people whether he was for or against the Klan and insisted that he was the "noble" organization's standard-bearer, carrying its flag against the onslaughts of Culberson, Thomas, the *Dallas Morning News*, and the Dallas and Fort Worth citizens' leagues.[33]

Mayfield, however, avoided comment on the Klan, saying that it was not an issue, and stressed instead the question of freight rates in Texas. He complained that the federal Interstate Commerce Commission had taken away most of the powers of the state railroad commission and that because of its high-handed methods rates on agricultural products were "extortionate" and "indefensibly high." The only way the people could obtain relief was for Congress to repeal the new Esch-Cummins Transportation Act and restore to the state railroad commissions all their original rate-making powers. He warned that no sweeping reductions in freight rates could be expected from the ICC. Syndicated columnist Bascom Timmons, however, a knowledgeable observer of the Washington scene, said that no one there took Mayfield's platform seriously: "The Esch-Cummins law may be modified, but when a half dozen of the most prominent Republican Senators have not been able to accomplish that, it is difficult to see how Mr. Mayfield could do it."[34]

Jim Ferguson knew that, to win, he must gain a large majority of the tenant-farmer and union-labor vote, and he directed his campaign toward these groups. Opening his canvass at Honey Springs on April 21, he prefaced the main part of his two-hour address with the candid admission that he was unable to pay his debts but that this very inability was a qualification for the Senate. "We are all in the same boat," he explained. "My condition financially fully identifies me with the great mass of people and qualifies me to represent you." Ferguson called for a free ballot, denounced the "tyranny and hypocrisy" of Sunday blue laws, and advocated keeping legal interest rates at no more than 6 percent, regulating rents, and reducing the federal government's payroll by at least 50 percent. He warned that the country would never return to prosperity until the "iniquitous" Federal Reserve System was abolished. With an eye to the union vote he declared himself in favor of the closed shop and against the open shop. Ferguson said that Prohibition was a failure and pledged, if elected, to do all in his power to repeal the Volstead Act and substitute a law that would permit the sale of light wines and beer under government regulation. This would drive the price down and force out of business the bootleggers and dope peddlers who were destroying the morals of boys and the virtue of girls. "Farmer Jim" was in fine speaking fettle and kept his audience laughing with his interpolated comments. At one point in his speech he remarked that the Texas legislature had tried to kill him politically, but, he said, "I am the liveliest corpse you ever saw and my opponents will find it out before this campaign is over."[35]

Then suddenly it appeared that the Democratic State Executive Committee might not place Ferguson's name on the primary ballot. An applicant for a place on the ticket had to certify that he had supported the Democratic nominees in the last general election, and Ferguson in 1920 had been an American party candidate. He argued that, while he had not voted the Democratic ticket, his name could legally appear because the law specified that twenty-five qualified voters could petition the state committee to place a candidate's name on the ballot. Twenty-five of Ferguson's friends in San Antonio submitted a petition. As a precaution he had his wife file as a candidate for the Senate on the primary ballot.[36]

When the state committee met in Austin on June 12, it was tightly controlled by Governor Neff's friends, scarcely one of whom favored placing Ferguson's name on the ballot. They regarded him as a bolter. Ferguson and his attorney, Luther Nickels, addressed the committee and ruffled a few feathers. Ferguson wanted a light-wines-and-beer referendum on the primary ballot, but the committee turned down his proposal with only one dissenting vote. Chairman Frank C. Davis of San Antonio, over the protest of many committeemen, who were eager to finish the job and go home, held the committee in session in a stifling hotel room while Marshall Hicks learned what Neff wanted done about Jim. Neff, Hicks, and Attorney General Keeling discussed the matter for hours at the capitol and finally decided that, while legally they had a perfect right to keep Ferguson from running as a Democrat, he would be able to do "a lot of stirring at the crossroads," and it would be more politic to place his name on the ballot and let the voters take care of him.

When Hicks returned to the committee with Neff's decision, hat in hand, breathing hard, and perspiring, the members voted 12 to 11 to permit Ferguson's name to go on the ballot, but only after adopting a party pledge that aimed to prevent his friends from voting in the primary. It excluded all those who had not voted for the Democratic nominees in the last election or who had given aid and comfort to the opposing parties. Ferguson was thus permitted to be a candidate but not a voter in the Democratic primary. The committee also placed Mrs. Ferguson's name on the ballot next to her husband's, and thus they were opposing candidates. Jim, however, had his wife withdraw her name. Her letter to Joe W. Hale of Waco, secretary of the committee, explained, "This action is taken in view of the fact that the Committee has certified the name of James E. Ferguson." Even then it required a ruling from the attorney general to omit her name from the primary ballot.[37]

Ferguson kicked off the last month of his campaign with an attack on Mayfield and Culberson in the *Forum*. He charged that Mayfield was the candidate of the railroads and the big corporations and was for the open shop and against the closed shop; that his scheme was to "set up a family aristocracy to control Texas with the House of Mayfield— Allison, Earle, and Billie" (Allison Mayfield, Earle's cousin, was chairman of the Texas Railroad Commission; Billie Mayfield, no relation, was a candidate for lieutenant governor); and that he had "gone in secretly with the Baptist politicians and the Ku Klux politicians who want to rule this state with a prohibition religious fanaticism that intends to strike down religious liberty which is guaranteed by the constitution." If Mayfield was not a klansman, let him say so: "The time has come when the people want to know who is who in this race."

As an antiprohibitionist, Culberson would attract "wet" voters who otherwise might favor Ferguson. Recognizing that the senator's health was his Achilles' heel, Jim launched a deadly thrust, announcing that he had "reliable information that Senator Culberson was not possessed of such mental powers as will enable him to attend and understand the deliberations of the Senate." After noting that the incumbent had not been in Texas in ten years and had not spoken in the Senate since 1919, Ferguson challenged him to come home in a Pullman car and let the people see him and make up their own minds about his mental condition. Ferguson promised, moreover, that if Culberson would make a twenty-minute speech in Dallas and a twenty-minute speech in San Antonio, he would withdraw from the race and support him. "Or, if he can't make a speech, then if he will come down to Dallas and San Antonio and sit in an arm chair unattended and pay attention while his campaign manager, Barry Miller, makes a two hours' speech to the people, . . . then I will withdraw from this race and support Senator Culberson." It was a challenge that the invalid could not accept. Tom Love admitted later that Ferguson's "reiterated charges as to Culberson's physical incapacity drove thousands of votes from him though most of them voted for some candidate other than Ferguson." [38]

After his statement early in April criticizing the Klan, Ferguson was not especially vigorous in his denunciation of the organization, referring only briefly to the question in his speeches. As Culberson faded and Mayfield showed surprising strength, however, he struck hard at the knights in the final days of the campaign, beginning with a Houston speech and during a swing through East Texas. "I had hoped," he said, "we would be spared the disgrace of having a fraternal organization entering politics with the purpose of trying to elect candidates it proposed." He called Neff the Klan's "kaiser" in Texas and Mayfield its "crown prince." He revealed that he had firsthand information from a prominent member of the Neff administration that the Klan wanted to drive the Jews and Catholics out of the country. "If this goes on you will have the worst revolution in this country you ever saw," Ferguson warned. "When you criticize another man's religion, you jeopardize your own. A man's religion is his own business." Noting that Jew, Catholic, and Protestant had fought side by side in the war, he said that he had never heard of a klansman "in the trenches." "The first time I ever saw one was when he turned up in this country with a bag of feathers in one hand and a tar bucket in the other, violating the laws of this country." [39]

Cullen Thomas tried to straddle the Klan question, since it threatened to split his following among Texas prohibitionists. He complained because it had become a campaign issue and reminded the voters that he was not a klansman nor a member of the Dallas County Citizens' League, whose leaders, he said, were not promoting his candidacy. In July, however, he took up the Klan issue, charging that Henry and Mayfield (whom he dubbed the "klandestine kandidate") were trying to use the organization to ride into office. In turn, Henry accused Thomas of shifting his attitude on the Klan question, which he had "found to be loaded" after he had declared that the Klan must die. Thomas, saying some bad things and also some good things about the Klan, reminded him of the snake

> Who wiggled in and wiggled out,
> Leaving all the people in doubt
> As to whether the critter that made the track
> Was going in or coming back. [40]

Thomas gave much time and attention to the Prohibition question. Of the six candidates only he and Mayfield were for Prohibition, and the Thomas camp sought to cast doubt on Mayfield's commitment to the sacred cause by taking up two charges made by Sterling Strong in his letter of withdrawal: (1) that Mayfield's name "stood A-One (A-1) in the Brewers' Blue Book while he was in the State Senate from Bosque County, Texas," and (2) that Mayfield had been selected to lead the fight for a bill outlawing racetrack gambling in the Senate in 1909 but that on the morning it was to be considered Mayfield "was charged with playing poker with a bunch of saloon lobbyists and the bill was taken out of his hands and leadership bestowed upon another Senator." Charles A. Leddy, a Thomas supporter, produced a certified copy of case no. 2978 in Justice of the Peace Court, Precinct 3, Travis County, showing that in February, 1909, "EBM" had entered a plea of guilty to gambling and had been fined ten dollars and costs. "It seems that Mayfield not only pussyfoots on the Klan issue, but pussyfoots in pleading under his initials instead of by his full name," Leddy jeered.[41]

Mayfield defended his record on Prohibition, offering to donate one hundred dollars to charity if any person could show from the record that he had ever voted against any Prohibition measure. Mayfield's headquarters distributed a one-page circular, "Prohibition Record of Actual Accomplishments," signed by the Reverend Ed. R. Barcus, of the First Methodist Church in Austin. Barcus declared that, "from the day he cast his first vote to this good hour, Earle B. Mayfield has supported, worked and voted for every prohibition measure." In reply, Thomas's backers claimed that Mayfield's votes for local-option measures in the Senate did not show any strong Prohibition record; practically every antiprohibitionist in that body had voted for them because they were "scared out of their wits" by impending statewide Prohibition. A Thomas circular bore the caption: "Mayfield Just as Good Pro as Any Anti in the Senate."[42]

In contrast to some of the other candidates, Clarence Ousley conducted what was termed "one of the more dignified campaigns of the year." In his addresses the Fort Worth man laid special stress on the South's adverse economic position when compared with New England's. He said that the cause was a tariff policy that taxed imported manufactured goods and admitted raw materials free. Ousley warned that the "free raw materialists" in the Democratic party were unwise in urging that the tariff should be removed on foreign cotton and woolen goods, since such an action would cripple if not destroy American cotton and woolen mills, whose operatives would not work for the low wages paid foreign workers. That would injure the South. Instead, he wanted tariff protection for the region's raw materials. "For 100 years the South has been producing a large part of the food and clothes of the world," he declared. "It seems that the producers should be given the same consideration as those who transport, transform and traffic in the product." When opponents charged that he had written a lot against Prohibition, Ousley replied that "no honest man who understands language could vote for any substantial amendment to the Volstead Act." [43]

From the beginning of Culberson's campaign his sponsors' strategy was to have him "show" in either first or second place in the July 22 primary and then win in the second primary in August as he had against Oscar B. Colquitt in 1916. The difficulty of his candidacy was that, with Mayfield, Ferguson, Thomas, Ousley, and Henry conducting energetic campaigns from one end of the state to the other, he was severely handicapped because he could make no fight at all except through his friends. Nevertheless, the Culberson men professed confidence that the "Old Guard" would neither surrender nor be called on to die and that the senator would be in the runoff. "His opponents have been making many speeches in North Texas & they are 'smaller fry' than before they began their speech making," Judge William H. Clark of Dallas wrote James B. Wells. "It is painfully evident even to the friends of Cullen Thomas, Mayfield, and Bob Henry that none of them are big enough for a United States Senator,—not all of them together,—in one bunch." Barry Miller predicted that Culberson would lead in the first primary by 50,000 or more votes. [44]

In March, C. W. Jurney asked Colonel House to obtain an endorsement for Culberson from Woodrow Wilson "to make his election certain," but considering the former president's coolness toward his former friend and confidant because of disagreements over policy at the Paris Peace Conference, it is unlikely that House made the attempt. On June 21, Culberson sent Wilson a copy of a public letter giving his reasons for having supported the woman-suffrage amendment. The senator probably hoped for a reply that could be used as an endorsement, but Wilson sent only a polite acknowledgment, expressing the hope that "the prolonged sessions of the Congress are not proving too burdensome to you." On the eve of the primary Tom Love made a last effort to involve Wilson in the contest, wiring him that Clarence Ousley had condemned Culberson for voting against the Farmers' Emergency Tariff Law in 1916 and had said repeatedly in his speeches that Wilson had favored the policy of the law as shown in a letter to Representative Claude Kitchin of North Carolina. "Primaries Saturday will appreciate it if you will immediately wire me or Dallas News whether Ousleys statement well founded." The ailing Wilson ignored Love's request.[45]

By abandoning Robert Henry and Sterling Strong for Earle Mayfield, the Klan assured him a big lead in the Democratic primary on July 22. The surprise in the voting was Jim Ferguson, who finished second, about 30,000 votes behind Mayfield. Commented the *Dallas Morning News*, ". . . it is doubtful if there are many who can sincerely say they expected ex-Governor Ferguson to disclose the strength which the returns witness." Culberson finished a poor third; ill health and a younger generation of Texas voters who knew him not ended a political career extending back to the Jim Hogg era. Thomas was fourth in the balloting, followed by Ousley. Henry attracted only a handful of Klan votes and finished last. "I was walking up the track toward Washington, when the Ku Klux train came along, and everybody knows what happened," Thomas said in a statement. "The intrusion of the klan question literally cut what would have been my vote in two."[46]

Three klansmen entered the runoff for statewide offices: Billie Mayfield of Houston, editor of a weekly Klan newspaper, for lieutenant governor; George D. Garrett of Dallas for state treasurer; and Ed R. Bentley of McAllen for state superintendent of public instruction. Many klansmen won either outright nomination or slots in the runoff in local races in Dallas, Fort Worth, Houston, Austin, Wichita Falls, Waco, Beaumont, and other cities. The Klan was ecstatic. On July 28, Grand Dragon Brown Harwood sent a letter to "all Exalted Cyclops, Terrors, and Klansmen," rejoicing over the triumph of "the native-born white Protestant Gentile who is standing in the way of foreign religious aggression, and who holds allegiance only to God, home and country." The victory, he explained, had been won on soil enriched by the Protestant blood that had been shed in wresting it away from the "priest-ridden tyranny that now encumbers and holds the remainder of what was once Old Mexico."[47]

Taking note of the Klan victories in Texas, the *New York Times* commented acidly: "If one likes to be ruled by 'Imperial Palaces,' Kleagles and that sort of thing, and the 'Invisible Empire,' one likes so to be ruled. The Texas primary is at least happy in the fact that it has put one Mayfield, a Klan man described as modest, even if guilty of being a 'newspaper man,' at the head of the poll." But because the total votes polled by the four anti-Klan candidates for the senate outnumbered the ballots cast for Mayfield and Henry by almost 2 to 1, a dozen Texas editors reached by *Literary Digest* magazine refused to recognize in the result a triumph for the hooded order. "The Klan has won no victory in Texas," wired the editor of the *San Angelo Standard*. "Unusual circumstances and not the Klan, have placed State Railroad Commissioner Mayfield in the lead for United States Senator over the veteran Senator Culberson." "The Klan's influence can not be counted as the one decisive factor in the Mayfield victory," agreed the *Corpus Christi Caller*. The paper maintained that "Texas has not surrendered to the 'invisible empire,'" while the *Denison Herald* asserted that "an analysis of the vote polled shows an anti–Ku Klux, rather than a Ku Klux victory." Democratic leaders in Washington were less sanguine, however. They feared that Mayfield's victory would bring the religious issue into the presidential election of 1924 and cost their party the Catholic vote in the northern states. "Mr. Mayfield, the inconspicuous of six months ago, is very conspicuous now," wrote Bascom Timmons. "And Mr. Mayfield is a nightmare to the national democracy."[48]

As Mayfield and Ferguson made preparations for a second campaign, followers of the defeated candidates had to decide whether to support an impeached and removed former governor or a man who had the backing of the Klan. "We are . . . in a sad political predicament down here," lamented a professor of history at the University of Texas, "with the choice between Ferguson on the one side and Earl [*sic*] Mayfield, a Ku Kluxer and a wind bag, on the other." As soon as Culberson's defeat was certain, his campaign manager, Barry Miller, who had supported Hobby in 1918, offered his services to Ferguson: "Reports show that you are 17,000 votes ahead of Senator Culberson, which will put you in the run-off. In view of this fact there can be but one place for a real Democrat to go." Miller's decision prompted Culberson to announce that he would take no part in the second primary but that "my friends as a matter of course should exercise their own judgment as to whom they would support."[49]

A large number of Texans chose to make their decision for Prohibition and other progressive issues and endorsed Mayfield. Jesse Daniel Ames, president of the League of Women Voters; Lily Joseph, president of the Federation of Women's Clubs; Alma Watts, president of the Women's Christian Temperance Union; and prominent clubwoman

Ann Pennybacker supported Mayfield over Ferguson. In response to a telegram from the *Houston Post*, Senator Morris Sheppard said that he favored Mayfield "because I believe his election would be in the best interest of prohibition enforcement, the eighteenth amendment and progressive Democratic legislation in general." Cullen Thomas also endorsed him, though his law partner and campaign manager, O. O. Touchstone, chose Ferguson because of the Klan issue. Thomas B. Love, who had supported Culberson, announced:

I am for Earle B. Mayfield for United States Senator, because I have no doubt whatever that he would make an infinitely better United States Senator for Texas than would James E. Ferguson, though I am unalterably opposed to the Ku Klux Klan. . . . I believe he would be a progressive, Woodrow Wilson, League of Nations, prohibition, woman suffrage Democratic Senator, and that James E. Ferguson would be the very opposite of this. To borrow the language of my friend, Judge Barry Miller, I feel that "there can be but one place for a real Democrat to go."[50]

William P. Hobby issued a statement that Mayfield's election would be "in keeping with the progress of democracy and the forward march of Texas" while Ferguson's election would be "a step backward." Joe Bailey said, however, that he was against both candidates: "One would give the government to the unions, the other would give it to the Ku Klux." General Crane, the prosecutor in Ferguson's impeachment trial and chairman of the Dallas County Citizens' League, faced a particularly difficult choice. Many Texans wanted to know what his attitude would be in the campaign as a guide to their own decisions. Crane considered staying out of the runoff primary but finally decided to vote for the anti-Klan candidates in the local and state races but not to vote in the senatorial race. Privately Crane hoped that Ferguson, "the less of two evils," would win and that the Senate would refuse to seat him. "We then would be rid of both evils, the ku klux klan and an impeached Governor, and could give a decent man a chance to run next time," he explained.[51]

An effort was made to keep Ferguson's name off the August ballot through a petition filed by Judge John W. Gaines of San Antonio with the State Democratic Executive Committee. The petition alleged that Ferguson was ineligible for the United States Senate under the argument that it was a state office and his impeachment conviction barred him from running for it. Ferguson charged that Mayfield was behind the move and branded him "as a contemptible political coward." Actually Judge Gaines favored the former governor over Mayfield but hoped that if he was disqualified the courts would put Culberson on the ticket as the next-highest in the July primary and he could then be elected. C. W. Jurney wired Gaines, however, that the senator would not be a candidate even if the courts held that his name should properly be listed. Mayfield indicated that he wanted Ferguson "until the finish—and I will finish him"—and offered to have his attorneys help him get his name on the ballot. When the state committee met in Dallas, supporters of the two men "jointly held the steering wheel of the steam roller" that snuffed out every objection to having Ferguson's name appear.[52]

Ferguson began the runoff campaign by making it plain that the Klan would be his big issue. "The question in this campaign is shall the Senator from Texas be selected by the order from King William the First from the imperial palace in Georgia, or shall the Senator be elected by the sovereign voice of the people of Texas," he told a cheering, hand-clapping, foot-stamping, overflow crowd in his opening address at Waxahachie. "It is now a question whether you want Prince Earle or Farmer Jim." He challenged Mayfield to debate the Klan issue with him on the stump "anywhere and anyhow." Alleging that the "Ku Klux politicians" had double-crossed Henry because the big corporations could not control him, while Mayfield had "always been on the side of the big railroads and big business in this country," Ferguson warned that the country's corporations were using the Klan to crush the laboring masses, rob the public with high railroad rates, and turn the nation over to "the most damnable set of political hijackers that ever cursed a free country." If left alone, the Klan would "bring on the greatest internal revolution this nation ever saw, and . . . plunge us into a condition far worse than Russia itself."[53]

In homely and vigorous language Ferguson asserted in his speeches that Mayfield was a "hypocritical wet pro" whose personal prohibition record belied his public one; he had drunk Scotch highballs at the Austin Country Club and later joined the club in his wife's name because he could not afford to be a member of a club that sold liquor. Jim invited his Georgetown audience to go to Austin, where he and Mayfield had lived for three and a half years, and ask one hundred men about their private lives. "If they don't tell you I was a sober man all of this time and that Earle B. Mayfield is not, then I will donate $100 to the Red Cross." He charged that his opponent and "Water Power Hobby" had attended a party near Jonah on the San Gabriel River three years before and that "they got drunk as boiled owls," and "he and Hobby got naked and run up and down the banks of this river in that condition until forced to stop by the local officers at Georgetown." At Giddings he accused Mayfield of "being guilty of conduct with the opposite sex that I can not, in decency, mention when ladies are present in the audience" and pleaded with the crowd to support him against "this contemptible libertine who is trying to pull the wool over your eyes."[54]

Mayfield began his campaign by emphasizing the railroad-transportation and Prohibition issues, but soon, stung by Ferguson's charges, he struck back. At Denton he said that his opponent "stands before the people of Texas as a perjurer," that Ferguson had testified at his impeachment trial that the $150,000 under investigation had not come from Texas brewers, and that the San Antonio brewers had later testified that they had given him the money. Declaring that he did not intend to be drawn into any "mudslinging contest," Mayfield said that his only response to the former governor's allegations was that "they come from the mouth of James E. Ferguson." He later changed his mind, however, and stated that neither he nor his wife had joined the Austin Country Club until more than a year and a half after the state prohibition law had gone into effect, and that since that time it had been absolutely against club rules to serve liquor on the premises. Ferguson in turn produced a witness who had seen Mayfield drinking Scotch highballs at the club while it still had a liquor license. "Why cannot the preachers of Texas find somebody to support who is not a poker player?" an irate Jasper man asked the Reverend E. L. Shettles:

I wish you would tell Mayfield for me to keep to the main issues and say nothing about his drinking bootleg liquor or playing poker if he is guilty, for as sure as he confesses it all the Methodist stewards and Baptist deacons from the "forks of the creek" will vote for Ferguson. . . . They will vote for any scalawag who makes no pretentions to morality before they will a man who runs on a reform ticket, and is unclean in his private life. And I think this is the last time I am going to vote for a man who cannot emphatically deny such acusations [sic] as Ferguson brings against Mayfield.[55]

When Mayfield charged that Ferguson had received 3,500 black votes in Bexar County in the first primary and was now making an effort to persuade the German Republicans in South Texas to vote for him in the runoff, Jim replied by producing a handbill that he said was being circulated in the border counties calling on all Mexicans to vote for Mayfield. He said that in North Texas his opponent was ranting about his "100 per cent Americanism" and opposition to foreign immigration while in South Texas "he sneaks around stealthily and tries to corral the Mexican vote by spreading around Spanish handbills promising the Mexican social equality." "Oh, he's a fine, 100 per cent American!" sneered Ferguson. "Oh, he's a lovely feller to go around bawling about white supremacy!"[56]

On August 21 a Ferguson rally at Houston was interrupted when someone near the auditorium door yelled in a loud voice, "Hurrah for Billie Mayfield!" At this prearranged signal several hundred men and women seated in the lower part of the hall and some in the gallery rose and, with catcalls and jeers, began forcing their way to the exits. In an instant the crowd was in an uproar. Ferguson tried to go on with his speech, but could not be heard above the hubbub. He appealed to the city and county officials to quiet the disturbance. When they made no move, he accused them of having Klan sympathies. Ferguson said later, "I knew if I sat down until they finished filing out, I would lose my entire crowd." After a twenty-minute delay he continued his speech and finished without further trouble. He tried to turn the incident to his advantage, declaring the next night in San Antonio that there could be but one issue until the end of the campaign: "Shall we be ruled by the mob, or shall we bow only to the dictates of constitutional Government?"[57]

The Klan had used the walkout plan before, trying but failing to break up an anti-Klan rally addressed by General Crane at Waco the previous July. Mayfield, however, claimed that the scheme to stampede the Houston meeting was "hatched up by Ferguson and his supporters for the purpose of gaining sympathy." Earlier in the campaign Mayfield himself had appeared on the stage at a Dallas rally with several known klansmen, including the Reverend A. C. Parker, the exalted cyclops of Dallas Klan No. 66. Ferguson challenged Mayfield to meet him in a joint debate, but Mayfield refused, explaining his reasons by telling a story about a possum that a polecat challenged to a fight. The possum declined, saying, "You know I can whip you and everybody else knows it, but think what a condition I would be in after the fight to go home to my wife and children."[58]

Just before election day Woodrow Wilson's name was injected into the campaign at Rockwall. After denouncing the Klan before a crowd, Ferguson read a telegram from the former president denouncing as "grossly false" a statement by the Reverend Mr. Parker that "eighty-five per cent of Wilson's appointees were Catholics." Wilson stated, "I thought it inconsistent with the principles of our Government to consider the church connection of anyone I appointed to office." Ferguson made no comment on the telegram, apparently satisfied with the crowd's response. Ferguson continued his attack on Mayfield. "Let me tell you, my friends, what Earle Mayfield is," Ferguson declared. "He is a low-down, stinking, contemptible, pussillanimous, gambling little upstart hypocrite. And that's not bad language I am using either. It is the only phrase that will describe Earle Mayfield in his true colors."[59]

In his last few speeches of the campaign Ferguson moved his audience to tears as he pleaded for vindication and for the chance to go home to his wife "and kiss her and say, honey, we're free again—the Democrats of Texas have said so." That plea, made in a closing speech at Fort Worth, produced absolute silence in a crowd that had greeted his denunciation of the Klan with wild cheering and noisemaking, "and," the *Dallas Morning News* reported, "as the ex-Governor's voice died out on the air, marking the close of one of the most vigorous and active campaigns he has made, many a face was tear stained, and many a man and woman, with handkerchief in hand pressed forward to shake the hand of the candidate."[60]

Ferguson predicted that he would defeat Mayfield more easily and by a larger majority than he had beaten Tom Ball in 1914. "My majority over Ball," he said, "was about 45,000. My majority over Mayfield will be about 75,000." He explained, "Ball had the united support of the prohibitionists of Texas, which Mayfield hasn't got, and Ball besides had many strong antis among his followers, and the women prayed for Ball and the preachers preached for him." "There has been a rising tide that started two weeks ago for me and it will roll high by Saturday," he predicted in the *Ferguson Forum*. It did not roll high enough, however; Mayfield defeated him by 52,358 votes—317,591 to 265,233.[61]

Mayfield led in 174 counties scattered throughout the state, but his largest majorities were in the blackland counties of Central, North, and Northwest Texas, where prohibitionists were numerous. "A vote against Mayfield is a vote for light wines and beer and for the return of the saloon," Collin County (county seat, McKinney) voters were told. Mayfield lost his home county, Bosque, by almost 400 votes (Ferguson carried Bell County by 20 votes) but swept all the counties with big cities except Bexar (county seat, San Antonio) and El Paso. He carried the Klan strongholds of Dallas County by 10,000 votes and Harris County (Houston) by more than 5,000 votes, the latter being almost exactly offset by a similar Ferguson majority in Bexar County. Ferguson led Mayfield in sixty-nine counties, including nine of the ten so-called German counties, where the beer-loving citizens approved his light-wines-and-beer plank. In a bitter postelection analysis in the *Ferguson Forum*, Ferguson blamed his defeat in the big cities on ballot-box fraud and "simply because the Klan induced a great majority of the labor union voters to quit me and vote for Mayfield." In retrospect, however, he saw a silver lining to his defeat, telling a reporter in 1932 that "though I didn't win the race I established myself as the anti-Klan candidate and that elected my wife two years later." [62]

Although the Klan had nominated a United States senator, its candidates for lieutenant governor, state treasurer, and state superintendent of public instruction (Billie Mayfield, George D. Garrett, and Ed R. Bentley, respectively) were defeated by their non-Klan opponents, T. Whitfield Davidson, C. V. Terrell, and S. L. M. Marrs, by majorities of 111,334, 71,680, and 21,990. Davidson's winning margin over Billie Mayfield, who had pledged to "drive modern evils from this land of ours," was double the margin of Earle Mayfield over Ferguson. The *Dallas Morning News* noted that in each of the three statewide contests in which both candidates were prohibitionists the non-Klan candidate won, while in the one race in which a Klan candidate was successful he triumphed over "an avowed and inveterate anti-prohibitionist." The *News* concluded "that a good many thousand prohibitionists who have no sympathy with the Ku Klux Klan and its works voted for its senatorial candidate." That Ferguson had been ousted from the governorship in an impeachment trial only accentuated that "the success of Mr. Mayfield was at once a prohibition victory and a Ku Klux Klan defeat." "So far as Mayfield was concerned," General Crane wrote, "the prohibitionists joined the Klansmen in the second primaries, and secured his victory." [63]

The eastern press generally accepted this thesis. "Viewed from a distance, the choice between Mayfield, sponsored by the Ku Klux and the Anti-Saloon League, and Ferguson, who was impeached while serving as governor, must have been a hard one," editorialized the *New York World*, adding that many thousands of Texans must have voted for Mayfield despite an aversion both to the Klan and to the

Anti-Saloon League and that Ferguson's presence in the race made the issue a personal one, "dwarfing every other consideration." "Had Earle B. Mayfield been opposed in the runoff by some Democrat without the stain of impeachment and the deep scars of an old party feud upon him, Mayfield would have gone the way of the three other favorites of the Ku Kluxers," said the *Philadelphia Evening Public Ledger*. "On the Klan issue Mr. Mayfield, like Brer Rabbit, 'lay low.' But he got the votes," was the comment of the *New York Times*.[64]

Still, the anti-Klan press could not explain away the striking success the organization had enjoyed in local races; in Dallas, Tarrant, Harris, Jefferson, McLennan, Wichita, and many less populous counties, Klan-backed candidates who had not won nomination in the first primary gained victories in the runoff. In Dallas, where Klan majorities ranged from 1,600 to 9,340 in seven races, klansmen celebrated with a night parade headed by the fiery cross to the tune of "Onward, Christian Soldiers." Shelby Cox, who had defeated District Attorney Maury Hughes, rode with exalted cyclops Parker, D. C. McCord, and George Purl, the last of whom won a seat in the Texas House of Representatives. Purl was one of an almost certain Klan majority in that house of the Thirty-eighth Legislature.[65]

Most of the state's congressmen tried to straddle the Klan issue, though U.S. Representative John Nance Garner said that the Klan was totally foreign to the American way of life—after which hooded klansmen gathered near his home in Uvalde to burn a cross and announced plans to defeat him, and he received threatening letters. Garner won reelection, but he lost counties, including Uvalde, that he had always carried before. He wrote Tom Connally:

Thanks for your telegram. My original friend was not far wrong when he said that the women, the soldiers and the K.K.K.'s were after my scalp. I was certainly surprised at the vote in this district—my friends were also, since the campaign was conducted in a secret like way—anyways it is all right, and I am glad all the boys are coming back with, as you know, one exception [Tom Blanton].

In the Fourteenth District, Republican incumbent Harry Wurzbach of Seguin won over a Jewish anti-Klan Democrat, Harry Hertzberg of San Antonio, in the November contest. Wurzbach carried his opponent's home county, Bexar, and won the election by about 3,000 votes.[66]

Arrayed behind Ed Westbrook, a former state senator, against

Sam Rayburn were the Klan, the Farm Labor Union, the American Federation of Labor, the railroad brotherhoods and the striking railroad shopmen at Denison, and the railroad companies. "I've lost this race," Rayburn muttered glumly as he watched the returns, but when the last vote was counted, he had won by the narrow margin of 1,254 votes. "My majority was not as big as I had hoped but if you could have seen first hand the real conditions in this district you would even wonder at as much majority as I got," the relieved candidate wrote Tom Connally.[67]

The Democratic State Convention opened in San Antonio on September 5 under the ominous shadow of a gun battle between the Klan and anti-Klan factions in Sealy, Texas, in which several people had been killed. The entire state was jittery with tension. No one knew how much strength the Klan had in the convention, and there was fear that it would take over. The Klan supporters themselves were uncertain and, in the bad blood of the moment, apparently more cautious than usual. They did not want the Democratic party to endorse their organization, but they wanted no condemnation either. On the other hand, the militant anti-Klan forces were demanding either a denunciation of the organization by name or a plank in the platform that everyone could understand as Democratic disapproval of the Klan's principles. Declaring that he was "for harmony if possible but for principle at any price," Ferguson, who did not go to San Antonio, wired Frank C. Davis, chairman of the Democratic Executive Committee, that the convention should declare for strict enforcement of all laws, condemn the Klan, and demand the passage of a law prohibiting a klansman from holding office. "Let us put Texas democracy in no false light before the national democracy," he urged.[68]

On the evening before the convention opened, the Bexar County delegation and anti-Klan delegates from other counties held a two-hour closed caucus and appointed a seven-member committee to prepare a strong resolution condemning the Klan by name. John C. Granbery of Southwestern University, Georgetown, presented the caucus with a resolution condemning religious intolerance and other principles that the Klan was alleged to support but not mentioning the Klan specifically; it was turned down by the other delegates as too mild. Seeing that he had "gotten in the wrong pew," Granbery left the meeting, saying that "their views are so drastic as to be insulting to many good men who have unfortunately been brought into the Ku Klux

Klan. I am convinced they will not be satisfied short of a determined effort to bust up the convention." [69]

When the convention opened on September 5, a steamroller went into operation in the interest of "harmony." Supposedly anti-Klan forces were steering the machine, though some thought that the Klan was behind it. Marshall Hicks was selected temporary and then permanent chairman, and both in his keynote address and in his handling of the convention he was for harmony. He was interested in securing the confirmation of Neff's nomination in the primary and in framing a platform that would elect his candidate with the least possible trouble. A motion was adopted that all resolutions submitted to the convention must be referred to the platform committee without being read or debated—thus precluding any floor fights. "Mr. Marshall [Hicks] elected temporary and permanent chairman without opposition. Convention running smoothly thus far," Hicks's law partner Charles M. Dickson wired another member of the firm. The platform committee met the next morning, September 6, and voted down both the Granbery resolution and the so-called Teagarden resolution, which was drafted by the committee appointed by the anti-Klan caucus and denounced the Klan by name. [70]

On the convention's second day "prolonged cheering and repeated ovations" greeted Neff and T. Whitfield Davidson, the nominee for lieutenant governor, when they asserted in their acceptance speeches that they were the servants of all the people and not of any clique or coterie and spoke of the need for peace and good will and the banishment of religious and racial hatred and turmoil. "While governor, I have not felt that I was called upon to commend every laudable undertaking nor to condemn every worthless enterprise that might have followers in Texas," Neff said. He continued:

That I might render the best service, I have not permitted myself since I became governor to become a member of or to align myself with any commercial, social, secret, sectional, racial or ecclesiastical organization that even had a tendency to separate our people into sects or sections. All men, Christian and pagan, Jew and gentile, Catholic and Protestant, rich and poor, black and white, those who speak classical English and those who articulate in a foreign tongue, the upper ten and the lower ten thousand, have looked alike and fared alike, and shall continue to look alike and fare alike officially.

In his address Davidson was even more severe about the Klan. Earle Mayfield was also cordially received and cheered when he spoke against the liquor traffic and foreign immigration. He said that he was going to Washington "to represent all the people, without respect of religion or creed." After the three speeches John Granbery jumped to his feet and moved that "the broad Democratic sentiments expressed this day by Pat Neff and T. W. Davidson be endorsed as the sentiments of the convention." Wild applause followed. Hicks shouted, "You are out of order!" and broke his gavel in an effort to be heard above the din. While Hicks refused to put the question, the crowd shouted its approval. The Dallas and Harris County Klan delegations sat quietly. Privately, however, they complained that Neff's speech had been "cold" and that he had "stuck a dagger in the organization." One klansman grumbled that if the governor had spoken thus before the first primary he would have been forced into a runoff.[71]

In an uproarious afternoon session the delegates by a roll-call vote of 691½ to 135½ shut off all debate on the Klan issue by tabling the Teagarden resolution and shouting through the majority platform report, which made no mention of the Klan. An attempt to introduce the milder Granbery resolution was ruled out of order by the chair. Barry Miller had arrived in San Antonio with a proxy from Delta County to lead the floor fight for the Teagarden resolution, but at the crucial moment Hicks ruled that his proxy had come too late to be acted on by the credentials committee and denied him a seat. After approving with a "wild roar of ayes" a klansman's motion thanking Hicks for the "masterly way" in which he had handled the proceedings, the convention adjourned.[72]

Some disgruntled anti-Klan delegates left the San Antonio convention prepared to nominate an independent candidate to run against Mayfield in the November election. After a conference at the Adolphus Hotel in Dallas on September 9, Barry Miller, Henry D. Lindsley, John H. Kirby, Joe Eagle, Scott Woodward, and about a hundred others from various parts of the state issued a call to "the Democratic voters of Texas" to meet in a statewide mass meeting in Dallas on September 16 to name "a real Democrat for United States Senator in opposition to the Ku Klux Klan nominee." George E. B. Peddy, a thirty-year-old assistant district attorney of Harris County, was selected to oppose Mayfield. E. P. Wilmot, an Austin banker, the Republican candidate for the United States Senate, withdrew from the contest, and the Republican state committee endorsed Peddy. R. B. Creager of Brownsville, the Republican state chairman, immediately wired President Harding of the committee's action. "Close coalition is thus formed between Republicans and anti-Klan Democrats who are now outside of and fighting the Democratic party," he reported. "This is a large and influential element. There is a good chance of electing Peddy and under any circumstances action today means great and permanent strengthening of Republican Party in Texas and making of it a real factor in State's affairs."[73]

The presidential election of 1920 had found the Texas Republican party once again divided into feuding "Lily White" and "Black and Tan" factions. A majority of the "Black and Tan" group, led by William Madison ("Gooseneck Bill") McDonald, a black, and E. H. R. Green, had supported General Leonard Wood for the GOP presidential nomination, only to see Creager and Frank E. Scobey of San Antonio move to the front by backing Ohio Senator Harding. Creager had made the only seconding speech for him at the Republican National Convention. Harding had met Creager, an oil-and-land speculator, through Scobey, one of the "Ohio Gang," who called Creager "my best friend in the South, and I believe the most influential Republican in the State of Texas." After the president chose Creager over Congressman Harry Wurzbach and National Committeeman H. F. MacGregor of Houston as his "referee" on patronage matters in Texas, Creager, called the "Red Fox of the Rio Grande Valley," assumed a leadership of the state party that would last for three decades. Under his control it developed an exclusive country-club image that hampered its numerical growth. Creager assured Harding in May, 1921:

I say to you that we are building on the most solid foundation on which the Republican Party can be built in Texas or any of the other Southern States. We have drawn in, and are drawing in others, of the most solid business element of the state, and are not relying on the negro and "pie hunting element." This latter element can always be controlled by the better element to which I refer, without giving it that controlling importance which Republican politicans of the South have heretofore given to it. It does not mean driving this element out of the Republican Party at all, but it does mean subordinating it to the better element.[74]

Henry D. Lindsley, who had supported Harding in 1920, was named Peddy's campaign manager, and a financial committee of twenty-five prominent Texans was organized to raise funds. Among its members were John H. Kirby and Joseph S. Cullinan of Houston, Frank Kell of Wichita Falls, Robert J. Kleberg of Kingsville, and James B.

Wells of Brownsville. Kirby and Cullinan together made contributions and loans to the Peddy campaign totaling $58,819.86. Mr. and Mrs. Richard Fleming and Rienzi M. Johnston, the former publisher of the *Houston Post*, were the mainstays of Peddy headquarters in Houston. Chesley W. Jurney, Culberson's secretary, pledged his support and scored the Klan.[75]

As a student leader at the University of Texas, Peddy, dressed in his officer-candidate uniform, had led a student march to the capitol in 1917 to protest Governor Ferguson's veto of the university appropriation bill. Peddy's presence in uniform had particularly irritated Ferguson, who later described the "insult" as one "which if offered to [Peddy's] commanding general would have secured his execution at sunrise." Peddy, however, had supported Ferguson against Mayfield in the runoff and as a result had been asked to resign the presidency of his Sunday-school class at the First Methodist church of Houston. Letting bygones be bygones, Ferguson announced that he would vote for Peddy. "God has given us a candidate," he told the readers of the *Ferguson Forum*. "He is good. He is able. He is fearless. All the gates of hell and the Ku Klux Klan will not prevail against him." But not all the Ferguson men were as forgiving as Jim. "Governor to think you would ask me to vote for a man that believed so much in mobs in 1917 in that he led a mob against the Governor of Texas," wrote an irate T. T. Thompson of Clarksville. "A man that stood for all the greed of the University. I am utterly shocked. I must say no. I can not think of voting for a man that had so little respect for the familey [*sic*] of the Governor of Texas that he wanted to forever destroy their husband and father." Fergusonite Alexander Dienst endorsed this letter: "*Thems'* my sentiments friend Thompson (*Dienst*)."[76]

Peddy's campaign suffered a setback when Attorney General W. A. Keeling ruled that no person who had voted in either Democratic primary in 1922 could have his name printed on the ballot for the November election as an independent candidate. Noted one historian, "That was but the beginning of an amazing series of filing of protests, injunctions, appeals, hearings, trials, and rulings which must have made the voters dizzy in regard to the candidates' eligibility." Creager certified to the secretary of state that Peddy was the Republican candidate for senator, only to have Keeling rule that his name could not go on the ballot because he had not been nominated for the Senate in a general primary as required by a 1913 law. For good measure, Peddy was also barred because he had voted in the Democratic primary. Peddy's attorneys appealed to the federal courts, but the Circuit Court of Appeals in New Orleans ruled on October 23 that it lacked jurisdiction to instruct state officials on the matter. Keeling announced that this decision meant that Peddy's name would not go on the ballot but that the voters had the right to write in Peddy's name. Thus, if Peddy was to win, his supporters must conduct a write-in campaign of enormous proportions.[77]

The independent Democrats and the Republicans counterattacked by beginning legal proceedings to bar Mayfield's name from the Democratic ballot. Attorneys for Peddy, including Bailey's law partner, Luther Nickels, went before Hawkins Scarborough, judge of the Thirteenth District Court, at Corsicana, on October 3 and secured a temporary injunction restraining the secretary of state from certifying Mayfield's name as the Democratic nominee for the United States Senate. They alleged that in his campaign Mayfield had spent more than the $10,000 allowed by a state law of 1919 and had not reported the additional funds. The attorney general appealed Scarborough's order to the Fifth Court of Civil Appeals, at Dallas, and with the appeal filed a motion to send the case to the Texas Supreme Court for quick and final action. Mayfield's attorneys filed a separate motion to suspend the proceedings at Corsicana. The appeals court denied Mayfield's motion and sent the case to Austin.[78]

Back in Corsicana, the case went to jury trial in a hearing on the petition for a permanent injunction to keep Mayfield's name off the ballot. Mayfield admitted on the witness stand that he was a member of the Klan until the latter part of January, 1922, when he resigned from the organization, and that he had received formal acceptance of his resignation about February 1. Under questioning by Luther Nickels, he said that he had attended four Klan meetings since his resignation—in Dallas, Longview, Aransas Pass, and Gainesville. But a Dallas man testified that the candidate had spoken at three Klan meetings in that city between February and April, 1922, and that at one of them Hiram Wesley Evans had introduced him as a "good klansman and our next Senator." Mayfield denied the testimony of another witness, Mike McNamara, a deputy oil-and-gas commissioner, that he had received from McNamara an unreported campaign contribution of $200 and had later instructed McNamara to deny sending him the money.[79]

On October 26 the jury at Corsicana decided twelve of the twenty-

one issues submitted by the court in favor of the plaintiffs, and Judge
Scarborough entered the judgment that Mayfield and his campaign
managers had not reported correctly all receipts and disbursements
and that $40,500 had been spent by Mayfield and others in his behalf.
The next day the judge signed a sweeping injunction denying Mayfield
a place on the ballot, and it now appeared that he too would have to
conduct a write-in campaign. However, after much running of attorneys from courthouse to courthouse, on the afternoon before the November 7 election the Texas Supreme Court cleared away all legal
obstructions to the appearance of Mayfield's name on the ballot. The
result of all this legal maneuvering was that Peddy's name did not appear on the ticket, either as an independent Democrat or as the Republican nominee, in any county. Mayfield's name was on the ballot in
thirty-two counties. Just before the election Hiram Wesley Evans,
worried that Mayfield might be ruled off the ballot, was said to have
given a delegation of Texas Klan officials $25,000 to use in instructing
klansmen how to write in his favorite's name.[80]

Although Peddy made a vigorous campaign against what he termed
the "Klan-controlled machinery" of the Democratic party, his chances
were doomed from the outset. The Texas voter's traditional loyalty to
the "party of the fathers" and his regard for the sacred primary pledge
worked against the young Houstonian. The Klan vote remained solidly
behind Mayfield, and most drys also supported him. Tom Love, in an
interview with the press on October 11, said that there was no valid
reason why a Texas Democrat should fail to heartily support Mayfield,
who was "eminently better fitted by training and experience than his
opponent and, if elected, will be free from any obligation to or influence by the stand pat Republicans and pseudo Democratic elements in
Texas which are so ostentatiously supporting his opponent." Love dismissed as "nonsense" the talk that Mayfield was the Klan nominee.
"He is the nominee of the Democratic party in its regular and legal
Democratic State primary. He could not have been nominated without
the votes of thousands of Democrats who like myself are opposed to
the Ku Klux Klan."[81]

The Reverend Atticus Webb, superintendent of the Anti-Saloon
League in Texas, threw his influence and that of *Home and State*, the
league's paper, behind Mayfield and against Peddy, whom he accused
of being in the hands of the liquor forces. Webb insisted that the Klan
issue was only camouflage and that the real meaning of Peddy's can-

didacy was an attack on the Eighteenth Amendment. John C. Granbery, a prohibitionist and a supporter of Peddy, scolded Webb for supporting Mayfield and coming very near to making the *Home and State* "a Ku Klux Paper" but failed to change Webb's mind. Granbery and Webb took the matter to the league's state Board of Managers, which gave its support to the superintendent. One of the members bluntly declared: "If Dr. Granbery is more an anti–Ku Klux than he is a prohibitionist (and there is quite a bit of evidence to that effect) you [Webb] can not take his protest seriously. I no longer believe in Dr. Granbery as a leader of our moral forces or as a democrat."

Granbery complained about the attitude of Webb and the board to P. A. Baker, general superintendent of the national Anti-Saloon League, who declared that as league superintendent he should remain neutral when the two candidates were both friendly to Prohibition. Granbery then publicly appealed to the drys not to be fooled by charges that Peddy, "a fellow-prohibitionist," had gone over to the liquor crowd. However, after attending the annual session of his Methodist conference in Lampasas, Granbery wearily admitted, "Political prejudice and Klan propaganda have so taken hold of the minds of the majority of the Methodist preachers and laymen that they can see only this: *Ferguson* and an alleged alliance with the liquor traffic."[82]

At the general election on November 7, Mayfield was elected over Peddy by a two-to-one majority, 264,260 to 130,744. Peddy carried twenty-seven counties, including nine of the ten German counties. He ran best in Southwest Texas, next best in the largest cities and in a number of West Texas counties, and, on the whole, poorest in East Texas. The anti-Klan press generally agreed that Mayfield's victory was a party rather than a personal triumph and demonstrated the Democratic party's hold on the people's affections. The *Texas Christian Advocate*, however, declared that Mayfield had won because "he had always championed the right side of every moral issue in Texas." "The election of Mayfield is among other things a tremendous victory for prohibition," the *Houston Post* claimed. "It insures not only another 'dry' Senator from Texas, but it spells the doom of the pro-liquor movement in the State."[83]

Governor Neff did not campaign in the November election and was an easy winner over his Republican opponent, William Hawley Atwell of Dallas, by a margin of almost five to one, 334,199 to 73,327. Atwell, a lawyer and former United States district attorney for the

Northern District of Texas, was in Europe when the Republican convention chose him for its nominee. He made some addresses during
the campaign and said that the Klan was "really the outgrowth of the
failure to properly enforce the law." After the gubernatorial election
President Harding named Atwell United States district judge for the
Northern District of Texas. Atwell served in that post until 1954. Judge
Atwell astonished New York City in 1927 and 1928 by taking the Prohibition law seriously during two summer tours of duty on the bench in
Brooklyn Federal Court.[84]

Peddy and his backers carried their fight against Mayfield and the
Klan to the United States Senate, filing a petition on February 22,
1923, contesting the election and asking for an investigation. Peddy
also requested a ballot recount and claimed that he was entitled to the
seat. The Republicans' interest in the case was not simply to see that
justice was done. R. B. Creager thought the Senate investigation
showing Klan dominance of the Democratic party in the nation's banner Democratic state would have an obvious effect on the Catholic,
Jewish, and foreign-born vote in doubtful states. "If this matter is handled properly through a contest in the Senate, a tremendous amount of
most valuable political capital can unquestionably be made out of it,"
he advised Harding. "It will far overshadow the Newberry case on the
financial side, and will taint the Democracy with Klan affiliation and at
least partial control."[85]

To counter the Peddy challenge, Mayfield conferred with Morris
Sheppard and other Democratic senators in Washington to ensure that
he was seated, employed Tom Love for the same purpose, and sought
unsuccessfully to have Love cooperate with a Dallas grand jury in an
investigation of the Peddy campaign management. "I am dead certain
that the files of the Western Union at Dallas will reveal some very in-
teresting messages between Creager and Lindsley," he wrote Love,
"and in my judgment an investigation of these things should be had at
the very earliest possible moment."[86]

Peddy's petition was referred to a subcommittee of the Senate
Committee on Privileges and Elections, which conducted hearings
from May 8 to December 13, 1924, on the 1922 senatorial campaign in
Texas, the Klan's role in Mayfield's election, and the charge that he and
his supporters had spent unlawful sums of money. After interviewing
a number of klansmen from Texas and Atlanta, who provided abun-
dant evidence that Mayfield had been the Klan's "official" candidate,

though giving conflicting testimony about its financial backing, the subcommittee voted unanimously to dismiss the contest. The Senate accepted the report without objection on February 3, 1925, nearly two and a half years after the election (Mayfield had been sworn in on December 3, 1923). While awaiting the outcome of the investigation, he voted on roll calls, offered petitions, and transacted routine business but did not participate in debate or offer bills or amendments.[87]

Mayfield's predecessor, Charles A. Culberson, had left the Senate on March 4, 1923. Always immaculately dressed, he continued to go to the Senate barbershop in the Capitol every morning to be shaved by his favorite barber and to meet former colleagues. With a heavy army cape draping his shoulders, he enjoyed being driven around Washington twice a day, accompanied by relatives or friends. Although he was not well enough to follow House's suggestion that he write either a history of Texas or a history of the Hogg and Culberson administrations, he did prepare what he termed "Personal Reminiscences," thirty-two "short letters"—one for each of his thirty-two years in public life. These were published serially in the newspapers. On March 19, 1925, he died in Washington of pneumonia and was buried in Fort Worth. "Charles A. Culberson for 40 years was the darling of Texas politics," said the *New York World*. "More than Bailey and longer than Houston, he was the beloved leader of the Lone Star State, and might have remained in the senate forever had he been able to attend to the duties of the office."[88]

In the words of one student of the Klan, "the election of Earle B. Mayfield to the United States Senate was a striking victory for the Klan, one of the best known and most spectacular of its numerous conquests in the 1920's."[89] With almost solid backing from his fellow klansmen, Mayfield had triumphed over five opponents in the first primary and had then gone on to win the Democratic nomination in the runoff by defeating a former governor who had been impeached and removed from office. Against any other opponent than Jim Ferguson the outcome might have been different. Still, Mayfield's victory and the stunning success of local Klan candidates allowed Lone Star klansmen to boast that Texas was, politically speaking, the banner Klan state in the nation. They looked forward confidently to playing a pivotal role in the presidential and gubernatorial elections of 1924.

CHAPTER 4

Pat M. Neff and the Battles of Peace

As Frederick L. Collins, a writer from New York, walked up the broad steps of the imposing Texas State Capitol one day in 1924 to interview Pat Neff, in the forefront of his mind was the popular impression of the governor as the "cowboy governor" who had recently presented his big black hat to Governor Gifford Pinchot of Pennsylvania on the condition that he wear it to the Republican National Convention—"Pat Neff, the Wild Man from Waco!" "And then," Collins wrote afterward, "I found myself shaking hands with a tall, fine-featured, iron-gray man of culture, dignity, and charm, a man who might have been the president of a New England university." "Fed on six-shooters and bell-spurs," laughed Neff, when Collins told him of his fears, "and reared on bear's milk—that's what some people seem to think about us Texans. Now, *we* think we have a pretty fine State." There followed an oration on the past, present, and future bigness of the Lone Star State, "without table-thumping, without gestures above the head, without raising the soft, velvety tones of the voice, but without missing a flower or a statistic."[1]

Neff had spent his four years in the governor's office, now drawing to a close, using his abilities as an orator and as an expressive and fluent writer to prod his fellow Texans into sharing his dream of "making Texas a better place to live" through a program of constructive legislation and joining him in "winning the battles of peace as the ideals of service possess us."[2]

On November 28, 1922, after his election to a second two-year term, Neff delivered at Brenham the first of nine addresses planned to influence public opinion in favor of the program that he intended to present to the Thirty-eighth Legislature. The address at Brenham was a plea for calling a convention to write a new state constitution to replace the one adopted in 1876, one of the planks in the platform of the Democratic State Convention. Noting that the constitution had been amended thirty-eight times, Neff declared: "This was patch-work. No one piece of cloth could be made to blend with or fit into the old garment. New goods have already been sewed on to forty sections of the old garment. Texas is entitled to a brand new suit from hat to boots." In later addresses the governor advocated educational reform, highway construction, revision of the tax laws, law enforcement, penitentiary reform, promotion of the establishment of factories in Texas, and conservation and reclamation programs. His second inaugural address was a plea for the legislature to give him its cordial cooperation in enacting "a big, constructive legislative program." "All for Texas and Texas for all should be the consuming thought and the constant slogan both of you and of me as we think and work together in an effort to make this commonwealth the best place in all the world in which to live," the governor asserted.[3]

Neff presented his ambitious program to the legislature in a series of eight somewhat oratorical messages from January 13 to January 30, 1923. In one of his most forceful messages he again urged better law enforcement and reduction of the crime wave by repeal of the suspended-sentence law, enactment of a law that would allow the removal of local officers who refused to enforce the law, and other changes that would make the state's criminal code easier to enforce. The governor quoted crime statistics to show that in 1922 Texas had averaged more than three murders a day and that London, with 8 million people, averaged twenty-four homicides a year, while Texas, with 5 million, "averages more than one thousand murders a year." He urged a constitutional convention, declaring that the present constitution was outmoded and obsolete, commenting that it had been said with some reason that "all of our good laws are unconstitutional." He made some general comments on highway matters, reviewed the work of the State Textbook Commission, and gave a detailed survey of prison conditions. Neff made twelve recommendations for an enlarged and more elaborate educational system, including the authorization of a "strong, active, aggressive" state board of education; an annual education expenditure of $50 a child, the state paying half and local districts half; guarantee of a nine-month school term; and provision of a definite income for the colleges that would "take these schools out of a political wrangle every two years."

The governor asked for a uniform, equitable tax system based on a standard valuation, an income tax, an inheritance tax, a tax on natural resources, a franchise tax, taxes on certain occupations and corporate privileges, and the separation of state and county taxes, the ad valorem tax to be collected by the county and used by it exclusively. "If there is any part of the Texas statutes that is rude and crude, inefficient, unjust and unfair, it is that part that contains the tax laws of this State," he told the legislature.

Like a latter-day Henry Grady, Neff urged the building of factories in Texas to keep the state's cotton, wool, cattle, and other farm and ranch products at home. "Let the whirl of wheels and the click of factories, as they consume our raw material, join the glad song of our natural prosperity," he said. "Let the sky that bends at night above our farms and ranches be lighted with the blaze from our factories' furnaces." He urged the legislature to encourage industrial development through measures that would safeguard investors against "radical" laws. He suggested tax legislation to encourage and protect infant industries, legislation to conserve the waterpower of Texas rivers, and legislation for deepening the Gulf ports to provide ample shipping facilities. Neff said that it would also be helpful to work out a better transportation system. He suggested the establishment of a department in one of the state's colleges to teach young men and women textile work. He warned that unless factories were built in Texas it would be necessary to write another "Paradise Lost."[4]

The legislature was not impressed by this free flow of special messages and failed to adopt most of the governor's recommendations. In his study of the chief executive office in Texas, Fred Gantt found that governors who "repeatedly aimed a barrage of verbiage at the legislators upon the slightest provocation" were less successful in achieving enactment of their proposals than were those who outlined their programs during the early days of a session, reserving special messages for emergencies. "Results would seem to indicate that the Legislature resents too frequent a display of 'gubernatorial influence' through the exercise of the message power," Gantt concluded.[5]

How did Neff's progressive program fare? Neff was disappointed in his hopes for a new constitution. On January 21, 1923, the attorney general delivered an opinion that the legislature did not have the authority to call a constitutional convention without first submitting the question to a vote of the people. Representative Lee Rountree of Brazos County, in introducing a convention resolution, had the Democratic platform convention plank printed in the *House Journal* and quoted liberally from Neff's speeches on the subject. As amended and finally passed, 77 to 43, the House resolution provided for an election to be held in November, 1924, at which the voters should decide whether or not a convention should be held and also elect ninety-three delegates to such a convention, three for each senatorial district. If authorized, the convention was to convene in Austin on the first Monday in May, 1925.

The Senate convention resolution, sponsored by Senator W. E. Doyle of Freestone County, died in committee. On March 10 the House resolution was lost in the Senate by a tie vote, 14 to 14. Senator R. M. Dudley of El Paso, who was serving as president pro tem, voted no and killed the resolution for the session. It could not be considered for another two years.[6]

Neff was vitally interested in prison reform. On January 23, 1923, he sent the legislature a long report on the prison system, "with the hope," he said, "that your honorable body will help in every way possible . . . to make the penitentiary a going, reformatory, worthwhile institution, worthy the great State it was instituted to serve." He spoke of the twelve prison farms scattered over Texas and the main penitentiary at Huntsville and announced that there were approximately 3,700 convicts in the system, 1,200 more than there were at the beginning of his administration. Of these prisoners, he said, 90 were illiterate, unskilled laborers; many were mental and physical misfits able to do only ordinary manual labor. For those prisoners able to perform industrial work he recommended the establishment of a tannery; cotton, shoe, and wagon factories; a cabinet shop; and a cannery inside the prison walls. About 250 selected prison-farm convicts would be put to work without guards on the public roads, under a "gentleman's contract" for commutation of time. Finally, he would designate one of the farms an honor farm and place prisoners there to work under the direction of a superintendent but without guards.

The governor also discussed the advisability of moving the penitentiary to a more central location than Huntsville; he said that, after studying the question for two years, he found himself unable to agree with the proponents of the proposition. The valuable improvements on the farms would be "practically a total loss" if the penitentiary was moved. Instead, he recommended keeping the seven prison farms in Fort Bend and Brazoria counties, totaling 53,853 acres, and building a new penitentiary plant near the center of this tract. The penitentiary at Huntsville would be converted into an insane asylum. In conclusion,

Neff said that he "would be pleased to have legislation in keeping with the recommendations herein made."[7]

The next day Jim Ferguson, in a letter to Neff, Lieutenant Governor T. Whitfield Davidson, and certain members of the legislature, said that he and a group of associates would lease the entire prison system from the state for a period of ten years and operate it under the supervision of the Board of Prison Commissioners. He offered to pay the state $260,000 a year for the lease. On January 25 the House voted 79 to 34 to return Ferguson's letter to him, after voting down, 57 to 47, a resolution by B. E. Quinn of Jefferson calling it a "brazen affront" to the people of Texas and a "reflection on their intelligence."[8]

On January 31, Lieutenant Governor Davidson told the Marshall, Texas, Lions Club that the "chief problems now facing the State are taxation, highway building and maintenance and the future of the penitentiary system." He opposed Neff's plan to erect a new penitentiary, proposing instead the establishment of cement and clothing plants and construction of a concrete highway through Texas with convict labor. Pointing out that the system had been running $1 million in debt each year, he declared that the farms would never pay expenses because of the annual floods in the counties where they were situated. Representative Claude Teer of Granger, chairman of the legislature's joint penitentiary-relocating committee, warned that ruin in the form of unavoidable deficits faced the prison system unless large-scale farming was abandoned and the system was concentrated somewhere near the center of the state. On March 3 the committee voted almost unanimously to remove the main prison from Huntsville and relocate it in the central part of the state, preferably within seventy-five to one hundred miles of Austin. At the same time committee members opposed Neff's plan to move it to a Fort Bend convict farm. With the governor and the committee at loggerheads the legislature was unable to take any action one way or the other.[9]

The governor continued his rigid policy of granting very few pardons, and that brought him into conflict with Davidson, who favored greater leniency. Neff was out of the state a number of times during his second term, on one occasion making a trip to Panama, and during his absences Davidson as acting governor had full power to act on pardon requests. He was flooded with letters, telegrams, and personal appeals for executive clemency. "Where there was one that might ordinarily have been presented at any time to the Governor I denied it," he wrote in his *Memoirs*. "But where they possessed merits I granted them even though the Governor may not have approved my action." Davidson's view was that Neff should appoint a conscientious board of pardon advisers made up of trusted friends who would not abuse their power but who would take the responsibility of details away from the governor's office. "I trust you understand my position," he wrote Neff on September 9, 1924, "simply to act in the future as I have in the past, that is, not to abuse the pardoning power, but on the other hand not to refuse to do that which I believe to be both merciful and proper, if such an occasion should arise." A piqued Neff replied that, in view of Davidson's determination to grant pardons whenever he thought it proper to do so, he had decided to cancel a campaign tour on behalf of the national Democratic ticket. "I could not enjoy my trip . . . out of the state realizing that pardons and paroles were being granted by you." [10]

When Neff became governor, the state's road-building plan was based on the idea that all roads were county roads and that responsibility for their construction and maintenance belonged to the county commissioners' courts. Under this plan some $100 million in county and district road bonds had been voted, and state and federal grants had been awarded to the counties. Yet Texas had no highway system worthy of the name. In 1923, Neff declared that scarcely one hundred miles of continuous pavement existed anywhere in Texas and that every good pavement ended in a mudhole. Meanwhile, the automobile was penetrating the remotest sections of the state. By 1925, Texas had 983,420 motor vehicles, and the one-million mark was reached in 1926. Chambers of commerce were regularly organizing automobile caravans and making tours to conventions or to points in their trade territories to advertise their cities.

In 1922, Texas was faced with the possibility of losing federal highway-construction aid because the Texas Highway Commission, as it was then constituted under the Texas Highway Act of 1917, could not comply with the requirements of the Federal Aid to Roads Act of 1921, administered by the United States Department of Agriculture. The latter provided that a state could designate 7 percent of its road mileage to receive federal funds and that the designated mileage must be under the exclusive control of a state agency in matters of design, construction, and maintenance. Moreover, the failure of a single county to maintain its portion of a state highway on which federal funds had been spent would furnish grounds for the secretary of agriculture to deny

the state further federal aid. To give states not in compliance a chance
to enact the needed changes, the secretary had the option of continuing projects until 1924.

On April 17, 1922, a group of about two hundred good-roads advocates met in the Senate chamber at the state capitol and organized the
Texas Highway Association. Neff addressed the meeting and declared
that he strongly favored good roads and supported the passage of legislation that would enable the state to secure federal aid for highway
construction. He called upon the organization to work out a "big road
building program for this State, not a little, sickly, puny one," and
promised to devote much of his time during the coming summer to
carrying the program to the people.

In June a legislative committee was appointed to work out a detailed plan of suggestions for the legislature, and at a meeting in Galveston on August 4 and 5, attended by nearly four hundred persons, a
legislative program was adopted, and plans were made for an educational campaign to arouse Texans to the need for good roads. The
Democratic State Convention, the County Judges and Commissioners'
Association, and the state Highway Commission endorsed the program
advocated by the association. As finally agreed upon by the association's board of directors and the legislative committee at a meeting in
Waco on December 21, the following recommendations were made to
the Thirty-eighth Legislature: (1) a constitutional amendment giving
the state the power to designate, construct, operate, control, and provide for the maintenance of a state system of public highways, (2) a constitutional amendment providing for a state highway commission made
up of three members appointed by the governor for a term of six years,
one member to be appointed every two years, (3) reimbursement to
the counties for improvements made by such counties on roads designated as state highways, (4) enactment of a practicable and constitutional headlight law, (5) appropriate penalties for violations of the highway laws, (6) assessment on every motor vehicle of a license fee of
$0.50 per horsepower and also of a graduated fee according to the
weight of the vehicle, (7) assessment on every commercial motor vehicle weighing more than 3½ tons of a large license fee, ranging from
$3.00 to $5.00 per 100 pounds, and (8) levy of a tax of $0.02 cents a
gallon on gasoline, the proceeds to go into the state-highway fund earmarked for the construction and maintenance of state roads.

The Thirty-eighth Legislature, in contrast to its predecessor, assumed a friendly attitude toward the highway department. Realization that it would be impossible to build a connected system of state highways under the 1917 law, which permitted gaps in counties unable or unwilling to vote road bonds, contributed powerfully to the movement toward centralization. Beginning on February 15, 1925, the term of office of highway commissioners was extended from two to six years, one member to be appointed by the governor every two years. This change allowed commissioners time to get to know their jobs. License fees for motor vehicles were increased to help provide funds to match federal aid and to maintain roads in those counties that could not or would not maintain federally aided roads. Automobile-registration fees were to be used for the maintenance of state highways under the control of the highway commission. An occupation tax of $0.01 per gallon was levied on wholesale gasoline dealers; three-fourths of the revenue was to go to the highway fund and one-fourth to the public school fund. The speed limit was raised ten miles, to thirty-five miles an hour. Finally, a proposed constitutional amendment authorizing the state to take over the construction, operation, and maintenance of the new state system of public highways was approved by the legislature for submission to the voters on July 28, 1923.

In the midst of the campaign for adoption of the amendment, the attorney general ruled that it could not be legally voted upon on July 28, since the state constitution provided that proposed amendments must be published in a newspaper in each county once a week for four consecutive weeks, beginning at least three months before the election. The highway amendment was not mailed to the newspapers for publication until after June 4. Although disappointed by the failure to secure adoption of the amendment, the State Highway Commission, through its chairman, R. M. Hubbard, announced that it would "carry on." As it turned out, the Texas Supreme Court in *Robins* v. *Limestone County* (1925) ruled that the ownership of public roads was vested in the state alone and that, "unless the Constitution forbids, it may exercise that right direct or by and through such agencies as it may designate." The ruling made a constitutional amendment unnecessary.

"During my administration there was laid in Texas the foundation for a broad and extensive road-building program," Neff wrote later. "The day is not far distant when we shall have a comprehensive system of arterial highways, free from railroad crossings, shaded by beautiful trees, adorned with attractive shrubbery, lighted with electricity, and appreciated by the people as a thing of beauty and joy forever." In 1937, D. K. Martin, a member of the State Highway Commission in three different administrations, echoed Neff: "In my judgment Governor Neff's administration . . . laid the foundation for the highway program that is now under way in Texas. . . . No other administration has meant so much in so many ways to highway building as that of Governor Neff's."[11]

Neff also deserves credit for the inception of the Texas state-parks system. Texas retained its public lands when it entered the Union but later sold or gave away practically all of them. The land given to forty-one railroad companies alone from 1852 to 1882 was more than 38,900,000 acres. In 1882 a block of 3,000,000 acres was sliced off and given in exchange for a new capitol building. The land was valued at fifty cents an acre—and officials thought the state was driving an excellent bargain to dispose of it at any price. At the beginning of 1923, Texas did not own the land for one park for camping or recreational purposes. In Neff's words, "She did not reserve one acre of land to be used and enjoyed by the public in the name of the State." On May 1, 1923, the governor sent a message to the legislature recommending the creation of a nonsalaried state-parks committee, to be composed of six members, with the task of soliciting donations of land of any size suited to public-park purposes and reporting all data concerning such tracts to each regular session of the legislature.

Neff was ever a purveyor of colorful phrases, and he rose to new heights when he challenged the legislators to come face to face with the automobile age and provide scenic beauty spots for the people "to go 'back to nature,' where the bees hum, the birds sing, the brooks ripple, the breezes blow and the flowers bloom." He declared, "By the establishment of a system of parks and camping places throughout the State we will make of Texas the Mecca for automobile tourists and bequeath to posterity a most valuable legacy."

Somewhat reluctantly the legislature went along with the governor and created the State Parks Board. The state was divided into five districts, each district represented by a resident of the district. Members were appointed by the governor for six-year terms. D. E. Colp of San Antonio was the first chairman. During his last year in office Neff, usually in company with members of the board, traveled 8,150 miles, visited 82 counties, and delivered 100 speeches in behalf of state parks. He was able to report in January, 1925, that private donors had given the board fifty-two tracts of land, ranging from the ten-acre Mother Neff Park near McGregor, mentioned earlier, to more than a thousand acres.

The legislature did not appropriate any money with which to buy parkland. When Neff requested an annual appropriation of $50,000 for the board members' traveling expenses and the upkeep of the parks, the lawmakers' answer was a resolution expressing gratitude to the donors but suggesting that, because of the needs of the state's educational institutions and public schools, the deeds should be returned to the donors unless they, or cities and counties, provided maintenance "so that the State shall never be required to make appropriations therefore." Some opponents of the appropriation argued that it would be equivalent to maintaining local tourist camps at state expense. Others urged that every dollar available for park purposes should be spent to acquire an extensive tract, such as the Davis Mountains, instead of scattering small parks over the state.

Happily, the resolution was no more than a delaying action, and in later years the park system grew to large proportions. "The park work in Texas is here to stay," Neff prophesied in *The Battles of Peace*:

The world moves slowly, but it never takes a backward step in a big, worthwhile cause like this. The work may be delayed now and then, but the day is near at hand when our highways will be lined, and Texas will be dotted, with State parks, camping places, and recreational centers, all of them beauty spots to be held in sacred trust by the State for the public good, now and forever.[12]

Another cause close to Neff's heart was the dual one of water conservation and land reclamation. According to the governor, about 12 million acres of Texas land, suitable for irrigation, was too dry, while another 4 million acres, subject to flooding, was too wet. Also the toll of life and property from flooding was becoming greater each year. During the past ten years the property loss resulting from floods had averaged $8 million a year. In 1913 no less than $75 million in property had washed into the Gulf of Mexico. In 1922 crop losses from floods totaled $20 million; 24,000 acres of corn and cotton belonging to the Texas penitentiary system were swept into the Gulf in one night. To dramatize the inter-dependent problems of flood control and land preservation and reclamation, in August, 1922, Neff called a conference of 250 engineers in Austin. This gathering was soon followed by a general meeting in Waco, at which the participants organized the Texas Conservation Association. The *Dallas Morning News* editorialized that the Waco meeting "marks the organized beginning of a public movement which, if successful, will be the most important ever undertaken in Texas."

The Thirty-eighth Legislature appropriated $600,000 for two years for topographic and hydrographic surveys of the upper reaches of the state's principal rivers by the State Board of Water Engineers. The purpose of the surveys was to measure streamflow and to determine sites where water could be stored for irrigation, generation of electricity, and other beneficial purposes. The Topographic Branch of the United States Geological Survey, recognizing the importance of this work, matched the state appropriation, furnished necessary scientific equipment, and promised to print all maps of the work free of cost. By the time the appropriation was exhausted, in August, 1925, a total of 6,500 square miles had been surveyed, and aerial photographs had been taken of 12,000 square miles, data from which were incorporated into maps. Tarrant and LaSalle counties had already formed water-improvement districts. "The work of water conservation and of land preservation and reclamation has just begun," Neff wrote in 1925. "Its ultimate value, no one can forecast. It will conquer the drouth. It will make our deserts blossom with vegetation. It will make along our streams numberless valleys of the Nile." In July, 1938, Neff said to Emma Shirley: "Giving the matter now the long look, the park work and the conservation of flood waters seem to me more far-reaching than anything else during my administration."[13]

Since 1917 the increasing cost of state administration had been a major legislative problem. After the Thirty-seventh Legislature refused to accept Neff's wide-ranging program for the reorganization of state government to promote efficiency and eliminate waste, the governor made no recommendations on administrative consolidation to the 1923 regular session. However, several bills were introduced to abolish or consolidate departments. None of these proposals was adopted. An act was passed abolishing all special funds in the treasury and transferring the moneys to the general-revenue fund. Indicative of the growing number of banks and insurance companies in Texas were bills separating state supervision of banking and of insurance. The commissioner of insurance and banking became the commissioner of insurance, and a banking commissioner was provided to head a new department of banking. Neff vetoed the bills, however.

During the second called session, Neff asked for the reorganization of the State Health Department to enhance its usefulness, scope, and effectiveness. He renewed his plea that the legislature take steps to prevent waste by consolidating or abolishing departments wherever possible, pointing in particular to duplication of functions in the Department of Agriculture; the Markets and Warehouse Department; Texas A&M College; the College of Industrial Arts, at Denton; the Department of Labor; and the Mining Board. Instead of reducing the number of state agencies, however, the legislature increased the number, creating seven new state boards and three temporary commissions.

The first attempt to provide an efficiency survey of state administration was a bill offered by Representative Homer Hendricks of Ellis County and Burke W. Mathes of Hale County. It proposed the creation of a committee on economy, to be composed of three senators appointed by the president of the Senate, and three representatives appointed by the speaker of the House. The committee was to have power to "direct an inquiry into the organization, structure, and the manner and method of administration of the various executive agencies of the State Government." The bill called for an appropriation of $25,000 for the work of the committee and authorization to "employ a reputable firm of management engineers fully experienced in the organization and administrative methods of government bodies, to conduct its investigations and advise in the preparation of its reports." The bill never came to a vote. Although two governors, two Democratic conventions, and four legislatures had endorsed administrative reorganization in principle, the results achieved were slight.[14]

Several important education bills were passed by the Thirty-eighth Legislature. In 1900, Texas had only three state-supported institutions of higher learning; by 1920 it had nine. During this period total student enrollment increased quickly by a margin of 582 percent, while the total population increased only 53 percent. Legislative biennial appropriations for higher education increased approximately 2,185 percent, while the state's wealth increased only about 265 percent. An immense increase swelled the number of students enrolled in the colleges. The large per capita cost of higher education in comparison with that of grade and high schools aroused much resentment and opposition among spokesmen for rural Texas. Moreover, rather than a single, unified system of higher education that would foster harmonious cooperation, by 1920 the state had developed no fewer than four systems with four separate boards of regents. Rivalry for students, programs, buildings, public favor, and legislative appropriations was keen among the heads of the schools.[15]

The Thirty-seventh Legislature by concurrent resolution had authorized the appointment of a committee of nine citizens to make a "thorough examination" of higher education in the state and had instructed the committee to recommend "a method of systemizing the work of higher education in Texas, together with an efficient plan for their support and maintenance." Rather typically, the legislature made no appropriation for the expenses of the committee, which was called upon, in one member's words, to "make bricks without straw." It was unable to do much but recommend to the next legislature that, inasmuch as the state's schools constituted a unity, a general survey of the entire educational system should be made as soon as possible. That accorded with the consensus of educational leaders. The Texas State Teachers Association, various women's organizations, and other groups urged it, and Neff "recommended whole-heartedly this step to the legislature."[16]

In 1923 the legislature appropriated $50,000 to defray the expenses of an educational survey. To ensure the strictest impartiality, the law provided that a large and representative committee of state officers, educators, and citizens was to set up a commission under whose direct charge an educational expert and his staff were to conduct the survey. The survey director and his staff must not be residents of Texas, but the director was authorized to call for the assistance of anyone in the state he chose. The commission appointed as director George A. Works, of the College of Agriculture of Cornell University, who had a broad experience in conducting school surveys in the United States and Canada. Works employed a number of leading specialists of Texas and other states.[17]

In addition to the $50,000 appropriation for the survey, the legislature appropriated $3 million to supplement the public-school fund, authorized the income from the available fund of the University of Texas to be used for building purposes for the coming fifteen years, established a normal school at Kingsville, in South Texas, permitted former servicemen to attend state colleges tuition-free, strengthened and extended the compulsory-school-attendance law, accepted federal aid for vocational training in the public schools, and approved the consolidation of all the rural schools of a county in one centralized county-unit system, if the county so desired.[18]

During his first term Neff had vetoed a $50,000 appropriation for the establishment of a college in West Texas, giving as his reasons the failure of the State Democratic Convention of 1920 to include a demand for the college in the party platform and the state's financial condition, which did not permit the formation of a new institution at that time. The initial short-lived reaction was a secession movement in West Texas, after which the West Texans renewed their demand for a college. During his campaign for reelection in 1922, Neff learned that H. T. Kimbro of the Lubbock Chamber of Commerce was winning the support of the "Bailey boys" by telling them that the governor was "a friend of Lubbock's" and that it was "important for Lubbock to remain the friend of Neff as the A&M College Bill is sure to be up again and that we must show our friendship for the Governor by making the majority in Lubbock County as big as possible." A delegation of West Texans secured a plank in the Democratic platform of 1922 calling for the establishment of a "branch Agricultural College in West Texas," to be governed by the Texas A&M Board of Regents. This provision met one of Neff's objections to the bill of 1921.[19]

When the Thirty-eighth Legislature convened in January, 1923, several bills calling for the creation of a college were introduced. Representative R. A. Baldwin of Lubbock County wanted an independent A&M college; Senator William Bledsoe of Lubbock was willing to accept a dependent branch of Texas A&M with the hope that the school's status might be changed as it grew. In addition, Representative Lewis A. Carpenter of Dallas had proposed the founding of a technological college somewhere in the state. To add to the confusion, there was the question of the size of the appropriation to be sought. Baldwin thought that the West Texans would not get more than half a million dollars, but some promoters declared that Neff had advised them to "make it a big one." Other questions were whether the school should be coeducational and what its curriculum should be. Baldwin told reporters that "West Texas has got a little away from a strictly agricultural college, and we want it on broad lines and co-educational as well—a big senior institution."

A "West Texas" meeting was held in Fort Worth, attended by about two hundred delegates from forty counties, to try to reconcile the serious differences. The delegates agreed on the need for "the immediate establishment in West Texas of a co-educational senior college of the first rank" but differed on the interpretation of that statement. Baldwin and Bledsoe went back to the capitol and promoted the bills they had introduced earlier. Meanwhile, a bill introduced by Carpenter and T. K. Irwin of Dallas for a college of technology and textile engineering received a favorable report from the House Committee on Commerce and Manufacturing. Carpenter seemed receptive to the idea of linking his bill with the West Texas college plan, and his influence as a klansman with other members of the Klan in the legislature would be a definite asset in passing a compromise measure.

The several authors of the conflicting bills met in the Senate reception room on January 25, 1923, the day before the West Texas college bills were to be called up for floor action. Present were Bledsoe, Baldwin, and Carpenter; Representatives Richard M. Chitwood of Nolan County and Burke W. Mathes of Hale; Silliman Evans of the *Fort Worth Star-Telegram*; and Homer Wade of the West Texas Chamber of Commerce. Wade was acting as "legislative representative" for the backers of the college. When everyone had entered the room, Wade closed the doors and said: "You have been invited into this room this morning for the purpose of reaching an agreement upon a West Texas college bill. I have the keys to the door in my pocket, and they will not be removed therefrom until such an agreement is reached." After a two-hour conference it was agreed that the college would be statewide in scope; that it would be independent of Texas A&M, with its own board of directors; and that an appropriation of a million dollars would be sought, though a lesser amount would be acceptable. Carpenter insisted that the name Texas Technological College must be adopted as the price of his support. He and Bledsoe then wrote a new bill, Senate Bill 103, which passed the Senate 24 to 5 and the House 95 to 26.

Neff waited several days before signing the bill, creating some suspense, but remarked to a visiting Dallas delegation that that he had been "'sitting on the lid for two years' and that he wanted something better in the future." The governor believed that the school's technical-training course would be a potential influence in establishing textile manufacturing in the state. He said later that the creation of Texas Tech heralded Texas producers' independence from eastern manufacturers. On February 10 he signed the college bill. It provided that the

institution was to be situated north of the 29th parallel and west of
the 98th meridian, was to be coeducational, and was to have a nine-
member board of directors. It was to give instruction in technology and
textile engineering and also offer courses in the arts and sciences. The
legislature initially appropriated $1,000,000 for the college and $2,500
to meet the expenses of the five-man board that would select the location for the new school. Thirty-seven towns submitted briefs supporting their requests for the college, and during July and August, 1923,
the selection board visited each of them in turn to inspect the proposed sites. On August 8 the board awarded the college to Lubbock.[20]

Thirty-eight tax bills were introduced in the House during the
regular session of 1923. The only major bills that negotiated the whole
distance were the Cowan bill, taxing gasoline one cent a gallon; the
Melson bill, imposing a 2 percent tax on sulfur production, and the
Sackett-McNatt motor-vehicle act, levying an annual pro rata tax on
trucks and passenger cars. A constitutional amendment proposed by
Senator W. E. Doyle, a Confederate veteran, to raise the Confederate
pension tax from five cents to seven cents was approved and scheduled
to be submitted to the voters in the general election of 1924.

Wright Patman's bill enlarging the scope of the intangible-assets-
tax law was killed. Also decapitated was the session's most controversial revenue proposal: a state-income-tax bill offered by C. E. Dinkle of
Hunt County, which would have taxed incomes of $5,000 and up, be-
ginning with 0.5 percent at the $5,000 figure and gradually increasing
until it reached 6 percent on incomes in excess of $12,000. Until the
last minute there was hope that an agreement would be reached on a
bill to increase the 1.5 percent tax on crude-oil production, but the
Senate conferees refused to go above a 2 percent tax and rejected a
House compromise of 2.5 percent. The House had favored 3 percent.
On his return home from Austin, Senator W. R. Cousins of Jefferson
County told his constituents that the legislature had "gone wild over
taxation." He said that it "may be surprising to the people of Texas to
know that 25 per cent of the members of the Legislature pay only a poll
tax, and no property tax whatever, and that 35 per cent of them pay
taxes in amounts under $10."[21] Implied in the senator's remarks was
the accusation that sansculottes were loose in the capitol.

It was no secret that the so-called Klan influence had organized
the House and controlled the election of officers. The ratio in the
House was said to be about two to one Klan or pro-Klan, and in the

Senate about one and a half to one anti-Klan. This meant, according to some legislative observers, that "no radical legislation will be put over by either side." The first stir of the session occurred when the senators voted to invite former Governor James E. Ferguson to address them. Those who feared that he would be fiery and denounce his political opponents were agreeably disappointed; his remarks were conciliatory.[22]

On January 11, Senator Joe Burkett introduced a resolution that would place the Senate on record as commending and endorsing the efforts of Governor John M. Parker of Louisiana "in behalf of the enforcement of law, the vindication of the constitutional rights of American citizens and against the rule of hooded mobs and masked political organizations." A motion to table failed 18 to 10, and the resolution was sent on a voice vote to the Committee on State Affairs. On January 16, after receiving a favorable committee report, the Senate endorsed the resolution by a vote of 18 to 8 with two pairs and one senator not voting, and it was telegraphed to Governor Parker at Baton Rouge. Burkett also introduced a bill by Representative V. D. Fugler of Harrison County, already submitted to the House, requiring the filing of names of members of all secret organizations. The measure was killed.[23]

Anti-Klan members of the Senate Committee on Nominations prepared a "questionnaire" to be signed under oath before a notary public. "Are you a klansman?" nominees were asked. "Are you a Knight of the Ku Klux Klan? Are you a member of the Invisible Empire? Do you believe in the imperial wizard and the teachings promulgated by him, including the lash, the tar bucket and tar and feather parties?" On February 26 the committee summoned all of Neff's recent appointees residing in Austin and awaiting confirmation to a closed meeting to answer questions about their affiliations, past, present, or prospective, with the Klan. Adjutant General Thomas Barton was said to have refused to answer one of the questions asked him in the committee room. In executive session on February 27 the Senate confirmed thirty of thirty-seven of the governor's appointees but held up for further consideration Barton; Labor Commissioner Joseph F. Myers; State Tax Commissioner John G. Willacy; State Health Officer J. H. Beazley; J. E. Boog-Scott, chairman of the Live Stock Sanitary Commission; Mrs. Charles de Groff, nominated to the Board of Regents of Texas Technological College; and Charles W. Row, nominated to the State Rate-making Board. On March 1 the Senate confirmed all these nominees except Mrs. de Groff.[24]

During the regular session of the legislature Senators Joe Burkett, I. D. Fairchild, Archie Parr, I. E. Clark, W. E. Doyle, and H. L. Darwin plotted a "quick trick" to relieve Jim Ferguson from the penalties of the impeachment resolution adopted in 1917. Ferguson's daughter Ouida was privy to the plan, and his friends thought that her presence in the Senate gallery when the question came up would have a good moral effect on some of their lukewarm brethren. On February 9, Burkett called Ouida on the telephone. He said: "The Lieutenant Governor has just asked Senator Parr to take the Chair. Hurry! The fireworks are about to begin!" As soon as she arrived in the gallery, Parr recognized Burkett, who offered Senate Resolution 57, which said in part: "That said James E. Ferguson be and he is hereby declared to be henceforth pardoned, relieved and released from the terms and provisions thereof; and he be hereafter qualified to hold any office under the State of Texas to which he may be elected by the people or to which he may be legally appointed."

As the chamber erupted in a bedlam of noise, a voice vote was quickly taken. Parr declared that the ayes had it. Fairchild moved to adjourn, and the motion prevailed. A short time later Davidson, who had been hastily summoned from another part of the capitol, returned to the chair. After about thirty minutes of wrangling, Senator John H. Bailey moved to expunge from the journal all the proceedings that had occurred from the time Davidson left the chair until he returned to it. The motion was adopted, and the Fergusonites found themselves back where they had started. The next day the *Fort Worth Star-Telegram* carried, in bold type, the headline "Ferguson Citizen for 30 Minutes!"[25]

On May 16, Ferguson's friends introduced a resolution to expunge the record of his impeachment from the *Senate Journal* and to restore his right to hold office, but it was defeated 16 to 6. Senators Parr, Fairchild, Clark, Doyle, Burkett, and Charles Murphy voted for the resolution. Commenting on the Senate's action, Ferguson said that he knew beforehand that he had only a "slim chance" for relief but wanted the matter put to a test so that his friends would know whom to support and whom to scratch in 1924. He declared that one reason for the Senate's refusal to restore his right to hold office was that there were too many candidates for governor in the Senate or candidates who had friends there. A prominent newspaperman had told him that if he would agree not to run for governor the resolution could be put over without any trouble. Jim admitted that he would like to be governor again, "and I would be if these fellers in the Senate will just turn loose so I can get my name on the ticket. But Lord God, how afraid they are."

Ferguson said, however, that the main reason for the Senate's defeat of the resolution was the fifteen senators, either klansmen or Klan sympathizers, who formed a majority of the twenty-four present. It was they who had slammed the door in his and the people's face. "Don't forget this, every Ku Klux present voted against me." "Everyone had just as well understand that the people are going to give me vindication sooner or later," he declared. "I shall not stop making my appeal for relief until my dying hour." [26]

As far as Klan-backed legislation was concerned, an "anti-parochial school bill," introduced by Representative O. L. Baker of Orange County, requiring the use of the public-school general curriculum in private and parochial schools, was killed in the House on February 13 by a vote of 72 to 53. Another Klan measure, however, sponsored by Lewis T. Carpenter of Dallas, requiring the teaching of the United States and Texas constitutions in the public schools and colleges passed the House on June 11. Unsuccessful attempts were made to amend the measure to require that two hours a week must be devoted to these subjects (defeated 75 to 30) and to include the study of the Bill of Rights, the right of trial by jury, religious freedom, free speech, and free press (defeated 81 to 27). The bill died in the Senate Committee on Education. [27]

On March 9, in response to a mounting demand by religious fundamentalists for a state antievolution law, the House passed 71 to 34 the Stroder-Howeth Bill, which provided that in tax-supported schools "it shall be unlawful to teach the theory of evolution as a fact, either Darwinian, or which involves that man evolved from the ape, as applied to the origin of mankind." A second section made it unlawful to use any textbook that taught evolution as a fact or "in any way discredits the Genesis account of the origin of man" or "advances the idea that man was evolved from the lower life." The bill's cosponsor, J. T. Stroder of Navarro County, denounced evolution as that "vicious and infamous doctrine . . . that mankind sprang from pollywog, to a frog, to an ape, to a monkey, to a baboon, to a Jap, to a negro, to a Chinaman, to a man." "H. G. Wells and every thing vicious was taught and practiced there," he wrote privately of the University of Texas the following year. Another representative, J. A. Dodd of Bowie County, declared:

The state forces me to pay taxes to support schools, then forces me to send my children to those schools and there shows my children the road to hell through teaching them the hellish infidelity of evolution. We owe it to our children and to our mothers who loved their Bible and taught us its meaning to abolish forever from our schools this iniquitous fallacy which holds that the Bible is a liar and that man is a monkey.

Lloyd Price of Morris County, Eugene Miller of Parker County, and J. Roy Hardin of Kaufman County were the leading opponents of the Stroder-Howeth Bill in the House. They argued that antievolution laws would restrict teachers unnecessarily, that they violated academic freedom, and that such restrictions were outside the authority of the state legislature. Some members claimed that prohibitions were unnecessary because Texas teachers did not teach evolution anyway. Although the Senate Committee on Education gave the Stroder-Howeth Bill a favorable report, it died on the Senate calendar when the regular session ended on March 14.[28]

One of the leaders of the fundamentalist crusade was William Jennings Bryan, whom the Democratic party had nominated for president in 1896, 1900, and 1908. Bryan had served as Wilson's first secretary of state, resigning in June, 1915, rather than sign the second *Lusitania* note to Germany. His interest in antievolution legislation had been aroused early in 1922; on January 19 of that year he had addressed the Kentucky legislature and pleaded for a law barring the teaching of Darwinism in any institution supported by state funds. He was invited to address the legislatures of Tennessee, Arkansas, Georgia, Mississippi, Ohio, Wisconsin, West Virginia, and Florida. "The evolutionary hypothesis," he proclaimed in 1923, "is the only thing that has seriously menaced religion since the birth of Christ and it menaces . . . civilization as well as religion." "Bryan's entire campaign for anti-evolution legislation was based upon his lifelong belief that the majority must rule in everything," wrote Lawrence W. Levine.[29]

On March 30, 1923, J. Frank Norris, the fiery and controversial fundamentalist minister of the First Baptist Church in Fort Worth, invited Bryan to speak in that city and in Dallas. "The State Legislature is going to be called in special session in sixty days, and under the influence of your address, the anti-evolution bill would pass at the special session," Norris said. "Mr. Bryan, we have given evolution a body blow here and you can give it a knock-out for the final count." The "Great Commoner" replied, however, that he would not be justified in making the trip unless he could also address the legislature.[30]

On May 8, Bryan wrote Representative Stroder declining for several reasons an invitation to come to Austin. One of the reasons was Neff's failure to lay the antievolution bill before the special session, which was evidence that he was opposed to it, "and my coming would have aroused criticism that would have neutralized the effect of my speech. It would have turned from a matter of principle to a personal fight on the governor—our opponents would resort to this in order to avoid a fight on the merits of the issue." Still, Bryan thought that even if Stroder did not succeed in this session he had laid the foundation for a successful fight two years hence. "The fact that the measure passed the House by more than two thirds vote will give it a standing that, I think, will insure victory. I hope to be able to make some speeches in Texas in support of the proposition." In the meantime, he had sent copies of two speeches, "The Menace of Darwinism" and "Science vs. Evolution," for all the legislators.[31]

Although they were unable to pass an antievolution bill in the Thirty-eighth Legislature, on May 28 the fundamentalists in the House did succeed in passing a concurrent resolution by Stroder and Dodd declaring it to be the sense of the Texas Legislature that the Darwinian theory should not be taught in the state's public schools. The vote was 81 to 9. In a letter to Bryan the following January, Stroder referred to the resolution as "your Resolution," suggesting that Bryan may have been the actual author. The Farm Labor Union of America drafted Stroder to run for the Texas State Senate in 1924 against J. Roy Hardin, and Stroder told Bryan that "any kind remark from you in that direction will aid us in trying to fill the Senate with our kind, instead of unchangeable aristocrats." Hardin, however, won the seat.[32]

A provision of the Terrell Election Law of 1903 declared that "the county executive committee of the party holding any primary election may prescribe additional qualifications necessary to participants therein." Under this provision the Democratic party of any county could bar blacks from voting in the primary if it so desired by having its county executive committee prescribe additional qualifications. In 1921, C. N. Love, long-term editor of the *Texas Freeman*, and five other black Houstonians filed suit against G. W. Griffin, chairman of the

Democratic Executive Committee of Harris County, attacking the white primary. The case was carried to the United States Supreme Court, which dismissed it as moot because the election had passed.[33]

In hotly contested Democratic primaries, such as the Neff-Bailey runoff of 1920 and the senatorial election of 1922, election officials sometimes allowed blacks to vote. Ferguson was said to have been the beneficiary of 3,500 black votes in Bexar County in the first primary. From 1918 to 1936, Charles Bellinger, a black with extensive real-estate holdings in San Antonio, controlled enough black votes to swing a county or city election. Bellinger made his start in politics by appealing to eleven black ministers to deliver the black vote to him in return for his promise to have the streets in front of their churches paved so that members could attend services more easily in rainy weather. He also lent money to other blacks. In exchange for the five to eight thousand votes that Bellinger controlled, his white political allies provided paved streets, water and sewer connections, schools, parks, playgrounds, firehouses, a library, and a public auditorium for the black section of town. Bellinger also had their tacit approval of his control of local bootlegging and gambling. In 1918, D. A. McAskill and John Tobin were candidates for district attorney in the Democratic primary of Bexar County. Both men had previously had the support of blacks in local primaries; however, this time most of the black votes swung to Tobin, who was elected. Thereupon McAskill, as a means of weakening Tobin's organization, began campaigning for a state law to bar blacks from voting in the Democratic primary.[34]

In 1923, Representative Douglas Davenport of Bexar County introduced a primary-election bill, which was referred to as the "white man's primary law." On March 2 it passed the House 89 to 23, in a considerably different form from the original draft. Struck out were provisions to make it a crime not to comply with a primary-election pledge, to authorize grand juries to look into ballot boxes, and to prohibit courts from issuing writs to restrain officers and other persons from performing acts required by election laws. Plainly, as the *Dallas Morning News* noted, the original bill "was an echo of the campaign and controversies over the office of United States Senator in 1922." As passed by the House, the bill required every voter to register his party affiliation when he obtained his poll-tax receipt or exemption certificate; authorized the state executive committee to prescribe qualifications for voters, in addition to those laid down in the statutes; and re-

quired the Republican party of Texas to nominate all candidates for
state, district, county, and precinct offices in primary elections or go
out of business. Thus the provision barring blacks from the Democratic primary was only one part of a punitive bill designed to prevent
any repetition of the Mayfield-Peddy senatorial contest of 1922. The
Dallas Morning News said that a fitting title for the measure would be
"An Act to give the Democratic party of Texas a political monopoly and
a strangle-hold on all offices." The Senate Committee on Privileges and
Elections reported the bill favorably with six amendments, but it died
on the Senate calendar.[35]

As passed in the second called session, Davenport's bill read as
follows:

All qualified voters under the law and Constitution of the State of Texas who
are bona fide members of the Democratic party, shall be eligible to participate
in any Democratic primary election, provided such voter complies with all
laws and rules governing party primary elections; however in no event shall a
negro be eligible to participate in a Democratic party primary election held in
the State of Texas, and should a negro vote in a Democratic primary election,
such ballot shall be void and election officials are herein directed to throw out
such ballot and not count the same.

This provision was known as Article 3093a, Acts of 1923. On June 1,
Neff filed the white-primary law, without his signature, with the secretary of state, to become effective ninety days after the adjournment of
the second called session.[36]

H. C. Chandler of San Antonio tested the new law in a federal
district court in 1924 (*Chandler* v. *Neff*), claiming that it violated both
the Fourteenth and the Fifteenth amendments. The court denied
both contentions; it ruled that the right sought under the Fourteenth
Amendment accrued from state citizenship only and that, in light of
the United States Supreme Court's decision in *Newberry* v. *U.S.*
(1921), the Texas primary was not an election within the meaning of
the Fifteenth Amendment. The San Antonio machine then secured a
revision of the city charter to allow a nonpartisan primary that would
include black voters.[37]

In the waning days of the regular session a minority faction in the
Senate led by Senators John H. Bailey and Alvin Wirtz used parliamentary tactics to kill the House quo warranto bill for the removal of
negligent peace officers. The legislature did provide that county judges
could remove drunken, incompetent, or uncooperative peace officers

but made a mockery of the law by requiring that drunkenness must occur on three successive occasions and providing that it must be shown that the intoxication was not caused by drinking liquor prescribed by a licensed physician.[38]

The House shifted the burden of proof to the accused in liquor cases by passing a bill that made possession of any "preparation" containing more than 1 percent alcohol by volume prima facie evidence of unlawful possession; however, the defendant had the right to introduce evidence showing the legality of such possession. Representative Frank H. Burmeister of Atascosa County, a former antiprohibitionist and one of the three coauthors of the bill, declared that it would "put teeth in the prohibition laws." The bill's opponents claimed that it would also put certain mouthwashes and hair tonics under a ban. The Reverend Atticus Webb, who sat at J. T. Stroder's desk during the debate, said that the Anti-Saloon League endorsed the measure.[39]

Stating that the Senate had "smothered to death" the quo warranto bill for the removal of local officers and had so far failed to act on the House bill "providing an effective method of punishing outlaws who openly and unfearingly manufacture and sell whiskey in Texas," Neff sent a message to the legislature on March 10, 1923, four days before the date set for adjournment, calling it back into session on March 15. The governor noted that the lawmakers had also failed to pass the appropriation bill or provide adequate funds for the proper support of the public schools and other eleemosynary institutions for the coming biennium and had not passed "some real constructive legislative measures . . . for the growth and on going of Texas."[40]

The Senate vented its anger on the governor, branding him narrow-minded for trying to dictate to the legislators. "I never thought that in free and Democratic America we would have a chief executive who would say 'If you don't do my will, I will keep you here, punish you,'" declared Alvin Wirtz. "The people of Texas did not elect Pat M. Neff to be Senator or to control the Senate of this State," said Charles Murphy, in moving a resolution expunging that portion of Neff's proclamation containing the reference to the quo warranto bill. Murphy was voted down 23 to 4. On March 12 the Senate adopted 18 to 6 a concurrent resolution already passed by the House 58 to 51, asking Neff to reconsider his proclamation and postpone the special session for thirty days. The governor refused but said that he would accept the legislature's verdict on a special session as final.

The verdict was swift in coming. When the special session convened at 10:00 a.m. on March 15, it remained in session just long enough to adopt the following resolution: "Resolved by the House of Representatives, the Senate concurring. That the First Called Session of the Thirty-eighth Legislature adjourn sine die March 15, 1923, at 11 o'clock a.m." The sine die resolution was the only business transacted during the one-hour session, the shortest in the state's history. When Neff was asked if he had any comment to make, he replied, "You can pull a horse to the creek, but you can't make him drink."[41]

The governor called a second special session for April 16 and laid out a program for taking care of an anticipated deficit of about $6 million and for laws to make Prohibition effective and for his officer-removal bill. Neff told the legislators: "Government and taxation are inseparably interwoven, are interdependent," adding, "There are two sources of revenue: one is property, the other is privilege." He asserted that government was "prone to look too much to property, and too little to privilege" and asked for eight revenue-raising bills, including a franchise tax on corporations, an inheritance tax, a state income tax, an increase in the crude-oil tax, and a delinquent tax.[42]

Another thirty days were spent in futile haggling over a varied assortment of revenue-raising proposals. The House voted 81 to 32 to reject a 2 percent gross-production tax on oil instead of 3 percent as fixed in the House bill. Neff's pet measure, the quo warranto bill providing for the removal of officers, passed the House 75 to 24 but was killed in the Senate, in part because several senators were hostile to the governor. Senator Archie Parr criticized Neff for submitting so many subjects for legislation during the special session. "If there is another called session the Governor will be to blame," he declared. "He has no right to submit all this 'junk' until we get through with the appropriation bills." The legislators approved appropriation measures totaling $39,207,931.33 but could not agree on tax measures to meet the increase in expenditures.[43]

On May 16, Neff called the legislature back for a third try "to adjust by appropriate legislation the wide discrepancy between appropriations heretofore made . . . and the estimated available revenues." Claiming that the deficit would be more than $8 million, he kept the appropriation bills on his desk and indicated that a veto was likely if the legislature did not come up with additional tax revenues. The House, where revenue measures originate, responded with a shower of bills; twenty-six were introduced on opening day, twenty-five of which proposed new or increased taxes. Wright Patman, an admirer of Neff, led off with eight bills levying new occupation taxes or increasing existing ones. Two of these, affecting pipeline operators, express companies, gas companies, electric power works, and waterworks, were passed; the other six fell by the wayside. There were bills proposing income taxes, a measure to tax lawyers who filed divorce suits, and a bill that would have levied an annual tax of twelve dollars on professional workers, including nurses, physicians, lawyers, civil engineers, and architects. Among the legislative moves was a proposal for taking over for general use all of the state's special funds except two, those of the Highway Department and the State Game, Fish and Oyster Department.[44]

A flood of telegrams and letters from the State Bankers Association, chambers of commerce, farm bureaus, and other organizations across the state inundated the legislators. The letters protested specifically the income-tax bill sponsored by C. E. Dinkle but also raised objections to all other tax measures. Proponents of new taxes said that the cry was "inspired propaganda" and did not represent "the voice of the folks back home." On May 23, however, the House voted 64 to 50 to kill the income-tax bill for the session. Another bone of contention was the crude-oil tax; the Senate refused to accept a tax above 2 percent, and the House sought a 3 percent rate (a 100 percent increase), though it was willing to settle for 2.5 percent. A 2 percent bill enacted in the second called session was on Neff's desk but had not been signed because the governor was hoping for a higher percentage. R. L. Robinson, a lobbyist for the Texas Farm Labor Union, which was supporting the 3 percent figure, accused the senators of listening "to the lobbyists of the big oil companies" and threatened to take the issue to the people in the 1924 campaign.[45]

Basically, the House wanted more revenue, and the Senate wanted to cut appropriations materially to avoid new taxes. A farm bloc in the lower chamber voted to stay in Austin "for Christmas dinner" to achieve an appropriation of $6 million for the public-school fund and an appropriation of $3 million for rural-school aid. On May 23, Neff was the target of criticism by Senator Bailey for his alleged failure to "stay in his office and attend to business." A newspaper report on the governor's visit to San Antonio that referred to his kissing "Lady Fort Worth" created much laughter among the senators. Neff, in turn, declared that the Texas Legislature "not only lacks courage but something else beside" and called Bailey's criticism "too picayunish to merit the dignity of a reply."[46]

On May 31, as the session passed the midpoint of its thirty days, with the Senate slaughtering House tax bills, Neff vetoed the pending appropriation measures. Quickly the Senate voted out four substitute bills totaling $35,960,099, reducing the original totals by $3,247,832. Rather than face a summer session in the capitol, the House voted 74 to 42 to accept the Senate's cut in the public-school appropriation from $6 million to $4 million. That cut, together with 2 percent gross-receipts taxes on oil and sulfur, a $0.01 per gallon gasoline tax, and other small tax bills, put the budget more nearly in balance. On June 14, Neff addressed the legislature again, this time accepting the new appropriation bills and an estimated $2 million deficit. The governor, who took pride in his metaphors, employed a figure of speech common in the horse-and-wagon days: he had decided, he said, that "so often have I submitted this proposition to you that I have no hope that you would make 'tongue and buckle meet' should I again reconvene you for this purpose in another special session." He concluded, "I do not feel that we should at this time spend more of the people's money in marching up the legislative hill and down the legislative hill in a futile effort to do the thing that ought to be done, but which it seems is impossible for you to do." He would have to reduce appropriations as best he could by means of the veto.[47]

The Thirty-eighth Legislature passed twelve bills creating new state courts. Neff vetoed them all, on the grounds that existing courts were not busy, but each time the legislature overrode him. Some observers contended that many of the lawmakers did so out of spite. "The Governor, it but states a painfully obvious fact to say, is not highly popular in either house of the Legislature," commented the *Dallas Morning News*. "With some members, indeed, he is singularly unpopular, and with such members the opportunity to repudiate his veto presented a temptation which their animosity could not resist." These were the only bills passed over Neff's veto in four years, however. In all he vetoed ninety-three measures.[48]

On December 4, 1922, the State Textbook Commission made wholesale changes in the list of free textbooks furnished to the children of Texas, voting to discard about 2,300,000 books already purchased and to buy new books at a cost of $1,800,000. Many citizens felt that these changes were unwise and warned that the 1923–24 school year might be shortened by a month or more because the money for the new books must come from the public-school fund. The legislature passed the Pope Bill nullifying the contracts, but Neff vetoed it on April 3, 1923. "In absence of fraud, corruption, or mistake, the Legislature has not the right in equity or in good conscience, to regard a contract made by the duly accredited agents of the State, as a 'scrap of paper,'" he declared. "Texas has not done so in the past. She should not begin it now." In May the House and the Senate adopted a simple resolution commanding state officials not to recognize the contracts as valid. Superintendent of Public Instruction S. L. M. Marrs then announced that he would not list the new texts on the requisition forms sent to the local school superintendents. It took a suit by the American Book Company, an order from the State Board of Education, and a decision of the State Supreme Court to force Marrs to recognize the contracts.

The hard feelings between Marrs and Neff, who defended the contracts, lingered. "I spent a good part of two days up there in the Text Book Commission room and listened to them wrangle about first one thing and then another," a book agent wrote the following year. "All the book people are so disgusted they don't know what to do. . . . Mr. Marrs and the Governor can agree on nothing and at one time during the Meeting when the Governor managed to gain his point all the Text Book agents nearly applauded." In view of the large sums of money involved, the decisions of the Textbook Commission would continue to be controversial during the next administration.[49]

Neff showed early in his first term that he intended to give recognition to women. It was his policy to appoint one or more women to all state boards, including the boards of regents of the state's institutions of higher education. He was the first Texas governor to have a woman as his private secretary; Mrs. Espa Stanford succeeded R. B. Walthall in that position. The governor also named three women attorneys—Hortense Ward, Ruth Brazzil, and Hattie L. Hennenburg—as special judges of the Texas Supreme Court to hear a case in which the Woodmen of the World was a party. All three of the regular Texas Supreme Court judges were disqualified because of their membership in the organization. Neff apparently made many attempts to secure men as special justices, but each time he offered an appointment to a prominent male member of the bar, the attorney declined because he too belonged to the Woodmen of the World. Finally the governor decided to appoint three attorneys who, because of their sex, could not be members of that organization. This was the first time in Texas and perhaps anywhere in the United States that women constituted the highest state court.[30]

During the Neff administration a coalition of women's organizations formed the Women's Joint Legislative Council to promote social and welfare bills and combat discrimination against their sex. The participating groups in 1922 included the Texas Federation of Women's Clubs, the Texas Congress of Mothers and Parent-Teacher Associations, the Texas League of Women Voters, the Federation of Business and Professional Women's Clubs, and the Women's Christian Temperance Union. The Texas Graduate Nurses Association joined the council in 1924. Dubbed the "Petticoat Lobby" by condescending members of the Thirty-eighth Legislature, the women were assigned Senate Committee Room 5, as their headquarters—an arrangement that current lobbyists might envy. From this room streamed press statements, telegrams, circular letters, and relays of women to lobby lawmakers and the governor. "Their work was a colorful and, to some, a disconcertingly effective experiment in Government by newly enfranchised citizens," wrote Mrs. Jane Y. McCallum, executive secretary of the council from 1923 to 1925.

All of the Petticoat Lobby's six proposed bills were passed during the Thirty-eighth Legislature and were signed by the governor. They included (1) an emergency appropriation for the public schools, (2) a bill strengthening the Prohibition laws, (3) a bill authorizing a survey of the prison system "with teeth in it," (4) a bill authorizing an educational survey to be made by out-of-state educators, (5) matching state appropriations for maternal- and child-hygiene work under the Sheppard-Towner Maternity and Infancy Protection Act, and (6) a birth-registration resolution. "Reasonable, did you say?" an old-time House member stormed at a colleague who had innocently complimented the brevity of the women's program when it was presented in January, 1923. "Why, you haven't read it. It is the most audacious piece of Bolshevism ever permitted to clutter up this chamber." "The irate lawmaker expressed a half truth," remarked Mrs. McCallum in relating this anecdote. "It was 'audacious' to advocate Federal 'interference' for mothers and babies in a section of as 'rock-ribbed States righters' and 'rugged individualists' as certain types of political orators gloried, killed time, and beclouded issues in claiming Texas to be."[51]

During his second term Neff kept up his private war against crime. In 1923 he sent the Texas Rangers to San Antonio to stop liquor traffic, gambling, and other forms of vice. Alamo City politicians bitterly resented the presence of the lawmen and sought to have them removed, but Neff, equally stubborn, kept them there. On August 6, Adjutant General Thomas Barton visited the five Rangers in San Antonio; he had previously announced that he would rid the city of vice even if he had to send in the entire Ranger force for an indefinite period. "San Antonio will be a clean town, when the rangers get through," he boasted. A year later, when historian Walter Prescott Webb visited the city, he found thirty Rangers commanded by Captain B. C. Baldwin quartered in an old house at 331 Garden Street, south of the Alamo. "On the whole they appeared to be the biggest men I had ever seen in one group, and they were about the most miserable. They spent their time between liquor raids in skylarking, a gay mask behind which to hide their longing for the home ranges."[52] San Antonio was not ready for reform.

There were sporadic acts of violence by the Klan in the Lone Star State during 1923. In January, at Goose Creek, an oil town near Houston, Mrs. Audry Harrison, recently separated from her husband, was sick in bed. A visitor, J. V. Armand, had brought her a basket of fruit. While her two daughters and two neighbor children were playing about, five masked men burst into the room with leveled revolvers. Amid the shrieks of the children and gunfire they carried off Mrs. Harrison and Armand after shooting out the tires of Armand's automobile. The men threw the woman to the ground and whipped her, and one of the men hacked off her hair close to her head with a pocketknife. They gave Armand twenty to thirty blows with a flail and poured crude oil over his hair and bleeding wounds.

The Harris County district attorney was a klansman and was not inclined to pursue the matter, and six months elapsed before indictments were procured in this and other Goose Creek cases. Several Houston citizens employed a private investigator and twenty-five Goose Creek klansmen were subsequently arraigned and fined after pleading guilty to a long list of floggings and kidnappings. What aroused public indignation even more was the revelation that for the preceding

eighteen months Goose Creek had endured a reign of terror with almost weekly whippings, virtually none of them reported to the grand
jury.[53]

On the night of July 2, 1923, a railroad worker, Otto Lange, was
sitting on the porch of his home in Somerville, Burleson County, with
his aged mother and his little daughter. Three klansmen came for him,
and, when he resisted, they clubbed his mother with a pistol. A stray
shot from a pistol hit his daughter in the hand; another bullet killed
Lange. Neff was on a trip to the Panama Canal Zone when the outrage
occurred, and Acting Governor Davidson sent the Texas Rangers to investigate. Earlier in the year he had denounced the Klan from the presiding officer's chair in the Senate chamber, following the appearance
of a body of masked men in the House during a concert by the Negro
Jubilee Singers of Saint John's Orphanage. When Neff returned to the
state, he approved Davidson's course and gave instructions to Frank
Hamer to continue the investigation of the Lange murder case along
the lines suggested by the lieutenant governor. The case was apparently allowed to lag, however, and when, a month later, Neff was again
absent from the state, Davidson pushed the investigation. He also sent
Rangers to investigate floggings in four Texas cities. "He has employed
with energy every force at his command to vindicate the law and constituted government," the *Dallas Morning News* noted approvingly,
"and in doing so he has earned the gratitude of every citizen who understands the subversive nature of the crimes that have moved him to
act." By his actions Davidson helped destroy the influence of the Klan
in Texas—and also perfected his anti-Klan credentials for the next
gubernatorial election.[54]

In Williamson County, just north of Austin, a traveling salesman
from Waco named R. W. Burleson was suspected of being something of
a Don Juan by klansmen in the Taylor and Georgetown klaverns. It
was rumored around the area that he and a young widow with whom
he had been living as a boarder were having immoral relations. In early
1923 Rev. A. A. Davis, a Baptist preacher who wore a "fiery cross"
on his watch chain, delivered a note to Burleson bearing the seal of
Georgetown Klan No. 178 and warning Burleson to cease his relationship with the widow. Burleson burned the note and then proceeded to
go around Taylor bragging that he would kill twenty-one "Ku Klux" if
they did not leave him alone. On Easter Sunday, April 1, 1923, Burleson was kidnapped from a car in which he was riding with the widow

and another couple by eight or ten men in klan robes and hoods. He was taken to a pecan grove near the community of Jonah and flogged almost to death with a leather strap. The bleeding salesman was loaded into a pickup truck and hauled to Taylor, where he was fastened with a chain to a tree on the courthouse lawn. The klansmen poured a bucket of creosote over his head, shoulders, and back and then departed.

Dan Moody, the young district attorney of Williamson and Travis counties, prosecuted five of the klansmen involved. The trial of Murray Jackson in September, 1923, in Criminal District Court in Georgetown on charges of assault with prohibited weapons attracted reporters from all over the state and made the handsome, red-haired Moody a new star in the Texas political firmament. Jackson was found guilty and was sentenced to five years in the penitentiary. Separate trials were held in January and February, 1924, for Olen Gossett and Dewey Ball; each pleaded guilty to assault with prohibited weapons and each was sentenced to one year in the penitentiary. Moody dismissed the case against Godfrey Loftus of Elgin so that he would be available as a prosecution witness. The Reverend A. A. Davis was tried in January, 1924, for perjury in connection with his testimony to the grand jury and was given a two-year sentence. With Ball's sentencing on February 1, what was generally known as the "notorious Burleson flogging case" was closed. "In my opinion it will be heard of and talked about in every State of the Union," wrote a Cherokee County man to Judge James R. Hamilton, who had presided at the trials, "and those people up north who think that Texas is noted for nothing, except lawlessness, will find out, in this case, that there is at least one County in Texas that is 'English' when it comes to executing and enforcing law." Another wrote, "God bless you the grand and petit jurors and district attorney. Real Americans without a mask." The *Williamson County Sun* of Georgetown endorsed Moody for the office of state attorney general on January 18, 1924, claiming much support for him throughout the state. A few weeks later Moody announced his candidacy for the office.[35]

In 1923, a political off year in Texas, the Klan, now numbering about 170,000 members, according to one estimate, took control of the city administrations in Dallas, Fort Worth, and Wichita Falls but lost municipal contests in San Antonio and El Paso. In El Paso, State Senator R. M. Dudley was elected mayor by 2,120 votes over P. E. Gardner, who had Klan backing, and the Dudley slate of aldermen won out over Gardner men. "The voting yesterday was for or against the Klan," editorialized the *El Paso Times*. "This was the only issue involved. The result showed El Paso was wholeheartedly against such a secret organization." The Klan made one more effort in the El Paso school-board election on April 4, but four candidates pledged "to end Klan domination in schools affairs" were swept into office. Although the Klan remained in existence for several years, it never again challenged in El Paso County.[56]

In February, 1923, Robert E. Vinson resigned as president of the University of Texas to accept a similar position at Western Reserve University, in Cleveland, Ohio. "We are deeply distressed at the resignation of Dr. Vinson, but you can not blame him," wrote Mrs. Percy V. Pennybacker. "He is to get a much larger salary, and he will not be humiliated and harassed by having to go to the legislature for money. This latter worry has caused us to lose our last three presidents."[57]

The search for Vinson's successor once more involved the university in state politics. Rumors flew through the capitol that Dean H. Y. Benedict would be named acting president and that Neff would be named president later—he would remain in office until all legislative matters had been disposed of and then resign the governorship. Following a meeting of the University of Texas Board of Regents on February 26, H. J. Lutcher Stark, chairman of the board, was closeted with Neff for more than an hour. He and Regent Fred W. Cook were said to be leaning strongly in the governor's favor. Neff's close friend Marshall Hicks had wired Cook: "I know of no one better qualified to perform the duties of president of the University than Governor Neff and I suggest that he be tendered this position by the Board of Regents."[58]

The governor's partisans declared that his scholarship was equal to Vinson's, since he held degrees from Baylor and the University of Texas; that he was familiar with university administration from his long service as chairman of the Baylor Board of Trustees; and that his selection would bolster the people's confidence in the university, which had been undermined by the Ferguson fight and by charges of unnecessary expenditures and a lax moral climate. A "close and intimate" friend of Neff's said that the governor would rather contribute to the building up of the University of Texas than be a United States senator. Neff himself maintained a discreet silence about the rumors. When pointedly questioned by reporters, he laughed and said, "I am like the old maid who was asked if it was true that she would marry a certain man, and who replied: 'I haven't been asked yet.'" To another inquirer the governor quipped, "I belong to the 'Know Nothing' party."[59]

The reaction of the University of Texas faculty to Neff's proposed appointment was strongly negative. An angry Eugene C. Barker, chairman of the Department of History, summoned his energy for a "bear fight"; he was determined to throw all of his talent and influence against the governor. In May, Barker wrote A. C. Kray, a member of the faculty of the University of Minnesota: "As you know we have lost Vinson and are in eminent danger of getting Neff to succeed him. I think the faculty for once is a unit in opposing the appointment of any politician, but being a unit in opinion means nothing as to method of procedure and action. As a matter of fact, we are doing nothing." "Is it possible that there is real danger of the Board selecting that damned politician?" his colleague Charles Ramsdell asked Barker:

I think that our great Board might do anything, almost, because few of them have any sense; but it seems incredible to me that the friends of the University over the state would allow that to threaten without a protest that would jar them into something like a sense of their duty and responsibility. If they even dare to think seriously of that they ought to be shaken over the pit of Hell.[60]

On May 9 the *Dallas Morning News* noted a "persistent report in State House circles" that Neff would be offered the presidency and that he would accept and resign as governor in the near future. Two days later the paper editorialized "Surely Not Mr. Neff," pointing out that he was not a man of scholarly distinction and was only a "tolerable" executive on the list of Texas governors; moreover, he would carry into the presidency the prejudices and hatreds with which he had been loaded down during his public career. "The University ought not to be forced to face the enemies of Pat Neff. The welfare of the University ought not to become a mere question of measuring out reward or revenge to Pat Neff." On June 5, the University of Texas Ex-Students' Association, at its annual business meeting in Austin, went on record as opposed to the selection as president of any man in high political office who had "political enemies." It was no secret that the resolution was aimed directly at Neff.[61]

A related rumor in circulation was that Neff, Davidson, and Stark, a wealthy businessman of Orange, Texas, had come to an agreement that the governor was to be appointed president of the university and would resign as governor, allowing Davidson to succeed him, but with the understanding that the latter would not be a candidate for governor in 1924 but would throw his support to Stark. Jim Ferguson made the story public in the *Ferguson Forum* on May 17, telling his readers:

Now here is what I predict: Pat will be elected at the June meeting of the board of regents. If T. W. Davidson will agree, and I think he will, to not become a candidate for governor, then I predict that Pat will resign as governor and immediately throw his feet in the university pay crib. If Davidson makes it known that he will be a candidate for governor then Pat's election will be to take effect some time after next summer's primary, or until such time as Davidson says he will be good. As soon as Pat is elected Stark will announce for governor and the university will, as usual, be in politics up to the neck and looking for the coin.[62]

A few days earlier Davidson had written privately to Edward Crane of Dallas, an active member of the Ex-Students' Association, denying that he had ever discussed a deal with either Neff or Stark:

It is my intention to be a candidate for Governor next year, regardless of who becomes President of the University. This report is of most insidious and contemptible character in that it gives me the appearance of being willing to take the title of the Governorship for a few months at the price of my honor, and waive any claim that I might have for a future election.

His private information was that Stark had no intention of running for governor, while "you know that Neff never consults with anybody about anything. So I most emphatically deny that any such arrangements as charged have been made." On May 24, Davidson wrote to Regent H. A. Wroe to deny publicly any three-cornered political trade. "And I may be pardoned for getting a little egotistical if I should further say to you that I believe I can be elected Governor next year and intend to run regardless of who else enters the field."[63]

Yet Davidson evidently favored Neff's election, for included in his letter to Crane was a two-page mimeographed statement: "Reasons Why Many Men Favor Neff for President of the University." It read in part: "Lieutenant Governor T. W. Davidson expects to be a candidate for Governor, and confidently expects to win if he can get into the run-off, or can avoid being stranded between the anti-prohibitionists and the clan [*sic*]. This condition may be avoided by Neff being President of the University."[64]

After postponing the selection of a new president until its meeting of July 10, at that meeting the Board of Regents again postponed the question until August 13. The university faculty was left in the dark about the final decision. "It is very strongly indicated that Neff has the job in his pocket but it is not absolutely hopeless," Barker wrote. "Up until recently it looked as if Neff's candidacy had petered out," Charles Ramsdell observed, "but about ten days ago he appointed three new Regents, all of them close personal friends of his. He is at present off on a trip to Cuba and the Panama Canal, and we do not know whether the new appointments mean that he has given up the fight for the presidency, or whether he is making a last desperate effort to get the job."[65]

Also at their July meeting the regents adopted a resolution that "no infidel, atheist, or agnostic be employed in any capacity in the University of Texas, and . . . no person who does not believe in God as the Supreme Being and Ruler of the Universe shall hereafter be employed or at any time continue in or be elected or appointed to any office or position of any character in this University." The acting president of the university, W. S. Sutton, opposed the resolution, but only Regent Sam P. Cochran voted against it. They held an inquisition on Dean H. Y. Benedict. As the story goes, Stark asked Benedict whether he believed in a deity. "Well," Benedict is said to have replied, "just recently I knew it would please my wife and I didn't think it would hurt our baby, so I consented to his being baptized." "Do you believe in God?" demanded Stark. "Do you mean an anthropomorphic God?" Benedict parried. "The interrogation was adjourned until Stark could find a dictionary," wrote Ronnie Dugger. "It was never resumed." Barker thought that a good deal of the anti-Benedict sentiment had been spread by persons who wanted him put out of the running for the presidency of the university and that his inclusion on a list of candidates prepared by a faculty committee chaired by Barker had had something to do with the regents' calling him in for a "conversation."[66]

The board's resolution did not attract much attention in the press; the campus newspaper, the *Daily Texan*, merely commented that it was probably designed to do no more than "reassure the people of the state as to the university's position on religion" and to "quiet" criticism of religious views at the school. The Orange County Ku Klux Klan endorsed the resolution, and David A. Frank, the editor-in-chief of the *Alcalde*, the magazine of the Ex-Students' Association, called it "not only justified" but "highly proper." Frank's editorial prompted a defense of the "University of Inquiring Minds" in the December issue by attorney Ralph Smith, whom everyone called "Railroad" Smith. He wrote:

The University of Inquiring Minds is not dependent upon the state for support, though the state is often dependent upon it; it asks no appropriations of a reluctant legislature nor bothers about the veto messages of intolerant executives; it brooks no limitations by a board of bigots and lays no limitations on the human mind, save the rule of reason.[67]

Smith later published his comments as *A Little Preachment and a Short Epistle to the Bigots of Texas*, which he offered "For Sale to Students of the University of Inquiring Minds and Ex-Students of the University of Texas, at 25 Cents the Copy, Prepaid." Smith was one of a colorful line of Texas iconoclasts that included William Cowper Brann, James ("Cyclone") Davis, Don Hampton Biggers, and Wilford B. ("Pitchfork") Smith.[68]

Before their August 13 meeting, a majority of the Board of Regents agreed informally not to elect a new president but to allow Sutton to continue as acting president for the 1923–24 year. Neff's supporters on the board were behind this move, for after a year his term as governor would have nearly drawn to a close, and the race for United States senator would have developed sufficiently to show the way the wind was blowing. Faced with this waiting game, the anti-Neff forces decided not to take any chances on a hasty appointment and countered with a plan to have the state's leading newspapers publish protest editorials on the first day of every regents' meeting. George M. Bailey, chief editorial writer for the *Houston Post*, initiated the plan. "I believe if this co-operation can be organized it may be possible to scare the Board and Neff off," he wrote Will Hogg. A statewide campaign to have every chapter of "Texas Exes" in and out of the state pass resolutions and send them directly to each member of the board and perhaps to the governor was also discussed. John A. Lomax, secretary of the Ex-Students' Association, fretted, "Unless we do something of this sort, I fear that things will rock along and the worst that can happen will be put over without the people of the State really knowing the widespread opposition."[69]

At last, on May 16, 1924, the Board of Regents met in Austin to select a permanent president. A number of former students from all over the state opposed to Neff planned to attend the meeting. John Lomax asked Richard Fleming to meet with Will Hogg, son of former Governor James Stephen Hogg, in Houston and ask him to attend. Hogg, who had served as a university regent from 1914 to 1916 and was active in the Ex-Students' Association, had captained the pro-

university forces in the struggle against Governor Ferguson (whom
Hogg called "Old Ukulele Jim"). Hogg had pitched camp in a suite at
the Driskill Hotel in Austin in the summer of 1917, put up money for
the fight, and published the stenographic record of Ferguson's impeachment. No governor, he declared, could "put the putrid paw of
politics on the University of Texas." Lomax called Hogg the "Watchdog
of the University."[70]

Hogg's brother Mike objected to Will's attendance at the regents'
meeting: "You know there's a lady on the board of regents and if you go
in there, you're gonna start cussin' just as sure as fate. You shouldn't
go." Fleming stepped in and told them how important the meeting
was, and Will finally said that he would go and promised Mike that he
would not "raise hell." The meeting was held on the ground floor of
Sutton Hall on the university campus. According to Fleming, "It was
one of the most ludicrous things in the world to see Lutcher [Stark]
going around and looking out the window to see if anyone was listening
in." Stark was looking in the wrong place; a freshman reporter for the
Daily Texan had secreted himself in a closet and got the whole story.

Hogg acted as spokesman for those opposing Neff's selection, and
he had not been talking five minutes when he forgot all the promises
he had made. "He just let loose," Fleming recalled. "Cussed old Pat
Neff and all of his cohorts. They promised then and there that morning
that they would not elect Pat Neff president. We left with that assurance." That afternoon, however, the regents, led by Chairman
Stark, voted 7 to 2 to offer Neff the presidency. The two dissenting regents, Frank Jones and Sam P. Cochran, promptly resigned from the
board. The governor, aware of the determined opposition of a majority
of the former students, university faculty, and students, declined the
position. Whether the offer was merely complimentary and the governor's refusal prearranged cannot be known with certainty. Stark said
later that the board had elected Neff in good faith and had had no prior
assurance that he would decline.[71]

Hogg and the members of the Ex-Students' Association who had
opposed Neff's appointment were so incensed by Stark's actions that
they wanted him to resign both as regent and as head of the fund-raising
drive for the construction of a memorial stadium on the University of
Texas campus. "If our association ever expects to teach our kind a fundamental lesson in University government now is the time by levelling
on Stark until he quits the Board," Hogg wired D. A. Frank. After

tempers cooled, the anti-Stark faction was persuaded to swallow its resentment and "string along" with the stadium drive. Stark remained on
the Board of Regents until 1943, serving six four-year terms, during
three of which he was chairman.[72]

On the same afternoon that Neff declined the presidency, the regents offered the position to Guy Stanton Ford, graduate dean of the
University of Minnesota. On the following day Ford declined the offer.
On May 28 historian Herbert Eugene Bolton of the University of California was offered the position, but, after visiting Austin on June 13
and 14, he too refused the post. Finally, on July 5, Walter M. Splawn
accepted the presidency. A former professor of economics in the university, the small, frail, intellectual-looking Splawn was serving as
chairman of the Texas Railroad Commission. His selection was not well
received by some members of the faculty who suspected that Neff, a
fellow Baptist, had probably exerted political pressure in his behalf. In
a letter to Barker, Frederic Duncalf expressed the opinion that "Splawn
is Neff's man and appointed by Neff's regents probably at his dictation." "Is it the sp(l)awn of the Devil, I wonder," another faculty member punned. Splawn, however, assured Barker that he did not believe
that the governor would in any way seek to put any friend of his on the
faculty. "In fact, I think such would be remote from his mind."[73]

While Neff was under consideration for the presidency of the University of Texas, his admirers were mentioning him as a dark-horse
candidate for the 1924 Democratic nomination for president of the
United States. "To-day, the only difference of opinion in regard to Pat
Neff is whether, when he gets through being governor, he should be
elected president of the University of Texas or President of the United
States," wrote Frederick L. Collins. "And this difference would not exist if there wasn't a strong element in Texas which considers the former
position the higher of the two honors." About the time he was first
elected governor, Neff had mentioned in a conversation with a Wichita
Falls man that he might want to go to the White House. Neff took his
supporters' talk seriously enough to challenge the Klan and the friends
of William Gibbs McAdoo for control of the Texas delegation.[74]

CHAPTER 5

"Seeing It Through with McAdoo"

THE 1924 Democratic National Convention, held in New York City, was the longest (seventeen days) and one of the loudest, most uncoordinated, and most divisive conventions ever held by the party. Arthur Krock, writing in the *New York Times*, described it as a "snarling, cursing, tedious, tenuous, suicidal, homicidal rough-house." It was a fierce internal battle between rural, mostly Protestant drys from the South and West who were supporting William Gibbs McAdoo of California, Woodrow Wilson's son-in-law and former secretary of the treasury, and eastern, urban wets who were backing the candidacy of New York's Governor Alfred E. Smith, a Roman Catholic. The Democrats balloted 103 times before, in a state of exhaustion, they selected John W. Davis of West Virginia, a Wall Street lawyer, to run against President Calvin Coolidge, the Republican candidate, and Senator Robert M. La Follette of Wisconsin, the nominee of the Progressive party. "Thanks," Davis said to a friend's congratulations on the day of his nomination, "but you know what it's worth." "He was doomed from the beginning and at that moment he knew it," noted his biographer William H. Harbaugh.[1]

Texas was a key state in the national campaigns of McAdoo and of his chief rival in the South, Senator Oscar W. Underwood of Alabama. Both men needed a win when Texas voters held their precinct conventions on May 3 to begin the delegate-selection process. McAdoo's sweeping victory in Texas gave him the momentum to go on to New York as the leading contender for his party's nomination; for Underwood, defeat in Texas left him as little more than Alabama's favorite son, ranking alongside nearly a score of other hopefuls.

Born in Marietta, Georgia, on October 31, 1863, McAdoo grew up in the straitened economic circumstances of the post–Civil War South. After attending the University of Tennessee, where his father was professor of history and English, he practiced law for a time in Chattanooga and organized the company that electrified Knoxville's streetcars. In 1892, after the business venture failed, he moved to New York City. Reputation and fortune came to him at the turn of the century, when he formed a company to connect Manhattan and New Jersey with four Hudson River tunnels. He next gravitated toward politics, supporting Woodrow Wilson for governor of New Jersey in 1910. The following year he joined the small group of men promoting Wilson's presidential candidacy. After Wilson's election in 1912, Wilson named him secretary of the treasury. In addition, he served as chairman of the Federal Reserve Board, the Federal Farm Loan Board, and the War Finance Corporation, as well as director general of the nation's railroads after the federal government took them over in 1917. His wartime patronage gave him the nucleus of a political machine.[2]

"McAdoo was the very epitome of ideological and political flexibility," wrote his biographer John Broesamle. "His surpassing joys came from solving difficult problems, preferably several at a time; and his constant search for new solutions was characterized more than anything else by a restless sidestepping of ideology." This characteristic led some observers to distrust what they thought was ideological shiftiness. Walter Lippmann wrote in 1920 that McAdoo "is not fundamentally moved by the simple moralities" and that "of all candidates he has incomparably the greatest sensibility to the prevailing winds of public opinion." He was, Lippmann said, "a statesman grafted upon a promoter." Yet McAdoo's six years of outstanding service in the cabinet (he resigned in 1919 to practice law in New York City) provided strong evidence of his progressivism, the specific thrust of which in the 1920s was anti-Tammany, anti–Wall Street, and dry—attitudes that were very acceptable to Wilsonian Democrats in the South and West.[3]

McAdoo might have won his party's nomination for president in 1920; Secretary of the Navy Josephus Daniels noted in his diary on January 29, 1920, that "McAdoo seems our strongest man." He ranked first in a poll taken by the Literary Digest before the convention. But the ailing Wilson, who apparently wanted a third term, would not endorse him. According to Daniels, the president told Postmaster General Albert Sidney Burleson soon after the election of 1918 that McAdoo was not fit for the presidency. By then his position as the now-unpopular Wilson's son-in-law (he had married Eleanor Wilson in 1914) and supposed political heir was a fatal handicap in the eyes of some Democratic leaders. "If you want to know how McAdoo would fare in the campaign read Matt 21—verses 33–39 [the parable of the wicked husbandmen]," wrote William Jennings Bryan in May, 1920. "Think the son in law argument would occupy so large a place in the campaign."[4]

McAdoo was constrained to shun any overt appearance of campaigning and hope for a draft at the San Francisco convention. Although he led in the early balloting, Governor James Cox of Ohio, aided by the Charles Murphy–Tom Taggart–George Brennan alliance of machine bosses, won the nomination on the forty-fourth ballot. Most of the dry progressives in Texas had supported McAdoo, and although the state convention left the national delegation uninstructed, his ardent supporter Thomas B. Love noted that it also "adopted a resolution declaring that any delegate from Texas who did not vote for McAdoo ought to be hung, or words to that effect, and elected a solid McAdoo delegation." The forty Texans, hoping to repeat their triumph in Baltimore in 1912, stayed with McAdoo until Cox was nominated and then left for home "dragging their tails behind them," as Joe Bailey acidly remarked.[5]

After Cox's smashing defeat by Warren G. Harding in November, 1920, a group of McAdoo's supporters began preliminary activity on his behalf, looking to 1924. The group included Daniel C. Roper of South Carolina, who had been collector of internal revenue under Wilson and was now a tax lawyer in Washington, D.C.; Thomas B. Love of Texas, assistant secretary of the treasury from 1917 to 1919; Robert W. Woolley, a Washington lawyer and former member of the Interstate Commerce Commission; Thomas L. Chadbourne, a wealthy New York lawyer who had served on the War Trade Board; financier Bernard M. Baruch, former chairman of the War Industries Board; and Angus W. McLean, formerly on the War Finance Board and soon to be elected governor of North Carolina.[6]

McAdoo was fortunate in having Tom Love as manager of his campaign in Texas and adviser on political strategy. A native of Missouri, where he was secretary of the Democratic State Central Committee from 1896 to 1898, Love transferred his law practice from Springfield to Dallas in 1899. He was elected to the Texas House of Representatives in 1902, 1904, and 1906, in his last term serving as speaker. An expert on taxes, insurance, and banking, Love played an important role in the passage of reform legislation relating to these issues, including the Robertson Insurance Law, which required all life-insurance companies doing business in Texas to invest 75 percent of their Texas

Left: William P. Hobby. *Courtesy Barker Texas History Center, University of Texas at Austin. Right:* Pat M. Neff. *Courtesy Barker Texas History Center, University of Texas at Austin*

Governors William P. Hobby and Pat M. Neff with Mexican delegation at Neff's inauguration, January 18, 1921. *File no. 2843, courtesy Austin–Travis County Collection, Austin Public Library*

Left: Robert L. Henry. *Courtesy Barker Texas History Center, University of Texas at Austin. Right:* Earle B. Mayfield. *Courtesy Barker Texas History Center, University of Texas at Austin*

Ku Klux Klan parade on Congress Avenue in Austin, September 2, 1921. *Courtesy Austin–Travis County Collection, Austin Public Library*

Left: Charles A. Culberson. *Courtesy Barker Texas History Center, University of Texas at Austin. Right:* T. Whitfield Davidson. *Courtesy Barker Texas History Center, University of Texas at Austin*

Left: Lynch Davidson. *From* Texans and Their State. *Right:* Cullen Thomas. *Courtesy Barker Texas History Center, University of Texas at Austin*

Left: Thomas B. Love. *From* Texas Parade. *Right:* Cato Sells. *From* Texans and Their State

Left: William B. Hanger. *From* Texans and Their State. *Right:* Marshall Hicks. *From* Texas under Many Flags

Campaign picture of Miriam A. Ferguson, in her bonnet, on her farm near Temple with her younger daughter Dorrace and her Democratic mule. *From San Antonio Light Collection, University of Texas Institute of Texan Cultures, San Antonio*

Left: Anti-Ferguson cartoon, 1924. The faint outline of a woman's skirt is a reference to Mrs. Ferguson's candidacy for governor as a proxy for her husband. *Courtesy Texas State Archives, Austin. Right:* Miriam A. Ferguson. *From Ouida Ferguson Nalle,* The Fergusons of Texas

Inauguration of Miriam A. Ferguson, January 20, 1925. *File no. 3045, courtesy Austin–Travis County Collection, Austin Public Library*

Will Rogers with Miriam and Jim Ferguson. *File no. 2909, courtesy Austin–Travis County Collection, Austin Public Library*

Governor Miriam A. Ferguson signing the Ferguson amnesty bill. *File no. 2898, courtesy Austin–Travis County Collection, Austin Public Library*

Left: Martin M. Crane. *Courtesy Barker Texas History Center, University of Texas at Austin. Right:* Will C. Hogg. *Courtesy Barker Texas History Center, University of Texas at Austin*

Left: Tom Connally. *From Frank Carter Adams, ed.,* Texas Democracy: A Centennial History of Politics and Personalities of the Democratic Party, 1836–1936. *Right:* Morris Sheppard. *From Frank Carter Adams, ed.,* Texas Democracy: A Centennial History of Politics and Personalities of the Democratic Party, 1836–1936

Left: Minnie Fisher Cunningham. *From* Texas Women's Hall of Fame. *Right:* Jane Y. McCallum. *From* Texas Women's Hall of Fame

Dan Moody opening his gubernatorial campaign in Taylor, May 8, 1926. *File no. 2822, courtesy Austin–Travis County Collection, Austin Public Library*

Inauguration of Dan Moody, January 18, 1927, with Governor Miriam A. Ferguson standing at far right. *Courtesy Austin–Travis County Collection, Austin Public Library*

Governor Dan Moody in his office. *From Biog—Daniel J. Moody file, courtesy Austin–Travis County Collection, Austin Public Library*

Left: Mrs. Claude De Van Watts. *From* Who's Who of the Womanhood of Texas. *Right:* Cone Johnson. *From* Principles and Policies Advocated by Cone Johnson

Seizure of illegal Mexican liquor, Marfa, 1928. *From Smithers Collection, Humanities Research Center, University of Texas at Austin*

Left: Jesse H. Jones. *From Bascom N. Timmons,* Jesse H. Jones: The Man and the Statesman. *Right:* Dan Moody. *Courtesy Austin–Travis County Collection, Austin Public Library*

Cartoon by Don Hampton Biggers critical of Prohibition Democrats supporting Al Smith. *Courtesy Texas State Archives, Austin*

reserves in Texas securities. He also helped assure passage of the Terrell Election Law. In 1907 Governor Thomas Campbell appointed him the first state commissioner of insurance and banking; in that capacity the administration of the Robertson Law was one of his principal duties. He resigned in 1910 to join a Dallas insurance company.[7]

Friends claimed that Love was the "original Wilson man" in Texas, and he did not dispute them. On November 8, 1910, the day Wilson was elected governor of New Jersey, Love sent him the following telegram: "I heartily congratulate you upon your magnificent campaign and the people of New Jersey upon your election as Governor. I am for you for President of the U.S. in 1912." Immediately thereafter Love began organizing Texas for Wilson, and he later felt that he deserved the credit usually given to Colonel House for gaining the Texas delegation for the New Jersey governor. McAdoo stated that as Wilson floor leaders at the Baltimore convention, Love and Albert Sidney Burleson "were of inestimable help in holding the Wilson forces together during the [Champ] Clark cyclone."[8]

An implacable foe of liquor, Love was the dry candidate for Democratic national committeeman in 1916. He lost, but in 1917 Wilson appointed him assistant secretary of the treasury, and McAdoo placed him in charge of the Division of War Risk Insurance and Internal Revenue. "It was a tremendously important job, and one that only a big man could fill satisfactorily," McAdoo wrote in his autobiography. "Love made a splendid record." It was then that Love's friendship with the "Chief," as McAdoo was called, was cemented. Returning to Texas in 1919, Love was one of the leaders of the anti-Bailey forces the following year, when he was elected Democratic national committeeman.[9]

"He had a bulldog expression," newsman Raymond Brooks said of Love. "He had red hair and a red, bristly mustache. These turned white, but the mustache stayed bristly, and somehow seemed a tangible picture of his disposition." Aggressive and tenacious and a ruthless, unforgiving political infighter, Love was also a hard worker with an infinite capacity for taking pains. When he had a campaign under way, all of the details were at his fingertips; seldom did any escape him. Many observers laid his success to his elaborate system of gaining information. He was said to have correspondents in practically every precinct in the state to keep him informed on public sentiment. As an organizer he had the faculty of selecting the right man for a particular job. Keeping himself in the background as much as possible, he devoted his energy to directing projects, leaving the details for his lieutenants to carry out. The primary reason for his success, however, was his knowledge of men and politics. "Especially of the latter, it is said there is nothing that he does not know," wrote Alex Acheson, a reporter for the *Dallas Times*, in 1928:

His political sagacity is marveled at by friend and foe alike. He has an intimate knowledge of political history, and there is hardly a fact or figure of even lesser importance during the past forty years of that history that he cannot recall off hand. This knowledge of the background of any issue, coupled with a knowledge of the voters that enable him to forecast the fashion in which most of them will treat such an issue, goes a long way in explaining what, to all appearances, is often little short of sheer wizardry.[10]

To prepare the way for McAdoo's campaign in 1924, his supporters sought to remove the ineffectual George White of Ohio, a Cox man, as chairman of the Democratic National Committee. Love and Robert Woolley were the leaders in the move to oust White and replace him with one of their own group. A majority of the national committee petitioned White to call a meeting in March, 1921, to consider his status, but his tenure was guarded by the anti-McAdoo faction in the party. "Somebody ought to entertain him with a private view of a steam roller filmed in action, the final flash being, 'This means you,'" Woolley grumbled to Love. "You may think he would then understand; I don't."[11] It was not until September 20, 1921, that the chairman finally resigned rather than be forced out. The McAdoo committee members wanted Daniel Roper or Breckenridge Long of Missouri to succeed White but accepted a compromise choice, Cordell Hull of Tennessee, who promised a strict neutrality toward the two antagonistic factions.[12]

Love wanted Woolley to travel over the country and keep the McAdoo "house fires burning," but the latter balked. "What he [McAdoo] wants to do is to keep quiet for a long time . . . and let the necessity for him become overwhelmingly obvious, without the slightest help of any kind," Woolley wrote Love. "If he is to be the Democratic nominee in 1924 he must deal in silence and a lot of it—and those who in the public mind are close to him, like you, Roper and myself, must do likewise." In the summer of 1921, McAdoo was reported to be "very unhappy in his present business and professional work" and was "restive under existing political conditions." Early in 1922 he moved from New York City, which was politically hostile to him, to Los Angeles, California. Although he denied that there was any political significance in the move, it was in fact a deliberate effort to identify himself with the dry progressive Democrats in the West and South. To many rural Democrats, New York City, the home of Wall Street and Tammany Hall, with its large foreign-born population, speakeasies, cultural attractions, and religious modernism, was the embodiment of all that was "alien" to American life—a fusion of Babel, Sodom, and Gomorrah.[13]

In the elections of 1922 the Republican majority in the United States Senate was cut by two-thirds, and the Democrats gained seventy-eight seats in the House—within a dozen of a majority. The people were turned against Harding and the Republican Old Guard, but astute observers thought that the voters' attitude was a negative one; there was no proof that they approved of the Democratic party's vague program. "We must not assume that the recent victory means that the people have turned Democratic and that they will remain so," warned McAdoo, who had spoken for local Democratic candidates in twelve western states. "The fact is that the victory is more anti-Republican than pro-Democratic. I know this from the spirit and temper of the people of the West."[14]

Historian David Burner noted that the elections of 1922 amounted to a permanent breakthrough for the Democratic party in urban areas —particularly in the Northeast and the Middle West—and thus strengthened the wing of the party that was hostile to McAdoo. But his Texas supporters saw the party's resurgence at the polls as portending his nomination and election in 1924. "We won a glorious victory, not only in Texas, but throughout the Nation," Love wrote to a fellow Democrat. "It means that if we nominate McAdoo for President in 1924 we will win. The candidate must be a dry, a friend of labor who is not afraid to say so, a Woodrow Wilson Democrat and must have no Tammany Hall taint upon him and McAdoo fills the bill." He told McAdoo that fifty to one hundred McAdoo-for-president clubs should be formed in every state within the next six months. "We folks down here in Texas are not thinking of any other nominee than McAdoo," declared Marshall Hicks, "and if he will come out of the 'West' with the dash of Knight Errant Lochinvar, we folks in Texas, with the other states of the South, will make his calling and election sure."[15]

McAdoo professed reluctance to return to public life but was flooded with demands that he become a candidate. He told Love in November, 1922, that a decision did not have to be made immediately; the more important question was proper organization of the progressive forces: "What we have got to do is to convince the people during the next two years that we are the uncompromising foes of all that Wall Street and Harding's hardboiled Administration represent and that we are the militant champions of liberalism, progress and righteousness."[16]

As early as February, 1923, however, McAdoo confided to Bernard Baruch his decision to enter the race for the Democratic nomination. The financier tried to restrain him from making his move too soon. "This is a time for the jockey to sit down and let his horse race along in the last bunch," he cautioned. "Some time in the early part of the next year is the time to give the horse his head." Throughout 1923, McAdoo and his friends quietly shaped their plans. There was no McAdoo headquarters in the literal sense, but Daniel C. Roper in Washington acted as campaign coordinator. Love assumed responsibility for Texas, Oklahoma, Arkansas, and Missouri.[17]

On March 7, 1923, the first statewide McAdoo for President Club was formed in Austin and adopted "Seeing It Through with McAdoo" as its slogan. More than half of the state legislators were charter members. Marshall Hicks was elected president of the club, and Larry Mills of Austin was elected secretary. "We purpose repeating for you all that we did with Mr. Wilson," Representative D. S. Davenport of San Antonio wired McAdoo. Through Zach L. Cobb, an El Paso lawyer who had recently moved to Los Angeles, McAdoo conveyed privately his deep appreciation for the action of his Texas friends, explaining that a telegram expressing that appreciation would be construed as an announcement of candidacy.[18]

People were already wanting to know where McAdoo stood on the Klan question. There were demands that he speak out against the order, demands that he dodged by stating that he stood for the guarantees of the Bill of Rights. A congratulatory telegram that he sent to Earle Mayfield following his victory over George Peddy in the race for United States senator brought a pledge of support for 1924 from the senator-elect and was interpreted by some anti-Klan forces as an endorsement of the Klan. Former Texas Congressman Joe H. Eagle warned McAdoo: "If that *Mayfield* letter stands, it is to my mind sure that you are throwing away a President nomination which, but for the Klan issue, would be the equivalent of election." McAdoo protested that he had sent similar telegrams to any number of other successful Democratic candidates and that it had never occurred to him that anyone would think he was endorsing the Klan by congratulating Mayfield.[19]

In March, 1923, Senator Thomas Walsh of Montana warned Mc-Adoo against allowing Love to become the "head and directing agent of the 'McAdoo forces,'" while he was at the same time one of Mayfield's chief boosters in the Senate contest. Said Walsh:

It may be embarrassing to you to signify to Mr. Love that his usefulness, so far as your candidacy is concerned, is at an end, as it was for Mr. Wilson to take like action touching George Harvey, but the Texas fight promises to be as bitter as any recorded in the political annals of any state and though I hold Mr. Love personally in very high esteem, there is but one course for you to take.[20]

After pondering Walsh's advice, McAdoo concluded that it would be "most unwise" for Love to take a prominent part in the Mayfield contest for the Senate. "I hope sincerely that he may be able to keep out of it as much as possible," he wrote Roper. "Of course I don't advise him to go back on a friend, no matter what happens to me." Roper agreed that Love had gained such a position in the public mind that his active interest in McAdoo's behalf "might not be very constructive"; he had discussed the matter with Love, who had promised to exercise the necessary discretion. Love told McAdoo that it would lessen complications if he served "as a private in the ranks and you may be assured that I am on the job all the time and am giving it my best attention with these things in view." The Klan presented the "most difficult phase of the situation," and he thought it best for McAdoo "to absolutely ignore all reference to this matter at least for the present."[21]

On July 14, 1923, sixty-five men and women from all over Texas "sounded their McAdoo preferences" in a two-hour conference at the Adolphus Hotel in Dallas. Marshall Hicks called the meeting to order. Principally it was a session of speechmaking, with Love, who could not stay "in the ranks" for long, "pitching the notes." That afternoon members of the advisory board met in Love's office to select an executive committee—one member from each senatorial district—and a finance committee. "Texas is going to be all right without any question," Love advised Roper. "I had no hand in calling the Dallas conference, but after it was called I was sure that it was desirable for me to take part in it and I am satisfied that the meeting did good. It was a better meeting than the meeting which initiated the Woodrow Wilson movement in Texas in 1911." McAdoo thanked Love for the "fine meeting" and asked him to let the rest of the participants know of his appreciation. "I think it is a wise thing now to proceed with the organization of these clubs. Such a movement will help immensely." "The Texas fellows are certainly taking hold with vigor," an obviously pleased McAdoo wrote a Massachusetts supporter. "They are a fine bunch." [22]

On the other hand, Jim Ferguson proclaimed the McAdoo meeting "a complete fizzle," because only sixty-five people had attended, despite weeks of advertising. It had been, Ferguson claimed, a coming together of klansmen and their tools to launch the McAdoo boom. Noting Hicks's warning to the gathering that serious opposition to McAdoo was developing in Texas, Ferguson declared flatly: "He's right. That opposition is so serious there isn't even an outside chance to put it over this time. T. Bunkum [Love] and his machine are doomed to certain defeat." [23]

Ferguson had been sniping at McAdoo (whom he derisively dubbed the "crum" [crummy] prince) for months, calling him the Klan's candidate. McAdoo had sputtered to Roper in April: ". . . this scoundrel Ferguson seems to be determined to create the impression in prejudiced minds that I belong to the Klan. Whether I should go at him with a sharp stick or ignore him is the question. I am inclined to the latter." Roper agreed, seeing no good to be gained from replying to libelous statements. After Ferguson's attack on the Dallas meeting, however, the hot-tempered McAdoo's anger boiled over in a letter to Love: "I see that impossible skunk and scoundrel, Ferguson, continues to lie about me and you. To h—— with him! He is not worth noticing, but he has the power of mischief. . . . Of course, I cannot and will not become involved in any recognition of or controversy with so base a creature as this fellow." [24]

McAdoo's Texas supporters wanted him to accept an invitation to make an address at the state fair, which was to open in Dallas on October 15. "It seems that it is going to be indispensably necessary to declare yourself upon the Americanism question and in good temperate language declare yourself against that proposition," Love advised, "and I believe that here is the best place to make the declaration." He also wanted him to make a statement about the increase in railroad workers' wages that took place while he was director general of railroads. McAdoo, however, declined to speak at the fair, pleading other engagements. "I am firmly convinced that I ought not to become mixed up in the issues you mention," he wrote Love. "I think it would be unwise from every standpoint. Of course, I should inevitably become involved if I went to Dallas." [25]

The sudden death of President Harding in San Francisco of a cerebral embolism on August 2, 1923, elevated Vice-President Calvin Coolidge of Massachusetts to the presidency. Pondering this unexpected development, McAdoo decided that his party's chances were not as good as they would have been if Harding had lived, and that it was all the more important that the Democrats nominate a strong man of progressive views on a distinctly liberal and progressive platform. "If we do that, we can win; I feel this strongly," he told Roper. "I am quite sure that if Coolidge is nominated or any other stand-pat Republican is nominated, and we nominate the right kind of a Democrat, we can carry the country without the East, although I think that we should have an excellent chance to carry some strong states in the East, and central west as well." [26]

For a time an ill-defined movement to boost the candidacy of automobile manufacturer Henry Ford was regarded as a threat to McAdoo. As Mark Sullivan put it, he was in danger of "being run down by a Ford." Ford drew his support from farmers and laborers, pacifists, prohibitionists, and anti-Semites. "His opposition to me is based upon narrow prejudices, created by a lying secretary who seems to dominate him completely . . . and his natural republicanism," McAdoo commented to Love in September. "In spite of his professions, I think he is one of the strongest standpatters in the Republican Party." On December 18, Ford announced his support for Coolidge and took himself out of the running as a candidate. [27]

On a trip to the East in October, McAdoo made final plans for his campaign, and on the return journey in November he opened headquarters in Chicago, with Judge David L. Rockwell, an Ohio lawyer, as campaign manager. His campaign formally opened in South Dakota in December, 1923, when delegates to a state party convention invited him to become a candidate. His affirmative reply to the convention officially launched him in the race. [28]

The only other announced candidate at the time was Oscar W. Underwood, the conservative senior senator from Alabama. He announced his decision to run on August 1, 1923, in a speech to the Alabama State Legislature, which in February had petitioned him to run. The sixty-one-year-old Underwood was a veteran congressman, having served continuously in the House of Representatives from 1897 to 1915, before taking his seat in the Senate, where he remained for two terms. A respected figure in the congressional hierarchy, he had acted as Democratic floor leader in the House from 1911 to 1915, but was best remembered as chairman of the powerful House Ways and Means Committee; the important tariff bill of 1913 bore his name. Politically a wet, Underwood invoked traditional southern political doctrine to condemn Prohibition because it "challenged the integrity of the compact between the States" and compelled men "to live their lives in the mold prescribed by the power of government."[29]

This was Underwood's second bid for the Democratic nomination. In 1912 he had been one of the principal candidates, along with Wilson and Clark, at the Baltimore convention, polling 117½ votes on the first ballot. He was bitterly opposed by William Jennings Bryan, with whom he had quarreled over the tariff, and never realized his potential strength. Initially Underwood expected to carry most if not all of the southern states, their delegates having been instructed to vote for him as long as his name was before the national convention. This sectional endorsement was crucial to his overall campaign strategy, for without the support of the South the senator doubted that he could gain further consideration. The Kentucky-born Underwood's credentials as a "real" southerner were suspect to some, however. Love wrote privately, "The wets and Wall Street interests are supporting Underwood, a Southern man with Northern interests, whose father was a colonel in the Union Army—in the hope of taking the Southern states and delegates away from McAdoo, the man they really fear and whom they are intent on destroying." The popular image of Underwood as a wet and a reactionary tool of machine politicians was given greater currency by Tennessee editor George Fort Milton in an article in *Outlook* in January, 1924.[30]

William E. Lea, the thirty-four-year-old mayor of Orange, Texas, who had been a wartime army friend of Underwood's son, sparked the senator's campaign in the Lone Star State. In September, 1923, Lea persuaded Joe Bailey, Oscar B. Colquitt, Judge Charles A. Pippin, and Dallas lawyer Louis Blaylock to join him in a call for an organizational meeting on October 1. Shortly before the meeting was convened, Lea discovered that there was a great deal of opposition to the movement, because most of the leaders were anti-prohibitionists and Bailey men. Sixty-five people attended and chose D. A. Frank of Dallas as chairman, Dabney White of Tyler as secretary, and Lea as campaign manager. Frank was known to be a strong prohibitionist and woman suffragist and to be opposed to "Baileyism," and Lea regarded his selection as a master stroke of political manipulation to avoid alienating any single faction in the state.[31]

In carrying out his southern strategy, Underwood decided to visit Texas during the fall of 1923, before Congress met and his campaigning time became limited. His health was not strong enough to permit him to speak in more than a few carefully selected cities. "I cannot travel every night and speak and shake hands with friends all the next day," he wrote Frank. There was trouble with his schedule because he did not want to sleep on the train. Still, his visit ranked among the more important events in the primary election of 1924, for in a speech in Houston on October 27, he took on the Klan. The senator was talking about class legislation, when he exclaimed:

Government must be free and in the open and not behind closed doors. It is all right to have organizations for purposes of amusements; it is all right to have fraternal organizations and civic clubs; but when men have secret organizations for purpose of governing them, they are striking at the very principle of free government. I know that in Texas I have reached the home of real Democracy. We citizens must grant to every man his individual rights and liberties as long as he stays within the law, but the law must not be made or executed by class or clan. I mean no reflection on any man or organization, but if there are men in organizations of that kind, they must give equal rights to all men who have a claim to American citizenship and real Democrats should not stay in any organization that denies that right to any man.

According to the *Dallas Morning News*, these were "totally unexpected statements," for earlier in the day, when a newspaperman asked Underwood to state his position on the Klan, his advisers in the room stopped him before he could say anything more than "I am not a member of the klan; personally I have no position." These advisers included Lea and former Congressman Robert Lee Henry, who had broken with the Klan when it refused to support him for the Senate in the 1922 election.[32]

Did he perhaps decide to denounce the Ku Klux Klan as an answer to the rumor that the Texas Klan would back McAdoo for the presidency? Regarding that question, Underwood later wrote Joe Eagle: "You know me well enough to know that I did not take my position in my Houston speech captiously or without careful deliberation and consideration." He added: "Of course my speech in Houston was directed directly at the Ku-Klux Klan and all other secret cliques and organizations that seek to control the politics of this country behind closed doors, and that are trampling upon the fundamental principles of the personal liberty, independence of action, and freedom of thought, of the great masses of American people." This statement was later incorporated into the platform adopted by the Texas Underwood organization.[33]

Reaction to the Houston speech was immediate. Klansmen, recognizing Underwood as a leading adversary, dubbed him the "Jew, jug, and Jesuit" candidate, while the *New York World* said that his chances of nomination had been immensely improved by his bold stand. During the week he was in Texas, the senator also spoke in Wichita Falls, Nocona, Dallas, San Antonio, Orange, and Beaumont. Leading McAdoo supporters in Texas disparaged his visit. "The opinion seems to be unanimous that a solid McAdoo delegation from Texas is an assured fact, especially since Mr. Underwood's tour of the state," Love wrote Roper. "The reports from everywhere are that he had poor crowds and made a poor impression." In an interview Colonel Tom Ball of Houston commented that Underwood's opposition to Prohibition, woman suffrage, and anti–child-labor legislation would make it impossible for him to go far.[34]

McAdoo's initial reaction to Underwood's candidacy was that he did not have the "ghost of a chance." His strategy was to concede Alabama to Underwood while seeking second-choice support in its delegation. He believed that if Mississippi and Georgia would endorse him their support would "destroy the force of Underwood's candidacy" and throw practically the whole South to him, except for Alabama and possibly Louisiana. To Thomas Chadbourne and others, McAdoo construed his own remarks against intolerance at a University of Southern California commencement in June, 1923, as a disavowal of the Klan. "My views on these points are far more direct and specific than Mr. Underwood's anemic statement in Texas, which has been heralded by his friends as such a display of courage," he wrote. "By the way, this speech [at the university] was quite widely published in the Catholic press, and a strong attempt is being made to use it against me, so I am told, with the K.K.K.'s."[35]

Underwood's attack on the Klan brought into his Texas organization several militant opponents of the Klan, some of whom hoped to convert the Underwood movement into an anti-Klan party or faction. Joe Eagle called for an organization that would crusade against the Klan and name candidates for offices from "President down to Precinct

Constable." Joseph S. Cullinan, a wealthy oilman, also believed that
Underwood should head an anti-Klan organization in Texas. However,
Lea and Houston lumberman John Henry Kirby were opposed to making Underwood secondary in the campaign; they wanted a militant Underwood organization with the Klan as one of the paramount issues but
not *the* paramount issue. The result was a call for a full-scale meeting of
Underwood's strongest supporters in Dallas on December 31, 1923, to
outline a definite policy on this subject. Lea wrote the senator, ". . . if
we can only act in moderation and wisely, I believe that the Underwood campaign will be put on such footing in Texas as to secure control
of the delegation at the Convention."[36]

When the meeting convened at the Oriental Hotel, most of Underwood's leading supporters in the state were present. It took almost
thirteen hours to thrash out the platform. As finally adopted, it was an
endorsement of the Constitution, the Bill of Rights, the three branches
of government, strict construction of the Constitution, the principle of
states' rights, tax reduction, enforcement of the provisions of both the
state and federal constitutions, opposition to government by "Boards,
Bureaus, Commissions and Surveys," and an unequivocal endorsement of Underwood's stand on the Klan in his Houston address and in
the letter to Eagle and of the senator himself as a candidate for the
Democratic nomination. A quotation from the Democratic platform of
1856 denouncing the nativist Know-Nothing party was also included.[37]

The executive committee was completed with the selection of a
chairman for each of the thirty-one senatorial districts, and an advisory
board headed by Cullinan was formed with an initial membership of
125 and plans for augmenting it to at least 250 persons. Frank Kell
agreed to lead the sixteen-member finance committee. Lea thought
that it would be best if Kirby, Cullinan, Bailey, Colquitt, and Louis
Wortham did not serve on that committee. He was somewhat fearful
because "about fifty percent of the men who signed the declaration of
principles are what is known as 'the old gang,' and subject to criticism
on that account," but he assured Underwood that "the situation in
Texas looks brighter all the time." The Alabaman replied that he thoroughly approved of the provisions of the platform. "They are sound in
principle, and in accord with my views," he asserted. "As to the Klan
issue, I do not think anybody in the country now has any doubt about
my position in regard to the Klan activities, and I think it helpful
rather than harmful to give them full publicity."[38]

One anti-Klan leader who did not attend the Underwood meeting in Dallas was James E. Ferguson. In 1923, the former governor beat the drum for Henry Ford in the columns of the *Forum*, telling his readers that "day by day Mr. Ford's candidacy for the presidency grows brighter and brighter and better and better." The Fergusonites met in Temple in late July and organized a Texas Ford-for-President Club, with John E. Morriss of Dallas as president and Frank Doering of Temple as secretary. "Ford is the only man with whom the democrats have a ghost of a show to win the presidency next year," Ferguson declared before 4,000 people in a speech in Austin opening the Ford boom. "I am not a candidate for anything, and am not trying to get on the ticket as the vice presidential nominee," he assured his audience. In November, Ferguson's preference was still Ford, if he would run, but he thought that Underwood had the best chance of winning the Democratic nomination because he had made a clear-cut statement against the Klan. He was "unalterably opposed to McAdoo because he is a Ku Klux sympathizer and possibly a member and is the candidate of the wall street federal reserve board crowd."[39]

Ford's endorsement of Coolidge in December left Ferguson without a candidate. "It is hard to tell whether Ford got in Calvin's limousine or Coolidge got in Henry's flivver," he noted ruefully. "Any how, they are riding together."[40] Lea invited Ferguson to attend the Underwood conference, but he declined, saying that he could be of no help since he had not yet declared for Underwood but that he would like to talk to Lea about the matter. He went to Dallas early in January and spent about ten hours over a three-day period in conference with Lea. When he offered to endorse the senator if the Underwood leaders would support him in the 1924 gubernatorial primary, Lea replied that, while they were inclined to be friendly, it was not good policy to favor one candidate more than another. Ferguson then asked Lea to discuss the matter with the other Underwood leaders in Texas. The campaign manager talked with Kirby, Cullinan, Kell, Bailey, and Colquitt, and the consensus was that, while there would be no alliance between the Underwood organization and Klan candidates, they could not tie themselves to any one of the anti-Klan candidates, even in return for as much help as Ferguson might offer.

When Ferguson heard this, he was "inclined to be quite bitter about it" and threatened to make alliances elsewhere. Lea pointed out that he would not dare align himself publicly with McAdoo's forces in

Texas, knowing that they had Klan support. Ferguson countered by warning that his friends would make local alignments with the McAdoo men to elect a McAdoo delegation in return for their support in the state election. It would be bad business to trade with the McAdoo forces, Lea suggested; Ferguson could not depend upon them, because the leaders had been bitterly opposed to him from the beginning. Friendliness to Underwood would be his best policy, particularly because of the Klan situation; a "mutual understanding" might then be reached at the state convention. Ferguson left in "a seemingly friendly frame of mind" but without committing himself to Underwood.[41]

With Texas political leaders taking positions on the McAdoo or the Underwood side, the position of Governor Pat Neff assumed critical importance. Should he refuse to support a delegation instructed for McAdoo, a wedge would be driven into the dry strength of Texas, which the Californian expected to have solidly behind him. There was some reason to believe that Neff desired a favorite-son endorsement. In June, 1923, R. B. Walthall, head of the oil-and-gas division of the Railroad Commission and Neff's former private secretary, addressed a letter to Texas newspapers in which he pointed out the governor's availability. Ferguson sneered that Walthall had "perpetrated the season's best joke" and predicted that everybody would laugh at his letter. The following month, however, Larry Mills informed Love that Neff was leaving soon on a speaking tour through the North and East and that "his friends here [in Austin], some of them at least, are taking him rather seriously."[42]

Meanwhile, William Jennings Bryan, who regarded Underwood as a wet, an opponent of woman suffrage, and a captive of Wall Street, was looking for a southern candidate to combat the Alabaman in the South. He was convinced that the wets and Wall Street were merely using Underwood as a stalking horse to line up votes that would eventually be switched to John W. Davis, "whose record is not known and upon whom they can rely." On August 1, after Underwood formally announced his candidacy, Bryan said that he had no objection to a southern candidate as such and mentioned as possibilities Josephus Daniels of North Carolina, former Governor Braxton Bragg Comer of Alabama, and Governor Pat Neff of Texas. "Every Southern State can furnish an available progressive Democrat who can poll several million votes more than Senator Underwood," Bryan declared. "He was not available in 1912 and is much less available now."[43]

Neff was highly pleased to be mentioned by Bryan. He wrote "the Commoner" a flattering thank-you letter, noting that "I have gotten much inspiration from your life and from your addresses." He enclosed a copy of a speech, "The Price of Civilization," which he was to deliver in Chautauqua, New York, on August 14, asking Bryan to look over that part which dealt with state-federal relations in connection with the enforcement of Prohibition. Bryan was "very much impressed" by the speech and sent a copy to the *Jacksonville* (Florida) *Observer*. He also included an encomium on Neff, hailing him as a leader who led in the right direction and could unite the South and West:

The Democratic Party has to choose between the exploited masses on one side and the exploiters on the other, just as the Children of Israel had to choose between God and Baal. Governor Neff's speech shows that he is the kind of man we need. There is no reason why the South should not have the Presidency, and the best way to secure the Presidency is to put up a man like Neff who is with the people and brave enough to wield the powers of government in their behalf. *Why not Governor Neff?* [44]

Bryan coached Neff on the need to win the support of his and other states. He told Neff that not only was he big enough to be president but he was sound on the two essential points, "namely, that you are against the Wall Street crowd and in sympathy with the masses, and second, that you are dry and in favor of enforcement of prohibition." The launching of Underwood's candidacy made Neff's candidacy opportune. "With you as a candidate representing the progressive Democracy and the dry side, Mr. Underwood would have to make his appeal to Southern wets and Southern reactionaries," he pointed out. "He would have no advantage over you on the Southern question and would be at a great disadvantage on the other issues." [45]

Bryan and his wife were going to California to visit their children, and he invited the governor to meet him on the train either in Houston on the night of August 26 or in San Antonio the next morning. Neff arranged to board the train at Liberty, about twenty-five miles from Houston, so that the two men could have an uninterrupted visit without making it necessary for Bryan to stay up late. Afterward Neff confided to a friend: "He was much stronger in his conversation concerning his advocacy of my cause for President than were the statements contained in his published communication." "I met Neff and was very much pleased with him," Bryan wrote an official of the Anti-Saloon League. The governor, he said, was a teetotaler who believed with

Bryan that Prohibition enforcement ought to be entrusted only to those who did not drink. "I think it is well to emphasize Neff's availability as a dry candidate, at the same time calling attention to drys in other states," was his recommendation. "It may be best for us to have a dry candidate in each state so that the states will be committed, and then these delegations will be available for the support of the dry candidate who has the largest following."[46]

Some of Neff's friends wanted him to head a strong favorite-son delegation to the national convention. Texas Secretary of State S. L. Staples corresponded with the governor's supporters in Texas, assuring them that Neff was receiving much encouragement both in and out of the state and that "his chances to secure the nomination are growing stronger each day." Staples also wrote to a Democratic National Committee member in Oklahoma, who promised to take up the Neff candidacy with the leading Democrats of that state and see what sentiment he could create. A Crockett lawyer suggested that the state convention, which would select the delegation to New York, might be held in Waco, Neff's hometown. "It is my opinion that this would be quite a 'strategic' move on the part of the Governor's friends for obvious reasons."[47]

Neff told inquirers that at present he had no definite political plans for the future. "Quite a number of my friends seem anxious that some aggressive steps be taken in regard to the Democratic nomination in 1924," he wrote early in December. "I am not sure just what will be the best course. I doubt the wisdom of taking any public stand just at this time. General talk by my friends . . . , of course, is the thing most helpful at present." Meanwhile, he attracted national attention by presenting Republican Governor Gifford Pinchot of Pennsylvania with a "Texas sombrero." He also asked Bryan to come to Texas for a duck-hunting trip on the Gulf Coast in January, 1924, and the Commoner tentatively accepted.[48]

To advance Neff's candidacy, his friends on the Democratic State Executive Committee endorsed him for the Democratic nomination at a meeting in Dallas on December 15. He was hailed as "one possessing the wisdom, strength, courage and sense of justice that would make a great President" and in whose personality "are happily combined all the elements of character, ability and magnetism that makes a successful and ideal leader, the safest, the wisest and the strongest leader in the ranks of Democracy today." On the same day Bryan announced that if he was elected to the Florida delegation he would nominate a southern Democrat for president. Although he would not name the man he had in mind, he did say that his choice was not McAdoo or Underwood and that he was dry and progressive. It was inferred that he would present Neff's name.[49]

The McAdoo managers in Texas professed not to be worried about the favorite-son movement for Neff. "The action of the Democratic State Executive Committee, which is dominated by the Governor, in endorsing him intended it as a sheer compliment and this will not affect the situation in this State," Love assured McAdoo. "There is no doubt that a solid McAdoo delegation will go from Texas." Love privately expressed regret at the movement to divide the anti-Underwood forces in order to pay the governor a compliment because of the injury it was bound to do Neff, "for it is certain that it cannot be successful enough to prevent a sweeping McAdoo victory in the State." In a public statement Marshall Hicks accused the governor's friends of "playing directly into the hands of the wets," who were trying to stop McAdoo from showing his real strength on the early ballots by encouraging each state in which McAdoo was strong to instruct for a favorite son or to send an uninstructed delegation. Declaring that "this is no time to be passing pretty compliments to even our best friends," Hicks urged Texas voters to send a delegation instructed to vote for McAdoo as long as his name was before the convention. The McAdoo state headquarters opened in the Southland Hotel in Dallas on January 1, 1924, and old Wilsonian Cato Sells of Fort Worth was named campaign manager.[50]

Underwood's followers in Texas were pleased by the rift in the ranks of the hitherto triumphant dry forces. John H. Kirby's *Austin Statesman* called the endorsement of Neff by the Democratic State Executive Committee "a severe blow" to the McAdoo cause in the state. William E. Lea regarded the endorsement as a "distinct victory" for Underwood in that it widened the breach between Love and Neff. Love was so incensed that he was openly abusive about the governor. Lea had information that when Neff returned from a northern trip in January he would probably open active work for an uninstructed delegation on the premise that Texas was tired of "bosses" and did not care to go to the next convention "hog-tied" as it had been in the past. "Of course we are making all the capital we can out of this friction," Lea told Underwood.[51]

Friends advised Neff either to make a serious fight for the delega-

tion or to get out of the race. To allow the McAdoo advocates to secure
the delegation, while the public supposed that Neff's supporters were
fighting for him, would advertise to the world that the governor was in
political eclipse in his own state. Neff temporized, saying privately that
he had not yet been able to work out to his own satisfaction any kind of
political program. "I have in mind what I think should be done along
the line of Texas politics," he wrote, "but I am not sure as to the best
means of obtaining the desired end." [52]

On January 12, Neff's friends in Waco effected the temporary organization of a statewide Neff-for-President Club in the office he had
occupied when he practiced law. J. T. Harrington, who was regarded
as being as close to the governor as any man in Texas, was elected president; and Joe W. Hale, secretary of the Democratic State Executive
Committee, was chosen temporary secretary. A mass meeting to establish a permanent organization was promised in the near future. The
meeting called upon the governor's friends throughout Texas and the
friends of democracy throughout the nation to join them "in an effort to
secure the nomination of this stalwart Democrat, one who is safe, wise
and a strong leader in the ranks of democracy, and one who hails from
an Empire State that is no farther southwest than Massachusetts is
northeast." [53]

Cato Sells, through Bryan's friend, C. M. Rosser of Dallas, warned
Bryan that a Neff favorite-son candidacy would help the Underwood
cause in the state. "I trust and anticipate when Mr. Bryan comes to
Texas he will forget the whole Neff-for-President propaganda," he
wrote another of Bryan's friends. [54] In fact, while Bryan was courting
Neff and mentioning him favorably to fellow Democrats and the press,
he began sounding out A. A. Murphree, president of the University of
Florida, on a possible favorite-son candidacy. Finding the educator receptive to the idea, on January 14 he announced that he would present
the obscure Floridian's name to the Democratic convention. According to Marshall Hicks, Bryan's announcement gave Neff's followers
"quite a jolt." "The Neff people had expected Bryan to present Neff's
name in the National Convention," Hicks told Love. "I know this to be
a fact and they feel very 'let down' after finding out that Bryan had
other plans." Ironically, because by law Murphree's position barred
him from entering a political primary, Bryan had no candidate to oppose McAdoo and Underwood in Florida and as a result found himself
pledged to cast a vote for McAdoo at the convention. [55]

Bryan came to Texas on a speaking tour at the end of January. Sells talked with him in Dallas and Fort Worth and assured Hicks that "there is no danger of his saying anything while in Texas to which we could seriously object." Bryan was not unfriendly to McAdoo, and Sells had reason to believe that he expected him to be nominated. While he was in Texas, Bryan spent two days with Neff on a duck hunt at the game preserve of W. L. Moody, Jr., on the Gulf Coast. As the party sat down for breakfast on the second morning, Neff observed a big wooden duck on his plate. Bryan, who was seated next to him, blandly explained, "It has been decided that each person is to eat for breakfast the duck killed by him on the previous day." Although Neff's poor marksmanship inspired the joke, the decoy duck was an appropriate symbol of his role in Bryan's effort to combat Underwood in the South.[56]

Just when McAdoo's candidacy seemed to be prospering, it received a crippling blow during the Senate investigation of the Teapot Dome scandal. In 1921, after arranging with Secretary of the Navy Edwin Denby to transfer naval oil reserves to the Department of the Interior, Secretary of the Interior Albert B. Fall of New Mexico promptly leased the properties to private oil companies. Edward L. Doheny's Pan-American Petroleum Company obtained the Elk Hills reserve in California, and the Teapot Dome reserve in Wyoming was turned over to Harry F. Sinclair's Mammoth Oil Company. The Senate hearings, conducted by Thomas J. Walsh, revealed that Doheny had "lent" Fall $100,000 in cash, handed over secretly in a "little black bag." Sinclair had given Fall more than $300,000 in cash and negotiable securities. Democrats rejoiced at the great storm over Teapot Dome—a storm that seemed certain to sweep the Republicans from office in 1924. "I think we have the republicans on the run," John Nance Garner wrote McAdoo. "We have 'Uncle Andy' [Mellon] and 'Cal' whipped on the tax question, and it looks like Tea Pot Dome is giving us sufficient fuel to heat up the entire country."[57]

On February 1, however, Senator Irvin Lenroot of Wisconsin, acting at the request of Senator Jim Reed, against whom McAdoo was campaigning in Missouri, asked Doheny for the names of all former cabinet officials on his payroll. The oilman replied that he had hired several, including Attorney General Thomas Watt Gregory, recently named by Coolidge special counsel in the Teapot Dome investigation (Gregory quickly resigned), and McAdoo. McAdoo's law firm, Doheny said, had been employed "to represent us in Washington in connection with Mexican matters." That had occurred while Wilson was president; afterward McAdoo "represented us in Mexico." Doheny testified that he paid him "about $250,000," a figure later corrected to $100,000. Beginning on March 1, 1922, McAdoo had been paid an annual retainer of $25,000 a year.[38]

By association with Doheny, McAdoo was stuck fast to the Teapot Dome scandal. Since the Democrats planned to make the oil leases a major issue in the 1924 campaign, it would be embarrassing to nominate a man who had worked for Doheny. McAdoo's enemies immediately proclaimed loudly that McAdoo was no longer available for the nomination. Senator Thaddeus Caraway of Arkansas asked rather brutally, "How are you going to put Doheny's attorney in the White House?" "The general consensus of opinion is that Mr. McAdoo is out of the running," the Reverend J. Frank Norris informed Bryan. "The people will never elect a man who has been found selling his influence to oil pirates." According to Frank Kent, of the *Baltimore Sun*, it would be a "joke" to see McAdoo on the stump denouncing his own employer's bribery of Albert Fall. A Republican paper in Boston commented: "'McAdoo'll do' is proposed as the Democratic slogan—but it looks now as if they were ready to make it 'McAdieu.'"[59]

Privately, Breckenridge Long of Missouri expressed a gloomy outlook: "It is unmistakable that the McAdoo forces are crumbling." Tom Love, who had been "his ardent supporter," was now "out for [Indiana senator Samuel] Ralston for President," wrote Long. Wilson's private secretary Joseph Tumulty now favored Senator Walsh, and Bernard Baruch, who had been helping finance the McAdoo campaign, was turning toward another candidate. "When Love, Tumulty, and Baruch . . . desert him," suggested Long, "it means a great deal. It means he is gone." Even Daniel Roper, "his supposed chief advisor and supermanager," was "awfully wobbly." Journalist Mark Sullivan described the immediate effect of Doheny's testimony:

Within one hour after the news flew out from Washington on a thousand wires, it was taken for granted, no less by McAdoo's supporters than by his opponents, that his political career was ruined. His opponents took heart and resumed vigorously the pushing forward of other candidates; his supporters, in dismay, turned to look for a substitute.[60]

McAdoo refused to give up. From Los Angeles he issued a statement declaring that Doheny was "wholly without justification of any sort" in mentioning his name in connection with the oil leases. Arriving in Washington to attend Wilson's funeral (the former president had died on February 3), he asked to testify before Walsh's committee. He met several times with Roper, Love, Baruch, Tom Chadbourne, David Rockwell, and other supporters, and the consensus was that he should withdraw gracefully from the race with an announcement that he would continue to work for progressive principles and would attend the convention as a delegate to help achieve these goals. In the event of a deadlock the convention might turn to him with a draft; in any case he would put himself in a good position for 1928. McAdoo refused to heed this advice. After calmly defending his reputation before the Senate committee on February 11, he announced his intention of staying in the contest at a well-publicized conference of his supporters in Chicago on February 18. "I sincerely believe that it would have been a mistake for me to have taken any other course than the one I took," he wrote Colonel House, who had advised him to withdraw. "The implication would have been terrible and the result, I am sure, would have been disastrous to my good name and professional standing. Moreover, nobody likes a quitter and I have never yet quit in the face of an enemy." He felt obliged to go on with the fight and to put the question to the test with the people in the March primaries.[61]

McAdoo's Texas managers stuck with him. Hicks, who was not able to go to Chicago because of a court case, wired Rockwell: "In my judgement our chief is the only democrat who can lead us to victory this year. Recent assault upon him is a smoke screen of predatory interests. Texas will stand for McAdoo at New York as Texas stood for Woodrow Wilson at Baltimore." "Hirelings of special interests have about quit talking of your being 'eliminated,'" Joseph Myers wrote McAdoo. "A few of the 'kept' newspapers are making themselves ridiculous in their attempts to defend Secretary Denby, and at the same time find fault with your perfectly legitimate connection with Doheny. On with the battle for good government and clean politics."[62]

McAdoo's connection with Doheny precipitated a financial crisis in his organization as campaign contributions dried up. In Texas the situation was so serious that Sells warned Love that "we cannot proceed much farther without substantial assistance. . . . Not a dollar has come in since I saw you in Chicago and obligations are fast piling up with our hands so tied as to practically stop organization activities." On February 16, William Lea reported to Underwood that McAdoo's Texas headquarters had been on the verge of closing up shop for the past two weeks because of lack of money. Larry Mills had resigned as secretary to take charge of Felix Robertson's gubernatorial campaign because there were no funds to pay him. Lea had invited Sells to have lunch with him. "I did not see any reason for ignoring the man when he was down," he explained, adding, "As a matter of fact, if Mr. McAdoo withdraws in Texas, I fear it will be a much harder battle because at present we have the Neff and McAdoo forces definitely split; and if Mr. McAdoo withdraws, we have no tangible thing to fight, in as much as the Neff forces are growing more and more friendly." [63]

With the separation of Neff's friends from the McAdoo group, the well-financed wet faction backing Underwood, strengthened by the revelations of McAdoo's relationship with Doheny, now posed a serious threat to capture control of the Texas delegation. After a conference in Austin on March 7 attended by Sells, Love, and Hicks, Sells telegraphed Brice Clagett, McAdoo's executive secretary, that the "Chief" should send the following wire: "If my candidacy in Texas might seriously divide progressive forces I do not desire my name used there. The vital thing is to elect a Texas delegation which will never support a reactionary candidate. I am sincere in the hope that my friends will leave nothing undone to that end." On the following day, March 8, Love advised Clagett that a union of all progressive forces in Texas was generally regarded as prudent if not necessary to defeat Underwood and that he, Hicks, and Sells had agreed that it was "imperatively necessary to join forces either for uninstructed or favorite son delegation." Said Love: "This certainly offers best possible solution of impossible situation and opportunity to obtain friendly delegation. Alternative is to close headquarters at once for lack of funds. Now largely in hole and impossible to raise any for Chief. Should wire Sells and Hicks by Monday." [64]

McAdoo was shocked by this sudden development on the eve of crucial primaries in Georgia and elsewhere. "Sells message great surprise," Clagett wired Hicks. "Such action grave error. Chief hopes you will hold fort." Clagett wired Rockwell to telephone Love immediately, adding: "I don't understand that situation. It would be ruinous in Georgia and other places if Texas status changed. Relying on you to do everything necessary." Love was also asked to get in touch with Rockwell by phone. He telegraphed back: "Acute financial difficulties and serious danger of division of forces on account of local candidacy

[Neff's] and extraordinary activity generously financed for Oscar [Underwood] make prompt compliance with Sells and Hicks suggestion wired yesterday indispensable to best result in Texas and necessary to avert embarrassing developments."[65]

McAdoo went east to campaign in Georgia before that state's primary on March 19 and arranged to meet Love in Saint Louis. In the meantime his Texas headquarters remained open. Love advised McAdoo that Texas could not be carried for a delegation instructed for McAdoo and that his friends should join forces with the Neff people to elect an uninstructed or a Neff delegation. If the progressive forces were combined, the delegation would not be unfriendly to McAdoo, but otherwise, Love said, he feared the election of either Underwood or a hostile Neff delegation. McAdoo agreed to be guided by the judgment of his Texas managers, though he admitted to Roper: "It would be a great pity . . . not to have Texas tied up to us from the outset."[66]

On March 17, Love told Hicks that definite arrangements should be made to bring matters to a head:

I am getting more anxious to see a consolidation of all the progressive forces because I do not like the lay of the land so far as the reactionary group in Texas are concerned. They have been helped by the result in Alabama and are spending a world of money and with no organization opposing them it may become dangerous. The progressive forces of the State ought to be told without delay, certainly not later than next week, what the program is and how it is to be pursued.[67]

Negotiations were going on with Neff at this time. "Our friend here saw the Austin party and he is agreeable to our plan," Hicks wrote Love cryptically from San Antonio. "He thinks with us that the chief should say something so as to give us the opportunity to announce our plan." The Austin party was still away and would not be back home for several days. "I think we should wait until after the 19th instant and we can then proceed to put our plan in operation," Hicks advised. "Maybe we should meet in Austin again to have a definite understanding all around." "Our friend here" was Frank C. Davis, the state Democratic chairman, and the "Austin party" was Neff. A story in the *San Antonio Express* of March 20, headlined "M'Adoo Supporters—in Texas Seeking New Horse to Ride," reported that the governor had been absent from Austin with the State Parks Board for more than a week and that in his absence his closest political confidantes at Austin have been filled with declarations to the effect "somebody must be found upon whom to concentrate." As related, the bulk of these statements come from men and women who had much to do with the McAdoo boom prior to its recent travail. They are now leading the chorus for Neff instructions and are saying that the entire McAdoo outfit, bandwagon, church wagon, steam roller, fleet of trucks and all will be found tenting on the Neff camp grounds and in a Neff park.[68]

Underwood had received almost two-thirds of the more than 100,000 votes cast in the Alabama primary on March 11 and now had twenty-four convention votes. McAdoo had not challenged Underwood in his native state, but both men were entered in the Georgia primary, to be held a week later. McAdoo made a last-minute tour of the state and appealed to native-son sentiment. In a speech at Macon on March 15, he was asked where he stood on the Klan and replied that he stood four square with respect to this and all other orders and organization on the immutable guarantees of liberty contained in the First Amendment. When McAdoo won a handsome two-to-one victory, the Underwood managers claimed that they had positive proof that on the eve of the election the Klan had been ordered to vote for him.[69]

Love thought that McAdoo's victory in Georgia had substantially put Underwood out of the running and that it had greatly improved the situation in Texas by giving heart to McAdoo's supporters. The Underwood vote in the state was a "wet reactionary Anti-McAdoo vote," however, and would not be lessened appreciably in numbers by his defeat in Georgia. It might still be necessary to forgo instructions or possibly to agree to favorite-son instructions. A great deal depended on the outcome of the South Dakota primary on March 25. Immediately after McAdoo won in South Dakota, Love, Hicks, Sells, Davis, and klansman William Hanger held a two-day conference in San Antonio. "We decided to go straight ahead and make a fight for McAdoo instructions in Texas," Love wrote Roper. "We are hoping to get the Governor's acquiescence in the plan but whatever he does, we will go ahead anyway. I believe we will win." "Situation improved. Will make hard fight for McAdoo delegation," Sells wired McAdoo. "Your telegram gratifies me very much," the candidate replied.[70] Love set out to raise the $5,000 he needed to keep the campaign going and asked Roper to find a financial angel willing to contribute $1,000 or $2,500. Roper sent his personal check for $1,000.[71]

Love and Sells asked McAdoo to make a speaking tour in Texas between April 9 and 14, beginning in Amarillo and continuing through Fort Worth, Dallas, Houston, and San Antonio. The candidate agreed. Buoyed by his recent victories, McAdoo was in a warlike mood; his letters bristled with military metaphors. "The preliminary battles we have already won have dumbfounded and discouraged our enemies," he wrote Roper. "They have received a fatal blow. What we have got to do is to follow up the victories with smashing attacks all along the front and administer a Waterloo to them on the 'field of carnage' in Madison Square Garden, New York City."[72]

Still, he wanted an understanding, if possible, with Neff. "He and I are friends and there is no reason that I can see why we should come into collision," he told Love on March 31. "I wish very much you would talk to him candidly and say to him, as coming from me, that I feel it would be a great pity to divide the progressive forces of Texas and allow the reactionary and wet element to control the state."[73]

And what of Neff? Following Doheny's testimony before the Senate Investigatory Committee, Silliman Evans, of the *Fort Worth Star-Telegram*, had wired the governor: "Final knock out delivered to McAdoo in senate [this] afternoon when proof made of his being attorney for Doheny during corrupt oil deals. Congratulations. Hit the Ball." Neff replied: "I am watching closely present developments in Washington. When the tenpins commence falling you cannot tell how many will fall. . . . Things are moving along nicely here." In February he had a long conference with Lea, who reported to Underwood that Neff "is still shaking in his shoes because of the fact that he nearly aligned himself with Mr. McAdoo early last fall." Confident that he held the upper hand, Lea intimated to Neff that the Underwood people might want him to speak in the senator's behalf after his nomination. The two men were to meet again, but the outcome of that session is unknown. On March 24, however, Lea wrote to Underwood's office manager in Washington: "Neff is still a doubtful element; and there is some talk now of Neff announcing as a favorite son from Texas. As I have said before, Neff has a following in the state that is not to be discounted, and I do not underestimate his strength."[74]

In a speech in Corsicana on March 5, Neff branded the bootlegger as a Bolshevist and anarchist who pulled down the nation's flag and trampled the Republic in the dust. He also advocated the use of the army and navy to keep rumrunners from landing their contraband goods on American soil. Breaking a long silence on political questions, he declared, without mentioning names, that the Texas delegation should never support any candidate who had, or who inherited as the convention proceeded, "the support of the corrupt powers or the wet influences," which seemed to rule out Underwood. As for the question of instructions, Neff said that state-convention delegates should be "definitely instructed as to the fundamental principles of the party" but that it should be left to their good judgment what further instructions, if any, should be given to the national delegation. [75]

"When do we move?" asked an admirer of the governor's address. "The stage is set, but there is no alarm clock." "The tenpins are falling rapidly now," Neff replied. "It is impossible to tell how many will fall, as each one falling seems to hit another. 'Watchful waiting' is a good policy just at present. The alarm clock, however, may be heard most any hour. I am glad you approved the Corsicana observation on National politics. We may add to it soon." At the end of March, however, all he would say privately was that Texas Democrats "should definitely instruct all delegates in reference to the platform, and the kind of nominee to place on it." Boyd Gatewood, in an editorial in the *Fort Worth Record*, said that Neff now had very little chance of receiving the nomination for president. "His boom reaching its peak at the time he was endorsed by the state Democratic executive committee, has been defeated if not punctured, by the sharp-pointed drive launched by Oscar W. Underwood's management in the state, and by McAdoo's resistance, lately aroused." [76]

On April 4, Love requested a meeting with Neff in Austin, and the governor readily agreed. There were conflicting reports about what passed between the two men. According to one story, Neff was offered a favorite-son delegation hand-picked by Love that would ultimately go to McAdoo in return for an introduction of the Californian by Neff in Dallas. The governor refused to make the trade. "It is untrue," Love said of the story. "I made no such proposition to Governor Neff." In turn Love later charged that the governor had proposed that, inasmuch as Bryan had mentioned him as suitable presidential timber, he would not make a campaign against McAdoo, provided the latter would agree to speak in Texas only along the lines of progressive democracy. Love said that this offer was declined, which angered the governor, and he began a campaign against McAdoo. A member of the Texas Railroad Commission reported that Neff thought Love should

have worked up the Texas endorsement for him. Love was told that
"Neff really wanted the endorsement."[77]

What seems to have happened is that before the Georgia primary
the discouraged McAdoo managers were prepared to back a favorite-
son delegation friendly to their candidate, that overtures were made to
Neff through Frank Davis, but that before a final agreement was worked
out Love and Hicks changed their minds and decided to seek an instructed McAdoo delegation. Neff was asked to acquiesce in this decision and to introduce McAdoo in Dallas. Miffed, he refused and made
a counterproposal along the lines set forth by Love, which was rejected, whereupon the negotiations collapsed. Neff then announced
that he would make a three-week speaking tour, beginning in Cleburne on April 14. He stated that the Texas delegation should not be
instructed to support either McAdoo or Underwood, since a third candidate was a possibility at the Democratic convention.[78]

By the time Neff began his tour, McAdoo had already made a
rapid swing through the state, beginning in Amarillo on April 9. "If
Governor Neff were not making it a three cornered fight, there would
be no doubt about Texas," he wrote from Oklahoma City, where he was
to speak before proceeding to Fort Worth on April 11. "This injects an
element of uncertainty. However, my friends are confident." In his
Fort Worth address McAdoo took issue with Neff, declaring that an uninstructed delegation would play directly into the hands of the party's
wets and reactionaries; although mentioning no names, he made it apparent that he meant Underwood and Al Smith. McAdoo asserted that
if the Texas delegation in 1912 had not been instructed for Wilson he
would not have been nominated, "and the whole destiny of America
and the world would have been changed." In Houston he put his plea
in brief form: "If you want me, say so," he told the crowd. "If you want
Underwood, say so. Be fish or fowl; be outstanding for something." His
attacks on Neff cheered the Underwood workers, and they doubted
that his presence would affect the ultimate outcome, which would be a
victory for Underwood.[79]

When asked by newspapermen how he stood on the Klan, McAdoo
repeated his Macon, Georgia, statement, which he had been using as
his answer to all questions about the Klan. It was noted that at Fort
Worth he had received State Senator William A. Hanger, who had directed the Klan forces at the last state Democratic convention in San
Antonio. W. L. Thornton of Dallas, a leading klansman and a member

of the Democratic State Executive Committee, told reporters that he regarded McAdoo as the outstanding leader of the Democratic party and took Neff to task for advocating an uninstructed delegation. "I have always had a very high personal regard for Governor Neff," said Thornton. "However, he has placed himself squarely in line with Brennan, Murphy and the other bosses of the party. His utterances will doubtless be hailed with delight by all the wet reactionary leaders in Texas and throughout the Nation."[80]

Following his speech in San Antonio on April 12, McAdoo met with Marshall Hicks and others to approve details of the Texas campaign and then left for North Carolina. He was delighted with his reception and asked Hicks and Love to provide for a vigorous follow-up speaking campaign right after the governor's.[81]

In his speaking tour Neff flung down the gauntlet to the McAdoo forces, repeatedly declaring that the Californian was unfit to be the Democratic standard-bearer because he had accepted Doheny's retainers and had represented corporations seeking tax refunds in cases arising while he was secretary of the treasury. Moreover, he had recently lost Missouri, Wisconsin, Arizona, Nebraska, Rhode Island, and Illinois. "Why tie up with a candidate who is defeated before he starts?" Neff asked his audiences. "Why does Texas want to tie the hands of her delegation for anybody? If she goes to the ball instructed there will be no body to dance with her. Underwood will be too wet to dance and McAdoo will be too oily." The Texas delegation, he said, should go to New York with iron-bound instructions on principles and platform but not on men, except that it should vote for no candidate "unless that man believes in the virility of the national and state prohibition laws and [is] one committed to their enforcement."[82]

Neff had a conference with publisher Charles Marsh of Austin, and the Marsh–E. S. Fentress newspapers in Texas got behind him. Hugh Nugent Fitzgerald, a political columnist for the *Austin American*, a Marsh-Fentress paper, accompanied the governor on his speaking tour. "Job Hunters of Texas Out to Beat Neff" was the heading of one Fitzgerald piece, in which he predicted that there would be no "party spoils" for politicans of the Hicks-Love-Sells stripe if the governor won his fight. W. L. Moody, Jr., had the *Galveston News* help Neff editorially.[83] The governor's friends throughout the state organized to carry out his program at the precinct and county conventions. R. Harper Kirby, chairman of the Prohibition forces in Texas when the state went dry, addressed a circular letter to his fellow drys, enclosing a draft precinct resolution for a national delegation instructed only on principles. Mrs. Claude De Van Watts, the president of the Texas branch of the WCTU, sent out an "S.O.S. America calls" to Texas women on Neff's behalf.[84]

In those counties in which the Underwood people were not strong enough to elect their own delegates, they worked for Neff. "The Underwood people are well organized and, of course, are encouraging Neff," a McAdoo supporter in El Paso informed Love.[85] This wet activity in turn caused some of the governor's dry friends to swing behind McAdoo. "I have always been a Neff man, but right here we part company," an East Texas man wrote the governor. "I do not want a *dark horse* for President. We want a prohibitionist for president, and East Texas will instruct for that matchless Prohibitionist and Statesman Wm. Gibbs McAdoo, the only man in the race worthy of support." Frank Davis broke with the governor and denounced his proposal for an uninstructed delegation. With the exception of Albert Sidney Burleson and Robert Lee Henry, practically all of the surviving Wilson leaders of 1912 were on the firing line for McAdoo. M. M. Crane and Cullen Thomas were for him, though they were not active. Cone Johnson was ill but got under the McAdoo flag with a telegram to Hicks on May 1. Because of Neff's unexpected role, the Texas Anti-Saloon League refused to take sides, but Atticus Webb, in a letter to the *Dallas Morning News*, declared that on the question of Prohibition enforcement league leaders throughout the country were "uniformly satisfied with William G. McAdoo. His stand on this question had been . . . uniform and unequivocal."[86]

The adage that "politics make strange bedfellows" was never truer than when Jim Ferguson lay down beside Neff and called for an uninstructed delegation. Ferguson's longstanding antipathy for McAdoo, whom he characterized as a "Holier than Thou, Longlegged, light fingered, Cadaverous, progressive democrat" who "can't tell anybody whether he is for the Ku Klux or against the Ku Klux," and his rebuff by the Underwood leaders prompted his action; there is no evidence that he and Neff had a formal agreement. Ferguson made his own speaking tour against McAdoo, charging that he was a "Klucker either in fact or in secret alliance" and that Love and Sells, in addition to securing the help of "Grand Wizzard Evans," had secured the support of

Colonel Mayfield's Weekly, "thus making unanimous and official the Klan support of McAdoo in Texas."[87]

Although Neff attracted good crowds, McAdoo's managers were confident that he made no impression. "Am in close touch with all sections of our state and confident that Texas will send solid instructed delegation for you despite efforts of Governor Neff," Hicks wrote McAdoo on April 17. "Your friends will hold the line." "There is no doubt but that the Underwood people and James E. Ferguson are working to throw all the wet reactionary strength of the state into a consolidation with Neff's forces," Love advised Atticus Webb, adding, "I do not believe they will succeed."[88]

Stung by the governor's contention that McAdoo was unfit for the presidency, Love offered to divide time with him during a speech in Dallas on April 28. Neff declined, saying that he was not a candidate for an office, was not urging the nomination of any particular candidate, and had not mentioned Love in his addresses.[89]

In his Dallas speech Love scored the governor for his fight against an instructed delegation. "It is somewhat surprising to find Ferguson and Neff yoked up together in this fight," he said, "and yet it is not surprising after all. The truth is they have never been far apart." "I am delighted to hear that you have skinned Neff," wrote McAdoo, who had been deeply angered by the governor's "contemptible calumnies." "He deserves it if any man ever did, and I hope the people will skin him." Later he added for good measure, "I had no idea that Neff was such a contemptible skunk as he has turned out to be."[90]

In contrast to McAdoo's and Neff's speaking tours through Texas, Underwood left his campaign in his managers' hands. Lea worked to enlist in every precinct in the state an Underwood chairman who would get out the senator's supporters on May 3, and an effort was made to "blanket the political women" through a Woman's Advisory Committee headed by Mrs. Hortense Ward of Houston, a militant suffragist and prohibitionist. "The political women of Texas are rather few but they exercise quite a crusading influence, and to muzzle them for the other side is tantamount to success among the more conservative women," he explained to Underwood. The campaign was well financed, with the Washington headquarters furnishing both workers and money. At Underwood's request B. F. Riley, who had been pastor of Houston's First Baptist Church before moving to Birmingham,

Alabama, and who had written a history of the Texas Baptists, visited the Lone Star State to overcome his coreligionists' distrust of the wet senator.[91]

Underwood's setback in Georgia left his Texas supporters "a little discouraged" because they had been led to expect that he would carry the state by a substantial majority. It caused them to adopt the strategy of demonstrating to Texans through the press that only a concerted effort by the Klan could defeat him. As Lea explained to Burleson:

The chief strategical reason for this is that if we must go to the New York convention with an uninstructed delegation, then we can lay the onus of it upon the Klan; because from the developments in Georgia, the complete cooperation of McAdoo and the Klan in that state, there has been a reaction in the North that rebounds intensely to the Senator's benefit. For the first time the political writers are beginning to realize the fact that the fundamental issue to be settled at the National Convention is whether the Ku Klux Klan will control the destiny of the country, and naturally, Senator Underwood is the foremost candidate for the presidential nomination who has assailed the undemocracy of the Klan.[92]

On April 23, Lea wired Underwood that his presence in Texas was the one thing necessary to ensure "absolute success" in the state and that if he would put himself in the hands of his Texas managers they would arrange an easy schedule that would crystallize the sentiment for him. "This will aid us to instruct the delegation for you and upon this probably depends the ultimate result," Lea coaxed. Underwood begged off, pleading urgent Senate business, but the truth of the matter was that he did not like to campaign and did not want to travel as far as Texas. One of the Alabaman's Washington advisers complained that his campaign lacked "pop and ginger." "He detests the ordinary fake business in politics and does not seem to even appreciate the advantage of a good slogan."[93]

On the day before the precinct conventions the *Dallas Morning News* reported that Underwood, Neff, and Ferguson leaders over the state had agreed to an anti-McAdoo resolution instructing delegates to the county conventions to oppose all measures or persons favoring his nomination. Questioned about the resolution, Lea insisted that it was of no concern to him: "If our friends wish to adopt such a resolution, we have no objection to offer, but we are taking no stock in such an enterprise." Said Lea: "We are fighting the battles of Oscar W. Underwood, and with us it is not an anti but a pro fight. We are for Underwood." Despite Lea's disclaimer, the Underwood, Neff, and Ferguson men did join forces in some counties.[94]

This fusion did not, however, prevent a majority of the delegates in the precinct conventions on May 3 from being pledged to support McAdoo. Three days later at the county conventions an even more overwhelming victory was recorded. Returns from 154 counties gave McAdoo 749 delegates and Underwood 84, with 41 uninstructed. "Our State Convention at Waco will be a 'love feast,' our friends overwhelmingly so in the majority as to be not only in complete control but able to enforce their every wish and will," Sells advised David Rockwell. "Hurrah for Texas. It is great news. Warm Congratulations," McAdoo wired Love. He was particularly pleased with the Texas verdict, "because it was a stinging rebuke to that cur Neff for his contemptible and unwarranted calumnies about me."[95]

Notwithstanding the fact that the uninstructed forces were victors in the precinct conventions in Neff's own McLennan County, a number of delegates headed by Klansman Alva Bryan defected to the McAdoo side, and the county convention instructed the state-convention delegates for McAdoo. Ironically, Neff, as chairman of the delegation, was bound to vote for the Californian. "There was nothing finer in the whole campaign than the actions of the McLennan County convention in instructing Governor Neff to vote for McAdoo," exulted Love. "It was a fitting climax." A disgusted W. E. Spell, who along with Walter Taylor had led the Neff forces in the convention, told the governor that his friends "were powerless to stem the tide of the Klansmen who had instructions from Atlanta . . . to do exactly what was done. . . . The whole program was pre-arranged and was not arranged in Waco, but was transmitted here."[96]

According to some observers, McAdoo's victory was as much a rebuke to Neff as a testimony of partiality for the Californian's candidacy. The governor's campaign had given groups like the Klan and the Farm Labor Union an opportunity to settle old scores against him, allowed McAdoo's supporters to exploit the resentment aroused when a governor sought to instruct the people in their political duties, and created the suspicion that Neff's opposition to McAdoo was animated by an ambition to carry Texas's vote to New York in his vest pocket. Moreover, Neff had based his argument for an uninstructed delegation on the curious proposition that the character of every one of the avowed candidates was so dubious that an instructed delegation might go to

New York only to discover that its candidate had become involved in a scandal. "It is not surprising that the Democrats of Texas were not much moved by an argument which put so many of the party's foremost leaders under suspicion," editorialized the *Dallas Morning News*. "We preached a good gospel to the Texas Democracy, but they voted otherwise at the precinct and county conventions," a rueful governor wrote privately.[97]

The only thing left for the Underwood forces to do was to analyze the causes of their defeat. Texas newspapers generally felt that the senator's Prohibition record was at fault; the state was predominantly dry, and Underwood was known as a wet. Furthermore, the impression was widespread that he could never be nominated and that his delegates would eventually go to Al Smith, who was totally unacceptable to Texas voters. Mrs. Hortense Ward felt that the opposition of the Klan and the prohibitionists, coupled with apathy among other voters, best explained the results. W. E. Lea charged that the Klan was responsible for McAdoo's victory on May 3. His campaign had been carried on in the order's secret klaverns, and two weeks before the precinct conventions meetings had been held and the knights instructed to vote for McAdoo, particularly in the larger cities, which went overwhelmingly for him. Lea offered as evidence handbills instructing klansmen to vote for a McAdoo delegation to the county conventions. A typical bill warned: "No Klansmen should vote with Jim Ferguson—the Arch Enemy of the *Klan*. Ferguson is for uninstructed delegates." A Klan handbill circulated in the Fort Worth area called upon Klan "delegates to the County Convention to vote as a unit, both for the above [dry] resolutions and for delegates to the State Convention who favor the nomination of William G. McAdoo in the National Convention."[98]

By linking McAdoo with the Klan, Lea hoped to advance Underwood's candidacy elsewhere. "It is true that we have not won; but it is also true, while it may be a defeat locally, I look for it to result in a victory nationally," he wrote an El Paso friend. Meanwhile, Underwood expanded his fight against the Klan. On May 12 he announced that he intended "to press the Klan issue" before the national convention's resolutions committee, and if that failed he would "carry the fight to the floor." In a later statement Underwood's campaign manager, Charles Carlin, vowed that the Underwood forces would "lead the fight against the machinations of the Klan" and hoped that "other aspirants for the

nomination will join hands with [them] in this movement." Campaign
managers in Tennessee and Mississippi were warned to expect a full
Klan assault on election day: ". . . it can be taken for granted that the
entire influence will be arrayed in solid opposition."[99]

On May 14, Love denied a report that the Klan had agreed to promote McAdoo's interests in the precinct conventions in exchange for
McAdoo-Love support of the Klan candidate for governor, Judge Felix
D. Robertson. "This 'political trade' report is entirely erroneous,"
Love declared. "I am not pledged to any candidate for Governor." But
he readily admitted that "in campaigning for McAdoo we have naturally sought the support of the people of Texas as a whole, regardless of
organizations or factions." "The Underwood crowd have a system
when they lose a state of blaming it on the Ku Klux," he wrote Tom
Chadbourne. "The truth is they couldn't beat a drum except by such
legislative aid as they had in Alabama."[100]

Yet some form of understanding was reached with the Klan. "Senator Underwood's positive declaration against the Klan has antagonized
their membership so positively that I have not found it necessary to do
otherwise than remain in a passive and receptive attitude," Cato Sells
advised McAdoo on January 30, 1924. "The Klan folks have not disturbed us in any manner. This attitude so far as we are concerned
seems to be friendly without any effort to embarrass." William Hanger
attended the San Antonio conference on March 25–26, when the decision was made to continue the fight for an instructed McAdoo delegation. When Joseph Myers informed Love in early April that the Underwood people were arranging to send special men over the state to pass
the word down the line "anything to beat McAdoo," Love replied that
"it would be a good idea if this information could be sent direct to
Hanger and [Z. E.] Marvin." Myers wrote McAdoo at this time that
"a great secret organization, which supported him [Neff] two years
[ago], have become offended because of his attack on them made right
after the election. (This organization is also bitterly opposed to Underwood)."[101] In his memoirs historian Claude Bowers recalled that Mc-
Adoo had talked to him on the eve of the national convention about the
Klan tag and had offered the following explanation:

In 1912 Wilson's candidacy in Texas had been managed by Cato Sells and Tom
Love, who had been remarkably astute in organizing the state, and McAdoo
had enlisted their support for himself. It was not until they had organized
Texas thoroughly for him, he said, that he learned of Sells's connection with

the Klan, which was powerful. He said that to have dismissed him at that juncture would have been to concentrate the Klansmen against him everywhere.

Nevertheless, the Klan had had much to do with his piling up of strength, and, in David Burner's words, "It could not be doubted that at least in some sense that McAdoo was the Klan's candidate." [102]

"The chief significance of this primary campaign in Texas was that it materially aided in the comeback of McAdoo following the February crisis in his campaign," noted Lee Allen. Just as McAdoo's primary victories in Georgia and South Dakota led his Texas managers to abandon their plan to unite with the Neff people behind an uninstructed or favorite-son delegation, his overwhelming victory in Texas, coming after a number of states went against him in April, provided the impetus for a series of victories that made him the leading contender when the national convention opened. [103] Without Texas his campaign would have been stopped in its tracks. "Now we have got such a momentum on the movement that I don't believe we can be stopped," wrote McAdoo two days after the precinct conventions in Texas. He added: "It is a curious thing that the impossible is always put up to me. I have never had anything easy come to me. But to smash down obstacles to victory is the most thrilling thing in the world, and I do not enjoy any other kind of a victory, I must confess. We are going to win." [104]

Underwood's campaign went steadily downhill after Texas, with decisive defeats in Tennessee, Mississippi, and Florida. His only remaining hope was that McAdoo and Smith would kill one another off in the convention and that he would emerge as the compromise nominee. [105]

When the Democratic State Convention was held in Waco on May 27, the outcome was a foregone conclusion. Perhaps one-half to two-thirds of the delegates were klansmen, klanswomen, and Klan sympathizers. William E. Lea, who characterized the gathering as "dominated by the klan," did not even bother to launch an Underwood fight. True to expectations, the convention chose a delegation of rock-ribbed McAdoo supporters ("about half Klan and half anti-Klan," according to Love), bound to him by ironclad instructions. The delegation included such prominent Texas klansmen as Earle Mayfield, Mike T. Lively of Dallas, and Marvin A. Childers of San Antonio. It contained six members of the Baltimore Convention of 1912. Marshall Hicks was chairman of the convention and of the delegation. Love was reelected national committeeman without opposition, and a klans-woman, Mrs. J. T. Bloodworth of Fort Worth, was elected national committeewoman.[106]

In a number of precinct conventions over the state Alvin M. Owsley of Dallas, a former national commander of the American Legion, had been endorsed for the vice-presidential nomination. Owsley had actively promoted his candidacy, which attracted the support of many former servicemen, sending telegrams to county Democratic leaders asking them to secure their county's endorsement. Love opposed the Owsley boom, arguing that to place his name on the ticket with McAdoo would weaken it because both were southern men, and on May 7 he announced that the opposition to Owsley would be carried to the Waco convention. A state employee told Love that "this crowd here in Austin is dying hard and is going to try to humiliate you at Waco by insisting on instructions for Alvin Owsley for Vice President." A compromise was finally worked out whereby the convention endorsed but did not give instructions for Owsley.[107]

At McAdoo's request a resolution was adopted favoring the substitution of majority rule for the two-thirds rule at the national convention. An anti-Klan resolution prepared by John C. Granbery, similar to the one that he had introduced in the San Antonio convention two years before, was tabled in committee without debate. "Harmony was the obsession of practically all hands," noted the *Dallas Morning News*. Not a single motion on any major issue was made from the floor. The principal motions were put from the platform by Bill Hanger, who occupied a seat at a small table at the left of the speaker's stand. Observers agreed that he was the "generalissimo," and under his leadership the harmony program was put through "with almost merciless efficiency."[108]

Neff came up from Austin with his "fighting clothes" on and told one of his close friends that he would fight if anyone "stepped on his toes." Although leaders of the McAdoo, Klan, and Neff factions agreed in a preconvention caucus to include the governor on the delegation, Love refused to go along. Neff's name was recommended to the convention, but he declined the post, telling the delegates that he had no apology to make for his stand against an instructed delegation and could not conscientiously serve on it. If he had not voluntarily retired, Love had a delegate ready to call for a convention vote to strike his name off the list; doubtless it would have passed. "Dirt dauber stays at home," Neff's onetime ally Frank Davis wired McAdoo. All in all, Love was well satisfied with the convention's work. "The State Convention at Waco went precisely as I desired it on every point," he wrote McAdoo. "It is my first one I ever attended that went that way." Neff had to be content with the titles "Game Sport" and "fightin' wah hoss." "Bill Hanger a Hero, Pat the Pious and Wah Hoss—And It Opened with Pra'r and Klosed with Kussing Kontest," was Don H. Bigger's characterization of what he termed "That Waco Ku Klux Kornvention" in his Fort Worth newspaper, the *Texas Tail Twister*.[109]

Neff went to New York as, in his words, a "private in the ranks," though he was accorded the honor of sitting on the speaker's platform because of his office. He may still have harbored dark-horse hopes if the convention deadlocked between McAdoo and Smith. "A dark horse is certain to be selected. You must come to the convention by all means," Chesley Jurney had wired him from New York. Publisher Charles Marsh also thought that a dark horse would be nominated and had suggested that Neff's "earliest possible arrival" was "desirable from every standpoint. Practically all important figures on ground by Thursday." He particularly wanted him to see Bryan early. After his arrival in New York, Neff infuriated the Texas delegation by giving out a statement warning that the selection of either McAdoo or Smith meant defeat for the party. "Smith is too wet. McAdoo is too oily," the governor stated. He mentioned John W. Davis, Senator Royal Copeland of New York, Samuel Ralston, Newton Baker, and Bryan as "abler and better fitted men." A cartoon by John Knott, "The Rough Rider in New York," which appeared in the *Dallas Morning News* on June 25, showed Neff in cowboy regalia, on a plunging bronco, firing two pistols into posters of McAdoo and Smith. "But he isn't doing much rough riding," Love remarked acidly. Neff looked at the cartoon and just smiled.[110]

The Texas delegation intended to make its forty votes the rock upon which McAdoo would make his stand for the nomination. They pointed with pride to their support of Wilson in 1912 and McAdoo in 1920. The early Texas arrivals were unwilling to discuss publicly a compromise candidate. "We are here to support McAdoo until the last note is sounded," declared Cato Sells. Marshall Hicks telegraphed McAdoo from the Texas-McAdoo special train en route to New York: "We will stand by you till the last galoot's ashore."[111] Some of the delegates, however, told reporters off the record that John W. Davis would be "a mighty good man to head the ticket in case Mr. McAdoo should not be designated."[112]

Imperial Wizard Hiram Wesley Evans and his Klan "board of strategy," which included Senator Mayfield and Z. E. Marvin, set up headquarters in the Hotel McAlpine, where the Texas delegation was staying, and began organizing their forces for the expected fight to denounce the Klan by name in the platform. "His [Evans's] dragons, cyclops and kleagles report to him there," noted the *Baltimore Sun*. "Klan delegates to the convention call on him for instructions." Alva Bryan, a klansman from Waco, was made a member of the platform and resolutions committee to try to head off any anti-Klan resolution that might be presented. The Underwood and Smith supporters saw in a Klan plank fight the opportunity to inflict enough damage on McAdoo to ensure his defeat. Illinois boss George Brennan was asked later: "George, why did you inject the Klan issue into the convention? It almost killed the party." Brennan replied, "It did, but it was the only thing we had left to stop McAdoo, and by God it worked."[113]

The majority report of the platform committee did not mention the Klan by name, containing only a vague condemnation of mob violence and religious and racial strife. The minority report pledged the party "to oppose any effort on the part of the Ku Klux Klan . . . to interfere with the religious liberty or political freedom of any citizen, or to limit the civic rights of any citizen . . . because of religion, birthplace, or racial origin." During the uproarious balloting on the minority report, fifteen New York City policemen took up stations around the Texas delegation, which had been characterized in the convention as a "klan delegation from a klan-dominated State." Indiana and other so-called Klan states were likewise provided with blue-coated protection. When the roll had been completed, chairman Thomas Walsh announced that the minority plank had been defeated by 1 vote, 542³⁄₂₀ to 541³⁄₂₀. Under the unit rule Texas cast its 40 votes against naming the Klan, though a poll of the delegation revealed that Mrs. Jesse Daniel Ames of Georgetown, Hal Brennan of Laredo, and Dwight Lewelling of Dallas favored the minority report. The switch of 1½ votes in the Georgia delegation prevented the adoption of the anti-Klan plan.[114]

Texas regularly cast its 40 votes for McAdoo, who for eight days led the field, with Smith second. The two men were hopelessly deadlocked. On July 4 the Californian's forces stood at their Marne when on the sixty-ninth ballot they pushed his vote to 530—within striking distance of a majority but far short of the 732 votes needed for nomination. If they could get a majority, they proposed to make a power play to abrogate the two-thirds rule. The McAdoo managers appealed to the twenty-four-member delegation from Virginia to come over, but it stuck to its favorite son, Senator Carter Glass. From that point the McAdoo vote steadily declined and recovered some of its former strength only when spurred on by the candidate himself. Baruch and other supporters urged him to withdraw from a contest that was destroying the party, but he insisted that the fight go on. "Don't think for a minute that I contemplate withdrawing from this fight," McAdoo told a rally of his delegates on July 6. "I would feel like the most contemptible traitor if I did. I have never yet run from a fight and I don't intend to now." "Texas will stand by you till hell freezes over!" shouted a delegate at the rear of the hall.[115]

In the last hours of the convention Love went to McAdoo and suggested that he throw his support behind Colonel House. "That's fine, go ahead," Love quoted the candidate as replying. It soon became evident, however, that it would be impossible to concentrate his delegates on anyone, except by gravitation. In any event, the frail House had repeatedly declined overtures to become a candidate, and he told Love later that "in no circumstances would I have considered accepting the nomination had it been offered."[116]

McAdoo finally released his delegates on July 8 after the 99th ballot. "The liquor interests and Wall street brought about the deadlock and succeeded in defeating Mr. McAdoo," Love asserted. The faithful Texans stayed with McAdoo on the 100th ballot, voted for former Secretary of Agriculture E. T. Meredith of Iowa on the next ballot, and then swung behind John W. Davis on the 102d ballot in preference to Underwood, who was at last getting the "run" promised him by the Smith forces. The exhausted and dispirited delegates nominated the West Virginian on the 103d ballot. The choice for vice-president rested between Alvin Owsley of Texas and Governor Charles W. Bryan of Nebraska. Party leaders decided that Bryan should be chosen to placate his brother and help the ticket in the West. Colonel Thomas H. Ball of Houston placed Owsley's name in nomination, but Texas withdrew his name and changed its vote to Bryan during the roll call.[117]

Texas Democrats were generally pleased with the choice of Davis and assured him that he would receive an overwhelming majority in the state. Love warmly endorsed his selection. Houston businessman Jesse Jones became director of finance for the Democratic National Committee and undertook to raise funds for the Davis campaign. Neff called Davis's nomination an "exceedingly wise choice" and in October made a number of speeches for the candidate in Kentucky. On his return from New York the governor told reporters that his opposition to the "unwise policy of the iron-bound instructions as to individuals" had been vindicated by events. His feud with Love continued, and the latter tried unsuccessfully to keep Neff from being invited to speak for Davis.[118]

None of the three leading presidential candidates—Coolidge, Davis, or La Follette—campaigned in Texas, though La Follette's running mate, Senator Burton K. Wheeler of Montana, made an address in El Paso on October 16. Davis condemned the Klan by name in a speech at Sea Girt, New Jersey, on August 21, but his utterance did him no evident harm in Texas. He polled nearly four times as many votes as Coolidge did in the state, a considerable improvement over 1920, when Cox did not quite double Harding's vote. Although the secretary of the Texas State Committee for La Follette had predicted that "we are going to poll the largest opposition vote ever polled in Texas," the senator received just 42,551 votes, chiefly from Union men and German-Americans.[119]

The Republicans, trumpeting the slogan "Coolidge or Chaos," rode to an easy victory nationally. Davis won the electoral vote of only the eleven former Confederate States plus Oklahoma, a total of 136. La Follette received the 13 votes of Wisconsin, and Coolidge the 382 of the other thirty-five states. In popular votes Coolidge had 15,719,021 to Davis's 8,836,704, and La Follette's 4,988,398. The nomination of Charles W. Bryan was highly unpopular in the East, and the third-party ticket hurt the Democrats in rural areas from the Middle West to the Pacific Coast and cut into the ethnic vote in eastern cities. Davis wrote Bryan that "the long wrangle at the New York Convention and the entry of La Follette into the field rendered it absolutely impossible for us to overcome the normal odds which exist against the Democratic Party."[120]

In Texas the presidential race was overshadowed by state politics. "We won a great and glorious victory in Texas on August 23rd. Our joy we share with you," a Graham lawyer wrote Davis on September 5. He explained:

The embattled hosts of the Texas democracy stopped the hooded legions at the Marne. At the high tide of the conflict a frail woman girt about with the traditions of the fathers and armed with the sword of the constitution summoned the good men and women of Texas to duty's call with the cry—"They shall not pass." She did not cry in vain. Our State Convention has just adjourned at Austin. If we left anything undone I do not recall it. We swept out the last vestige of the bed-sheet brigade who had sought to turn the American eagle into a night-owl. [121]

What the exuberant lawyer was celebrating was the outcome of one of the most colorful and exciting elections in Texas history—a contest of "the Bonnet or the Hood," in which Mrs. Miriam Amanda Ferguson defeated Klan-backed Judge Felix Robertson for the Democratic nomination for governor less than three months after the Klan had "probably reached the zenith of its political power in the state" [122]— during the Democratic presidential primary. How this swift change in the fortunes of the Texas Klan came about is the subject of the following chapter.

CHAPTER 6

The Bonnet or the Hood

THE state elections of 1924 in Texas were for the most part fought on the Klan issue. It was assumed that the Texas Klan, with a membership now numbering between 97,000 and 170,000, would have a candidate for governor. "It is going to be the greatest and fiercest political battle ever waged in Texas," predicted the Klan paper in Houston. "The fight is between the K.K.K.'s and the J.J.J.'s—Jew, Jug, and Jesuits." "By 1924 the Klan in Texas was a highly organized, efficient minority," wrote Charles Alexander. "Working quietly and mysteriously, this minority nearly controlled the political life of the state." It would demonstrate its power in the Democratic presidential primary that spring, dominating the precinct, county, and state Democratic conventions and the Texas delegation to the national convention.[1]

The Klan, however, continued to have internal difficulties in Texas, and early in 1924 dissension arose over the choice of a gubernatorial candidate. According to the *San Antonio Express*, the order would have "reveled in glee if either Marshall Hicks or Congressman Tom T. Connally had agreed to stand and receive its blessings and tenders of aid at the polls," but both men declined to make the race. In Houston, Klan editor Billie Mayfield, who had been the order's unsuccessful candidate for lieutenant governor in 1922, boomed Dallas attorney V. A. Collins in the columns of his weekly newspaper. "All of the talk right now in klan circles in this neck of the woods is Collins for governor," he announced. A former state senator and charter member of Dallas Klan No. 66, Collins had entered the race for governor in December, 1923, without consulting or asking permission of the Klan hierarchy. He opened his campaign with a speech in Beaumont—a Klan center—on January 5, 1924.[2]

Grand Dragon Z. E. ("Zeke") Marvin of Dallas, a wealthy native of Indiana who was a good friend and a leading disciple of Imperial Wizard Evans, had his own candidate in mind for the governorship: Criminal District Court Judge Felix D. Robertson, a member of the

Dallas Klan and, like Collins, a prohibitionist. The executive commit-tee of the realm, composed of seven officials from each of the five prov-inces plus five additional klansmen from each province chosen by the grand titans in Texas—making a total of sixty—met in Dallas in the early part of January and endorsed Robertson. Collins tried to discuss this action in a meeting of the Dallas Klan; four days later he received a registered letter notifying him of his suspension from the Klan. Ac-cording to Collins, "This letter was mailed to every klan in Texas for the seeming purpose of creating the impression that I had been guilty of improper conduct on the floor of the klan. In fact, the statements contained in the letter were inaccurate to an extreme, and tended to prejudice good klansmen in Texas against me."[3]

"Felix Robertson is known as the call boy of Zeke Marvin of Dallas," exploded Mayfield in Houston, "and I won't vote for any man for governor of Texas who is put out, controlled and dictated to by any one man, even though that man be a high ranking klansman." He be-gan a running editorial fight with Marvin and with the *Texas 100 Per-cent American*, the organ of the Dallas Klan. "His [Mayfield's] conduct has been a vicious and unbecoming display of disloyalty," sputtered the *100 Per Cent American*. Worried by Mayfield's assault, the grand dragon visited the Waco, Fort Worth, Houston, and San Antonio Klans to assure the knights that Robertson had been selected in a democratic manner. While Fort Worth and Waco klansmen endorsed Robertson, the Houston and San Antonio chapters rejected him. Calling Marvin a "yankee republican" and a "whiskey prescription druggist," Mayfield accused him of selling 2,120 gallons of whiskey through his chain of drugstores the previous year, for which he had received $67,340, and called for a statewide Klan elimination primary. Marvin yielded and told the three hundred or more local Klans to decide between Collins and Robertson. "Will Hold Primary within the Klan, It's All Harmony Now," Mayfield crowed in a headline in his *Weekly*: "Slip me your hand, Zeke, it's all over now. We are going singing into the battle, together, and the fighting can't start any too soon for me. Lemme at 'em!"[4]

Texas klansmen, perhaps fearing that Marvin and his friends would bolt the Klan if they rejected Robertson, overwhelmingly approved him by standing vote in the local elimination primaries in March. May-field was summoned to Dallas for a conference and spent the better part of a day talking with Marvin and the leaders of the Dallas Klan. Afterward he saw Collins and told him that Marvin had offered a "great inducement" to the editor to stop supporting Collins and swing to Robertson in his editorials. Back in Houston, Mayfield condemned Collins for promoting strife and told his readers that he would not follow the Dallas attorney in a bolt: "Within the klan camp, the outlook is that Felix Robertson of Dallas will be the klan entry and if Felix is the man this paper is going down the line for him."[5]

Born at old Washington-on-the-Brazos in 1872, Felix Robertson was the son of one of the Confederacy's youngest generals, Felix Huston Robertson, who served as a brigade commander in the Army of Tennessee. His grandfather, General J. B. Robertson, commanded Hood's Texas Brigade in Lee's Army of Northern Virginia. He was licensed to practice law in 1896 and served for six years as an assistant attorney general of McLennan County under Cullen F. Thomas. He moved to Dallas about 1911 and later served three years as judge of the Corporation Court. Judge Robertson had also had a military career of sorts. During World War I he had served as a major in the 132d Field Artillery of the Thirty-sixth Division. He had later been assigned to the First Texas Cavalry, which he helped organize. At the close of the war he was discharged as lieutenant colonel of the Third Texas Cavalry.[6]

According to Robertson's platform, the "three vital questions uppermost in the minds of the people of Texas" were "Taxation, Public Education and Law Enforcement." He promised, if elected, no new offices or increase in taxes; strict economy in state government; more and better schools and $15 per capita for education; and the "prompt, vigorous and impartial enforcement" of all laws, including those against the manufacture, transportation, and sale of liquor, the laws against gambling, and the Sunday laws. He pledged to use "the entire police power of the State to prevent lynchings, whippings and any other form of mob violence." He favored the gradual reformation of the prison system, careful and prudent use of the pardon power, the repeal of the open-port law, homes for tenant farmers and city workers, a "square deal" for farmers, improved roads, conservation of natural resources, a tax on gasoline, an absentee-voting law, and the admission of former servicemen into state educational institutions free of tuition, fees, or charges. The candidate stood for the separation of church and state, an end to foreign immigration, the suppression of every foreign-language newspaper, the deportation of criminal foreigners, white supremacy, and America for Americans. "I have been a prohibitionist in practice and belief and have for more than thirty years supported woman suffrage," he declared.[7]

Robertson, a Baptist, later added the spiritual question to his list of vital issues facing the state. Claiming to be a "praying judge," he declared that "America and Texas have forgotten God and are drifting toward the same materialism that caused the decay and ruin of Rome and Germany" and of all the nations that had fallen since the beginning of time. "And above all those ghastly ruins there stands but one thing, the rugged cross of Christianity, the cross on which our master was sacrificed." He pleaded for a return to Christianity, the Bible, the Golden Rule, and the Ten Commandments, saying that if America, and Texas especially, would do this the material issues would take care of themselves.[8]

Like Bob Henry in 1922, Collins refused to accept the outcome of the elimination primaries and stayed in the race. According to the *San Antonio Express*, he owned "all the fervor of the Gael" and had "a vocabulary that rolls out like the surge of the sea against the headlands of Kerry." "A few men are trying to manipulate the entire Klan organization and vote its membership like white-faced cattle," Collins charged in a Dallas speech:

Now, I want the people of Texas to know who these eliminators in the Klan are. I charge that three of the Grand Titans of Texas and the Grand Dragon of Texas, constituting a majority of those who engineered and effectuated the so-called nomination of Judge Robertson, are old-time anti-prohibitionists, and are anti-prohibitionists today.

Collins said that he asked no quarter and expected to give none: "My fight is not against the published principles of the Ku Klux Klan, but it is against the bunch which hold the high offices in the Klan."[9]

Another candidate, Adjutant General Thomas B. Barton of Amarillo, a former druggist who had won his spurs and shoulder leaves fighting in France and who was given to raiding with the Texas Rangers, was also considered part of what the *San Antonio Express* called "the klan political entente." He made a definite decision to run in June, 1923, asking his supporters to form Barton-for-governor clubs in their hometowns and to write letters to twenty-five friends telling them of his candidacy and asking them to get busy on his behalf. In a speech in San Antonio, Robertson referred to Barton, without naming him, as a "saber rattler" who was "guzzling whiskey" while he (Robertson) was a prohibitionist. In turn Barton referred to his fellow officer as "the bottle-scarred veteran" and got off this punishing quip: "He's the only general who ever made this record in a war: He enlisted in Dallas. He was discharged in Fort Worth. He went home from the war on a street car."[10]

With the Texas Klan united behind Robertson, both Collins and Barton were doomed to also-ran status in the first primary. Also in that category were the other minor candidates—State Senator Joe Burkett of Eastland, who scored the Klan in his speeches; State Representative W. E. Pope of Nueces County, whose slogan, according to the *San Antonio Express*, was "No more taxes—no time, no place, against nobody nor nothing," and who seemed content to rise or fall on that, leaving the Klan issue to the other candidates; and George W. Dixon of Harris County, who made no canvass.[11]

James E. Ferguson offered a more serious challenge to Robertson's candidacy. In February, 1923, Ferguson moved the *Ferguson Forum* to Dallas. Jim announced that he had moved to Dallas because it was a great city, and he was going to help make it greater. He was going to make the *Forum* a great agricultural and livestock paper with a statewide circulation. He made contact with the city's Jewish merchants and asked them to advertise in the paper. One firm gave him a $25.00 advertisement, and he bought $37.50 worth of floor covering in return, only to have the firm refuse to buy any more advertising. Another firm gave $8.00 and the same day bought $400.00 worth of advertising in the *Texas 100 Per Cent American*. Outraged, Ferguson came out with a blistering anti-Semitic editorial, "The Cloven Foot of the Dallas Jews," in the March 15, 1923, issue of the *Forum*, charging that "there is now hatched in Dallas an unholy alliance between the Big Jews and the Big Ku Klux, whereby the Ku Klux are to get the big offices and the Big Jews are to get the big business. In other words the Jews of Dallas now think the Ku Klux are on a paying basis and they have took over the business end of it."[12] In a second editorial, published on March 29, headlined "The Ku Klux Jews of Dallas," Ferguson warned that "me and my friends are getting damn tired of these Jews running to us and asking us to defend their liberties and then running to the Ku Klux to sell them dry goods." And he vowed: "Nineteen hundred years ago the Jews formed themselves into a mob and lynched the Savior of men on the Cross of Calvary. By the eternal that reigns above, they shall not again be allowed to hook up with another mob and lynch religion and political liberty on the Cross of Greed and Gain."[13]

After a five-month sojourn in Dallas, Ferguson moved the *Forum* back to Temple. "The year 1923 has been a hard struggle for the *Forum*" he admitted. "It will show little or no profit." On January 1, 1924, he announced an increase in the individual subscription rate from $1.50 to $2.00 a year and in the club rate (five or more) from $1.00 to $1.50 and warned that if subscribers withdrew their patronage the *Forum* would have to quit.[14]

In 1923, Ferguson made an off-year talking tour, speaking twenty-nine times between June 1 and December 3. His "very short platform" called for the national government to issue one-third more cash money, and to levy and collect one-third less taxes and for the voters to elect two-thirds of the Texas Legislature and the United States Congress from the ranks of farmers and ranchmen. At the end of the year he told *Forum* readers, "I will be so busy getting two small chicken farms in operation that I will not do any more speaking until about the time the grass rises next spring."[15]

On January 19, 1924, Ferguson formally announced as a candidate for governor in the July primary. He declared that the action of the court of impeachment in 1917 was invalid and that there was no legal barrier to his holding the governor's office. He served notice, however, that should partisanship prevent his name from going on the ballot, his wife would make the race, for "if the State has a Governor Ferguson we need not fall out about who signs on the dotted line." He promised to reduce appropriations by $15 million, to keep the prison system free of debt and self-sustaining, to reduce taxes and then reduce interest and rents, and to veto all liquor legislation pro or anti. Ferguson proposed changes in the highway act so that the greater portion of the money collected would remain in the counties where it was paid to be used for road building under county supervision and for the support of the public schools. While promising liberal aid to rural schools, he repeated his familiar complaint that "there are too many people going hog wild about higher education." "I am not opposed to higher education if it does not get too high," he declared. "And that is what is the matter now." He promised to cut the appropriations to the University of Texas and Texas A&M by $1 million each and to reduce the total appropriation to all other institutions of higher education by $500,000.

"If a man is so narrow and so intolerant that he wants to believe in the principles of the Ku Klux, that is his right and his business," Ferguson stated. "But when he covers up his face and goes out in disguise to whip and assault some woman or murder and maim some man, then that is mine and every other good citizen's business." He said that, therefore, he favored a strict antimask law that would punish by a term in the county jail any person over twenty-one found in a public place wearing a mask or other disguise. Three or more masked or disguised persons over twenty-one found together in a private place would each receive a sentence of one year in the penitentiary. Any church property used by such persons should be put on the tax rolls at full value. He also favored a strict law requiring all secret or fraternal organizations to file the names of their members in the county clerk's office, to be kept in a bound volume open to public inspection. Failure to file such names and proper certification would be a misdemeanor with heavy fine and revocation of charter.[16]

In 1932, Ferguson told an interviewer for the *Houston Press* that he had made the decision to have his wife announce if his name was kept off the ballot as he sat on the back of a wagon with T. H. McGregor at Lometa waiting for a train. "T. H., I may run my head off and then get thrown out of the race," Ferguson said. "What do you think about running through my wife if that happens?" "Well," answered Mc-Gregor, "if a man can run a grocery store in his wife's name I don't see why he couldn't run a state that way." "By gosh, I believe I'll try it," Jim declared. There was nothing really new in the idea, however; as mentioned earlier, Mrs. Ferguson had filed for the United States Senate in 1922, withdrawing after the State Democratic Executive Committee placed her husband's name on the ballot.[17]

Hugh Nugent Fitzgerald, of the *Austin American*, predicted that Ferguson's entry would seal the doom of many candidates early in the race. He recalled William Hanger's prediction on the day the Texas Senate ousted Ferguson from office: "This is a crucifixion. Fergusonism will be an issue in the politics of Texas every year there is an election held until Ferguson dies." Remarked Fitzgerald, "Hanger must be a prophet or at least the son of a prophet."[18]

Ferguson opened his campaign in Kerens, Navarro County, on May 10. A suit had already been filed in Houston district court by John F. Maddox, seeking to restrain the State Democratic Executive Committee from placing Ferguson's name on the ballot. The committee was to meet on June 9 to certify the names of candidates for state offices to the various county chairmen. On May 17, Judge Ewing Boyd of the Fifty-fifth District Court, in Houston, ordered that Ferguson's name could not appear on the Democratic primary ballot. Ferguson's attorney, W. G. Love, had made his defense on the argument that the impeachment proceedings were illegal because Ferguson had filed his resignation as governor before the verdict, that the Senate had no right to inflict punishment because impeachment offenses had never been prescribed by law, and that the impeachment proceedings were brought in one term of the legislature and terminated in another term, with new members who had not heard the evidence in the first session. Attorneys for the Democratic Executive Committee stayed neutral throughout the hearing, which lasted a day and a half. Ferguson announced in Waxahachie on May 28 that his wife's name had been sent to the Executive Committee. "If that Democratic body persists in its refusal to place my name on the ticket, then Mrs. Ferguson's name will be placed on the ballot, that the family name may be vindicated before the good people of Texas," Ferguson declared. While his attorneys appealed to the Texas Supreme Court, he continued his speaking tour.[19]

Neff was out of the state, and two members of the Texas Supreme Court who were to hear the Ferguson case were either disqualified or unable to serve. Acting Governor T. Whitfield Davidson appointed Alexander S. Coke of Dallas and Howard Templeton of San Antonio to serve with William Pierson, the regular associate justice. The case was set for June 9. Meeting in Dallas the same day, the Executive Committee put Mrs. Ferguson's name on the ballot but took no action on her husband's name pending the outcome of the Supreme Court hearing. There was some opposition to placing Barry Miller's name on the ballot for lieutenant governor because he had supported Peddy against Mayfield in 1922, but in the end he was certified. On June 12, in an elaborate opinion, all three members of the State Supreme Court upheld Ferguson's impeachment in all particulars, ruling that the Senate had acted within its constitutional powers in the impeachment; that its decisions therein were final; that in an impeachment it was a court of original, exclusive, and final jurisdiction; and that, therefore, Ferguson could not hold office as long as the Senate judgment stood.[20]

Miriam A. Ferguson, who would now run in her husband's place, was forty-nine on June 13, 1924. A quiet, home-loving woman, the mother of two daughters, Ouida and Dorrace, and a grandmother, she had taken no part in the fight for woman's suffrage and had no interest in clubs. "Personally, I prefer that men shall attend to all public matters," she replied, when questioned about woman suffrage in 1916. Now she issued a statement approving her husband's platform but adding to it an appeal to the voters "for the vindication of our family name":

Mother, father, son or brother, won't you help me? Jim and I are not seeking revenge; we are asking for the name of our children to be cleared of this awful judgment. If any wrong has been done, God in heaven knows we have suffered enough. Though we have lost most of our earthly possessions in these years of trouble, we shall not complain if the people will keep us from losing our family name which we want to leave to our children. We are passing on, and fast, and most of us are tipping over the summit of life's journey and next time may be too late and that is why we are so anxious now.

She spoke of her qualifications for office, saying:

I know I can't talk about the Constitution and the making of laws and the science of government like some other candidates, and I believe they have talked too much, but I have a trusting and abiding faith "that my Redeemer liveth," and I am trusting in him to guide my footsteps in the path of righteousness for the good of our people and the good of our State.[21]

"Governor Jim" did all the campaigning for his wife, wearing his usual stump costume—a black alpaca suit with a long-tailed coat and a dust-covered black slouch hat. Mrs. Ferguson contented herself with saying a few words to the crowds before introducing her husband. She pleaded for votes as a matter of fairness to her as well as to her husband and their children. Jim took frequent digs at "highbrow" education, telling a Corsicana audience that "A&M College turns out mechanics that won't work and farmers that won't farm. Just as long as they take $400 and give it to the University highbrow and only $13 for the little children that hoe the cotton in the springtime and drag the heavy sack in the fall, just so long will Jim Ferguson continue to raise hell about it!"

Ferguson said that he did not hate the Klan but did hate its principles. "Our daddies set up a Republic and the voice of the people!" he shouted. "The klan would set up an empire and the voice of a grand gizzard. We are not going to bow to the voice of any dern gizzard that ever set on any dern throne!" He scathingly referred to the "klan delegation" to the New York convention that voted for "Mac-a-doodle-do" and became the "laughing stock of the country." The Texans had changed their name in history from the "Immortal Forty" to the "Long-horn Texas Koo-Koos." [22]

Confusion was sowed in some voters' minds by the presence of two candidates named Davidson in the race: Lynch Davidson of Houston, a wealthy lumberman and former lieutenant governor, and T. Whitfield Davidson of Marshall, the present lieutenant governor. Confusion worse confounded—Lynch was from Harris County, and T. W. was from Harrison County. One of the "Immortal Forty" delegates to the Baltimore Convention of 1912, T. Whitfield Davidson had entered the race for lieutenant governor in 1918 and had run a close second in a field of six. In the runoff, however, he had been defeated by W. A. Johnson, a long-time state senator. Two years later, having been elected to fill an unexpired term in the Texas Senate, T. W. Davidson did not run for lieutenant governor, and Johnson was defeated by Lynch Davidson. Lynch did not run for reelection in 1922, announcing that he would be a candidate for governor in 1924 and that it was his duty to vacate the lieutenant-governorship during the time he would be running. The real contest in 1922 was between T. Whitfield Davidson and Klansman Billie Mayfield. Mayfield led in the first primary by about 25,000 votes, but in the runoff election Davidson defeated him quite decisively. As mentioned earlier, on several occasions while serving as acting governor during Neff's absences from the state, Davidson had sent the Texas Rangers to investigate Klan outrages. A furious Mayfield dubbed him "Tiddely Winks Davidson, the publicity hound." In 1924, Davidson's campaign strategy was to make the Klan issue, in the words of the *San Antonio Express*, "not only the 'paramount issue,' but the never-absent issue, the screaming issue, the issue that can not be lost." The paper estimated that he would command from 75 to 90 percent of the anti-Klan strength in the Democratic party. [23]

In February, in a letter to John C. Granbery, Davidson discussed the 1924 campaign:

The Ku Klux Klan fears me more than any other candidate. Their papers are denouncing me more vigorously than any other candidate. They want a runoff between James Ferguson and their man. They want a repetition of the Earle Mayfield–Ferguson race. . . . Our forces . . . should get together early, and let the people know that I am the man to enter the second primary to make the race with the klan champion. If Lynch Davidson gets in the runoff, organized Labor will join hands with the klan and help to beat him. If Ferguson gets in the runoff, higher education, prohibition, women, and everybody else will help the klan to beat him. I have incurred the displeasure of the klan by doing

my duty, and those who do not sympathize with it should rally around my standard, and they are.[24]

Davidson struck hard at the Klan in his speeches. "It is no concern
of the Governor of Texas what organization you join," he told an audience in Edna. "But this idea that there are crimes the law can not
reach and may be reached by tar and feather parties and vigilante committees must stop in Texas." He declared in another speech: "As John
H. Reagan won a glorious victory against Know-Nothingism, so shall I
win against Ku Kluckism. I am conducting a campaign against mob law
and secrecy in politics, fighting conspiracy aimed at subversion of justice in the courts and the rights upheld in the Constitution."[25]

Lynch Davidson had served in the Texas House and Senate before
being elected lieutenant governor in 1920. Ruddy-faced, red-haired,
and dynamic, he bristled with energy. He was credited with saving the
state more than $1 million in the administration of the state railroad.
Calling for "more business in government and less government in business" and promising "an economical business administration," he
summed up his candidacy as "based largely upon economic reforms,
education and the enforcement of the law." He opposed the Klan, having voiced his views in October, 1921, while he was lieutenant governor. Davidson had the support of more than one hundred newspapers
and of large business interests, such as were represented by chambers
of commerce, and bankers. The Hogg brothers, Will and Mike, endorsed his candidacy.[26]

In February, Ferguson warned his followers that the Klan had gotten its hands on two-thirds of the union labor leaders in Texas and intended to control the rank-and-file workers through them and then lay
their hands on his friends, the farmers, who had in good faith joined
with them for cooperative marketing purposes. On March 4 Ferguson
wrote a letter to W. D. Lewis, who had been chosen to put his name in
nomination at the Farm-Labor Political Conference then in session in
Dallas, asking him not to present his name. The conference had, he
said, "openly endorsed three known members of the Ku Klux Klan,"
and he intended to ask his friends to vote against these klansmen and
would do so himself.[27]

The Farm Labor Union, the Texas State Federation of Labor, and
the four railroad brotherhoods had delegates at the conference. The
roll call showed fifty-five counties represented and 375 voting dele-

gates. T. Whitfield Davidson was endorsed for governor on the first ballot over W. E. Pope, H. L. Darwin, and V. A. Collins. The vote was Davidson, 228; Pope, 106; Darwin, 29; and Collins, 24. Davidson was supported by the farmer delegates, while the labor delegates lined up behind Pope. Barry Miller was endorsed for lieutenant governor, Dan Moody for attorney general, and Fred W. Davis for United States senator.[28]

Lynch Davidson made over two hundred speeches before July 1, directing most of his fire at the other Davidson, whom he referred to as "T. W. (The Wrong) Davidson." He warned the "conservative, home-loving, home-owning farmers and laborers of Texas" that the Non-Partisan League of North Dakota was trying to gain control of Texas government. In a statement issued at Cisco on March 29, he declared that "if nothing else is accomplished in Texas in 1924 than defeat of the socialistic program of the Farm-Labor political conference, written in Dallas, March 3, it may be counted a valuable year in the progress of this Commonwealth." He told audiences that he wanted to "distinguish myself from my namesake opponent, T. W. Davidson, who is carrying this socialistic banner throughout Texas, advocating among other things, that the constitutional restriction of 35 cents ad valorem tax be eliminated and that the sky be the limit for taxation on Texas farms and property." "The Wrong" Davidson had traded around with so many groups, cliques, and blocs, he said, that people were beginning to ask whether he belonged to the Klan.[29]

T. Whitfield Davidson defended his endorsement by the Farm-Labor Political Conference, saying that he and the other men it had endorsed were not radicals or extremists. "Charles Culberson and Tom Campbell had each enjoyed the confidence of these men and I hope to enjoy it as long as I live," he declared. "There are 40,000 railroad men in Texas in the brotherhood; 175,000 farmers, with their dues paid up, besides innumerable craftsmen, and I am proud to be their standard bearer in this fight." Speaking in Wichita Falls, he warned klansmen that Lynch "was fishing for the klan vote, but he'll double-cross you if you do elect him." Left high and dry by his failure to face the issue squarely, he said, the Houston man was trying to cover up his own shortcomings by telling the people in a loud voice that the Klan was going to support Whit Davidson and give Robertson the "double cross." "The statement attributed to this gentleman . . . that I have made a trade with that organization is laughable and untrue," T. W. stated.[30]

In early July, T. W. Davidson challenged Lynch Davidson to a debate or a series of debates on campaign issues, but the latter declined, saying that the challenge had come "from the hit dog as a howl of defeat." Whit retorted that Lynch was the "militant Ku Klux" candidate to go into the runoff against Robertson because the klansmen thought they could beat him. T. Whitfield Davidson's campaign manager had earlier told W. N. Jones of Mineola that, in Jones's words,

some of the more sensible Klansmen like Bill Hanger wanted to take Robertson out of the race and put [Lynch] Davidson in, but the rank and file objected, then there was called a conference of some 40 Cyclops at Fort Worth and it was there determined to fight the battle through with little Felix. I know that while these propositions were pending for some 10 days, Lynch laid off of the Klan in his speeches and after the meeting at Fort Worth he give them the devil again.

The two Davidsons had criticized each other so pitilessly that observers predicted that it would be impossible to get the friends of either one to support the other should one of them make the runoff.[31]

As the first primary drew closer, it was conceded that Robertson would be in first place because of his Klan backing. Nearly all the candidates agreed that Mrs. Ferguson had "come up" surprisingly in the last few weeks and would run a strong race, though they were willing to concede her only a third-place finish. Her husband said that she was a "cinch" to go into the second primary. "Last week I spoke to more than 30,000 people and the political storm that I predicted two weeks ago is now sweeping Texas like a cyclone," he told his *Forum* readers on July 24. "Already my good wife and I have heard the voice of the people which to us is like the voice of the Savior appearing to his disciples walking on the waters saying to them, 'Be ye not afraid, It is I,' and with feelings of deepest gratitude we are thankful for this expression of our friends everywhere which means sure and certain victory."[32]

In the first primary, on July 26, the vote of the four leading candidates was Robertson, 193,508; Mrs. Ferguson, 146,424; Lynch Davidson, 141,208; and T. W. Davidson, 125,011. All the other candidates together received 96,972. The total vote cast—703,123—was the largest in Texas's history. As the votes came in, Mrs. Ferguson and Lynch Davidson were in a seesaw race for second, with final returns giving the former a margin of 5,216 votes.[33] Fate had favored the Fergusons again. With either of the Davidsons out of the race, the other would have led the ticket, with Robertson second and Ferguson eliminated. As T. Whitfield Davidson explained in his autobiography: "Lynch Davidson and I, having the same name and similar political views of the Klan, divided a substantial vote which if given to either of us would have put us in the second primary by a hundred thousand votes, but we divided the vote so evenly that Mrs. Ferguson and the Klan candidate, Felix Robertson, entered the second primary."

According to Davidson, a year or more after the election Robertson's campaign manager, Larry Mills, told him that he had spent more than two weeks before the first primary working for Mrs. Ferguson. "We had a conference among ourselves, men like Zeke Marvin and others, and we came to the conclusion that if there was a runoff between you and Robertson that you would win. We sought to prevent that by boosting Ma Ferguson," Davidson quoted Mills as saying. Mills continued: "In touring the State I would leave the message from Klan to Klan, Felix Robertson is safe for entry into the second primary. Do all you can for Ma Ferguson. . . . The effort we think turned many who were voting for Whit Davidson into the Ma Ferguson column without losing any to Felix Robertson." In another campaign "What if?" General Jacob F. Wolters advised Lynch Davidson to seek the support of Mayor John W. Tobin of San Antonio and the mayor's "behind-the-scenes power," John Boyle. Wolters set up an appointment with the two men. When Davidson arrived in San Antonio, however, he met some foes of the Tobin-Boyle organization, who convinced him that Wolters's advice was all wrong. Therefore, instead of keeping his appointment, he went to the *San Antonio Express* office and made a statement denouncing the two men. T. W. Davidson then rushed to the Alamo City, won their endorsement, and carried Bexar County with 11,666 votes to Robertson's 8,262, Lynch Davidson's 2,629, and Mrs. Ferguson's 1,173. The Bexar machine vote would have put Lynch ahead of Mrs. Ferguson in the statewide returns.[34]

Whether Mrs. Ferguson or Lynch Davidson would finish second was not immediately known. Returns from many counties were incomplete. According to Ouida Ferguson Nalle, her father thought that "somebody was holding out on us. Klan skulduggery in the county election boards." Grimly Ferguson said to his wife: "We have worked too many years and too hard for this victory to have it taken away from us at this late date. If the Dallas Election Bureau can't find out how the counties voted, I can." He sent a telegram to a Ferguson man in each county, asking him to telegraph the county vote to him immediately.

He received about two hundred answers. The next morning he boarded the train for Dallas, where the Democratic Executive Committee was meeting to canvass the returns. He walked in on the group with the rolled-up reports. Lynch Davidson was present to contest the election. "What's that under your arm?" one of Davidson's lawyers asked. Ferguson decided to run a bluff. He slammed the papers down on the table. "That's the evidence to ruin any damn fool who tries to steal this election," he told him. Davidson did not bring any contest. "You didn't fool me any," he told Ferguson later, "but you damn near scared my lawyers to death." [35]

"If I am elected I am going to be Governor," Mrs. Ferguson said in an interview in Temple on July 31. "To Jim belongs only the honors that go with being the husband of the Governor. He will be my right-hand man, that's all just like I was his when he was Governor." A slight sadness flitted over her face before she said exultantly: "I feel that through the good women and fine men of Texas, my craft will again sail on sunny seas. The vote by which I am now leading, though the governorship may not be my portion, has vindicated my Jim, my big, fine Jim, and has in part removed the stigma of the blow that swept us from the gubernatorial mansion in 1917."

In a public statement Mrs. Ferguson declared that if she was elected she would endeavor, with the aid and advice of her husband and patriotic citizens, regardless of past controversies and affiliations, to bring about a constructive administration of state affairs and that she would not be a candidate for a second term "if our prayers for vindication are answered." No institution of higher education "from the University on down" need fear her administration as long as it was efficiently and economically maintained within the limits of public revenues. The Prohibition laws would be strictly enforced. Although she did not mention the Klan, she appealed for a reconsecration to the Constitution's provisions guaranteeing freedom of religion and political thought, adding, "Let us spend a little more time living up to our own religion, rather than complaining about our neighbors' religion, and maybe we will get along better." "For two years I want to give the people of Texas a devoted service," she concluded. "Mothers, won't you help me?" [36]

The gubernatorial race far overshadowed the contest for the United States Senate, in which Senator Morris Sheppard was a candidate for reelection. The forty-nine-year-old senior senator from Texas

had excellent credentials as a dry Wilsonian progressive. After succeeding to the seat in the House of Representatives vacated by his father's death in 1902, he had taken Bailey's seat in the Senate in 1913.
He had supported nearly all of the New Freedom legislation and had
favored many of the social-justice concepts embodied in the Keating-
Owen Child Labor Act, the La Follette Seamen's Act, and the Adam-
son Act regulating the workday of railroad workers. Called the "Father
of National Prohibition" because of his authorship of the Eighteenth
Amendment, he had also voted for the woman-suffrage amendment. In
international affairs he had favored American membership in the
League of Nations and in the 1920s had advocated entry into the World
Court. He had been the Senate sponsor of the Sheppard-Towner Act,
which provided federal aid to the states for maternity and infant health
care, and had resisted the Old Guard Republicans by helping organize
the farm and progressive blocs in Congress.[37]

Two organizational pillars of Sheppard's electoral successes were
the Woodmen of the World, of which he was "sovereign banker," and
the Anti-Saloon League of America. "Other Texans, casting an eye at
the senatorship, turn pale when they think of Morris with his two organizations and his neat little black book with its accurate record of his
faithfulness in Washington," wrote "The Gentleman at the Keyhole" in
an article on Sheppard in *Collier's* in 1929. The "Gentleman" concluded: "He is not a great senator, but he knows more about the fine
art of being the little senator than anyone else in the world." Sheppard's opposition to the return of the railroads to private ownership
as embodied in the Esch-Cummins Act of 1920 also won him "generous" endorsements from a number of the railroad labor organizations
in 1924.[38]

Sheppard's opposition was insignificant. A few trial balloons had
been sent up in 1923 in behalf of Alvin Owsley, Pat Neff, Jim Ferguson,
and O. B. Colquitt, but only two minor candidates entered the race.
Fred W. Davis of Austin, a former state commissioner of agriculture,
was the choice of the Farm-Labor Political Conference. He advocated
states' rights and warned against the invasion of those rights through
such federal legislation as Prohibition, child labor, and the "dollar
matching" Sheppard-Towner and Smith-Lever acts. The other candidate, John F. Maddox, advocated federal aid in improving the state's
ports and rivers, modification of the Volstead Act, pure securities, conservation of natural resources, and better credit for farmers and cattle-

men. He was also opposed to increasing the jurisdiction of the federal
courts and opposed the Klan. Sheppard spent $3,724 on his campaign,
had no outside contributions, and was nominated in the first primary
by 200,000 votes.[39]

In the runoff, Mrs. Ferguson got all the publicity a candidate
could want. "Next morning early we were awakened by the ringing of
the telephone, followed by the ringing of the doorbell," her daughter
Ouida recalled. "Reporters and more reporters; telegrams, long distance calls from papers as far away as New York. Every few minutes a
taxi would deliver another eager news gatherer at our door." They
wanted interviews and human-interest pictures. Jim had not yet returned from Dallas, but Ouida, who seems to have possessed her father's political savvy, persuaded her slender, dignified mother to let
them photograph her peeling peaches in the kitchen. The rest was
"dead easy." Would she go to her farm—eleven miles south of Temple—and pose in front of her birthplace? She refused at first—she had
to put up those peaches—but finally yielded. A family friend, Harry
Fisher of Houston, plotted pictures with Ouida while they were driving Mrs. Ferguson to the old Wallace farm. One of the farm women
lent the candidate a sunbonnet. It was dirty, but after turning it wrong
side out, Ouida and Fisher persuaded her to put it on. From these
widely circulated pictures came the idea of using as her campaign song
"Put on Your Old Gray Bonnet with the Blue Ribbon on It." New lyrics
were composed to fit the music:

> Get out your old time bonnet
> And put Miriam Ferguson on it,
> > And hitch your wagon to a star.
> So on election day
> We each of us can say
> > Hurrah! Governor Miriam, Hurrah!

The candidate was photographed feeding a flock of white leghorn
chickens, hoeing her garden, and standing beside a brace of mules,
"Major and Mrs. Hoople, who sauntered along in time to get into the
picture." "Yes," Mrs. Ferguson said afterward, "Mules, chickens, cows,
pigs and a sunbonnet! You and Harry Fisher certainly made me make a
fool out of myself that day."[40]

The caption with the picture showing Mrs. Ferguson peeling
peaches called her "Ma" Ferguson. Her initials were M. A., and if one
added the initial of her maiden name, it became "MAW." Jim Ferguson

automatically became "Pa." Mrs. Ferguson believed that Frank Gibler, a reporter for the *Houston Press*, gave her the "Ma Ferguson" label. "It was hard for me to get used to being called Ma," she said later. "Yet I think the nickname got me a lot of votes." It reinforced her image as a traditional wife and mother. That was what Ocie Speer meant when he noted the political value in the fact that she was not an "aggressive woman." Soon stickers bearing the slogan "Me for Ma" began appearing on automobiles and wagons all over the state. Some of them added, "And I Ain't Got a Dern Thing Against Pa." The Robertson supporters countered with "Not Ma for Me. Too Much Pa." Still another slogan appeared: "A Bonnet or a Hood." One poem, borrowing from Harry Holcomb Bennett's "The Flag Goes By," began:

> Hoods off!
> Along the street there comes
> Patriotic daughters and loyal sons,
> A crowd of bonnets beneath the sky,
> Hoods off!
> Miriam Ferguson is passing by.[41]

With the field narrowed to Mrs. Ferguson and Robertson, the supporters of the losing candidates had to make the difficult choice of the Fergusons or the Klan. A few Texans wanted Will Hogg to run for governor on an independent ticket. "I know that you must love your state as your father did," a San Antonio lawyer appealed to Hogg. "You made the fight against Ferguson when he tried to destroy the University. If you will now come as an Independent, anti-Ku-Klux and anti-Ferguson, you will sweep this state and be elected governor." "As between Miriam and Felix, give me carbolic acid," wrote the editor of *Holland's Magazine*. But Hogg sailed for Europe. When Robertson solicited his support in the runoff, he was told that Hogg could not be reached. Hogg later scrawled a note to his secretary in pencil across the bottom of the carbon of the letter, "Why the hell didn't you answer such letters to effect that I was absent *indefinitely etc.*"[42]

Mrs. Ferguson was supported by the two Davidsons and most of the other candidates who had been eliminated in the first primary. Joe Burkett said privately that he was supporting her "with the sincere hope that we shall be able to drive the 'invisible empire' beyond the borders of Texas, *never to return.*" Former Senator Joe Bailey, who had long hated Jim Ferguson and had opposed woman suffrage, declared in an address at Plano on August 8 that he expected to support Mrs.

Ferguson, though he had had no change of heart or attitude on the woman-suffrage question. Said Bailey:

If Judge Robertson were a candidate as a Democrat alone against Mrs. Ferguson, I would vote for Robertson. But he is not running as a Democrat. Instead he is running as the indorsee of the Ku Klux Klan. Thus has the issue been raised. And I do not propose to cast my vote for the nominee of a secret oathbound party that seeks to control the Democratic party of the State, and through it the State.[43]

Other anti-Ferguson Democrats rallied to Ma's standard, including Mrs. Jessie Daniel Ames, a leader in the fight for woman suffrage in Texas; John C. Granbery, a professor at Southwestern University at Georgetown; Mike Hogg; Alvin C. Owsley; Cato Sells; and General Martin M. Crane, who had represented the Texas House of Representatives in Ferguson's impeachment trial. Crane announced his support only after Jim Ferguson "expressly agreed" with him, Senator V. A. Collins, and others that nothing would be said about "vindication" in the campaign. Many people, mindful of Ferguson's past record, hesitated to vote for his wife for fear that he would dominate her. In a statement to the *Dallas Morning News*, Crane said that it would be unjust to make Mrs. Ferguson vicariously atone for any sins, real or imaginary, that her husband might have committed seven years earlier. While admitting that Jim would be influential in her administration, Crane tried to allay any fears on that point:

It will be so much to the advantage of the people of Texas. No man who knows Gov. Ferguson believes that he is a fool. No man believes that Gov. Ferguson, or any other man with his brain and past experience, will advise his wife, as Governor of Texas, to pursue any course that would subject her to just criticism. The coarsest of men are sensitive on that point. Instead of being a liability to her administration he will be a positive asset. The people of Texas will be much more fortunate in having her as Governor with him and others that she may call to her assistance as advisors than if Judge Robertson, without any legislative or governmental experience, should be elected Governor, with the crowd of klan leaders . . . present as his advisors and directors.[44]

"They say Jim will run the State," declared one former Ferguson opponent. "All right, I'd rather have it run by James and Miriam Ferguson than by Evans, Marvin, Butcher, Robertson and gang." The people of Texas, Ferguson men promised, would have "two governors for the price of one."[45]

Anti-Klan prohibitionists were reassured by Mrs. Ferguson's lifelong opposition to whiskey and her pledge not to weaken the liquor laws and to stop the sale of drugstore whiskey. They felt that Prohibition enforcement would be safer in her hands than in those of Robertson and his Klan advisers. Z. E. Marvin, they charged, was "the largest drugstore seller of liquor in the State at this time." When the Robertson camp tried to make it appear that all the "whiskey men" were for Mrs. Ferguson and the pros for Robertson, Crane replied in the *Dallas Morning News* that such distinguished pros as Cone Johnson, Judge Joseph E. Cockrell, Judge S. C. Padelford of Fort Worth, T. N. Jones of Taylor (a member of the Prohibition campaign committee in 1887), and Epps G. Knight of Dallas were supporting Mrs. Ferguson while wets W. A. Hanger ("the convention manager of the anti-prohibitionist forces in Texas for years"), John M. Mathis of Houston, and Z. E. Marvin were in Robertson's corner. Said Crane: "Felix and his Ku Klux preachers . . . need to read that divine command again, 'Thou shalt not bear false witness against thy neighbor.'" [46]

Crane also soothed the fears of nervous friends of the University of Texas who recalled Jim Ferguson's remark that "there are too many people going 'hog wild' over higher education" and his pledge to cut the university and A&M appropriations. "I do not believe that Jim Ferguson will permit his wife, if he can help it, to stain her name by any vicious attack on the educational institutions of this State," Crane wrote Judge Victor Brooks of Austin. "He knows that will provoke the same old fight." In a speech at Waco on August 19, Crane declared that if Robertson was elected the university would become the plaything of the Klan leaders: "The chairs will be filled by men of the hooded order. And what is true of the State University is likewise true of all other State colleges and institutions of learning." When D. A. Frank of Dallas mailed a broadside to the "Ex-students and Friends of the University of Texas," expressing opposition to Mrs. Ferguson, General Crane's son Edward made a statement taking issue with Frank and echoing his father's warnings. A militant Klan majority on the University of Texas Board of Regents would see to it that "the professors at the University will bow their knees in allegiance to the invisible empire, or go elsewhere. The ablest, the independent thinking members of the faculty will resign, and there will only remain and be added thereto second-rate, cowardly time-serving salary takers." [47]

Opponents of the Klan held mass meetings throughout the state, at which participants endorsed Mrs. Ferguson, scored the Klan, and formed county organizations "to repudiate every candidate who seeks a Democratic nomination through Ku Klux membership or by catering to Ku Klux support." Speakers at these rallies included Crane, Jed C. Adams, Oscar B. Colquitt, Judge C. F. Greenwood, C. C. Renfro, all of Dallas, and John C. Granbery. Some of the Klan element tried to interfere with the meetings by wiring or phoning the speakers and canceling their engagements. "We have no intention whatever, of calling off your speaking engagement for next Monday night," T. S. Henderson of Cameron, in Milam County, wrote Granbery, "and if you receive wires, telephone messages or letters, do not pay any attention to them; but just make your arrangements to be here . . . and 'pour it on 'em.'"[48]

Many of the state's largest newspapers supported the Fergusons. George B. Dealey, owner of the *Dallas Morning News*, which had opposed the Klan for several years, hesitated to endorse the Fergusons, but his son Ted, who was covering the campaign as a correspondent, urged his father to have the paper take a positive stand in the campaign: "Now is the time for us to *reap the fruits* of the seeds we planted two or three years ago. . . . Mrs. Ferguson . . . will undoubtedly make Texas a good governor. Felix Robertson is an avowed Klansman. . . . Now is the time to wop him where it will do the most good." The paper's editorial council was not unanimous in its opinion, but Dealey and the majority sided with Ted. Even so, it was not until August 17 that the *News* openly endorsed Mrs. Ferguson: "Soon or late we shall be compelled, as a means of saving the principles of popular government, to rid ourselves of the klan as a political power. We can do it now by electing Mrs. Ferguson. Her election will sound the death knell of the klan as a political power in this State." The following day Robertson, in a speech in San Angelo, called the *News* "that scarlet woman of Texas journalism," which "is always on the wrong side and always loses."[49]

In addition to his Klan supporters, Robertson had the backing of the group Jim Ferguson classified as "political preachers," which included Atticus Webb, of the Anti-Saloon League; H. D. Knickerbocker, the presiding elder of the Dallas district of the Methodist Episcopal Church, South; and many dry progressives, such as Tom Love and Colonel Thomas Ball, Ferguson's opponent in 1914. These men insisted that Prohibition, not the Klan, was the real issue, with Ferguson leading the antis. "In Texas more than anywhere else a bitter fight has been made on the Klan," Webb advised the national superintendent of the Anti-Saloon League. "While some pros have taken part in this fight, the backbone of it has been the wet element. They have done their best to force everybody to quit the prohibition fight, and join them in their anti-Klan fight. I have persistently refused to do so, and supported dry candidates whether Klansmen or anti-Klansmen." "Ferguson has a rotten platform and a rotten record," Knickerbocker wired Robertson. "If the klan were twice as bad as its worst enemies charge, it couldn't be half as bad as Ferguson. No reasoning voter will forget that Mrs. Ferguson is only a dummy representative of Jim and is running on his platform." The San Antonio chapter of the WCTU endorsed Robertson, but the state board, reflecting the attitude of Mrs. Claude De Van Watts, president of the Texas WCTU, refused to endorse either candidate.[50]

Governor Pat Neff remained aloof from the increasingly bitter campaign, believing that it would be both bad taste and bad policy to use the prestige of his office in an effort to name his successor. "For this reason I did not deem it wise or expedient to make any public statement at any time in regard to the governor's race," he wrote after the runoff. This hands-off policy irritated some of the Fergusonites. In the M. M. Crane papers is a small booklet with the title *What Pat Neff Said During Ferguson-Robertson Campaign.* Inside are four blank tissue-paper pages.[51]

The second primary resembled in some ways the senatorial contest of 1922. Again a Klan-backed prohibitionist was opposing an anti-Klan antiprohibitionist. Viewing the first primary figures and sensing their impending defeat, klansmen sought to break up the anti-Klan forces by raising the Prohibition issue. Robertson delivered his opening address of the runoff in Wichita Falls on the night of August 5. During his speech he made a number of references to the "old-time whiskey politicians" who were "fighting tooth and nail" to defeat him in order to bring "comfort and cheer back into the minds and hearts of men who have always stood as uncompromising foes of temperance, sobriety and prohibition." Alluding to Mrs. Ferguson's candidacy, he declared that the people of Texas were in no mood to place the state government back in the hands that had held it in 1917. He pledged if elected to do all in his power to further the cause of Prohibition and promised to ask the legislature to pass a law prohibiting the sale of pre-

scription liquor in drugstores. Robertson complained that he was not
receiving a square deal from the daily papers, with the exception of the
Dallas Times-Herald. "The daily papers carry, in no uncertain terms,
their song of hate against me." [52]

In later speeches Robertson declared himself against mob law and
whipping. "If any one man or set of men in Texas when I'm Governor
undertake to override the law I'll suppress them if it requires the
whole police force of Texas. So help me God," he pledged, adding that
he would "kill every durn member of the mob if necessary." He also
solemnly promised to conduct the office of governor without domination by "any unholy clique or crew." "I am master of my own soul
and no man can make me do anything I don't want to do," he said in
answer to the charge that he would appoint only klansmen to office. "I
wouldn't put a partisan klansman on the bench for anything in this
world."

Robertson denied charges that he was publicly a prohibitionist
and privately a wet in his own drinking habits. He admitted that at one
time he had been a wet prohibitionist but that he had heard a bar-
tender in Dallas speak contemptuously of the drys who slipped in the
side doors of saloons to get a drink and his conversion to a dry pro became complete. "No human being ever saw me intoxicated," he told a
Dallas audience. "I am 53 years old and I have never been drunk in my
life. It's been years and years, so long I can't remember how long, since
I took a drink." [53]

Anti-Ferguson literature was distributed at Robertson rallies and
at some of Ferguson's rallies. One of the broadsides had a cartoon of
Jim Ferguson in a skirt on his way to Austin. He was labeled "$156,000
Jim." Over his head hung a dark cloud with a leering face labeled "Liquor Traffic." The banner at the top read, "Same Old Gang Back of
Him!" Below the cartoon was the legend "Fall got $100,000 in a black
bag from Doheny. Ferguson got $156,000 in a black bag from the
brewers." On the back of the broadside were excerpts from the *Ferguson Forum* bearing on Ferguson's attitude toward the Democratic party
in 1920, when he had bolted and organized his own American party.
Another broadside showed Ferguson in a bonnet with the caption "The
bonnet's all right, but look who's in it." "Vote solidly against Jim Ferguson" urged the *Texas 100 Per Cent American*: "They say 'scratch a
Turk, and you find a Tartar.' You swat that old Mother Hubbard, and

underneath you will still find the odoriferous Jim Ferguson who sold his soul and his state to the brewers, and who became a yellow dog, taking them as his master."[54]

For more than two years the slogan of some klansmen had been "Down with the Jew, Jug, and Jesuit." In the runoff the slogan was somewhat emasculated, and the sole cry was against the "Jug." In an appeal for Jewish votes the Robertson forces distributed reprints of Ferguson's March 17, 1923, editorial, "The Cloven Foot of the Dallas Jew," with the caption "Ferguson Vents Spleen on Jewish People."[55]

Unhappily for Felix Robertson, Grand Wizard Hiram Evans arrived in Texas with a black body servant just as the runoff campaign was beginning. It was alleged that, while traveling from Shreveport, Louisiana, to Fort Worth, Evans had permitted his servant to occupy a lower berth in a Pullman car reserved for whites. The man, half-dressed, left the car when threatened by other passengers and went to the black car. The incident furnished ammunition for the Klan's opponents. One authority on Texas politics, after saying that it would not have been so bad if there had not been women in the car, predicted that the incident would cost Robertson between 50,000 and 100,000 votes. Said Jed Adams in a speech to a mass anti-Klan meeting in Kaufman on August 4: "This Evans now rides in staterooms and carries with him a negro masseur. This negro, who is an ex–prize fighter, rides in the Pullman car with white women at Dr. Evans's order. Dr. Evans denies that he told the Negro to stay in the Pullman. But who, I ask you, bought the ticket?"

"Now, Mr. Klansman, it's up to you," Ferguson declared in a signed editorial in the *Forum*. "All along you have said that you were in favor of white supremacy and you took an oath to observe klanishness and employ only klansmen and then you talked about respect for womanhood." But could he now say that the Klan stood for the same principles? "It seems that your last two, ex–Grand Emperor Simmons and Clarke, were whore lovers and now your present grand gizzard is a 'nigger' lover. Which is the worst?" Ferguson continued:

Just think, Mr. 100 per center, of your old mother having to climb away up into a pullman hay loft to get a little rest while a big buck nigger is allowed to snore at ease and luxury in a lower berth along side of the great Ku Klux god, Evans, as his personal servant. If you boys in the Ku Klux want to still follow your "nigger loving" boss, all right; but you ought to stop all that "bull" you have been handing out about white supremacy and respect for womanhood. . . .

Don't forget how that Felix Robertson is being run by a nigger lover and everybody knows it. . . .

I don't believe you boys will stay with this nigger loving gang any further.[56]

The Fergusons opened their campaign at a meeting in Dallas on August 6. Mrs. Ferguson was introduced first. "Ladies and Gentlemen, I thank you for this expression of appreciation, and I hope that I may be able to render service to our State in justification of the confidence that you impose in me," she said in a quiet voice that scarcely carried beyond the first twenty rows of the audience. "As you know, I am inexperienced as a public speaker, so I shall leave that to my husband, who has done the talking for us, while I have been working at home." As Ferguson arose, the crowd cheered for several minutes, and as the cheering gradually died down, there were cries of "Hook 'em, cowpuncher!" and "Hurray for Jim!"

Ferguson denied that he had ever attempted "by word or deed" to destroy the University of Texas and stated that in his wife's administration higher education would not be called upon to make any more sacrifices than any other department in reducing appropriations. "Equal rights to all and special privileges to none is the slogan." He also pledged that in the appointments of regents and directors his wife would call upon the Ex-Students' Association for counsel and cooperation. "This she feels is not only a proper reverence for sentiment, but also an official duty." Although he had no desire to see the race pitched upon the Prohibition question, viewing it as settled, he would not back away from it. He challenged Robertson to lay his liquor record side by side with Mrs. Ferguson's and let the people decide which was the better prohibitionist. Ferguson closed with his usual promise to fight the Klan "from Hell to Haw River."[57]

Ferguson's condemnation of Robertson's Prohibition record was the outstanding feature of his second address the following day in Waco. He declared that the Klan candidate was the "biggest prohibition hypocrite that ever climbed aboard the prohibition band wagon in this State." He had been drunk "a dozen times since he was elected District Judge in Dallas two years ago," said the former governor, "and yet he has the nerve to go parading around this State as a prohibitionist. He has drunk enough liquor in the last twenty years to float a battleship and nobody knows this better than you people here in Waco." Noting that he had given Robertson a commission as a major in the national guard when he was governor, Ferguson charged that he had not been in camp three months before he had lost the title and was known to officers and men as "Tanlac Robertson." Ferguson offered the following challenge:

If I can't prove that he drank more tanlac while in the army than my wife has drunk cistern water during her whole life, then she will withdraw from this race, hold her nose and vote for him. Or if he can show where my wife has had one single drink of intoxicating liquor from the cradle to this good hour, then again I say she will withdraw from the race and vote for him.

After Ferguson had been speaking for more than an hour, and just before he began his excoriation of the Klan, several hundred people rose from their seats and made for the exits. It was mildly reminiscent of the scene in Houston two years before, when Ferguson was running against Mayfield and the Klan tried to break up his meeting, or when a premeditated attempt was made to disrupt an anti-Klan meeting in Waco at which General Crane was the featured speaker.[58]

As the campaign heated up, Ferguson drew large, excited crowds to his meetings. At Cooper automobiles and spring wagons from Delta and half a dozen or more neighboring counties made their way to town, and long before the time set for the meeting, between five and six thousand people, many of them women–elderly women in gingham dresses and sunbonnets and younger women with babies in their arms or small children by their sides—jammed their way into a spacious cotton shed that was being used for the occasion. When the wooden platform collapsed while Ferguson was being introduced, a bale of cotton was stood on end, and he delivered his address from that improvised dais. The heat was intense under the tin roof of the shed, and Ferguson spoke in his shirt-sleeves and with his collar loosened. "The crowd was on a hair-trigger tension during the whole two hours of the speaking," reported the *Dallas Morning News*:

"Pour it on 'em" was the slogan of the occasion. Sunburned farmers yelled this homely bit of slang at each dramatic point of Ferguson's address. When he was denouncing the klan, men in the crowd yelled to him continually, suggesting other things he should say, all this apparently in anxiety lest the former Governor should fail to "pour it on 'em" to the entire satisfaction of everyone.[59]

Mrs. Ferguson joined her husband in Greenville later that day for an evening rally. About ten thousand people were present; all four streets surrounding the courthouse were completely blocked, and it was almost impossible to push through the throng. From the platform the eye could not reach into the murky darkness of the night to discern the extreme limits of the crowd. In answer to Robertson's charge that he would be the real governor of Texas, Ferguson stated in farmers' phraseology: "Of course, I am going to help my wife if she is elected Governor. Every man helps his wife. While she is running the main show, I'm going to bring in the wood and water every day." Mrs. Ferguson shook so many hands in Greenville that she injured her right hand and had to put iodine and bandages on it. Her husband was kept busy explaining to a disappointed crowd in Decatur two days later why his wife could not be present: "She hasn't caught the idea of how to shake hands yet. Instead of shaking hands herself and beating people to the grip, she lets them shake hands with her. Her hand is just torn all to pieces as a consequence."[60]

By the last week of the campaign the only thing in doubt was the size of the Ferguson majority. Speaking in Lubbock before a crowd of ten thousand or more from the South Plains country, Ferguson predicted that his wife's majority would be at least 75,000 but asked his cheering audience to make the majority 200,000—"so that we may forever settle this Ku Klux Klan nonsense and have time once more to attend to the business of the State." He scathingly denounced the "trading and truckling" tactics of the Klan and the Klan candidate as revealed in the present race, adding: "But, oh, bless god, we've got this Ku Klux bunch running. Now, don't cheer, boys; the poor devils are dying."[61]

While Jim campaigned in West Texas, Mrs. Ferguson and her daughter Dorrace were in Houston on August 20 for an all-day program culminating in a monster evening rally in the city auditorium. She was awakened in the morning by two bands, the members dressed in farmer costumes, who paraded for her. All day throngs greeted the candidate. She was a guest at a luncheon, preceded by an informal reception. With the runoff just three days away Mrs. Ferguson was more confident than ever of success. "In case you should lose, Mrs. Ferguson——," a reporter started to ask her a question. "You need not consider that hypothesis," she interrupted. "I am not going to lose. I am going to be the next Governor of Texas." In a statement to the United Press, Mrs. Ferguson said there was only one real issue in the campaign—"whether the attempted domination of this State by a little group of klan politicians will be successful."[62]

On the eve of the runoff election, presidential candidate John W.

Davis came out against the Klan in a speech at Seagirt, New Jersey. Jim Ferguson immediately issued a statement calling his position against the Klan "the utterance of a great Democrat on a great Democratic principle, one of the greatest utterances of modern times. The Democratic ticket now has more than a chance to win in November and the test of a candidate for office has now been prescribed and defined by the leader of our party." The people of Texas, he predicted, "will not be so foolish as to elect a klansman Governor of this State when such action would do more to hinder the national Democratic success than any other one thing."[63]

For his part Robertson expressed confidence that he would defeat Mrs. Ferguson by at least 90,000 votes. "I notice Jim Ferguson says I have given up," he commented. "But he will find that I'm about the livest thing he's been up against." He continued to insist that the "great issue" in the race was not the Klan but "whether you will turn the State of Texas over to the whiskey ring. All the bootleggers and all the old-time members of the whiskey ring are against me." His supporters staged their own all-day program in Houston on August 21, including a rally at the auditorium that evening. Colonel Tom Ball and the candidate spoke. Robertson brought his runoff campaign to a close in a hometown speech in Dallas on August 22, in which he reviewed Ferguson's record, assailed the *Dallas Morning News* and the *Dallas Dispatch* for their partisanship, and called once more for a state government of "common sense, common honesty and Christianity."[64]

The red-hot, picturesque, vituperative campaign came to an end on August 23 with a total vote larger than the one in the July primary, a most unusual occurrence, and it was also the largest vote polled in a Texas election to that time. Mrs. Ferguson defeated Robertson by 97,732 votes, 413,751 to 316,019. She led in 173 of the 249 counties reporting. In 1922, Ferguson had had a majority of more than 4,000 votes over Mayfield in 222 rural counties, but the Klan candidate had overcome this majority from "the forks of the creek" by polling an enormous vote in the big cities and had won by 52,000 votes. Robertson hoped to do the same thing, but the large urban majorities failed to materialize. Dallas, Tarrant, and Jefferson counties voted for Robertson by majorities of 7,673, 4,453, and 1,804, respectively. Bexar County, however, gave the Fergusons a majority of 4,278, Travis gave them a lead of 866, and El Paso gave them a majority of 40. Harris County, formerly a Klan stronghold, favored Robertson by only 761 votes. "The whole story of the primary election lies in the failure of the big cities of Texas, normally klan strongholds, to rally to the support of Robertson," commented the *Dallas Morning News.*[65]

Barry Miller of Dallas, a foe of the Klan who had managed Culberson's campaign for reelection in 1922, was nominated for lieutenant governor over Will C. Edwards of Denton, the Klan candidate. Young District Attorney Dan Moody of Taylor, who had successfully prosecuted flogging cases in Williamson County in 1923–24, won his race for attorney general from Edward B. Ward of Corpus Christi, who had Klan backing. During the runoff the Klan circulated stories that in the flogging cases Moody "had a negro jury in full; also a statement that you had a negro jury in part; that you had a full Catholic jury, and a mixed Catholic and negro jury." After the runoff primary Dallas and Tarrant counties were the only major counties in Texas still under Klan control, for slates of anti-Klan candidates were nominated in many counties, large and small. In Dallas the district attorney's race was strictly a Klan and anti-Klan affair, with incumbent Shelby S. Cox the Klan-endorsed candidate and Calvin Muse the anti-Klan standard-bearer. Cox polled 22,155 votes against Muse's 16,494, gaining a majority of 5,661 votes.[66]

On the day after the election Mrs. Ferguson received more than one thousand telegrams congratulating her upon her victory, some of them facetiously offering "bed sheets and pillow cases" at bargain prices. In a statement to the Associated Press the candidate declared that her selection was "a victory for the masses as distinguished from a victory of personality." She continued:

The verdict Saturday tells plainer than words what the people think of the Ku Klux Klan after they have had opportunity to observe its workings and purposes. Texas people do know and ought to know from their opportunity more about what the klan means than any other State in the Union, and just as soon as other States have time to learn the real purposes of the klan and its secret desire to set up here a supergovernment they will do just like Texas did Saturday and repudiate it in terms unmistakable.[67]

The *Dallas Morning News* agreed with Mrs. Ferguson that personal considerations played but a small part in the election outcome. The majorities for her and the other anti-Klan candidates were a judgment against the hooded order as a political organization: "It handwrites on the wall a warning to anyone and everyone who may be seized of the evil ambition to make Texas a satrapy in an invisible empire. It is an outcome which vindicates the cause of popular government." Declared the *Galveston News*, "The Klan suffered a decisive defeat." The Ferguson victory, according to the *Houston Press*, "sounded the death-knell of the Klan as a political organization." Just before the election the *Houston Chronicle* asserted that the ballots would be cast "not with reference to the two individuals, but to determine whether Texas shall be governed by a constitution or by a ritual gotten up and peddled by a citizen of Georgia." After the voting was over, it said, "the open season for the Ku Klux Klan as a political force in Texas ended on August 23, 1924." [68]

Outside Texas the view of Mrs. Ferguson's victory was that it marked the recessional of the Klan as a dominating political power in a state where it had been outstanding and potent in recent months. Texas had been known in the East as the most powerful Klan state in the Union, causing the runoff to be viewed with more than the usual interest. "With Texas lost to the Klan," remarked the *Cleveland Plain Dealer*, "the power of the secret organization will be very sensibly diminished, for Texas is the greatest of the Southern States and also the State in which the Klan was most confident of its power." No other state than Texas, said the *Brooklyn Times*, could have given the Klan a drubbing "with the same shattering effect on the morale of the hooded organization." The Klan's crushing defeat gave the *New Haven Register* hope that "this insidious force is declining everywhere in the United States." The *New York Times* commented that the "smashing defeat suffered by the Klan in Texas ought to be a signal to start a warfare against it all over the country." [69]

Charles Ferguson (not related to the Fergusons), a Methodist minister of Fort Worth, offered a thoughtful dissent from the universality with which the Ferguson victory was heralded as an unqualified repudiation of Klanism. Writing in the October, 1924, issue of the *Southwest Review*, Ferguson claimed that the Texas verdict was a political defeat for the Klan but not a renunciation of Klanism as a philosophy of life. "Its basic tenets were not even ostensibly impugned. The antagonism which the former governor and his comrades manifested was directed only against the aspirations of the Ku Klux Klan for office." After recounting Jim Ferguson's exploitation of the incident involving Evans's body servant, Ferguson remarked: "If Shakespeare had not been overperverted, it would be well to observe that so far as the Klan was involved, Ferguson and his cohorts triumphed simply because they outkukluxed Ku Kluxism." [70]

Newspaper comments, while featuring the defeat of the Klan, also recognized the importance of Mrs. Ferguson's victory as the first woman elected governor by popular vote in American history. The *Washington Star* printed a front-page cartoon by Clifford Berryman, picturing a rugged pioneer whose hat was labeled "Texas" and who said, "Come on, fellows; give the girls a chance." The *Star* said editorially that "Texas gives the woman in politics the most brilliant recognition she has yet attained. Go West, young woman, and grow up with the country." Texas, admitted the *Waxahachie Daily Light*, is "certain to be the cynosure of the eyes of the nation, a nation curious to know what will be the result of a feminine gubernatorial administration." Georgia, observed the *Troy* (New York) *Herald*, had appointed the first woman United States senator (Mrs. Rebecca Latimer Felton); Texas would have the honor of possessing the first woman governor. It was a curious fact, the paper commented, "that the South, long the bulwark of the anti-suffragists, should be the first section of the country to put women into high positions."[71]

The Klan press in Texas put the best face it could on the defeat of its candidates. *Colonel Mayfield's Weekly* was delighted because Robertson had polled a larger vote than had been given to any previous candidate and was defeated only because "the Republicans dumped their entire party strength of 150,000 votes against the Klan nominee"; it expected a bigger vote the next time. There were combined against the Klan, declared the *Fort Worth American Citizen*, "all the political rings and brewery gangs that have been in control of the election machinery for many years." Grand Dragon Marvin announced that "the approval of around 275,000 clean-cut American votes for the principles of which the Ku Klux Klan stands is a very great victory." He continued:

The klan of Texas knows no personality, is not a political organization, and was never intended to promote the personal interest of anyone, political or otherwise. The klan stands for and will fight for good government. Its immediate mission in Texas should be to fight Fergusonism. When the klan ceases to fight Fergusonism, . . . it deserves to die. If those who would fight the principles of the klan feel free to gloat over last Saturday's election, their glee will surely turn to remorse. The result is inevitable.[72]

Tom Love thought that the election result was due to the fact that "about 200,000 of our old crowd concluded that even Fergusonism was better than Ku Kluxism. While I am against both, I think they were wrong and that Fergusonism is ten times worse." On August 28, Love announced that he did not intend to vote for Mrs. Ferguson in the November general election, though he would "earnestly and heartily" support every other candidate on the Democratic ticket from Davis and Bryan down. He hoped to be able to support an able, honest, incorruptible independent Democrat who was opposed to both Fergusonism and the Klan but indicated that he was prepared to support "any candidate on any ticket," even a write-in, "whose candidacy in my best judgment offers the best assurance of keeping the banner of Fergusonism off the battlements of the State Capitol at Austin." In keeping with the course he intended to pursue, Love announced that he had forwarded his resignation as Democratic national committeeman from Texas to the party chairman, Clem Shaver. The following day Love held a conference in San Antonio with Marshall Hicks, Frank C. Davis, and Hicks's law partner, Charles M. Dickson. Dickson had filed a protest with Davis a few days before against the State Democratic Executive Committee for declaring Mrs. Ferguson the nominee on the ground that she was not qualified to hold the office of governor because she was a woman. "Many Democrats are in favor of running the Ku Kluxers out of the party," Love told reporters. "I am not. The main reason is that we cannot do it. There are too many of them. Another reason is that there are some good men among them who have fought with us against Fergusonism for the last ten years and we have yet to find one of them guilty of any crime." Love insisted that his visit had no political significance, that he was on an automobile trip to the Davis Mountains, was simply seeking a rest, and would not attend the state convention.[73]

On the eve of the state convention, which was to meet in Austin on September 2, the Ferguson campaign headquarters completed a canvass of 249 counties, which showed that the former governor's forces would control the convention by a majority of 121 votes, 624 to the Klan's 503. The Klan contingent, through J. W. Blake of Houston, a member of a Klan-dominated "rump" Harris County delegation, asserted that the Klan would have a 150-vote advantage. Corrected figures from the Ferguson headquarters later raised the anti-Klan majority to 215 votes, 662½ to 447½. What tactics the Klan forces would employ became a question of increasing interest as party leaders, delegates and visitors milled about hotel lobbies and gathered in caucuses and conferences. A Klan coup was feared, with a host of knights arriving at the eleventh hour and the Dallas County delegation was closely watched for some expression of the order's strategy.[74]

Jim Ferguson and his political lieutenants had been preaching party harmony since the runoff, and when Mrs. Ferguson was quoted in the *Austin American* as saying that she would not appoint klansmen to office and would clear state departments of them where she had the power to do so, Ferguson, in a telephone call from Temple to the *Austin Statesman*, vigorously denied the interviews ascribed to his wife. "If the newspapers wish to re-open old quarrels and revive past bitterness, they should do so upon their own responsibility, and not seek to place my wife in a false attitude," declared Farmer Jim. Ferguson leaders in Austin called off a big jubilee meeting to celebrate Mrs. Ferguson's victory after Jim expressed concern that something might be said that would antagonize Robertson voters.[75]

The first day of the convention was marked by victories for the anti-Klan forces in every controversial matter. The Klan took its worst political drubbing to date. All the old-guarders of the Colquitt and Ferguson regimes, some of whom had not been seen in a state convention in ten years, were among the victors, and Joe Bailey scored a comeback, being chosen as the convention's permanent chairman. The position of temporary chairman, however, went to Ferguson's one-time nemesis, General Crane. Reporters again recalled the adage about politics making strange bedfellows. The convention rejected selections for credentials- and platform-committee appointments made by the Dallas County delegation and approved by an overwhelming vote the men favored by the anti-Klan minority on the delegation. "Give us more raw meat!" yelled a delegate after the vote was taken. The delegates also replaced Klan-backed nominees for the new executive committee with opponents of the order. Klan leaders sitting with the Dallas delegation wilted after the first fire, and some of them left the convention hall. The next morning the convention approved a plank criticizing the Klan as "an un-Democratic, un-Christian and un-American organization," condemned its political activities, and called on those who had joined "this dangerous order" to withdraw to stop strife. Davis's condemnation of the Klan's deeds at Seagirt was adopted in full. A demand was made for the public registration of secret organizations and an anti-mask law. The convention also adopted a resolution offered from the floor providing for the removal of Mrs. J. T. Bloodworth of Fort Worth as national committeewoman because of her Klan activities and affiliations and favoring Mary Wade Smith, a prominent clubwoman from Sherman, as her successor. Ferguson had earlier persuaded the platform committee not to call for her resignation. Probably a large number of the delegates did not realize that Mrs. Smith was a Catholic when they voted for her (one of her five children was a priest). In a letter to Mrs. Percy V. Pennybacker she acknowledged that she might not get the committeewoman position because of her religion, for

some weak kneed Brethren have announced that in the interest of harmony they will not insist on Mrs. Bloodworth's removal—not that they hate the klan less but *Rome* more. I understand that Farmer Jim will oppose any effort to unseat her. Naturally he wants to stop the fight now that "Ma" is seated, and I made speeches against him in my county several years ago.

Mrs. Smith was right. The executive committee did not replace Mrs. Bloodworth.[76]

Governor Neff was not invited to address the convention or even to appear before it. He was seen in the hall only once, and that was for only a short time. No reason for the failure to invite him was given. The governor's order to law-enforcement officials to make Austin and Travis County "as dry as the Sahara Desert" during the convention stirred resentment among thirsty delegates, who saw Texas Rangers wearing large black hats on duty in the hotels, watching hand luggage, looking over persons entering elevators, and listening for invitations to "have one." Neff's failure to endorse Mrs. Ferguson may have been a factor, as well as the antipathy antiprohibitionist leaders felt for "Pat the Pious." The Fergusons and the Neffs spent a pleasant twenty minutes in the executive offices in the State Capitol after holding a levee in the Senate chamber after the convention adjourned. "Governor Neff pledged his hearty cooperation both before and after Mrs. Ferguson's nomination to make her administration a complete success," said a member of the Ferguson family. "And Governor Ferguson complimented Governor Neff on the high ideals of his administration and its success."[77]

Texas Republicans were jubilant at the prospect that the Democratic party would be torn apart by internal dissension over the Klan issue. Meeting in Fort Worth on August 12, the Republican State Convention adopted a short platform, including an anti-Klan plank, and nominated a complete state ticket headed by Thomas P. Lee, a Houston businessman, for governor and Thomas M. Kennerly, a Houston attorney, for United States senator. "Mr. Lee will not be the next Governor of Texas, and he knows it, probably, as well as anybody in the State," commented the *Dallas Morning News*, adding: "It is a pity that

it is so. It is unfortunate for the Democratic party that it is so. With a
Republican party that had a real chance in Texas we would have a rectitude and a careful leadership in the Democratic party such as we have
not known since the days of the Populist uprising." Lee agreed with
the News's assessment of his prospects. From Colorado Springs, Colorado, he wired Jim Ferguson to express "my sincere desire that your
good wife receive the Democratic nomination Aug. 23 primary, in
which event I shall be thoroughly content with the usual empty Republican honor." [78]

Lee's telegram so angered Texas Republican leaders that there
were demands that he withdraw as a candidate. National Committeeman R. B. Creager complained that the Republicans had an excellent
chance to elect a governor until "Lee spoiled it all by his telegram to
Mrs. Ferguson." On August 18, in a statement to the Republicans of
Texas, Lee declined to be the party's candidate for governor, referring
to public statements made by "one of our people [Creager]" which
made it impossible for him to remain in the race. [79]

After Mrs. Ferguson's victory in the runoff primary the State Republican Executive Committee met at the Rice Hotel in Houston to
name Lee's replacement. Henry Zweifel of Fort Worth, the federal district attorney for the North Texas District, received extensive boosting, but the question of lining up with the Klan to attract Robertson
voters caused a tie-up in the committee. Old-line Republicans wanted
a Republican nominee, arguing that to nominate a Democrat would
ultimately weaken the Republican state organization. A fusionist element favored naming a Democrat who could draw Klan votes. This
group was divided into two classes, Republican klansmen who did not
want a fight made on their organization, and new recruits who believed a victory with a Democratic nominee was better than no victory
at all. A decision was finally reached not to nominate anyone until
after the Democratic State Convention. It was rumored that if the
Democrats condemned the Klan the Republicans would side with it,
but Creager denied that postponement meant that a klansman would
be selected to oppose Mrs. Ferguson. "The anti-Klan plank will remain in our platform," he asserted. Meanwhile, black Republicans
held a separate convention in the office of the Texas Freeman, a black
weekly. They pleaded for a strong party organization and endorsed the
Coolidge-Dawes ticket. [80]

When the Republican Executive Committee met in Dallas behind closed doors on September 5, only two men were considered as possible nominees: Henry Zweifel and George C. Butte, dean of the University of Texas Law School. Colonel William E. Talbot of Dallas, who had the backing of the Dallas County Republican organization, declined to permit his name to be presented. After two hours' deliberation, Butte was the unanimous choice on the first ballot. Characterizing Butte as a Christian gentleman of the highest type, Creager predicted that he would poll not only the normal party vote but an enormous Democratic vote in the general election.[81]

Butte, homeward-bound from Europe aboard the steamship *Rotterdam*, was notified of his selection by wireless. "I was overwhelmed," the candidate declared on his arrival in New York City on September 12. "I am virtually a nobody in Texas politics. Why, I wouldn't recognize the State's political leaders if they strolled down the pier to meet me." Back in Austin, he announced his resignation as dean of the law school and gave out a platform which he said had only one plank: "It is Art. XVI, Sec. 1, of the Constitution of Texas, which contains the Governor's oath of office. I promise the people of Texas that I will support the Constitution and will faithfully and impartially execute the laws of Texas—all of them." He declared: "I am not now and have never been a member of the Ku Klux Klan. I have not now and never will have any alliance with it. The constitutional guarantees of religious liberty and security of person are sacred, and I will enforce them to the uttermost of my powers."[82]

Butte was born in San Francisco, California, in 1877, and moved with his family to Hunt County when he was nine years old. He was reared on a farm near Commerce and attended the public schools there. He received the B.A. degree from Austin College, in Sherman, in 1895 and the B.A. and M.A. degrees from the University of Texas in 1903 and 1904. From 1904 to 1911 he practiced law in Muskogee, Oklahoma, and in 1910 was an unsuccessful candidate for district judge there on the Republican ticket. Retiring from law practice, Butte went to Europe to study and received the J.D. degree from the University of Heidelburg in 1913. He was professor of law in the University of Texas from 1914 to 1918. Early in 1918 he volunteered for army service and was named head of the Foreign Intelligence Division of the General Staff with the rank of major. In 1919 he took a year's leave of absence from the university to organize the Pipe Line and Conservation Department of the Texas Railroad Commission and write its regulations. He also drafted a public-utilities bill at the request of the League of Texas Municipalities. In 1920 he resumed his duties in the law school. John C. Granbery described him as "a fine man to put on the stump" against Ferguson in 1922. "The ablest man in the State University and so far as I know the ablest man in the Republican party in Texas is Dr. George C. Butte," he wrote. Following the death of John C. Townes in 1923, Butte was named dean of the law school. [83]

Opening his campaign in Sherman on October 1, Butte explained at the outset that he regarded former Governor Ferguson, not his wife, as his opponent. He asserted that there was no essential difference between the Democratic and Republican state platforms and that it mattered little whether the voters elected a Democratic or a Republican governor; they should vote for the man and not the party. "We shall have a government by proxy," Butte asserted, warning that, if Mrs. Ferguson was elected, "it will be the greatest example of irresponsible personal government that history records." The former governor would have the power without the responsibility, "and never was there an example of power without responsibility but that tyranny arose." [84]

Butte pursued the strategy of Neff and Ferguson in their first races and tried to cover as much territory as possible and make as many speeches as possible each day. During the campaign he traveled about three thousand miles and made one hundred speeches. His supporters claimed that he was drawing larger crowds than had any other Republican candidate in recent years and that he was expected to carry the San Antonio area, was especially strong in West Texas, and probably would win the race. "My heartiest congratulations on the magnificent campaign you are making," Creager wired Butte on October 15. "Reports from all sections of state are most highly pleasing and indicate your election." [85]

A number of anti-Ferguson Democrats bolted the party before the general election and founded an organization known as the Good Government Democratic League of Texas in Dallas on September 27. Among those present were Tom Love; Dr. C. C. Selecman, president of Southern Methodist University; Dallas attorney D. A. Frank; former State Senator H. Bascom Thomas; the Reverend Arthur W. Jones of Arlington, former head of the Anti-Saloon League of Texas; and Mrs. John D. Claybrooke of Austin, president of the Women's Democratic Association of Texas. John Marshall of Sherman was elected president, and S. A. Fishburn of Dallas was elected secretary. Butte, whom various speakers characterized as "a good Independent Democrat," was nominated for governor. "I have the impression that the Good Government Democrats of Texas are going to elect George C. Butte Governor," Love wrote Daniel Roper. "There is a ground swell on at this time."[86]

Democratic party loyalists warned voters that under the election laws a Democrat could not vote for Butte without voting the entire Republican ticket. The Good Government Democrats therefore concentrated their efforts on instructing Texans how to vote the Democratic ticket generally and also vote for Butte. The state attorney general ruled that they could do so by scratching out Mrs. Ferguson's name and either writing Butte's name below it in the Democratic column or scratching all the names on the Republican ticket except Butte's.[87]

Broadsides compared Ferguson's war record unfavorably with Butte's, commended Butte's services as chief oil-and-gas supervisor, and appealed to women, Jews, and drys by reminding them that Ferguson had opposed woman suffrage, had published anti-Semitic editorials in the *Ferguson Forum*, and was politically wet. The race question was injected into the campaign when Judge Joseph E. Cockrell charged Love with following Republican leaders "regardless of their color." The latter retorted that the only black leadership in the campaign to date was that of Gooseneck Bill McDonald, "the black and tan boss of Texas, who has declared for Ferguson, and a number of Brazos bottom negroes who got together at Marlin the other day and likewise declared for Ferguson." Butte also raised the matter of McDonald support for his opponent in his speeches, saying that he, Butte, stood for the social and political supremacy of the white race and that "Jim Ferguson can take him [McDonald] and go in peace."[88]

In an effort to keep Mrs. Ferguson's name off the general-election ballot, Charles M. Dickson, after his rebuff by the State Democratic Executive Committee, filed a suit on September 10 in the Fifty-third District Court of Travis County. He argued that if Mrs. Ferguson was elected she would be a "figurehead or Governor in name only," since Jim Ferguson was the real candidate; that Ferguson would be entitled to half her salary as community property, though he was barred from receiving any emolument from the state; and that a woman was ineligible to be governor of Texas, because only the masculine pronoun was used in the Texas Constitution. Judge George Calhoun ruled, however, that there was nothing in the state constitution that disqualified a woman from holding office. On appeal the Texas Supreme Court unanimously held that Mrs. Ferguson was eligible to hold office since the state and federal woman-suffrage amendments had removed any pre-existing sex ineligibility and ordered her name placed on the ballot.[89]

At first the Fergusons were inclined to let nature take its course, since in previous Texas primaries the Democratic nomination had been equivalent to election. Isolated as much as possible in her home in Temple, Mrs. Ferguson said on September 6 that she was taking a "rocking-chair vacation." No speaking dates were arranged for either of the Fergusons, and both declined to discuss the Republican ticket. By the end of the month, however, Butte's campaign had achieved enough momentum to cause the Democrats some concern. "It is quite evident that there is a move on that must not be minimized and I am already passing the word out to our friends as to the necessity of getting out to vote," Ferguson advised General Crane. "The Ku Klux–Butte ticket is hoping to win, not by their large number of votes, but by hoping that the Democrats will go to sleep," the former governor wrote a San Antonio supporter. "For that reason it is necessary that our friends be warned what they intend to do."[90]

On October 6 the State Democratic Executive Committee issued a ringing appeal to Texas Democrats to honor their pledge to support all the party nominees. It denounced "a certain disgruntled element in the party" that was now aiding the Republicans and "who we now charge to be in secret alliance with the infamous Ku Klux Klan to announce the doctrine that a Democrat has the right to bolt simply because the party nominee was not his choice in the primary." Speaking in Sherman, Joe Bailey launched an attack on those holding "this strange doctrine of violating party pledges." "What would the Savior of the world say if told that a pledge was not binding on a man's conscience?" he asked. "A man may be honest, but ignorant, but he can not be honest unless he keeps his word. Whenever any people forsake their fundamentals either in politics or religion nothing but trouble comes to pass."[91]

Jim Ferguson again campaigned for his wife, opening a statewide tour with a speech at Hillsboro on October 23. He ridiculed Butte's selection as the Republican candidate. After looking around and failing to find anybody on land, he said, the "Republican–Ku Klux" crowd had "finally jumped on one poor ignorant professor away out in the middle of the ocean and thrust upon the poor devil the Republican–

Ku Klux nomination for Governor." He warned that the Klan was not to be put down without another struggle. "They must make another trial to get control of the Government of Texas so that they could seat a king and a wizard on the throne to control the politics and patronage of the State of Texas." He jabbed at Tom Love and the Good Government Democratic League, which, he said, included many prominent klansmen and Klan sympathizers. Becoming more personal, he accused Butte of running off to Europe when his law partner in Oklahoma was sent to jail for embezzlement, attacked his war record as "just another one of those swivel-chair warriors who stayed over here while the boys went over yonder," and claimed that Butte had received seven dollars for every hour that he had worked for the University of Texas. The only thing to Butte's credit was his resignation from the university, which had relieved it of the embarrassment of his employment.[92]

Ferguson predicted in the *Forum* that Butte would not carry twenty counties and said that it was "a lead pipe cinch that he will not begin to be as strong as Felix Robertson was." His wife would beat Butte 2½ to 1. Asked if he had any statement to make on the eve of the election, Ferguson replied: "Yes, you can say that the boys have licked 'em to a frazzle and my good wife has gone clean over the top. Our friends throughout Texas deserve the credit." Ferguson men were confident that most Democrats would remain loyal to the "party of the fathers." "Butte will, of course, by reason of the alliance made with the Klan, receive a much larger vote than any Republican has received in a long time, perhaps," wrote a Quitman attorney, "but I cannot think that there are enough Democrats who will tear loose from their ancient Democratic moorings and vote for the Republican nominee as to land that theoretical scholar, fastidious pedagogue of camouflaged and spectacular piety, in the Governor's chair."[93]

The November 4 election, according to the *New York Times*, signaled "the greatest political revolution that ever took place in Texas." Although Mrs. Ferguson defeated Butte by 127,588 votes, 422,558 to 294,970, the former law-school dean carried fifty-five counties, most of them in West, Southwest, and Southeast Texas, and received almost three times as many votes as any previous Republican candidate for governor in Texas. He polled about 165,000 votes more than the national Republican ticket of Coolidge and Dawes.[94] Democratic election judges were said to have thrown out thousands of ballots with Butte's name written in the Democratic column, and for a time Republican leaders considered contesting Mrs. Ferguson's election for that reason, but as the rural returns came in, her majority climbed steadily. "It looks as though the Ferguson majority will now go over one hundred thousand," Butte's campaign manager, W. E. Talbot, reported to him. "Personally, I am willing to conceed [*sic*] the election, but I be dog-gone if I am going to congratulate him." On November 18 the Republican leaders announced that they would not contest the result. Butte declined to talk about the election or the decision against contesting it. "I am now going home," he announced, "and, like our genial friend, Mr. Pickwick, I am going to 'reflect on the mutability of human affairs.'" [95]

Butte showed his greatest strength in counties with large cities: Dallas, Tarrant, Harris, El Paso, Jefferson, and McLennan. Bexar County went for Mrs. Ferguson, and she carried the ten German counties 27,632 to 8,231, as loyalty to Jim Ferguson outweighed their growing tendency toward Republicanism. "The Republican Germans and negroes (about 75,000 of them) voted solidly for Ferguson," Love informed McAdoo. "If they had voted for Butte, he would have been elected." "Ma" won Bell County but lost her own precinct by about 15 votes and Temple by 500 votes. Most klansmen, it appears, voted for Butte, as did thousands of die-hard Ferguson haters. [96]

In other contests, Barry Miller received 526,100 votes for lieutenant governor, while the Republican candidate, J. H. Kurth, received only 175,546. Republican Harry M. Wurzbach was reelected to Congress over D. S. Davenport by an almost two-to-one majority. Julius Real, who had served in the State Senate as a Republican from 1909 to 1914, defeated his Democratic opponent T. H. Ridgeway to return to the Senate. [97]

The wife of a Ferguson man on the State Democratic Executive Committee commented about the outcome of the election: "All I know about the political situation is, that 'Ma' is in, and that we helped put her there, and have pledged ourselves to see that 'Jim' keeps in proper bounds, and we believe and hope, that Texas will not suffer from this administration, but that the Ku Klux will not only suffer but die the death." [98]

And "die the death" it did. The Klan's failure to nominate Robertson or to defeat Ferguson in the general election, together with the loss of all the counties it had formerly dominated, signaled the withering away of the order as a force in Texas politics. "It was all over," recalled a former klansman. "After Robertson was beaten the prominent men left the Klan. The Klan's standing went with them." Noted the historian of the order in the Southwest: "By the end of 1924 Texas, once the most cherished prize of the men who ran the Klan, was no longer the number one state in Klandom. Other states—Indiana, Ohio, Alabama—became more important than Texas in Klan affairs."[99]

As much as the Fergusons had fought the Klan, they had reason to be grateful to it, for it was through his fight against the organization that Jim Ferguson found the vindication he had sought for seven years. George Fort Milton of the *Chattanooga News*, reflecting on the Texas election, wrote:

The big trouble with the Klan politically is that its mere existence allows a vicious band of reactionaries to shelter behind the anti-Klan charge. . . . They offer a choice of two evils, and I will confess it is a terrible choice. Had it not been for the Klan Jim Ferguson never could have elected his wife (which means himself) in Texas.[100]

Only time would tell if the "Governors Ferguson" would realize the hopes of their friends or the worst fears of their enemies.

CHAPTER 7

The Governors Ferguson of Texas

A CARNIVAL atmosphere pervaded Austin on January 20, 1925, as thousands of people from all parts of the state came to the capital to see the inauguration of the first woman governor of Texas. In the morning hours Congress Avenue was a moving panorama of limousines and Lizzies, mule-drawn wagons, and here and there a buggy of a past era. Reported the *Austin American*: "High-heel boots kept step with square-toe Oxfords. Calico and gingham rubbed elbows with satin and silk. Lanky plainsmen jogged by on cow ponies. Men of the military swaggered along beside tall figures in the inevitable Prince Albert coat and black felt hat." Bands paraded up and down the street. "Not since the funeral of [gunman] Ben Thompson [in 1884] had the city of Austin seen anything like the inauguration of Mrs. Ferguson," wrote one observer.[1]

Shortly before noon a band played "The Eyes of Texas Are upon You" as the incoming and outgoing governors, with entourage, marched into the packed House of Representatives chamber and took their places on the speaker's stand. The crush of people was so great that senators had to shift for themselves, and many were lost in the shuffle. In addition to the five thousand people in the hall, thousands more stood outside the closed doors, milled around in the capitol corridors and rotundas, and spilled out onto the terraced grounds. The "Ma" Ferguson of gingham-apron and sunbonnet and jam-preserving pictures was absent. In her stead was a woman handsomely gowned in a black-satin dress trimmed with chinchilla, a deep-ivory feather boa, and a feather-decked black hat. Jim Ferguson's smile was one of supreme satisfaction. After an operatic soprano, dressed in cowgirl costume, sang "Put on Your Old Gray Bonnet," accompanied by the Old Gray Mare Band from Brownwood, Mrs. Ferguson took the oath of office. In introducing his successor, the courtly Pat Neff told her that he had left in the governor's office a portrait of Woodrow Wilson; a white rose, the symbol of pure motives; and an open Bible, in which he had marked the 105th verse of Psalm 119: "Thy word is a lamp unto my feet, and a light unto my path." This Book of Books, he said, would prove a chart and compass to her and succeeding governors as they directed the ship of state. "He seemed at times to be looking over and beyond the crowd straight into the eyes of posterity," wrote Harry Benge Crozier of Neff's innovation. Since that day the outgoing governor's marking of a passage in this Bible has become a tradition.

Governor Ferguson made a short acceptance speech in a barely audible voice. "Recognizing and freely admitting my inexperience in governmental affairs, I must ask the advice and counsel of others," she stated. Everyone knew what that meant: Jim Ferguson was to be her principal adviser. She said that what Texas needed was a long pull, a strong pull, and a pull all together. The new governor pleaded for more heart in government, proclaimed political equality for women, and assured the audience that many women would be invited to take an active part in her administration. "As the first woman governor of our beloved state, I ask for the good will and the prayers of the women of Texas. I want to be worthy of the trust and the confidence which they have reposed in me. . . . With love for all, with malice toward none, trusting in God, I consecrate my life to my state," she concluded. When the governor and her husband entered her office and found Neff's marked Bible, Jim closed it and tossed it over to the window ledge with the remark: "Sunday School is dismissed. The Governor's office is now open for business."[2]

In 1917 the Fergusons had driven away from the executive mansion in a Packard Twin-Six with Mrs. Ferguson at the wheel (Jim did not drive). As they left the grounds, she had predicted that there would be a brighter day and that they would return in the Packard. Two years later they stored the car in a Temple garage, and there it remained until November, 1924, when the governor-elect, remembering her prediction of seven years before, had it repaired and polished and drove it back to Austin for her inauguration. With Mrs. Ferguson again driving, the family returned to the mansion in the Packard. As they arrived under the portecochere, she said, as if addressing the old car: "Well, we have returned! We departed in disgrace; we now return in glory!" Walking in the grounds that afternoon, Mrs. Ferguson was struck dumb to find that her name had been removed from a block of concrete at the threshold of the greenhouse that had been built in 1915 during her husband's first administration. It had been her pride and joy. Summoning a concrete man, she had her name and the date restored.[3]

The Thirty-ninth Legislature had convened on January 13, a week before Mrs. Ferguson's inauguration. Not many representatives had been returned to the House from the previous Klan-dominated one. Of the 150 members only 59 had served in the Thirty-eighth Legislature. Sixteen new members had served in legislatures before the Thirty-eighth. Thus 75 members, or exactly half of the House, had no previous legislative experience. Lee Satterwhite, a newspaper editor and Panhandle farmer of Carson County, was elected Speaker on the sixth ballot over T. K. Irwin of Dallas and J. W. Hall of Houston in what observers called "one of the closest and most exciting races ever held in the House." Irwin, who had the backing of the Klan, made a bid for Jim Ferguson's support by announcing that he would favor a proposal to remove Ferguson's disqualification, but the former governor, while expressing pleasure at Irwin's statement, announced that he had no choice in the contest. Some observers looked upon Satterwhite's election as evidence that the House was declaring its independence of both Ferguson and the Klan.[4]

In contrast to the House, the Senate, where Lieutenant Governor Barry Miller would preside after January 20, had an unusually high percentage of experience; sixteen senators were returned, and eight of the new senators had served in either the House or the Senate, which left only seven inexperienced members. The Senate had been reapportioned, and sixteen senators would draw four-year terms, and fifteen senators two-year terms. West Texans fared especially well in the lot drawing for long terms: six were winners, including the lone Republican in the upper house, Julius Real of Kerrville.[5]

During his last week in office Governor Neff had sent the legislature messages on the state-park and prison systems, the Highway Department, the Live Stock Sanitary Commission, reclamation and flood control, and the Texas Rangers. He also recommended that the legislature adopt "Texas, Our Texas," by W. J. Marsh and Mrs. Gladys Yokum Wright of Fort Worth, as the state song; it was the winning entry in a contest the governor had sponsored.[6]

On January 16 the Senate Committee on Nominations overturned predictions by favorably reporting on most of Neff's recess appointments. The Senate later confirmed many of them, including reappointment of R. B. Walthall, the governor's former private secretary, to the

Board of Control for the remainder of the six-year term beginning January 1, 1924, and Mrs. Espa Stanford, also a former private secretary to the governor, as a member of the Industrial Accident Board. Ferguson had earlier announced that Roy I. Tennant of Temple was his choice for the Board of Control, and Walthall's confirmation gave rise to newspaper stories that the Senate was breaking with Ferguson and would refuse to remove the stigma from his name. However, Senator J. G. Strong, the chairman of the Committee on Nominations, declared in a Senate speech that he knew of no break with the former governor. "As to the removal of the impeachment disqualifications of James E. Ferguson, personally I am in favor of it," he commented afterward, "and shall fight for such a procedure and I am of the opinion that a large majority of the Senate feel as I do about it. I know a large majority of the Committee on Nominations are very much pro-Ferguson." Ferguson, after paying a social call on Neff, said that there had been no quarrel with the retiring governor on the question of recess appointments "or anything else."[7]

In its final consideration of Neff's appointments on January 19, the Senate saluted the rising and not the setting sun by making a virtual clean sweep of his six recess appointments to the University of Texas Board of Regents. Only two members—R. G. Storey of Dallas and Tuckett Royall of Palestine—were confirmed, and Royall's term ended in 1925, leaving seven appointments to be made by the incoming administration. Mrs. H. J. O'Hair of Coleman, whose term expired in 1927, was the only regent not affected by the change of administrations. The Senate also withheld confirmation of Neff's entire list of appointments to the State Textbook Commission, seven in all, and declined to confirm Charles E. Baughman as commissioner of markets and warehouses, though John M. Scott was confirmed as commissioner of insurance against Ferguson's wishes. Appointments to the Board of Optometry, the Board of Directors of Texas Tech College, the State Board of Pharmacy, the State Board of Medical Examiners, and the State Board of Veterinary Medical Examiners were also turned down. On his last day in office Neff appointed T. W. Davidson, Mrs. Florence Sterling of Houston, Cullen Thomas of Dallas, and W. W. Woodson of Waco to the University of Texas Board of Regents and Lynch Davidson to the Texas Tech board, but the Senate declined to act on them, and all but Mrs. Sterling withdrew their names.[8]

In contrast, the Senate Committee on Nominations took "scarcely more than one minute" to approve unanimously ten state officials named by Mrs. Ferguson on January 23, while the Senate confirmed the entire list in as much time as was required to call their names. Perhaps the most noteworthy appointment was Mrs. Emma Grigsby Meharg as secretary of state, the first woman in Texas to hold that office. There were only two women among the next 109 appointees. Meanwhile, the Fergusons met with members of the University of Texas Ex-Students' Association and asked the organization to submit twenty or twenty-five names from which the Board of Regents could be chosen. "The results were entirely satisfactory," Harbert Davenport, a Brownsville lawyer, wrote historian Eugene Barker, "and if the ex-students act harmoniously and through the council of the association, we shall have a board of regents which will include [T. S.] Henderson, either M. M. Crane or Ed Crane, Dexter Hamilton, Mike Hogg, Logue Carlton, Judge R. L. Batts, and one or two others of the same caliber." "There will be no vindictiveness on the Governor's part toward any member of the University's faculty," he assured Barker.[9]

The Ex-Students' Association opposed the reappointment of H. A. Wroe of Austin and H. J. Lutcher Stark of Orange, the chairman of the board, because they had voted for Neff for president of the university, and Wroe resigned from the board after Ferguson failed to reassure him that he would be asked to serve again. On January 29, Mrs. Ferguson submitted the names of Marcellus E. Foster of Houston, Ted Dealey of Dallas, George W. Tyler of Belton, S. C. Padleford of Fort Worth, and L. J. Truett of McKinney. Truett and Dealey declined, and Mart H. Royston of Galveston and Edward Howard of Wichita Falls were appointed along with Stark and Sam Neathery of McKinney. Despite a vigorous fight against him by the Ex-Students' Association, Stark was confirmed on February 11 by a vote of 24 to 6 (4 votes to spare) in a three-hour closed executive session. After the debate had waxed warm for over two hours, a senator left the chamber and entered the governor's private office. He soon returned bringing a strong plea from Mrs. Ferguson for Stark's confirmation, which quickly followed.[10]

Governor Ferguson named Frank V. Lanham of Dallas to a two-year term as chairman of the State Highway Commission along with former State Senator Joe Burkett of Eastland for the four-year term.

John H. Bickett, Sr., of San Antonio was reappointed for the six-year term. Lanham, a road contractor, was the son of the late governor S. W. T. Lanham and the brother of Congressman Fritz Lanham of Fort Worth. Burkett had been a candidate for the Democratic nomination for governor in the first primary and had supported Mrs. Ferguson in the runoff. The members of the Highway Commission would hold office under the new highway law, which went into effect in February.[11]

Governor Ferguson's first message to the legislature called for economy and reform in state government. She predicted a two-million-dollar deficit in the general revenue fund and noted that the requested appropriations totaled $43 million while the expected revenue for the next two years was only $38 million. The governor suggested that the major appropriation bills should be taken up at once and disposed of and that the total sum voted should not exceed $30 to $35 million. The legislature was asked to investigate the State Banking Department, said to be in a "deplorable state of confusion," and the governor added that the powers of the State Insurance Department should be clarified. She thought that the work of the adjutant general's department should be expanded by building armories but that the number of Texas Rangers should be reduced and that they should not be "arbitrarily" sent to any section of the state to perform the duties of local law-enforcement officials. The laws against murder, robbery, speeding, and sale of liquor should be strengthened; serious attention should also be given to cattle-tick eradication, and the lawmakers should heed the demand of the Democratic State Convention and put the bootleg drugstores out of business.

Turning to penitentiary matters, Mrs. Ferguson announced that the Neff honor farm would be continued "until such time as reason and discretion will require its discontinuance." She would appoint a board of pardons to hear clemency applications and would adopt "a most liberal policy in the matter of pardons." The legislature might consider confining no prisoner in the penitentiary whose term was less than two years; such prisoners could be working on the county roads at less expense. Not all punishment could be abolished, and the prison commissioners must retain some effective and persuasive mode of punishment that would be humane as well. While the physical condition of the prison system could be made very much better, and more than $3 million had been lost in operating the system during the last five or six years, "a fairly good condition" now existed. Commissioners Herring and Sayle, whose terms ran concurrently with hers, appeared to be working for the system's best interest, she said, and had promised to cooperate in every way possible with the governor and the new commissioner. The system was running a deficit and was buying supplies on time. The sum of $600,000 would tide it over until the crops went to market, saving 25 percent on purchases, or $150,000. The legislature could either permit the commission to execute a chattel mortgage on its current crops and livestock or make an emergency appropriation.

The governor had some constructive suggestions on highway and education legislation. Pointing out that the State Highway Department had spent $40 million in 1924, she suggested a motor-vehicle tax averaging $6, the funds to remain in the counties collecting them, to be used in maintaining lateral roads, and a gasoline tax of 3 cents a gallon that would produce a minimum of $12 million. A fourth of the tax should be turned over to the common- and country-school fund, and the rest should be used for building and maintaining permanent roads. A small tax on factory-made cigars and cigarettes, designated the "Educational Tax," was suggested, three-fourths of the money to go to higher education and one-fourth to the common- and country-school funds. The governor also recommended the construction of a new $500,000 insane asylum at Sweetwater, in Nolan County. She concluded her message by wishing the lawmakers "God speed in your labors." [12]

The legislature carried out about half of the Democratic party's demands and half of the legislation suggested by the governor. When the session opened, the *Dallas Morning News* reported that many legislators felt that there were already too many laws on the books. "We are law confused," said one newly elected representative. "I believe in the principle as enunciated by Thomas Jefferson, that 'the country governed least is governed best'!" Another new member succinctly commented: "——— new laws, let's enforce a few of our old." With very few exceptions the legislators stressed the need to reduce the cost of state government and declared for tax relief. [13]

"There were almost no bills passed by the 1925 Legislature of outstanding public interest," according to State Librarian Octavia F. Rogan. The State Highway Commission was given jurisdiction over the construction and maintenance of all state highways, and Texas's highway-construction regulations were made to conform to federal regulations, thus enabling the state to continue to receive federal aid.

The State Warehouse and Market Department was made a part of the State Department of Agriculture, and major changes were made in the tick-eradication law. A new textbook commission was created, and some changes were made in the laws governing its work. The life of the Education Survey Commission was extended for two years. Oil royalties that had gone into the University of Texas permanent fund were now to be paid into the building fund. The antipollution law was strengthened to forbid the draining of crude oil and other harmful substances into streams. "Foreign" corporations having no permit to do business in Texas but holding stock in Texas corporations were authorized by Senate Bill 180 to vote their stock and participate in the management and control of said corporations, just as other stockholders could, without violating Texas's antitrust laws. This measure, which occasioned little discussion at the time, was to become an issue in the gubernatorial election of 1926, because it legitimized the control of Humble Oil Company by Standard Oil of New Jersey. In 1919 Humble had sold 50 percent of its stock to Jersey Standard for $17 million. Later this was increased to 60 percent. "These gentlemen did not use brass bands while they were hunting legislative ducks," the *Austin American* said of the corporation lawyers who quietly lobbied the measure through the legislature. "They stated their mission briefly and they were given what they asked." The Senate approved Senate Bill 180 on February 16, by a vote of 15 to 8, with eight senators absent; the House passed it on March 11, by a vote of 97 to 27; and Governor Ferguson signed it on April 7.

From a social viewpoint, the most constructive law was the one carrying out the recommendations of the Texas Eleemosynary Commission, established by the previous legislature, for improving the commitment, parole, discharge, care, and custody of the mentally ill. The legislature also submitted four constitutional amendments, all of which were adopted at the general election in November, 1926.[14]

The administration openly opposed the federal child-labor amendment, and the legislature overwhelmingly rejected it by a vote in the Senate of 19 to 2 and a vote in the House of 111 to 16. Although some opponents simply objected to any legislation, federal or state, on the subject, the majority, though favoring regulation of child labor, did not want it regulated by the federal government. As dear as the child-labor amendment was to the members of the Petticoat Lobby, they realized the hopelessness of the fight and for the sake of harmony and the rest of their program did not push for its adoption. When, however, Senator John Davis of Dallas introduced a bill to repeal Texas's part of the fifty-fifty Sheppard-Towner Maternity Act, agreed to by the previous legislature after a fierce struggle, the lobby went on the warpath. The executive secretary of the lobby, Mrs. Jane Y. McCallum, warned that the women would not "passively submit to a tearing-down process. We enter no protest when the lawmakers become so fervent over the welfare of the 'little fishes,' of our roads, fish, oysters, game, pig, cattle and ticks. Then why, in the name of the Most High, should they object when we, the women of Texas, ask for this pitiful little sum to alleviate the sufferings of mothers and babies?"

Davis's bill came close on the heels of the Senate Finance Committee's decision to eliminate the appropriation to the Bureau of Child Hygiene—$72,000 for the biennium—an appropriation that would allow the state to receive a like amount from the federal government under the Sheppard-Towner Act. On February 9 the Senate overruled the committee, voting 24 to 5 to restore the $72,000. Davis's motion to appropriate the money without accepting the federal funds was defeated. "If Texas can spend millions for the health of its cattle," said Senator Floyd, "it can surely spend this $72,000 for the health of its babies." The press gave the Petticoat Lobby credit for having influenced retention of the appropriation.[15]

The Thirty-eighth Legislature had authorized a joint House-Senate committee and the Texas Committee on Prisons and Prison Labor, a division of the National Committee on Prison Labor, to make a survey of the prison system without cost to the state. Persistent reports of "numerous irregularities, grafts, extravagances, waste and brutal treatment of prisoners in connection with the State Penitentiary System" prompted the House of Representatives to authorize a five-member investigation committee. The *Dallas Morning News* had earlier editorialized that Mrs. Ferguson faced no more urgent task than that of overhauling the prison system, which the paper termed "a standing disgrace." Committee hearings revealed graft and brutality, stills inside the prison walls, barns burned after prison officials had removed all their contents, and bribes given for pardons. In addition, several days were devoted to spicy testimony concerning a relationship between a prison official and a convict's wife. "The investigation of the prison system has unearthed a condition of affairs that smells to Heaven," a woman advocate of prison reform lamented. T. K. Irwin, one of the members of the investigating committee, demanded that J. A. Herring, chairman of the Board of Prison Commissioners, resign or he would ask the House to impeach him. He also demanded resignations from a number of other prison officials and prison-farm managers. Irwin did not, however, carry out his impeachment threat when Herring stayed on.

In its report the investigating committee made seventeen recommendations for reforming the system, including centralization and a change to one-man control, continuous and searching publicity at all times of its operation, improvement of the parole laws and system, a workable indeterminate-sentence law, extension of the honor system, a civil service for guards and employees, abolition of the bat and other severe forms of corporal punishment, improved medical and religious services, a statewide organization to help former convicts adjust to civil life, and restoration of citizenship to all prisoners upon their release.[16]

In March the legislature passed the Teer bill, which provided for the sale of the prison system and its relocation in Central Texas, and appropriated $200,000 to purchase land. Most of the money was to come from the sale of the existing prison farms. The Petticoat Lobby supported the measure. Jim Ferguson criticized the bill because it provided insufficient funds to effect removal and because the five-member committee that was to have charge of selling the farms, buying new land, and fixing the location might overrule the view of the governor and himself. On April 2, Mrs. Ferguson's veto ax fell on the Teer bill. In explaining her veto, she stated that $10 million would be required to relocate the system and that the condition of state finances would not permit such an undertaking at that time. The governor promised to cooperate with the legislature at the appropriate time in taking up the prison-removal matter in "a practical and business way." She added: "There has been recent abuses in the prison system which can not be justified and are justly condemned, and I shall do my best to meet the views of those who are calling for reform along these lines."

The lawmakers appropriated only $100,000 of the $600,000 required to tide over the prison system until its crops were marketed. After conferring with the prison commissioners, who candidly admitted that the system was "broke" and needed money, the Fergusons arranged on June 2 to borrow $200,000 to carry it for three months. Judge W. L. Hill of Houston refused to disclose who advanced the funds, saying that "one of my clients loaned the money to the prison system." Presumably it came from a Houston bank. The terms also were unknown.[17]

Senator Alvin Wirtz's bill to repeal the provision of the Robertson Insurance Law requiring life-insurance companies to invest no less than 75 percent of their Texas reserves in approved Texas securities was killed by the Senate after a stubborn fight, 20 to 8. In an unusual move Lieutenant Governor Barry Miller left his chair to plead for the bill's defeat. "They in their arrogance walked out of the State and threatened us with destruction," he said of the insurance companies. "They would have us buckle the knee, would browbeat us and dictate to us." Legislation aimed at the drugstore liquor traffic, a platform demand, also went by the boards. The Senate passed a bill, but the House refused, 70 to 40, to take it up.[18]

Revenue-producing measures never had a chance. A "big lobby" representing wholesale tobacco jobbers opposed the proposed 10 percent sales tax on cigarettes and cigars, a pet Ferguson measure, and the House Committee on Revenue and Taxation killed it. The same fate befell a 10 percent tax on soft drinks and ice cream. An automobile license fee bill and a bill to increase the gasoline tax from $0.01 to $0.025 per gallon passed the House, but the Senate applied the ax. "I want to charge that the oil and gasoline companies are the ones opposing these measures," declared Senator Walter Woodward of Coleman. "Their lobby has been present here on the floor of this Senate and elsewhere. An attempt has been made here to assassinate these bills, to shoot them in the back." Ferguson told reporters that the "gas tax bill had been killed by the oil lobby." Yet the fact that two houses were able to agree on the major appropriation bills in just sixty-six days was considered a remarkable achievement—"one which would memorialize it for a long time to come," predicted the *Dallas Morning News*. Total appropriations, however, despite campaign pledges of economy, exceeded those made by the Thirty-eighth Legislature by almost $750,000.[19]

Governor Ferguson then went to work with her blue pencil, cutting $1,243,560 from the education appropriation bill, which totaled $14,410,728. The Department of Journalism, the Department of Music, and the School of Library Science in the University of Texas were abolished, along with the office of business manager and $200,000 for two summer-school sessions. There had been a long-standing political feud between Jim Ferguson and Will Mayes, chairman of the journalism department and a former lieutenant governor. Mayes was one of the five university faculty members whose resignation Ferguson had demanded in 1917, saying that Mayes was "editor of a paper [the *Brownwood Bulletin*] that skinned me from hell to breakfast." The Texas A&M Publicity Department was likewise obliterated. Some faculty positions were eliminated at that and several other state schools, and heavy cuts were made in new construction projects. Anticipating "strenuous and outspoken opposition and condemnation" to her vetoes, Mrs. Ferguson declared, "I am sure that before the people condemn me, they will remember that I was elected upon a platform of tax reduction and economy, and my action in this instance is in obedience to that promise." The governor also squeezed $767,338 from the appropriation for state administrative departments, making a total savings of $2 million.[20]

Senator Archer Parr, a loyal Fergusonite, secured passage of a bill allowing legislators and their families to accept free railroad passes, a privilege denied them since 1901. Mrs. Ferguson vetoed it. "While I do not question the sincerity of those who voted for this measure," she declared, "yet I feel that if this bill was to become a law that the sainted Jim Hogg has lived in vain. Though I regret to differ with some of my friends whose purpose I do not question, yet in my opinion the free pass proposition is wrong in principle." The acceptance of a pass was equivalent to accepting money, she said, and was therefore not good public policy. Senator J. D. Parnell of Wichita Falls threatened to pass the free-pass bill over her veto. He grumbled: "Some of us might question the bulging packet of passes which James E. Ferguson carries around as a result of being attorney for the Sugarland Railroad." The veto stood, however, to the satisfaction of the state press. Editorialized the *Dallas Morning News*: "The News would have rejoiced over the decapitation of that sinister measure, regardless of the fashion of the weapon employed, but it is infinitely preferable to have it done with the principle of righteousness."[21]

Klansmen in the legislature marshaled their forces to resist most administration measures passively but to wage a desperate fight on outright anti-Klan laws. "The klan," said a Klan leader in Austin, "may be submerged, but it's not sunk." Representative Luke Mankin, an austere lawyer of Georgetown, introduced an antimask bill and another bill requiring secret organizations to file membership lists with county clerks. The membership-registration bill died on the Senate calendar. The antimask bill as drafted carried the death penalty for one convicted of attacking a person while masked or disguised, but the House Committee on Criminal Jurisdiction substituted a prison sentence. On February 16 the House engrossed the bill by a vote of 79 to 38 after adopting an amendment exempting the Shrine from the prohibition on parades by masked or disguised persons. There was some facetious horseplay as J. W. Stell of Paris offered an amendment exempting "Halloween ghosts and Santa Clauses"; the amendment was turned down by voice vote. Another fun-provoking amendment, ruled out of order by the Speaker, provided that nothing in the act should apply to "deep-sea divers within three miles of shore." An amendment offered by Representative Nathaniel Jacks of Dallas to say that the bill did not apply to Shriners, Knights of Columbus, or any other secret order except the Klan was tabled 56 to 49.

The Senate antimask bill, sponsored by T. J. Holbrook of Galveston, differed from the Mankin bill in not exempting the Shrine. Both measures provided minimum prison sentences of five years for assault by "any two or more persons acting in concert, or aiding and abetting each other" while masked or disguised. Appearance at any public place masked or disguised so as to make identity difficult carried a fine not exceeding $500 or confinement in a county jail for one year or both. Appearance near a private home or the attempt to enter a private home while masked was punishable by imprisonment for a term of one to ten years. Entry into a church by a masked person carried a sentence of two to ten years. Parades by any secret society of masked persons "along any public road or any street or alley of any city or town in this State" was punishable by a fine of $100 to 500 or a county-jail sentence of six months or both, but local Klans still had the right to wear disguises on their own property.

On February 25 the House passed the Mankin bill 84 to 22, and the Senate adopted the Holbrook bill 26 to 1. The House voted 89 to 30 to concur in the Senate's revision of the Mankin bill eliminating the provision exempting the Shrine. As sent to the governor, House Bill 67 covered all secret societies, exempting only social gatherings and church entertainments. Mrs. Ferguson signed the bill on March 9, with a pen that had been fashioned from a steer's horn. "We hope that in doing this we are literally taking the bull by the horns and breaking his neck," she remarked.[22]

In 1929 the State Court of Criminal Appeals held a part of the Mankin law invalid, on the grounds that the disguise was not described by any standard that was specific. In any event, the decline of the Klan had already begun before the law was passed, and two former klansmen interviewed by Charles C. Alexander in May, 1959, denied that it had any effect on membership. Alexander thus found it "doubtful that the Mankin law had a significant part in the denouement of the Texas Klan." According to one estimate, the number of Texas klansmen in mid-1925 stood at under 80,000, a drop of perhaps 50 percent from the previous year. Fort Worth's new Klan auditorium had been burned by incendiaries in 1924, and in 1925 attempts were made on the Klan's Beethoven Hall in San Antonio. The blazing electric cross atop Sam Houston Klan No. 1 headquarters in Houston was taken down, and the building was sold to the city for $187,000. By 1926 the Dallas and Fort Worth chapters were in the hands of Klan receivers. In October, 1924, Dallas Klan No. 66 ousted Zeke Marvin after he failed to be elected exalted cyclops. At the beginning of 1926 the former grand dragon estimated that the Dallas chapter was down from 13,000 members in 1924 to 1,200 and that membership throughout the whole state was less than 18,000. Not a province in Texas could pay its help.[23]

On January 28 the Senate authorized the appointment of a five-member committee to investigate the procedure necessary to restore Jim Ferguson's political rights. Four members of the committee recommended an amnesty law; the chairman, Lloyd E. Price of Daingerfield, submitted a minority report calling for a constitutional amendment. On February 10, after more than three hours of argument over the two plans, the Senate by a vote of 21 to 6 passed General Amnesty Bill 252 restoring Ferguson's political rights. The Fergusons were present on the floor of the Senate chamber during the vote. Attorney General Dan Moody ruled, however, that the measure was invalid because the legislature did not have the power to pardon a person convicted on articles of impeachment by the Senate.

Jim Ferguson then told his friends that he wanted the House to pass the Senate amnesty bill and the Senate to resolve itself into a high court of impeachment to remove his disqualifications and restore his political rights. "I think either is legal," he said, "but in view of the Attorney General's opinion and to be on the safe side I hope both methods will be pursued and then no doubt will exist." On February 18, Ferguson announced that Moody had told him that "the Senate in thirty minutes can turn itself into a court of impeachment and reverse the judgment of 1917." The authority was furnished in the case of *Maddox* v. *Ferguson*, wherein the Texas Supreme Court had held the Senate to be a continuing body. The next day, however, Moody denied that he had committed himself to the legality of such a proceeding. "I did not intend to be understood as giving a committal," he stated. "The suggestion would require an investigation that I had not made."

"The war is on and I do not know where it will end," retorted Ferguson, opening wide the breach between the Fergusons and Moody. He charged that the power and prestige of the attorney general's office was against the goal that was "dearest to our hearts and the thing which we fought for [for] the last seven years and which my wife won so magnificently in the last campaign and election."

"Were you present when Mr. Moody made the statements to your husband?" reporters asked the governor. "Yes, I was," came the prompt reply, "and heard it all." Jim added: "We are fighting a strong combination and fighting for our very lives. We are fighting the Butte press, the Attorney General Dan Moody, and his crowd, all aligned against us, and they are attempting to deny us and the people the right we have won and are entitled to."[24]

The House Judiciary Committee tied on the amnesty bill with 9 members in favor and 9 against and passed the measure out on February 17 without any recommendation other than it be printed. It was the first time in Texas legislative history that such a situation had arisen. The bill was placed on the House calendar, but, with nineteen other Senate bills ahead of it, it stood little chance for prompt consideration. Opponents led by Robert Lee Bobbitt of Webb County, W. D. McFarlane of Young County, and J. W. Hall of Harris County, among others, tried to delay proceedings to prevent the House from reaching it. Proponents had a clear majority of about 15 votes but could not muster the two-thirds majority needed to consider the bill out of its regular order. A group of amnesty supporters then decided to lay every Senate bill on the table subject to call until the Ferguson amnesty bill was reached. Finally, with Speaker Satterwhite acting as peacemaker, the two sides agreed to consider the bill on March 10. After almost seven hours of bitter debate the House passed the bill to a third reading by a vote of 79 to 53, and the following day the bill was approved 78 to 50. Since the measure failed to receive a two-thirds vote, it would not take effect for ninety days after the legislature adjourned. The Senate, however, refused 16 to 13 to resolve itself into a high court of impeachment to modify the 1917 order and restore Ferguson's political rights.[25]

On March 31, Mrs. Ferguson signed the amnesty bill with a gold pen given to her by her Temple friends. In addition to her husband and friends, President Splawn of the University of Texas and two university regents, George W. Tyler and Edward Howard, who had been in conference with the Fergusons, were invited to witness the signing. A battery of cameras was set up, and as the governor finished signing the amnesty bill, the blinds were drawn, there was the blinding glare of a flashlamp, and the closing scene of the eight-year political battle was recorded in photographs. Mrs. Ferguson "was radiant with unconcealed joy and beamed with smiles on those grouped about her for one of the happiest events of her life." Not until Jim again sought office, however, would it be known whether the courts would uphold the bill.[26]

The Thirty-ninth Legislature ended on March 19, and members lost no time making their exit. The pay—two dollars a day for the last six days—sent them home in a hurry. "Probably less time was wasted, more attention concentrated and more sincerity displayed on the public business in this session than in any session in years," the *Dallas Morning News* noted approvingly. "On the whole the Legislature has done well and neither the Governor nor the State has reason to complain. The Governor has already given voice to praise and the State is likely to concur in that praise." Except for the bitter fight over the amnesty bill, Mrs. Ferguson had gotten along with the legislators without serious friction and without truckling or truculence on one side or the other. Her vetoes had been sparing but firm. "The session of the Anti-Klan Legislature was about the most successful that we have seen in Texas," concluded John C. Granbery:

The administration of Mrs. Ferguson has so far been about what we expected—not so very bad and nothing brilliant. The absurdity and falsity of the charges that Selecman, Knickerbocker, and other preachers made all over the State to the effect that her election meant bringing back liquor into Texas, etc. are apparent, as it should have been to them. The platform demand for economy has been rigidly complied with, so that schools and other good causes have not in some instances gotten all they want. Taking it altogether, I would say that the Ferguson administration has been rather better than most that I have known.[27]

Mrs. Ferguson was governor in name only. Her husband set up an office next to hers and was the real power. He attended the meetings of state boards, agencies, and commissions with or without her, received political callers, and "advised." The legislature passed a bill for the disposal of iron-ore properties in East Texas, and Jim found that, busy as he was, he could sandwich in the chairmanship of the board of managers of those properties. The bill provided that the governor must approve any transaction agreed upon by the board. Texans said, "Jim's the Governor, Ma signs the papers." Was Jim present a good deal of the time when Mrs. Ferguson transacted business? Ma's private secretary, Ghent Sanderford, was asked in an interview in 1967. He replied: "Lots of times. That's right. Most all the time. That was true. If he hadn't—if the people hadn't thought that Ferguson would be the governor *himself*, they never would have elected Mrs. Ferguson." He continued: "On the all-important things where there's lots at stake, Ferguson was the controlling . . . he controlled that. But small matters, small matters, routine of the office and like that, she did it. As far as shaping the policies of the governor's office, Governor Jim did it. I think it's fair for me to say that."[28]

Occasionally Jim forgot to maintain the pose of adviser. Once he remarked, "In the first primary I ran second." He quickly corrected himself: "I mean my wife ran second." He added, "We haven't decided whether we will run for governor next year or not." In explaining why an interview must not last too long, he said to a visitor: "I have to leave Austin in about an hour to go to New Braunfels, to talk to some of my constituents." One day Ferguson told Sanderford that he was going to fire Nola Wood, an employee in the secretary of state's office, for disloyalty to him. Sanderford, who thought the disloyalty charge was the work of "a bunch of gossiping women," was furious and shook his finger at Ferguson, saying, "Governor, you are not going to fire Mrs. Wood!" Jim jumped up from his chair, doubled up his fist and hit the top of the desk. "*Who* in the *hell* is *Governor of Texas—you* or *me*?" he demanded. Sanderford shot back, "Neither one of us is Governor!"[29]

There were times, however, when Mrs. Ferguson asserted herself in no uncertain terms. Shortly before she was to take office, Rhea Starnes, a staunch Ferguson backer, found her and Jim in a hot debate over an appointment he wanted made. She declared that the man might have all the qualifications in the world but that he drank liquor and ran around with wild women and she would not have him in her official family. On her first day in office the governor overruled her husband emphatically when he told a reporter that he was going to have a milk cow at the executive mansion. Mrs. Ferguson looked squarely at the reporter and said firmly: "No, there is not going to be any cow at the mansion. I am the Governor and you can say there will be no cow at the mansion." Abashed, Jim said nothing. According to their daughter Ouida, the Fergusons often had "heated arguments" over pardon cases that they took home to review in the evenings.[30]

Mrs. Ferguson had promised in her campaign and in her first message to the legislature to adopt a most liberal pardon policy, and 239 convicts were released in the first seventy days of her administration. By the end of 1925 the number of clemency proclamations had reached 1,201, including full pardons; conditional pardons; paroles; restorations of citizenship; remissions of jail sentences, bond forfeitures, and fines; commutations of death sentences to life imprisonment; and reprieves. During her first twenty months in office she signed more than 2,000 grants of executive clemency, and the final total was 3,595, including 1,318 full pardons and 829 conditional pardons. Nola Wood, who made out the pardons and proclamations, recalled Jim Ferguson's role in a 1977 interview:

Lots of times on the pardons and things—on the commissions—he'd write a memorandum on there: "Issue so and so. Issue so and so." In his handwriting. Why, I wouldn't no more write that up than a thing in the world. Send me to the penitentiary. I'd just roll them back out and say, "Have Governor Miriam write the memorandum on these," and he'd write it out in pencil. Then Governor Miriam would write the same words on there—but in her handwriting. I went through mental agony working for them.[31]

This generous pardon policy soon aroused sharp criticism from press, pulpit, and platform. Every day the *Fort Worth Star-Telegram* published on the front page a prominent box marked "Pardon Record," in which Ma's cumulative executive-clemency totals were listed for all the state to see. The Dallas District Conference of the Methodist Episcopal Church, South unanimously adopted a resolution condemning the governor's wholesale pardoning of criminals as "a menace to law and order and the good of society." On April 28, 1925, in a statement to the people of Texas, Mrs. Ferguson invited her critics to make a personal inspection of the record in each instance, asserting that it was not how many pardons were issued that was important but the worthiness of the cases. "Rave on, ye critics, if you think you can explain your action to your God," she declared. Nothing would deter her from a course of mercy. Notice was given that between fifty and seventy-five pardons would be issued to tubercular convicts in the next thirty days. In addition forty-five "penniless and friendless" black prisoners later received "Juneteenth" pardons. "A lot of politicians are trying to scare up an issue to run for governor on next year," Jim Ferguson told the *Houston Chronicle*. "But if they want to make that the issue, I am willing to take them on and I'll promise them they can't win on it. They are out of accord with all our ideas of mercy and civilization." Ferguson men explained that since Governor Neff had freed very few prisoners Ma was merely "catching up" on a backlog of worthy cases. "Practically all of the pardons granted have been to short-term convicts and all of them with clean records," Ghent Sanderford advised one critic.[32]

The penitentiary was full of short-term liquor-law violators, and since Jim Ferguson was politically "wet," he did not consider these violations serious offenses. In an address to the Texas Bar Association in Austin on July 2, he defended his wife's pardon record and accused the lawyers of not doing their full duty in assuring that the courts administer "even-handed justice" in Texas. He charged that "they knew and he knew hundreds of lawyers in Texas who are violating the liquor laws daily and go unpunished, yet in the courthouse they are sending hundreds of poor men to the penitentiary for committing the same offense and these poor devils have a wife and four or five children unable to make a living like the 'hightoned' lawyer."[33]

On November 28, 1925, in a bold counterattack on their critics, the Fergusons announced that the governor was offering a $500 reward from state law-enforcement funds for the arrest and conviction of liquor-law violators who were worth at least $5,000. Without mentioning names, the proclamation singled out two millionaire newspaper publishers who along with other wealthy Texans had violated the liquor law with impunity while poor people were put in jail for having a pint on their hip or making a little liquor for home consumption. Former Governor Hobby was one of the publishers, and the other was Amon G. Carter of the *Fort Worth Star-Telegram*, with whom the Fergusons were feuding. At the recent University of Texas–Texas A&M Thanksgiving football game in College Station, Carter had paraded in

back of the Ferguson box yelling "Hurray for A&M; Hurrah for Dan
Moody." A policeman escorted him from the grandstand. Jim told reporters that Carter had given a big party for some oilmen in Fort
Worth the previous winter, when his garage had been fitted up like a
saloon; six hundred guests had received three hundred souvenir imita-
tion Bibles (fakes, each with a cavity to hold a pint of liquor) and three
hundred hollow canes with a pint of liquor in each. "We've got one of
the Bibles and one of the canes," chimed in Ma. She added that Carter
had been "drunk as a biled owl" at the football game. "He was waving a
cane and it looked just like one of these canes he had at that dinner. He
probably had it full of liquor."[34]

Shortly thereafter, Governor Ferguson demanded Carter's resignation from the Board of Regents of Texas Tech on the ground that his
behavior had not been an appropriate example for the rising generation. In a letter that several newspapers refused to print, Texas libel
laws being stringent, Carter labeled her charges "without justification"
and refused to resign. "As a matter of fact," he declared, "the accusation of the Governor is so egregious and absurd that it might well be
classed with farce-comedy, but for the evident resentment that lay
back of the charge." Jim Ferguson reportedly remarked, "If Tech's
Board of Directors want to keep him, of course they can," and the incident was closed.[35]

Whispered stories of "purchased pardons" were spreading over
the state. According to one famous anecdote, the father of a convicted
criminal pleaded with Jim Ferguson to intercede with Ma and get a
pardon for his son; Ferguson kept changing the subject to a horse that
he wanted to sell for $5,000. Finally the exasperated father demanded,
"What on earth would I want with a $5,000 horse?" The former gover-
nor replied: "Well, I figure your son might ride him home from the
penitentiary if you bought him." In other versions of the story the ani-
mal was a dried-up cow or a bull, but selling pardons was always the
point. Ouida Ferguson Nalle admitted that the "pardon-selling lie"
brought many offers of payments for pardons. She reported that a lawyer friend of the family offered to split a $5,000 fee fifty-fifty with her if
she would get her mother to grant a pardon to one of his clients. Ferguson's friends avowed that money was needed "to set everything
straight at Austin." Indeed, Dorrace Ferguson Watt said in a 1964
interview: "You know what started all the trouble, don't you? Our

friends. They'd try to get money out of the prisoner, and they'd say: 'Give me $5,000 and I'll give half to the governor. She is a good friend of mine.'" Dan Moody was told of a case in which a Waco man applied to Ferguson for a pardon for a friend and Jim referred him to John Shelton, who told him that it would cost $5,000. The man went back to Waco, and a few days later, so the story went, Shelton wrote him that he could arrange the pardon for $2,500. Ghent Sanderford recalled that a policeman tried to offer Ferguson some money in return for a pardon, placing several bills in his palm when they shook hands. Ferguson was so furious that he ordered the man out of his office with instructions never to return. Sanderford said that it was commonplace for legislators to ask the governor to grant a pardon to a constituent or a client in return for a vote on an administration measure.[36]

Undoubtedly some pardons were granted as political favors and not for merit. B. Y. Cummins of Wichita Falls, a close personal and political friend of Jim's who had secured a number of pardons, stated under oath that he considered it perfectly proper for the governor to grant pardons to the clients of attorneys who were friends of the Fergusons and that such friendship was a sufficient reason for clemency. During the 1926 campaign a Limestone County judge asked Jim Ferguson to restore a Mexia man's citizenship, "as he wants to cast a vote for Mrs. Ferguson in the coming Primaries." The restoration was granted. Jim once insisted that the dean of students in the University of Texas give clemency to the son of a close political friend who faced automatic suspension for being jailed on a drunk-and-disorderly charge. When the dean stood firm and told him that no exception could be made, "Jim didn't like it a bit." An investigating committee of the Thirty-ninth Legislature reported that many of the governor's pardons had been granted on the recommendation of her husband, some even before the criminal reached the penitentiary. (According to one joke that went the rounds, one day when Mrs. Ferguson was in an elevator in the capitol, a man stepped on her foot. "Pardon me," he said. She replied, "You'll have to see Jim.") Yet no clear-cut evidence was ever offered that money actually changed hands. In 1955, Ralph Steen, a student of the Ferguson era, wrote Sanderford, "In my opinion no pardons were sold." In 1979 he wrote:

After more than fifty years these rumors remain rumors. It would be most unusual for a person who bought a pardon to admit it, and certainly no one associated with the administration ever conceded that pardons were sold. It can be added that a person seeking a pardon needed an attorney and that it was good judgment to choose an attorney who was in good standing with the governor.[37]

Critics of the Fergusons also alleged that they profited directly from state textbook adoptions, though, again, the charge was never proved. At a meeting of the State Textbook Commission in Austin on October 12 to 14, 1925, Governor Ferguson recommended that the group meet in executive session and that she appoint a clerk to serve in an administrative capacity. The commission, a majority of whose members were appointed by the governor, concurred, and she named her husband as clerk. Said the *San Angelo Standard* of the action: "If anyone—Jim Ferguson included—can make the voters of this State believe that Jim Ferguson exercised only the insignificant position of a 'humble clerk' in the deliberations of the Textbook Commission, we'll give him the brown derby for being the greatest explainer of all times."[38]

At the meeting Spanish, physiology, biology, general-science, math, and spelling texts were to be adopted, and such large publishing companies as the American Book Company, Ginn and Company, Macmillan, J. B. Lippincott, and World Book had submitted bids. It was advantageous for the state to deal with such firms because of their ability to fulfill their contracts and the attractiveness of their quantity prices. State Superintendent of Education S. L. M. Marrs had earlier written Governor Neff: "There is one thing very confusing to any textbook board, no matter how competent that board may be and that is a lot of these little gnats representing nondescript houses that are getting into the eyes, mouths, and nostrils of these board members. They are here today but tomorrow fly away."

The Textbook Commission received fifteen bids to furnish a two-part speller for six years, with the American Book Company submitting the highest bid. The Fergusons endorsed that company's speller, and on the second ballot, their friend H. A. Wroe voted to adopt it, achieving the necessary majority. In the other five basic categories four books either nominated or supported by Governor Ferguson were eventually adopted. The American Book Company was also to supply one of the five high-school general-science books. Only in the selection of the Spanish book was the governor overruled, and she finally changed her vote to be included in the majority. The contract with the American Book Company called for the sale of thousands of copies of a speller to Texas at a price that was five cents a copy higher than the retail price of a single copy in Cincinnati, Ohio, the location of the company's home office. The selection of the highest-priced speller brought charges of favoritism. "It is understandable that the merit of a particular book may be so great that the fact that it costs most does not interfere with the fact that it is also worth most," editorialized the *Dallas Morning News*. "But it is difficult to imagine that the genius and originality entering into the editing of a textbook on spelling is so great as to require the favoring of the most expensive book offered over less costly competitors."[39]

It was common knowledge that the Fergusons and members of their staff were close friends of Frank R. Adrian, the field agent for the publishing company. "I went to both of them," Adrian later told a House investigating committee. "I recognized the fact that the power of both——." A legislator interrupted: "You recognized the fact that Governor James E. Ferguson had influence over the Board, didn't you?" Adrian replied:

As an agent, I thought he would have something to say perhaps about what his wife might do, but I met them both, just like every other book agent in Texas did. If I could meet Mrs. Ferguson, I did it; if I had a chance to talk to James E. Ferguson, I did it. I was out after a contract. . . . I put up my side of the story. When these Text-book boards meet it is always the American Book Company against Superintendent Marrs.[40]

The State Textbook Commission created a subcommittee made up of Governor Ferguson, Wroe, and Marrs to sign the book contracts after they had been examined and approved by Attorney General Moody—in fact, with his "advice and consent." When Moody ruled on a technicality that the American Book Company had not submitted a valid bid, Mrs. Ferguson and Wroe decided to ignore his ruling and proceed with the execution of the contracts, valued at $600,000. However, Superintendent Marrs, the third member of the subcommittee, refused to go along and omitted the American Book Company's texts from the list of approved titles sent to local school officials.[41]

In what the *Dallas Morning News* called "one of the stormiest sessions ever held by a Texas State Textbook Commission," the body on February 9, 1926, voted 4 to 3 to sustain the subcommittee's action in signing the contracts. During the discussion Marrs charged that agents of the publisher had written the contracts signed by Mrs. Ferguson and Wroe and that the attorney general had never seen them. Jim Ferguson, who was sitting across the table from the superintendent, suddenly jumped to his feet and, striking the table a heavy blow with his hand, shouted loudly enough to be heard in the Capitol corridor: "You know that is an untruth! You know that D. A. Gregg [chief clerk in the secretary of state's office] prepared that form." Ferguson then charged that the attitude of Marrs and Moody toward the American Book Company was "purely political." Ferguson was furious and loudly exclaimed that insinuations and innuendoes of "corruption and irregularities" must cease. Adrian later contradicted Ferguson, however, telling the House investigating committee that "we drew the contract and it was approved by Judge Gregg" with "very slight changes."[42]

The publisher then filed a motion in the Texas Supreme Court for a mandamus against Marrs to compel him to recognize and enforce its contract with the state. The company won a victory when the court held that its contracts were valid and enjoined Marrs "from making any derogatory or damaging statements regarding the validity of relator's contracts." He was further required to include the names of the American Book Company's texts on the requisition blanks sent to local school officials. The attorney general sent one of his assistants to Cincinnati and New York City to investigate the publisher's records, but apparently nothing incriminating was found against the company.[43]

In those days Texas paid the governor only $4,000 a year. A poor man had no business taking the job. Lynch Davidson could afford it (humorist Will Rogers said of him, "Lynch is so rich he can afford to be honest"), but the Fergusons were in straitened circumstances. Two weeks before his wife's inauguration Ferguson remarked: "I am a poor man; in fact worse than poor. We figure our expenses will be increased $20,000 when we move to the capitol, so there was nothing for me to do but to look around for something to do."

The statement related to his employment on December 31, 1924, by W. T. Eldridge of Houston as attorney and adviser at an annual salary of $10,000 plus traveling expenses. Eldridge, president of the Sugarland Railroad, had recently acquired a substantial interest in three other small lines. He also owned sugar and mattress factories. Ferguson had not practiced law for some time, and what service he had agreed to render Eldridge was not precisely detailed. A San Antonian sputtered, "We have a man constitutionally impeached as a felon and forever barred from acting in any official capacity in reality the governor of the state and at the same time on the payroll of the railroads at $20,000 [sic] a year. He openly proves that *law* is impotent when a dic-

tator so declares." According to later testimony by Eldridge, his principal purpose in employing Ferguson was to have him make speeches in
communities to which he hoped to extend his railroad lines. He also
testified that he had a long-standing quarrel with the Prison Commission over a sugar-cane contract.[44]

Apparently finding this annual retainer insufficient for his needs,
Ferguson devised other means of augmenting the family income. Mrs.
Ferguson organized herself into the Capitol Syndicate, Inc., and employed a well-known newspaperwoman, Clare Ogden Davis, as press
secretary to ghostwrite a series of articles under Ma's name offering an
"intimate, woman's angle" on the business of being governor. These
were sold to the newspapers. Jim Ferguson tried to fix a price for the
governor's interviews with writers for eastern magazines and newspapers. "You see, we are very busy here, and we have this thing all
systematized, with a syndicate of our own," he told one writer. "You'd
want us to talk to you, and pose for pictures, and then O.K. what you
wrote. Well, there'd have to be a satisfactory financial arrangement
made first. It cost us $400,000 and many tears to git here, and we ain't
givin' nothin' away!" This practice was soon abandoned, however.[45]

The Fergusons' daughter Ouida Nalle, acting as an agent of the
American Surety Company, wrote surety bonds for road and other contractors and for public officials. "Ouida is her father's own daughter,"
was the way Austin people described her business activities. She established the Capitol Insurance Agency in partnership with Mrs. Ruth
Yett. Later Mrs. Yett sued her for one-half of the $1,878 commission on
a $939,000 surety bond written for a highway contractor plus $1,500 in
damages. She alleged in her petition that Ouida had secured lucrative
highway bonds because she was the governor's daughter and "through
the personal influence and direction of her father" and that she had
expressed a determination to dissolve the partnership and write bonds
singly. Ouida was also a partner in a real-estate firm that was pushing
development at the Colorado River Dam, near Austin. Her husband,
George S. Nalle, promoted stock in the Frank Pavitte Mining Company, which had a twenty-year lease on 128 acres of land in Burnet
County on which lead ore had been found. He wrote letters to prominent friends of the administration, including some legislators, inviting
them to buy stock and to send their checks to him "care Governor's
Mansion, Austin, Texas."[46]

The Ferguson Forum proved an excellent source of revenue. The circulation was no more than 20,000, and it had never carried enough advertising to pay mailing costs. On December 18, 1924, after his wife had been elected governor, Ferguson printed 50,000 copies of a special edition of the paper. It was a twenty-eight-page, seven-column issue, with 2,674 inches of advertising and 1,246 inches of reading matter. In big red type across the front was the line "Good Will Edition of the Forum," underneath which appeared in bold black type: "To Unite All Political and Religious Factions, To Pull Together for a Greater Texas and a Greater Prosperity." All but 19 inches of the advertisements were for firms that would have occasion to seek business or favors from the state government.

Among the companies buying full-page ads (at $250 a page) were the Southern Pacific Railroad, the Paramount Motion Picture Corporation, the Humble Oil and Refining Company, the Southwestern Bell Telephone Company, the Uvalde Rock Asphalt Company, and two road-contracting concerns. Half-page ads were purchased by the *Houston Chronicle*, the Houston Gas and Fuel Company, the Houston Creamery Company, the First National Bank of Houston, the Houston Power and Light and Houston Power Company, Clark and Courts (a Galveston stationers firm), the New Braunfels Brewery Company, and six road contractors and highway-material and machinery companies. Nineteen other firms bought less expensive ads. Several companies, including the Texas and Pacific Railroad, declined to purchase advertising but bought multiple $2 subscriptions to the *Forum*. On January 1, 1925, there was another "Good Will Edition" of twenty pages, twelve of them advertising, mostly for different companies but in the same lines of business as those advertising in the earlier issue. An advertising solicitor for the *Forum* estimated that about $17,000 was collected from these two issues. [47]

Jim followed with "Farm to Mill" and "Great Development" editions and a full-page ad in each weekly issue described as "part of a series to promote the building of more good roads in Texas, and . . . contributed by the undersigned public-spirited citizens who have at heart the best interests of this great state." The signatures represented twenty-six firms, including four road-material companies and twenty-two road contractors. Wrote journalist Don H. Biggers: "To a discerning person every one of those ads cried out loud: 'Influence for sale,' on one hand, and 'we are buying influence,' on the other." [48] Or, as the heading of Jim's front-page editorial aptly expressed it, "Good Will Is a Tangible Asset."

Whittaker Broadnax, of the American Road Company, quoted Ferguson's advertising solicitor, Joseph Furst, as assuring him:

"I understand that you people gave twenty thousand dollars to the Ku Klux. We are going to bury the hatchet, and get together and put this good roads campaign over, and have lots of money to build good roads. I don't mean to say by this, that you are going to get contracts, but if you will advertise, you will get work and everything will be on the square."

A Houston contractor said that Furst told him that "Jim needed the money badly." Ferguson first approved the names on the solicitation list and then gave Furst a letter directed to them personally. A photostat of the following letter, dated February 27, 1925, from Ferguson to D. T. Austin, of Haden and Austin, a Houston contracting firm—on State Executive Department stationery—is in the Oscar B. Colquitt Papers:

Dear Mrs. Austin:

I want to ask your co-operation in a movement to promote the building of "*More and Better Roads*" in Texas.

To that end, I have devoted a section of my paper, "*The Forum*," to an instructive campaign of "*Facts and Figures*"; that the people of our great state may be awakened to the urgent need of "*Good Roads*" and take the action to build them.

I have asked Mr. Furst to call on you and explain our plans more fully; and I assure you that I shall appreciate your support in this matter.

"In all my solicitations . . . I didn't do much talking; I did a lot of listening," Furst told a House investigating committee. "I would walk in and present my letter, and they would right immediately go into their song about their life-long loyalty and devotion to Jim Ferguson." He was asked, "You attributed a good deal of that to the fact that Mr. Ferguson had gone through the lists and given you the names?" He answered, "No, I just attributed it to the fact that they were lying."[49]

Road contractors told the committee about purchasing space in the *Forum* to "please Jim." C. E. Hoff, of the San Antonio firm Colglazier and Hoff, said that his company agreed to pay $1,000 for advertising to "avoid the ill will of Jim Ferguson, and get an even break on highway contracts to be let." W. A. Boyett of Bryan testified that he had paid $1,500 for advertising, believing that "Jim would feel more friendly than if I had refused to buy space," and added that he appreciated Ferguson's help in getting a $76,000 maintenance contract in Brazos, Robertson, Waller, and Madison counties. "I didn't think it would make him mad," Holland Page, a Lockhart contractor, replied when asked whether he had felt that buying $1,200 in advertising would win Ferguson's goodwill. Page testified that before he left the office of the State Highway Department, after having been awarded a $65,000 maintenance contract for Guadalupe and Gonzales counties, Joe Furst approached him, and he agreed to buy advertising, paying $600 down and the rest within thirty days. Jim Ferguson was present when the contract was awarded, Page testified, "but didn't say anything." Immediately after his conference with Furst, and within thirty minutes after the contract was awarded, Page went to the governor's mansion, where he arranged with Ouida Nalle to buy a $65,000 surety bond costing $650 through the American Surety Company. H. T. Rainey, a farmer near Lockhart and an "old friend of the Fergusons," had asked Page to let her handle the bond.[50]

Practically all the state employees in the capitol subscribed to the *Forum*. In June, 1925, W. B. Shoe, head of the Workmen's Compensation Division of the State Fire Insurance Commission, announced that he had been asked to resign because he had refused to subscribe to the paper. A circular signed by Jim was mailed to University of Texas faculty members asking them to subscribe in anticipation of the coming campaign of 1926. Former State Representative Sam E. Johnson, Jr., a highway-section foreman in Blanco and Gillespie counties, told the investigating committee that during the campaign a man named House, the maintenance engineer, had asked all the men working on the road to subscribe to the *Forum* so that Ferguson could defend himself. Johnson never asked any of the men to do it, but twelve or fifteen thought it was "all right," and each gave him a dollar to send to the *Forum* office.[51]

No one could say how much money Ferguson made after his wife became governor. His close friends said that he frankly felt that the state had made him the victim of ghastly and conscienceless persecution in the course of which it had stripped him of all that he had and that his comeback gave him an ethical and moral right to make all the money he could, as long as he made it within the law.[52]

At the end of Neff's administration Texas had 16,445 miles of designated state highways. Its revenues for highway construction and maintenance—derived from federal aid, a gasoline tax, and the vehicle-license system—amounted to about $20 million a year. This was a greater sum than the state spent for higher education, eleemosynary institutions, and the judiciary combined. The State Highway Department employed 3,500 persons directly and 5,000 more indirectly. The state was divided into sixteen highway districts, and in each one a division engineer supervised both construction and maintenance. The state highway engineer selected the division engineers with the approval of the highway commissioners. Each of the three part-time highway commissioners was paid the small annual salary of $2,500, but together they exercised nearly absolute administrative powers.

At their first meeting on February 16, 1925, the commissioners—Frank V. Lanham, Joe Burkett, and John Bickett, Sr.—divided the state into three parts, each with six districts (two new ones were created); each commissioner was to supervise one part. Lanham's territory embraced north and northeast Texas; Burkett's, West Texas and the Panhandle; and Bickett's, South and Southeast Texas. Bickett was in ill health and seldom attended meetings, and Lanham and Burkett awarded most of the highway contracts. The spoils system was inaugurated when the custom of allowing the division engineer to select his maintenance superintendent and section foreman was discontinued and the commissioners filled these positions themselves. The new appointees often lacked road experience. "Many of them were what I would call broken down war horses and second rate politicians, with some influence in their communities," noted maintenance engineer Leo Ehlinger, who resigned in February, 1925. He added, "Some were men who would do what they were told to do, regardless of whether it was ethical or not, and some were not exactly honest." R. J. Hank, who replaced Gibb Gilchrist as state highway engineer, was merely a figurehead; during his whole tenure he selected only one division engineer, and that was in an emergency.[53]

J. Harvey Briggs of San Antonio, a crushed-rock salesman who had known Lanham for years, wrote the legislators on February 15, 1925:

It is the firm belief of the greater majority of the men who built the roads in Texas,—the engineers, contractors and material men, that under the newly appointed Highway Commissioners the fine department we have had in the past will be entirely wrecked or very badly crippled, there remaining only a Department that will function mostly as a political machine.

Because Briggs would not tell a legislative committee the names of engineers and contractors he claimed to represent, he was not permitted to present his case against the State Highway Commission.[54]

The highway commissioners invited Jim Ferguson to sit with them at their meetings. "I though I ought to accept their kind invitation so as to bring about an effective and economical administration," he explained. He never missed a meeting; and on one occasion when it was not convenient for him to attend, the meeting was postponed. Before Mrs. Ferguson's inauguration all commission meetings had been open to the public; now they were held behind closed doors. N. R. Sinclair, of the *San Antonio Express*, told O. B. Colquitt, "[Alvin] Wirtz, I heard, attended a meeting of the highway commission at which Ferguson presided and slit open envelopes containing bids and decided who would get contracts."[55]

Contracts were awarded to men or firms who had never before built or maintained roads. Merchants, doctors, lawyers, politicians, farmers, ranchers, ginners, and others became contractors overnight. To receive these contracts, they formed road-building firms, such as the Houston County Construction Company, the Marine Construction Company, the Panola Construction Company, and the South Texas Construction Company. It was difficult for the public to learn the identities of the real owners of the new firms. For example, the Washington Construction Company was Joe Baker, a farmer, and L. W. Hensley, another farmer, was the Franklin Construction Company. One thing they all had in common: they either were loyal Ferguson men or had advertised in the *Ferguson Forum*.[56]

Huge sums were spent in Ferguson's native Bell County—a total of $721,169.18 from February 15, 1925, to October 11, 1926. Frank Denison, a Temple hardware merchant and one of Ferguson's closest friends, was awarded a $23,450 contract for maintaining the highways in the county and an indefinite contract to build what came to be called the "Invisible Highway," a five-mile road between Temple and Belton that consisted of two strips of brick about eighteen inches wide for each lane laid on a crushed-rock base. Under the agreement the more the pavement cost, the more Denison would make, since he was to receive cost plus 10 percent profit. Denison, not being a contractor, promptly hired the General Construction Company of Fort Worth to do the work. Much of the equipment used in building the road was purchased from Denison's store. S. B. Moore of La Porte, the patentee of the In-

visible Highway, was employed at a salary of $375.00 a month to super-
vise construction and was given the title "Consulting Engineer to the
State Highway Commission." The Invisible Highway, which proved to
be completely worthless, cost $49,022.40 a mile, including under-
passes and culverts. Denison also received a $25,248 contract for Falls
County, a $30,702.00 contract for Milam County, and a $40,085.00 contract for Williamson County.[57]

Charles Hurdleston, who had been a railroad commissioner under
Jim Ferguson, was awarded a contract for approximately $112,000 to
maintain the roads in four counties. He organized the Marine Construction Company and assigned the contract to it. The capital stock of
the company was $5,000—half of which had to be put up as a bond—
and that half was paid out of the first monthly payment received from
the state under the contract. Hurdleston had been Ferguson's choice
to fill the vacancy of the 1924 Democratic state ticket occasioned by
Splawn's withdrawal as a candidate for railroad commissioner to become president of the University of Texas. When friends remonstrated
with him that Hurdleston was a klansman, Ferguson said: "Yes, Charlie
Hurdleston has a perfectly good explanation of all that and I am going
to have him go before the committee and make his explanation tomorrow. Charlie Hurdleston is in the contracting business in Fort Worth,
and he joined the Ku Klux Klan so that he could get some contracts. Of
course, nobody could blame him for that." Despite the explanation,
however, C. V. Terrell received the nomination. "In reference to the
support of Hurdleston for Railroad Commissioner," Ferguson wrote
M. M. Crane afterward, "I beg to advise, that I never agreed to support him until he had furnished me an official certificate from the
Cyclops of the Fort Worth Klan that he, Hurdleston, had resigned
from the Klan on June 10th of this year."[58]

As early as December, 1924, General Crane had warned Ferguson
that his enemies were whispering that "some one or more unworthy
men would be put in as Road Commissioners, in the disbursement of
the large funds that come into their hands." Tom Love, who called Ferguson the "outstanding corruptionist of all time," advocated a policy of
"watchful waiting" for the friends of good government, looking to the
Democratic primary of 1926. When he heard rumors that Ferguson
was granting pardons in his wife's name and had been employed as an
attorney by road companies to represent them before the Highway
Commission, in the last hours of the session Love tried unsuccessfully

to have the House of Representatives appoint a committee to "sit in vacation and investigate from time to time the action of the Governor along these lines."[59]

In July, 1925, Silliman Evans, a staff correspondent of the *Fort Worth Star-Telegram*, told his employer, Amon Carter, that he had information that highway contracts had been let to friends of Highway Commissioners Lanham and Burkett without competitive bidding, without bonds, and at excessively high prices. Beginning on July 16, Evans conferred several times with Louis W. Kemp, executive secretary of the Texas Highway and Municipal Contractors Association, about graft in the State Highway Department. Evans explained that the *Star-Telegram* planned to run a series of articles on road building in Texas and publicize some of the irregularities in the department. Kemp was new to his job, having resigned as general manager of the Texas Rock Asphalt Company on July 1, 1925. He gave Evans what information he had and suggested some questions to ask R. J. Hank, the state highway engineer, but neither man was in a position to make open charges against the commissioners. Hank passed the questions on to Lanham, whose answers were published on August 11, 1925.[60]

On August 10, Kemp had breakfast in Austin with D. T. Austin, whose Houston firm, Haden and Austin, was a member of the Municipal Contractors Association. Austin complained that the Sherman-Youmans Construction Company of Houston, which had a state contract to maintain the highways in Harris and Galveston counties, was using state-owned equipment on a private paving job in Goose Creek. He said that it was Kemp's duty to have such practices stopped. Kemp agreed and asked Austin to find out whether the equipment was still in use in Goose Creek or in any other cities and report his findings. On August 13, Haden and Austin wired Kemp: "They are doing the same thing here on Boundary Street in Houston today that they did at Goose Creek." Kemp went to Houston, and after talking with members of the association and with E. S. Atkinson, the division engineer, decided to report his findings to Jim Ferguson. E. J. Hussion, a staunch Fergusonite, gave Kemp a letter of introduction to the former governor.

Kemp called at the governor's office on the morning of August 15 and thanks to Hussion's letter reached Ferguson's desk without delay. When he explained his errand, Ferguson first asked whether he was representing "that Ku Klux crowd down at Houston." He demanded three or four times, "Are you (the association) for or against this administration?" When Kemp replied that the association was nonpolitical, Ferguson persisted: "You can't be that, you have got to be on one side or the other. Are you for or against this administration?" He continued, "If you are lining up with that bunch of Klu Kluxers and grafters down there to persecute these boys [Sherman-Youmans], the war is on." The conversation lasted thirty or forty minutes, and Kemp left without knowing what action the former governor would take.

Kemp walked from Ferguson's office to Attorney General Dan Moody's office and told him about his visit. Moody promptly replied that he would see to it that state equipment was removed from Boundary Street in Houston. The *Houston Chronicle* of August 16 carried an interview with contractor L. W. Sherman in which he said: "Of course I know him [Kemp]. I care nothing about him. If he keeps on I will tell how he and others have told me that they were organized to freeze out every little contractor. . . . I will call the Attorney General's attention to their activities." Sherman's statement prompted Kemp to ask Moody to investigate the activities of the Texas Highway and Municipal Contractors Association. Moody remarked, "It looks like someone else needs to be investigated." That night, August 17, in Silliman Evans's room in the Stephen F. Austin Hotel, Kemp met with Moody, Assistant Attorneys General George Christian and Ernest May, and a stenographer and told them about irregularities in the State Highway Department.[61]

The next morning Moody filed an injunction suit in the Fifty-third District Court to restrain the Sherman-Youmans Company from using State Highway Department equipment on private contracts. Lanham scored the attorney general for his suit and for what he termed Kemp's "strong-arm methods." Referring to the controversy as an "excellent example of raising a tempest in a teapot," he charged that the Texas Highway and Municipal Contractors Association was harassing an independent operator who had submitted the lowest bid in Harris County. "The whole thing started with a bunch of Ku Kluxers and a few sore-head contractors who have been kicked away from the pie counter," Ferguson told the *Houston Chronicle*. Moody's request for an injunction was denied after the attorney for Sherman-Youmans gave assurances that the firm would no longer use state equipment on private contracts.[62]

On August 20, Kemp called on Lanham at his office and told him that the price of 30 cents a square yard to resurface highways provided

for in many of the contracts the commissioners were awarding was ex-
orbitant and that even 11 cents a square yard would be high. Lanham
replied that if Kemp knew of any contractor willing to do similar work
at the lower price he would be given all the work he could handle.
"Mr. Kemp seems to think that the members of his association are
going to have a little barbecue here tomorrow and that he is to furnish
the goat meat," the chairman told Raymond Brooks, of the *Austin
Statesman.* Kemp interpreted Lanham's statement as an ultimatum to
the association to fire him.

Jake Doyle telephoned R. J. Potts of Waco, president of the association, and several directors, to protest vigorously Kemp's actions in
the Sherman-Youmans controversy. Doyle was vice-president of the
Uvalde Rock Asphalt Company, a firm known to be close to the Ferguson administration. Potts hurriedly called a meeting of the board of directors, most of whom had lucrative contracts with the Highway Department. Meeting in Lanham's office on the morning of August 21,
they heard Kemp tell the highway chairman that the commission was
engaging in corrupt practices. Lanham insisted that all remarks be
confined to Boundary Street in Houston and threatened to adjourn the
meeting if Kemp kept "butting in."

The directors went to the Stephen F. Austin Hotel to consider the
case and later returned to the Highway Department without Kemp for
another meeting with Lanham. At about five o'clock Potts told Kemp
that it appeared that his resignation would be requested. Kemp replied: "I am guilty of offending Frank Lanham but I refuse to resign. I
want to be *fired.*" It was then announced that the office of executive
secretary had been declared vacant effective September 1. Potts, however, later telephoned Kemp and asked him to remain until September
10, and Kemp agreed.

Potts wrote Kemp on August 25 that "it would be desirable both
from your standpoint and ours for you to make some reference in your
daily letter to recent action of the Board." Kemp decided to mention
the matter in not only one but all of his newsletters. Inasmuch as he
felt himself the "goat," he decided to head future letters: "Goat Bleats,"
and instead of confining the mailing list to association members, he
added other names as well. Much of the information on irregularities
in the State highway department that he had previously given to
Moody he now intended to furnish to the general public. "The First
Bleats," run off on a duplicating machine in Kemp's room at the Elks

Club, appeared on August 26, with the details of his firing, and other "Bleats" followed daily. Potts, who was vacationing in Atlanta, Georgia, wired Kemp to "discontinue these statements entirely and immediately" and ordered him to vacate his office by September 1.[63]

According to Kemp, many of the state's major newspapers were afraid to publish his charges against the State Highway Commission because in past years they had been forced to pay Jim Ferguson thousands of dollars for statements they had printed about him. "An odd situation existed in Texas," he noted later. "The State was being robbed of millions of dollars in broad daylight while the newspaper reporters helplessly looked on." On September 3, however, Don H. Biggers of Fredericksburg called on Kemp. Biggers, a crusading free-lance journalist, had made many earnest but unsuccessful attempts to establish a periodical to carry his views of current Texas politics and events. He had kept up with Kemp's row with Ferguson, writing him: "It seems to me that there are elements of real interest and front page stuff in this scrap. . . . For some time the atmosphere throughout the state has been putrid with 'counsellor' Jim rumors. Where there is so much smoke there must be a few smouldering embers, and this little match may start a conflagration." He hoped to give Kemp's data wide publicity and gain some financial backing through an anti-Ferguson movement. Biggers showed Kemp the proofs of a number of articles compiled from the "Goat Bleats" he was going to publish in the weekly *Johnson City Record-Courier*, of which he was associate editor, and stated that he would print anything Kemp would write. Kemp agreed to furnish copy at no cost and to discontinue "Goat Bleats."[64]

After the *Johnson City Record-Courier* began running Kemp's articles, the little weekly's circulation jumped almost overnight. "Every mail brings more subscriptions," the paper noted on October 16. "Nearly 200 since last issue. Honestly we don't know how so many people heard about the *Record-Courier*, and the fight we are making." According to Biggers, fifteen people had made a donation of approximately $100 each to send the paper to every county judge in Texas, many county commissioners, all members of the legislature, and a number of interested individuals. Meanwhile, Silliman Evans continued to offer Kemp encouragement. "You are doing us a great service, and I personally appreciate your kindness," he wrote on September 6. "We are optimistic at the developments now under way. . . . Keep it up." To publicize his charges and force the big daily papers to notice them, Kemp addressed the annual meeting of the County Judges and County Commissioners Association in Amarillo on September 28; he told of irregularities in the administration of highway department business and charged that exorbitant prices had been paid for road surfacing.[65]

Meanwhile, Moody had continued his highway investigation, and on October 16, he wrote Lanham directing the cancellation of contracts in thirty-three counties because they had been let for sums substantially higher than the lowest bids. It was not within the State Highway Commission's discretion, he said, "arbitrarily to reject the lowest bid for one substantially higher, especially when it is awarding to such rejected low bidders contracts covering other counties." Moody gave figures showing that accepted bids totaled $1,034,112, while lower bids totaled $872,976.25, a difference in favor of the lower bidders of $161,135.75. Lanham refused Moody's request and defended the commission's policy of awarding contracts to what it considered the best if not always the lowest bidders. He characterized the attorney general's letter as "giving an opinion dictating the policy of the Highway Commission, which was not requested," adding that "it was evidently done with the intention of creating in the public mind the thought that the Highway Commission was simply dealing out contracts in the nature of plums and with no other basis to work upon."[66]

Some legislators were urging the governor to call a special session to deal with tick eradication, an outbreak of hoof-and-mouth disease in the coastal counties, and relief of the drought-stricken central portion of the state and to investigate state departments. On October 17, Mrs. Ferguson announced that she would not put the taxpayers to the expense of a special session, since "nine-tenths of this talk about a special session, is either inspired by some prospective candidate for Governor or his intimate friends, or it is some disappointed county official who wants me to call a 'they say' legislature and open it so that the gossipers may come down and air 10,000 rumors not based on one fact." She invited those who thought that the laws were being violated to take their complaints to the courts or before the grand juries. "I have no one to protect and if any appointee under my administration is guilty of any wrong or violation of any law, just report that fact to me by any credible testimony and it will not be necessary to call the Legislature or anybody else to remove such appointee from office," she promised.[67]

On October 23, Governor Ferguson asked the State Highway

Commission to withhold payments to contracts for surfacing or topping work until the contracts had been fully completed and final disposition had been made of any suit that Moody might bring to cancel them. Promising to comply, Lanham stated that when all the facts had come to light "the wind will have been taken out of the wild reports concerning State Highway matters." Moody immediately retorted: "This letter was written by James E. Ferguson for 'political reasons' he has occasionally attributed to me, and is a belated effort to save his administration from the condemnation that may result when the people of Texas know the extent of the extravagance practiced in awarding contracts for surfacing State highways." On October 26 the three highway commissioners sent a letter to Moody's office, hand-carried by a secretary, Eugene T. Smith, pointedly refusing to cancel road contracts in thirty-one counties as the attorney general had directed in his October 15 letter. Only in Camp and Limestone counties were steps taken to cancel contracts.[68]

It was revealed at this time that $436,800.26 in state payments for road work, deposited in a Kansas City, Missouri, bank by the American Road Company, had been returned to Dallas and placed in escrow in the American National Bank, subject to the orders of Moody and the company president or the final judgment of the courts in any suit arising out of the highway investigation. Of this money, $319,000 had been voted in dividends to stockholders, and their endorsed checks were turned over to the bank. Returning from Dallas, where he had received reports from the company and from auditors who had examined its books as well as those of another firm, whose name was not revealed, Moody told reporters that he intended to protect the state from "grossly improvident contracts let for an unconscionable price."[69]

On November 5, Moody filed suit in the Fifty-third District Court of Travis County against the American Road Company for cancellation of contracts to surface highways in a number of counties, forfeiture of its permit to do business in Texas, and recovery of $650,000 in excessive profits. He alleged that the state had paid $1,719,480 to the company under these contracts and that the company had furnished the asphalt and subcontracted the work at a cost of $603,768—the state furnishing the cover materials—leaving a profit of $1,115,712. According to the petition, when it was chartered in Delaware solely for the purpose of contracting with the Texas Highway Commission, the American Road Company had as assets one Merriam railroad asphalt plant (purchased from Frank Lanham's Texas Road Company), three Ford automobiles, one Buick automobile, one Studebaker automobile, and $10,000 in cash in the bank. Discussing the figures, Moody said that the contracts had run one-third of their course and that if costs remained the same during the last two-thirds the total profit would be in excess of $3 million on state payments of approximately $6 million. Former State Highway Engineer Gibb Gilchrist advised the attorney general on the technical aspects of road engineering, providing information on excessive per-yard asphalt costs, reasonable weather conditions for roadwork, the advisibility of second-course asphalt treatments, and other engineering-related matters. In addition, he appeared as an expert witness for the state in the American Road and Hoffman suits.[70]

Mrs. Ferguson instructed the State Highway Commission to resist the suit by intervening with the assistance of attorneys paid out of the state treasury. She contended, in defense of her stand, that the attorney general had no authority to bring suit in the name of the state unless so directed by the governor. According to Lanham, the 30 cents per square yard specified for asphalt surfacing provided in the contract was understood by all parties to mean a two-course treatment. This argument was seriously weakened, however, because the American Road Company had been paid not only for work done but for work yet to be done and had not been required to give a surety bond for the performance of its contract obligations. Moreover, to justify the prices paid, Lanham assumed that there was to be a second-course treatment in every instance, whereas the terms of the contract showed that that was not contemplated. In a belated attempt to legitimatize its position, the Highway Commission ordered the American Road Company to make a $500,000 bond to ensure faithful performance of its contract and asked for a complete second-course application of asphalt. W. K. McIllyar, the president of the company, replied that "in acknowledgement of your authority to so order, the American Road Company, in keeping with the contract, stands ready, able, and willing to begin the work ordered by your maintenance engineer not later than December 1, 1925."[71]

Moody resisted the plea of intervention, and the district judge hearing the suit, George Calhoun, denied it, holding that the attorney general had authority to sue the American Road Company. The ensuing settlement, reached after counsel for both sides had been closeted with the judge in his chambers for several hours, was a notable victory for the state. Officials of the road company accepted cancellation of all existing state highway contracts, agreed to cancellation of their permit to do business in Texas, and confessed to judgment for $600,367.90, less a credit of $314,342.79 representing approved but unpaid estimates on work already done. They also agreed to return $285.025.41 to the state treasurer. The state press hailed the attorney general's "splendid victory." From Austin, Silliman Evans wired Louis Kemp, who had accepted a position with the Texas Company in Iowa: "Dan Moody had a barbecue today. Frank Lanham furnished the goat meat."[72]

The sequel to the American Road Company suit was the resignation of Lanham and Burkett from the State Highway Commission. Asked about a successor, Lanham replied, "I don't know, but either Jack Dempsey or Red Grange is needed, for the job demands a man who can either fight or run." Bickett, who was still in ill health and had not approved the American Road Company contract, escaped most of the criticism and was allowed to remain. It was alleged that Burkett had been instrumental in the awarding of large noncompetitive, non-bond contracts at the 30-cent rate to the Hoffman Construction Company of Eastland, which was composed of his friends. Moody sued in the Fifty-third District Court for cancellation of the company's road contracts and asked for damages in the amount of $100,000 and the withholding of further payments of $351,047 in state funds, making the total amount sought $451,047. The petition also asked that a receiver be appointed to take charge of the company's property. This suit was not settled until December, 1926. Trial testimony revealed that Joe Burkett had received a $19,000 loan from the president of the company, as well as $400 or $500 from a stockholder for a trip to California to investigate paving and $200 more when he investigated paving in New Jersey. After the state had concluded its testimony to show that the contract price and profits were excessive, the defense elected not to offer testimony and confessed judgment for $412,000. All state highway contracts held by the company were canceled. Only the suit against the Sherman-Youmans Construction Company remained to be tried. On March 6, 1927, the state received a judgment against the firm for $7,198.56.[73]

In the meantime, renewed demands were heard that Governor Ferguson call a special session of the House. Some anti-Fergusonites considered the American Road Company deal grounds for ousting her

from office. "Let's impeach Ma!" they cried. Following a conference in
the Stephen F. Austin Hotel on November 23, forty-five members of
the legislature issued a virtual ultimatum to the governor; unless she
announced by December 10 that she would convene the legislature on
January 4, they would meet without her call. Alfred P. C. Petsch of
Fredericksburg, who had been House floor leader of the Ferguson amnesty bill, delivered the ultimatum to Mrs. Ferguson's private secretary, Ghent Sanderford. Fifty-two legislators, two more than the necessary number, signed a petition asking Speaker Lee Satterwhite to call a
session in the event Mrs. Ferguson refused to act. Satterwhite immediately announced that, "in event the Governor does not call a special
session of the Thirty-ninth Legislature by Dec. 15, by the power
vested in me through the petition by the members of the Legislature I
shall call the session." [74]

Jim Ferguson hit back at his critics, declaring that both Satterwhite and Moody wanted to be governor of Texas. The present trouble
in his wife's administration was caused, he said, by "disgruntled contractors, County Commissioners who had lost their clabber on highway
contracts and men with political bees in their bonnets." "We have skinned the Ku Klux Klan, and so few are left that they are afraid to come
out into the open and fight," the former governor declared, daring
enemies to produce evidence before a grand jury. He declined to say
what the governor was going to do about the special-session ultimatum. Lieutenant Governor Barry Miller later told a reporter for the
Dallas Journal that he talked to Jim about a special session. "His
friends were all advising him to call a special session. He felt that it
ought to be called, although he didn't come right out and say that,"
Miller said. Mrs. Ferguson asked what the two men were talking
about. Her eyes flashed, and she pounded the table with her fist. "I
won't do it," she told them: "They can't make me do it. That's what
caused all the trouble for Jim and I'm not going to let them get me
in the same mess. They got him to call a special session and bought
enough votes to impeach him. There's a lot of money behind this fight
on us and they'll do the same thing to me."

When the Travis County Grand Jury, which had devoted much of
its time since October 5 to a highway investigation, adjourned on November 28 without returning any indictments in connection with state
departments, Ferguson laughingly remarked, "Now some of the pa-

pers which have been headlining 'another Moody victory,' should
come across and proclaim 'another Moody defeat.'"[75]

It was at this time that the Fergusons announced that the governor was offering a $500 reward from state law-enforcement funds for
the arrest and conviction of liquor-law violators who were worth at
least $5,000. This was soon followed by a demand that Amon Carter
resign from the Texas Tech Board of Regents. Will Rogers joked that
Jim reminded him of his first car, an old Overland:

It had some of the most terrible noises and knocks. People would say, "Will,
get that noise fixed." But I wouldn't. I would just keep on and in a few days a
worse one would drown out that one, and that's what Jim did. He made the
highway drown out the pardon scandal, and now he has made the "Liquor Enforcement for the Rich" drown out interest in the highways.[76]

The anti-Ferguson camp announced that Will Hogg and T. K. Irwin (the latter had been the Klan candidate for speaker against Satterwhite) would undertake to raise $300,000 to underwrite the cost of a
special session, since many representatives were too poor to pay their
own expenses. Asked about the report, Hogg indicated that he would
join in such a guarantee at the request of the Speaker and a majority of
the House of Representatives, "who now seem impelled by patriotic
duty and an aroused public opinion to investigate the Ferguson administration." "However," Hogg continued, "I would heaps rather join a
syndicate to pension Jim and turn him out to grass with plenty of
money which he appears to love very much."[77]

The Ferguson forces seized upon this underwriting scheme to
launch their counterattack. Making the most of his opponents' "slush-
fund" blunder, Farmer Jim declared that rich men, aligned with the
Klan, were trying to bribe the legislature to get at him through his wife
because he had fought the hooded order and beaten it and because he
had been "agin high rents, agin high taxes, and agin high interest."
Some of the petitioners for the session were klansmen, and Senator
Earle Mayfield had asked the United States Department of Justice to
launch a "sweeping investigation" of the highway situation in Texas.
Ferguson also began pulling political strings behind the scenes, and
there were many conferences at the capitol and in Austin hotels. Virtually everyone in the state, except the most violent anti-Ferguson partisans, sided with the Fergusons on the underwriting issue. Moody is-

sued an opinion holding that it would be against public policy for private or individual sources to underwrite the expenses of a special session for impeachment purposes and that there was no authority for issuing warrants against the legislature's exhausted contingency fund. In view of the lack of funds and the strong possibility that Ferguson could control at least eleven votes in the Senate—even if the House did vote to impeach—the belief spread that it would not be worthwhile to try impeachment proceedings.[78]

There were other reasons for the ebbing of the impeachment tide. The more moderate elements of the anti-Ferguson group argued that it would be a serious mistake to maneuver themselves into a position where they might be charged with sacrificing a woman to their desire for vengeance against Jim Ferguson. "Ferguson," warned the *Houston Press*, "has turned one impeachment to his advantage." Strengthening this attitude was the fact that investigation had not fixed any personal responsibility on Mrs. Ferguson for the highway "scandals," except that she let her husband run things for her, and he held no official position. Texas feminist leaders felt sorry for Ma, declaring that she was a "slave wife" and a mere figurehead and blaming everything on "Governor Jim." Still another factor in the reaction was that Texans were beginning to be embarrassed by the nationwide publicity given to their troubles with the Fergusons. There had not been many impeachments of governors in American history, and they did not like the idea of having two chalked up against them.[79]

Some people were hoping for a compromise that would keep things "clean" for the rest of the present administration and then get rid of the Fergusons, forever, if possible. Jim was reported to have promised that he would keep his hands off highway contracts during the next fourteen months and that neither he nor his wife would run in the next gubernatorial campaign. Arthur B. Eidson, chairman of the State Democratic Executive Committee, announced after a conference with the Fergusons that he did not think either would be a candidate in 1926. Jim, however, was said to have his eye on running for Mayfield's Senate seat in 1928.[80]

Attorney General Moody's apparent success in reaching an understanding with the State Highway Commission was partly responsible for the belief that "things would go on all right" with state affairs. He conferred with the two new members, Chairman Hal Mosely of Dallas, a civil engineer and graduate of A&M, and John Cage, a Stephenville businessman, and indicated his approval of their attitude. Reportedly they gave assurances that they would cooperate with him to protect the public interest in highway matters. However, in mid-January, 1926—three months after his original request—Moody was still vainly demanding cancellation of one-year road contracts in twenty-nine counties. "The boys have straightened out some in the Department since Lanham and Burkett got out, but there are no angels fluttering around up there yet," a consulting engineer wrote Louis Kemp in March, 1926. "The party is still just as rough as it dare be. The gang are pretty badly scared, and the close insiders are issuing orders to complete all pending work before the first of January, 1927, which is a good indication that they expect to be outsiders after that date."[81]

On December 8, Mrs. Ferguson announced that she would not call a special session for reasons of economy but that "should it subsequently appear that there is urgent need for a special session of the Legislature, I will not hesitate to take the legislature into my confidence and ask their aid in the solution of any matter involving the public good." It was now up to Satterwhite to carry out his threat to call the House into session. On December 21 he announced that conditions were not propitious for a special session because of financial difficulties and the unfinished state of Moody's suits to cancel road contracts and the Travis County Grand Jury's investigation into highway matters; he would therefore, he said, "await further developments." The former lawmen retired discomfited from the field of battle.[82]

Despite widespread doubts about the administration's honesty, the Fergusons were far from beaten as 1925 drew to a close. Their bitterest enemies did not deny that the tide of family fortunes was flowing back after the ebb following the highway revelations. The grand jury's investigation was a "dud," as far as the criminal phase was concerned. The only indictments returned were against F. G. Hoffman, vice-president of the Hoffman Construction Company, for perjury and swindling in connection with a $46,000 state payment for asphalt on or about October 1, 1925.[83]

Talk of impeachment had melted into thin air. If the political outlook seemed dubious, as it invariably did for the Fergusons three or four months before the primaries, that thought apparently did not worry Jim or his wife. Finishing her first year in office on January 19, 1926, the governor was "all smiles" as she declared that extending mercy to several hundred unfortunate convicts and raising the state prison system from debt during a lean, dry year were her outstanding accomplishments. "Believing that a cheerful, happy outlook is the best antidote for gloom," she proclaimed January "Laugh Month" in Texas. The *Fort Worth Star-Telegram* commented bitterly: "We can expect the Fergusons to laugh just as long as Texas stands for it; and we can expect the nation to laugh as long as we stand for it. The Fergusons say laugh, so let's do it. The joke is on us."[84]

Anti-Ferguson leaders felt that the only sure way of getting rid of Ma and "*Tainted* or *Slippery Jim*" was to unite behind one candidate. "Do not have too many candidates against him or her for there is a certain element that would go to Hades for him," a Navasota banker warned Will Hogg. "That element while small cannot be broken and evidently his hope is to get in by scattering the voters of the opposition and all good men should unite on the most available man next election and also see that some one from the *tenant ranks comes out to divide Ferguson's following.*" Dan Moody seemed to have the inside track on the nomination for governor, because of the favorable publicity he had been receiving for his highway investigations and recovery of $1,012,000 in state funds. Most anti-Fergusonites regarded the personable thirty-two-year-old attorney general as the man to wage war on "Fergusonism" and hoped that an already-announced candidate, Lynch Davidson, would gracefully withdraw from the race.[85]

CHAPTER 8

"Dan's the Man"

ALTHOUGH Mrs. Ferguson had promised in 1924 to serve only one term instead of the traditional two, she had been in office only eight months when her husband began lining up the Ferguson men for the 1926 race. He sent them letters asking them to compile information and furnish it to "our manager," Guy R. Holcomb, a former Wichita Falls attorney who was managing the *Ferguson Forum* business office in Austin. Supplementing those letters were letters from Holcomb asking for county poll-tax lists and the "name and address of at least one good Ferguson friend for each 25 votes in each voting box, who are generally active in public affairs and well-informed on public issues." Holcomb ended his letter with the suggestion that "the matter be kept quiet for the present at least." Ferguson had recently declared in effect that, if the Ferguson pardon record and administration were attacked, another campaign would be pitched on the record of his wife's administration. His own entry as a candidate would have forced a test of the amnesty act passed by the Thirty-ninth Legislature. Should the Texas Supreme Court find the act void, then the solace of its enactment would be largely nullified. Family friends saw another advantage in Mrs. Ferguson's running. She could make the race on her administration's merits while striving to remove the turbulent past ten years from the picture.[1]

According to Ouida Nalle, Mrs. Ferguson decided to run again because she had not completed certain important tasks that she had started. She also considered that her first term completed her husband's second term, which he had not been allowed to finish. The question whether or not the governor should run again was thrashed out in family council over many evenings. Ouida's husband, George, listened but offered no opinion. Finally Jim asked him, "George, what do you think of Mamma's running for governor again?"

George tactfully evaded the question: "My goodness alive, don't ask me, Governor Jim, I never would have had the nerve to run her the first time."[2]

When Mrs. Ferguson was threatened with impeachment in the fall of 1925 following the State Highway Department revelations, it was rumored that she would not be a candidate to succeed herself. This was almost certainly a tactical ploy to stave off a special session, for on February 27, 1926, she announced for reelection, declaring that the stigma of impeachment had not been removed from the Ferguson family because no name had been mentioned in the amnesty act.[3]

On April 24 the governor released her platform. She claimed that she had reduced appropriations by more than $10 million, had placed the prison system on a self-sustaining basis, and had enforced the law. She would, she said, oppose any attempt to move the prison system from its present location. She was in favor of a minimum seven-month school term for the lower grades and an eight-month term for the higher grades, a $15 per capita annual apportionment for every school-child, the building of county high schools wherever needed, the building of at least six junior colleges during her next term, and the equitable distribution of the Permanent University Fund between the University of Texas and Texas A&M.

The Ferguson platform proposed a gasoline tax of $0.03 a gallon, a $0.01 tax on each cigar and on each package of twenty cigarettes, and a reduction of at least one-third in the automobile tax. The state property tax rate for 1926 would be reduced from $0.35 to $0.25 per $100 valuation—a reduction of a little under 30 percent. Mrs. Ferguson defended her pardon record, contending that she had been actuated only by "mercy and forgiveness" and that the number of pardons had nothing to do with the issue. While admitting that part of the criticism of the State Highway Commission had been justified, she declared that the department had made a good record and would have made a better one had it not been hampered by unnecessary litigation. "That this litigation is prompted more by political ambition than patriotic motives is quite evident to anyone who wants to know the facts," she said in a slap at Attorney General Moody. "If Fergusonism be treason, then make the most of it," was the governor's defiant challenge to her critics. "It is a deft campaign document," the *Dallas Morning News* admitted.[4]

The first announced candidate in the race was former Lieutenant Governor Lynch Davidson of Houston, who had narrowly failed to gain a runoff spot with Felix Robertson in 1924, falling 5,216 votes behind Mrs. Ferguson in the first primary. On September 3, 1924, Davidson announced on the liner *Berengaria* in New York City, just before sailing for Europe, that he would be a candidate for governor in 1926. Commenting on the recent Texas primaries, he said, "I do not regard the result as a 'Ma' Ferguson victory, but it was an antiklan victory." In the summer of 1925, Davidson enlisted Don H. Biggers in his cause; a reproduction of an article by Biggers in the Johnson County newspaper endorsing Davidson's candidacy was sent to every newspaper in Texas at his expense. The letters were mailed from Fredericksburg so that they would not be linked to Davidson's Houston headquarters. The former lieutenant governor also encouraged his friends to write to Moody asking him to run for attorney general again. "A lot of that sort of thing would do good," he told Biggers.[5]

Davidson himself advised Moody not to enter the governor's race, telling him plainly that he had already announced and warning that if Texas had two more years of Fergusonism it would be because the attorney general had entered the contest and divided the anti-Ferguson vote (he later questioned whether Ferguson would have run if Moody had not). In his speeches Davidson declared that what Texas needed most was the business administration of state affairs by a businessman and that to elect either Moody or Mrs. Ferguson would mean a continuation of disturbance at the state capitol and consequent unsettled business conditions.[6]

The other Davidson, former Lieutenant Governor T. Whitfield Davidson, had announced on June 30, 1925, that he would not renew his unsuccessful candidacy of 1924 the next year but intimated that he might do so in 1928. He warned that if a large number of candidates entered the field the runoff primary would be between the Ferguson forces and a Klan-supported candidate. "If we had a preferential primary at which the voter might record his second choice, while all the candidates were before him, or a convention, where eliminations might take place, the condition would be wholly different," he said. "Our double primary is a great failure."[7] On September 15, 1925, Speaker Lee Satterwhite authorized a statement that he would not be a candidate for either governor or lieutenant governor in the 1926 primaries but would instead seek reelection to the House. The following March he announced his support for Moody's candidacy. Seventy-five-year-old James H. ("Cyclone") Davis was eager to run for governor as the Klan candidate, but stated in March, 1926, that he would join with the order's other leaders to prevent any klansman from entering a state race, adding that, since Lynch Davidson's opening speech "rings clear and sound on the prohibition question, as the case now stands, I expect to support him." "To hear our Klux friends talk one might conclude that they intend to vote for Moody," wrote a Ferguson man in Mineola, "but if you know a fellow pretty well and can get down under his skin it is easy to see that he does not intend to do so. In my judgment unless some new man enters the race, . . . the klan will line up behind Davidson. He has been playing with them for some months."[8]

Meanwhile, Moody was receiving many letters urging him to announce as a candidate for governor. "Everyone is saying, 'Well, I would like to see Dan Moody run for Governor, for we have lots of confidence in his ability, his honesty and his integrity,'" Eugene Sanders of Nacogdoches informed the attorney general, "so old boy, it now looks as if the people of Texas are going to draft you as their governor." "Not for my sake or your sake but for God's sake run for Governor," Shearn Moody (no relation to Dan) pleaded. "You can count on the support of the Moody branch of the family in Galveston, newspaper and all." Moody had no money of his own to finance a campaign; in fact, he told Colquitt that he was $5,000 in debt, but, according to the former governor, he had advised his uncle in Dallas that he was going to run but wanted to wait to announce until he tried the Hoffman case. "I think if he announces his friends will be willing to come forward and finance the campaign for him," Colquitt wrote Don Biggers.[9]

Sanders had a talk with Moody at the end of January, and, while the attorney general did not say in so many words that he was going to run, he left it up to him whether to tell friends that he was going to be a candidate. Taking the hint, Sanders immediately began lining up support. When Fred Acree, a Moody, Texas, businessman, asked Moody for a definite announcement about his intentions, the attorney general broke his silence on political questions to say: "First, I believe that Mr. Ferguson should be retired to private life, and second, I doubt the other man's [Lynch Davidson's] fitness for the office or his ability to take care of himself in the campaign that will be waged against him." As he explained:

This man declared himself in a newspaper interview following the results of the American Road Company case. As I understood that interview, he has left himself in a position where he is vulnerable to either side. You very likely read the editorials of the Dallas News on this interview which he gave out. I am

certain that one of the issues in the coming campaign will be the road question, and certainly the man opposed to Mr. Ferguson should be in a position to
take care of him on this question. I am not right sure that the Houston man is
in that position.[10]

Moody's friends in Taylor—Harry Graves, Richard Critz, James
Shaw, and others—were quietly working on his behalf. In January,
Shaw, vice-president and cashier of the City National Bank in Taylor,
talked to bankers in Houston and Galveston "and other men of influence" and reported to Moody that, while the Houston men were naturally for their fellow townsman Lynch Davidson, "they are unanimous
in saying that you were the logical man, and that you above all others
can make the campaign a real overthrow of Jim Ferguson and what he
and his crowd stand for." In reply Moody suggested in confidence that
an organization of Moody clubs should be started, beginning with one
in Taylor. "If such a thing would spread generally it would be a tremendous advantage and would furnish an organization to start with."[11]

At a gala mass meeting in Georgetown on March 2, the anniver-
sary of Texas's declaration of independence from Mexico, his supporters formally commended Moody, the "favorite son" of Williamson
County, to the people of Texas as their next governor and petitioned
him to become a candidate upon the principles of "honesty in office,
economy in the expenditure of the public money, and fair equal enforcement of the law." Veteran Democrat Marshall Hicks, one of the six
out-of-county speakers, intoned, "You have sounded a call that hear-
kens back to the olden days, for Dan Moody has the courage of Hogg,
the polish of Culberson and solid integrity of Joe Sayers, and he would
lead us back to the high position Texas occupied before the evil days
came upon us." Introducing himself as one of the original vindicators
for the amnesty bill, Representative Alfred P. C. Petsch of Fredericksburg told the crowd that it would be "foolish to vindicate Pa again."[12]

The next day Moody wrote privately that "I am going to have to
dispose of this question [of announcing for governor] in the immediate
future. The situation has got to such a place as that I must answer before long." Calling the meeting "a decided success," Richard Critz advised the attorney general that "the boys here" had talked the matter
over and thought that his announcement should not be delayed for
long, for "continued suspense at this time might do harm."[13]

Moody formally announced his candidacy for governor on March
6. He made the Texas road contracts, the textbook adoptions, and

other current charges against Jim Ferguson direct issues and took them straight to the former governor. He also flayed Ferguson for the place he held in his wife's administration. "For more than a year one man, a private citizen, has exercised a position of greater power and influence than any public official and that man has been, and now is, free from the restraints and responsibilities which the law places on public officials," Moody charged. "As a result of this situation we have had and now have the exercise of official authority by proxy." The attorney general also fired at Lynch Davidson, declaring that there was no issue between Ferguson and the Houston businessman on the highway question. Davidson had accepted "the lame explanation of these contracts given by the mouthpiece of the present Governor and adopted the figures of the resigned chairman of the Highway Commission, and says that my effort to compel road contractors who had wrongfully taken from the public funds unconscionable and excessive profits, to return such profits, was a mistake."

Moody pledged that if he was elected he would expose and bring to justice the guilty parties in the road-contracts matter; restore honesty in the state government; appoint "clean, high-class, honest and capable men and women" to office; enforce the laws; curtail the issuance of pardons; put the state prison system on a business base and eliminate waste, extravagance and graft; encourage a system of connected highways; maintain the public schools in the highest state of efficiency; support higher education; make corrections in the free-textbook law; and work for election and judicial reform.[14]

The red-haired young attorney general whom anti-Fergusonites were hailing as a political Moses was born on June 1, 1893, in Taylor, Williamson County, the son of Daniel James and Nancy Robertson Moody. The family had a background of preaching, teaching, and the law. Moody's paternal grandfather was a hard-shelled Baptist preacher who moved from Virginia to Tennessee and then to Missouri. His maternal grandfather was a doctor and a Methodist minister in Tennessee. In 1876, Moody's father, "Dan'l" Moody, as he always wrote his name, moved to Taylor, where he was a claims agent for the Illinois and Great Northern Railroad. In his youth he had served in the Confederate Army and as a Baptist preacher and a cattle drover between Texas and Missouri. When Taylor was incorporated in 1892, Dan'l Moody was the town's first mayor. Later he served as justice of the peace, helped establish a building-and-loan association, and ran an insurance business. He was sixty when Dan was born and died when the boy was fifteen. Moody's mother was a schoolteacher who moved to Texas from Tennessee with her widowed mother and family in 1883. Four of her brothers became lawyers, including Judge James H. Robertson, a law partner of Jim Hogg and the author of the Robertson Insurance Law.

When Dan was two years old, family reverses brought the family hardship, and when he was nine, he had to go to work delivering milk from 4:30 A.M. until time for school and again in the evening. At an early age he decided that he would become a lawyer. He worked in a coffee-roasting plant and as a delivery boy for a grocery store, a cashier in a store, and a lineman for the Citizens Light and Power Company of Taylor. In 1909, at the age of sixteen, he became a member of the International Brotherhood of Electrical Workers. He attended the University of Texas from 1910 to 1914, the last two years in law school, working summers as an electrical contractor to pay his expenses. He passed the bar examination without graduating and established a practice in Taylor, soon forming a partnership with Harris Melasky.

When the United States entered World War I, Moody volunteered for the Army Air Service but was rejected. He was put on the deferred list because his mother was an invalid but, notwithstanding that, served as a second lieutenant in the Texas National Guard and volunteered as a private in the army. He was in a training camp in Little Rock, Arkansas, when the war ended. He resumed his practice in Taylor, and in 1920, at twenty-six, was elected county attorney of Williamson County.[15]

A Klan organizer came to Taylor and asked Moody and another citizen to aid him. "He told us frankly of the whippings," Moody recalled later, "and we told him we didn't need anything like that in Taylor." The man found others more amenable, and the Taylor Klan was organized. One morning a friend met Moody at the door of his office. "What do you think of the Klan?" the friend asked.

"I think it incipient anarchy," Moody replied. "Why? Are you a member?"

The friend replied: "I was until last night, when I resigned. They talked about your enmity to the Klan at the meeting, and they are looking for a lawyer to oppose you for re-election."

Moody went to the Klan leader. "Now you haven't much of a Klan in Taylor," he told him. "You probably couldn't get a lawyer to run against me. So I'm going to enlarge the territory from which you may draw your candidate, and run for district attorney." Meanwhile, Ben Robertson, the incumbent district attorney and Moody's cousin, resigned from office in 1922, and, without consulting Moody, Governor Neff appointed him to fill the vacancy. Neff had attended a law banquet at which Moody spoke and had been impressed by the young prosecutor. Moody said that he learned about his appointment when he read the headlines in the *Austin American*. His district included Williamson and Travis counties, but even with Austin to draw upon, the Klan did not find a suitable candidate, and Moody was unopposed for election to a full term.[16]

Moody's successful prosecution of four klansmen implicated in the flogging of R. W. Burleson gained him widespread publicity at a time when the hooded order was a power in the state. "Now I know that was the incident that started me in public life," Moody said later. "I believe it broke the Klan's back in Texas." The *Houston Chronicle* first suggested Moody for attorney general. He recalled that, when he started his race, "I was about the only person in Texas who thought I could be elected." He polled 315,107 votes, or 49 percent of the total, in the first primary, and piled up 463,411 votes in the runoff against the Klan candidate Edward B. Ward, who received 211,783 votes. He thus became the youngest man ever elected to the office and, in the words of one admirer, the "Idol of Texas." Veteran Democrat Barry Miller referred to Moody as "that red-headed whirlwind from Williamson County" and predicted that he would go far in public life. At first many believed that he was a Ferguson adherent, because the *Ferguson Forum* endorsed him, but it was not long before they found out that they were very much mistaken.[17]

Tall, rather thin, boyish-looking, with reddish hair inclined to curl, Moody had a hearty, ruddy complexion and a pleasing, soft drawl. He was not an eloquent speaker, but his seriousness carried conviction. He had the habit of seeming to pause to grope for the precise word, often changing the form of a phrase, which made his oratory seem a bit difficult for him and taxing upon his listener. He was credited with an unusual memory. As district attorney, Moody would question each of twenty-four or thirty-six prospective jurors; then, after both prosecutor and defense had ruled out names until the list was down to twelve, he would call each of the twelve by name. Years later he could still recall small details of his political campaigns.[18]

In addition to Mrs. Ferguson, Davidson, and Moody, there were three minor candidates in the field: Mrs. Edith E. Wilmans of Dallas, the first woman to serve in the Texas legislature; Mrs. Kate M. Johnston of San Antonio, who ran on a wet platform; and the Reverend O. F. ("Zim") Zimmerman, who had formed a "partnership with God" and pledged himself to "run every agency of the devil out of the State."

Zim promised the farmers thirty cents cotton and said that if he was forced to support either Ferguson or Moody he would support Ferguson because "we can rid Texas of Ferguson within two years, while Moody's election means ten years of Colquitt–Crane–Barry Miller-ism." Colquitt suspected that the "Ferguson crowd" had brought Zimmerman out through Milton Farrier of Naples, who was connected with Bank Commissioner C. O. Austin. "I will bet a dollar against a doughnut that Ferguson, [T. H.] McGregor and Farrier either wrote or furnished the thoughts for Zimmerman's speech," he wrote Moody after the minister announced his candidacy. "I look for it to appear in full in the Ferguson Forum with favorable comment."[19]

Former Democratic supporters of George Butte and anti-Klan backers of Mrs. Ferguson in 1924 forgot their bitter factional disputes and united to organize the Dallas County Moody-for-Governor Club. Cullen F. Thomas, who had made more speeches for the Fergusons than any other man, was named chairman of the Moody forces. He said that in this campaign the paramount issue would be not the Klan but civic righteousness and purity in government. Among the other followers of Ma in 1924 who recanted and came down the sawdust trail to the mourners' bench were General Martin M. Crane, Judge C. A. Leddy, H. Bascom Thomas, Epps G. Knight, and the Reverend Charles S. Fields. Tom Love was present and declared that Moody's work of the last six months was "a sight draft on the patriotism of every Texan" and that the only issue before the voters was Ferguson versus anti-Ferguson. "In any event, get on the stump at the earliest possible moment and tell the people the truth about Fergusonism," Love wrote the candidate. "Don't have any fears of being considered a one-idea-ed man. Talk about Fergusonism and nothing else. Tell all you know and try to tell something new every day."[20]

In Harris County, Stephen L. Pinckney and Alvin Moody quietly organized for the attorney general under the name the Responsible Government League, lining up precinct leaders, selecting a central committee and various chairmen, and arranging for spacious headquarters in the old *Houston Post* building. Moody was office manager, and Mrs. Richard T. Fleming was in charge of women's work. "By the time Dan makes his opening speech at Taylor we will be on our toes and ready to go, which I think will be time enough," Pinckney informed the Austin headquarters. "The sentiment in this county in favor of Mr. Moody appears to be so overwhelming that it frightens me."[21]

Moody had added romance to the race when he married Mildred Paxton, the daughter of an Abilene banker, on April 20. Jim Ferguson lost no time asking Moody whether he was going to make his bride promise at the altar that she would never in any way advise him in regard to his political conduct. The prospective bridegroom ignored the question, and the former governor went joyfully to the people with the announcement, "If you elect Moody you will have a Jiggs in the Executive Office and a Maggie running him with a rolling pin." The new Mrs. Moody accompanied her husband on some of his speaking tours, prompting Ferguson to comment that the attorney general was "a candidate with nothing to recommend him save a lipstick, a new wife, and a big head."[22]

Although Moody was invited to "open up" in Moody, in McLennan County, he chose to launch his campaign in Taylor on May 8. Hundreds of well-wishers from all over the state joined the homefolks, and a special train came up from San Antonio, picking up passengers along the way. The crowd, estimated at between eight and ten thousand, heard Moody deliver perhaps the longest opening speech ever made by a candidate for governor of Texas. He dedicated his candidacy to the repudiation of what he, in common with many others, denominated "Fergusonism." Other speakers included O. B. Colquitt, who was applauded when he remarked that the three features of the Ferguson history and administration were the American party, the American Road Company, and the American Book Company. Mrs. Jesse Daniel Ames of Georgetown said that Mrs. Ferguson was not the choice of Texas women and that her incumbency was not properly chargeable to them. "I now pledge to Mr. Moody the support of a majority of women of Texas and make him the promise that the women will work so hard there will be no need for a second primary."[23]

Texas women rallied under the Moody banner. Mrs. Jane Y. Mc-

Callum was named state chairman of the Texas Women Citizens' Committee, Dan Moody for Governor. "It turns my heart to lead to think about it," she confided to her diary. "I'd much rather do the publicity and head the committee on literature." Her own choice was Minnie Fisher Cunningham. Of Moody she wrote, "He is certainly one fine, clean, straight thinking person, but *such a boy.*" Mrs. McCallum overtaxed her strength and ran some fever every day, and her doctor ordered her to bed shortly before the first primary. Mrs. Percy V. Pennybacker, a prominent clubwoman of Austin, endorsed Moody, and Mrs. Ames made speeches for him. The women formed county Moody clubs. In Austin, in a meeting in the Driskill Hotel, more than two hundred women organized a women's Dan-Moody-for-Governor Club. The group sponsored a speech by Senator V. A. Collins in Eastwood Park on July 14. Ladies were assured that they would hear "no vile epithets, no vituperation, no profanity, and no vulgarity"—a slap at Jim Ferguson's well-known platform antics.[24]

Moody made the mistake of not designating a campaign manager, and Colquitt and other backers were soon complaining that no one was in charge, and organization was lagging. "The people of the State are for Moody in my opinion," wrote Colquitt, "but Moody's friends are badly in need of organization and it is going to take quick and active work to draw them together in the various counties and arouse enthusiasm and get out his supporters at the polls." Steve Pinckney closed his Houston office and spent several weeks in the Austin headquarters, but he did not have full authority, and it was hard to make the office function properly. Practically all of the office workers were donating their services free of charge and paying their own expenses. "It is nothing short of criminal to have to run a headquarters like this one is having to be run," Pinckney complained to Will Hogg, "but I am going to stay here until I drop, however much I would like to do otherwise." Pinckney left at the end of June to undertake some organization work in the field, and Judge D. W. Wilcox was placed in charge, though it was too late to designate him as campaign manager.[25]

Moody was expected to run well in the large cities and to carry most of the North, West, and South Texas counties. His managers recognized that his hardest fight would be in East Texas. "Around here we hear nothing but Moody," wrote an Austin woman, "but over in East Texas they seem all to be for 'Ma.'" While the towns were expected to give the attorney general good majorities, Ferguson was strong among the rural voters, who, Moody partisans affirmed, never read anything but the *Ferguson Forum*. A Houston County man urged Moody to visit the rural districts and out-of-the-way places in East Texas:

I am fully confident that the people who read and the more intelligent of our people will support you in the July primary. There are so many from the forks of the creek, the hill billies, I call them, that are not posted, who perhaps never heard of the American Road Company or of Hoffman Road Company. This class will no doubt support Ferguson, at least he is looking to them to win this race. He is depending upon their ignorance of the affairs of state to support him. . . . This problem of ignorance is your only difficulty in your campaign. Just how many are of this class the Lord only knows. But there are thousands of them.[26]

Ferguson's anti-Prohibition stance further strengthened his appeal in East Texas. "Without exception, the men of any influence or prominence at all, who are supporting Ferguson, are rabid and uncompromising anti-prohibitionists," a Lufkin lawyer told Moody. "It is impossible to change them. If Ferguson were to burn the Capitol and loot the treasury, it would not matter to them." In Liberty County everyone interested in the whiskey business, as manufacturer, middleman, or buyer, was said to be for Ferguson, with a "Me for Ma" sticker on the windshield. "Unfortunately we have a large number of such people in the Trinity river bottom, a great place for making illicit whisky," lamented a Rayburn doctor. "This county is a Ferguson Co. and every blind tiger and their sympathisers will vote for 'Ma,' as they do not know how long it will be before they will want a parden [sic]," was the grim prophecy of a Moody backer in Sabine County, on the Louisiana line.[27]

The piney-woods counties of East Texas—Shelby, San Augustine, Sabine, Newton, Orange, Angelina, Jasper, Nacogdoches, and Trinity—were conceded to be "dyed in the wool on Fergusonism," "a red hot Ferguson bed." A common sight in those counties was "Me for Ma" signs on the backbands of the mules of highway-maintenance crews. "Sabine County will give old Jim more votes than all of the rest of the candidates put together," Moody was advised. "There is no question about the local voting box—it will go for you four to one," a Jasper County supporter assured Moody, "but the forks of the river here are still favoring any man who will denounce the University's 'ammonia-spraying high-brows.'" Moody supporters in Jasper County hesitated to organize a club for fear it would stir up the rural voters and result in an even heavier vote for Ferguson.[28]

Prison-system employees in Walker County were active for Ferguson and had trustee convicts distributing photographs and literature on the streets of Huntsville, but in spite of that, W. L. Dean, Moody's county manager, thought that Walker would go for the attorney general. "The women are active for you, as are also a great many of the men."[29]

Moody's chances were brighter in Northeast Texas, with supporters in Anderson, Harrison, Henderson, Houston, Panola, and Rusk counties predicting that he would garner more votes in those counties than the other candidates. Klan and anti-Klan leaders in Smith County buried the hatchet and selected Tyler newspaper editor Carl Estes, a veteran wounded in the war who had spent the past four years in hospitals, to take the lead in organizing the county for Moody. The wife of veteran Democrat Cone Johnson was in poor health, but Cone agreed to deliver a speech at a Moody rally in Houston that would be broadcast over Radio KPRC and was expected to reach at least 50,000 people.[30]

Most of the state's largest daily newspapers, including G. B. Dealey's *Dallas Morning News*, Amon Carter's *Fort Worth Star-Telegram*, Jesse Jones's *Houston Chronicle*, Ross Sterling's *Houston Post-Dispatch* (which Jim Ferguson called the "Pest Disgrace"), and the Marsh-Fentress chain of papers in Waco, Austin, Wichita Falls, and Port Arthur, assured their readers early and late that "Dan's the Man." Boyd Gatewood, a brilliant reporter for the *Post-Dispatch*, served as Moody's unofficial press agent and publicity adviser, helping him plan his strategy and his speeches. According to Ed Kilman, "No Texas newspaperman ever distilled more poison for the opposition or more effective publicity for his candidate into straight news stories than Boyd Gatewood did in that campaign." The financially hard-pressed county weeklies generally reflected the views of the most of their subscribers. "As the sentiment of the people here seems to be for Ferguson I believe that if I were to take any stand I would be courting financial loss," the editor of the *Forney News-Messenger* explained frankly to Moody. Most Ferguson weeklies were in East Texas, while Moody had the editorial support of most of the papers in the rest of the state. At the Panhandle Press Convention in Amarillo in April nearly every editor was his "strong supporter."[31]

O. B. Colquitt published in Dallas several issues of a campaign paper called the *Free Lance*. "Ferguson has all the newspapers bull-dozed with fear of libel suits," he had earlier written Don H. Biggers, "but I am in favor of finding a way to print the truth and put it into the hands of every citizen in the state." Colquitt wanted to reach Texas farmers with Moody literature to counteract the *Ferguson Forum*. He saw to it that 200,000 copies of the June issue of the *Free Lance* were mailed to rural-route boxholders. "We are receiving a large number of letters from farmers wanting the Free Lance and from all I can learn, they are crying for it like a baby cries for Castoria," he wrote Will Hogg. He complained, however, about the shortage of funds. "Our friends in Dallas have succeeded in raising about one day's postage."[32]

In an extra edition of the *Free Lance* dated June 26, twelve pages were devoted to "57 Varieties of Fergusonism"—a headline in big red type across the top of the first page. The anonymous author, described as "a man of extensive knowledge and experience in public affairs," was Tom Love, who at the request of Moody leaders had prepared this doc-umented review of the Ferguson record beginning with his impeach-ment trial. Biggers called it "altogether the hottest political document ever turned loose in Texas."[33]

Will Hogg took an active part in Moody's candidacy. His diary re-cords nine meetings with the attorney general between April 2 and June 26, and he discussed the campaign with John Boyle of San An-tonio in Houston on April 21; with Boyle, Hicks, Pinckney, R. L. Bob-bitt of Laredo, and others at the Gunter Hotel in San Antonio on May 22 and 23; and with Sawnie Aldredge, Colquitt, Love, and others in Dallas on June 13.[34] Hogg introduced the candidate to a mass meeting in the Houston City Auditorium on June 8 in what Thomas W. Gregory wrote Colonel House was "a very lurid speech such as Will usually makes and which may or may not help his candidate. Will is the most pronounced rough-neck I know but he has a great heart which is in the right place and he is certainly built along very large lines." Hogg dis-tributed his remarks in a printed circular, prompting one angry Fer-gusonite in Sulphur Springs to reply rather incoherently on the back of one: "We use Toilet paper at our house so we can use this. . . . 'We are for Ferguson' Can't you be white and not a *yellow heart*, and a *pink liver*, Curr. Watch Ferguson snow your Honest as you call it under."[35]

The Hogg brothers, Jim's sons, accompanied Moody through East Texas on June 25 and 26 to, as they expressed it, "interview" their father's old friends on his behalf. Will spoke briefly at several points, saying, "If my father were alive he would be for Dan Moody."[36]

Moody rarely referred to his platform in his speeches, insisting instead that the real issue before the voters was Fergusonism. "The question in this campaign is whether this man Ferguson shall be made to take his hands off public affairs in Texas," he declared, adding:

The most zealous advocate of Ferguson will in candor admit that the power of the highest office in the State is held and exercised for the last eighteen months by one only a private citizen. He doesn't have the qualifications to hold any public office in Texas, but he administers the Governor's office de facto. This is contrary to the principle of democracy and of free government. He exercises power without accountability to the law or to the people of Texas. My campaign is committed to correcting that evil.

Discussing the *Ferguson Forum*, Moody stated that a one-page advertisement in the paper had sometimes cost more than an ad in any of the state's fifteen largest daily newspapers which had a combined circulation of 680,190. Instead of being a wood-and-water bearer, Ferguson had shown that he wanted to be a "purse bearer at the expense of the people." He was the salaried employee of a railroad company, had actually supervised the work of the State Highway Commission and attended its meetings until Moody began his investigation, and had directed the awarding of textbook contracts worth millions of dollars. Moody attacked the road contracts, noting that the American Road Company, chartered in Delaware, had been "brought to a balmy Southern climate when four days old, and when only eight days old was given road contracts involving a million or more dollars." Answering Ferguson's charge that he was too young and inexperienced to be governor, Moody retorted, "If I'm elected Governor I'll be old enough to ask the Legislature to conduct an investigation, and I'll be old enough to give them a start on the facts." The attorney general did not once mention Lynch Davidson by name in a campaign speech, referring to him as "the other candidate" and as "Ferguson's second choice."[37]

Moody's youth stood him in good stead. He often made as many as five speeches a day and stopped to shake hands in a dozen towns yet never appeared tired. His method of scheduling speeches was haphazard; he would promise to speak at points hundreds of miles apart, regardless of transportation facilities, leaving it to good luck to be able to fill his engagements. "Moody should devote the balance of this campaign in the large populace sections of the State," Colquitt advised at the beginning of July. "I cannot understand the purpose in wearing him out making long jumps like that from Sherman to Texarkana and from the Panhandle to points in Central Texas." In his campaigning and at political conventions Moody almost always wore a carefully pressed white linen suit and white shoes. How he managed to remain immaculate-appearing in the heat was a mystery to newsmen. "He could walk along a muddy road and never get a splotch on his white foot gear," Walter Hornaday recalled in wonder.[38]

Moody was criticized at times for talking too long. "People are no longer willing to sit for two hours to listen to a lot of speeches when they can get in their Fords and stir up a little breeze," he was told. He was advised to conserve his strength in the long campaign and to hold his audience better by condensing his speeches so as to cover all his points in an hour. Still, Colquitt, a veteran campaigner, thought that Moody's speeches were having "a wonderfully good effect. He is growing stronger on the stump each day, in my opinion, and is fully able to handle 'Ukelele Jim' on the ground." "While he is not a speaker who carries much enthusiasm and is not brilliant in his utterances, he is giving them the cold facts and the people are thinking," said another observer after attending a Moody rally in Waco. Moody thrived on heckling. While Ferguson seemed to be irritated by hecklers, the attorney general never lost his head, and his retorts were apt and rapid.[39]

Jim Ferguson announced that his wife would not open her campaign for reelection until sometime early in May in North Texas. "The farmers are six weeks behind with their field work," he explained, "and can not leave the land at this time to hear political speeches." Moody was told that "Jim is going to indulge in the nastiest kind of attacks on you and 'smoke you out' in a personal fight."[40] A crowd estimated by the *Ferguson Forum* at 25,000 greeted the Fergusons when they opened their campaign at Sulphur Springs, Hopkins County, in Northeast Texas on May 22. Mrs. Ferguson spoke first, briefly reviewing the accomplishments of her administration as set forth in her platform and taking Moody to task for his opposition to the amnesty bill, his efforts to set aside the action of the textbook board in adopting textbooks, and his attack on the State Highway Department. Then she issued a challenge to Moody:

The primaries come on July 24th. Regardless of the result, he and I could stay in office until the second Tuesday in January, 1927. But I will agree that if he leads me one vote in the primary that I will immediately resign without waiting until next year, if he will agree that if I lead him 25,000 votes in the primary on July 24th he will immediately resign. If the Attorney General is brave, a great service can be rendered to the people by getting rid of a very bad Governor as he claims, or getting rid of a very incompetent Attorney General, as the people may decide. Come on, Mr. Attorney General, and let us stop the pain.

Then Mrs. Ferguson asked the crowd to "hear my husband, your friend, in his own defense." Pledging not to throw mud in the campaign ("I am going to throw rocks"), Jim poured it on the attorney general, charging that "Moody's campaign was daddied in the evoluted monkey end of the Baptist church and boosted by the Ku Klux Klan and supported by the big oil companies opposed to the gasoline tax." Elaborating on this statement, Ferguson, in an appeal to fundamentalists, declared that the evolution Baptist preachers who had forgotten the old-time religion were preaching for their newfound hero, "Daniel Jiggs Moody." They had supported Felix Robertson and George Butte in 1924 and were now telling people that Moody was the Thomas Jefferson of the age and the savior of all mankind. "But what could you expect from a crowd that had denied God and admit that they come from a tadpole?" he shouted.

In an effort to resurrect the Klan issue, Ferguson declared that "Dan Moody is either a member of the Klan or he is in sympathy with them, and the last would be just as bad as the first if not worse." Imperial wizard Hiram Wesley Evans and Larry Mills, Robertson's campaign manager, were supporting Moody. Ferguson said of Mills, "If the truth was known I am sure Dan has requested him to visit the klan lodges and keep him posted on the political situation." Jim challenged Moody and his group to name any person who was "*now*" (italics added) a member in good standing of the Klan in the Ferguson administration, promising that if they could prove their charge his wife would remove "any active klansman from office."

Reviewing the big oil companies' opposition to the gasoline tax, Ferguson charged that oil lobbyists Jake Wolters, Julius Germany, Will Francis, and Joe Laney were supporting Moody. "The oil companies reap a golden harvest from the pockets of the people with the profits from the sale of their products and they ought to be willing to have some part of the prices which they fix for the people to pay to be given to the upkeep of our roads and our schools," Ferguson asserted. "Let us have no pussy footing and no side stepping and political dodging on this issue."[41]

Answering Mrs. Ferguson's challenge the following night in San Antonio, Moody said: "So eager am I to rid the state of everything they stand for, that I accept the challenge of Jim issued in his wife's name. . . . It makes it impossible and unnecessary to discuss anything else than Fergusonism; it assures the State of a short, quick, and decisive engagement, with a final result on the night of July 24th." Many of Moody's friends initially criticized him for accepting the bet, which they regarded as one of Jim's bluffs. "I am of the opinion that you have lost votes by accepting Ferguson's challenge," one of them fretted. "Anyone knows that if he loses he will never resign. There are quite a few Lynch Davidson men here that had agreed to vote for you thinking Davidson has no chance that have gone back to him now claiming Davidson has a good chance since the bet." The *Dallas Morning News* editorialized against Moody's "indiscretion"in making a side bet with Mrs. Ferguson. Even Moody's wife "was afraid it was that 'fool move' predicted by oldtime Politicians he'd make because of his youth!!" [42]

Davidson rapped Moody's "betting covenant with Jim Ferguson by which he attempts to rob the people of their right to name the Attorney General and also to name the Governor of Texas in the coming election," compared it with a "negro crap game," and said the only honorable course left to him was to withdraw from the race. Moody's reply to the criticism was that he had done the people of Texas a favor in making it possible to free the state from the blight of Fergusonism within sixty days. "I regard it as a public duty," he told a Houston audience, "to return Jim Ferguson to his Bosque County ranch." [43]

Colquitt, who had urged Moody to accept the challenge, defended his decision in the *Free Lance*. "Moody did right in accepting the Ferguson challenge and submitting the issue squarely to the people. It is a solemn referendum to the people and they will determine whether they approve Fergusonism or condemn it." Moody's friends soon came to believe that, in Mrs. Moody's words, it was "Dan's Smartest Move," because it narrowed the issue to one between him and Ferguson. A vote for Davidson, he could argue, was a vote to have Ferguson remain in power from July 25 to January 18 with an attorney general of his own choosing. [44] Probably no man in Texas was more surprised than Jim Ferguson when Moody accepted the challenge. If the attorney general had declined, he would have made the refusal a major issue. Still, he professed to be delighted. "The governor," Ferguson exulted, "has got the attorney general in the political electric chair, and she is going to electrocute him on July 24."[45]

Early in June, Ferguson announced that he would make forty-three speeches before the first primary, beginning in Beaumont on June 2 and closing in Austin on July 23. Mrs. Ferguson would make no more speeches, since "no attack has been made on her administration and none can be made." As far as her strength would permit, however, she would visit as many places as possible and personally thank the people for their continued loyalty and support.[46]

Country folk made up the bulk of Ferguson's audiences. More than half the crowd in Cisco were farm women, who sat all day with their families in the stifling tent eating lunches they had brought with them. Ferguson spoke for two and a half hours in the muggy heat and, encouraged by shouts of "Pour it on!" divested himself of his coat, waistcoat, and finally his collar and tie. "Our hardest fight in this section is with the farm vote," a Milam County attorney wrote James Shaw. "They have always supported Ferguson, and while we are breaking a few away, a large majority of the farm vote is still with him." Plows and middle busters were placed on the platform when Ferguson spoke in Marques, Leon County, in answer to a statement in a Houston newspaper referring to Fergusonites as "cultivator jockeys."[47]

Ferguson tried to make fundamentalists believe that Moody denied the biblical story of creation and that the textbook controversy was over evolution rather than the price the taxpayers had to pay for free books. In Lufkin, "under the spreading pine trees of Angelina County," he held an anti-evolution meeting on July 8. There Jim put more stress on evolution than he had in any previous speech, denouncing the "monkey-faced Baptists" who were supporting Moody. "I am not talking about the old time Baptists," he hastened to explain, "but about those who are like Dr. S. P. Brooks of Baylor University, who about two months ago said that men used to have a tail and wore it off by squatting down. When they tried to put such stuff in Texas school books Mrs. Ferguson kept it out, for she is a Christian mother." There were yells and hurrahs for Ma and a chorus of amens. Ferguson continued: "God made the world in six days and created man in His own image, the Bible says, and I agree with you Baptists who believe that. But your monkey-faced Baptists are more dangerous than any group of anarchists. You fellows are worse than the Ku Klux Klan and we're going to wipe you out." "Give it to 'em, Jim!" the crowd shouted. "Sure we will!"

The Lufkin meeting was held in Lake Park, and near the platform was a cage with two little rhesus monkeys. When Ferguson shouted "Monkey-faced Baptists!" his audience roared in glee. When about a score of his hearers in the nearby trees hung by their legs and clapped their hands in wild fervor, the monkeys became frightened and shrieked in terror, adding a shrill, piercing note to the din. It was in response to the "monkey-faced Baptist" onslaughts that Moody declared his confidence that the whale swallowed Jonah.[48]

As the primary campaign was beginning, the United States Supreme Court handed down a decision in the Archer County case invalidating Texas road-district bonds. The Texas Highway Association and other interested parties pressed Mrs. Ferguson to call a special session to pass bond-validation measures that had been prepared by a statewide committee, but the governor was afraid that a special session would give her enemies in the legislature an opportunity to launch an investigation of state departments. She wanted any special session to be delayed until September or the first part of October, after the primaries were over. The Fergusons wanted a law passed "at a convenient time" allowing the people of the road districts to vote on validating their bonds; the *Fort Worth Star-Telegram* ascribed to Jim a statement that "if the bonds which the Supreme Court has said the people 'don't owe' are saddled back upon them, 'your children will curse the day.'"[49]

Ferguson's enemies immediately accused him of repudiation. "Jim Ferguson wants to turn Texas into a Bolshevik Russia by trying to repudiate the bond debts of nearly $80,000,000," Moody charged in a speech in Snyder on June 19. "These debts are just and I believe that the people of Texas will pay them despite any technicality which they may now have." As criticism of his stand mounted, Ferguson denied that his wife favored repudiation. "She never was and never will be for repudiation," he said. "She wants validation by the people. She has more confidence in the people of Texas than the other candidates have."[50]

From the beginning Lynch Davidson was overshadowed by the Moody-Ferguson contest. "The present situation does not look the best in the world from the standpoint of publicity," he admitted when his campaign was almost two months old. "On the other hand wherever I go, particularly through the central and north-central part of

Texas, my strength among the every day people is seemingly better than it ever was." "I measure the situation this way," he continued. "Moody's candidacy is largely a newspaper candidacy. Of course, that makes a very strong situation, but it is not the ruling situation by any manner of means."[51]

Davidson directed most of his fire at the attorney general. Promising to speak out on all the issues, he declared that the state's interests would be served by plain talk and not by trying to cover up in a cloak of anti-Fergusonism. He thought the Ferguson administration "the blackest stain on Texas' political history" but said, "I am not trying to ride into office with no qualification but my anti-Fergusonism." He challenged the Moody newspapers to explain why the attorney general had allowed the Magnolia Petroleum Company in the fall of 1925 to tear down the barriers against trust domination which former Attorney General B. F. Looney had set up. Looney had won a $500,000 fine against the Standard Oil Company in 1913 and put Standard's Magnolia Company stock in the hands of a trustee, whose duty it was to prevent violation of antitrust laws. When the stock passed from Standard of New Jersey to Standard of New York, Moody had made no effort to show that this was "a subterfuge of the rankest kind" but had "accepted the facts represented to him" and asked the courts to pass on them. "Perhaps Moody will explain why Looney was able to secure a $500,000 fine and a trusteeship, but Moody wasn't able to even hold the trusteeship," Davidson taunted.[52]

Davidson also called on Moody to tell the voters his stand on Prohibition. The only enlightenment on this matter was Moody's San Antonio speech, in which he referred to the tick law and the Prohibition law and said that he favored the tick law. Moody claimed always to have been a prohibitionist, but Colquitt had told him, "If you talk about whiskey you can't get any of the votes we got," and he was now silent on the liquor question. The attorney general denied the inference that he was a dry in North Texas and a wet in South Texas, reminding Davidson that he had made a speech on Prohibition in Houston only a few months before. "I have always spoken and voted for prohibition whenever given an opportunity," he said. Privately Moody complained that Davidson was trying to inject the Eighteenth Amendment and the Volstead Act, "which are purely national issues," into the campaign as part of his "consistent attempts to distract the attention of the people from the iniquities of the Ferguson administration."[53]

In his opening speech in Palestine on March 13, Davidson had promised to let the people know the facts about the enactment by the last legislature of Senate Bill 180, which permitted a foreign corporation lacking a permit to do business in Texas but lawfully owning or acquiring stock in Texas corporations to vote the stock and participate in the management and control of its business affairs. In a speech in Bonham on April 24, Davidson charged that the bill's known purpose was to legalize Standard Oil's return to Texas and thus repudiate the work of Hogg, Culberson, R. V. Davidson, and Looney. He promised, when elected governor, to urge the repeal of Senate Bill 180, which he referred to as the corporate merger or oil act, and to insist on a rigid enforcement of the state's antitrust laws.[54]

Elaborating on this charge, Davidson said in a speech in Newcastle that the bill had "slipped through before any one not in the conspiracy realized its sinister effect," that it "was read once and hurriedly passed," and that "its sponsors were afraid to have it come up to three regular readings." When Senator Charles Murphy showed from the legislative journals that none of these statements was true, the *Dallas Morning News* editorially chided Davidson "for the propogation of a calumnious idea which has been proved to be unfounded in fact and which is defamatory of honorable men." Davidson fired back: "Do you deny that hundreds of lobbyists were sent to Austin to get Senate bill No. 180 passed?" Meanwhile, other lawmakers entered the fray. Senator J. D. Parnell defended the bill, quoting former Attorney General W. A. Keeling on the effect of the measure, while Representative Newt B. Williams of Waco charged that "Senate bill 180 turns foreign corporations without authority to do business in Texas scott free, to own, manage and control every pipe line, every refinery and every production company in Texas without any limit whatever."[55]

In fact, John A. Mobley, a Houston attorney whose firm acted as general counsel "on larger matters" to the Humble Company and represented Standard Oil Company of New Jersey in Texas, wrote Steve Pinckney that he had prepared the arguments used in the legislature in favor of Senate Bill 180 and had helped draw up the bill. Declining to speak for Moody in Henderson on July 21, Mobley explained: "Lynch Davidson knows of my firm's associations and connections, and he would at once misrepresent any appearance I might make; and while I am not thin skinned and would care naught for such misrepresentation, I feel quite sure that it would cost us more votes than it would gain." Julius A. Germany accepted an invitation to make two speeches for Moody in Van Zandt County but promised Wilcox that he would not "have a news reporter present."[56]

During the last month of the primary campaign, Davidson hammered on the theme that a combination of oil and liquor interests was attempting to defeat him for the governorship. "The Houston oil interests are against me, so is O. B. Colquitt and other North Texas political has-beens," he declared in a speech in Mineola. "This is the line-up against me. This is the picture of Texas politics as it now stands—oil and booze in an unholy alliance to put the young man, Moody, into office, so that they can run things to suit themselves. I have the highest personal regard for Dan. He's a nice boy, but he's fallen in with the wrong crowd." Speaking in Honey Grove on June 25, Davidson singled out the Hogg brothers for attack, charging that they were having Moody put up a smoke screen of anti-Ferguson oratory while they and Standard Oil and the whiskey men carried on the campaign's real business, which was to snipe at Davidson because he had uncovered their scheme to monopolize oil in Texas. "Dan is the knight on the white horse cavaliering against Ferguson, but the heavy work is being done by the Hogg brothers, the Houston Post-Dispatch, Oscar B. Colquitt and others who are mixing oil and liquor in their political sentiments."[57]

Stung, the Hogg brothers took note of Davidson's charges in a statement released to the press on June 29, pointing out that there was such "a striking note of similarity" between his present tactics and "Old Jim's early political efforts" that "Lynch's East Texas nickname of Loblolly Lynch is liable to be changed in the cut-over districts to Little Jim, and we fear it might stick." In a letter to Davidson dated July 13, the brothers indignantly denied his charge that they were in combination with oil and liquor interests in contributing to a slush fund for Moody and offered to open their books, checks, vouchers, and files for a public audit provided Davidson would do likewise. Davidson characterized their letter as "typical of Jim Ferguson–Colquitt politics," called attention to the "flood of money" being spent in Moody's campaign, and offered to report his campaign expenditures if Moody would do likewise. "If my campaign expenses amount to one-fourth of Moody's total campaign expenses, I will offer a public apology for whatever I may have said."[58]

Beyond charging that Davidson had always been in favor of "large interests" and that his attitude was influenced by a desire not so much to drive them from the state as to appeal to popular prejudice against a large oil company for political advantage, the Moody camp made no effective reply to the candidate's charges concerning Senate Bill 180 and corporate support for Moody. Don H. Biggers later stated that "beyond question corporations contributed thousands of dollars to his [Moody's] campaign fund" and that Davidson's proof of his charge that the attorney general was the candidate of corporations "should have received far more serious consideration than it did." Although they were provided with advance copies of Davidson's speech in Bonham, neither the *Houston Post-Dispatch* nor the *Houston Chronicle* carried a word in their news columns about his attack on Senate Bill 180. Four years later, however, when J. Frank Norris demanded that Moody give the people of Texas the names of the "big oil companies" that had put up $105,000 to elect him governor, Moody fired back, "I am pleased to say to you that no oil company has ever at anytime contributed any sum of money or anything of value to any campaign fund of mine."[39]

Drawing on his personal wealth, Davidson distributed statewide 70,000 free copies of the *Magnolia Park News*, a small weekly that he converted into a campaign paper; advertised extensively in weekly county newspapers; sponsored a nightly radio program; paid salaries to many county and district campaign managers; and employed what the Hogg brothers called "his clan of compensated claquers and emissaries now traveling throughout the state." Davidson's full-page advertisements in J. Frank Norris's *Searchlight* and the nightly broadcasts of his speeches over Norris's radio station in Fort Worth attracted a great deal of attention and brought a plea from Moody's North Texas manager that something be done through the Fort Worth headquarters to counteract these activities.[60]

The Ferguson and Davidson camps tried to persuade anti-Klan voters that Moody had an understanding with the "bed-sheet brigade" and was a klansman at heart. In a letter to Judge R. V. Soloman of La Grange that was released to the press, Moody branded as "absolutely false and not having the semblance of truth" rumors circulating in Fayette County that he had some connection with the Klan. He said: "My attitude on the Klan question has been established by my record in the courthouse and that record has considerable to do with the campaign issues of two years ago. I campaigned for office and stated many times my attitude on this question. That attitude remains unchanged to this day."[61]

Although relatively few voters other than die-hard Fergusonites were persuaded that Moody was in league with the Klan, his organization was careful to keep him free from any taint by association with the knights. A Palestine speech was canceled when it was learned that the local Klan was holding its annual barbecue the same night. "Jim Ferguson would say all over the country that Dan addressed the K.K.K. Barbecue here and lots of people would believe it as Jim's appeal is to the ignorant and he is not trying to reach the intelligent voters of the State," warned the president of the Anderson County Moody club. Plans for the attorney general to attend a private chicken-barbecue dinner in La Grange before he spoke were canceled when the host was accused of being a klansman.[62]

Undoubtedly many klansmen and former members preferred Moody over Jim Ferguson, despite his anti-Klan stance. In Smith County they were said to be "lining up almost to a 'man'" for the attorney general, and a Rusk lawyer complained to Colquitt that the self-appointed Moody leaders in Cherokee County were "a coterie, all of whom were for both Robertson and Butte . . . two years ago and have assumed that they are the sole custodians of the Moody campaign . . . , and in this way are undertaking a revival of Ku Klux prestige at the expense of Moody's popularity." In 1928 a klansman wrote Tom Love that "my friend M. A. Childers, then highest officer in the Ku Klux in Texas," had "made speeches in every part where the Klan had lodges, urging all us Klansmen to vote solidly for Moody as the lesser of two evils . . . , he seeming the strongest with the best record with which to defeat Fergusonism."[63]

Moody-for-governor clubs were not organized in a number of counties because it was feared there would be friction between his Klan and anti-Klan supporters. For example, a Hillsboro lawyer, George W. Dupree, warned Moody that a club in Hill County would be "the worst politics that could happen" because it would have to include both klansmen and anti-klansmen and would give both groups an excuse for voting against the attorney general because the other side was supporting him. Moody agreed with this analysis but added, "Of course, if the Klan following should undertake to assume the reins of organization in your county, I would appreciate your doing all you can to offset this by having a balanced organization including the best men of both sides of the question."[64]

Moody supporters accused Jim Ferguson of giving the Klan hell in

the *Forum* and on the stump but at the same time giving jobs to all of
them that he could with the intention of getting as many Klan votes as
possible. As an example they pointed to Mike Lively, Ferguson's chief
lieutenant in Dallas County and an attorney for the Fuller Construction Company, which had received contracts from the State Highway
Commission. According to Colquitt, Lively was one of the three men
who had forced Felix Robertson on the Klan in 1924.[65]

Davidson was reported to be putting forth a "terrific effort" to line
up the Klan in Dallas County, and Zeke Marvin, Dr. A. C. Parker,
Alec Pope, and a few of their immediate followers were for him, though
Pope was not putting forth any great effort in his behalf. When Davidson spoke in Dallas on June 21, Marvin and Parker were on the speaker's
stand. In Paris, Texas, three active Klan leaders made arrangements
for Davidson's speech. "The only votes that I can find Davidson is getting here are the 'died-in-the-wool' klansmen who are dying hard and
pick Davidson as the least of three evils," a Timpson man told Moody
headquarters. A San Saba editor declared that "Lynch Davidson has
bought the leaders of the klan just like a cattle man would drouth
stricken cattle, with range delivery."[66]

Rumors increased in July that the Klan was going to throw its support to Davidson. The secretary of the order in Port Arthur was quoted
as saying that the Klan was lining up for the Houston man and would
throw its entire strength to him in the last week of the campaign,
though the informant reported that the leading klansmen in Beaumont
said that they had no such word. A Dr. Kirby from Arlington, claiming
to be a knight, visited a number of klansmen in Cleburne on July 6 and
stated that there would be a stampede of klansmen for Davidson in the
primary. There was considerable talk in Houston about the Klan's
swinging its influence in favor of Davidson. "In my opinion an earnest
effort is being made to accomplish this, but the situation did not seem
alarming to the executive committee when we talked it over at a meeting last night," reported the secretary of the Moody organization in
that city. The *Fort Worth American*, a Klan paper, recommended Davidson to the order, and an issue of Norris's *Searchlight* containing a
Davidson ad charging that a "conspiracy of oil and booze was going to
elect Dan Moody" and a cartoon showing the attorney general sitting
on Colquitt's knee with a whiskey bottle pouring money into his hand,
was sent to all *American* subscribers.[67]

The campaign of 1926 was colorful and frequently dirty. The Ferguson camp viciously attacked Moody's war record. One campaign card read: "You hear much of *'Fighting Dan' But!* When red battle stamped its foot and Nations felt the shock—where, oh, where was your 'Fighting Dan'? Invincible in Peace and Invisible in War 'Dan's the Man.'" Another card, printed in red, that was mailed from Ferguson headquarters read: "'Fighting Dan'? 'Southern Chivalry'? 'First in Peace, Last in War, First to Run against a Woman Governor.' 'Dan's the 'Reclassified Man.'" Moody supporters responded that, while their candidate made no claim to being a war hero, his military record was one of which no man need be ashamed; he had been honorably discharged from the army in February, 1919, and was a past post commander of the American Legion and a Legion member in good standing. They contrasted Moody's record with that of Ferguson, who had made a speech against the draft in Dallas in April, 1917, and had publicly and repeatedly attacked President Wilson. The Moody camp also reminded voters that Ferguson had been twenty-six and unmarried at the time of the Spanish-American War but had not enlisted.[68]

Moody's opponents spread the story that, while serving as district attorney in Williamson and Travis counties, he had used blacks as jurors in the trials of white men and had gone out of his way to do so. Travis County used the jury-wheel system, by which property-owning blacks were occasionally drawn in the panel. In one or two cases defense counsel refused to excuse them, and they were seated as jurors. Moody headquarters hastened to squelch this story, instructing backers to tell inquirers that Moody had a standing offer to lawyers representing defendants to excuse all blacks who might be selected as jurors. In another instance Moody was asked not to speak in Hillsboro on June 19, Negro Emancipation Day in Texas, for fear that Ferguson would make capital of the coincidence.[69]

"I am a member of organized labor," Moody had declared in his opening speech in Taylor, basing his claim on a card issued to him on November 30, 1910, by Union Local 199, International Brotherhood of Electrical Workers, Temple, Texas. The Moody camp circulated among labor men a card showing a copy of his union labor card on one side and his photograph and a statement that he was a member of organized labor on the other side. To counteract this, a circular headed "Union Labor Record of General Moody" was distributed in union towns like

Galveston. It reproduced a letter from the secretary of the Electrical
Workers Union, dated April 9, 1926, stating that "we find no record of
any member by the name of Dan Moody." The circular charged:

"General" Moody's main activity in connection with organized labor consists of
his military service at Galveston, during a strike, when he stood with gun and
bayonet against union men who thought they had a right to strike for better
wages and better living conditions, and in his guarding those who had taken
their jobs, and in patronizing a non-union barber shop at Taylor. This is the
record of "General" Moody upon which he is asking the support of organized
labor.[70]

The Moody managers used two of Ferguson's editorial diatribes
against him. On December 16, 1920, he had written in the *Forum* that
"the Mexican people have not improved one bit in civilization and they
are more blood thirsty than ever. I had rather have a hundred Japs
than a dozen Mexicans in Texas. The Mexican hordes coming into this
country must be stopped by law right now." This piece was printed in
both English and Spanish under the title "Ferguson to Drive Mexicans
from Texas." The manager of the Moody Club in Wichita Falls requested and received a copy of Ferguson's attack on the Jewish merchants of Dallas, which he wanted to have printed in pamphlet form.[71]

Efforts were also made to shake the consistent loyalty of German and Czech voters to the Fergusons. Colquitt was popular with
these voters because of his anti-Prohibition views, and copies of the
Free Lance were circulated along with Moody literature in German
and Czech. The Czech fraternal lodges were reminded that Ferguson
wanted to repudiate the Texas road bonds that they had purchased.
Czech speakers were recruited, and Moody ads, including an endorsement by Williamson County Czechs, were published in Czech-
language newspapers. Judge Augustine Haidusek of La Grange,
publisher of *Svoboda*, was "strong for Mr. Moody" and printed the endorsement without charge. All the other papers were reluctant to accept the ads and charged regular rates. Moody's men hoped, at best, to
"hammer down" Ferguson majorities. "This county has always been
strong for Ferguson, and I can not say that he will not carry it, but we
will do our best," promised a supporter in Guadalupe County.[72]

As primary day neared, partisans of the three major candidates
sought to outdo one another in public professions of devotion. Stickers
reading "Me for Ma," "Lynch Is a Cinch," "Dan's the Man," "More
Men like Dan Moody," and "Thinking of Ma Makes Me *Moody*" ap-

peared in every section of the state. The most popular slogan, "Dan's the Man," was painted on fences and barns, pasted on automobile windshields and in windows of stores and homes, and posted everywhere else where glue or nails would stick. Learning that highway employees were tearing down Moody signs along the roads, Moody's San Antonio headquarters sent out two men at night to paint "Moody" across area roads every half mile or so. "No one can come in or out of this territory without seeing *Moody* very often," the office manager proudly reported.[73]

It was soon evident that the Ferguson campaign was in trouble. Almost alone of the anti-Ferguson leaders who had rallied to Mrs. Ferguson's side against the Klan in 1924, Joe Bailey remained loyal and made a number of speeches in Ma's behalf.[74] At the end of June it was rumored that Mrs. Ferguson was contemplating withdrawing from the race. A report circulated that Jim had kidney trouble that would kill him in thirty days if he kept campaigning and that her own kidneys were bad. Publicly branding such rumors as "absolutely untrue and a rank falsehood," the governor declared that she had entered the race to stay and to win and that Jim's health was excellent. Her husband at first predicted in the *Ferguson Forum* that she would lead Moody by at least 242,000 votes but a month later revised her majority downward to 105,000. Yet he claimed that "poor Dan is a blowed out sucker that is weakening every day. His friends know it, his opposition sees it, the dogs know it, the children know it, the women know it and Lynch Davidson is shouting about it and Moody is paying the penalty for sponsoring a hate campaign in Texas politics."[75]

Mrs. Ferguson unexpectedly joined her husband at Brownwood on July 14, telling the crowd that her opponents wanted to deny her a second term because she was a woman and had a husband. "I call on the wives and mothers to withhold this attack on our sex. I am claiming my rights and the rights of all women as well when I ask for re-election. As for my husband, he is able to take care of his rights himself." The governor warned that if she lost the election "the cause of woman's rights will be set back 100 years."[76]

Throughout the campaign Ferguson was bothered by hecklers, to whom he made bitter responses. In his closing speech at Wooldridge Park in Austin, Ferguson offered a heckler fifty dollars to come to the speaker's stand to "fight it out" and waited ten minutes while a youth in the audience who had yelled out a question was jostled by a dozen Fergusonites and rushed partway out of the park. Cheers for Moody, which started mildly fifteen minutes after Ferguson followed his wife in addressing the crowd of 18,000—the largest crowd ever to gather in the park—grew in volume as Ferguson bitterly denounced the hecklers as "ku klux cowards," "dirty scoundrels," "damn scoundrels," and "low-down idiots." "In Wooldridge Park everyone said it was the 'wildest political rally' ever," Mrs. Moody wrote later in the family scrapbook. "Newspapers said next day Ma fanned Jim & encouraged him. Those near the bandstand said she told him to 'shut up' & 'sit down'!!!'" [77]

Moody was extremely confident about the outcome of the election, especially in the closing days of the campaign. All over the state he was told he would win a clear majority, making a runoff unnecessary. Jim Ferguson predicted that his wife would lead all the others and win the nomination in the first primary. Lynch Davidson's manager said that his man would run first, Moody second, and the Fergusons third, that 100,000 votes would go to "Zim and the ladies" (a reference to Zimmerman and the two obscure women candidates, Edith Wilmans and Kate Johnston), and that a runoff would be necessary. "As the German butcher said to his customer, 'you pays your money and you takes your choice,'" commented H. N. Fitzgerald, veteran political reporter of the *Austin American*. [78]

The "Texas Twister" that political weather prophets had predicted as far back as the previous November visited the Lone Star State in the form of the July 24 primary, and when the dust had cleared, Moody, with 409,732 votes, lacked only 1,771 votes of receiving a clear majority over all his opponents. Mrs. Ferguson with 283,482 votes, trailed him by 126,250. Davidson was far down in third place with 122,449 votes. Zimmerman received 2,962 votes, Mrs. Wilmans 1,580, and Mrs. Johnston 1,029. For a time it appeared that Moody's total would exceed that of the other five candidates, but the correction of an error of 3,000 in tabulating the Milam County returns wiped out his majority and made a runoff necessary—unless Governor Ferguson withdrew. [79]

Mrs. Ferguson had a majority in only thirty counties, chiefly in East Texas and the ten German counties, where she carried 61 percent of the totals. Moody received majorities in ninety-eight counties, including Dallas, Harris, Bexar, Tarrant, and Travis counties. Davidson had majorities in only two counties, Kenedy and Winkler. The attorney general carried the Fergusons' home county, Bell, by 5,076 to 4,020 for Mrs. Ferguson and won her home ward in Temple 405 to 192. [80]

"This means the end of 'Fergusonism' in public affairs," telegraphed the *Austin American* in response to the *Literary Digest's* request for comment on Moody's victory. The *El Paso Times and Herald*
was convinced that "Texas has recovered her self-respect." "Texas
might have stood for Governor 'Ma' Ferguson a while longer from
considerations of chivalry," added the paper, "but former Governor
'Jim' was too much of a load, particularly after he advocated repudiation of the outstanding road district bonds of the State, aggregating
$80,000,000." The verdict of the primary was "clear and unmistakable"
to the *Fort Worth Star-Telegram*: "It means the immediate restoration
of Texas credit." Furthermore, "The vote for Dan Moody is the most
stinging rebuke ever given any State Administration, with the possible
exception of that which resulted in the impeachment of Governor 'Jim'
in 1917." "Young, fearless, and aggressive, Moody is to-day the strongest man politically that Texas has had in a long time," declared the
Dallas Dispatch, an opinion echoed in the national press, which gave
extensive coverage to Moody's victory.[81]

McAdoo supporters in Texas saw Moody's victory as a portent of
success for their beloved Chief in 1928. Marshall Hicks, Frank C.
Davis, and George D. Armistead sent McAdoo the following telegram:

Texas has set her house in order and restored responsible government and
what Texas has done she will join with the nation in repeating in November
nineteen twenty-eight under your leadership. Tom Love has been elected to
the State Senate and will be administration leader and Robert L. Bobbitt
Moody's classmate and Marshall's law partner will be Speaker of the House.
Wherefore we send you love and greetings.

Tom Love also thought that Moody's "glorious victory" meant "McAdoo
for President in 1928." McAdoo was pleased by the recent political developments. "I am overjoyed that Fergusonism in Texas has been uprooted," he wrote Thomas Watt Gregory. "Our friends have been doing some good work lately in Texas, Oklahoma, Tennessee and Iowa."[82]

Texans waited to see whether Mrs. Ferguson would honor her
pledge to resign if Moody led her in the first primary. On July 26 she
authorized a special session of the legislature for September 13 to validate the road-district bonds and to conduct an investigation of state departments. At the same time she announced her withdrawal from the
race for governor, whether or not Moody had a majority, and said that
she would resign her office "no later than November 1." Moody immediately declared that her pledge to resign was not in compliance with

the challenge made at Sulphur Springs and accepted by him. He added that he was powerless to force her to comply and said that only the people could do that. The consensus among Texas newspapers was that the governor had welshed on the bet.[83]

In the *Forum* of July 29, an editorial by Jim Ferguson appeared under a bold black headline, "How It Happened." In the editorial he admitted: "I don't know. I am just beginning to find out. I hope in due course to be able to learn the real reason for the results of last Saturday's election. I think the opposition in their desire to gloat over the defeat of a woman will aid us in getting the evidence." The direction his private investigation was taking was indicated by his warning:

Nobody need be surprised to see the fiery cross in evidence and this crowd is so wild with victory that we need not be surprised to see a Ku Klux parade in the next sixty days and perhaps some good American will fall a victim to the lash. Some prominent politicians are claiming that the antimask law from this time on is a nullity and that a strong demand will be made for the repeal of the search and seizure law.[84]

The county Democratic conventions met on July 31, and a large majority—perhaps as many as two-thirds—adopted resolutions calling for Mrs. Ferguson's immediate resignation. When the State Democratic Executive Committee met in Dallas on August 9 to canvass the vote in the first primary, both Jim Ferguson and Moody were present with their followers, and both groups were at sea about what the other side was planning. At the committee meeting Mrs. Ferguson asked in a petition that Moody's name not be certified to the various county chairmen and committees because he had received unlawful campaign contributions from two legislators, Lee Satterwhite and R. L. Bobbitt, and had received but not accounted for large sums, some of them unlawfully accepted from firms, associations, and corporations, and that the money had been used to perpetrate election frauds. Chairman Arthur Eidson ruled that the committee was not a judicial body and should not consider the petition, and the members voted unanimously to sustain him. The names of both Moody and Mrs. Ferguson were certified for the second primary. An angry Moody told the committee that her petition was presented "for a sinister political purpose. It was presented before this committee for the benefit of these newspaper reporters and I denounce the representations of fact and the conclusions drawn."[85]

Meanwhile, Moody supporters in Austin claimed that the governor's failure to file an expense account twenty-five days before the runoff was a violation of the election law punishable by the barring of her name from the ballot. They also revealed that her campaign had received $25.00 from a county judge in La Salle County. Moody's own campaign expense account showed contributions amounting to $9,938.50 and expenditures totaling $9,009.44, leaving a balance of $929.06, which would be prorated among all the contributors to his campaign. Obviously, this was just the tip of the iceberg.[86] Although by law candidates for governor and U.S. senator could not spend more than $10,000, the limit applied only to those expenditures actually made by the candidates or their campaign headquarters. It did not include money spent by friends, by state, district, or local committees, or by other interested parties.

Any doubts that there would be an active runoff campaign and that Mrs. Ferguson would resign were removed on August 11, when she announced that she was in the contest to the end and that Moody had never accepted her proposition to resign—that he had sidestepped by calling it "Jim's bluff" and would not have resigned if the vote had been in her favor, and that, in addition, the pledge was based on the two primaries and not a single election. The governor said that she had obtained a majority of the Democratic votes of Texas but that the oil companies with their money coupled with the Klan and the "Love stripe of bolting democrats" had backed Moody and given him the vote he received. She pointed to the Klan's gloatings over his victory as partial proof. "In other words, my proposition was based upon a Democratic primary and not a bolting Ku Klux Klan primary. Even if Mr. Moody had accepted my proposition directly to me, I would have been released by reason of political fraud and illegal election."

Mrs. Ferguson virtually served notice that the Klan and the oil companies would be the principal issues in the second primary, promising, if elected, to curtail Klan activities further and to urge a law requiring them to register their membership in each county and intimating that the coming special session would be called upon to raise the tax on crude-oil production from 1.5 percent to 3 percent. Replying to Moody's charges of government by proxy and irresponsible government, she asserted, "Invisible government is a lot worse than irresponsible government."[87]

It is difficult to understand why Jim Ferguson had his wife make the runoff race when defeat was certain. Saying that there were only three issues in the runoff—"Fergusonism vs. Ku Kluxism; Moodyism vs. legal elections; Moodyism vs. gasoline tax for schools and roads"— Jim compared the August campaign to the recent Jack Dempsey–Luis Firpo prizefight, vowing that, "like that of Dempsey over Firpo, this will be a triumph of brain and courage over youth and ignorance."[88]

Suffering severely from recurrent attacks of hay fever, Mrs. Ferguson appeared with her husband only at the campaign opening in Temple, just a week before the August 28 runoff. But she gave out several statements to the press attacking her opponent. Declaring that she was still opposed to any attempt to relocate the state prison system, she charged that Moody planned to move the state penitentiary to 10,000 acres of mostly worn-out land near Round Rock in Moody's home county, Williamson. "The scheme to relocate the penitentiary system will tax the people of Texas at least $8,000,000 more for land alone," she said, "and it will cost $2,000,000 additional to erect buildings to take care of the prison population." In her second campaign statement of the week the governor reiterated that the Klan was the real issue in the campaign and charged that Moody was trying to dodge the issue "to deceive and divide our friends." "If Mr. Moody should be elected the Governor all his crowd would be invisible and he would be responsible more to the Ku Klux Klan than to the Democrats of Texas," she warned. "Let's have no quibbling and dodging of the real issue in this campaign."[89]

In speeches in Galveston, Sealy, and Groesbeck, Ferguson stressed that there was an alliance between the Klan and Moody and said that he would devote his life to fighting invisible government. "Dan Moody is not attacking the Klan," he asserted, "and it makes no difference whether he belongs or not. Just as soon as the Governor got back into the race, they quit making demonstrations they had when they thought Moody was nominated." Noting that Moody's lead came from twenty-five cities and towns controlled by the Klan, he accused Klan election officials of stuffing the ballot boxes and warned that if there was any corruption in the second primary he would ask for an investigation of the oil companies' books; they had spent large sums of money in the first campaign and had enlisted the support of the Klan in hopes of getting an administration that would defeat the gasoline tax. "And we'll put more people in the pen than Ma Ferguson could pardon out in a 1,000 years," he vowed.[90]

Moody spent two weeks campaigning in every part of the state except the far-western section and the Panhandle. He said in Houston that Ferguson's issues were all "clap-trap," including the prison relocation story, which he said Ferguson had made up "out of whole cloth," and that his cries of election fraud only showed that he was a poor loser. The Klan issue had been settled "two years ago," and the people were going to get rid of "proxy government." The attorney general, in a "joyous mood," closed his campaign in Austin, speaking in Wooldridge Park, where Ferguson had made his last speech in the first primary; his militant attack on Ferguson was greeted with cheers and laughter.[91]

Lynch Davidson and most of his supporters moved into the Moody fold. A number of Fergusonites, disgusted by the governor's failure to resign or discouraged by Moody's huge lead in the first primary, indicated that they would vote for the attorney general or would not vote at all.[92] Surprised by the Fergusons' decision not to open their campaign until August 21, Moody's friends concluded that Jim believed that his one hope of success was to keep the vote small on election day and that a more active campaign would only bring out Moody voters in greater numbers. "It seems that the slogan for the Ferguson bunch is to keep their dogs tied under the wagon till the morning of the twenty eighth and they will be cut loose and rushed to the polls, while the Moody supporters will be careless and not turn out," warned a Moody man. "That is the way they aim to elect Mrs. Ferguson."[93] The Moody headquarters in Austin advised his friends to avoid overconfidence and to turn out a record-breaking vote. The Texas Women Citizens' Committee urged its members to put on an intensive campaign: "Let us once and for all place the stamp of every intelligent woman's disapproval on the growing tendency of scheming, unscrupulous politicians who try to place feminine 'cats-paws' or 'figure-heads' in office, through a hypocritical appeal of 'chivalry for the weaker sex.'"[94]

Mrs. Ferguson was buried beneath a deluge of Moody ballots, receiving 270,595 votes to her opponent's 495,723. The attorney general made an almost clean sweep of the counties in North and West Texas, and all the large-city counties gave him huge majorities—a lead of 23,704 votes in Dallas, 16,290 in Harris, 15,823 in Tarrant, and 8,946 in Bexar. He won his home county by a large majority and also led in Bell and Bosque, the two Ferguson home counties. Travis County gave Moody 9,046 votes; Mrs. Ferguson, 2,541. She practically doubled the votes for her opponent in the ten German counties, 16,636 to 8,572, and led in twenty additional counties, mostly in South and Southeast Texas. "Don Archee" Parr refused to desert the Ferguson standard, and Duval County gave her 1,210 votes to Moody's 25, but Starr County switched its allegiance from the first primary, when Mrs. Ferguson had polled 848 votes to Moody's 21 and Davidson's 4. This time around Moody received 1,007 votes, and Mrs. Ferguson 3.[95]

When asked how his wife considered her defeat, Ferguson replied proudly: "My wife is a good sport," and told newsmen, "We are just trying to decide which calf the train ran over." He talked of his political philosophy, saying: "One must play the game philosophically. When one is crowned with the laurel wreath of victory, reflection will convince one he has not gained one-tenth of what he thought. Similarly when one has lost, he has not lost one-tenth of what he had first thought." On reflection, however, the bitterly disappointed former governor editorialized in the *Forum* that all but 131,735 of Moody's votes had come from "Ku Klux or Ku Klux lovers" while his wife had received 275,000 Democratic votes. "I am really amused at the situation already," Ferguson commented. "When Mr. Moody tries to hold Earle Mayfield, John Tobin, O. B. Colquitt, Tom Love, Atticus Webb and Hiram Evans in the same bed—Boy, he will be some fixer if he can put it over. We already hear the rumblings."[96]

The gubernatorial campaign had overshadowed a hotly contested race for the nomination for attorney general, in which twenty-seven-year-old James V. Allred of Wichita Falls (a future "Centennial governor" of Texas) was a candidate, along with Charles L. Brachfield, Thomas B. Christopher, John W. Hornsby, T. K. Irwin, and Claude Pollard. To almost everyone's surprise Allred, who crisscrossed the state in a secondhand Model T Ford, entered the runoff against Pollard, a former assistant attorney general under R. V. Davidson. Pollard led in the first primary with 149,204 votes to Allred's 144,820.[97]

Although privately for Moody, Allred tried to stay out of the governor's race, but during the runoff his enemies in Wichita County circulated rumors that he was a strong Ferguson man.[98] Jim Ferguson was provoked by Allred's disclaimers to come out in the *Forum* with a story blasting Allred for denying that he had sought Ferguson's help in the campaign. Ferguson's attack helped Pollard among the dyed-in-the-wool Ferguson men but helped Allred among Jim's enemies.[99] Allred lost to Pollard in the runoff, but his opponent's victory margin—4,046 votes—was so small that there was no stigma attached to defeat, and he would have to be reckoned with in the future. Allred analyzed the outcome as follows:

My opponent was pretty experienced in the game and had the support of about ninety per cent of the lawyers of the state and all of the newspapers, and my campaign was a personal one in which I appealed to the great common people. The result was that my vote is an expression of personal popularity and his the result of a campaign principally of advertising.

Deciding that it was best to accept defeat as gracefully as possible, Allred did not demand a recount. Returning to Wichita Falls to open a law office with his brother Raymond, he bided his time.[100]

Moody's forces were in complete control of the State Democratic Convention, which met in San Antonio on September 7. Neither the governor nor her husband attended, though Lavaca County had named them as delegates. The platform adopted with a lone dissenting vote was similar to the draft that Moody submitted, the chief difference being that he proposed to denounce the Klan by name and call upon it to disband in Texas, while the platform deplored the activities of secret societies in politics but did not name the order and eliminated the call to the Klan to disband. Moody wanted to take the fight to name the Klan before the convention, but John Boyle of San Antonio and other anti-Klan leaders dissuaded him. Moody, however, mentioned the Klan issue in his acceptance address, saying that he had taken a public position from the start of active and outspoken opposition to "any hampering of liberty and constitutional government for members of any creed or race."[101]

"This awful State convention," Ferguson called it, declaring that it "did not have the nerve to call the Ku Klux by name." I told you so, Ferguson chortled:

Mr. Moody says he is now fighting the Ku Klux, but when the Governor was fighting the Ku Klux before the people and I was denouncing their activities in this campaign, Mr. Moody said I was using a last year's bird nest for an issue in this campaign and he said in the campaign that the Ku Klux question was settled. I am just wondering that if he believed he was right then why didn't he tell the convention that they were talking about a last year's bird nest when they put in a plank in the platform condemning secret societies in politics. Ma Ferguson can now say, "I told you so" on one proposition at least.[102]

Ferguson had a point. While Texas was no longer the banner Klan state in the Union, politicians were still wary of its invisible influence. Boyle, a Roman Catholic, had declined the permanent chairmanship

of the convention and had stayed out of the limelight for fear of arousing anti-Catholic feelings, and the convention, like the 1924 Democratic National Convention in New York City, failed to condemn the
Klan by name. The strongly anti-Klan *Dallas Morning News* took the
meeting to task for its timidity. Republican National Committeeman
R. B. Creager severely criticized the convention for not denouncing
the Klan by name and called the selection of klansman W. L. Thornton
of Dallas as a member of the state committee a direct slap in the faces
of the anti-Klan forces, especially since an anti-Klan delegate had been
suggested for the office. When, however, Creager was reminded that
the Republican State Convention had also failed to name the Klan in
its condemnation of secret societies of all kinds, he replied lamely: "We
didn't boast, however, that we were going to pan the klan, while the
Democrats did."[103]

The special session of the legislature passed 556 bills validating
the road bonds, plus a general-bond-validation act and another measure providing for the issuance of valid bonds in the future and appropriated $5,469,000, including $3,500,000 from the general fund for the
schools to ensure the $14 per capita apportionment. The House cre-
ated a recess committee of anti-Ferguson members to investigate the
State Highway Department, the State Textbook Commission, and the
State Board of Pardons. The committee was to start work immediately
after adjournment and was to report its findings to the Fortieth Legislature, after Mrs. Ferguson had left office. The Senate approved 22 to 8
an investigation of "contributions to campaign funds during the recent
primary elections," but reversed itself the next day 16 to 12, after Senator A. E. Wood objected that the purpose of the investigation was to
embarrass Moody. The House passed 118 to 2 a measure lowering the
motor-registration fee and the companion Dale Bill, increasing the
gasoline tax from one to three cents a gallon, as recommended by the
governor, 102 to 14; but the Senate voted 12 to 8 with unseemly haste
to shelve these bills until the next legislature before the Senate Committee on State Affairs had held its hearings on the two measures and
made its report.[104]

The Senate refused to confirm Hal Moseley and John H. Cage as
highway commissioners. After the vote (22 to 7) was announced, there
were exclamations that "the Ferguson hold on the Senate is forever
broken." When Judge E. L. Pitts of Mineral Wells declined appoint-

ment to the commission and Senators James G. Strong of Carthage and Charles Murphy of Houston found they could not be confirmed to it, Mrs. Ferguson waited until the legislature adjourned and then appointed Eugene Smith, secretary of the commission, to succeed Moseley as chairman and Scott Woodward of Fort Worth to take Cage's place. Commissioner John H. Bickett resigned on account of ill health, and George P. Robertson of Meridian was appointed to succeed him. In the Fortieth Legislature the Senate took no action regarding these three recess appointments, and thus Moody was able to name three highway commissioners, just as Mrs. Ferguson had suggested one and appointed two others when she took office.[105]

On October 7 by a vote of 56 to 47 the House adopted a concurrent resolution asking Governor Ferguson to resign in compliance with her campaign wager with Moody. Before the excitement in the House had died down, word came that Senator H. L. Lewis, presiding in place of Lieutenant Governor Barry Miller, had ruled that the resolution was out of order because it did not come within the governor's call or within any legislation submitted by her. Senator A. E. Wood, Moody's recognized leader in the Senate, announced that the ruling would not be appealed. The legislature adjourned on October 8, and on the following day Representative Rube Loftin of Henrietta, House floor manager for the administration, after a visit to the governor's office, flatly denied capitol gossip that she would resign before her term expired on January 18, 1927.[106]

The House Investigating Committee took testimony between October and December. Headlines in the *Dallas Morning News* told the story: "Ferguson Demanded 10% on Bid, Says Contractor," "Contractors Testify They Paid for Ads in Ferguson Forum," "Nephew of Jim Ferguson Offered to 'Split Commission,' Witness Informs Investigators," "Three Testify of $750 loans to Joe Burkett," "Jim's Brother Asked $2,500, Contractor Says," "'Want Salary Doubled' Book Agent Asks Yoe, He Says," "Prison Official Says He Wasn't Drunk and Never Sold Pardons," "Ferguson Dictates Award of Road Job, Witness Testifies," "Prison Farm Theft Told to Probing Board," and "10,000 Paid Jim to Aid in Railway Plan." The *Ferguson Forum* dismissed all these charges, saying that the House Investigating Committee was stacked with Ferguson's political enemies. It was all pronounced to be "hearsay evidence" and old tales that the grand jury had earlier rejected. Ferguson said that he did not even know the witnesses who made the charges and described their testimony as "infamous cheap political falsehoods" and "damnable lies." [107]

Republican George Butte's 294,970 votes for governor in 1924 against Mrs. Ferguson required the Republicans to hold their first party primary in Texas since the passage of the Terrell Election Law. [108] Both R. B. Creager and Congressman Harry M. Wurzbach sought control of the state party machinery and appealed to national party leaders for assistance. President Coolidge was flooded with letters testifying to the good character of Creager and his Texas organization, while Congressman Will R. Wood of Indiana and John Q. Tilson of Connecticut, the chairman and first vice-chairman, respectively, of the National Republican Congressional Committee, of which Wurzbach was second vice-chairman, received "a packing case of letters" testifying to the contrary. Wood and Tilson told the White House that federal patronage should not be used to destroy a Republican majority in the House of Representatives, as was being done in Texas, and that all the rest was a smoke screen to obscure the real issue. In turn, Creager charged that Wurzbach, under the encouragement of Tilson and Wood and in combination with George F. Rockhold, the leader in 1920 of the Texas presidential efforts for Republican Frank O. Lowden of Illinois, and "Gooseneck" Bill McDonald, the black political boss, was making an open and avowed fight for control of the state organization. According to Creager, the Wurzbach headquarters, run by Rockhold, had been financed by unknown parties outside Texas in the amount of $10,000. [109]

Creager's one-time friend Frank Scobey of San Antonio was now allied with Wurzbach and was trying to interest Vice-President Charles Dawes in making a race for the Republican presidential nomination in 1928. "We have a Primary for the first time in the Republican party this year, and if my friend, the General, is going to get in the 1928 race, now would be a fine time for some of his friends to set the pins for him here," he wrote Dawes's brother Beeman. Beeman, however, did not bother to answer Scobey's letter. [110]

Judge E. P. Scott of Corpus Christi, an old Bull Mooser, was the Wurzbach faction's candidate for governor and carried Bexar County in the congressman's home territory, but Harvey H. Haines of Houston, who had the backing of Creager and the party organization, won the primary, 11,215 to 4,047 for Scott. Wurzbach was an easy winner over

Fred M. Knetsch of Seguin in the Fourteenth Congressional District race. After the primary Wurzbach said that the vote was a decisive repudiation of the Creager–State Chairman Eugene Nolte faction in the Fourteenth District. "It means that a decided drift away from the tactics pursued by the present patronage dispensers in Texas has set in. It will not end until both Creager and Nolte are shelved and the party management put in other hands."[111]

Creager and his friends dominated the Republican State Convention in Dallas on September 7. The Republican State Executive Committee limited the Wurzbach faction to less than 5 percent of the available seats. Creager issued a statement saying that, despite Wurzbach's efforts, 95 percent of the delegates were "regular organization men, and that the Texas party would be behind the national administration."[112]

The general election in November attracted even less interest than usual in a non-presidential-election year. Neither Moody nor Haines bothered to campaign. Haines, general manager of the Houston Chamber of Commerce, was said to have been the first American soldier to land in France from the First Division of the American Expeditionary Force. The *Dallas Morning News* described him as "a veteran Texas Republican." Moody scored the Republicans for advertising their state ticket in the *Ferguson Forum*, terming it "the usual attempt of the republican leaders to gain partisan profit from supposed democratic factional differences. It is true to republican party form and in keeping with republican tactics." Jim Ferguson denied that he had given instructions to his leading supporters to work for the Republican ticket and stated that the Haines ad had been accepted as paid political advertising and did not reflect the attitude of the *Forum* publishers. He and the governor had cast absentee ballots in Temple and had voted the Democratic ticket from top to bottom. In the statewide vote, which equaled about one-third of that cast in the runoff, Moody received 233,068 votes to 31,531 for Haines and 908 for M. A. Smith, the Socialist party candidate.[113]

Wurzbach was reelected by a sizable majority over his opponent, A. D. Rogers, and once more carried Bexar County. After the general election Scobey summarized the Wurzbach faction's charges against Creager and the regular party organization in a letter to a friend in California:

Under the Creager machine the Republican Party in Texas has become almost extinct. Less than twenty-five thousand votes cast in the entire state and when

McKinley ran in 1896 we had one hundred thousand. You know, too, how many Republicans have come into the state since then. But you cannot play against the Ku Klux one time and be for them in the next campaign. All the organization Creager has is on paper. . . . Wurzbach and a Republican representative from his county to the Legislature are the only two Republicans elected in the entire state, and at least forty percent of the entire vote was cast in this district. Creager is in bad with the leaders in the house, but he is in good with Coolidge because Coolidge thinks he can deliver the vote in 1928.[114]

Texans as a whole seemed content to have Moody as the actual as well as titular leader of the Democratic party in the state, and some editorial writers and party chiefs in other states had begun to see him as a potential leader in the national party. Referring to Moody as "the courageous and fighting young attorney general," the *Kansas City Star* added that he had "shown himself aggressively honest" and that "he should be one of the coming men in the democratic leadership." "Out of the Lone Star State has emerged a new figure in national politics," said the *Philadelphia Inquirer* in a front-page story. "Dan Moody, . . . smasher of the power of the Ku Klux Klan, today stands out as the Al Smith of the South, the finest campaigner that section has produced in twenty years." Admirers pointed out that the thirty-three-year-old Moody would be just old enough to serve as president by the time 1928 rolled around and that it would not take the South, the West, and the Middle West long to decide between him and Smith or the "aged McAdoo." Should Moody turn loose his "far-reaching and magnetic voice" in a Democratic convention like that of 1924, "it would be the Chicago convention of 1896 over again, with the red-haired Moody taking the place of the black-haired Bryan."[115]

In contrast, editorial post mortems on the Fergusons struck an elegiac note. "Moody was the logical candidate of the new day in Texas against the 'Fergusonism' of the older day," the *New York Evening Post* explained to its readers. The *Post* writer continued:

A new Texas of the public schools, of the universities, of growing industries, of immigration and of a widening future is doing its best to turn its back on the demagogy and "hill-billyism" of the old Texas. There may be other chapters to come in the dramatic tale of "Fergusonism," but sooner or later "hill-billyism" will lose its grip on Texas. The Lone Star State is entering a new phase in its development in which "Fergusonism" can hardly hold its place.[116]

In a similar vein Duncan Aikman, the discerning El Paso journalist, wrote in the *Southwest Review* that Texans had failed to view Fergusonism for what it really was—"a slice of Americana cut raw from the flank of the almost extinct but still vivid and galumping beast." They did not yet realize that if Jim Ferguson had died fifty years earlier "all the Zenith Lytton Stracheys would even now be begging their publishers to write snippy biographies of him. They have ignored the pointed possibility that in Vermont and Oregon the sophisticates of 1976 may be pawing over his memory to remind themselves sadly that American politics has lost its zest." [117]

Most Texans agreed that the political death knell of Ma and Pa Ferguson had sounded in the election returns, but the Henderson County merchant who warned Moody before the second primary that "Old Jim will never be out of the political arena in Texas until he is placed four feet under sod" was the better prophet. On the last day of Mrs. Ferguson's administration Jim, standing by the desk of her private secretary, remarked: "They did not bluff us after all. When we were criticized for pardoning 20 prisoners we answered them the next day by pardoning 40." "Don't worry," he added, "it will all come out in a washing." The Fergusons would indeed return to the executive mansion, though not until January, 1933, in the depths of the Depression. [118]

CHAPTER 9

A Daniel Come to Judgment

TEXAS's first woman governor relinquished the reins of state government to the state's youngest governor on January 18, 1927, when Dan Moody took the oath of office. The inaugural ceremonies, the first in the state held outdoors, under the arch of the south entrance to the State Capitol Building, was witnessed by what was said to be the largest crowd in Texas history—50,000 people. The Cowboy Band of Simmons College, Mrs. Moody's alma mater, was the inaugural band. Five earlier governors—Joseph Sayers, Oscar B. Colquitt, James E. Ferguson, William P. Hobby, and Pat M. Neff—were present for the ceremonies. Moody sat between Mrs. Ferguson and Lieutenant Governor Barry Miller; the outgoing governor's husband sat on the other side of the improvised platform. Mrs. Moody, who had refused to follow protocol by entering on Jim's arm, occupied a seat with her family immediately in front of the platform. "It went in the newspapers all over the U.S., perhaps I was wrong," she noted in her diary. "But I felt we owed him no courtesy, time for that to stop and justice be done. I was commended by many and I am sure many thought me 'little,' but I felt right."[1]

Both the outgoing and the incoming governors showed by their remarks that the campaign had not been entirely forgotten. In her speech of presentation Mrs. Ferguson made this statement:

If I am condemned and criticized I shall not murmur because I remember that Sam Houston, the Father of Texas, paid the same penalty. If I am hated and abused I shall forgive my enemies and find comfort in the recollection that Jim Hogg, when he laid down the reins of power, was also hated and abused.

"Frankly, he was not my choice for governor," she said disparagingly of Moody. "He may not have been your choice. But be that as it may, whether you like it or not, he is now your governor." She ended by asking the people to support Moody in the interest of the public good. "If he makes a success we all ought to be pleased—if he makes a failure some of you can be pleased." Noting that Moody's election as a "34-year-old governor [he was actually thirty-three] was about as novel as my election as a woman governor," she declared. "Time alone will prove whether the people have acted wisely in either instance." Moody laughed with the crowd.

In his brief address the new governor said that the people "commission us to place their government upon a plan which will restore public confidence in existing forms and receive the respect of all men." "I recognize that the people of Texas hold their public offices in sacred trust," said the man who during the campaign had charged the Fergusons with fostering "irresponsible government."[2]

Mrs. Ferguson seemed in good spirits and said to friends, "I'm sitting on top of the world." Following the precedent set by Governor Neff, she marked the Golden Rule (Matthew 7:12) in the Bible for her successor's guidance: "Therefore all things whatsoever ye would that men should do to you, do ye even so to them; for this is the law and the prophets." Before she left office, Mrs. Ferguson filed 304 additional clemency proclamations with the secretary of state, 147 of which were full pardons, bringing the total of her clemency proclamations for two years to 3,595.[3]

Few Texas governors had assumed office under such auspicious circumstances—youth, victory in a memorable political campaign climaxing a notable record in the attorney general's office, a record majority in a gubernatorial election, and a host of enthusiastic followers. "Because of these facts, it is all the more important to the new Governor that his administration should be the success to which Texas looks forward," cautioned the *Dallas Morning News*. "A young man whose pleasing personality found him friends in a heated race is no longer the picturesque campaigner. He is Dan J. Moody, Governor of Texas."[4]

Moody knew that he had a big job on his hands. He had many things to do and many other things to undo. The problems of Texas government held his chief interest as he talked to an interviewer for the *New York Times* about taxation, good roads, administration of justice, civil service, and the libel laws. He wanted to make taxation uniform throughout the state and absolutely fair to rich and poor alike, adding that that also involved the public-school system—which, if he had his way, he intended to make the equal of any other in the nation. He wanted country boys and girls to receive a full nine months of instruction a year, just as urban children did. "I want to see Texas a State of splendid schools, a system in which every child, no matter how humble, will get the very best advantages that a State with the wealth of Texas can supply," he declared.[5]

Making his first appearance before the legislature since his inauguration, Moody delivered his initial message at a joint session of the House and Senate on January 20. The galleries and the floor of the House chamber were filled with spectators, who frequently applauded his various recommendations. He suggested to the lawmakers the development of a scientific system of taxation; judicial reform so as to make justice surer, speedier, more economical, more equitable, and more nearly within the reach of rich and poor alike; the enactment of a classified civil-service law; enactment of a corrupt-practices act prohibiting members or officers of one department from accepting employment with other departments; reasonable increases in the salaries of some state officers; and establishment of a unified system of accounting for all state departments.

In other recommendations, he favored placing the prison system on a self-supporting basis, creating a prison board empowered to select a manager for the system, and passing laws, or constitutional amendments if necessary, to protect the public from the indiscriminate pardoning of criminals and to ensure that both sides of every pardon application would receive a full and complete hearing. The governor also recommended the efficient and economical development of a system of interconnecting state highways and the appropriation of adequate revenues for the State Highway Department. He also advocated improvement of the state's election laws, amendment of the libel laws to protect newspapers and other publications in conveying fair and accurate information to the public, and an alimony law for married women. He urged liberal funding of the state's public schools, coordination of the institutions of higher education to eliminate duplications, and provision for a stable income for public schools, based on the state's taxable wealth, to assure uniformity of school terms throughout the state, "so that every child shall have an equal opportunity to secure instruction for the same period or term." The further development of Texas ports should be encouraged so that the state's producers could enjoy the savings of water transportation for their goods.[6]

Moody's message, which established him as an advocate of business-progressive reform, together with a few proposals that he made

later, set forth what came to be known as the "Moody Program." The
state press applauded the governor's words. "Governor Moody has
given the Legislature a lead," editorialized the *Dallas Morning News*.
"It will not fail greatly nor go far astray if it follows along the courses he
would lead it." A Knott cartoon, "A Job Well Done!" showed an approving Old Man Texas reading Moody's message. Said another paper:

All of us expected an honest message, wherever reform in judicial procedure
and pardons might be touched upon. But the 5,000,000 people of Texas today
reading the first message of governor Moody will realize as they read, that a
constructive, broad-gauged and fearless mind sits within the head of the 33-
year-old red-headed smiling youngster who until a few years ago had never
been out of his native state. Texas has seen the dawn of a splendid legislative duty.[7]

   The Fortieth Legislature had sixty-four freshmen members—fifty-
nine in the House and five in the Senate. The new senators were Mar-
gie E. Neal of Carthage, the first woman elected to the Texas Senate;
Julian P. Greer of Athens; Thomas B. Love of Dallas; J. W. Hall of
Houston; and W. D. McFarlane of Graham. There was "practically no
contest" in the election of Speaker of the House. Opposition to Robert
Lee Bobbitt of Laredo, a Moody partisan, faded considerably when
W. S. Barron of Bryan announced that he would not be a candidate.
On January 8, F. A. Dale of Bonham, who had been leading the anti-
Bobbitt forces, announced that his group would not field a candidate.
Old-timers could not remember when a legislature had not had at least
two candidates for Speaker, and the contest had always provided some
excitement as the session opened. Its absence meant a tame start. Bob-
bitt's friends declared that no resentment would be shown toward
House members who had sided with the Ferguson administration during the special session and even said that a few committee chairman-
ships would probably be given to them.
   On January 11, Bobbitt was unanimously elected Speaker, and
Senator A. E. Wood, another friend of Moody's, was named president
pro tem of the Senate, over which Lieutenant Governor Barry Miller
would preside. A reporter for the *Dallas Morning News* noted that
Moody's friends were "in undisputed control of both the House and
the Senate." The opening session of the House was also unique in that
a woman, Secretary of State Emma Grigsby Meharg, presided and declared the House ready for business. "She ruled over the House for

fully an hour, directing its temporary organization and wielding the gavel with the poise and confidence of a veteran presiding officer," the reporter commented.[8]

One of the highlights of the opening days of the session was Tom Love's proposed amendment to the Senate rules requiring lobbyists to register with the Senate Committee on Legislation before interviewing senators. The lobbyists were to fill out forms, under oath, showing the names of their clients, the legislation they were interested in and whether they were for or against it, and such information as the committee might require. Moreover:

It shall be its duty to make such examination and investigations as it shall deem advisable, or as may be requested in writing by an Senator, for the purpose of ascertaining and informing the Senate of the facts pertinent to the employment or compensation of any legislative representative, agent or attorney or of the methods used by any such representative, agent or attorney, to influence legislation, including any contributions heretofore made by any such agent, representative, or attorney, or by any such person, firm or corporation represented by them, to campaign funds in this State.

Love explained:

It is not my purpose to convict any person of dishonesty or to reflect on any person, but I want to turn the spotlight of publicity on lobbying, the same as Woodrow Wilson did when Washington swarmed with lobbyists who were endeavoring to smother some of his great constructive programs. It had a highly salutary effect and that is what I would do for Texas and the Texas Legislature.

"Pitiless publicity," as Wilson had called it, was a great deterrent to wrongdoers, Love added, and a great aid in passing "wholesome" legislation.

When his proposed rule change received a 3-to-1 adverse committee report, Love promised to press it as soon as the inauguration was over. On January 21, however, after appealing to his fellow senators to "assist in an honest and sincere effort" to put a stop to alleged lobbying practices "before the oil interests of this State go the way of the breweries," Love lost the fight on the Senate floor. The vote killing the proposition was 20 to 6, with only Fairchild, Floyd, Greer, McFarlane, and Neal joining Love. Senator Hall, present, who would have voted yes, was paired with Senator Bledsoe, absent, who would have voted no. It is worth noting that all five freshman senators favored Love's proposal.[9]

On January 21, Lee Satterwhite read to the House the report of the House Investigating Committee, which had been looking into the activities of state departments during the Ferguson administration. The committee reported that the testimony it had been able to obtain was "sufficient to establish the fact that the power and prestige of the Governor's office of this State, during the years 1925 and 1926, have been practically usurped and dictated by a private citizen, the husband of the Governor, for political favoritism and financial gain, and the fact that he was a private citizen has placed him beyond the pale of the law." After hearing the report, the House was apparently at a loss about what to do with it. The view of Satterwhite and Claude D. Teer was that no action was needed, since no recommendation had been made. After some discussion that view prevailed, and the report was ordered printed in the *House Journal*, subject to resolutions at any future time.[10]

Soon afterward Jim Ferguson issued a statement, entitled "My Answer to the Probing Committee," denying the allegations. Referring sarcastically to the document as the committee's "great report," Ferguson said:

I have not raised my voice against the committee for fear that somebody might say that I was afraid of their investigation of me and the acts of the Governor. . . . I was willing to let them have their way and do their worst, knowing that, like the proverbial calf, if given enough rope, they would break their own necks. The report filed fully verifies my opinion.[11]

"Jim Ferguson," observed Will Rogers, "has 150,000 voters in Texas that would be with him if he blew up the Capitol building in Washington. They would say, 'Well, Jim was right. The thing ought to have been blowed up years ago.'" Ferguson knew that he could count on the loyalty of his vest-pocket vote in the rural counties. To the surprise of few, he remained in politics, moving from Temple to Austin to be nearer the front line. In October, 1927, he took the *Ferguson Forum* to the capital city, announcing "We Are Here." When he found the financial going difficult, he appealed to the faithful: "Send us at least one subscription and if you do not know whom to send it to, send us the $1.00 and we will get a new reader." In Reinhart Luthin's words, "Soon Governor Moody and his administration were frying on Jim's editorial grill."[12]

Despite their public statements, the Ferguson haters knew that he was neither politically dead nor buried as deep as they claimed.

To keep him on the defensive, Tom Love introduced a bill repealing the Ferguson amnesty law of 1925. After speeches lasting nearly four hours, the Senate approved Love's measure 19 to 7. Three senators present did not vote. Declaring that the Senate was "dominated by the oil companies, Ku Klux and prohibition fanatics of Texas," Ferguson charged that Love was trying to put an end to him and his friends politically so that they could ensure a Texas delegation pledged to McAdoo in 1928. He announced:

I accept the gage of battle and here and now call to arms every liberty loving voter of Texas to give battle to this Love, McAdoo crowd run by the Ku Klux, special interest, and prohibition fanatics. I here and now denounce national and state prohibition as the biggest farce and fizzle of this age and I boldly declare that it has produced more fanaticism and more crime and more little men in office than any law that was ever put on the statute books.[13]

On March 14 the House passed the amnesty-repeal bill to third reading 90 to 24, and that night the final vote was 78 to 25. "The bill is finally passed and I hope we shall never hear of it again," said Speaker Bobbitt. On March 31, Moody signed the measure, entering on it a notation that he adhered to his original belief that the amnesty bill was unconstitutional and that in such an event it was wiped from the statute books. The governor also noted, however, that if the amnesty act was valid it had conferred rights that the repealing act could not take away. This was tantamount to holding that if the amnesty law was constitutional it irrevocably removed Ferguson's disabilities.[14]

During the legislative session Texas Ranger Captains Tom Hickman and Frank Hamer arrested two members of the House, F. A. Dale of Bonham and H. H. Moore of Cooper, for accepting $1,000 in marked bills from Willis W. Chamberlain, a lobbyist for the State Optometric Association. It was alleged that the transaction had taken place on the night of February 2 in an alley behind an Austin hotel in which Moore had a room. The two Rangers had been informed that the "delivery" was about to be made and were nearby when Chamberlain handed the money to Dale after the two men had left Moore's room. The House quickly voted to open an investigation of the bribery charge.

Moore had introduced House Bill 270 proposing to place a $50 annual occupation tax on every Texas optometrist, whether itinerant or stationary, and Chamberlain was in Austin to work against the measure. When he became suspicious that Dale and Moore were in collu-

sion to "shake down" the optometrists, demanding cash to kill the
measure, he laid the matter before Bobbitt. The Speaker talked with
Governor Moody, who authorized the Rangers to begin an investigation and arrest the parties, if they concluded that the accusations were
true. Dale admitted accepting the money, but only as a "retaining fee"
to defend Chamberlain if contempt charges were brought against him
in the House for writing letters soliciting funds to defray his lobbying
expenses. Moore categorically denied knowing anything about a bribe.

The investigating committee recommended that the two men be
expelled from the House, and Bobbitt, in an impassioned speech, declared them to be "as guilty as hell itself." On February 8 the House
voted 133 to 4 to expel Dale and 119 to 14 to expel Moore. "I hope you
vote in fear of no man, but in fear of Almighty God," Bobbitt announced
from the chair as the vote was taken. Both men appealed to their constituents for reelection but were defeated by large majorities.[15]

Lobbyists were also prominent in the discussions surrounding a
bill to place a tax on tobacco in all forms on the basis of one cent for
each ten cents or fraction thereof of the retail price. W. S. Barron, the
floor leader for the tax in the House, scored the tobacco lobbyists in
Austin, saying that they were literally "covering us up with their messages to defeat the bill," camouflaged so as to appear to be in the best
interest of the state. "Even the great newspapers have taken up the
fight, it seems, and are opposing so-called 'nuisance taxes' in their editorial columns," Barron complained. Bobbitt left the chair to make a
strong appeal for the bill. "To tax tobacco entirely out of existence
would be a service to society," he said, declaring that its use was inju-
rious to the human system. John H. Kirby of Houston, who led the
opposition to the tax, took sharp issue with Bobbitt, saying that he believed that tobacco was helpful, not harmful, to the system.

In the Senate, Tom Love introduced a resolution calling for an investigation of lobbying practices, declaring that "common talk" was
"that several thousand dollars is being spent each day to defeat the
House tobacco tax measure." The debate spread over a wide range of
subjects, including Love's relationship with the Ku Klux Klan, an earlier tiff with Walter Woodward over the latter's textbook bill, and
Thomas Jefferson's taste for liquor. Critics charged that Love's purpose
was to bring himself into the limelight. The Dallas senator admitted
that he did not know of any unlawful or dishonest proceedings of lobby-

ists in the Senate but stated that there "was no single question in
which the people of Texas are so much interested as in knowing the
facts as to the representatives of special interests." On March 8, after
an all-morning debate, the Senate voted 19 to 12 to refer Love's resolution to the Committee on State Affairs.

That night the House engrossed the tobacco-tax bill 67 to 40, after
five hours of debate. On March 12 the bill passed the House 61 to 53,
after two hours of the utmost confusion and disorder, but was "smothered beneath a pile of bills in the Senate" following a shrewd exercise
in parliamentary tactics by its opponents. Representative Adrian Pool
of El Paso predicted:

Financially, this state is going to be in a hell of a fix for the next two years. They
will have just $3,700,000, less to spend the next two years than they have had
the last two years. That is going to mean a cut on everything in Texas from top
to bottom. We passed the tobacco tax in the House, which would have pulled
us out of the hole, but it will never get to a vote in the Senate. No other revenue bill has been passed.

On March 15 the Senate voted 17 to 10 not to take up the tobacco-tax
bill, and the bill died when the legislature adjourned on the following
day.[16]

Representatives of Texas road interests had met in Austin on December 2, 1926, at a conference called by Representative W. A. Williamson of Bexar County and had unanimously voted to recommend to
the Fortieth Legislature an increase in the gasoline tax from one cent
to two cents a gallon, a 40 percent reduction in passenger-car registration fees, and a constitutional amendment authorizing the placing of all
gasoline-tax revenues in the state highway fund and giving to the available school fund all gross-receipts taxes on mineral production. Under
existing law one-fourth of the gasoline tax went to the school fund,
which was made up of annual monies earmarked for support of the
public school system and prorated to local districts according to scho-
lastic attendance. Lee Satterwhite said that placing the gross-receipts
taxes in the school fund would yield nearly $5 million a year. The con-
ferees agreed that if the legislature would adopt the proposed program
the highway-funding and school-appropriation problems would be
solved: the Highway Department would be placed on a higher plane of
efficiency and taken out of politics, and the legislature would save considerable time and trouble by eliminating the necessity of making sup-
plemental appropriations to the school fund.[17]

In his first message to the legislature, Moody had suggested a gasoline tax of $0.02 per gallon. Claude Teer told the House that he too recommended that sum, thinking that the Senate would not pass a $0.03 tax, but said that the higher tax "will not be offensive to the Governor, I assure you." Two bills were introduced: the Dale-Wallace bill increased the gasoline tax to $0.03 a gallon, and a companion measure reduced the motor-vehicle license fee and gave the counties all the revenue from passenger-car registration. Both bills passed the House overwhelmingly, the gasoline tax 118 to 3 and the registration bill 115 to 0. The Senate Committee on State Affairs, however, recommended a $0.02 gasoline tax and offered a substitute motor-vehicle-license-fee bill striking out all except the apportionment clause and giving 30 percent of the weight tax to the counties with a $50,000 limit per county. The *Ferguson Forum* editorialized: "The oil company lobby has killed the 3-cent gasoline tax very dead and only the fear of the people would make the senate recede from its position. But the fact still remains that the oil lobby is one of the most powerful ever assembled at the capitol."

On March 15 the House concurred in Senate amendments to the gasoline-tax bill 110 to 9. As finally passed, the measure raised the $0.01 gasoline tax to $0.03 per gallon until September 1, 1928, when it would drop to $0.02. A conference committee deadlocked on the motor-vehicle-license-fee bill, but a revision was accomplished reducing the cost to the owner and giving the counties more money to spend in building and maintaining lateral roads that were not designated as units of the state highway system. [18]

Civil-service reform in Texas faced a formidable barrier in a provision of the state constitution that "the duration of all offices not fixed by this Constitution shall never exceed two years." All 254 Texas counties operated without a single county civil-service commission. The Democratic State Convention of 1912, which had been dominated by Governor Colquitt's supporters, gave the first unequivocal endorsement of a civil-service system. Plank 12 of the platform of 1912 read: "All clerical positions in any of the departments or state institutions should be filled on the test of merit, and the rules of civil service applied to them." Nothing came of the plank, and no succeeding governor stressed the need for civil-service legislation until "Governor Moody became the staunchest, most persistent advocate of a classified civil service who has ever occupied the governor's office." [19]

Moody had asked for a civil-service law placing subordinate state officials on a merit basis. A bill by Representative Leonard Tillotson of Sealy creating a civil-service commission was killed in a House committee. A bill was introduced prohibiting members of the legislature and certain other officials from practicing before state departments, a Democratic platform demand and a Moody administration measure. The bill stipulated a penalty of one year in the penitentiary and removal from office.[20] It was killed in the House 61 to 54.

The Fortieth Legislature could point to a creditable record of achievement in its regular session, though it did not comply with many of Moody's recommendations. Among its achievements were the first real improvement in the Texas libel law in thirty years or more, reorganization of the State Textbook Commission and legislation requiring successful bidders to maintain depositories in Texas, and authorization of the State Railroad Commission to supervise and regulate motor-bus companies. Some progress was made in judicial reform. A two-member Commission of Appeals was created to assist the State Court of Criminal Appeals. The State Supreme Court was authorized to make semiannual equalizations of the dockets of the eleven courts of civil appeals. In an effort to facilitate speedy trials, the state was organized into nine administrative judicial districts. A bill of concern to women was passed providing that if a husband disappeared and his whereabouts was unknown to his wife for a period of twelve months the wife could, with the permission of the district court, administer the community property. An act was also passed accepting the provisions of the federal Sheppard-Towner Maternity and Infancy Welfare Act as amended in 1927, and providing that the Bureau of Child Hygiene of the State Board of Health should carry on the work in Texas. The guaranty-fund law, which had been part of the state's banking code for years, was repealed.[21]

In keeping with the requirements of a constitutional amendment approved by the voters, the legislature abolished the old three-member prison commission and created the Texas Prison Board, to consist of nine members appointed by the governor and approved by the Senate for six-year overlapping terms, one-third of the members retiring each second year. It was the board's duty to establish general prison policy and to employ a manager. The manager had general charge of the entire prison system and was responsible to the board for its operation. One of the board's first acts was to appoint W. H. Mead to that post. The legislature also passed laws requiring that all prison-system revenues were to be placed in the state treasury to the credit of the general-revenue fund and that all accounts were to be paid through the offices of the treasurer and the comptroller. At Moody's request the legislature appropriated money to pay the system's debts and stipulated that it was to operate in the future under a budget to keep it on a cash basis. An auditor was provided for the system. No reference was made to buying new land for relocation of the system or selling any of its 80,000 acres.

As a reaction to the liberal Ferguson pardon policy, the legislature passed a bill requiring that when a prisoner made application for a pardon the clerk of the Board of Pardon Advisers was to notify the prosecuting officers and the sheriff of the county in which the prisoner had been convicted. At any time within thirty days these officials might register their opposition to the granting of the pardon.[22]

Unlike its predecessor, the Fortieth Legislature did not act on the general appropriation bills during the regular session. Members objected that some bills were passed too hurriedly, others were neglected, and still others were defeated because of the rush to adjourn. Moody, therefore, issued a proclamation on April 18, convening the legislature in special session on May 9. Three subjects were mentioned in the call: appropriations, a selective civil-service act, and efficient and economical development of a system of correlated state highways. Although many bills had been introduced to change the organization or the policies of the State Highway Commission, and some of them had been pressed, none had been acted upon. With appropriations still to be made—which determined taxation—the *Dallas Morning News* warned the departing lawmakers that "the approval which it may safely be assumed the Legislature has won by its conduct during the session just ended is in a high state of jeopardy."[23]

In those areas of government in which he had the power, Moody did well. He quickly reorganized state departments and saw to it that they operated honestly and efficiently, and in his appointments he maintained a commendably high standard. It was inevitable, however, that in filling vacancies he would create hard feelings and bitterness among some of his followers, thousands of whom applied for state jobs. On January 10, 1927, Mrs. Moody fretted in her diary:

The surge of office-seekers, almost smothering, swarming over the lobby so that Dan can scarcely beat his way out. They track him to his hiding place if he gets another room in the Hotel where we live, trying to get work done. . . .

Then the cocksure "intimate" or pseudo *friends* who demand and make it hard
to work things out for the best interests of the state. . . . And always the buzzing of the insect "Fergusonism" to annoy. The Highway Commission and slip-
ping by confirmations, etc.[24]

Some older Moody partisans felt that his younger backers were
trying to monopolize his administration. The *Dallas Morning News*
had grumbled after the runoff primary that "to the many existing kinds
of Democrats there is to be added—and has been, indeed—a variety
whose sole distinction is that its hair is ungrayed, and whose members
see in that a prescriptive right which none of the criteria of merit may
be allowed to abate or qualify." Wrote R. B. Cousins of Moody: "His
strength came out of his university friends and their influence—the
younger set which is now in charge of things, politically in Texas." Colquitt told Moody that he feared that "Will Hogg feels cold because you
have not written to thank him for the work he did." Hogg himself
warned the governor that he was "assuming an unnecessary risk in
not conferring with numerous disinterested friends of your own and
of Texas who, entirely from motives of affectionate patriotism, enlisted under your banner in the last campaign to free the State from
Fergusonism."[25]

Among Moody's women backers, Mrs. Jane Y. McCallum disliked
Mrs. Jesse Daniel Ames, whom she suspected of planning to run the
Joint Legislative Council and install herself as dictator. "It is a great
relief to know that Dan understands Mrs. A," she noted in her diary
after a phone conversation with the governor-elect, "because I've
never known a more insincere woman, and she is brainy enough and
attractive enough on short acquaintance to be dangerous. Because she
couldn't run Dan and his campaign she seems to be out for revenge,
and I am reliably informed is saying that the women (including myself)
have fallen out with him." Moody named Mrs. McCallum secretary of
state, the second woman in succession to hold the office (in 1931, Governor Ross S. Sterling reappointed her).[26]

Moody's first two appointments to the University of Texas Board of
Regents—Will Hogg and Robert L. Batts—were hailed by alumni and
faculty as signs of better days for the school. John Lomax wrote to
Hogg: "Governor Dan's two appointments to the Board of Regents of
the University meet my hearty approval. If we will now make two others equally as good, we will have a breeze that will clean out the last

vestige of putridity on the inside of the University." Lomax wrote to Batts, "With you and Will Hogg on the Board will come to an end the days of small politics in the administration of University affairs." Roy Bedichek, director of the Interscholastic League Bureau in the university's Division of Extension, told Batts, "It will give all of us new heart if you and Will Hogg agree to serve."[27]

Moody then appointed to the board Robert Holliday of El Paso and reappointed H. J. Lutcher Stark, the latter over Hogg's vigorous objections, expressed personally to the governor. Hogg informed Moody before the board's meeting of February 24, at which Stark was elected chairman, that he would not serve. Hogg denied to Stark that his refusal had been prompted by Stark's election in his absence, as the *Houston Post-Dispatch* reported on February 25. "I resigned or really declined to serve *before* that meeting of the board; not having qualified I couldn't resign and I simply declined to serve." This was disingenuous, for the hot-tempered Will confirmed to Holliday that he would not sit on the board with Stark:

If you and Steve [Pinckney], either or both of you, kept your ears open during that day in Austin, you know I not only warned Governor Moody but predicted the eventuation which you witnessed as a member of the board. I will say this—perhaps if you and Steve and some of the other boys had been as firm as I was in the matter, he might not have made the mistake he did—the mistake was not a mistake so far as I am concerned and I bear no ill-will; it was certainly a mistake from which the University will not recover during the next two years at least.

A few sentences later Hogg's anger got the better of him: "The mistake was to make the reappointment *under any conditions whatsoever*—you will recall that all loyal ex-students sincerely applauded Mr. Frank Jones and Mr. Sam Cochran for resigning when Stark, O'Hair et al elected Neff President. How in the hell Moody had the *heart* to make the reappointment, I have never been able to comprehend—he didn't hurt my feelings by doing it; he befouled an ideal of University government for which some of us have been fighting at least 16 years."[28]

Moody was eager to keep Hogg on the board, and he suggested to Holliday that the three men go over the matter together in Austin. Hogg was adamant, however, and Moody promised to appoint Thomas Watt Gregory of Houston, president of the Ex-Students' Association, in his place. After he talked with Gregory, however, it "popped into" Holliday's head that the former United States attorney general would be the best man to succeed Splawn, who had resigned as university president. When Gregory declined the office for personal reasons, Eugene Barker of the History Department and Dean Harry Y. Benedict of the College of Arts and Sciences were the two faculty members most frequently mentioned as Splawn's successor. Batts wrote:

So far as I can see things have been run exclusively by Stark and Splawn and Bellmont [the athletic director] and Fergusonian methods have not been looked upon with disfavor. If we can get the right man to succeed Splawn the rest ought to be easy. . . . The consensus is that we should go into the University for a president. I think highly of Benedict and Barker and they are the people usually mentioned.

In October the board chose Benedict, beloved by faculty and students alike as "Dean Benny." He headed the university until his sudden death on May 10, 1937.[29]

  Gregory also took himself out of the running for the regential appointment, and Holliday fretted, "I am very anxious, of course, that we have a Regent appointed before the next meeting of the board, and Dan has to be pushed or he will let it wait until mañana." Moody conferred with Batts, Gregory, and Holliday and decided to consult with Hogg, who was then in New York. Hogg would not be placated. "I am frank to say that you are not helping that institution solve its many pressing problems by postponing appointments regardless of geography or political values to confer with me or anyone else," he wired the governor. "Then too you know how much I value my advice to you as you have already proven just what it is worth so please don't waste your time messing with me." Moody finally acted and appointed Edward Crane of Dallas, the son of General Martin M. Crane, to the board.[30]

  Early in his administration Moody had a falling out with Amon Carter, the publisher of the *Fort Worth Star-Telegram.* "It seems that when I refused to appoint the man recommended by Mr. Carter for a place on the Highway Commission that I incurred his endless enmity," Moody noted at a later date. Mrs. Moody wrote in her diary on January 30, 1927: "The break with Amon Carter who would 'rule or ruin' and desired and tried to dictate to Dan weighed heavily on Dan; Silliman's part in it hurt most because Dan likes Silliman [Evans] personally and he had all Dan's confidence (yet *he* was so patently sold, body and soul, to Amon). Such things are jarring." Carter, who resigned as chairman of the Texas Tech Board of Regents, was a bad enemy for the new governor to make. To the end of his life Carter feuded with rival Dallas, with the Fergusons, and later with Lyndon B. Johnson (one of Carter's deathbed pleas was that the *Star-Telegram* never support LBJ)—feuded, in fact, with anyone who attempted to derail his mission in life—selling Fort Worth and West Texas. "Amon Carter," said John Nance Garner, "wants the whole Government of the United States to be run for the exclusive benefit of Fort Worth and, if possible, to the detriment of Dallas."[31]

Under Carter's leadership the *Star-Telegram* had become Texas's largest and most powerful newspaper and ultimately became the largest newspaper in the South. Its special domain was West Texas, where it circulated from the Panhandle to the Rio Grande and from Fort Worth to towns two hundred miles west of El Paso. For four years the paper assailed Moody, sometimes misrepresenting his position, the governor felt. "I should think that the average reader of the Fort Worth *Star-Telegram* would realize that its editorial policy is favorable to large interests and apparently shows no concern in the welfare of the average man," Moody wrote in June, 1929. "The news columns also, at times at least, carry forward the apparent editorial policy. I have absolutely no objection on earth to its opposition to anything I may advocate or to its support of anything which I oppose. I do feel, however, that a newspaper ought to correctly state the facts in its news columns."[32]

The Senate's rejection of the three highway commissioners appointed by Governor Ferguson gave Moody the opportunity to name the three members, and it was there that he experienced some of his most serious problems in exercising the appointment power. Oscar B. Colquitt wanted the chairmanship of the commission, and Love recommended him to Moody, commenting, "I know that Jim Ferguson and the crooked road contractors of the State are strongly opposed to it and I believe there can be no safer criterion than this."[33] Although Moody had written privately to Louis Kemp that he had been "a wonderful help" in the highway investigation "and your services have contributed largely to the success we are having," he publicly gave credit to Colquitt as "the first man in Texas" to suggest the road-contract investigation, saying, "From first to last he has co-operated with me, and rendered all the assistance he could."[34]

During the 1926 campaign Colquitt had been one of Moody's inner circle of advisers. Publication of the *Free Lance* had cost him nearly $24,000, with a deficit of $7,700 at the end of the campaign. Privately he took much of the credit for Moody's victory. "I suppose

the Fergusons would think it a piece of ignorance in me to think that
my influence was sufficient to defeat them, but it so happens that it
turned out that way," he boasted. In a conversation with Colquitt in
September, 1929, Moody remarked, "If you have not had the prominence in this campaign I don't know who has." Silliman Evans, however, told Colquitt that Moody had stated to him that "more than a
thousand people" had been to him and told him not to let Colquitt control him and that he was embarrassed about Colquitt. Both Ferguson
and Davidson had predicted during the 1926 campaign that Colquitt
would be rewarded with the chairmanship of the State Highway Commission and that he would use it to build an organization for a United
States Senate race against Mayfield in 1928, and it was true that the
former governor was thinking of becoming a candidate. "At this time, I
have no plans with reference to it—except that I shall do all I can in
any event to defeat either Ferguson or Mayfield, and I would not support Patrick Neff," Colquitt wrote a supporter. "It is quite natural for
the friends of each one of these gentlemen, to knock me, however, and
I will not now say that circumstances might not arise to induce me to
make the fight." [35]

Moody discussed with Colquitt an appointment to a tax-survey
office that the legislature would be asked to create, but the only position Colquitt would consider was the chairmanship of the State Highway Commission: "The salary is small, the responsibility great. But the
opportunity for an honest man to build a monument for himself, and do
real service for his state is worth the sacrifice one would have to make."
For the other two commissioners Colquitt recommended Ross S. Sterling of Houston and J. A. Kemp of Wichita Falls. [36]

Tale carriers told Colquitt that Moody intended to pull away from
"such men as Colquitt, Hogg Bros., Sterling, Cone Johnson," that the
"Williamson County Kitchen Cabinet" around Moody was opposed to
Colquitt's appointment because he might have more influence than
they. Love told Colquitt that Senator Wood had informed Moody that
eight Ferguson senators, two Davidson men, and Wood himself would
oppose Colquitt's confirmation and that the Senate would not confirm
him. According to Love, Wood had gone to Edgar Witt of Waco, a
Davidson man, while the Senate was considering the Ferguson highway appointments in the special session and, without authority from
Moody, had assured Witt that "Moody would not appoint Colquitt to
anything, and if he did he [Wood] would vote against his confirmation

or resign." With this assurance the Davidson men in the Senate had voted to postpone action on the Ferguson appointees. Wood exonerated Moody from any connection with the trade but said that he knew about it later.[37]

Although Colquitt obtained signed statements from all the Ferguson senators except one stating that they would vote for his confirmation, he failed to receive the appointment, and his rejection left him embittered. He accused the governor of ingratitude. "Moody, when I was helping him develop his road suit cases, characterized me as '*a patriot!*'" he wrote angrily to Love. "But at the time I was helping him in two ways—to make a success of his suits and an available candidate for governor." Brooding on his failure, he soon concluded that the "real cause" of Moody's attitude was not the "unholy" trade between Wood and Witt but rather the campaign charge that he had promised Colquitt the position in exchange for his support. The governor "'has leaned backwards on me' to convince his enemies that there was no truth in the lies they told," he lamented, recalling the lines from Shakespeare's *King Henry VIII*:

> And my integrity to heaven, is all
> I dare now call my own. O Cromwell, Cromwell,
> Had I served my God with a half the zeal
> I served my king, he would not in mine age
> have left me naked to mine enemies.

Further reflection and additional reports suggested another motive for his rejection. On February 18 he informed Love: "Within 48 hours after our joint conference with him [Moody], he told another man whom he had sent for to discuss his application, that he had just turned down Colquitt and Tom Love; that he was going to run the governor's office and didn't want any bosses." Colquitt warned: "You [Love] are on the 'list of bosses' to be shuned [*sic*]. He will temporize with you, however, because he don't want your active official opposition. He has no leadership, because he does not want any one else to."[38] Love himself, anticipating that enemies would try to turn Moody against him, had earlier written the governor-elect that his pledge to help make his administration a great success "in *your way*" was "absolutely dependable regardless of what the shoulder-shrugging trouble makers and crooks may tell you."[39]

On January 25, 1927, Louis Kemp was summoned to the gover-

nor's office and offered a place on the State Highway Commission. He
declined with thanks, saying that he did not care to enter politics and
could not afford the financial sacrifice. Moody then named Ross S.
Sterling chairman of the commission and also named Cone Johnson.
Johnson's appointment was a surprise, for his name had not been
mentioned in all the speculation. Sterling announced that he would
give his full time to the State Highway Department, which left William
Hobby virtually in charge of the *Houston Post-Dispatch* and the newspaper's radio station. Hobby was also publisher of the *Beaumont
Enterprise-Journal.* Cato Sells of Fort Worth was mentioned for the
third spot on the commission, but Thomas Watt Gregory wrote Moody
that his appointment "would be an extremely unfortunate one and I am
quite sure would be deeply regretted in the future." West Texas won
its claim for representation on the commission when Moody chose District Judge W. R. Ely of Abilene.[40]

On February 3, Moody told Kemp that he had asked the new commissioners to consult him regarding appointments in the department.
Moody also said that he would like to see Kemp accept the position of
state maintenance engineer—that by doing so he could save the state
millions of dollars. Kemp firmly refused the position. The three commissioners asked him to appear before an executive session and recommend for discharge employees whom he knew to be unfit. They, together with State Highway Engineer R. A. Thompson, met twice in
Kemp's room in the Stephen F. Austin Hotel on February 9 to discuss
highway matters. The following day Moody asked Kemp to call at his
office to discuss the selection of division engineers and other highway
employees. With Moody's permission Kemp consulted with former
State Highway Engineer Gibb Gilchrist, who happened to be in Austin, and the two men drew up a list of recommendations. The governor
promised to submit the list to the commission and ask that the men
named be appointed.[41]

On April 28, Moody had to spend an hour as a peacemaker between the highway commissioners and members of the Senate Finance
Committee, following a clash that erupted between Cone Johnson and
Senators Westbrook, Parr, Fairchild, and Holbrook because he had removed the division engineers appointed by the previous commission
and appointed their successors without consulting the senators. Johnson said that the removals were the result of a complete reorganization
and a determination to "bring the Highway Commission into the confi-

dence of the people." He declared emphatically that lawmakers, chambers of commerce, or others could not use influence with the commissioners in obtaining aid for roads and that "merit alone will control." While the commissioners were glad to receive legislators, their presence was unnecessary, he said, since the county judge was best able to present his county's needs, and the commission was best able to decide whether it had funds for the work.

Johnson's candor affronted senatorial dignity. Moody told the angry committee members that the commissioners had a hard job with much responsibility and that for that reason they should bear with them. He admitted that some of salary figures requested by the commission were possibly too high but said that he had left the whole highway administration to the commissioners and that he had every confidence in them. As for the division engineers, only three had been selected, he said, and they appeared to be capable and well recommended.

The *Dallas Morning News* chided Moody for asking the committee to be "forbearant" with the commissioners: "He would have spoken more appositely, it seems to the News, if he had demanded for it the full freedom from political interference which Mr. Johnson had declared to be its right." This prompted Mrs. Moody to some reflections on politics in her diary:

First rumblings of criticism over Highway commission's failure to use any patronage and steady determination to clean the whole thing out, and let merit rule. Of course the criticism is in reality a compliment; but the vultures of the old Ferguson gang unscrupulous, always hover near. A queer game politics, and it is a game; because in order to put through any constructive legislation Dan has to employ tact and not antagonize this old entrenched gang, for they can block things. I loved Cone Johnson's and Sterling's spunk in telling them to "go to——." Then Dan had to pour oil on the troubled waters. Then comes the good old stodgy Dallas News, not understanding the tireless, endless fighting and maneuvering it requires to hold varying factions together, in a working whole, and hints in an editorial that Dan was not quite as strong as he ought to be, maybe because he did pour oil on the waters. Thanklessness, thy name is politics.[42]

On the day after the legislature convened in Austin for the first special session, Representative Alfred P. C. Petsch, an "original Moody man," made what he termed an authorized statement: "It is now safe to say that Gov. Dan Moody will be a candidate for the United States Senate in the 1928 primaries." "It is not only a fact that Moody is sure to make the race," he said, "but his friends are cognizant of it and are already preparing to organize his campaign." Neither Mayfield nor Ferguson was satisfactory to the "great body politic" of Texas, and this majority must have a candidate who reflected neither the Mayfield nor the Ferguson grouping. "The choice is Dan Moody and he can easily be elected."

Was Petsch's statement a trial balloon? Moody waited for five days before puncturing it with a statement that the use of his name in the discussion of possible candidates for the Senate was without his authorization or encouragement. "My mind is occupied with other subjects at present, and questions of partisan politics are not giving me interest," he stated. "I have enough to engage my attention in the duties of the office to which the people have elected me and I have more than enough to take my time and energy in endeavoring to give the people of Texas a good administration." Still, gossip persisted around the capitol that, in one newspaper's words, "the young governor may leap over the second term legend and hitch his political flivver to a Washington-found star." [43]

At this time the governor assumed an economy stance. Pork-barrel politics drew his fire in a speech in Marlin on April 9. Later he announced that he was opposed to any large state-bond issue, such as $150 million, for the construction of public highways, pointing out that only about five thousand miles could be built with that sum and that half of the mileage would be taken in trunk lines across the state from east to west and north to south. He also said that having large sums of money to spend encouraged waste and beclouded economy. The State Highway Commission's present expenditures were about as much as could economically be spent on the highways, and there was therefore no just cause to vote large amounts of bonds. Moody was also against more taxes and said on May 2 that he thought the appropriation bills should remain within the anticipated revenues for the biennium beginning September 1, 1927. His statement indicated that he did not expect to submit additional revenue measures to the special session and that if he adhered to that position there would be no tobacco tax. [44]

Pledging themselves to a pay-as-you-go policy to keep disbursements within anticipated revenue, on May 10 more than fifty House members formed a bloc to trim appropriation bills. The tone of the caucus, presided over by Representative W. R. Poage of Waco, who had called the meeting, forecast stormy weather ahead for the bills reported out by the House Appropriation Committee. Three members of the committee, John H. Kirby, Henry B. Dielmann of San Antonio, and Ray Holder of Lancaster, sat in the caucus, and Kirby, who took an active part, made the motion for the pay-as-you-go policy.[45]

On May 19, however, the full House voted 76 to 41 to table Poage's motion to keep appropriations within a revenue based on an ad valorem rate not to exceed $0.23 on $100.00 valuation and went on record as favoring a rate of $0.35. Although Moody in his address to the legislature again exhorted that body to practice economy, he was reconciled to a return to the $0.35 rate, at least for the next year. "Apparently that idea has made its way as an unwelcome visitor to the Governor's office," noted the *Dallas Morning News.*[46]

In a vigorous message to the special session Moody urged the enactment of a classified civil-service law. A bill to provide for "certain civil service examinations" passed the House after many amendments, one of which gave responsibility for administration of the act to the State Board of Control. Some senators laid a basis for opposition to the measure by presenting petitions from their constituents opposing it. Representatives of some affected state departments were active in "a quiet campaign" against the bill. On May 26, Moody personally urged the merits of civil service for state employees before the Senate State Affairs Committee, and the measure was reported favorably, 6 to 1.[47]

Tom Pollard of Tyler was in charge of Moody's civil-service measure in the Senate. He had introduced a civil-service bill in each of the last three regular sessions but had never moved it beyond the committee room. On June 3, by a vote of 15 to 11, the Senate moved to reconsider the vote of approval given to the special order of the bill the previous day. At 2:00 in the afternoon Pollard had the floor and conducted a filibuster to prevent the reconsideration of the special order. The bill's opponents admitted the truth of his argument that to eliminate the special order would kill the bill. The filibuster only postponed its defeat for a day, however. The fatal shot was fired at 2:00 P.M. on June 4 by Senator R. S. Bowers of Caldwell, who moved that the Senate adjourn to 9:00 Monday morning, June 6. This motion carried 18 to 13. All contested bills were practically dead, since according to the Senate rules no bill, except conference reports, could be voted on during the last twenty-four hours before adjournment, which was scheduled for June 7. Since a two-thirds vote was required to suspend the rules, the motion spelled death for the civil-service bill. Despite the defeat Pol-

lard was jubilant. "We'll pass it next time," he predicted. "The bill to
be presented will be in somewhat different form, so as to overcome
objections of several opponents of the measure at this session. In fact,
it now looks to me as though civil service will have a working majority
at the next session of the Legislature."[48]

"There was nothing of Moody or anti-Moody in the vote" to adjourn, the *Dallas Morning News* contended. "Several senators who
voted to adjourn have been supporting civil service and others had
about made up their mind to do so. Everybody saw, however, that a
fight was on which would have been almost sure to take the entire afternoon—and time was needed for free conference [of committees
working on appropriation bills]." Senators feared that if the money
bills were not passed Moody would immediately call the legislature
back for another special session, and most of them wanted to go home.[49]

Moody also met defeat on his plans for the prison system. Lee Satterwhite persuaded the House to pass a bill requiring the approval of
the legislature before any prison lands could be bought or sold, thus
giving the lawmakers a veto power in relocating the prison system.
Moody was committed to a policy of relocation and wanted that power
placed with the newly created Texas Prison Board, subject to the governor's approval. He told Satterwhite, chairman of the House Committee on Penitentiaries, that he "hoped to jar him loose from his present
position in that connection." The former Speaker replied, "It can't be
done." Opponents of the administration's prison bill won the first victory of the special session on May 26, when the Senate Penitentiary
Committee amended the measure to make it conform to the Satterwhite plan. It was then reported favorably.[50]

In the House the Satterwhite amendment, providing for legislative approval of sale, was adopted on June 2, 65 to 57, over the Teer
plan, which would have given the State Prison Board plenary power.
The House's action was a victory for those who favored concentration
of the system on the South Texas farms and a defeat for the faction
favoring sale of the present lands and the relocation of the system in
Central Texas. The *Dallas Morning News* predicted that if the selection of a location was left to the legislature it would keep things as they
were for another two or three years, since it would be almost impossible to get a majority of the lawmakers to agree on any location.[51]

The special session also had to deal with the state's white-primary
law. In 1923 the legislature had passed a law making blacks ineligible to

participate in a Democratic party primary in the state and directing election officials to throw out their ballots and not count them. In 1924, Dr. Lawrence A. Nixon, a black dentist of El Paso, attempted to vote in a Democratic primary election. Although he had voted regularly in previous primaries and general elections, this time he was denied a ballot. He filed suit for damages against C. C. Herndon, the election judge. The NAACP chapter in El Paso retained a local white title lawyer, Fred C. Knollenberg, to handle the case and appealed to the national organization for assistance. Arthur B. Spingarn, chairman of the Legal Committee of the NAACP; Moorfield Storey, president of the NAACP; and James A. Cobb and Louis Marshall, NAACP attorneys, closely supervised Knollenberg's work. After the Federal District Court at El Paso and the Federal Circuit Court of Appeals at New Orleans dismissed Nixon's suit, it was carried to the United States Supreme Court. On March 7, 1927, in the case of *Nixon* v. *Herndon*, the Court in a unanimous decision delivered by Oliver Wendell Holmes declared the Texas statute unconstitutional as a violation of the Fourteenth Amendment.[52]

On the day the decision was handed down, Moody announced that "new legislation will be necessary to protect the ballot" and that, "since the Democratic Party is a voluntary organization, certainly a law can be passed giving the committee of the party authority to prescribe rules as to who can participate in a party primary." The *Dallas Morning News*, however, viewed the decision in a different light:

As a matter of fact, . . . the specter of negro domination in Texas is utter foolishness. It is likely to become more and more foolish as the proportion of white population continues to rise. Such negroes as choose to vote the Democratic ticket are in no sense a menace to white supremacy or to good government, and their participation prior to the enactment of the statute declared unconstitutional never amounted to either menace or emergency.[53]

When a bill was introduced in the legislature "to empower any political party in the State to prescribe the qualifications of its members and determine such qualifications," the *News* declared that such a statute was unnecessary because every political party had an "inherent power" to determine its membership. "What the Legislature needs to do in this regard is precisely nothing at all, unless it be to cease its interference with political parties." Somewhat more surprising was Jim Ferguson's characterization of the *Nixon* v. *Herndon* decision as "timely." Perhaps with an eye to mending his political fences with the state's Jewish and Mexican-American voters, he warned that if a law could be passed denying the Negro race the vote then it would not be long until an attempt was made to exclude the Jewish race from elections, followed by laws excluding Bohemians, Mexicans, and Germans, "and then, in truth and fact, the Constitution will become a scrap of paper. Every good citizen should rejoice in the fact that the Supreme Court has stepped in and promptly declared for the perpetuation of the God Given Right of Suffrage." [54]

The legislature repealed Article 3107—the white-primary provision—and enacted a new Article 3107, whereby

every political party in this State through its State Executive Committee shall have the power to prescribe the qualifications of its own members and shall in its own way determine who shall be qualified to vote or otherwise participate in such political party; providing that no person shall ever be denied the right to participate in a primary in this State because of former political views or affiliations or because of membership or nonmembership in organizations other than the political party.

This proviso was added to the original bill to prevent the State Democratic Executive Committee from using its new statutory authority to bar party bolters and klansmen from the Democratic primary. Pursuant to the statute, the Executive Committee passed a resolution allowing only qualified white Democrats who took the pledge "I am a Democrat and pledge myself to support the nominees of this primary" to participate in the Democratic primary elections on July 28 and August 25, 1928. [55]

The legislature in the regular session passed a bill drafted by Tom Love entitled "An Act Providing for the Segregation or Separation of the White and Negro Races and Providing for the Conferring of Power and Authority upon Cities to Pass Suitable Ordinances Controlling the Same. . . ." Cities were authorized to deny building permits to blacks who intended to build in white communities, and vice versa. In addition they were empowered to define "the negro race, negro community, white race and white community." The measure was intended to promote "peace, quiet, and tranquillity . . . as well as the public health." Moody allowed it to become law without his signature. [56]

The special session was marked more by what it failed to do, outside of appropriations and the white-primary law, than by what it accomplished. Like Neff, Moody was more progressive than most of the lawmakers, and his program was an almost complete failure. He submitted legislation on civil service, prison reform, highways, textbook changes, higher education, and a number of minor, local matters. The civil-service bill was killed; there was no prison legislation; no highway bills of any consequence were passed; the textbook law was not materially changed; a bill providing for a board of higher education was killed in the House; there was no judicial reform of great importance; and the bills for the strengthening of the criminal laws were lost in committee. Some progress was made in education. The per capita apportionment for the public schools was raised from $14 to $15 a year, the rural-aid appropriation was increased from $1,500,000 to $1,600,000 for 1927–28 and to $2,250,000 for 1928–29, and the university and most of the state colleges received special appropriations for a substantial building program.[57]

As sent to Moody, the four major appropriation bills would require a rise in the ad valorem tax rate from $0.23 to $0.30 for the first year of the biennium, with a reduction to $0.27 during the second year. Holding the rate to $0.23 would have required him to cut between $1,500,000 and $2,000,000 from the budget. He decided against that, vetoing only $442,503 in the budget. Still, despite "the kindly humor of the Governor's operation," the cuts hurt, eliminating new positions and dashing hopes for expansion at some state colleges. Lamented the president of Texas A&I in Kingsville:

The Legislature was pretty drastic and to a degree reactionary in making appropriations. They left us very little room for expansion during the next two years, but gave us about enough to take care of the institution on the present basis. Evidently the Governor was in sympathy with the chief committeemen, Senator Wood and Claude Teer, because after they had cut to the bone, the Governor took his little rip saw and went in a little deeper, being nothing left to cut.[58]

Invited to address the House before adjournment, the governor told the representatives that he "wasn't mad at anybody" who did not agree with him on the administration bills that had failed to pass and that he would submit them again at the next special session, with stronger reasons for their enactment. Moody said philosophically:

I found long ago that I can't always get every one to agree with me. And I don't fall out with any one that wouldn't agree with me. I also discovered some time ago that you could not get anywhere by driving any one. The only way to win is to appeal to their reason, and if that doesn't win, wait until another time. I think this has been a successful session, leaving out the appropriation measures, which I have not yet seen.

The governor had second thoughts, for the following day he issued a statement that read in part:

In all candor, and it is my duty to be candid with the people whose trust I hold, quite a deal was accomplished at the regular session, but lamentably little at the special session, called with high hope that so much might be done. Essential appropriations were made, and aside from that, no major constructive measures were adopted to fulfill the pledges of the Democratic platform.[59]

The newspapers differed on the reasons why the Moody program had not been more successful. Terming the governor's explanation that the wreckage of his program was the result of intellectual disagreements in which lawmakers had a right to indulge "a sportsmanlike, a gracious, and, one might add, a charitable explanation—so charitable, indeed, as to be perhaps a bit disingeneous," the *Dallas Morning News* went on to declare that in the Senate, especially, some of his recommendations had been blighted by the political and factional animosities engendered during the 1926 campaign. Certainly Jim Ferguson waxed wroth over the increase in the ad valorem tax rate. "If I was right mean I could have the best 'I told you so' alibi that anybody ever had but I am not going to do so now," he gloated in the *Forum*. "I think as soon as the people learn the facts and what has been done and what is proposed to be done in the future it will be unnecessary for me to make any further defense of Fergusonism." The *Houston Chronicle*, however, insisted that the defeat of the governor's program was not caused by any personal opposition to him. "In fact, Governor Moody probably is more popular with the legislators now than he has ever been." During the sessions he conferred frequently with members, and it was a rule in the governor's office that a senator or representative took precedence over other callers. Unlike the days of the Neff administration, they knew after talking with him just what to expect on legislative subjects. "But the Moody legislative program was a bit too advanced for the legislators, especially on the subject of civil service," the *Chronicle* commented. "There was no particular opposition to the governor, except for a small bloc in the Senate. Some of his friends opposed some of his measures and supported others."[60]

Friends of the governor offered another explanation, pointing out that some of his important legislation failed because it was submitted late in the session. He had pursued the policy of waiting for the appropriation bills to get far on their way before tendering other proposals, with the result that the latter suffered. If they had been submitted at the start of the session, the outcome would have been different. Representative W. A. Williamson of San Antonio, however, had predicted early in the session that little legislation would be passed except the appropriation bills. "In my legislative experience I have never seen a session with such an evident sentiment of 'thumbs down.'"[61]

With the wholesale defeat of Moody's recommendations another special session was regarded as inevitable. Some of his friends, led by Petsch, insisted that the logical time was immediately following the adjournment of the first special session, but others, including the leaders, Teer and Wood, stated positively that it would not be called that soon. October was considered the most likely date, but in fact the Fortieth Legislature did not meet again, and further consideration of the "Moody Program" had to wait for the convening of its successor in January, 1929.[62]

Preoccupied with work, Moody did not play golf or cards, did not dance, and rarely went fishing. He like hunting and shooting, and once a year he went on a deer hunt. He was a regular patron of shooting galleries and when he was going away on a trip, he often left home early enough to do a little shooting at a gallery near the railroad station. On other occasions he asked three or four friends to accompany him in the evening to the gallery, "where the governor shows boyish glee when he beats his friend in the shooting matches. And he frequently is the high gun, for he is a very good rifle shot."[63] Moody also enjoyed his hops over Texas in National Guard planes—open two-seaters with one engine. Mrs. Moody noted in the family scrapbook: "He loved those airplane trips (as Gov. he could call on them anytime) *until* late one evening 'they gave out of gas'—& *got lost* over East Texas & Dan was told by his pilot to 'get ready to jump' (all wore parachutes) Dan got busy at once on the terrain below, discovered Bryan Texas & they landed on *main street!*" Taking cognizance of Moody's fondness for flying, Jim Ferguson sneered in the *Forum*: "The only time when Moody is above [Tom] Love's dictation is when he is up in that flying machine and that don't last very long although it now occurs often."[64]

A nationally known figure, Moody was the subject of much speculation about his future political plans. Justice Louis Brandeis of the United States Supreme Court had been impressed by his "admirable presentation" of a case before the Court just before he became governor. Brandeis wrote Thomas Watt Gregory that Moody "knew his case; his manner was most tactful; and he proved himself a wise advocate. He looked to me as having been developed and ennobled by the experiences of the last year. If he goes forward on the straight and narrow path—he should be a great power for good in our political world in course of time."[65]

On June 19, 1927, Moody left Austin to accompany 125 Texas businessmen on the "All-Texas Special Good Will Tour" to the North and East, for the purpose of advertising investment opportunities in the state. The governor was a fervent booster of Texas in conversations with journalists. "She is an empire of virgin wealth as yet barely touched by Eastern capital," he told Robert Field of *Outlook* magazine. "She needs funds for building. Any one seeking to develop the resources of this State will be welcome here." He continued in an almost rhapsodic vein:

There are latent sources of wealth scarcely known to the investing public. Oil has been our advertiser; yet discerning economists know well enough that it represents but a fraction of our potential wealth. It is the development of agriculture—especially its diversification—in the building of good roads, and in the generating of electrical power that I am interested. What North Carolina with amazing rapidity has done in her borders we are eager to undertake in our own. No honest dollar that enters this State will ever be disturbed or threatened. The people have been educated to the uses of corporate wealth and do not fear aggregations of capital. Their only concern is that the money shall be free of taint and that it shall seek legitimate channels of expansion. The day of the political trust breaker is gone.[66]

The tour itinerary included: Kansas City, Saint Louis, Chicago, Cleveland, Buffalo, Niagara Falls, Boston, New York, Philadelphia, Baltimore, Washington, Pittsburgh, Cincinnati, and Memphis. Lieutenant Charles Pedley of Corsicana flew over the train in an airplane, christened the *Texas* for the trip, and announced the party's arrival at each stop by flying over the city. The idea of the tour was to advertise Texas, but, as it turned out, the eastern press seized hold of Moody and played him far above the goodwill part of the program. The Texans were cordially received in each of the cities they visited, and on June 29 in New York City Moody was introduced to Governor Al Smith at a luncheon at the Whitehall Club. Smith entered the room in the midst of a speech by Cullen Thomas and was greeted with "Hurrah for Al

Smith!" from the Texans. According to the *New York World*, "The manner of Gov. Moody was a study in coolness. As he sat at the speakers' table after the meal his face did not brighten when the New York Governor entered amid cheers from the diners."

"Political wiseacres" in the Texas delegation explained that Moody's lack of cordiality was a bit of Texas political wisdom. If he displayed positive friendship or sympathy with Smith, he would alienate a large number of home-state admirers at one stroke, whereas if he held the attitude he showed at the luncheon and attained the vice-presidential running place alongside Smith in 1928, the ticket would have the support of the Texas variety of the dry, Protestant southerner and of Smith's own followers. "The meeting of a strong man from the East with a strong man from the West" was how Cullen Thomas described the encounter.

Other members of the delegation told reporters that the favorable impression that Moody had made on the trip impelled them to plan to make him the Democratic candidate for president. Moody would head the Texas delegation to the convention and would be a serious favorite-son candidate. He was the only man in sight upon whom all factions could unite, and he would have the support of the McAdoo men from all over the Southwest. "It is apparent to this writer that Moody does not want the suggestion that he is a candidate for vice president, or for president for that matter, to get abroad," wrote Martin Andersen to the *Austin American* and *Statesman*. "It is doubted if the governor ever gets a thrill out of the thought and while he has not said so, one traveling with Moody for two weeks can easily ascertain that he wants none of the national dish at this time."[67]

Back in Austin, Acting Governor Barry Miller confirmed informally that he would not be a candidate for reelection in 1928. Should Moody become a candidate for the United States Senate, Miller would be a candidate for governor; otherwise, he would run in 1930. Miller's friends immediately started a movement to have him sent to the House from Dallas County if Moody sought a second term. They further suggested that he be elected Speaker. As it turned out, Miller changed his mind and was reelected to his third term as lieutenant governor in 1928.[68]

Moody suffered a political setback at home that summer. The Fortieth Legislature submitted four constitutional amendments to the voters. One amendment sought to separate the objects of taxation so as to allow all ad valorem taxes to go to the counties, another proposed to raise the salaries of the governor and the legislators, a third would increase the number of State Supreme Court justices from three to nine, and a fourth would permit the legislature to place district and county offices strictly on a salary basis in lieu of the fees, commissions, and perquisites prescribed by the Texas Constitution. Moody endorsed them all, and they would have had a good chance of success but for Jim Ferguson, who raised the cry of "Agin 'Em All" in the *Forum*:

Do the voters want to go to the polls and vote for four distinct radical changes in the Constitution, everyone of which will raise taxes? It does not make any difference what the merits of any of the amendments are because in the present tax-ridden state of the people the adoption of four constitutional amendments that will permit the raise [*sic*] of taxes simply means the last straw that broke the camel's back and bankruptcy to the people must follow.

The daily papers that had earlier expressed favorable comment on the amendments backed off, with the exception of Jesse Jones's *Houston Chronicle* and Ross Sterling's *Houston Post-Dispatch*—owned, Ferguson jeered, "by these accidental millionaires who deluded themselves into the idea that possession of their millions can take the place of brains to put these amendments over." The *Dallas Morning News* fretted about a corporation tax on intangible property, warning: ". . . once we adopt a taxation system which enables the State to satisfy its needs, and fancied needs, by levees on the corporations, Legislatures will be freed of the only restraint that is now put on their impulse to be extravagant. Extravagance, then, will manifest itself only in taxes levied on corporations." State Comptroller Sam H. Terrell issued a statement opposing the taxation amendment as "a dangerous experiment in that it would open an avenue for wide discrimination and provide a fertile field for exploitation by predatory interests." [69]

On August 1 all four amendments were defeated by 3-to-1 majorities in a vote that was much larger than the vote that had been cast on constitutional amendments in the last general election. Calling their defeat the most important victory of all his political battles, Ferguson rejoiced, saying that "four distinct and radical changes in our constitution were proposed without rhyme or reason. The people rose up in their might and majesty and said 'Thou shall not pass.'" "There are many side lights upon this election," he announced. "One is that Dan is *not* the man.'" [70]

Moody had contemplated making a speaking tour on behalf of the amendments, but a supporter warned him to give the idea a second thought, "for these amendments are foredoomed to defeat: you will not win any new laurels by leading such a forlorn hope. *Beware-Beware-Beware.*" The governor reconsidered and contented himself with a statement advocating the adoption of the judiciary amendment but not the other three. He admitted privately after the election that he had foreseen some weeks before that all the amendments were doomed. "The judiciary amendment was really important, and certainly there was no valid objection that could be presented against its adoption," he wrote. "The natural objection which seems to exist in the public minds [*sic*] to amendments to the constitution and the fact that some of the amendments were very bitterly fought is responsible for the fact that all went down." In 1929 he told Governor Harry Byrd of Virginia that the taxation amendment "met with the opposition of all of the corporate interests and they waged a very bitter fight against it."[71]

Those political observers who thought that Ferguson's relentless editorial attacks on Moody in the *Forum* were leading up to another Ferguson race in 1928 were mistaken. Moody was a candidate for a second term, but for the first time since 1914 neither Ma nor Pa was on the ballot for a state or federal office. Instead they supported for governor Louis J. Wardlaw, a Fort Worth lawyer and stock raiser and a friend of Jim's. A native of Falls County, Wardlaw was reared on a Runnels County farm. He had ranches on the Edwards Plateau and in Erath County and was a large producer of sheep, goats, cattle, and hogs. In announcing his candidacy on January 17, 1928, he promised a campaign for tax reduction, elimination of excessive appropriations, election of state highway commissioners from districts and one at large, and correction of widespread violations of the law. His entrance into the campaign came as a surprise even to close friends. He charged Moody with inefficiency; ridiculed the governor for his claim to honesty, saying that he had "broken most of his promises"; criticized him for vetoing a $66,000 appropriation to enforce the liquor-prescription law; and attacked the State Highway Commission for wasting millions, alleging that Sterling showed favoritism for the Houston area and Ely for the Abilene region.

Mrs. Edith Wilmans of Dallas was again a candidate for governor, as was Judge William E. Hawkins of Breckenridge, but neither made an active campaign.[72] "The disgruntled element headed by the *Star-Telegram* will probably center on Wardlaw as the man to try and beat you," Representative Ray Holder advised Moody. "The gamblers are behind him strong. I mean by that the race track gamblers who want to bring horse racing back. I have heard it rumored that Waggoner will spend a hundred thousand dollars to elect him. This will probably be one time that money can't buy enough votes."[73]

There was never any doubt of Moody's reelection. Except for a Fourth of July address to a large crowd at Waxahachie, he actively campaigned only during the two weeks before the first primary on July 28, 1928, describing his administration's accomplishments and practically ignoring his opponents, though once more he hammered on the theme of Fergusonism. He told of removing graft from the Highway Department, turning a losing prison system into a profitable one, wiping out debts, and lowering taxes. "Fergusonism is attempting a comeback this year," he warned, "through the candidacy of Louis J. Wardlaw. Wardlaw has no positive Wardlaw vote. He is appealing to an anti-Moody vote and to a pro-Ferguson vote. Despite what others say, Fergusonism and the danger of his return to control Texas politics is the one big issue in this campaign."

"He seems to think he is running against Jim Ferguson for Governor," Wardlaw replied. "Moody said Ferguson is going to vote for me. I hope he does, but I say let Moody and Ferguson settle their differences in the arena and let me alone."[74]

Moody won a majority of the 737,904 votes cast in the first primary, receiving 442,080 votes. Wardlaw received 245,508 votes; Hawkins, 32,079; and Wilmans, 18,237. The Wardlaw vote was impressive as an anti-Moody expression, yet the governor led him by approximately 200,000 votes and carried more than 200 counties, including all the counties with large voting populations. Wardlaw, in addition to carrying seven German counties because of the Ferguson influence and opposition to Moody's prohibitionism, won a number of West Texas counties in the neighborhood of his old home, including Runnels. He narrowly lost Tarrant, his home county, 14,482 to 13,620. The boss-controlled Mexican-border counties were as unpredictable as usual but in general gave Moody the advantage. Hidalgo gave Moody 4,462, Wardlaw 272; Starr voted for Moody, 896 to 4; Willacy, 681 to 79; and Zapata, 281 to 0. On the other hand, Duval gave Wardlaw 1,161 votes to only 28 for Moody, and Maverick favored Wardlaw 143 to 104.[75]

In the general election in November, Moody easily defeated his Republican opponent, W. H. Holmes, an Amarillo oil operator,

582,968 to 123,337. L. L. Rhodes, the Socialist candidate, received
787 votes, and 109 Texans had the temerity to vote for Communist
J. Steadman.

Putting the best face on the primary returns,[76] Ferguson boasted
that "we have slowed him [Moody] down like the devil." No informed
man, he said, would now contend that anybody believed very much in
the governor or his ability. "He may think he has destroyed me, but if
he has, he has destroyed himself in doing so. If he is not destroyed I
think I will be able to complete the job in the next few months—even
before he starts his second term."[77]

Mrs. Moody penned a favorable assessment of her husband's campaign in her diary:

Immediately after Houston Dan plunged into his campaign for re-election
(made necessary by the diabolical forces of "Rule-or-Ruin" Amon Carter.
There was another "Dan Moody the laundryman" put on the ticket from Fort
Worth. Also Jim Ferguson as always buzzing around, this time with poor old
Wardlaw). Dan made a rapid-fire campaign; even old Jim grudgingly admitted
that there never such "such a campaigner." The first primary saw Dan "vindicated"—hate the term as it smacks of Fergusonism—something like 150,000
majority over all opponents, so the run-off was eliminated. It also showed the
[Al] Smith super-zealots, with their dire predictions, that Dan stood solid with
the "people" that they at least appreciated honest stands for convictions. These
latter have been noticeably shut-up since the election.[78]

"Spanked and Accoladed" was the summary of the *Dallas Morning News* of Moody's victory in the first primary. The paper concluded
that only a small part of the opposition to him had been animated by
dissatisfaction with his performance as governor. "It was animated,
rather, by dissatisfaction with his performance in the political arena."
The opposition was in part made up of those who felt that he was pre-
sumptuous and gratuitous to make himself a leader in the factional
quarrel between the Al Smith and anti–Al Smith Democrats in Texas,
but, perhaps more largely, it comprised those who were pained by his
"flounderings, compromises and equivocations" in that role. "And certainly it must be granted that, however lofty the motives which enticed
the Governor into that contest, he came out of it ingloriously," the
paper concluded.[79] The presidential election of 1928 in Texas and
Moody's role therein—a role that, as the editorial quoted above indicates, brought him severe criticism–will be discussed in the next
chapter.

CHAPTER 10

How Dry I Am

UNTIL 1928, Texas was one of only two southern states that had never voted Republican in a presidential election. "Imperial Texas with her imperial domain and her imperial Democratic majority" was how Thomas H. Ball proudly described her in the Democratic National Convention that year.[1] Yet that November, Texas gave Herbert Hoover almost three times as many votes as it had given President Calvin Coolidge in 1924 and joined four other "solid South" states in the Republican column.

The campaign of 1928 was based on issues that were termed the "three P's"—prosperity, Prohibition, and prejudice.[2] The fact that the Democratic candidate, Al Smith of New York, was a Roman Catholic, a wet, and an honorary sachem of Tammany Hall has obscured some of the infighting that went on at the state level, where the election was actually decided. In Texas the control long exercised over the Democratic party by veteran prohibitionist Thomas B. Love of Dallas and his friends was challenged by a group of young, self-styled liberal Democrats who wanted to end what they saw as an era of fanaticism that had held the state in political bondage. Governor Dan Moody and a number of older anti-Love Democrats were persuaded to join this revolt against the bossism of the old machine. Dethroned, Love, after Smith's nomination, led his ultradry ("bone-dry") followers into the Hoover ranks—a defection that was to end two years later in the downfall of the "Dry Moses."[3]

The Democratic National Convention of 1928 seemed to be shaping up as a repeat of 1924, with William Gibbs McAdoo of California representing the rural, dry, Protestant South and West, and Governor Alfred E. Smith of New York, the urban, wet, Catholic Northeast. Love, McAdoo's chief lieutenant in Texas, believed that the Californian could win the nomination if the two-thirds rule was repealed, with a better-than-even chance to be elected by the Wilson states of 1916. "From the present outlook I have no doubt whatever that the delegation from Texas to the next National Convention will be a McAdoo delegation," he wrote McAdoo in September, 1926, "although I am sure it is not good politics to be quoted as saying this at this time." Love dismissed reports in the New York press that Moody would favor an uninstructed delegation. "No governor of Texas has made a successful effort to dominate the situation of the delegation from Texas to a National Convention and only one [Neff] has made any such effort during the twenty-five years I have lived in Texas," he informed columnist Mark Sullivan. "The Governor generally has 'other fish to fry.' While I am not speaking by authority, I predict that the new Governor of Texas [Moody] will lay off the job of controlling the situation of the Texas delegation in 1928." A note of disdain for the young governor intruded into a letter of March, 1927, from Love to McAdoo:

While I was very closely associated with Governor Moody during the session and we are very friendly, I do not know what his attitude is going to be except I am sure he will not support Smith—but it involves no reflection on anyone to say that it makes no difference what his attitude may be. My judgment is that he will not oppose any efforts our friends may make.[4]

If both Smith and McAdoo stood firm, it meant sure defeat, if not complete disaster, for the Democratic party. McAdoo, however, in the interest of party harmony, withdrew from the contest on September 17, 1927, in a letter to one of his Tennessee supporters, George Fort Milton, the editor of the *Chattanooga News*.[5] The Californian's withdrawal left Smith in a commanding position over two other wet candidates, Senator James Reed of Missouri and Governor Albert Ritchie of Maryland; a belated dry entry, Senator Thomas Walsh of Montana; and the usual crop of favorite sons. "It looks like it is getting more and more of a 'dirty mess' every week," Milton lamented to McAdoo in mid-October, 1927. "I have been trying to stimulate some sentiment for [Edwin] Meredith, Walsh, or [Vic] Donahey, but there seems to be practically no answering echo at all. You know I told you when you got out of it it meant Smith and I can't see anything to change my conclusion on this point. If he is beaten, it will be at the polls and not at the convention."[6]

In Texas political leaders assessed the impact of McAdoo's withdrawal on national and state politics. "Smith will be nominated," Albert Sidney Burleson declared flatly. "The Democratic party has no one to put up against him. How can 'no one' beat 'some one?' I am still for Smith. He is the most available candidate we can nominate." Jim

Ferguson said that Burleson's statement would "carry great weight with many prominent people of Texas." Another former member of Wilson's cabinet, Thomas Watt Gregory, who probably would have supported McAdoo if he had run, now leaned to Smith and made a firm commitment to the New Yorker in February, 1928. Marshall Hicks lamented that McAdoo's followers in Texas were "at sea." "We do not know what to do," he wrote McAdoo. "I am glad, however, to inform you that Texas will not submit to this [wet] program but will stand by her colors and send a delegation which will fight this crowd to the very end." Oscar B. Colquitt, a dry convert, and Cullen Thomas thought that Smith should follow McAdoo's example and voluntarily eliminate himself as a candidate for president in the interest of party harmony.[7] "To nominate Al Smith or any other wet will mean the downfall of the party," Tom Love predicted in January, 1928, after he returned from a Jackson Day dinner in Washington, D.C. "There are several Southern states that will break the ranks if that is done, and many Texans have assured me that this State will break from the solid South."

In an article on the political situation that he prepared for the February, 1928, issue of *Bunker's Monthly*, a magazine published in Fort Worth, Love contended that the major issue in the coming campaign was "the question of the enforcement of the law, local and State, as well as National, including our liquor laws." To prevent a wet president from paralyzing enforcement of Prohibition for four years, the Texas delegation should be instructed to vote as a unit, "first, last and all the time," against the nomination of Smith, Reed, Ritchie, or any other wet candidate. The battle must be fought and won in the precinct presidential primaries on May 5, 1928. He warned that if the liquor interests captured the Democratic party "there could be little doubt that the great host of moral voters . . . who have enthusiastically fought its battles since the first Woodrow Wilson campaign, and who re-elected him in 1916, would leave it never to return, or not for a generation at least."[8]

It was the strategy of Smith's managers to obtain uninstructed delegates from states like Texas where opposition to him was centered. It was easier to switch uninstructed delegates than pledged ones at the convention. In October, 1927, a group of influential young antiprohibitionist Democrats organized the Texas Uninstructed-for-President Club, with Charles I. Francis of Wichita Falls as president and Connie C. Renfro of Dallas as secretary. Other members included

Steve Pinckney, Richard T. Fleming, and Allen V. Peden, all of Houston; W. K. Hopkins of Gonzales; Paul D. Page of Bastrop; Robert L. Holliday of El Paso; Frank Culver, Jr., of Fort Worth; and T. J. Ramey of Sulphur Springs. These men had just begun to take part in politics in 1924 and had come together under Moody's "throw-the-rascals-out" banner in the campaign of 1926. To them Moody was a romantic figure.[9] Renfro, the group's spokesman, attacked the "disgraceful display of provincial narrowness and intolerance" that had characterized the Texas delegation of 1924; he wanted Texas to send to the next convention a group that would support any candidate, wet or dry, who was considered by two-thirds of the delegates to offer the best hope of victory. That was likely to be Al Smith, but Renfro denied that the club was particularly favorable to him. "This organization is not formed to promote the candidacy of Governor Smith," he wrote privately. "It is organized primarily to overthrow the Love-Sells-Hicks domination of the party in this State. . . . While we have no set immediate goal other than a purpose to take advantage of such opportunities as may come our way, we believe that we can do more for the party than the Love crowd can."[10] Bone-dry leaders, however, regarded the uninstructed organization as a disguised move to deliver the Texas delegation to Smith.[11]

The uninstructed group regarded Moody as the logical man to lead their fight to head off Love and the "old guard." They wanted to draft his leadership if he did not offer it voluntarily, and twenty-five of them gathered in Austin for that purpose, offering Moody their support in a fight against Love for control of the Texas delegation. "Dan was pleased and things started out grand," recalled Allen Peden, the publisher of the *Houston Gargoyle*. "Most of those young men, all but one or two in fact, were for Al Smith, and while they did not ask Moody, an announced dry, to openly advocate the New Yorker's candidacy, they at least expected him to say nothing against it." Renfro wanted the governor to announce that the Texas delegation should be instructed to work for a pro–Eighteenth Amendment plank in the national platform but should be left free to choose the nominee to run on such a platform. Moody, however, was personally opposed to Smith, Reed, and Ritchie and was unwilling to go as far as the uninstructed group wished in giving the delegation freedom of choice.[12]

Chesley W. Jurney, who had previously been Charles A. Culberson's private secretary and now filled the same office for Senator Royal

Copeland of New York, was given a leave of absence and visited Texas in the late summer and fall of 1927 to further Smith's candidacy. "Mr. Jurney, Secretary to Senator Copeland, is here," a Dallas attorney wrote Franklin D. Roosevelt. "He is doing good work." Copeland sent a copy of Jurney's report to Smith along with a newspaper account "showing that the plan for uninstructed delegation is progressing nicely." Smith read it with "a good deal of interest." Unfortunately, the report has been lost.[13]

The following year, when R. L. Henry of Houston advised Jurney that a Harris County Smith Club had been organized, the latter replied that the Smith people were carrying on an undercover campaign:

The opinion among our friends is 100 percent for this character of work, as we do not feel anything can be gained by great publicity and a hot campaign. The Democrats of Texas pretty generally understand the situation, which makes it possible to do this. It will be very helpful to our movement if you will do this also. In other words, hereafter hold "executive meetings" of your club and do not let the proceedings of your club be published. The point is, the only way we can win this campaign is not through the newspapers, but through precinct organizations. Whether you agree with this or not, I am sure you will be willing to do as the rest of us think is best.

Jurney asked Henry to tell people who wrote from over the state asking his help in forming Smith clubs that the governor's friends were not encouraging the organization of clubs "and that it would be better if they would simply get key men in every precinct who will fight for uninstructed delegations and who will see that the 'right' men go to the county and state conventions." Carbon copies of this letter were sent to Charles Francis, Connie Renfro, Steve Pinckney, John Boyle, George E. B. Peddy, Walter Woodul, and William A. Kirkland, indicating that they were all privy to the Smith strategy for Texas.[14]

Added interest in the election began to develop when Houston was chosen as the site for the Democratic National Convention. It would be the first time since 1860 that the party had met in the lower South. Jesse Jones, treasurer of the Democratic National Committee, won the convention for Houston by offering his own certified check for $200,000 and promising to build a hall that would seat 25,000 people. Frank Hague of New Jersey, Thomas Spellacy of Connecticut, and other Smith adherents on the national committee voted for Houston from the first ballot. Political observers saw the selection as a gesture to the South to support Smith as well as an attempt to allay anti-Smith prejudice in Texas by making the state host to the nation's Democrats. They also thought that it would give the Smith Democrats an opportunity to go even further in appeasing Texas and the South and West by naming the handsome thirty-five-year-old Moody for vice-president. The *Houston Post-Dispatch* suggested that "dry Dan Moody would make an ideal running mate for moist Al Smith."[15]

Both the Smith and the bone-dry forces in Texas saw Moody as a central figure in the struggle to control the state's delegation to Houston, and each dangled a tempting prize before his eyes. Albert Sidney Burleson and Thomas Watt Gregory, both pro-Smith, thought that the state should compliment Moody by instructing for him for vice-president. Jurney had sounded out Moody during his visit to Texas in 1927 to learn whether he was avilable as a dry running mate for Smith. Now he wrote the governor: "In 1936, after (8) years in the Vice Presidency, a certain friend of mine can win the Presidency (at 43)." Meanwhile, Marshall Hicks and former Texas Attorney General Walter Keeling started a movement to have the Texas delegation instructed for Moody for president. Claude Teer told Jesse Daniel Ames that he had advised Hicks to start the Moody-for-president boom because he believed that it was the only way to prevent Texas from voting for Smith and maintain a united front. That Keeling was the general attorney for the American Book Company prompted Jim Ferguson to comment acidly that "it was a great crime in the minds of Moody and his cohorts for anybody to represent the American Book Company during the Ferguson administration, but lo and behold it is a great virtue now for Keeling to represent the American Book Company while he is managing the campaign for Moody for president." Love advised Moody through Keeling to announce immediately for reelection as governor and declare his opposition to the nomination of a wet for president or vice-president. The way would then be open for the "good government Democrats" of Texas "not only to instruct against a wet nomination but also to instruct for Governor Moody for President."[16]

In November, 1927, Moody told reporters that published reports that he had been approached to become a candidate for a national office and "had answered favorably inquiries" could be discounted "at just exactly 100 per cent." "The Democratic party is not in the habit of nominating people from the South and, in my judgment, it is neither advisable nor likely that they soon acquire such a habit," he declared. He disclaimed any definite future political plans and reiterated his stand for a "ringing" Prohibition plank in the Democratic platform. On January 23, 1928, the Houston Democratic Executive Committee endorsed Smith for president and Moody as his running mate. The next day Moody told reporters that he had no intention of becoming a candidate for vice-president. Asked whether he would accept a draft, the governor answered, "That will never be done." He also refused to lend his name to the Hicks-Keeling movement to have him nominated for president and at the end of February announced that he would seek a second term as governor.[17]

A boom then developed for Jesse H. Jones as Smith's running mate. The ponderous, genial white-haired Houston timber magnate, builder, and financier was one of the richest men in Texas, owning nearly forty large buildings in his hometown, among them the Rice Hotel, and a thirty-five-story office building that was nearing completion. In addition, he was the publisher of the *Houston Chronicle*, the leading afternoon newspaper. He had been known outside Texas at least since 1917, when he worked with the Red Cross in Washington, D.C., and Paris. Sidestepping the question of the vice-presidency, Jones said that "the only thing I'm a candidate for is, the love, friendship, and confidence of the people of Texas."[18]

Edward S. Villmoore of Kansas City, Missouri, treasurer of the Reed organization, established a Reed-for-president state headquarters in Houston in January, 1928. "Fighting Jim" opened his campaign for the Democratic nomination with a speech in Dallas on February 20. Calling for a "united and militant Democracy," the Missourian declared at the outset that the "most important question before the American people is to drive the Republican party from power." He demanded a "return to honesty in government" and denounced the Coolidge administration and the oil scandal. He was against "centralized, bureaucratic government" and expressed the view that the United States should carry on a program of "defensive" rather than "offensive" preparedness. His defeat in Texas was presaged by the support of Joe Bailey and Jim Ferguson, both of whom were in political eclipse. Wilsonian Texans resented his betrayal of the president in the conflict over the League of Nations. Commented the *Dallas Morning News* after Reed had departed:

Texas is politically dry. Texas still worships at the shrine of Woodrow Wilson and will do so, for all anybody knows, through many years to come. Reed distinguished himself fighting prohibition and at fighting Wilson long before he achieved distinction as a fighter of corruption under Harding's regime. The political memory of Texas isn't very long. But it is long enough to recall that.[19]

Jim Ferguson wanted the Texas delegation to be instructed to vote for the nomination of Smith, Reed, or Ritchie as long as any of their names were before the convention. "Let us meet the enemy," he exhorted his followers. "Let us instruct our delegates. Let that instruction be against the Tom Cat crowd." (Tom Cat was Ferguson's nickname for Tom Love.) He challenged Moody and Love to join in a request to the state Democratic Executive Committee for a state primary to elect delegates to the national convention. Although Jim stated that "I'm for Reed first, and if he can't be nominated I'll be for Smith," Mrs. Ferguson announced on March 13 that she had decided to support the New York governor because "his heart beats in unison with the great toiling masses of our people." The press carried stories that she was not in line with her husband, but harmony was restored the following month when Ferguson also came out for Smith in the *Forum*:

My friends, I have come to love Governor Smith for the enemies he has made. When I see political scamps like Moody, Johnson and Love, and others of that kind, begin to tell lies on a good man like Governor Smith because of his religion and his independent political views then he begins to tug at my heart strings, and I begin to champ at the bit to get in the fight to give battle to this bunch of malicious devils that would take every liberty away from the American people in the name of a vicious fanaticism.

Ferguson issued a call for the names of those who were willing to support a statewide meeting to form a Smith-for-president club. He received four hundred names, mostly farmers, from one hundred counties, but many stated that they could not attend because of the expense and loss of time. So Ferguson called off the meeting and advised Smith's friends to work together at the precinct level. In point of fact, most of the open Smith leaders in Texas as well as the covert Smith supporters wanted nothing to do with the discredited former governor.[20]

The State Democratic Executive Committee voted on February 28 to bar from the Democratic precinct, county, and state conventions anyone who would not pledge to support party nominees, an action construed as favorable to the uninstructed-delegation idea favored by the Smith forces. Cone Johnson, who had served as chairman of the Texas delegation in 1912 and in 1920, voiced the outrage of the bone-drys when he characterized the committee's action as "a reflection on Texas Democracy and part of a scheme to deliver the Democracy of

Texas to Tammany Hall." Moody took no public stand in the pledge
fight, though he considered the pledge a blunder, but pointed out that
the state convention was the sole judge of the qualifications of delegates. Since the state committee would have to meet again before the
May 5 precinct conventions to exclude blacks formally from participation, it could at the same time, if it cared to, reconsider its action in
imposing a pledge. When Attorney General Claude Pollard ruled that
the committee had exceeded its legal powers in requiring the pledge
and that the test was not legally binding on precinct and county chairmen, Love announced that the decision had ended the hopes of those
favoring an uninstructed delegation. But State Democratic Chairman
D. W. Wilcox declared that Pollard had exceeded his authority in the
ruling and swore to enforce the pledge. "What is the use of having a
party without party lines and party loyalty?" added Wilcox's law partner, Harry Graves. "The test hurts no sincere Democrat."[21]

On March 3 the County Dry Democratic League was organized in
Dallas County by Love and others pledged to the nomination of "a dry
progressive Democrat for President of the United States on a dry, progressive platform." One possibility was Senator Thomas Walsh of Montana. Like Smith a Catholic, Walsh was a strong dry and a long-time
McAdoo supporter. A "smallish man with the heavy, drooping mustache of a poker player of Bloody Gulch" and "gimlet-like eyes," he was
much admired for his masterful conduct of the Teapot Dome investigation. His selection, some drys believed, would demonstrate to northeastern Democrats that their opposition to Smith was due not to his
religion but to his views on the Eighteenth Amendment. Walsh himself had a "distinct averson" to running as a dry candidate against a wet
candidate. "If I have in any measure earned or enjoyed any favor
among the people of America," he wrote, "it is because of services rendered, other than in promoting the cause of prohibition, and principles to which I have evidenced my attachment quite unrelated to that
subject." On March 4, 1928, he announced his candidacy.[22]

McAdoo, who was working for Walsh in the California primary
against Smith and Reed, wrote to his Texas friends asking them to do
everything possible for the Montanan. "The Texas movement, with
Tom Love, Frank Davis, Marshall Hicks, George Armistead, and others at the front, ought to be formidable," he assured the senator. "I
hope sincerely that it may succeed." Love wrote a Maine Democrat:
"Of course, Senator Walsh will be a most acceptable candidate to me

and to all our group, I am sure, but this is confidential as we are not playing any candidate up but simply making the fight against the nomination of a Wet candidate." Davis and Armistead wrote Walsh: "We are whistling up the rising tune. Watch Texas instruct for you."[23] Former State Senator W. J. Townsend of Wichita Falls invited the senator to make two or three speeches in Texas at an early date, but Walsh replied that it would be impossible for him to come because of his duties in Washington.[24]

Following the organization of the Dallas County Dry Democratic League, Love conferred in San Antonio with Hicks, Davis, and Cone Johnson and on his return to Dallas told reporters: "We were all agreed upon the imperative necessity of the dry progressive Democrats centering their efforts upon preventing the nomination of Reed, Smith or Ritchie or any other wet candidate, at the Houston convention." Yet, he denied a story by George Armistead in the *San Antonio Express* that the four men were launching a statewide campaign to carry the Walsh banner into the state convention in Beaumont on May 22. He also corrected the impression that he was personally committed to Walsh. While he had the highest admiration for the senator, he said, and believed that he would make an excellent candidate, that was likewise true of Cordell Hull of Tennessee, Edwin Meredith of Iowa, Governor Vic Donahey of Ohio, and other dry Democrats whose names were being urged. "Any one of them would make a better candidate and a better President than either of the wet entries," he insisted.[25]

Walsh's first clear-cut contest was in South Dakota. The state's Democratic convention endorsed Smith for president over him and unanimously expressed a preference for Moody as his running mate. "I didn't imagine they ever heard of me," was Moody's only comment. The next day he remarked that, while he appreciated the compliment, he felt certain that they had not seen his statement that he was candidate for reelection as governor and had no intention of becoming a candidate for any other office. Most Democrats in Austin believed that his selection in South Dakota with Smith was part of the same political strategy that had brought the national convention to Houston, namely, "to palliate the dry South and assure its support of the ticket with Smith at the head." It was now believed that other Smith states would also instruct for Moody.[26]

Five hundred Prohibition Democrats from seventy counties met in Dallas on March 15 and, under the leadership of Love, Sells, Hicks,

Johnson, and Davis, organized the Texas Constitutional Democrats with R. Harper Kirby of Austin as chairman. The organization adopted a resolution urging Democrats to attend their precinct conventions on May 5 and adopt resolutions favoring Prohibition and its strict enforcement and the election of a dry delegation to the Houston convention instructed to vote "as a unit at all times for only a candidate for President and Vice President whose record is 'openly and positively' for effective enforcement of our prohibition laws." Cone Johnson told Mrs. Jesse Daniel Ames that the resolutions were read to Moody over the telephone long distance and that he approved them. Speakers singled out Smith for attack; Cullen Thomas quipped that "Al Smith's candidacy hasn't a leg on which to stand unless it be bootlegs." Love wanted to instruct against Smith, Ritchie, and Reed by name but yielded to promote the fullest cooperation of all those who were opposed to turning the Democratic party over to the "outlawed liquor traffic." Afterward he wrote McAdoo: "I do not think there is any doubt about our whipping the fight in Texas." He explained why the Constitutional Democrats had not proposed an alternative to Smith: "Our policy in Texas is to consolidate by all possible means the support of all dry Democrats by avoiding emphasis on any particular candidate." But W. J. Townsend, a member of the platform and resolutions committee, assured Walsh that "you had a majority of those present at the meeting."[27]

Moody was invited to address the meeting of the Constitutional Democrats but instead spoke that evening at a Jackson Day dinner arranged by the Democratic women of Dallas County. His position was that the Texas delegation should not be instructed by name or inference against anyone, which would only engender bitterness and disunion, but should be instructed to work for a Prohibition plank in the national platform and the nomination of a candidate in sympathy with the plank. Charles I. Francis told reporters that Moody's speech was in complete harmony with the movement for an uninstructed delegation. He stated:

I am not for or against Al Smith. I do not believe any candidate will receive serious consideration at Houston who is not in favor of a plank in the party platform endorsing the Eighteenth Amendment and its strict enforcement. That is what our organization is for, but we do not favor tying the hands of Texas delegates with instructions except on this principle.

Another member of the uninstructed club, however, Robert Holliday of El Paso, wanted to know whether Moody was going to make an "active campaign fight" against Love. "You can win this fight if you want to and if you will select some of your younger friends from each Congressional District or Senatorial District," he told Moody. "They can organize this state with you making a few speeches in the central portion of the state, and can defeat Tom Love and his crowd."[28]

Back in Dallas on March 23, Moody said that he was personally opposed to Smith, Reed, and Ritchie and thought that the Texas delegation should be "firmly and unalterably bound by its instructions until a dry candidate is nominated." This statement caused some members of the uninstructed group to conclude that there was in fact no difference between Moody's position and Love's. Holliday complained:

It seems to us that you are now opposed to Smith, Reid [sic], and Richey [sic], and for a dry candidate only. Then, why shouldn't the democracy of this state, if it agrees with you and Mr. Love, let you and Love mail the vote of Texas to the Houston convention. Of course, we will follow you anywhere, right or wrong, but I must say that we do regret to see you throwing in with Tom Love. Please advise your revised position to date and whether it will be changed again in the future.[29]

In a long conversation with Jesse Daniel Ames and Jane Y. McCallum on March 30, Moody asserted that if Texas did not instruct against anyone by name the Smith forces would not be offended, that Smith could not be nominated, and Texas would then be in a position to act as an arbiter and offer the compromise candidate. "The Smith people would get behind the Texas offering if Texas had not offended by being too obviously against Smith now," he said. If a strong Prohibition plank was included in the platform, Smith could not accept such a plank and run on it without making himself and the party ridiculous. When Mrs. Ames suggested that Smith might come out and say that he favored such a plank and then run on it, Moody laughed and said that Smith could not do that because he would stultify himself and it would be too obvious.[30]

The governor now stepped in to make peace between the Constitutional Democrats and the uninstructed group and to prevent Love from controlling the Texas delegation. At his instigation Texas Democratic leaders were invited to attend a statewide harmony mass meeting in Dallas on April 7 in support of the program suggested by Moody in his Jackson Day speech in Dallas. Moody showed no disposition to confine himself to such "young" Democrats as Renfro, Francis, and Holliday and selected Thomas H. Ball, William P. Hobby, T. W. Da-

vidson, Martin M. Crane, and Lynch Davidson, among others, to help
work out a harmony plan. "Dan . . . conceived the idea that he could,
by going a little further, corral the dry crowd and leave Tom Love out
on an island by himself—a perfectly childish delusion," wrote Allen
Peden. "Forsaking his tried friends, he turned to such men as V. A. Collins, a Love henchman, Lynch Davidson, who had fought Moody for
the governorship, a strong dry, Tom Ball of Houston, an old prohibition war-horse." A synopsis of a letter of April 3, 1928, from Silliman
Evans to a man named Hand in Al Smith's private papers in Albany,
New York, is revealing. It reads in part:

Plea for uninstructed delegation was best policy at the time it was started, but
Gov. Moody has proven to be an impossible local politician unable to rise
above local issues. Had been relied to stay hitched, but has given cross to those
who relied on his pol. bravery. Serious danger of anti-Smith's grabbing the
play for the uninstructed delegation, taking charge of the movement and manning the delegation with anti-Smith men.[31]

The Constitutional Democrats were also suspicious of the governor's political motives and decided not to attend the April 7 meeting.
Cone Johnson warned grimly that if the meeting adopted a "milk and
cider" program with a loophole to help Smith win the nomination he
would denounce every man connected with it. Presiding over a Dallas
meeting of the Constitutional Democrats on the eve of the harmony
gathering, Love declared caustically: "The Democratic party can not
serve God and Booze; either in Texas or in the Nation. I believe this
sort of harmony will not only defeat but degrade the party for which I
have battled all my life, and I can not escape the conviction that it
ought to."[32]

The harmony meeting organized the Democrats of Texas (also
called the Harmony Democrats), with Lynch Davidson as permanent
chairman. Resolutions were adopted favoring a plank in the national
platform "unequivocally indorsing prohibition as written into the Constitution," opposing repeal, and demanding the "strict and efficient enforcement by the national government" of all Prohibition laws. The
Texas delegation should be instructed "to vote as a unit at all times and
upon all questions and for candidates for President and Vice President
who each favor and support the foregoing plank." Moody promised to
support the national nominees and made a strong plea for a dry plank
in the national platform but urged that the delegation should not be
instructed against any candidate. He said:

If the predictions of the political writers are true, the negative instructions
would be against the position of a majority of the votes in the convention. We
can effectively oppose their candidate without destroying our influence in the
convention, but we can hardly give a negative instruction without making our
delegates the victim of a steamroller and nothing more.

When by inference Moody charged Love with using Prohibition to his
personal advantage, he raised the loudest cheers of the day.[33]

The Texas Uninstructed-for-President Club was not active after
the Dallas harmony meeting, its members generally subscribing to the
program adopted there. After reviewing the results of the harmony
meeting, the Constitutional Democrats decided to go forward with
their organization to accomplish the adoption of their program at the
precinct conventions on May 5. "We think that we are 'sitting pretty,'"
Cone Johnson wrote R. Harper Kirby, after conferring with Love,
Cranfill, and others. "The erection of the harmony meeting, together
with ours, has put an end to the effort to swing Texas into the wet column and has put a quietus on the more adroit movement to aid Governor Smith by an Uninstructed delegation." The only thing to be
avoided now was a wrangle between the two groups. Johnson urged
Constitutional Democrats to participate in the precinct conventions in
spite of any pledge that they might be forced to take. "The pledge is
absurd, illegal and consequently not binding upon anybody which is
imposed upon him with authority of law," he argued.[34]

Joe Bailey cited the whispering campaign against Smith as his reason for switching from Reed or Ritchie to the New York governor. At a
meeting of his friends in the Baker Hotel in Dallas on April 16, the
former senator outlined his plan for a third Democratic group that
would "demand" enforcement of the party pledge, while the Constitutional Democrats opposed it and the Democrats of Texas merely "appealed" for its enforcement. He defined his meeting as that of Democrats, while terming the other two organizations "bolting Democrats,"
referring to the resolutions they had adopted and principles their leaders had proclaimed. The Bailey meeting issued a challenge, through
Chairman Oscar Calloway, for a debate at Nacogdoches among Bailey,
Love, and Moody. Lynch Davidson, after talking with Moody and others, replied that no debate was necessary or called for at the present
time. The reply was in line with Moody's wishes. As he read press reports of Bailey's speech at the Dallas meeting, Davidson remarked to
reporters that "the only difference, as far as I can see, is that Joe Bailey

wants to be dictator of Texas Democrats, while we want to walk shoulder to shoulder with Texas Democracy."[35]

In mid-April, Moody tried to bring the Democrats of Texas and the Constitutional Democrats together behind a common program. "It looks like things are going pretty good," he wrote Renfro, "and some of our friends of the Constitutional Democrats are favoring a meeting for the purpose of harmonizing such differences as exist." He met with Cone Johnson, Cullen Thomas, and V. A. Collins, who had replaced the deceased Kirby as chairman of the Constitutional Democrats. Afterward Johnson and Moody submitted a unity statement to Collins and Lynch Davidson, which the two chairmen published over their signatures on April 24. The Constitutional Democrats agreed to take the party loyalty pledge on May 5 "in good faith," to support resolutions under which the Texas delegation's vote at Houston would be "cast continuously as a unit for a dry platform and the nomination of a candidate who is in harmony with such a platform," and to cooperate with the Harmony Democrats in selecting delegates to the county, state, and national conventions "who are known to favor such a program and will faithfully carry it out."[36]

At a meeting in Dallas on April 26 attended by Moody, leaders of both groups "fully approved and ratified" the Davidson-Collins statement and pledged "full and complete cooperation" in executing it. Moody told reporters that the "contest narrows itself down to those who favor Gov. Smith's nomination and those who are supporting a dry platform. . . . All friends of prohibition should go into the primaries and make their wishes known." On May 2 the governor told four thousand Houstonians, "If Al Smith is nominated for president, the State of Texas is not going to be responsible."[37]

Tom Love was not brought into the harmony fold. He said later that Connie Renfro had invited all the Dallas conferees "and was careful not to invite me." Love told his friends that he would approve any agreement that did not prevent him from urging the adoption of resolutions instructing against wet candidates by name. "They all told me this was understood and Cone Johnson told me that he would continue to urge such resolutions as a safety first measure, which he did," Love later recalled. Since negative instructions were contrary to the Moody program, the Democrats of Texas were soon complaining that they had been "double-crossed." Despite the agreement, both factions pressed ahead with efforts to elect a majority of delegates to the upcoming state convention in Beaumont. In a press release the Harmony Democrats asserted that "a comparatively new element" was now in control of state politics: "Tom Love and his lieutenants, who have ruled the party for many years, were nearly all left out in the new controlling group, at the head of which is Moody, ably seconded by Lynch Davidson." Meanwhile, the Smith forces concentrated their delegate hunt in East and South Texas.[38]

Frank C. Davis, who was heading the Walsh campaign in Texas, planned a meeting of the senator's friends in Fort Worth or Austin, with the date and place tentatively set for May 12 in Fort Worth. But California held its presidential primary on May 1, and Walsh lost disastrously, finishing a poor third behind Smith and Reed. He immediately withdrew from the race, writing one of his chief supporters that the result in California "quite clearly indicates that the Democrats desire Gov. Smith as their candidate."[39]

The similarity of the resolutions offered in the May precinct conventions by the Constitutional Democrats and Democrats of Texas confused many voters and produced a situation in which both sides claimed victory. When the county conventions met on May 8, however, the Constitutionalists did better than expected, capturing the Dallas, Tarrant, Denton, and Wichita County delegations, among others. Their biggest victory was in Dallas County, where they elected Love convention chairman over the opposition of a Harmony–Al Smith coalition and named eighty-six delegates with instructions to vote as a unit at all times against Al Smith. Love presided with a brick as his gavel. The Moody managers charged that he had gained control of the convention with the help of the old Ku Klux Klan leaders. "The Dallas County Convention was so surcharged with the 'invisible spirit,' that you could see it," complained T. Whitfield Davidson. The Love men countered that they had gone to the Moody leaders and offered to combine forces against the Smith delegates but had been told, "We will not treat with you unless you throw down Tom Love." Moody managers confirmed that the governor had instructed his supporters to refuse any trading that involved Love or in any way interfered with the original Democrats of Texas program.[40]

"Rock-ribbed pros" dominated the Travis County convention, and a move by Smith supporters to endorse Thomas Watt Gregory as a delegate-at-large to the national convention was defeated 225 to 214. A plan to exclude Mrs. Claude De Van Watts, president of the Texas

WCTU, from the list of delegates to the state convention was abandoned when it developed that the drys were in the majority. While endorsing the idea of an uninstructed delegation, the delegates demanded a dry plank in the platform and "a dry candidate to stand on it."

In Harris County the Ku Klux Klan combined with the Moody forces to steamroll the Smith supporters. A Moody leader confessed to the governor that, "while on the surface your victory in this county was complete in every detail, and while our Delegation was instructed against no one by name, nevertheless the Klan element is in control." Harmony leaders were apprehensive that klansmen in "harmony" delegations such as Harris County's might count noses at Beaumont and find strength enough, in cooperation with the Constitutional Democrats, to take command of the convention and instruct against Smith by name.[41]

The state press predicted a heated contest in Beaumont between the Moody and Love groups. A *Houston Post Dispatch* story quoted Steve Pinckney of the Democrats of Texas as saying that the Constitutional Democrats were "a gang of Ku Kluxers." Personal relations between Moody and Love worsened when the latter publicly expressed anxiety that the governor might trade with the Smith supporters at Beaumont as his friends had done in the Dallas County convention. Stung by this "bitter injustice," Moody replied that he regarded Love's statement as "a base and insincere effort to create the impression that some one other than himself is willing to betray public confidence." The Harmony Democrats rejected a proposal by V. A. Collins and George C. Purl of the Constitutional Democrats that the two groups caucus the night before the Beaumont convention opened to agree on a solid anti-Smith delegation to the national convention. This put the Constitutionalists on notice that the Harmony men would have their own program and slate of delegates to Houston. With both groups opposing Smith and favoring a dry plank in the national platform, a staff writer for the *Houston Press* declared that "the subsurface issue is whether Tom Love and the Ku Klux Klan will dominate the convention, as they did at Waco four years ago, or whether the anti-klan faction of the state's prohibitionists will control."[42]

The three groups were about equal in delegates when the convention opened on May 22. John Boyle of San Antonio, the Smith floor leader, joined forces with Moody to elect W. L. Dean, the author of the Texas Prohibition law, as temporary chairman over V. A. Collins, the Constitutional Democrats' candidate, 573⅝ votes to 180⅔ votes. Judge E. A. Berry of Houston, placed in nomination by Jim Ferguson but without the support of the Smith caucus leaders, received 16½ votes. In seconding Dean's nomination, Moody told the delegates: "We are faced with about the same situation as in 1924. There is an effort to control the politics of the State by forming some kind of klan coalition. I stand for the Democrats of Texas managing their own affairs. I am opposed to any sort of boss rule in Texas." Moody said that he would rather be defeated five hundred times and walk out of Texas barefooted than win for the benefit of any sort of political gain. "They say I've made a trade with the Smith people," he declared, "but I've never made a political trade in my life and so help me God I never will make one."[43]

Aiding in the governor's complete victory was the last-minute debacle in the ranks of the Constitutional Democrats, with Cone Johnson and Cato Sells unwilling to fight Dean's nomination for temporary chairman. Dallas County, instructed against Smith and standing steadfast with Love, cast 86 votes for Collins, almost half the votes that Collins received. Sells's Tarrant County delegation, however, also instructed against Smith, voted for Dean, as did Grayson County. The Smith County delegation, headed by Johnson, voted first for Collins but then switched to Dean. Johnson told the convention that he had voted for Collins with the understanding that he was to withdraw at the proper time and second Dean's nomination. Cries of "Good-by Tom!" were heard when Love left the platform for a moment to talk with a delegate on the floor. George Purl shouted across to Moody, sitting near the front row, that Sells had turned state's evidence. "And he gets immunity when he does," the governor replied, "smiling broadly and happy over the outcome of the vote on the temporary chairman." Love passed within a few feet of Moody; the two men did not speak.[44]

Later the Harmony–Al Smith coalition defeated Oscar B. Colquitt's attempt to instruct against Smith by name, 511 to 203, and adopted the Moody program for a strong dry plank and a candidate in sympathy with such a plank. Then Boyle, by invoking the principle of local government and congressional-district selection of delegates, nearly succeeded in sending a wet delegation to Houston. It was believed in the convention that the Smith delegates were so distributed in the district caucuses as to allow them to name a majority of the Texas delegates. "It appeared that in every precinct in the State almost, some one or more Smith delegates of the hand-picked variety, got on the delegation and were present at the convention," Frank C. Davis wrote McAdoo. "The unsuspecting dry delegates seemed to have lost interest and failed to attend the convention, feeling that as there was in fact no real difference between the dry elements, that there was no necessity of attending the convention." Moody, who had earlier supported the principle of district selection, suddenly saw the consequences of its application. He interrupted a roll call to swing his support behind Tom Ball's resolution to have Dean appoint a committee to screen the delegates selected by the congressional districts. Amid cries of "Double-cross!" hurled at Moody by the outraged Smith delegates, the Harmony and Love groups passed Ball's resolution.[45]

As it turned out, most of the districts got the delegates they wanted, after their choices were given a private quizzing by the screening committee in Moody's presence. It was claimed that there were twenty or twenty-one Smith votes on the delegation. Under the unit rule twenty-one delegates could cast the state's entire 40 votes. "I anticipate an ugly time with the Texas delegation at Houston unless the matter is handled with great care," Cato Sells wrote Love. The latter wired McAdoo: "Texas delegation very close. Possibly for Smith resulting from treachery in the state convention which was two thirds against him." Moody was reported to have received assurances from the Smith delegates that they would stand solidly with the majority and not embarrass him. Robert M. Field of New York City, however, formerly a resident of Texas, made an early canvass of the Texas delegation and discovered that "19 ot its 40 votes were avowedly for Smith and that 2 or 3 others could have been whipped into line if occasion had demanded." Fortunately for Moody, the Texas delegation's vote was not needed to nominate Smith, and its solidarity was never tested.[46]

"I was between the horns of a dilemma," Moody confessed of his roll at Beaumont. "Either one I took meant I was gored and I took the one my conscience dictated to me to be the correct position. I feel humiliated over the situation, but I could not help it." Mrs. Moody wrote in her diary: "Dan stumbled off the train, a haggard lad, and said briefly, 'Well Mildred, I have been through Hell.'"[47]

Moody came out of the Beaumont convention with all the spoils of victory, but he also bore the brunt of the displeasure at the outcome. That resulted from his choice of tactics. He first accepted Boyle's aid to defeat Love and then was forced to use Love's followers to discomfit his allies of the first contest. That a victory so won should give rise to a charge of bad faith was inevitable. Love told McAdoo that "the cause of prohibition and good government was betrayed shamelessly by Dan Moody in this campaign and in the State Convention."Frank C. Davis commented:

The Harmony Democrats . . . were in fact supported by a large number of Smith wets parading as dries. There is no doubt that Governor Moody, consciously or otherwise, was greatly influenced by the activities of this wet element in his organization; and his organization formed a coalition with the wringing wet Smith element to defeat the Love element of the party.

Jesse Daniel Ames, however, believed that Moody had been "an innocent dupe in the hands of the astute Smith politicians," though he had done "a big thing" when he reversed himself at Beaumont at the last minute and tried to save the day.[48]

It was now said of Moody in Texas that he changed his opinions too frequently, that he misled his friends, and that he was not a leader. "The Governor knows nothing about the game of politics," was Mrs. Ames's opinion:

He does stand in awe of the political leaders, such as Crane and Mr. Ball. He cannot even bare [sic] to think that if the political situation demands a change in tactics or even commitments, they will change to meet new situations. . . . He is honest, sincere and ignorant. No political leader can afford to be innocent. He makes me feel like a low down critter nevertheless.

The governor knew that he had been hurt but hoped the wounds would heal in time. Veteran dry Dr. J. B. Cranfill thought otherwise. "On March 15, when we held the convention of our Constitutional Democrats, . . . you had not, so far as I know, outside of Jim Ferguson and his little contingent, a political enemy in Texas," he told Moody. "Now their name is legion. You emerged from the Beaumont convention smudged with political hostilities that will last as long as you live."[49]

After expressing appreciation for Jesse Jones's party activities the state convention resolved that "without presenting him as a candidate we commend him to the democracy of the nation as suitable in every way for the highest office in the gift of the people, and endorse him as the choice of the Texas democracy for the presidency." Jones's admirers interpreted the resolution to mean that he had been endorsed for the nomination, and W. L. Dean, chairman of the convention, said that it made support of Jones at Houston mandatory for the Texas delegation. Following a conference with Jones in Houston, Moody said, "Mr. Jones undoubtedly will be placed in nomination." He declined to expand his statement other than to say that the state convention's action was "a nice and very deserved compliment." The governor added that if Jones so desired he would be glad to make the nomination.[50]

Letters to newspapers, press releases, editorials, and even poems eulogized "Democracy's Miracle Man." According to a brief campaign biography by Paul Wakefield, "Jesse H. Jones has no magic lamp, but his Aladdin-like achievements suggest the possession of a magical mind and an attendant genii." Tom Love thought that Jones was the "best rallying point for the anti-Smith forces in the Convention, all things considered." Will Hogg, however, wrote a vigorous, plainspoken letter to Moody in which he attacked Jones without mercy or reserve for his "stalwart avarice and piratical trading spirit" in business transactions. "So, please don't proffer as President this ill-fitted pseudo-statesman who is now a talented gambler with buildings-and-banks as he formerly was with pitch-and-poker," Hogg pleaded.

He is always using the other fellow's chips to his own advantage—if that qualifies him to be President of this country, say so, but for your own sake don't stand on the platform of our first Southern session of the National Democracy since secession and make yourself and your friends ridiculous by referring to Jesse Jones' great heart, his great humanity, his great accomplishments, and his great spirit.[51]

Hogg sent a copy of his letter to John Boyle, who showed it to the press. A printed copy was prepared and circulated. "Hot as it is in fair Houston, this letter has lifted the temperature of the city at least twenty degrees," reported Edwin C. Hill of the *New York Sun*. Jones's friends bitterly resented Hogg's letter. They said that there was absolutely nothing to the charges and that a rivalry in Houston civic activities had engendered Hogg's antagonism. The row among the Texans threatened to cause an explosion in the convention. Moody was warned not only by Hogg but also by many other Texans that if he nominated Jones he need never expect another office within the gift of the people of Texas. When the time came, the governor failed to nominate Jones, and Tom Ball of Houston did the honors. A tired Moody belatedly arrived from the platform committee to give a seconding speech that lasted less than three minutes. "He came out and yawned, said three or four words, yawned again and retired," said klansman Billie Mayfield of Moody's address. "I never knew what Private John Allen meant when he said 'Don't let the awkward squad fire over my grave' until I heard Moody talk."[52]

At the Houston convention Moody again stated his opposition to Smith's nomination, which, he warned, might lead to a revolution within the Democratic party in the South, "wherein is the very life and soul of Democracy." He then added a personal objection to Smith: "The Democratic candidate must be of the evangelistic type to go over the nation and convince the people that the government is in the hands of corrupt and grafting men. Governor Smith does not fit in that situation." He flatly refused, however, to become the presidential candidate of the anti-Smith bitter-enders who were groping for a leader. He was reported to have confided to close friends that there seemed no chance of depriving the New Yorker of the nomination. Moody's refusal overshadowed the political importance of a statement he issued that in effect warned the Smith forces against disregarding southern Democrats in drafting the Prohibition plank. "No attempt should be made to draw an overdraft on the Democratic loyalty of the South," he said. "We want the Democratic party to have a forward position on the great moral issue of prohibition upon which the public mind feels with intensity. Any quibbling upon these matters is unthinkable." But nondelegate Tom Love, who arrived in Houston determined to "fight Smith in every possible way," dismissed such worries about the wording of the Prohibition plank. "There is no use in adopting a dry plank if Smith is nominated, for Smith will be his own plank."[53]

When the platform committee turned down Moody's bone-dry plank, he threatened a floor fight; wishing to avoid this, the Smith members accepted a less arid plank proposed by Senator Carter Glass of Virginia pledging "the party and its nominees to an honest effort to enforce the eighteenth amendment and all other provisions of the federal constitution and all laws enacted pursuant thereto." "It is a dry plank of a kind," a weary Moody commented as he left the committee meeting. Dry leaders brought intense pressure on him to accept the committee plank without making a losing and disruptive fight on the convention floor, and he finally yielded to them. He told the delegates, "I occupy the rather unfortunate position, not of representing the minority, but rather of being the minority myself." As he later explained his decision:

I would have even further contended for my proposition and have carried the fight to the floor, but when Senator Glass' plank was approved by such men as former Secretary Josephus Daniels, Bishop Cannon of the Methodist Church, and other leading and outstanding prohibitionists, I knew that I did not have a hope. In the end I could have gotten the votes of Texas and Georgia, and a few scattered votes here and there.[54]

While Moody was before the microphone addressing the convention, Senator Glass, Chairman Clem Shaver, and other high party officials nervously paced the hallway behind the speakers' stand—still fearing and distrusting him. Some of these leaders were dry, while others were wet, but all of them wanted party harmony. One of them was heard bitterly accusing the Texas governor of having double-crossed both the Smith workers and the drys. Governor Ritchie of Maryland had been selected to reply to Moody in case he presented a minority report. Seeing Moody on the rostrum and not troubling to listen to what he had to say, Ritchie arose at the conclusion of his remarks and began to protest against the minority dry resolution that he assumed had been presented. The audience rocked with laughter.[55]

Smith easily won the nomination at the end of the first ballot. Texas cast its 40 votes for Jesse Jones (Alabama gave him 3) and did not hop on the bandwagon during the stampede to Smith. Many people thought that the Texas delegation was demonstrating an aloofness bordering on hostility to the nominee. That night Judge George W. Olvany, the Tammany Hall chieftain, sent his and Jesse Jones's friend Colonel Joseph M. Hartfield to ask Jones whether he would accept the nomination for vice-president. Jones declined. Before the balloting began, the Texas delegation caucused behind the speakers' platform. Several World War I veterans favored Major General Henry T. Allen, the commander of the Nineteenth Division, while many others wanted Senator Alben Barkley of Kentucky. One delegate said that "the Powers of the Convention" had wanted Smith and that he thought it was high time the Texas delegation got behind the ticket and showed New York and the Democratic party that Texans were true Democrats. Following this, its was unanimously agreed that Texas would vote for Smith's choice, Senator Joseph T. Robinson of Arkansas—the Democratic minority leader in the Senate and the convention's permanent

chairman. Robinson was duly nominated. North Carolina gave Moody
9⅓ of its 24 votes at the request of Josephus Daniels, who had served
with the Texas governor on the platform committee.[56]

All was not harmony in the Texas Republican party either, as the battle
for control between Congressman Harry Wurzbach and National Committeeman R. B. Creager continued. Creager enjoyed President Coolidge's favor, as he had Harding's.[57] In the summer of 1927, Coolidge released an enigmatic statement to the press: "I do not choose to run for
president in 1928." Whether he meant that he would not actively seek
the nomination but would accept a draft or whether he really meant to
withdraw remains a mystery. Creager, fresh from the national capital,
said that Coolidge, despite his statement, would in all probability be
offered and urged to accept the Republican nomination, adding: "If the
convention were held tomorrow, I have no doubt but that the Texas
delegation would vote as a unit for Coolidge. He is the overwhelming
choice at this time." When Secretary of Commerce Herbert Hoover
began his campaign for the nomination, however, Creager joined other
"experienced and shrewd vendors of southern delegations" like Rush
Holland, a Washington, D.C., attorney; Bascom Slemp of Virginia;
Perry Howard, the black Mississippi leader; and Ben J. Davis, Republican national committeeman from Georgia, in lining up their delegations for Hoover. Creager did not even bother to consult with the
Texas state chairman, Eugene Nolte, before announcing that Hoover
would receive all the votes of the Texas delegation to the national convention. According to Frank Scobey: "At 3 o'clock he was in Congressman Garner's office and declared for an uninstructed delegation. The
White House called him at seven o'clock and he then said 'Texas' would
be for Hoover." Although Creager sent conciliatory explanatory letters
to the members of the headquarters and state executive committees,
he had aroused considerable resentment in party ranks.[58]

Wurzbach and his allies, Scobey, C. C. Littleton, Captain John E.
("Jack") Elgin, and William ("Gooseneck Bill") McDonald, set out to
capitalize on this discontent, traveling around Texas and meeting with
local Republican leaders who were unhappy with Creager. Scobey favored Vice-President Charles G. Dawes for the Republican nomination and tried to persuade him to challenge Hoover. "The situation in
Texas is looking good," he assured Dawes in February, 1928. "My late

friend, Creager, said everyone had to be for Hoover and the people did not like that. We are going to try to have an uninstructed delegation. If it was so you could become a candidate we could muster your strength more effectively, especially with the American Legion." But the vice-president refused to cooperate; he told Scobey that he favored Governor Frank O. Lowden of Illinois for the nomination. "If you can urge any of Lowden's friends or the friends of the other candidates to get busy in Texas, I believe all of them will get some delegates," Scobey coaxed, but to no avail.[59]

At the State Republican Convention in the Dallas City Hall auditorium on May 22, the Wurzbach forces made an unsuccessful attempt to gain control. Captain Elgin and C. C. Littleton, members of the State Executive Committee, were removed from the convention hall by Dallas policemen. After a plate-glass door leading into the auditorium was broken, Littleton was charged with defacing public property but was soon released on a $200 bond. He vigorously denied responsibility for breaking the door and called his arrest "a concocted scheme to get me out. If I had been allowed to stay we would have taken that convention."

Wurzbach left the hall when Littleton was arrested. Immediately thereafter Harry Beck of Hillsboro, a leader of the "Black and Tan" faction, shouted: "All Republicans follow me!" Fifty or more delegates followed him into a corridor just outside the hall. The rump meeting shortly moved to the Odd Fellows Hall nearby and named a full slate of convention delegates. The Wurzbach faction ordered its delegates to be uninstructed for president, while the Creager group in the auditorium instructed its delegates to vote for Hoover "so long as there is a reasonable chance of his nomination." Creager's faction endorsed him for vice-president. A resolution adopted by the regular convention expressed the belief that Texas would swing into the Republican column in November, because there were too many Texans "who have conscientious scruples against bowing their necks to the brass collar yoke to make a Tammany holiday."

Both Republican factions claimed that they had been the victors in Dallas. Wurzbach called it "the dawn of a new era for Texas Republicans," while Eugene Nolte said that "it meant death for the insurgents." Predicted Orville Bullington, a Creager lieutenant from Wichita Falls: "We gave them a bath, tossed them in Lake Michigan in 1916; we tossed them in again in 1920; we gave them a bath in Lake Erie in

1924; and in 1928 we are going to give them a bath in the old waters
of the Missouri. Do you know that gang still have their mind fixed back
in 1912?"[60]

The Republican National Convention met in Kansas City, Missouri, on June 12, 1928. The national committee had placed the
Creager delegation on the temporary roll before the opening session.
The contesting delegations appeared before the credentials committee. Gooseneck Bill McDonald kept interrupting the proceedings with
comments, and Orville Bullington asked that the sergeant-at-arms
"throw that nigger out of here." McDonald was ejected. Wurzbach once
again levied charges that Creager's organization aimed at controlling
patronage and losing elections. As evidence he offered signed deposi-
tions from the clerks in 128 Texas counties that there was no legal Republican organization in their counties. Oddly, the Creager spokesmen
did not bother to answer this damaging charge. Still, the majority report favored Creager, while a minority report recommended the seat-
ing of the Wurzbach group. On a roll-call vote the convention rejected
the minority report 659½ to 399½, and the Creager delegation was
seated. Only one roll call was required for Hoover's nomination. The
Texas delegation cast all 26 votes for him. Senator Charles Curtis of
Kansas was nominated for vice-president on the first ballot.[61]

"Our friend Wurzbach is absolutely a mess as a leader," a disgusted Scobey complained to Dawes upon his return from Kansas City.
"He couldn't lead a horse to the trough and have him drink!" The congressman was expected to challenge Creager's control of the party machinery again at the Republican State Convention in Fort Worth on
August 14, but the gathering was harmonious; not a single contest for
seats reached the floor. In fact, C. C. Littleton was cheered enthusiastically when he mounted the platform and pledged his support for
Hoover.[62] Wurzbach conferred with Hoover in Washington and assured him that there would be no breach in Texas Republican ranks
because of the squabble, but two members of his faction, J. M.O'Hara,
organization manager for the Republican State Committee, and Gooseneck Bill McDonald, claimed that 250,000 white and black Republican
voters belonging to the group would bolt their party and vote for
Smith. McDonald's change of front was due to the recognition of
the Creager "lily white" delegation at the Republican national convention. In announcing his withdrawal from the Republican organization,
O'Hara charged that "under the leadership of R. B. Creager patronage

peddling in Texas has been more pronounced than has been shown in the Senate investigation in Mississippi."[63]

The presidential campaign of 1928 reflected a deep antagonism between old and new America that went beyond any single issue. New York City symbolized the East to the farmers and small-town dwellers of the South and West. "To these the vast metropolis on the Hudson was a slum-crowded center of peoples whose derivation and habits excluded them from the vision of all that American had been founded to perpetuate," wrote Edmund Moore. "To many Americans, Al Smith's native city seemed more like Babylon than Main Street." Native Americans loyal to traditional values were dismayed by Smith's Catholicism, wet position, Tammany credentials, and personal mannerisms, and it was easy to paint him as the personification of the city's worst features. Walter C. Hornaday, a reporter for the *Dallas Morning News*, foresaw after the Houston convention that the fight against Smith in Texas and the South would not be entirely on account of Smith's views on alcohol. "It will be based in no small degree on the idea that he and the elements now in control of the party are not 'truly American,' according to the standard of the South and West," he predicted. "The idea will be advanced that Smith and his New York henchmen represent the Old World influence that has gained complete control of the party in the East and that this influence is hammering at the door of the South and West, where the eagerly American strain has been kept comparatively pure." Cone Johnson declared in Dallas on July 3:

There is a deeper significance to Smith's candidacy than even the liquor and religious issues. It is the fact that the Democratic convention was not an American assembly except here and there it contained elements of Americanism. In the main, it was a consolidation of Old World elements tempered with a little of America. I sat by the central aisle while the parade passed following Smith's nomination and the faces I saw in that mile-long procession were not American faces. I wondered where were the Americans.[64]

According to one student of the campaign, David Burner, "Al Smith not only failed to do an adequate job of presenting his case; there were moments in which he was almost arrogant in his refusal to meet Protestant America half way." He shattered the good feeling in Houston when, after he had been nominated and the convention was virtually over, he sent a telegram calling for "fundamental changes in the present provisions of national prohibition." Newspaper extras proclaimed that "Al Smith Will Carry Wet Fight to Voters." Drys saw his statement as a rejection of the moderate Prohibition plank in the Democratic platform. Josephus Daniels characterized it as "unnecessary and ill timed." To head his campaign, Smith named John J. Raskob of New York, chairman of the Democratic National Committee. Raskob was a devout Roman Catholic, who had contributed more than a million dollars to the church and had been made a Knight of the Order of Saint Gregory the Great by Pope Pius XI. He was also a director of the Association against the Prohibition Amendment and a Republican who had voted for Coolidge in 1924. Vice-president of E. I. Du Pont de Nemours and chairman of the finance committee of General Motors, Raskob listed himself in the current *Who's Who* as "capitalist." His appointment seemed an affront to the dry, rural, Protestant South and West and to the Democratic party's anticorporation, progressive wing. The party of Jefferson and Wilson had become the party of "rum, Romanism, and Raskob." James J. Hoey, George R. Van Namee, Belle Moskowitz, and other Smith managers concentrated on the East and neglected the South and West.[65]

In contrast, Hoover had a much broader appeal throughout the country. His public image represented a highly successful blend of modern and traditional themes. "As one of the 'new era's' heroes, he typified organized and efficient industrial America," wrote Kent Schofield. "As an orphaned farmboy who worked his way through college achieving success in his profession and in relief activities, Hoover appealed to an informal and individualistic rural America." He could appear as the "Great Engineer," businessman, administrator, humanitarian, political leader, Iowa farmboy, hero of the American success story, and guarantor of prosperity, without compromising any of these roles. "He is one 'Yankee' whom the Southern people believe understands and sympathizes with their problems," the Reverend J. Frank Norris wrote. "There is a tremendous amount of sentiment around his name because of his quick and wonderful work in connection with the Mississippi flood. All there is of bigness gathers around his name. And in addition to his many qualities as a statesman his name is like Theodore Roosevelt's, a household word. Every farmer boy knows him and every housewife, too."[66]

Leaders of the Methodist and Baptist churches called a conference of prohibitionists to meet in Asheville, North Carolina, on July 19 to plan their fight against Smith. It was attended by about three hundred delegates representing fourteen southern states and was spearheaded by Arthur J. Barton of Atlanta, a leader in the Southern Baptist church and the Anti-Saloon League, and by the Southern Methodist bishop James E. Cannon, Jr. After listening to a number of speeches attacking Smith as a wet and a Tammany man, these "embattled Prohibitionists," as J. F. Essary of the *Baltimore Sun* termed them, called upon all dry Democrats to vote for Hoover. In the meantime, Texas bone-dry Democrats moved to organize the state against the Democratic nominee. Among those participating in the bolt to Hoover were Tom Love; O. B. Colquitt; Cato Sells; Marshall Hicks; V. A. Collins; Dr. J. B. Cranfill; Atticus Webb of the Anti-Saloon League; Mrs. Claude De Van Watts, president of the WCTU; J. D. Sandefer, president of Simmons University in Abilene; and Methodist Bishop John M. Moore. A call was issued from Colquitt's office in Dallas for a mass meeting of anti–Al Smith Democrats in that city on July 17. The three hundred persons who attended the meeting formally organized as the Anti–Al Smith Democrats of Texas and selected Alvin Moody of Houston (no relative of the governor) as chairman. The group resolved that "the purpose of the organization shall be the defeat of Gov. Alfred E. Smith for President and the wresting of Democracy from the grip of Tammany Hall." The method of selecting electors and putting them on the ballot was left to the discretion of the campaign committee. After the meeting adjourned, Alvin Moody had a conference with R. B. Creager and found that Creager wished to cooperate "in every way possible." The Republican leaders had already decided that to obtain the support of "bolting Democrats" it would be necessary to concentrate on carrying the state for Hoover and to sacrifice the state Republican ticket and most county tickets. "I think we should concentrate all of our efforts on Hoover and not antagonize the quiet Democratic vote in any way," Orville Bullington advised the Republican State Executive Committee. "If a man like Ferguson were running, it would be different, but Moody seems to be well liked." As Captain J. F. Lucey of Dallas, a Creager ally, explained to Hoover's assistant, Lawrence Ritchey:

If we run Dr. Butte [for governor], as originally contemplated, then we lose the support of the "dry" vote and it will be construed as an attack upon [Dan] Moody. But, if we only work for the National Ticket it makes it very easy for all of the voters who are dissatisfied with the Smith candidacy, and they are not all anti-Smith, a very great number of them—perhaps a majority—are pro-Hoover and are looking for an opportunity of going over to our side because of Hoover and his accomplishments.

For his activities against Smith, Alvin Moody was asked to resign from the State Democratic Executive Committee by Chairman D. W. Wilcox. He replied that, while he was under no obligation to accept Wilcox's demand, "since you and others on the State committee are engaged in trying to force the honored name of Texas behind this political platform bolter, I hereby withdraw from the committee, but not from the Democratic party." [67]

A fusion electoral ticket was agreed upon at a conference in Dallas on September 8, attended by the steering committee of the Republican State Executive Committee and leaders of the Anti–Al Smith Democrats of Texas. The Republicans practically financed the "Hoovercrats." "They raised a little money themselves," Leonard Withington, director of organization at Republican State Headquarters, later told United States Senator Smith Brookhart's committee investigating the dispensing of federal patronage. According to a postcampaign report of expenditures, the Anti–Al Smith Democrats spent $29,157.04 of the $59,805.68 raised for the Hoover campaign in Texas. "The Republicans spent a great deal of money," Smith leader John Boyle of San Antonio told the committee. "The Democrats did not have the money. I think the Republican organization spent what they said, but I think there was spent in Texas at least $250,000." There had been a lot of "side organizations," he said. Asked whether he thought it took more than $29,000 to organize the Hoover Democrats, Boyle replied: "Absolutely; yes, sir." [68]

"The Republican campaign for Herbert Hoover in 1928 was a model of business-like organizations," noted Roger Olien. Texas had Hoover-Curtis Victory Club chairmen in 249 of the 254 counties, and these clubs enrolled about 60,000 members. Clubs were organized on seven college campuses, and 2,461 "Hoover Hostesses" brightened political rallies. "Business and trade organizations produced dozens of Hoover-Curtis Clubs; they included everyone from aviators, clay products manufacturers, chiropractors, and harness and saddle makers to doctors, lawyers, teachers, and advertising executives. On paper, at least, the campaign in Texas produced a record number of voluntary organizations and volunteer workers." [69]

Imperial wizard Hiram Wesley Evans had promised that the Klan would oppose Smith to the death. "Our work in the coming campaign will be like that of an evangelist: to spread the truth," he explained in a magazine article in January, 1928. "We shall show how Smith is inextricably allied with bossism, ['wet'] nullification, with alienism, with priest-rule. We shall show what all these mean, what danger they carry." The Klan hierarchy in Texas had still been intact in 1927, when Shelby Cox, former district attorney of Dallas County, served as grand dragon; but by 1928 only twenty-five hundred or so knights were left in the state, and, as far as Charles Alexander was able to determine, the state Klan organization had no official connection with the Hoovercrats. Yet many klansmen and former klansmen were active in helping swing Texas into the Republican column in the presidential election. V. A. Collins and Shelby Cox of Dallas, Marvin A. Childers of San Antonio, Lloyd P. Bloodworth of Fort Worth, Edward B. Ward of Corpus Christi, and Alva Bryan of Waco joined the Anti–Al Smith Democrats of Texas. Cox, Childers, and Bloodworth were present or past grand dragons in Texas. Among those elements supporting Hoover, Captain Lucey included "either the present or former Klan members, estimated to control from 200,000 to 250,000 votes."[70]

The task of the Anti–Al Smith Democrats was to persuade Democrats to vote for Hoover for president while at the same time supporting their Democratic local, county, and state tickets. As Colquitt explained the problem to Lawrence Ritchey:

At this time it is my deliberate judgment that a large majority of the voters of Texas are for Hoover and against Smith. But they have voted the Democratic ticket so long they are reluctant to vote any other ticket. Many of them will tell you they are for Hoover but they do not want to vote for him on a ticket headed Republican. This is the job we have in this State—getting the voters to overcome this prejudice in their own minds.[71]

Some of the county Democratic committees refused to permit the names of "bolters" to appear on the Democratic primary ticket. The Cameron County committee, headed by Judge Volney W. Taylor, omitted the names of Mrs. Edith Wilmans and Judge William E. Hawkins, candidates for governor, and Tom Love, a candidate for lieutenant governor, because they would not support Smith. Taylor vowed to "make Christians out of them, or clear them out of the party." Love, who went to Brownsville to make a personal plea, sought a court mandamus to force the committee to place his name on the Cameron ballot, contending that the county group had acted beyond its authority. His fight ended in defeat on July 21, when the Texas Supreme Court, on vacation, refused to accept jurisdiction. That left in force the decision of the Fourth Court of Civil Appeals in San Antonio affirming the judgment of Judge A. M. Kent of the 103d District Court at Brownsville, which held that the Cameron County committee had authority to leave Love's name off the ballot. Attorney General Claude Pollard then ruled that Love's name could be written on the ballots in the six or so counties that had omitted his name. "I don't know what the effect of this will be upon the vote," Love wrote McAdoo. "It is not unlikely that it will cause my defeat." Whatever the result, he had "kept the faith and shall be content. By saying that I would 'support the nominee' or by pussy-footing on the subject there is no doubt that I could have been elected, but I would rather have been defeated than to have to despise myself the rest of my days."[72]

In Albany, Smith showed little concern over the Hoovercrat movement in the South. Asked to comment on the situation in Texas at a news conference on July 18, he replied: "I don't know anything about it. That's for the national committee to worry about." With that he dismissed the subject. Smith's friends believed that defections in the South would not jeopardize his success there in November and that he would more than make up for any votes lost there by gains in the northern states.[73]

The regular Democrats in Texas seem not to have realized at first the strength of the anti-Smith sentiment and depended too much on the state's Democratic tradition to swing it into his column. The results of the first Democratic primary, held on July 28, were largely favorable to the Smith forces. Moody won renomination for a second term without a runoff, while Love ran 100,000 votes behind the incumbent lieutenant governor, Barry Miller, though he gained a spot in the second primary on August 25. Under the caption "No Balm in Texas," the *New York Times* saw the Texas result, and particularly Love's defeat, as indicating that "Texas must be lifted out of the Hoover hope chest." The *Dallas Morning News* thought the primary election showed that "Texas will go Democratic as usual," since if an additional 100,000 Republican votes were added to Love's anti-Smith tally the total Hoover vote would not be large enough to carry the state in the general election in November. Fort Worth editor Peter Molyneaux warned Dan Moody, however, that many voters who had cast ballots for Miller intended to vote for Hoover. "What I intend to convey is that Texas is really in danger unless a campaign is put on. The vote must be brought out in order to win."[74]

"Things got pretty lively around the 'house of the fathers' in 1928,"

Don H. Biggers recalled.[75] Besides the presidential sweepstakes, Texas voters had to pay some attention to the free-for-all senatorial campaign, which overshadowed the races for governor and lieutenant governor and other contests. Earle B. Mayfield had been elected to the United States Senate in 1922, defeating Jim Ferguson in the runoff primary and George E. B. Peddy, the candidate of the anti-Klan Democrats and Republicans, in the general election. The opposition to Mayfield both before and after his election, the belief that the Klan had lost most of its bullying power in Texas, and a conviction among many Texans that Mayfield did not measure up as a senator made it certain that he would have serious opposition for reelection in 1928. Among those mentioned as possible candidates who did not choose to run were Pat Neff, Cullen Thomas, O. B. Colquitt, Jim Ferguson, William Hobby, Sam Rayburn, John Nance Garner, and Dan Moody. Five candidates ultimately opposed Mayfield: Congressman Tom Connally of Marlin, Colonel Alvin M. Owsley of Dallas, Congressman Tom Blanton of Abilene, Mrs. Minnie Fisher Cunningham of Huntsville (a leading suffragist and the first woman to run for the United States Senate in Texas), and former Congressman Jeff McLemore of Laredo. Since it was generally conceded that Mayfield would lead but fail to win a majority in the first primary, the other candidates' main goal was to gain enough votes to enter the runoff with him.[76]

Connally quickly emerged as Mayfield's chief opponent. In his speeches he hammered at the senator because he had been elected by the Klan and had then denied it. As Connally's campaign manager, Robert F. Higgins, explained: "The idea that Mayfield repudiated the klan after they put him in the Senate may have driven quite a number of his supporters from his camp. And it is his course of deception that Mr. Connally has made his major attack upon." When the incumbent offered a suit of clothes to anyone who could show that Connally had accomplished anything in Washington, Connally told his audiences: "Make him give you a good suit, and not that old second-hand thing he ran in in 1922—that sheet and pillow case. Make him give you a good suit that can be worn in the daytime as well as at night." He asked the people to "turn out the bedsheet-and-mask candidate."[77]

Mayfield led in the first primary with 200,246 votes, followed by Connally with 178,091. Owsley was in third place with 131,755 votes, followed by Blanton with 126,758. Mrs. Cunningham trailed with 28,944 votes, and McLemore was in last place with 9,244. Mayfield carried 106 counties; Blanton, 79; Connally, 43; Owsley, 24; and Mrs. Cunningham her home county, Walker. Blanton led in all 19 counties of his congressional district and in 60 others, most small-vote counties in West Texas. He polled a small vote in the large cities and apparently was not well known except in his own section of the state. The larger counties were more favorable to Connally and Mayfield, but Owsley got a good vote and led the field in Dallas County, where he was practicing law. Harris County, a former Klan stronghold, gave Mayfield 45 percent of the vote, with Connally as the runner-up. The South Texas counties divided between Mayfield and Connally. Connally polled 270 of the 271 votes cast in Zapata and 874 of the 898 votes in Starr. Mayfield won three-fourths of the vote in Hidalgo and polled 1,173 of 1,195 votes in Archie Parr's Duval fiefdom.[78]

In the 1922 senatorial runoff between Mayfield and Ferguson, Ferguson had abused his rival, in Don H. Bigger's words, "as no other Texas candidate had ever been slandered and abused." On August 9, 1928, however, Jim, who had supported Owsley in the first primary, announced in the *Forum* that he was going to vote for Mayfield as the lesser of two evils. While Mayfield was an "open Ku Klux," Connally was a "secret Ku Klux lover." Subsequently the Connally camp was advised that before Ferguson came out for Mayfield the two men had met with A. P. Barrett, of the Louisiana Power and Light Company, in Barrett's hotel room in the Austin Hotel in Austin. Barrett was one of Mayfield's chief boosters and had contributed a large amount of money to his campaign; one estimate was as much as $60,000. "Room 428!" (the number of Barrett's hotel room) became the battle cry of the Connally forces. "Ferguson and the power magnate and Earle are all in the same bed, and it's a single bed at that," Connally told a San Antonio crowd. In another speech he referred to Ferguson's declaration that he had healed old sores with Mayfield. "Was it electric power ointment or Hiram Evans' Klan salve that healed those sores?" he asked his audience. Ferguson and Mayfield admitted visiting Barrett, but each denied that the other was present. "They may not have seen each other," Connally taunted. "When they brought in old Jim, they might have hid Mayfield in the bathroom. Or else Mayfield had on his Ku Klux robe and mask and Jim didn't recognize him."[79]

In the runoff Connally received 320,071 votes to Mayfield's 257,747—a majority of 62,324. Mayfield gained only a little over 50,000 votes in the second primary, while Connally almost doubled his previous vote. He carried 169 counties; Mayfield led in 67. All the large urban counties except Jefferson, a Klan hotbed, gave Connally substantial majorities. Mayfield's counties were primarily in East and Northeast Texas. Practically all the Blanton counties in Central West and West Texas went for Connally. He carried all the German counties, outpolling Mayfield 6,739 to 2,523. "The results in the German counties would seem to indicate a trend away from the championship of Jim Ferguson," wrote Seth McKay. "Or possibly they give added proof of the German dislike of any politician seeming tainted with any connection with the Ku Klux Klan." South Texas was divided as usual. For example, Duval County gave Mayfield 700 votes and Connally 6 votes; Zapata County gave Connally all 120 votes cast.[80]

Connally's impressive victory was interpreted as marking a new era in Texas politics. The voters had used him "as an instrument to start a recovery from a spell of sickness that held on like a leach." It was proof that the Klan was becoming as impotent in Texas as elsewhere and that, for the third time in 1928, Ferguson had ingloriously failed in his efforts to deliver his following to any candidate other than himself or his wife. "Candidates in the future will run from Ferguson support," predicted the "Political Analyst" of the *Austin American*. "We have killed two birds with one stone," crowed a newspaper editor in Wise County, "annihilated Earle B. and put the quietus on Jim Ferguson. Best thing that has happened in the Texas political arena in a century." "Earle Mayfield was the last of the old Ku Klux Klan regime," General Crane noted with satisfaction. "His defeat will practically eliminate that organization, as such, in Texas politics. There of course will be spots here and there where the vote will be influenced for or against a man by reason of his attitude on that question." In fact, the Texas Klan had been dying since Mrs. Ferguson's victory in 1924 and was only a shadow of its former self. It had made a halfhearted rally around Mayfield, and his defeat was the final nail driven into its coffin.[81]

In the meantime, leaders of the regular Democrats had met in Austin on August 11 and made plans to carry the state for Smith. Steve Pinckney took a hard line with the Hoovercrats. "The party has lagged along for several years in Texas and it has needed reorganization," he said. "It is to come Saturday after which there will be no place in its ranks for bolters and Republicans. These bolters will find no position in the party after the November election and they will be out for years to come." A central campaign committee was created and given power to organize the state down to the precinct level. Former Congressman James Young of Kaufman County, a lifelong dry and a Baptist, was named campaign committee chairman. The meeting favored barring from the August 25 runoff election voters who did not pledge themselves to support all the party nominees, including Smith, and asked that the next State Democratic Executive Committee take steps to prevent persons who bolted in November, 1928, from participating in any Democratic primary either as voters or as candidates until they had purged themselves by voting the regular Democratic ticket in November, 1930. Thomas Watt Gregory expressed the opinion of many Democratic loyalists when he remarked that "you might as well talk about a white negro or a green blackbird as to speak of a man as a 'Hoover Democrat.'"

The State Democratic Executive Committee met in San Antonio on August 13 and voted to put Love's name on the runoff ballot. Pinckney, who replaced Alvin Moody on the committee, had moved to strike Love's name from the list, saying that Love had forfeited his right to a place as a Democrat and that he favored "purging the party of rubbish." The motion failed, but the committee did adopt with but one no vote Pinckney's resolution calling upon voters in any Democratic primary to "bind and obligate themselves" to vote for all party nominees from president down, "to the end that the integrity and purity of the Democratic party may be maintained."[82]

The next day Love withdrew as a candidate for lieutenant governor. He charged that the executive committee had "changed the rules in the middle of the game" by requiring a pledge to support Al Smith in violation of the law and Democratic practice in Texas. Regular Democratic leaders interpreted Love's decision as prompted by the wish to avoid disclosing in the runoff how weak the Hoover forces actually were in Texas. Smith's cause in Texas got another boost when Senator Morris Sheppard, the "father of national Prohibition," announced for the national ticket on August 23, the day after the publication of Smith's nomination acceptance speech. "In my judgment, it is absolutely beyond the power of Governor Smith, or anyone else to destroy the Eighteenth Amendment," declared Sheppard. "I regard prohibition as safe and secure." "Governor Smith has a right to his personal views and has a right to submit them to Congress. I also have a right to oppose them within and not outside the Democratic party."[83]

The Democratic State Convention met in Dallas on September 11 to ratify the primary results and adopt a party platform. The State Democratic Exectutive Committee replaced anti–Al Smith delegations from Dallas, Tarrant, Harris, Bosque, and Palo Pinto counties with rival Smith groups and wound up eliminations by unseating an uncontested delegation from Erath County. When the convention approved the committee's report, Colquitt, to the accompaniment of four fist fights, led an exodus of Hoovercrats from the hall. The bolters organized on the steps of the Fair Park Auditorium. "In what hall shall we meet?" someone asked. "Let's meet here in God's open," suggested Love. "We have had enough of halls—Tammany Halls!" was the answering cry. Under Love's leadership the meeting adopted resolutions denouncing Smith's candidacy but approving the Democratic candidates for state offices.[84]

During September and October the Republicans and anti-Smith Democrats carried on a strenuous campaign in Texas, flooding the state with millions of pieces of literature. "Loyal Democrats who wish to see the prohibition plank in the Democratic platform adopted as a policy by this nation can, with confidence, vote for Herbert Hoover and commit that task to his hands," Marshall Hicks assured undecided Democrats in a pamphlet entitled *Which? Hoover or Smith?* The Republican party paid for 500,000 copies of a special edition of J. B. Cranfill's weekly *Southern Advance* carrying a sample ballot showing Democratic voters how to vote for Hoover electors and the remainder of the Democratic ticket, which were mailed to all the rural-mail-delivery boxes in Texas.[85]

The issue of Smith's Catholicism remained important until election day. Cranfill admitted to Hoover: "Quite unhappily the Catholic question obtrudes itself here constantly and perhaps more persistently than any other part of the United States. It is so throughout the South. It is not intolerance here, but fear of papal domination if Al Smith and Raskob enter the White House." One student of the campaign, Allan J. Lichtman, found evidence that "Hoover and the Republican leadership did not shrink from sponsoring personal attacks on Al Smith and probably took part in efforts to gain anti-Catholic votes."[86]

Church gatherings urged Smith's defeat, and ministers delivered political speeches under the guise of temperance sermons. "Governor Smith comes to us borne of solid Tammany, solid wets, solid Roman Catholicism, solid South," Methodist Bishop John M. Moore declared. "This is an unfortunate, unhappy and abnormal alliance. I do not believe it can be maintained. These will furnish major issues for the campaign whether the political leaders so choose or not." J. Frank Norris stumped Texas against the "wet-Catholic Smith" and on behalf of "that Christian gentleman and statesman, Herbert Hoover," speaking 119 times in thirty cities over a span of three and one-half months. Although he opposed Smith because of his wet position, "pork-barrel" politics, and Tammany Hall ties, Norris boldly asserted that the basic issue was Smith's Catholicism. He feared "foreign control," the destruction of religious liberty, and the threat to popular morals that a Roman Catholic president would bring. He talked about the Roman hierarchy, the persecution in the Dark Ages, and Smith's devotion to the dictatorial authority in Rome. At the end of his speeches he stepped forward and pleaded for all who were for "mother, flag, God, the Bible, and Herbert Hoover, to please stand up." The crowd would clap, yell, and in a moment stand.[87]

Another element of the anti-Smith whispering campaign was the accusation that the New York governor was a drunkard. He had been seen "dead drunk," "disgustingly tight," "staggering" at one place and time or another. Bishop Moore asserted: "Last November the statement was made in the periodical, 'The Nation,' that Governor Smith 'drinks every day, and the number of his cocktails and highballs is variously estimated at from four to eight.' This has never been denied." When John D. Freeman, editor of the *Baptist Reflector*, the official publication of the Tennessee Baptist Convention, made a reference to Smith's being drunk in Asheville, North Carolina, Norris made it the leading article in the *Fundamentalist* and broadcast it over his radio station. "If that one thing can be understood by all southern people it will be doubtful if Al Smith will carry one single southern state," he wrote Freeman. He asked the editor for proof of the allegation, but Freeman admitted that his information was hearsay. In a speech in Dallas vice-presidential nominee Joseph Robinson tried to silence this whisper. "The statement has been made that he is a drunkard," said Robinson, and paused for effect. Then he shouted: "*There's not one word of truth in it!*" Tom Love denied that there was any whispering campaign in Texas as charged by Robinson. "It's a thundering campaign," he declared. "Nobody heard of Governor Smith being drunk at Syracuse until he denied it. His denial of it was the first we heard of it."[88]

Smith's friends admitted that he took an occasional drink but denied that he had the "habit." But *Time* magazine asked: "If nominee Smith drinks, where does his drink come from? Is none of it procured in violation of the Federal Law? If he went to the White House, would he continue drinking there? If so, how would the drink be procured? Would it, as in the well-known case of President Harding, be kept for him in the White House?"[89]

Not all the whispering was directed against Smith. The Hoovercrats complained that the Democrats were trying to prejudice Texas voters and those of the other southern states against the Republican candidate by picturing him as an advocate of social equality for blacks. They thus hoped to gain a palliative against Smith's wet position and his other political defects in the South by erecting "a great bogey of Herbert Hoover and the negro question." "In the South it seems as if the chief weapon which has been used against Mr. Hoover has been the Democratic charge that he is a 'negro lover,'" George Fort Milton complained. It was charged that as secretary of commerce Hoover had canceled an order for the segregation of white and black clerks in the Bureau of the United States Census, had compelled them to sit at the same desk, and had generally "intermingled them." Congressman Sam Rayburn declared at a Democratic rally in Fort Worth's First Baptist Church in September, where he appeared with James H. Young:

As long as I am a white man, live among white people and respect the white womanhood of the Southland, I will never vote for Herbert Hoover, the advocate of racial social equality and the man who forced white girls working in his department, to share with negro women the lavatories and comfort stations. As long as I honor the memory of my Confederate father to our Southland and wear his name, I will never vote for the electors of a party which sent the carpet bagger and the scalawag to the prostrate South with saber and sword to crush the white civilization of the South to the earth. If he is elected President, he will undertake to carry the same policy of abolition of the segregation of the races to all of the departments of our government.[90]

O. B. Colquitt denied Rayburn's charges, explaining that the NAACP had asked the Census Bureau for special statistics on Negroes and that eighteen blacks had been assigned to these duties in a separate room "in the belief that the negro clerks would take pride in the work." Colquitt added that when the segregation became known to Coolidge he called Hoover's attention to a provision of the Civil Service Law against segregation, and the Negro clerks subsequently were restored to their desks "as had been done in all previous administrations." "Therefore, any segregation ever made, was by Secretary Hoover, which is the reverse to what Mr. Hoover is charged with doing," Colquitt concluded.

Colquitt charged Smith with responsibility for New York laws that allowed "mixing of whites and blacks" and interracial marriages, and even prohibited closing public places to blacks. He added, "If the leaders of the Tammanyized Democrats in Texas desire to bring forth the racial question, we will drown them with the stuff that they are attempting to use to create hatred and prejudice of the white citizenship of Texas and the South." He was as good as his word. His campaign paper, the *Constitutional Democrat*, carried such story headlines as "Tammanyizing the Colored Voters of St. Louis," "Al Smith's Tammany Nigger in the Woodpile," "Smith Appoints Negro," "Miscegenation," "Voting for Negro Congressman," "$30,000 to Colored Committee," and "Jack Johnson for Smith." (Johnson, a black, had been heavyweight champion from 1908 to 1915.) A picture of "the $7,500 a Year Tammany Negro Boss and His White Secretary" appeared in the *Constitutional Democrat* and was widely distributed in circular form. It showed Ferdinand Q. Morton, a New York City civil-service commissioner, seated at his desk dictating letters to his secretary. "Your photograph of the $7500. a year Tammany boss is a knock-out," J. Frank Norris wrote the editor of the *Fellowship Forum* (subtitled "A National Voice for Protestant Fraternal America"). "If you will send me this photograph I will have cuts made and sow the state down with them. This will mean 100,000 white votes for Hoover if we can get it before the people."[91]

The early optimism of the Texas regulars had evaporated by the middle of September. A delegation headed by Lieutenant Governor Barry Miller went to Oklahoma City to meet Smith, who sent a special message to Texas Democrats: "Texas has a foremost place in the front line in this fight. The eyes of Democracy are upon Texas, to paraphrase your own state hymn." Following conferences with members of Smith's train party, telegrams were sent to Texas congressmen releasing them from speaking engagements in other states so that they could campaign in Texas. Returning from Oklahoma City, Smith's Texas campaign manager W. A. Thomas announced that the Democratic party's message would be carried continuously and insistently to every voter in Texas by radio and from the platform until election day. Connie Renfro took charge of the speakers' bureau at the Smith headquarters in Dallas and promised more active and better-organized campaigning by Democratic speakers.[92]

Both party regulars and Hoovercrats showed keen interest in Dan Moody's role in the campaign. Having stated before the primaries that he would vote for the Democratic nominees, he made no further public utterance of his views. On August 8, Smith wrote him to express his appreciation for the "fine work you are doing for the Democratic ticket" and his hope that "sometime during the campaign I may have the opportunity of conferring with you." Party Chairman Raskob invited Moody to visit the Smith headquarters in New York, while Millard Tydings, chairman of the speakers' bureau, asked him to participate in the national speechmaking campaign that was to begin in early September. Moody did not acknowledge these communications for six weeks and then replied that "Texas does not require much campaigning for the Democratic Party. I know that items occasionally appear in the papers indicating that Texas might be a doubtful state, but, in my judgement, it is Democratic by a decisive majority."[93]

Moody told the state convention that he would support the Democratic ticket "from top to bottom," but he refused to mute his opposition to Smith's anti-Prohibition stance, nor would he make any speeches for the candidate in Texas. To a close friend the governor complained that the "speaking business has caused me no end of trouble":

A thing that I cannot understand is the fact that the folks who wanted to push me in a hole at Beaumont and leave me, and those who wanted to force the delegation at Houston to go contrary to the desires of the conventions that sent it there, are the most insistent; and they want me to make a speech which would require that I either forget a good many of my past expressions, or else put my ideas about some issues on the shelf for the time being.[94]

Moody was also under heavy pressure from anti-Smith Democrats to play a passive role in the Smith campaign. B. D. Sartain, campaign manager of the Anti–Al Smith Democrats of Texas, let him know that "I appreciate the fact that you are not making any speeches for Al Smith and his whiskey crowd. I trust that you will continue to do this." One result of the governor's silence was that angry Smith supporters retaliated in the state convention by emasculating his draft platform. They substituted milder words for his strong Prohibition plank, deleted a civil-service proposal, and incorporated the opposite of Moody's views on prison reform. Bereft of much of the dry support that he had manipulated against the wets in the Beaumont convention, Moody had lost control of the state party to the Smith element.[95]

In the last month of the campaign, party leaders bombarded Moody with requests for speeches on behalf of the national ticket. He finally yielded and agreed to introduce James Young at a local Democratic rally in Austin on October 12. He argued that the best way to keep the Democratic party "right" on Prohibition was for drys to stay in it. "I have always voted the Democratic ticket and in this election I will vote the Democratic ticket from top to bottom," he declared. When Republican Senator William E. Borah of Idaho spoke in Dallas on October 22, the Smith managers thought that Moody was the "trump card" to counter his efforts. The governor responded with an address in Dallas on October 27, carried by radio, in which he attacked Borah for attempting to "Republicanize" Texas.[96] As expected, the Hoovercrats were outraged. Wrote one angry woman: "I note that you have allowed Raskob and the wet bunch to take you over, will say that all God loving and decent people will tell you good by. . . . Raskob Dan."[97]

Just before the election D. W. Wilcox warned the Hoovercrats that the State Democratic Executive Committee "can and will" bar all bolters from the Democratic primaries in 1930. "Wilcox must think we are living in Russia instead of in Texas, founded and peopled by individuals and free, courageous lovers of good government," Alvin Moody retorted. "He cannot shackle free Texans. Santa Anna tried that in 1836 and failed." James Young predicted a 200,000 majority for Smith, adding that, as a churchman, "I can not but look with dismay on the harm that has been done to churches as institutions of Christianity in this campaign." W. A. Thomas complained that the Klan and the anti-Smith Democrats were continuing "covertly to fan the embers of bigotry," distributing tracts and letters throughout Texas that were, he said, a "rehash of the same goblin stuff with which the Ku Klux Klan has assaulted the decencies of the United States for the last eight years." Love retorted that "a Smith victory Tuesday would be a victory for Jim Ferguson and for all that he stands for and has stood for. . . . Hoover's victory in Texas will not be a partisan victory. It will be a great Democratic victory over Tammany Hall."[98]

Moody's belated entry into the election came too late to change its outcome. Even his wife, Mildred, voted for Hoover. On November 6 the combined Republicans and Hoovercrats gave Hoover 27,162 more votes than Smith and put Texas into the Republican column in a presidential election for the first time in history. "We have smashed the brass collar in Texas and have destroyed Tammany and liquor domination of the Democratic Party," Love exulted. Mrs. Moody wrote in her diary:

After the election joyous relief from the ding-donging of ardent Smithites; deadly silence from former brags; Steve [Pinckney] silent as the tomb, a greatly subdued and effacing Paul Page; for which we have given thanks! Naturally Dan got some blame for Texas Republican vote, and there was Tom Love gloating; but Dan had maintained a difficult position—his Democratic loyalty and then his principles. I believe time will prove him right.[99]

Nationally, of course, Hoover won in a landslide. He received 21,392,190 popular votes to Smith's 15,016,443 and 444 electoral votes to Smith's 87. Smith carried only Massachusetts and Rhode Island outside the traditionally Democratic states of the Old Confederacy, and even there he won only South Carolina, Georgia, Alabama, Mississippi, Louisiana, and Arkansas. Hoover carried Virginia, North Carolina, Tennessee, Florida, and Texas. "The only thing that stands out clearly above everything else is that all old party lines as they have hitherto existed are smashed, perhaps permanently," wrote Nicholas Murray Butler, president of Columbia University. "It is certainly a relief to find the South divided on almost everything, even if it be bigotry."[100]

In Texas, Democratic defections to Hoover were principally in the dry, rural northern and western counties and in metropolitan Harris, Dallas, and Tarrant counties, where the Klan had been strong and Republican prosperity had won many converts. The few urban counties that Smith carried gave him only a small margin. Bexar (San Antonio) went for Smith by only 149 votes, and El Paso by only 64. Most of the women activists in Texas politics were prohibitionists. There were klanswomen among them and some who were, indeed, Protestant bigots, but Smith's attitude and record on Prohibition were enough in themselves to send into the Hoover camp a large number of recently enfranchised women with no long-term habit of party regularity. The border counties with their large Mexican-American populations generally supported Smith, as did all but two of the ten traditionally Republican German counties. Leonard Withington thought that the Republicans "probably lost 50% of our usual German-American vote" and that "the loss was almost entirely due to wet sentiment." East Texas, which contained most of the state's blacks, remained faithful to the party traditionally respectful of white supremacy. According to political scien-

tist V. O. Key, Jr., "Only one of 22 counties with more than 35 percent
Negro population went Republican while 113 of 150 counties with less
than 5 percent Negro population turned Republican."[101]

At a meeting of the Independent Colored Voter's League in March,
1928, several blacks, including the president of the league, had advocated backing the Democratic party. Prominent blacks throughout
Texas eventually endorsed Smith, and, as already noted, William M.
McDonald was actively for him. According to Leonard Withington,
about 60 percent of the blacks voted for Smith, and 40 percent for
Hoover. "The negro vote was once all Republican but has been swinging the other way for some time," he noted, "but is falling in volume
and is a very small factor in Texas. Most of it wants a monetary consideration, which we will not give."[102]

Historian Seth S. McKay, familiar with the political history of
Texas, concluded that "in Texas as a whole the 1928 Presidential campaign was just another prohibition contest. . . . In practically every
county in the state there was a return match staged between the old
time dry and wet leaders as had been the case in several former prohibition elections." Governor Moody also thought that Prohibition was
the "determining factor" in the outcome. He wrote:

There is no doubt but that Senator Walsh of Montana, would have carried this
state by the usual Democratic majority. While other questions played their
part, I feel that it is certain that the nominee's stand on the prohibition question was responsible for the great defection from the Democratic Party.

"Religion did not cut the figure popularly supposed," Leonard Withington insisted. "Some loud mouthed persons made such a noise it
seemed to be prominent. Prohibition, Anti-Tammany, Prosperity, Hoover's record, Immigration, probably affected more actual votes."[103]

Yet the shift in traditional voting patterns was most marked in
those areas where the "political preachers" concentrated their efforts.
James Bryan Storey has compared the returns for the presidential elections of 1924 and 1928 in Tarrant, Dallas, Taylor, and Lubbock counties, "all of which were the scenes of major drives by anti-Catholic
forces" in 1928. In Tarrant County, the home of Norris and the politically active fundamentalist faculty of Southwestern Baptist Theological
Seminary, John Davis had received 61.7 percent of the total vote in
1924, while Smith polled only 30.9 percent in 1928. This was a 5.2 percent greater loss than the state average of 25.6 percent. In Dallas

County, the home of Methodist Bishop Moore and of Southern Methodist University, which Norris visited almost weekly in the final months of the campaign, the Democratic vote fell from 76.9 percent in 1924 to 38.8 percent in 1928. Smith lagged 38.1 percent behind Davis. In Taylor County, a center of the Church of Christ and home of rabid anti-Smith minister J. W. Hunt, the Democratic presidential vote dropped from 86.3 percent in 1924 to 31.7 percent in 1928—a drop of more than 54 percent. In Lubbock County, a center of Baptist and Church of Christ strength, which Norris and Hunt often visited, and which was also influenced by resident "political preachers" like D. B. Doak, the Democratic presidential vote plummeted over the years, from 74.3 percent in 1924 to 39.1 percent in 1928, a drop of 35.2 percent. Hoover, who carried Texas as a whole by less than 4 percent, carried Tarrant, Dallas, Taylor, and Lubbock counties by majorities of 38, 23, 36, and 23 percent, respectively.[104]

Smith's supporters believed that the Prohibition issue was hypocritically used to veil anti-Catholicism. In a letter to the *Dallas Morning News* in August, 1928, a Protestant observer of the campaign stated: "None of these wild drys objected to James M. Cox, who was as wet as Smith. Nor did they object to John W. Davis, who was even wetter than Smith. But it happens that both were Protestants. . . . They oppose our candidate because he happens to be born a Catholic." Editor Pitchfork Smith called the cry raised against Smith because he was a wet the biggest piece of hypocrisy in American politics in a hundred years. He wrote, in his usual colorful style: "Every day I hear some old tomato-nosed, booze-buster bellerin' about Al Smith 'bein' a wet.' Everybody knows he's lying. He's against Smith because he is a Catholic; and when he opposes him on that score he becomes a traitor to the constitution and not fit to black Al Smith's boots."[105]

"My opinion is that in a large number of instances, the prohibition revulsion was but a smoke screen," General Crane wrote after the election. "Some of my best friends . . . have such an intense prejudice against Roman Catholics that they cannot complacently think of electing one of them President of the United States or to any other important office." Thomas Watt Gregory was surprised by the outcome of the election in the state but was not entirely unprepared for it. He understood that on the Sunday before the election Hoover sample ballots were distributed in every Baptist and Methodist church in Texas and commented that the intolerance and bigotry displayed throughout the

state were very humiliating to men like him who loved what the
Democratic party stood for. He concluded: "Unquestionably, the catholicism of Smith lost him far more votes than all the other objections
to him combined. Out of 1,500,000 registered voters in this state I
think there were less than 700,000 cast, which shows that several hundred thousand democrats stayed away from the polls and did not vote
at all." [106]

On the other hand, historian David Y. Thomas of the University of
Arkansas contended that the Democratic orators, spellbinders, and
editorial writers won no votes for Smith by going up and down the land
denouncing as bigots all those who failed to make the distinction between the Catholic church as a religious body and the Catholic church
as a secular organization with political aims. "They called those who
objected to Governor Smith for his stand on prohibition hypocrites,
alleging the real reason was that he was a Catholic, and this too won no
votes," he stated. "There were thousands who would have voted for a
dry Catholic on a dry platform, but they knew that the plea for religious toleration was largely a smoke screen to hide the wetness of the
candidate; and that combination was too much for them." [107] It was not
Smith's religion per se that made him unacceptable to thousands of
Texans and caused them to desert the "party of the fathers" but the
combination of his conspicuous Catholicism, pro-wet stance, personal
mannerisms, Tammany Hall ties, and role as a spokesman for the new
immigrants. Undoubtedly, Senator Thomas Walsh of Montana, a dry
Catholic from a western state, would have carried Texas handily against
Hoover and would have had the support of most if not all of those who
became Hoovercrat leaders in the state. Moreover, Hoover's 27,162
majority did not really measure the extent of anti-Smith sentiment in
Texas; thousands of voters stayed home on election day because they
would not vote for Smith but could not bring themselves to vote for a
Republican. The ballots of Hoover voters who crossed out the list of
Democratic electors but forgot to mark out the Socialist and Communist tickets were invalidated. [108]

For the country as a whole, prosperity, not religion or Prohibition,
was the key issue. As Richard Hofstadter pointed out in 1960: "There
was not a Democrat alive, Protestant or Catholic, who could have
beaten Hoover in 1928." [109] In June, 1927, Franklin Delano Roosevelt
confided to Josephus Daniels that he was very doubtful whether any
Democrat could win in 1928 if "the present undoubted general pros-

perity of the country continues." His view was shared by most informed observers. "Smith is the only democrat, in my opinion, who
has a chance of election and he hasn't enough to worry over," Colonel
House wrote Thomas Watt Gregory in October, 1927. "This is a republican country by a very large majority and, barring accidents, they
will win." "As a matter of fact I do not believe the democrats will get
control of the national government until hard times come," said Gregory in reply.[110]

Smith probably got as many votes as any Democrat would have
won in 1928. The Democratic vote rose by 6,631,000 from Davis to
Smith, and the GOP vote rose by 5,673,000 from Coolidge to Hoover.
Smith thus gained almost a million more votes for his party than
Hoover did. He turned the normally heavy net Republican plurality in
the twelve largest cities into a slender Democratic plurality. Noted
Hofstadter:

He brought into the voting stream of the Democratic party ethnic groups that
had never taken part in politics and others that had been mainly Republican.
He extricated his party from its past dependence on agrarian interests and
made it known to the great urban populations. He lost a campaign that had to
be lost, but in such a way as to restore his party as an effective opposition and
to pave the way for the victories of F.D.R.[111]

Of course, without the jarring effect of the Great Depression, Republican control would in all probability have continued, and Hoover would
have been reelected handily in 1932.

The result in Texas was a bitter struggle for control of the Demo-
cratic-party machinery that seriously threatened the political fortunes
of party leaders, including Governor Moody and Senator Morris Sheppard, and even presaged a permanent partisan division in the state.
Angered by the epithets "party traitors" and "religious bigots" hurled
at them by the regulars, Hoovercrat leaders wanted revenge. They demanded that state chairman D. W. Wilcox resign in favor of a Hoover
Democrat and thus recognize the bolters' claim that they were the majority in the party. Moody and Sheppard must "explain" their support
of the Smith ticket. The state legislature was to repeal the official
pledge binding voters at the state Democratic primaries to support
party nominees and make it a criminal offense to try to bind any voter
to remain partisan against his conscience. Equally embittered by defeat and by the epithets "party wrecker" and "brass-collar Democrats,"
the regulars refused all concessions. National Committeeman Jed

Adams estimated that the Hoover Democrats in Texas were the minority faction of the party by more than 100,000 votes and declared
that efforts by the faction's leaders to take charge of the party would be
"silly and absurd."[112]

At least one voice was raised to urge that Smith run against Hoover
in 1932. Albert Sidney Burleson said, "Apparently the teachings of
Jefferson, Jackson and Wilson have been forgotten by the Southern
people." But he was drowned out by a chorus of other voices in the
South calling for the resignation of National Chairman Raskob. Dan
Moody called Raskob "a cynical commercialist with an alcohol complex." In the same breath in which he condemned Raskob, he hailed
the man to whom Smith's political potency had obviously passed: "The
tremendous vote [for governor] given Franklin D. Roosevelt by the
citizens of the Empire State attest the esteem in which he is held by
the people of the State and mark for him a continuous and growing
place among the leaders of thought in national affairs." Commented
Time: "It was as though Governor Moody, himself just re-elected by a
whacking majority in the South, had said to Governor-elect Roosevelt
in the North: 'It's going to be either you or me in 1932, old boy, and I'm
a good enough politician to see that it had better be you *and* me. We'll
decide later which of us gets first place on the ticket.'"[113]

Moody's "whacking majority" over token Republican opposition
might impress outsiders, but within Texas he was regarded as "practically non-existent politically." He had further alienated both the wets
and the drys by his halfhearted support of Smith. As a *San Antonio
Light* editor wrote Franklin Roosevelt after the election:

Perhaps you are wondering about my friend, Mr. Dan Moody, Governor, and
for your information, I believe you can easily forget him for from every source
it is apparent that he has killed himself politically. The Protestants who elected
him are all now against him because he voted for Mr. Smith, and the Catholics
are all against him because he would not defend and make speeches for Mr.
Smith; the dries are all against him because he backed Mr. Smith and those
were the people who were the backbone of his following, and the wets never
did have any use for him.[114]

At a victory dinner in Dallas on November 9 the Anti–Al Smith
Democrats made plans to continue their fight inside the Democratic
party under the name Anti-Tammany Democrats of Texas. Love wanted
"a real, virile organization" perfected in every county. "Nothing has
been worse needed in Texas in her whole history than a permanent or-

ganization of the moral forces in the Democratic Party," he wrote Alvin Moody. "We have such an organization built up as a result of this great campaign and we must maintain and strengthen it." If necessary, he said, he would run for governor in 1930. Looking beyond Texas, Love wanted the anti-Tammany forces to capture the Democratic party in the southern states, gain control of the national convention in 1932, rescind the two-thirds rule, and nominate "clean," dry candidates.[115]

The headquarters of the Anti-Tammany Democrats of Texas would be maintained permanently in Dallas, Love announced on November 12. "It will be our purpose to fight the domination of the democratic party by the liquor interests both in state and national politics," he explained. "We will oppose the nomination of Franklin D. Roosevelt, who was elected governor of New York on a pledge to veto all state liquor law enforcements legislation and all other wets." Legislation would be introduced in the next Texas legislature allowing the people to select all party executive committee members. That would relieve Texas Democrats "of their present illegally chosen committee."[116]

The first real test for the Anti-Tammany Democrats of Texas would come when the battle for control of the party state machinery opened in the Forty-first Legislature and in the 1930 primaries and conventions. The outcome of that struggle would either confirm the Hoovercrat triumph of 1928 or give a verdict of "Love's Labor's Lost."

Conclusion

BUSINESS progressivism had a substantial impact on Texas in the 1920s
even if the two progressive governors of that decade, Pat Neff and Dan
Moody, had more ideas than the legislature could comfortably assimi-
late. If the central themes of business progressivism were efficiency
and public services, including good roads, educational expansion, public health, and business methods in state government, then George
Tindall's interpretation of southern politics in the 1920s holds up well
for Texas.

Neff manifested the spirit of a crusader in vigorously advocating
his ideas. In frequent messages to the legislature, he recommended
such business-progressive reforms as abolishment or consolidation of
all unnecessary state boards and bureaus in order to eliminate extravagance and duplication of effort, prison reform, rural-school improvements and facilities for vocational education, improvement of the state
highway system, state parks, water conservation, laws to attract industry to Texas, a better public-health program, and a constitutional convention. He asked the legislature to raise gross receipts and corporate
franchise taxes; enact a state income-tax law designed to reach those
who had little or no physical property to be taxed; and levy at least a 5
percent severance tax on oil, natural gas, sulphur, quicksilver, and all
other minerals taken out of Texas soil.

The legislature was not impressed with the governor's ambitious
program. Although some offices were eliminated or consolidated, the
lawmakers refused to modify greatly the organization of state administration, no constitutional convention met, and there were no fundamental changes in the state tax system. Relocation and centralization of
the prison system were considered but not accomplished. Neff thought
that the chief cause of what he termed the worst "crime wave" in Texas
history was the suspended-sentence law, and he asked for its repeal—
to no avail.

Neff's obsession with law enforcement limited his effectiveness as chief executive, and relations between the governor and the legislature, never cordial or close, were sometimes downright choleric. Austere in manner, Neff was inclined to adopt a rather lofty tone toward the lawmakers, was secretive about his future plans, and had no spokesman or contact men on the floor of either the House or the Senate. T. Whitfield Davidson, lieutenant governor in Neff's second term, felt no obligation to sponsor or push the governor's program in the Senate. Another reason there was a breach between the governor and the legislature was that Neff disbanded the Board of Pardon Advisers, made his own investigations, and granted very few pardons (none for prisoners represented by attorneys). In this respect his administration was in striking contrast to those of Hobby and the Fergusons. Neff ran into difficulty with the legislature on money matters, and during his two terms a total of five extra sessions were necessary to pass appropriation bills.

Despite Neff's difficulties with the legislature, it did pass a number of measures that he favored and which broadened the state government's outreach to the people. It voted the largest appropriation for rural schools that had ever been made, provided funds for vocational education, voted $1.3 million for the enlargement of the University of Texas campus, established Texas Technological College in West Texas and South Texas State Teachers College at Kingsville, provided building and operating funds for Stephen F. Austin State Teachers College at Nacogdoches, legalized the formation of cooperative farm-marketing associations, authorized the creating of water and irrigation districts, authorized the licensing and supervision of maternity homes, created a tubercular hospital for ex-soldiers at Kerrville, and established a board to regulate the licensing of optometrists. The work of the Petticoat Lobby resulted in the enactment of still more progressive measures.

Neff strongly favored good roads, and he must be given a share of the credit for the expansion and improvement of the highway system. During his administration the Highway Commission was reorganized, a gasoline tax of one cent per gallon was levied for the highway and public-school funds, license fees for motor vehicles were increased, and the legislature approved a constitutional amendment authorizing the state to take over the construction, operation, and maintenance of a state highway system.

Neff also deserves credit for the beginning of the state parks system in 1923. Upon his recommendation, the legislature created a non-salaried state parks commission, with the duty of soliciting donations of land of any size suited to public-park purposes. Neff was able to report in 1925 that the state had received more than fifty tracts of land from private donors. Looking back from the vantage point of 1938, Neff rated his state-park work and the conservation of floodwaters as the most far-reaching contributions of his administration.

Still, Neff's accomplishments fell far short of his initial high expectations. Shortly after leaving office, he reflected upon his administration in words whose pessimistic tone was very different from the confident note he had struck in his first inaugural address:

As I now look back on my four years in the Governor's office, it is difficult to know just how much worthwhile service was rendered. Early in my administration I discovered that it was impossible to do the things that I had dreamed I would do. Many things hindered. Numberless contending and opposing forces had to be reckoned with. Frequently a Governor is helpless to do the things that, as a matter of fact, should be done. At times he feels that about all he can do is to write proclamations that no one reads, and give advice that no one heeds.[1]

Dan Moody sponsored an even broader reform program than Neff, including the reorganization and consolidation of state departments, a civil-service law, judicial reform, the centralization and industrialization of the prison system, a complete overhaul of the tax system, highway legislation, the elimination of unnecessary duplication in the state colleges, and a public-utilities commission. Historian Ralph Steen wrote in 1937: "The Moody recommendations were in keeping with the best thought in political economy, and if adopted would have replaced the present government with a more modern government."[2]

How did the ambitious "Moody program" of nonpartisan reform fare? The legislature carried out no more than half of the governor's recommendations, and few of the major organizational changes he proposed were adopted. The determined opposition of state officials to any change in the status quo had a tremendous influence upon the legislature; there was a natural hesitancy on the part of the legislature itself to deal with the complex problems; and necessary constitutional amendments were rejected by the voters. The greatest difficulty to overcome was the argument that administrative reorganization would concentrate too much power in the governor's hands. In addition, no genuinely constructive reforms were achieved in the tax system; no fundamental changes were made in the cumbersome judicial system; civil service based on merit was turned down; no unified system of accounting was imposed; the prison system was incompletely reorganized; and money was not appropriated for the comprehensive development of a modern state highway system.

On the positive side, the legislature made special appropriations for construction at the state colleges and universities; increased per capita apportionment for the public schools from $14.00 to $17.50 per year; increased the rural-school-aid appropriation; began judicial reform; provided for a state auditor and efficiency expert; improved the libel law; set up a Board of Prison Commissioners who, in turn, chose a general manager of the prison system; placed the prison system on a self-supporting basis; organized a state board of education; helped reform textbook selection; gave the Texas Railroad Commission more complete control over motor buses; and built hundreds of miles of improved highways on the basis of an increase in the gasoline tax to three cents per gallon.

Moody's record as governor was more noteworthy for its administrative than for its legislative endeavors. He reversed the Fergusons' liberal pardon policies, corrected the state textbook situation, and reformed the Highway Department—three areas which had been subject to much criticism during the previous administration. His demand that the Highway Department operate above the slightest suspicion of financial irregularities, his appointment of Ross Sterling (who succeeded him as governor in 1931), Cone Johnson, and W. R. Ely to the Highway Commission, and his selection of Gibb Gilchrist as state highway engineer laid the foundation for the department's "remarkable record of rectitude" in the years that followed. A historian of the Texas prison system, Herman L. Crow, wrote that Moody's conception of prison reform "exerted a powerful influence upon the policies of the Texas prison system, although the changes, impressive as they were, fell far short of the complete realization of his ideal."[3]

When Moody left office in January, 1931, reporter Alonzo Wasson of the *Dallas Morning News* noted that his record fitted well into the circumstances of his first election:

His candidacy for Governor was not a response to the call for great legislative enterprise needing a leader. He did improvise a program of legislative projects. But they were the surplusage of his appeal which brought him but few of the votes he got. His candidacy was primarily, and almost exclusively, a pledge to rescue public services from the grievous state into which they had been brought by maladministration.[4]

All Moody had talked about in the 1926 campaign was "Fergusonism," which was enough to win. His mandate in that sense was a negative one—to destroy Fergusonism.

As governor, Moody became known for his uncompromising honesty, and admirers gave him the nickname Honest Dan. He left office as he had entered it, a poor man financially. He was blind to the trading power of patronage or vetoes and would not "swap votes" with the legislature. A story is told of a legislator who offered to vote for an important administration measure if Moody would promise to sign one of his bills. He refused the trade, and the administration measure lost by a single vote. Then the legislator's bill came to Moody's desk; he signed it, as he had planned to do all along. He would not threaten to discipline those who opposed his program. "It is a question of ethics whether a Governor ought to be willing to sandbag a Senator or Representative into line," noted the *Dallas Morning News*. "Mr. Moody answers that question in the negative."[5] Still, his critics charged that he was unable to see the viewpoint of others. It was also said that he procrastinated and found it difficult to make up his own mind.

During his four years in office, Moody had eight legislative sessions (setting an all-time record with six sessions during his second term), vetoed fifteen bills during the sessions, and used the post-adjournment veto 102 times—a record which earned him the title of "Veto Governor of Texas." Only one veto was overridden.[6]

Some Moody supporters attributed his difficulties with the legislature to the animosity of political rivals like Jim Ferguson, State Senator Tom Love, and Lieutenant Governor Barry Miller, who hoped to succeed Moody and feared that he might seek an unprecedented third term. "I saw how Tom Love and Barry Miller acted with the rest of them just like a bunch of Monkeys," one indignant visitor to the Senate chamber wrote Moody. "Old man Jim Fergerson [sic] was sitting in the back tickled to death because the Senate would not do anything." In a 1975 interview, former state senator and lieutenant governor Walter F. Woodul offered three reasons Moody's legislative program was not more successful: the "legislature didn't have as good sense as he [Moody] did; . . . Ferguson had lots of friends in the legislature;" and

Moody "picked up enemies along the way." He added that "Barry Miller was not interested in Moody's program."[7]

Moody's failure to mediate the bitter fight between Al Smith and anti–Al Smith Democrats in Texas in the election of 1928 left both factions dissatisfied with his leadership and embittered his relations with the Forty-first Legislature. "All the time the Legislature was in session, a crazy 'wild' group, and Dan sweating so hard to put over constructive measures," Mrs. Moody noted in her diary on May 25, 1929. "Reactions were deadly, to the recent Smith-Hoover fight, with Dan the 'goat,' both sides." Jim Ferguson was "still working his hate" at the state capitol.[8]

Personal animosities, however, do not by themselves explain the failure of Moody's program, because during his first six months in office, when his popularity was still high and the only organized opposition was a small Ferguson clique in the Senate, his program was still rejected. According to the *Houston Chronicle*, it "was a bit too advanced for the legislature, especially on the subject of civil service. . . . Some of his friends opposed some of his measures and supported others."[9]

A partial explanation for why Moody's program was thought to be "a bit too advanced" must be sought in the attitudes of Texas lawmakers and of the voters who sent them to Austin. The 1920 Federal census showed that Texas was continuing to gain in population at a rate far above the national average, and rapid population growth continued in the 1920s, with a 24.9 percent increase (from 4,663,228 to 5,825,715) by 1930. Cities continued to grow more rapidly than rural areas. Rural Texas gained only 9 percent in population, while urban Texas increased 58 percent. In 1920, 32.4 percent of the state's population was classed as urban (living in incorporated towns of 2,500 or more); in 1930, the figure was 41 percent. But even this did not give the complete picture for the 59 percent of the population classified as rural in 1930 included all the people living in towns of less than 2,500. According to one estimate made in 1929, only 38.5 percent of the people of Texas lived outside cities and towns of some kind.[10]

The discovery of Spindletop Oil Field near Beaumont in 1901, the first of a long series of petroleum and natural-gas discoveries in Texas, had marked the beginning of the chief impetus to the state's economic expansion and population growth. The 1920 census reported that petroleum refining was Texas's leading industry, with $241,757,313 of products in the preceding year. In 1923, socialist George Clifton Edwards of Dallas wrote in the *Nation* that the spirit of present-day Texas was best exemplified by the cities to which the rich "black waxy" land counties and the oil counties were tributary:

Here are no arid plains, no wind-swept plateaus, no forests, rice fields, no cowboys. The rich little city of Waco has one twenty-story skyscraper sticking up like a totem pole among the Baptists. Houston has more skyscrapers; Dallas more and higher; all modern machine made, as much like the north as may be; crammed with offices, bankers, lawyers, oil men, "realtors"—effective Texas of today.[11]

Yet while Texas was undergoing marked changes economically and in the distribution of its population, to a very great degree it was unchanged psychologically—its characteristic habit of thought was rural. Besides the minority of Texans who lived on farms, a large portion of the city and town population had rural origins and antecedents. Peter Molyneaux, editor of *Texas Monthly*, gave the following definition of the term *rural*: "In general it is a habit of thought to which almost anything which transcends a purely agricultural form of society is in some degree alien. In its most narrow form the rural habit of thought is a neighborhood habit of thought, prescribed in its outlook by the interests and horizons of a rural countryside."[12]

The tenant farmer working on shares stood near the bottom of Texas agriculture and presented one of the most serious social problems the state had to face. In 1880 tenants constituted 37 percent of all Texas farmers; by 1910 this figure had grown to 52.6 percent, and by 1920 to 53.3 percent. In 1920, 66.1 percent of all farms, or nearly two out of three, in nineteen black land counties of Texas were operated by tenants. Agricultural expert William B. Bizzell wrote in his 1924 book *Rural Texas*: "It is impossible to build a prosperous and progressive rural civilization with more than half the farmers cultivating the land on some basis of cash or share tenancy." The rise in cotton prices from 1922 to 1925 after a sharp price break in 1920–21 muted agrarian discontent but did not solve the farmers' basic problems, stemming from unscientific farming, the crop-lien system, tenancy, a less than satisfactory marketing system, and overproduction. From 1919 to 1926 Texas increased cotton acreage from something over ten million to over eighteen million acres and her production from three million to almost six million bales.[13]

Little wonder then that when financially strapped rural voters participated directly in the legislative process through referenda on constitutional amendments those who bothered to vote turned down proposals for the general welfare if no apparent local benefit would result, even if each amendment involved the expenditure of a relatively small amount of money annually. In 1927, rural voters decisively defeated two proposed amendments to the state constitution which would have raised the salaries of the governor and the legislators and increased the number of judges on the state supreme court from three to nine (the present number). Out of a total of 200 counties reporting, only 51 gave majorities in favor of the amendments, while 149 gave majorities against them. One-third of the total vote in their favor was supplied by 9 counties in which larger cities and towns were located: Bexar, Dallas, El Paso, Galveston, Harris, Jefferson, Tarrant, Travis, and Wichita. McLennan County gave a small majority against the amendments, but Waco returned a favorable majority.[14]

To some extent, rural voters held an attitude of antagonism toward the cities and everything pertaining to them. In a letter to a Texas newspaper, a resident of a small town gave as one of the reasons for the rural vote against the amendments the fact that the big cities favored them. "The boys at the forks of the creek," he said, "see the cities becoming big and wealthy, commercial and financial interests merging for their own benefit . . . and they doubt the disinterestedness of their political friends and register their disapproval of anything they sponsor . . . on the theory that no good thing can come out of Nazareth."[15]

This same rural habit of thought among lawmakers almost untouched by the economic changes going on all around them put roadblocks in the path of those business-progressive reforms advocated by Neff and Moody which would have increased state expenditures. A look at the districts the nay-voting representatives hailed from shows a pattern of rural counties and small towns—places with names like Mercury, Rosebud, Paradise, Paint Rock, and Gap. In the 1921 Legislature, there were 4 representatives from Dallas and 3 from Houston. Fifty-two years later, in the reform legislature of 1973, the Dallas and Houston delegations totalled 33 members.

Peter Molyneaux told a pointed story about one rural East Texas representative during the Neff administration. When another member, Frank Burmeister of Atascosa County, supporting a small appropriation to promote reforestation, remarked that the man who made two blades of grass grow where only one grew before was a benefactor of society, the rural legislator objected on the ground that "you don't eat grass." Burmeister shot back at him: "Ah, my friend, but you are mistaken. You do eat grass. But you don't eat it until after it is fed to a calf." Friends of higher education lamented the animus against academic excellence among rural Texans, who, like their hero Jim Ferguson, were for higher education if it didn't get "too high." "Ignorance of the crassest kind, and arrogant beyond rivalry, is everywhere rampant," Richard F. Burges of El Paso complained in May, 1922. "The men who founded the Texas Republic did not pause to wipe the blood off of their swords before making what provision they could for 'a university of the first class,' and Representative [George W.] Dayton, of Cooke, since senator, informed me somewhat proudly that in his opinion the people of Texas would be glad to see the University closed."[16] In defense of rural legislators, however, it must be said that the farmers' most urgent problems were not the concerns of business progressivism.

Big corporations opposed some of Neff's and Moody's tax and regulatory proposals. After World War I, a corporate mood descended upon urban Texas, and the state's leading newspapers warned that strict regulation and higher taxes on business would hinder economic development. Journalist Bryan Mack wrote smugly in a 1929 article in *Review of Reviews*: "Years ago the legislature, urged by an unwise governor, enacted laws that were unfriendly to outside capital and made it a hardship to do business. But that day is gone and almost forgotten. Now capital from any state is eagerly welcomed and treated fairly."[17]

The inevitable crowd of lobbyists at the state capitol representing the state's oil and gas, sulphur, and lumber companies throttled severance or income-tax proposals. In an address to the second called session of the Forty-first Legislature, Moody suggested that the state adopt an income tax on individuals and corporations in partial substitution for the state ad valorem property tax. Opposition was formidable, with critics as expected charging that it would retard industrial development. "A Texas shunned by expanding industries and being rapidly denuded of those it now has is a by no means improbable result of its adoption of such a tax measure," warned the *Houston Gargoyle*. "We suggest to Dan Moody, Senator [Edgar] Witt, et al. that they re-read the fable of the goose that laid the golden eggs."[18] The special session took no action on Moody's tax proposal.

The powerful utilities lobby blocked in the Forty-first Legislature bills supported by Moody to create a utilities commission with rate-fixing powers. According to the *Dallas Morning News*, in a July, 1929, speech at Round Rock Moody charged that "the utilities have maintained a powerful lobby in Austin during the sessions of the Legislature to defeat utility regulation. He likened it to the lobbies of fifteen years ago by brewery and liquor interests." When John C. Granbery wrote Moody commending his 1929 message to the legislature, the governor replied pessimistically:

Some parts of it, as you would imagine, have not met with any great amount of enthusiasm at the hands of the Legislature, and likely will not be enacted into law. I believe the time will come when some of these matters will be enacted into law. I have sometimes felt that our attitude in Texas is a little too reactionary and that we were not ready to accept progressive measures which worked successfully in other states.[19]

If "progressive measures" include welfare aid, improved health-care delivery systems, urban mass transportation, pollution control, better regulation of utilities, a more equitable educational system, repeal of the Sunday blue laws, tax reform, campaign-finance reform, and a new constitution to replace the now 107-year-old document, Moody's assessment of the Texas attitude remains essentially valid after a further half-century of rapid industrial and urban growth.

Other important aspects of 1920s politics have also persisted or recurred in Texas. Both the Klan and the Fergusons were in political eclipse in 1928, but for "Ma" and "Pa" the loss of public favor was not permanent. When Mrs. Ferguson was defeated for governor in the 1930 Democratic runoff primary by Ross Shaw Sterling, the millionaire chairman of the State Highway Commission, the *New York Times* expressed pleasure that the people of Texas "in a time of economic discontent and even distress, refused to follow adroit and popular demagogues."[20] By 1932, however, many Texans were ready for a change. Jim Ferguson again entered his wife in the gubernatorial race, telling the voters: "Two years ago you got the best governor money could buy, this year you have the opportunity to get the best governor patriotism can give you." Mrs. Ferguson led Sterling by a wide margin in the first primary, but in the runoff she beat him by less than 4,000 votes—477,644 to 473,846. The Sterling camp charged that voter frauds in East Texas had given her the victory but were unable to overturn the result.[21]

Mrs. Ferguson's second administration was generally regarded as up to the average in Texas and met with less criticism than did her first one. When she announced on November 15, 1933, that she would not seek reelection in 1934, the issue of Fergusonism did not confront Texas voters for only the second time since 1914. The *New York Times* described Lone Star State voters as "apathetic" and called the gubernatorial contest (won by Attorney General James V. Allred) "the quietest in more than twenty years." *Texas Weekly* offered the following explanation for the public's apathy: "It takes a mob-rousing issue like that of Ku Kluxism, prohibition as it used to be, Fergusonism, or something of that kind—a single issue which divides the people into sheep and goats, according to one's point of view—to get the voters excited during the heat of summer. Fortunately, we think, no such issue looms at present."[22]

The Fergusons in retirement were shortly replaced in the affections of Texas's poorer whites by the greater showmanship and more lavish promises of W. Lee "Pass the Biscuits, Pappy" O'Daniel, called by V. O. Key, Jr., "a mountebank alongside whom old Jim looked like a statesman—and was."[23] O'Daniel was a Fort Worth flour merchant who advertised his "Hillbilly Flour" on a regular radio program that attracted a wide following. He campaigned for governor in 1938 on a platform of the Ten Commandments, adjustment of taxes, opposition to a sales tax, abolition of the poll tax, and pensions of thirty dollars a month for all persons over sixty-five. He said his motto would be the Golden Rule and announced a slogan of "Less Johnson grass and politicians; more smokestacks and business men." The old-line politicians openly laughed at the country music O'Daniel peddled on his campaign swings, but his crowds increased. People jammed the highways, sometimes waiting hours to catch a first hand glimpse of the famous radio salesman. His showmanship and pension promises brought out to the polls thousands who had not voted since 1928, when they had joined the moral crusade against Al Smith. O'Daniel was nominated in the first primary with 50.9 percent of the votes.[24]

In 1940, Mrs. Ferguson challenged the anti–New Deal O'Daniel as a pro-Roosevelt candidate. She assailed the musical campaigner as a "medicine man governor" who had put the state "under the shameful banner of the flour sack." Jim called the governor "a wandering minstrel." O'Daniel, he said, "is blowed-up, for the people are fed up on banjo-picking, bull fiddling statesmen." But the Fergusons were no match for Pappy, who was now the hero of the Texas underprivileged. Ma came in fourth in the primary, which O'Daniel won with 54.3 percent of the vote. Friends of the Fergusons blamed the radio for Ma's defeat; Pa, they explained, was a stump speaker who could not adjust his free-swinging style of oratory to the new method of vote collecting. "Jim Ferguson," declared his lieutenant Fisher Alsup, "was a man who had to be seen to be appreciated."[25]

The Fergusons had run their last race. On February 28, 1944, Jim, who had been in ill health for some time, suffered a severe stroke from which he never fully regained consciousness. He lingered for seven months, dying in his Austin home on September 21, 1944. The Austin bureau of the *Dallas Morning News* declared that Ferguson "was matched in his influence on state political history only by Sam Houston."[26]

Miriam lived for seventeen years after Jim's death. As she aged, the people of Texas seemed anxious to find ways to pay tribute to her. In 1953, the Texas Senate passed a resolution honoring her as "an example of noble and gentle womanhood, an ideal wife, and a devoted mother." On her eightieth birthday, June 13, 1955, about three hundred persons, including Governor Allan Shivers and U.S. Senate Majority Leader Lyndon B. Johnson, attended a dinner in her honor. Mrs. Ferguson was escorted to the speakers' table to the strains of her 1924 campaign song, "Put on Your Old Gray Bonnet."

This was her last formal public appearance. Her remaining years passed peacefully. She told a reporter that she felt no bitterness toward former enemies of Fergusonism, adding "most of them have seen the error of their ways, anyhow." On November 30, 1960, Miriam suffered a heart attack from which she seemingly recovered. But a little less than two weeks after her eighty-sixth birthday, she suffered a second attack and died on June 25, 1961. A simple funeral service at her home was followed by interment alongside Jim in the State Cemetery.[27]

The Ku Klux Klan, close to dormancy nationally since the civil rights struggles of the 1950s and 1960s, has risen again in recent years, riding the wave of racial and economic tensions in American society. With an estimated national membership of 10,000 in the various Klan factions and with about 100,000 more supporters, the modern Klan is a far cry in numbers from the 1920s Klan, which took on the trappings of a full-fledged political movement. In recent years, Texas klansmen have operated "paramilitary" training camps at several places in the state and have harassed immigrant Vietnamese fishermen on the Gulf

Coast. A group of 100 Ku Klux Klan members, including women and children, paraded through Seabrook on June 12, 1982, to protest the activities of the fishermen. About 150 people attended an August, 1982, Klan rally and cross-burning in a grassy field six miles southeast of Bastrop. In December, 1982, 50 klansmen gathered before thirty onlookers to torch an eighteen-foot wooden cross at a rally at Vidor, a Beaumont suburb. The Klan was blamed for the cancellation of a Christmas parade in Vidor.[28]

On September 2, 1921, probably 30,000 spectators watched 519 white-robed Knights of the Ku Klux Klan, headed by a Klansman carrying a fiery cross, parade on Congress Avenue in Austin. Sixty-two years later, on February 19, 1983, about 50 Klan members, surrounded by helmeted police carrying plexiglass shields, marched to the Texas Capitol from nearby Waterloo Park to protest the influx of illegal aliens and illegal drugs into Texas and to promote the Klan's belief in a "white Christian America." Up to 2,000 hecklers, a mostly young crowd of Anglos, Hispanics, and blacks, lined the parade route and pelted the marchers with rocks and bottles.

Eleven people—four law enforcement officers and seven spectators—were injured in the melee; twelve people were arrested on charges ranging from assault to inciting a riot, and one Klansman was taken into custody for carrying a prohibited weapon. Most of the injuries and arrests occurred at the end of the march when the crowd that had been flanking the Klan threatened to break through the line of police officers but was forced back with billy clubs. In sharp contrast to the Klan march, a diverse collection of anti-Klan groups marched peacefully on Congress Avenue that morning and staged an afternoon rally at Rosewood Park.[29]

During the Depression, Texas's militant drys waged a losing battle against the wet movement in the state. Texas joined in ratifying the Twenty-first Amendment to the United States Constitution, which ended national Prohibition, on December 5, 1933. Then the Forty-fourth Legislature submitted an amendment repealing state prohibition, and the voters ratified it on August 24, 1935, by a vote of 297,597 to 250,948. Yet the wet victory turned out to be drastically limited. At the same time that the voters rescinded the sixteen-year-old state prohibition amendment, they approved a constitutional ban on "open saloons." Many Texas counties remained dry under local-option laws, while many others permitted only the sale of light wines and beer. The sale of liquor by the drink was illegal everywhere in Texas; in wet areas restaurants and night clubs could serve beer and wine and provide ice and mixers for patrons who brought their own bottles, usually in brown bags. Beginning in 1961, it was legal for private clubs to serve mixed drinks to their members. Soon restaurants, hotels, and motels, most of which maintained private clubs on their premises, latched onto the idea of a temporary membership that allowed guests to belong to the club for a single night. These private clubs were essentially open saloons, and their blatant circumvention of the state's alcoholic-beverage code was what eventually brought liquor by the drink back into Texas. In November, 1970, heavy urban majorities produced a narrow victory for an amendment repealing the ban on liquor by the drink. The following year the legislature authorized the serving of alcohol in public establishments; and on May 18, 1971, elections in wet areas restored the public sale of mixed drinks in the state for the first time since 1919.[30]

Even now, however, the wet victory is not complete. In rural Texas the battle between wets and drys continues. At the present time, a third of the state, chiefly above a line from El Paso to Orange, is dry by law; and about thirty-five times a year a local option liquor election is held somewhere in the state.[31]

As rural counties have steadily legalized liquor sales and the price of corn whiskey has exceeded the cost of the store-bought variety, moonshiners have dwindled to a very few. "Moonshining has just about died out," said an agent for the Texas Alcoholic Beverage Commission in April, 1982. Harrison County on the Louisiana border remains one of the few places in Texas where at least two or three stills are seized each year. Moonshine still sells because people like it. "As long as there be a world, there will be some moonshine made and some moonshine sold," a Harrison County moonshiner remarked philosophically.[32]

The persistence of the Prohibition controversy on the turf of North Texas drys and the revival on a small scale of the Ku Klux Klan in Texas are not the only reasons why a student of the state's politics in the 1920s might have some sense of *deja vu*. There are lingering echoes of the controversy between modernist and fundamentalist Protestants and the anti-evolution crusade. Proponents of "creation science," which takes the biblical account of human origins as a basis for biology, want their theories to enjoy equal classroom standing with evolution.

The Texas State Board of Education has been under pressure to open its textbook selection process to both positive and negative comment. The current system allows only critics of texts to testify. Without discussion, the Board of Education agreed at a meeting on February 12, 1983, to give textbook supporters a spot at hearings.

As noted earlier in this chapter, the powerful utilities lobby blocked Governor Dan Moody's efforts to create a state commission with rate-fixing powers. The Texas Public Utility Commission was finally established in 1975, but now lawmakers face pressure to do something about the commission, which has become the focus of public anger over rising electric and telephone bills. Reformers charge that the three-member appointive commission has become a pro-utility body indifferent to rate-payers' interests. The major proposed changes are to elect the commissioners from geographical districts and to expand their number.

For the first time in a dozen years, Texas state government has a money problem, and in response the legislative battle cry of "no new taxes" is being revived. "In Texas, 'No New Taxes,' may not be as sacred a slogan as 'Remember the Alamo,' but it comes close," Dave McNeely of the *Austin American-Statesman* wrote recently. "Texas legislative history suggests that any move to increase taxes will leave some political blood on the floor of the Capitol, as powerful interest groups fight among themselves to keep from being taxed, and try to hold down state spending."[33] Every attempt in the legislature to raise the severance tax on oil in the last thirty-two years has failed (the natural-gas tax was last raised fourteen years ago), and the energy lobby is prepared to battle any severance-tax increase now as it did in the 1920s and after. Meanwhile, teachers, state employees, colleges, highway interests, and others try to have more state money spent on their areas.

In sum, issues seem to reappear in Texas politics, and conflicts in public values are not finally resolved but only advance and recede in prominence.

Notes

Introduction

1. Dewey W. Grantham, Jr., "The Contours of Southern Progressivism," *American Historical Review* 86 (December, 1981): 1057.

2. *Public Papers of the Presidents of the United States, Lyndon B. Johnson: Containing the Public Messages, Speeches, and Statements of the President, 1965 (In Two Books). Book I—January 1 to May 31, 1965*, pp. 195–96.

3. William Harmon, ed., *The Oxford Book of American Light Verse*, p. 106; Richard Jackson, ed., *Popular Songs of Nineteenth-Century America: Complete Original Sheet Music for 64 Songs*, pp. 116–18, 274.

4. V. O. Key, Jr., with Alexander Heard, *Southern Politics in State and Nation*, p. 265.

5. Dewey W. Grantham, Jr., "Texas Congressional Leaders and the New Freedom, 1913–1917," *Southwestern Historical Quarterly* 53 (July, 1949): 35–48; Alexander Graham Shanks, "Sam Rayburn in the Wilson Administrations, 1913–1921," *East Texas Historical Journal* 6 (March, 1968): 63–76.

6. Lewis L. Gould, *Progressives and Prohibitionists: Texas Democrats in the Wilson Era*, pp. xiii, 276; Jeanne Bozzell McCarty, *The Struggle for Sobriety: Protestants and Prohibition in Texas, 1919–1935*, pp. 6–7. On the Prohibition movement in the nation at large, see James H. Timberlake, *Prohibition and the Progressive Movement, 1900–1920* (Cambridge, Mass.: Harvard University Press, 1963); Joseph R. Gusfeld, *Symbolic Crusade: Status Politics and the American Temperance Movement* (Urbana: University of Illinois Press, 1963); Robert A. Hohner, "The Prohibitionists: Who Were They?" *South Atlantic Quarterly* 68 (Autumn, 1969): 491–96.

7. George B. Tindall, *The Persistent Tradition in New South Politics*, p. 58.

8. Love to Mark Sullivan, August 7, 1922, Thomas B. Love Papers, Dallas Historical Society (hereafter cited as Love Papers).

9. George B. Tindall, "Business Progressivism: Southern Politics in the Twenties," *South Atlantic Quarterly* 62 (Winter, 1963): 92–106; George B. Tindall, *The Emergence of the New South, 1913–1945*, pp. 224–33. See also H. Clarence Nixon, "The Changing Political Philosophy of the South," *Annals of the American Academy of Political and Social Sciences* 153 (January, 1931): 246–50; H. Clarence Nixon, "The Changing Background of Southern Politics," *Social Forces* 11 (October, 1932): 14–18.

10. Tindall, *Emergence of the New South*, p. 230.

11. Key, *Southern Politics in State and Nation*, p. 265.

12. O. Douglas Weeks, "The Texas Mexican and the Politics of South Texas," *American Political Science Review* 24 (August, 1930); 606–27; Evan Anders, "Bosses Under Siege: The Politics of South Texas during the Progressive Era" (Ph.D. diss., University of Texas, 1978); Evan Anders, *Boss Rule in South Texas: The Progressive Era*; Evan Anders, "Boss Rule and Constituent Interests: South Texas Politics during the Progressive Era,"

Southwestern Historical Quarterly 84 (January, 1981); 269–92; Evan Anders, "The Origins of the Parr Machine in Duval County, Texas," *Southwestern Historical Quarterly* 85 (October, 1981): 119–38.

13. A. Elizabeth Taylor, "The Woman Suffrage Movement in Texas," *Journal of Southern History* 17 (May, 1951): 194–215; Emma Louise Moyer Jackson, "Petticoat Politics: Political Activism among Texas Women in the 1920's" (Ph.D. diss., University of Texas, 1980).

14. *New York Times*, April 3, 1928.

15. *Dallas Morning News*, July 4, 1928.

Chapter 1

1. *Austin Statesman*, January 1, 1921; Audray Bateman, "Austinites Whooped It Up on Congress Avenue in 1921," *Austin American-Statesman*, January 1, 1977.

2. *Austin Statesman*, January 1, 1921; *New York Times*, September 7, 1920, quoted in Charles Merz, *The Dry Decade*, p. 56; Owen P. White, "Dripping Dry Dallas," *Collier's* 84 (July 20, 1929): 8–9, 38.

3. *Austin Statesman*, January 18, 1921; *Dallas Morning News*, January 19, 1921.

4. *Dallas Morning News*, January 20, 1921.

5. "Inaugural Address," in Pat M. Neff, *The Battles of Peace*, pp. 13–17.

6. Emma Morrill Shirley, *The Administration of Pat M. Neff, Governor of Texas, 1921–1925*, p. 41; Mary D. Farrell and Elizabeth Silverthorne, *First Ladies of Texas: The First One Hundred Years, 1836–1936, a History*, pp. 311–12.

7. There is no published biography of Neff. This biographical sketch was compiled from the following sources: S. P. Brooks, "Biographical Sketch," in Pat M. Neff, *A Collection of Twenty-three Addresses*; Hugh Nugent Fitzgerald, *Governors I Have Known*, pp. 44–57; Shirley, *Administration of Pat M. Neff*, pp. 1–6; James T. DeShields, *They Sat in High Places*, pp. 423–30; Paul Bolton, *Governors of Texas*; Joseph Martin Dawson, *A Thousand Months to Remember*, pp. 180–81; Betty Ann McCartney McSwain, ed., *The Bench and Bar of Waco and McLennan County, 1849–1976*, pp. 362–63; Lois Smith Murray, "Pat Morris Neff," in Walter Prescott Webb, H. Bailey Carroll, and Eldon Branda, eds., *The Handbook of Texas*, 3:642. See also Loise Moore, "Pat M. Neff and His Achievements" (master's thesis, Texas College of Arts and Industries, 1941); Reuben Bryan Nichols, "Pat M. Neff: His Boyhood and Early Political Career" (master's thesis, Baylor University, 1951).

8. Fitzgerald, *Governors I Have Known*, p. 44; "View and Review" (typescript), Harry Benge Crozier Papers, Capitol Legislative Reference Library (hereafter cited as Crozier Papers); Frank M. Locke to author, February 10, 1976.

9. Lola Matthews Laughlin, "The Speaking Career of Pat Morris Neff" (master's thesis, Baylor University, 1951), p. 119.

10. Neff, *Battles of Peace*, pp. 7–12.

11. Ibid., pp. 273–98.

12. On the election of 1920 in Texas, the best account is Lewis L. Gould, *Progressives & Prohibitionists: Texas Democrats in the Wilson Era*, pp. 249–77. See also Ralph W. Steen, "A Political History of Texas, 1900–1930," in Frank Carter Adams, ed., *Texas Democracy: A Centennial History of Politics and Personalities of the Democratic Party, 1836–1936*, 1:415–18; Shirley, *Administration of Pat M. Neff*, pp. 13–40; Seth S. McKay, *Texas Politics, 1906–1944: With Special Reference to the German Counties*, pp. 87–103. Statewide returns are in Alexander Heard and Donald S. Strong, *Southern Primaries and Elections, 1920–1949*, pp. 134–36. For Bailey, see Sam Hanna Acheson,

Joe Bailey: The Last Democrat; Bob Charles Holcomb, "Senator Joe Bailey: Two Decades of Controversy" (Ph.D. diss., Texas Tech University, 1968).

13. *Journal of the House of Representatives of the Regular Session of the Thirty-seventh Legislature (1921)*, pp. 6–10, 333–59, 447 (hereafter cited as *House Journal*, 37 Leg., reg. sess. [1921]); *Dallas Morning News*, January 10–12, 16, February 11, 1921.

14. Fred Gantt, Jr., interview with H. G. Perry, Stephenville, Texas, April 8, 1968, Oral History Collection, North Texas State University; E. L. Covey to author, February 20, 1976.

15. *Dallas Morning News*, January 12, 1921.

16. Fitzgerald, *Governors I Have Known*, pp. 66–68; Davidson to James B. Wells, May 6, 1920, James B. Wells Papers, University of Texas Archives (hereafter cited as Wells Papers).

17. Hobby's message is in *House Journal*, 37 Leg., reg. sess. (1921), pp. 18–23; *Dallas Morning News*, January 13, 16, 20, 1921.

18. *House Journal*, 37 Leg., reg. sess. (1921), pp. 157–62; Fred Gantt, Jr., *The Chief Executive in Texas: A Study in Gubernatorial Leadership*, pp. 302–303.

19. *Dallas Morning News*, January 24, 1921.

20. For the early history of state reorganization in Texas, see Frank M. Stewart, "The Movement for the Reorganization of State Administration in Texas," *Southwestern Political and Social Science Quarterly* 5 (December, 1924): 230–45; Frank M. Stewart, *The Reorganization of State Administration in Texas*, University of Texas Bulletin no. 2507 (1925); J. Alton Burdine, "Shall Texas Reorganize," *Southwest Review* 18 (Summer, 1933): 405–16.

21. *House Journal*, 37 Leg., reg. sess. (1921), pp. 259–62. See also Shirley, *Administration of Pat M. Neff*, pp. 44–45.

22. *House Journal*, 37 Leg., reg. sess. (1921), pp. 406–407.

23. Ibid., pp. 469–70; S. G. Reed, "Texas State Railroad," in Webb, Carroll, and Branda, eds., *Handbook of Texas*, 2:763–64.

24. Fitzgerald, *Governors I Have Known*, p. 66; Raymond Brooks, *Political Playback*, p. 12. The Eugene C. Barker Texas History Center compiled Brooks's articles from the galley proofs in the offices of the *Austin American-Statesman*. Brooks served as secretary of the State Railroad Board during its first year. The Texas State Railroad's lease with the Texas and New Orleans Railroad expired in 1962, and on November 1 of that year the Texas South-Eastern Railroad Company took up the lease. James M. Day, "Texas State Railroad," in Webb, Carroll, and Branda, eds., *Handbook of Texas*, 3:996.

25. *Dallas Morning News*, January 28, 31, 1921.

26. *House Journal*, 37 Leg., reg. sess. (1921), pp. 315–17.

27. Brooks to Neff, February 12, 1921, Atticus Webb to Neff, February 7, 1921, Reynolds to Neff, February 28, 1921, Neff to Reynolds, March 7, 1921, Pat M. Neff Papers, Texas Collection, Baylor University (hereafter cited as Neff Papers). See also Thomas S. Henderson to Mrs. Waller S. Baker, March 15, 1921, Thomas S. Henderson Papers, University of Texas Archives (hereafter cited as Henderson Papers); *Home and State*, April 1, 1921 (clipping), Pat M. Neff Biographical File, Barker Texas History Center (hereafter cited as Neff File).

28. *House Journal*, 37 Leg., reg. sess. (1921), p. 476; *Austin Statesman*, February 14, 1921. Neff inadvertently omitted his reasons for wanting the suspended-sentence law repealed, but that afternoon he sent a message to the legislature on the subject. *House Journal*, 37 Leg., reg. sess. (1921), pp. 482–84. Neff's warning about lobbyists was well taken. Roy C. Coffee, who represented Wise County in the Thirty-seventh and Thirty-eighth legislatures, wrote: "I would also say that the 3rd House of the lobbyist for busi-

ness groups and organizations was very strong during this period. They had some very strong men in state politics who spent considerable time in Austin, one of which was John Darrouzet of Galveston, Judge Elkins of Houston, and several able men representing the oil companies." Coffee to author, Feburary 10, 1976.

29. *Dallas Morning News*, February 18, 1921.

30. *House Journal*, 37 Leg., reg. sess. (1921), pp. 467, 624–35; *Dallas Morning News*, February 25, 1921.

31. *House Journal*, 37 Leg., reg. sess. (1921), pp. 710–12; *Dallas Morning News*, February 26, 1921.

32. *Dallas Morning News*, February 26, 1921; Robertson to Neff, February 26, 1921, S. M. Adams to R. B. Walthall, February 25, 1921, Neff Papers.

33. *Dallas Morning News*, February 26, 28, 1921.

34. *Journal of the Senate of Texas: Being the Regular Session of the Thirty-seventh Legislature (1921)*, pp. 608–609, 620 (hereafter cited as *Senate Journal*, 37 Leg., reg. sess. [1921]; *Dallas Morning News*, March 1, 1921.

35. Rupert N. Richardson, *Texas: The Lone Star State*, 2d ed., p. 315; Gantt, *Chief Executive in Texas*, p. 151; Herman Lee Crow, "A Political History of the Texas Penal System, 1829–1951" (Ph.D. diss., University of Texas, 1963), pp. 256–57. See also Stuart A. MacCorkle, "Pardoning Power in Texas," *Southwestern Social Science Quarterly* 15 (December, 1934): 218–28.

36. Neff to Board of Pardon Advisers, January 22, 1921, Neff Papers; Neff, *Battles of Peace*, p. 168. There is a file of letters in the Neff Papers commending his action in abolishing the State Board of Pardons and his recommendation that the suspended-sentence law be repealed. For examples, see Lee Simmons to Neff, January 24, 1921, the Rev. Martin Quill to Neff, January 25, 1921, Atticus Webb to Neff, January 25, 1921, W. T. Allen to Neff, February 2, 1921. Neff's most famous pardon was the one granted in January, 1925, to Huddie Ledbetter ("Leadbelly"), the black folk singer and twelve-string guitarist. In 1918, under the name of Walter Boyd, Ledbetter was convicted of murder and sentenced to thirty years in the Texas penitentiary. The story goes that Ledbetter sang a petition to Neff that secured his freedom. John Henry Faulk played Neff in the Paramount film *Leadbelly*, directed by Gordon Parks, in which the meeting between Neff and Ledbetter is a key scene. See Christine Hamm, "Huddie Ledbetter," in Webb, Carroll, and Branda, eds., *Handbook of Texas*, 3:513–14; Richard M. Garvin and Edmond G. Addeo, *The Midnight Special: The Legend of Leadbelly*, pp. 144–52; Charlayne Hunter, "'Leadbelly' Speaks for Every Black Who's Catching Hell," *New York Times*, July 4, 1976; *Daily Texan* (Austin), May 25, 1939, clipping in John A. Lomax Biographical File, Barker Texas History Center (hereafter cited as Lomax File).

37. *House Journal*, 37 Leg., reg. sess. (1921), pp. 373–74.

38. Ibid., p. 372; *Dallas Morning News*, February 4, 1921. The Texas Federation of Women's Clubs, which had been agitating for a prison survey as a first step to penal reform, kept a close watch on the committee and wanted to be informed about its findings. See Mrs. Florence C. Floore to Mrs. Henry F. Ring, February 11, 1921, J. A. Herring to Ring, February 15, 1921, Floore to Ring, March 7, 1921, Mrs. Henry F. Ring Papers, University of Texas Archives (hereafter cited as Ring Papers); J. A. Herring to Pat M. Neff, April 5, 1921, Neff Papers.

39. Tom Finty, Jr., "Our Legislative Mills, IV: Texas Makes Haste," *National Municipal Review* 12 (November 19, 1923): 649–54; Marvin Pierce Baker, "The Executive Veto in Texas" (master's thesis, University of Texas, 1933), pp. 64–65. Interviewed in 1968 by Joe B. Frantz, Congressman W. R. (Bob) Poage, who served in the Thirty-eighth and Thirty-ninth legislatures, recalled: "Back in those days we had sixty day ses-

sions at $5.00 a day and $2.00 a day thereafter; we served there twelve days at $2.00 a day. Even in those days, you could hardly make it. F: That discouraged lengthy sessions. P: Discouraged lengthy sessions." Congressman W. R. (Bob) Poage interview, November 11, 1968, Oral History Collection, Lyndon Baines Johnson Presidential Library.

40. *House Journal*, 37 Leg., reg. sess. (1921), pp. 718–20; *Dallas Morning News*, February 26, 1921.

41. *House Journal*, 37 Leg., reg. sess. (1921), pp. 1078–79; *Dallas Morning News*, February 26, March 1, 3, 13, 1921.

42. W. C. Binkley, "Notes from Texas," *Southwestern Political Science Quarterly* 1 (March, 1921): 426; *Dallas Morning News*, February 14, March 13, 1921.

43. *Dallas Morning News*, February 3, 24, March 13 (cartoon), March 15, 1921; Wesley Sisson Chumlea, "The Politics of Legislative Apportionment in Texas, 1921–1957" (Ph.D. diss., University of Texas, 1959), pp. 44–52.

44. Binkley, "Notes from Texas," pp. 426–27; *Dallas Morning News*, March 13, 1921; W. M. W. Splawn, "A Review of the Minimum Wage Theory and Practice, with Special Reference to Texas," *Southwestern Political Science Quarterly* 1 (March, 1921): 347–49, 368–69; Frank M. Stewart, "Notes from Texas," *Southwestern Political Science Quarterly* 2 (September, 1921): 198–200; Mary Thames, "A Study of the Texas Industrial Welfare Commission" (master's thesis, University of Texas, 1922); Gould, *Progressives & Prohibitionists*, pp. 251–52.

45. Shirley, *Administration of Pat M. Neff*, p. 64; Binkley, "Notes from Texas," p. 426; *House Journal*, 37 Leg., reg. sess. (1921), pp. 966, 1032–33; *Senate Journal*, 37 Leg., reg. sess. (1921), p. 462; *Dallas Morning News*, April 2, 1921.

46. Binkley, "Notes From Texas," p. 427; *Dallas Morning News*, March 13, 1921.

47. *House Journal*, 37 Leg., reg. sess. (1921), pp. 108–12, 220–21, 399–401; *Senate Journal*, 37 Leg., reg. sess. (1921), pp. 279–80; *Austin American*, February 7, 8, 1921; Robert E. Vinson, "The University Crosses the Bar," *Southwestern Historical Quarterly* 43 (January, 1940): 292–94; Walter E. Long, *"For All Time to Come"*, pp. 41–82; J. Evetts Haley, *George W. Littlefield, Texan*, pp. 272–76; William C. Pool, *Eugene C. Barker: Historian*, pp. 120–22; Kaye Northcott, "Be held permanently for education purposes . . . ," *Texas Observer* 64 (September, 1973): 1, 3–4. For a three-part series examining the controversy surrounding the Brackenridge Tract to 1973, see *Daily Texan*, April 19, 20, 23, 1973.

48. Long, *"For All Time to Come"*, p. 78. W. H. Folts, E. H. Perry, and H. A. Wroe were the three members of the Board of Regents from Austin.

49. *Dallas Morning News*, April 3, 4, 6, 9, 1921; Weston J. McConnell, *Social Cleavages in Texas: A Study of the Proposed Division of the State*, pp. 127–33; R. C. Crane, "The West Texas Agricultural and Mechanical College Movement and the Founding of Texas Technological College," *West Texas Historical Association Year Book* 7 (June, 1931): 20–28; Homer Dale Wade, *Establishment of Texas Technological College, 1916–1923*, ed. Elizabeth Howard West, pp. 47–58; Lawrence L. Graves, *A History of Lubbock*, pp. 518–19; Jane Gilmore Rushing and Kline A. Nall, *Evolution of a University: Texas Tech's First Fifty Years*, pp. 12–14.

50. Rushing and Nall, *Evolution of a University*, p. 13.

51. *Dallas Morning News*, April 5, 1921; Hicks to Neff, April 7, 1921, Neff to Campbell, April 30, 1921, Neff Papers.

52. Crane to the Rev. D. B. Doak, December 7, 1927, Royston Campbell Crane Papers, Southwest Collection, Texas Tech University (hereafter cited as Royston Campbell Crane Papers).

53. Gantt, *Chief Executive in Texas*, p. 95.

54. *Dallas Morning News*, March 15, 1921, January 14, 1925; Neff to Sam Neff, March 7, 1921, Neff to Pat Neff, Jr., April 28, 1921, Neff Papers; James A. Clark with Weldon Hart, *The Tactful Texan: A Biography of Governor Will Hobby*, p. 150.

55. Neff to F. F. Criswell, June 7, 1921, Neff Papers; Vernen Liles and Marjorie Seidel, "State Parks," in Webb, Carroll, and Branda, eds., *Handbook of Texas*, 3:703.

56. *Dallas Morning News*, Mary 29, June 3, July 21, 1921; J. A. Herring to Neff, May 16, 1921, Neff Papers.

57. *Dallas Morning News*, June 7, 10, 1921.

58. Ibid., June 7, July 5, 21, 1921 (interview with Herring); Herring to Neff, September 19, 1921, Neff to Herring, September 23, 1921, Neff Papers. Neff sent Herring proclamations revoking the paroles of seventy-one prisoners who had not reported to the State Prison Commission in 1920. Neff to Herring, June 17, 1921, Neff Papers.

59. *Dallas Morning News*, March 8, 10, 1921; Walter D. Taylor to Neff, April 19, 1921, Neff Papers.

60. *Dallas Morning News*, June 8, 9, 1921.

61. Ibid., June 18, 1921.

62. Ibid., July 5–7, 9–11, 1921.

63. Ibid., July 11, 12, 1921.

64. *Journal of the House of Representatives of the First Called Session of the Thirty-seventh Legislature (1921)*, pp. 4–6 (hereafter cited as *House Journal*, 37 Leg., 1st called sess. [1921]; *Dallas Morning News*, July 18, 19, 1921.

65. *Dallas Morning News*, July 20, 21, 1921. Neff's message is in *House Journal*, 37 Leg., 1st called sess. (1921), pp. 29–30.

66. *Dallas Morning News*, July 22, 23, 27, 1921. The joint legislative committee's report is in *House Journal*, 37 Leg., 1st called sess. (1921), pp. 409–12. The committee found that an employee had stolen $15,149.10 from the State Treasury Department but that he had been arrested, and the stolen money would be repaid by his relatives, friends, and bondsmen; that the padding of the school census in certain counties was under investigation by the State Department of Education; that the state would not be responsible for payroll irregularities in a Houston venereal clinic jointly supported by the federal government, the state, and the city of Houston; and that there had been some padding of expense accounts by traveling employees in the Fire Insurance Department but that it was believed that there was no intent to defraud the state.

67. O. Douglas Weeks, "Election Laws," in Webb, Carroll, and Branda, eds., *Handbook of Texas*, 1:552; Stewart, "Notes from Texas" (1921), p. 197. For the history of constitutional amendments submitted since 1876, see Irvin Stewart, "Constitutional Amendments in Texas," *Southwestern Political Science Quarterly* 3 (September, 1922): 145–58.

68. *House Journal*, 37 Leg., 1st called sess. (1921), pp. 182–84.

69. Ibid., pp. 116–24; Stewart, "Notes from Texas" (1921), pp. 195–96. The state chairman of the Texas League of Women Voters had this comment on the report: "If we could centralize our prisons as to location, create a Board of Advisors, one of this should be a woman to serve without pay but with expenses paid, I believe that we could bring about the prison reform for which we are all working. The inaccessibility of all the farms and the fact that they are scattered all over East Texas is one of the greatest hinderances [*sic*] to effective and permanent reforms." Mrs. Jesse Daniel Ames to Mrs. H. F. Ring, August 1, 1921, Ring Papers.

70. *Dallas Morning News*, August 5, 6, 16, 30, 1921; Stewart, "Notes from Texas" (1921), p. 196; Hertzberg to Ring, August 16, 1921, Mrs. S. M. N. Marrs to Ring, August 26, 1921, Ring Papers. See also Shirley, *Administration of Pat M. Neff*, pp. 56–57;

Crow, "Political History of the Texas Penal System," p. 238. Captain J. A. Herring had recommended that Neff veto the punishment bill, "as it is the most harmful one of the bunch." Herring to Neff, August 22, 1921, Neff Papers. See also Herring to Neff, October 20, 1921, Neff Papers. For Neff's defense of his veto, see Neff to Judge W. M. Tidwell, October 7, 1921, Neff Papers.

71. *Dallas Morning News*, May 18–21, 31, July 21, 31, December 16, 1921; W. G. Pryor, *Correspondence between W. G. Pryor, Prison Commissioner, and Pat M. Neff, Governor of Texas, concerning the Texas Prison System, Together with a Letter to the Texas Legislature*; Shirley, *Administration of Pat M. Neff*, pp. 57–58; Crow, "Political History of the Texas Prison System," pp. 236–37. Neff's comment is in Neff to Judge W. M. Tidwell, October 7, 1921, Neff Papers. On the prison loan, see Frank M. Stewart, "Notes from Texas," *Southwestern Political Science Quarterly* 2 (March, 1922): 350; J. A. Herring to Pat M. Neff, October 27, 1921, Neff Papers; Mrs. J. E. King to Mrs. H. F. Ring, March 15, 1922, Ring Papers.

72. *Dallas Morning News*, November 24, 1921; Neff to Herring, November 7, 1921, Hertzberg to Neff, December 2, 1921, Neff Papers. On one occasion, Neff revealed a flippant attitude toward his clemency power, writing Frank Davis of San Antonio: "Dear Davis: You wanted the negro at San Antonio to hang. He was hanged. You wanted the death penalty at Marlin commuted to life imprisonment. It has been commuted! It is beautiful to dwell together like brethren." Neff to Davis, March 3, 1922, Neff Papers.

73. *House Journal*, 37 Leg., 1st called sess. (1921), pp. 10–19, 94–96; *Dallas Morning News*, July 30, 1921.

74. *House Journal*, 37 Leg., 1st called sess. (1921), pp. 164–65, 198–99, 647; *Dallas Morning News*, August 3, 5, 11, 17, 1921; *Austin American*, August 16, 17 (poem), 1921. John H. Veatch was the representative from Johnson County.

75. *Journal of the House of Representatives of the Second Called Session of the Thirty-seventh Legislature*, pp. 2, 15–16 (hereafter cited as *House Journal*, 2d called sess. [1921]); Chumlea, "Politics of Legislative Apportionment," pp. 53–65.

76. *Dallas Morning News*, August 7, 9, 1921; Stewart, "Notes from Texas" (1921), pp. 193–94.

77. *Journal of the Senate, State of Texas Second Called Session Thirty-seventh Legislature*, p. 23 (hereafter cited as *Senate Journal*, 37 Leg., 2d called sess. [1921]); *House Journal*, 37 Leg., 2d called sess. (1921), pp. 10, 107–108; *Dallas Morning News*, August 18, 20, 24, 25, 1921; *Austin Statesman*, August 20, 21, 24, 25, 1921; *Austin American*, August 25, 1921; Stewart, "Notes from Texas" (1921), p. 193.

78. *Austin American*, August 21, 1921; Hogg to Alvin M. Owsley, October 24, 1921, William Clifford Hogg Papers, University of Texas Archives (hereafter cited as Hogg Papers).

79. Chumlea, "Politics of Legislative Apportionment," pp. 65–81. Neff is quoted in Mrs. Percy V. Pennybacker to Mrs. R. S. Thompson, December 6, 1921, Mrs. Percy V. Pennybacker Papers, University of Texas Archives (hereafter cited as Pennybacker Papers). For press criticism, see *Dallas Morning News*, August 12, 1921; *San Antonio Express*, August 19, 1921. See also J. M. Simpson to Senator R. P. Dorough, August 12, 1921, Dorough to Simpson, August 19, 1921, Simpson to William H. Bledsoe, August 22, 1921, William H. Bledsoe Papers, Southwest Collection, Texas Tech University (hereafter cited as Bledsoe Papers).

80. *House Journal*, 37 Leg., 2d called sess. (1921), pp. 22–23, 25, 121–24; *Austin Statesman*, August 23, 1921; *Dallas Morning News*, August 11, 24, 25, 1921; J. P. Anderson to R. B. Walthall, August 25, 1921, Neff Papers.

81. Neff, *Battles of Peace*, p. 268; Shirley, *Administration of Pat M. Neff*, pp. 63–64; Richardson, *Texas*, p. 315.

82. *Dallas Morning News*, July 20, 1921.

Chapter 2

1. For further information on the second Klan, see Charles O. Jackson, "William J. Simmons: A Career in Kluxism," *Georgia Historical Quarterly* 50 (December, 1966): 351–65; Robert L. Duffus, "Salesmen of Hate: The Ku Klux Klan," *World's Work* 46 (May, 1923): 31–38; Stanley Frost, *The Challenge of the Klan*, pp. 170–71; Arnold S. Rice, *The Ku Klux Klan in American Politics*, pp. 1–8; Charles C. Alexander, *The Ku Klux Klan in the Southwest*, pp. 1–19.

2. Thomas L. Stokes, *Chip off My Shoulder*, p. 121.

3. Ralph McGill, "The South Has Many Faces," *Atlantic* 211 (April, 1963): 90. The unidentified Atlanta man is quoted in McGill's article. See also Hiram Wesley Evans, "The Klan: Defender of Americanism," *Forum* 74 (December, 1925): 801–14.

4. Boyce House, *Oil Field Fury*, pp. 100–101.

5. John M. Mecklin, *The Ku Klux Klan: A Study of the American Mind*, pp. 107–108. See also Frank Tannenbaum, *Darker Phases of the South*, pp. 24–34.

6. Alexander, *Ku Klux Klan in the Southwest*, pp. 36–37; David M. Chalmers, *Hooded Americanism: The First Century of the Ku Klux Klan*, p. 39; Max Bentley, "The Ku Klux Klan in Texas," *McClure's Magazine* 57 (May, 1924): 14–15.

7. Mecklin, *Ku Klux Klan*, p. 40. For the riot, see Robert V. Haynes, *A Night of Violence: The Houston Riot of 1917*.

8. *Houston Post*, October 9, 1920; Bentley, "Ku Klux Klan in Texas," p. 14; Alexander, *Ku Klux Klan in the Southwest*, pp. 37–38. On the Klan in Texas, see Charles C. Alexander, *Crusade for Conformity: The Ku Klux Klan in Texas, 1920–1930*.

9. Alexander, *Ku Klux Klan in the Southwest*, pp. 38–39, 53, 108; Alexander, *Crusade for Conformity*, p. 6; Chalmers, *Hooded Americanism*, p. 40. I am indebted to Louise Moyer Jackson for this information on the women's Klan.

10. Edward T. Devine, "More about the Klan," *Survey* 48 (April 8, 1922): 42; Thomas E. Kroutter, Jr., "The Ku Klux Klan in Jefferson County, Texas, 1921–1924" (Master's thesis, Lamar University, 1972), p. 160; interview, July 28, 1947, name withheld on request, quoted in Lois E. Torrence, "The Ku Klux Klan in Dallas (1915–1928): An American Paradox" (Master's thesis, Southern Methodist University, 1948), p. 52; Brooks, *Political Playback*, p. 26; Alexander, *Ku Klux Klan in the Southwest*, p. 94.

11. Duncan Aikman, "Prairie Fire," *American Mercury* 6 (October, 1925): 214; interview with Glenn Pricer, August 22, 1947, quoted in Torrence, "Ku Klux Klan in Dallas," p. 53; Frost, *Challenge of the Klan*, p. 158. For a business directory of the Beaumont Ku Klux Klan, see Kroutter, "Ku Klux Klan in Jefferson County," pp. 179–80. It was supposedly posted in the meeting hall of Klan no. 75, but Kroutter does not attest to its authenticity.

12. Robert L. Duffus, "How the Ku Klux Klan Sells Hate," *World's Work* 46 (June, 1923): 183; *Dallas Morning News*, August 1, 1922.

13. George Clifton Edwards, "Texas: The Big Southwestern Specimen," *Nation* 116 (March 21, 1923): 337; Duffus, "How the Ku Klux Klan Sells Hate," p. 183; *Ferguson Forum*, March 15, 1923. See also *Ferguson Forum*, March 29, 1923.

14. Alexander, *Ku Klux Klan in the Southwest*, pp. 87–91; Bentley, "Ku Klux Klan in Texas," p. 16; House, *Oil Field Fury*, p. 100; J. B. Cranfill to J. D. Sandefer, April 29, 1922, J. B. Cranfill Papers, University of Texas Archives (hereafter cited as Cranfill Pa-

pers); Norman Murphy, "The Relationship of the Methodist Church to the Ku Klux Klan in Texas, 1920–1928" (seminar paper, University of Texas, 1970). See also Robert Moats Miller, "A Note on the Relationship between the Protestant Churches and the Revived Ku Klux Klan," *Journal of Southern History* 22 (August, 1956): 355–68.

15. Duffus, "How the Ku Klux Klan Sells Hate," p. 183; A. V. Dalrymple, *Liberty Dethroned*, pp. 28, 91. On Camp, see *Dallas Morning News*, April 23, 1922; Helen Gardner Lloyd to George B. Christian, Jr., April 25, 1922, John DeBerry Wheeler to Warren G. Harding, April 26, 1922, Will W. Alexander to George B. Christian, Jr., May 3, 1922, Warren G. Harding Papers, Ohio Historical Society (hereafter cited as Harding Papers).

16. Alexander, *Ku Klux Klan in the Southwest*, p. vii.

17. Edward T. Devine, "The Klan in Texas," *Survey* 48 (April 1, 1922): 10; Devine, "More about the Klan," p. 42; Walter C. Hornaday, "Klan Once Flourished in Many Texas Cities," *Dallas Morning News*, April 17, 1966; interview, July 28, 1947, name withheld on request, quoted in Torrence, "Ku Klux Klan in Dallas," p. 66; *Dallas Morning News*, May 31, 1921. Dr. Caleb A. Ridley, pastor of the Central Baptist Church of Atlanta and an imperial officer in the Klan, during a speech in Temple, Texas, turned to a large crowd of blacks who were assembled behind the speaker's stand and warned them that if they "kept on listening to insidious propaganda of mongrel negro uplift societies and followed these unprincipled leaders on and on, the modern Knights of the Ku Klux Klan will have to rise up as our fathers did and throw themselves between you and damnation or everyone of you will be swept from the face of the earth." Ridley asserted that the Klan was the best friend the Negro ever had, and he said there were men within the sound of his voice who knew that to be true. *Temple Daily Telegram*, August 15, 1921, clipping in Ku Klux Klan Subject File, Barker Texas History Center. See also Department of Education Knights of the Ku Klux Klan Realm of Texas, "The Klan's Attitude Toward the Negro," two-page broadside, dated May 18, 1924, in Campaign Materials—Ku Klux Klan, Texas State Archives.

18. The number of whippings is given in Mecklin, *Ku Klux Klan*, pp. 78–79. The cases are taken from a six-month summary published in the *Houston Press*, August 2, 1921, under the title "Thanks to the Ku Klux!" clipping in KKK Scrapbook, University of Texas Archives (hereafter cited as KKK Scrapbook). The near race riot in Houston is discussed in Bentley, "Ku Klux Klan in Texas," pp. 16–17. See also Chalmers, *Hooded Americanism*, p. 41. For the violence in May–June, 1922, see *New York Herald*, May 29, 1922, clipping in Ku Klux Klan File, Administrative Files, NAACP Papers, Manuscripts Division, Library of Congress (hereafter cited as Ku Klux Klan File, NAACP Papers); *Dallas Morning News*, May 25, 27, June 4, 1922.

19. Bentley, "Ku Klux Klan in Texas," p. 17; Alexander, *Ku Klux Klan in the Southwest*, pp. 57–59. A photographic copy of a Ku Klux Klan notice from Edna Klan no. 27, dated September 7, 1921, is in Oscar B. Colquitt Papers, University of Texas Archives (hereafter cited as Colquitt Papers).

20. Bentley, "Ku Klux Klan in Texas," p. 16; Rice, *Ku Klux Klan in American Politics*, p. 55; Kenneth T. Jackson, *The Ku Klux Klan in the City, 1915–1930*, p. 84; "The Ku-Klux Klan," *Catholic World* 116 (January, 1923): 440; Duffus, "How the Ku Klux Klan Sells Hate," p. 182.

21. Chalmers, *Hooded Americanism*, p. 41; Crane to Neff, May 2, 1922, Martin M. Crane Papers, University of Texas Archives (hereafter cited as Martin M. Crane Papers); interview with Glenn Pricer, August 22, 1947, quoted in Torrence, "Ku Klux Klan in Dallas," p. 66–67. According to Pricer: "The Klan really terrorized Dallas County for a while. They had a committee which heard complaints on personal conduct and then sup-

posedly decided whether or not certain persons should be whipped. This scared some people so that they stayed in their homes at night with guns beside them."

22. Grand Jury Report, December 5, 1921 (manuscript), James R. Hamilton Papers, Southern Historical Collection, University of North Carolina (hereafter cited as Hamilton Papers); *Austin Statesman*, 1921, newspaper clipping in KKK Scrapbook.

23. *Austin Statesman*, 1921, newspaper clipping in KKK Scrapbook; Rice, *Ku Klux Klan in American Politics*, p. 53; *Dallas Morning News*, March 30, 1922.

24. Bentley, "Ku Klux Klan in Texas," pp. 17–18.

25. *Dallas Morning News*, July 27, August 1, 1921; Duffus, "How the Ku Klux Klan Sells Hate," p. 180; *Dallas Morning News*, October 5, 1921.

26. *Dallas Morning News*, October 16, 1921; John O. King, *Joseph Stephen Cullinan: A Study of Leadership in the Texas Petroleum Industry, 1897–1937*, p. 212.

27. Bentley, "Ku Klux Klan in Texas," p. 19; Richard Henderson, *Maury Maverick: A Political Biography*, p. 30. See also Maury Maverick, *A Maverick American*, pp. 143–45.

28. Rice, *Ku Klux Klan in American Politics*, pp. 52–53; John Middagh, *Frontier Newspaper: The El Paso Times*, p. 196. When the Knights announced they would stage a masked parade in Farmersville in eastern Collin County, a broadside headed "Ku Klux Klan Parade" and signed by a group calling itself "The Ding Dang Gang" ordered local residents in honor of "this occasion on this doleful night, of this desolate day, of this weeping week, of this terrible month," to "disguise and mask yourself in the most ridiculous make up you can conceive. Wear anything from union-alls to night shirts, with or without tails. The real object of this great coming together of the Ding Dangers, is to see which can make the biggest fools of themselves—us or THE KU KLUX." "Ku Klux Klan Parade," one-page broadside in Broadsides—653, Texas State Archives.

29. *Austin American*, October 3, 1921; Alexander, *Ku Klux Klan in the Southwest*, pp. 50, 99; Rice, *Ku Klux Klan in American Politics*, p. 55. Saye is quoted in a *Dallas Morning News* editorial, January 2, 1922.

30. Chester T. Crowell, "Journalism in Texas," *American Mercury* 7 (April, 1926): 478. The *Houston Chronicle* editorial is quoted in full in Bentley, "Ku Klux Klan in Texas," pp. 18–19. Black's editorial is quoted in Middagh, *Frontier Newspaper*, p. 195. See also William J. Hooten, *Fifty-two Years a Newsman*, p. 9; "Klan Controls Early '20s EP," *El Paso Times*, April 2, 1981. The characterization of Aikman's pen as "pungent" is in Virginius Dabney, *Liberalism in the South*, p. 403.

31. *Dallas Morning News*, May 24, 1921.

32. Ibid., August 4, October 8, 1921, January 6, 1922.

33. Crowell, "Journalism in Texas," pp. 477–78. Pricer is quoted in Torrence, "Ku Klux Klan in Dallas," pp. 55, 67. When the Klan paraded in Bay City, Matagorda County, "a doctor and a businessman, who had a good occasion to know the favorite footwear of the town's citizens, were observed peeping out a window as the paraders in their white robes and hoods marched by. When asked what they were writing down, they replied they were making out a list of the secret organization's membership, identifying the members by their shoes!" Junann J. Stieghorst, *Bay City and Matagorda County: A History*, p. 167, citing interview with Mrs. A. S. Morton.

34. Torrence, "Ku Klux Klan in Dallas," p. 57; Ernest Sharpe, *G. B. Dealey of the Dallas News*, pp. 199–201. Camp is quoted in the *Dallas Morning News*, April 23, 1922.

35. *Dallas Morning News*, May 24, June 23, 1921; Kroutter, "Ku Klux Klan in Jefferson County," p. 19.

36. *Austin American-Statesman*, June 27, 1921; *Dallas Morning News*, June 28,

1921; *Hamilton for Congress Newspaper*, Hamilton Papers; unidentified newspaper clipping in KKK Scrapbook.

37. Tom B. Bartlett to Hamilton, June 28, 1921, Hamilton Papers. See also Houston citizen to Hamilton, June 28, 1921, D. A. Gregg to Hamilton, July 2, 1921, C. W. Webb to Hamilton, July 15, 1921, Hamilton Papers. A thirteen-page typescript of Hamilton's charge to the Travis County Grand Jury, October 3, 1921, is in the Hamilton Papers. See also *Dallas Morning News*, October 4, 1921; *Austin American*, October 4, 1921. For commendatory resolutions and letters, see the resolution signed by 150 citizens of Round Rock, October 24, 1921, printed in *Hamilton for Congress Newspaper*; Jno. B. Thomas to Hamilton, October 4, 1921, Lea Beatty to Hamilton, October 5, 1921, Jno. M. Sharpe to Hamilton, October 7, 1921, S. B. Branch to Hamilton, October 8, 1921, W. P. Connally to Hamilton, October 17, 1921, Hamilton Papers. Mention of the other seven district judges' charges is made in Max Bentley to Hamilton, October 5, 1921, Hamilton Papers. For warnings, see unsigned, undated message on line notepaper, anonymous to Hamilton, March 31, 1922, Hamilton Papers.

38. *Dallas Morning News*, July 26, 1921.

39. *House Journal*, 37 Leg., 1st called sess. (1921), pp. 163, 181; *Dallas Morning News*, July 28, August 2, 3, 6, 16, 1921.

40. *House Journal*, 37 Leg., 1st called sess. (1921), pp. 200, 230, 292–93; *Dallas Morning News*, August 11, 1921; Wright Patman interview, August 11, 1972, Oral History Collection, Johnson Library. Patman spoke of his harassment by the Klan: "Oh yes. And they threw bricks on my little home down there on 6th Street. I had a wife and two sons, little kids. Bill wasn't even born then. They'd throw bricks up on the house at night. Once they burst a window in the car and one time they cut a tire, did little old things like that to just express annoyance and displeasure in what I was doing. And they'd call at odd hours of the night to give me the devil and say they were going to kill me if I didn't stop that jumping on the best people in the world, the Ku Klux. And of course I paid no attention to it and went ahead." Patman wrote General Martin M. Crane: "We have very few klan sympathizers in this town [Linden] and the fewer that come here the better it will suit us." Patman to Crane, May 13, 1922, Martin M. Crane Papers.

41. *Dallas Morning News*, June 18, October 7, 12, 13, 16, 1921. One irate Texan sent Neff a clipping of the woman tarred and feathered at Tenaha with the red-penciled comment: "Why dont you resign and let the K. K. K. run Texas. Perhaps you and Dr Brooks could carry out your chivalry under masks with nobler results." Neff sent the clipping to Brooks with the comment: "I am getting various and sundry kinds of communications now a days. You may also be receiving some of a similar character. . . . In this connection desire to say that one of the State Senators advised some days ago that he thought the Klu [*sic*] Klux Klan was a Baptist organization." Neff to S. P. Brooks, July 23, 1921, Samuel P. Brooks Papers, Texas Collection, Baylor University (hereafter cited as Brooks Papers).

42. Foster to Neff, November 10, 1921, Neff to Foster, November 12, 1921, Neff Papers. The chief editorial writer for the *Dallas Morning News* believed that Neff "had trained your heaviest oratorical guns on forms of lawlessness which, although they merited all the denunciation you had visited on them, were nevertheless less menacing than others against which you had only fired occasional shots from the smallest of the guns in your arsenal." Alonzo Wasson to Neff, February 7, 1922, Neff Papers.

43. *Dallas Morning News*, January 13, 14, 1921; Neff, *Battles of Peace*, pp. 71–73. See also Kyle W. Shoemaker [Walter Prescott Webb], "How Mexia Was Made a Clean

City," *Owenwood Magazine* 1 (May, 1922): 19–26; John H. Jenkins, "Martial Law in Mexia," *Texas Military History* 6 (Fall, 1967): 175–89; H. Gordon Frost and John Jenkins, *"I'm Frank Hamer": The Life of a Texas Peace Officer*, pp. 102–12; Harry Krenek, *The Power Vested: The Use of Martial Law and the National Guard in Texas Domestic Crisis, 1919–1932*, pp. 59–83. For a private defense of his decision to declare martial law, see Pat M. Neff to Editorial Department, *Dallas Morning News*, February 2, 1922, Neff Papers.

44. Neff, *Battles of Peace*, p. 73; *Dallas Morning News*, February 19, 23, 25, March 15, 1922. The Mexia Klan meeting is discussed in Devine, "More about the Klan," p. 43.

45. *Dallas Morning News*, January 15, 18, 1922. The Navarro County Ranger raids of 1924 led by Marvin ("Red") Burton stopped lawlessness and vice activities in the Navarro field. James R. Ward, "Establishing Law and Order in the Oil Fields: The 1924 Ranger Raids in Navarro County, Texas," *Texana* 8 (1970): 38–46.

46. *Dallas Morning News*, March 24, 25, 1922.

47. Ibid., March 25, 26, 1922.

48. Ibid., April 2, 4–6, 11, 1921; Torrence, "Ku Klux Klan in Dallas," p. 72; pamphlet, Martin M. Crane Papers.

49. Rice, *Ku Klux Klan in American Politics*, p. 53; M. M. Crane to John Davis, April 15, 1922, Crane to Dan Harston, April 29, 1922, Martin M. Crane Papers.

50. Crane to Neff, April 24, May 10, 31, June 2, 14, 21, 1922, Neff to Crane, May 8, June 19, 1922, Martin M. Crane Papers; *Dallas Morning News*, May 11, 1922. Portions of the Crane-Neff correspondence dealt with the league's request that Neff furnish it with the names of klansmen in the Adjutant General's Department, the Texas Rangers, and the Texas National Guard. The governor promised an inquiry and later sent Crane letters from Adjutant General Thomas D. Barton, Brigadier General Jacob F. Wolters, and Major General John A. Hulen. Wolters said that he had not found any Klan officers in the Fifty-sixth Cavalry Brigade, while Hulen said that he was not a member of the Klan and did not know of any officers of the Thirty-sixth Division of the National Guard who were members. Barton had interviewed "either personally or by written inquiries, the Captains of the companies, all Rangers and all members of the Adjutant General's Department, and have failed to find any who are members of the Ku Klux Klan." Wolters to Neff, June 6, 1922, Hulen to Neff, June 17, 1922, Barton to Neff, June 17, 1922, Martin M. Crane Papers.

51. *Dallas Morning News*, April 7, 10, 1922.

52. Ibid., July 25, 1922; Torrence, "Ku Klux Klan in Dallas," pp. 75–76; Crane to Hugh J. Cureton, June 5, 1922, Martin M. Crane Papers. Rogers is quoted in Rice, *Ku Klux Klan in American Politics*, p. 53.

53. Kroutter, "Ku Klux Klan in Jefferson County," pp. 41–43; *New York World*, March 31, 1922, newspaper clipping in Ku Klux Klan File, NAACP Papers.

54. Kroutter, "Ku Klux Klan in Jefferson County," pp. 45–46, 48–49.

55. Ibid., pp. 71–81; Rice, *Ku Klux Klan in American Politics*, p. 52; B. E. Quinn to Pat M. Neff, July 17, 1922, Neff Papers. See also Stuart R. Smith to Neff, July 12, 1922, T. G. Roddy to Neff, July 12, 1922, Neff Papers.

56. Alexander, *Ku Klux Klan in the Southwest*, pp. 109, 125; Frost, *Challenge of the Klan*, pp. 23, 25. When Evans and his rebels prepared to oust Simmons on the charge that he along with E. Y. Clarke had looted the Klan, they found that the Klan name, property, and everything it owned were copyrighted and registered in Simmons's name. Evans formed a syndicate and bought out Simmons for $140,000. McGill, "South Has Many Faces," p. 90.

57. Testimony of Erwin J. Clark in U.S. Congress, Senate, *Senator from Texas: Hearings before a Subcommittee of the Committee on Privileges and Elections United States Senate Sixty-eighth Congress First Session Pursuant to S. Res. 97 Authorizing the Investigation of Alleged Unlawful Practices in the Election of a Senator from Texas*, p. 116.

58. Testimony of W. H. Castles in ibid., p. 992; interview, July 28, 1947, name withheld on request, quoted in Torrence, "Ku Klux Klan in Dallas," pp. 64–65.

59. Testimony of H. M. Keeling in U.S. Congress, Senate, *Senator from Texas*, p. 467; Bob Barker to M. M. Crane, 1922, Martin M. Crane Papers; Alexander, *Ku Klux Klan in the Southwest*, p. 125; Torrence, "Ku Klux Klan in Dallas," p. 65. Crane had written Barker: "I trust that you will organize in Fort Worth because I regard the Ku Klux obligation and the indifference that our people have manifested to it as the greatest danger that confronts us. It overshadows all others." Crane to Barker, April 15, 1922, Martin M. Crane Papers.

60. Shirley, *Administration of Pat M. Neff*, p. 65; Owsley to Will C. Hogg, September 30, 1921, Hogg to Owsley, October 24, 1921, Hogg Papers. Neff kept tabs on Owsley. The president of the College of Industrial Arts, Denton, wrote the governor: "The latest reliable information here is that Alvin M. Owsley is a candidate for congress from this district, and that he will not be a candidate for Governor." F. M. Bralley to Pat M. Neff, June 8, 1921, Neff Papers. On Owsley, see Wayne Gard, "Alvin Mansfield Owsley," in Webb, Carroll, and Branda, eds., *Handbook of Texas*, 3:680–81; Marion S. Adams, *Alvin M. Owsley of Texas: Apostle of Americanism*.

61. *Dallas Morning News*, April 28, June 4, 1922; Shirley, *Administration of Pat M. Neff*, p. 66.

62. *Dallas Morning News*, June 5, 27, July 5, 1922; Shirley, *Administration of Pat M. Neff*, p. 66.

63. *Dallas Morning News*, June 9, 1922; Joseph S. Myers to Thomas B. Love, May 22, 1922, Love Papers; Joseph W. Bailey to James B. Wells, July 7, 1922, Wells Papers; Steen, "Political History of Texas, 1900–1930," pp. 425–26. See also Atticus Webb to Pat M. Neff, June 12, 1922, Neff to Webb, June 30, 1922, Neff Papers. For Ferguson's support of Rogers, see *Ferguson Forum*, May 4, 1922; *Dallas Morning News*, July 4, 1922.

64. W. H. Cousins to Mrs. Espa Stanford, July 5, 1922, Neff Papers. See also C. M. Stocker to C. F. Goodridge, May 3, 1933, C. F. Goodridge Papers, University of Texas Archives (hereafter cited as Goodridge Papers).

65. *Dallas Morning News*, April 30, June 8, July 1, 2, 1922; *Pitchfork* (Dallas) 181 (July, 1922): 11, Wilford B. ("Pitchfork") Smith Papers, University of Texas Archives (hereafter cited as Wilford B. Smith Papers).

66. *Dallas Morning News*, June 4, 25, 28, 1922.

67. Steen, "Political History of Texas, 1900–1930," p. 426; Shirley, *Administration of Pat M. Neff*, p. 67–69. Neff sent a copy of his Plainview speech, along with some other literature, to Texas newspaper editors, with an accompanying letter, saying: "I am in hopes you will do me the honor to read these articles, and if, during the coming weeks, you see fit to make reference to the thoughts contained therein, I shall be glad. I assure you any consideration shown my candidacy for reelection as governor for a second term will be highly appreciated and gratefully remembered." A large file of these letters, marked "Editors Letters Campaign 1922," is in the Neff Papers.

68. Steen, "Political History of Texas, 1900–1930," p. 426; W. W. Searcy to Pat M. Neff, June 22, 1922; R. G. Storey to R. B. Walthall, June 23, 1922, Neff Papers. For criticisms of the Neff administration, see J. A. Herring to Walthall, June 20, 1922,

Creed G. Engledow to W. W. Sanders, June 22, 1922, Roy Butler to Sanders, June 22, 1922, G. E. Hamilton to Neff, June 27, 1922, Arthur L. McKenney to Neff, July 6, 1922, J. J. Dermody to S. L. Staples, July 8, 1922, Neff Papers. For reports on the Rogers and Neff campaigns in East Texas, see Storey to Neff, June 29, July 5, 7, 8, 14, 17, 20, 1922, Storey to Walthall, June 27, July 13, 1922, W. S. Parker to Neff, July 17, 1922, C. H. Machen to Mrs. Espie [sic] Standford, July 17, 1922, Neff Papers. Prison commissioners J. A. Herring and H. W. Sayle made trips to various parts of the state to make contact with Neff's friends. See Herring to Walthall, July 8, 1922, H. W. Sayle to Walthall, July 10, 1922, Sayle to Neff, July 11, 1922, Neff Papers.

69. *Dallas Morning News*, June 27, 1922; Ben G. Gross to Pat M. Neff, June 24, 1922, Neff to Gross, July 3, 1922, Neff Papers. Neither Neff nor Rogers answered the Dallas Citizens' League questionnaire. Warner did answer it. M. M. Crane to J. L. Winder, July 14, 1922, Martin M. Crane Papers.

70. Fred R. Baker to Pat M. Neff, July 6, 1922, B. E. Quinn to Neff, July 17, 1922, T. W. Davidson to Neff, July 24, 1922, Neff Papers. See also Rice, *Ku Klux Klan in American Politics*, pp. 56–57.

71. Ralph W. Steen, *Twentieth Century Texas: An Economic and Social History*, pp. 115–16.

72. *Dallas Morning News*, January 16, 1921.

73. Ibid., July 13, 1922; Neff, *Battles of Peace*, p. 73; unidentified newspaper clipping in William Pettus Hobby, Sr., Scrapbook, 1912–29, Barker Texas History Center, University of Texas (hereafter cited as Hobby Scrapbook). See also Paul Douglas Casdorph, "The Texas National Guard and the 1922 Railroad Strike at Denison," *Texas Military History* 3 (Winter, 1963): 211–18; Krenek, *The Power Vested*, pp. 33–58. The *Dallas Morning News* called on Neff to enforce the open-port law; see issues of July 14 ("What Governor Neff Can Do"), July 18 ("The Need at Denison"), and July 23, 1922 ("Where the Responsibility Rests").

74. *Austin Statesman*, July 14–16, 1922; *Dallas Morning News*, July 20, 1922; Neff, *Battles of Peace*, p. 74.

75. *Dallas Morning News*, July 25, 1922; Heard and Strong, *Southern Primaries and Elections*, p. 133, Edwards, "Texas," p. 336.

76. J. L. Chapman to Pat M. Neff, July 28, 1922 (references to "intolerant Bailey forces" and "poison venom" handed the "poor ignorant people"), J. E. Boyd to Neff, August 9, 1922, Jacob F. Wolters to Neff, July 24, 1922, Neff Papers. For explanations of the anti-Neff vote, see Frank J. Ford to Neff, July 22, 1922, John P. Marrs to Neff, July 24, 1922, F. F. Downs to R. B. Walthall, July 24, 1922, M. S. Munson to Neff, August 1, 1922, J. L. Ward to Neff August 8, 1922, Neff Papers.

77. Neff to F. F. Downs, July 29, 1922, Neff to "Dear Friends," July 5, 1922, Neff to R. G. Storey, July 27, 1922, Neff Papers. See also Neff to Pat Warner, July 17, 1922, Neff to Fletcher Lane, July 28, 1922, Neff Papers.

78. Neff, *Battles of Peace*, p. 73; *Austin Statesman*, July 17, 22, 1922. See also Shirley, *Administration of Pat M. Neff*, p. 59. Commissioner of Labor Joseph S. Myers, whom Neff had sent to Denison on July 23 to watch the strike situation, telegraphed his resignation to the governor "as a protest against the Federal authorities forcing the State of Texas to put troops in a peaceful city like Denison." After further consideration, however, Myers asked to be allowed to withdraw his resignation, and Neff granted his request. *Dallas Morning News*, July 27, 30, 1922. "We have an 'Open Port Law,' so named because it was designed, it was said, to keep 'open' the port of Galveston," wrote Socialist George Clifton Edwards of Dallas. "The day before election our young Baptist Governor would not use it, seeking union votes. He got them, and the day after election, it was

put into effect to break the railroad strike at Denison four hundred miles from any port. He estimated rightly our capacity for being fooled." Edwards, "Texas," p. 335.

79. *Dallas Morning News*, July 25, 26, 29, December 30, 1922; *Austin Statesman*, July 30, 1922; *Austin American*, November 7, 1926, newspaper clipping in Hobby Scrapbook. The martial-law authorities turned over 297 law violations to the local courts, but, according to Neff, "the county peace officers were in sympathy with the strikers. One hundred and sixty-one of these cases were dismissed from the court docket. No prosecution of any kind was had. One officer of the court can always block the enforcement of the law if he desires to do so." Neff, *Battles of Peace*, p. 76.

80. George K. Butcher to Neff, July 21, 1922, Z. E. Marvin and George K. Butcher to Neff, July 23, 1922, Hiram Wesley Evans to Neff, July 25, 1922, Neff to Butcher, July 26, 1922, Neff to Marvin, July 27, 1922, Neff to Evans, July 27, 1922, Neff Papers; *New York Times*, July 25, 1922.

Chapter 3

1. Gould, *Progressives & Prohibitionists*, pp. 13–14; Walter Prescott Webb and Terrell Webb, eds., *Washington Wife: Journal of Ellen Maury Slayden from 1897–1919*, p. 284. There is no scholarly biography of Culberson. James W. Madden, *Charles Allen Culberson: His Life, Character, and Public Services as County Attorney, Attorney General, Governor of Texas and United States Senator*, is an authorized biography. See also Seth S. McKay, "Charles Allen Culberson," in Webb, Carroll, and Branda, eds., *Handbook of Texas*, 1:443; Charles W. Ramsdell, "Charles Allen Culberson," in Allen Johnson and Dumas Malone, eds., *Dictionary of American Biography*, 4:585–86; Fitzgerald, *Governors I Have Known*, pp. 14–16; Robert L. Wagner, "The Gubernatorial Career of Charles Allen Culberson" (Master's thesis, University of Texas, 1954); Pollyanna B. Hughes and Elizabeth B. Harrison, "Charles A. Culberson: Not a Shadow of Hogg," *East Texas Historical Journal* 11 (Fall, 1973): 41–52.

2. Gould, *Progressives & Prohibitionists*, pp. 174–83. On Barry Miller, see *Address of Senator T. J. Holbrook at the Memorial Service Commemorating the Life and Public Career of the Honorable Barry Miller (1864–1933), Senate chamber, Austin, Texas, October 19, 1922*, an eight-page pamphlet in Barry Miller Biographical File, Barker Texas History Center, University of Texas (hereafter cited as Miller File); "Barry Miller," in Webb, Carroll, and Branda, eds., *Handbook of Texas*, 2:195; *Dallas Morning News*, July 4, 1930.

3. Mark Sullivan, "Midsummer Politics and Primaries," *World's Work* 44 (July, 1922): 299–300; Charles A. Culberson, "To the Democrats of Texas," in Charles A. Culberson Biographical File, Barker Texas History Center, University of Texas (hereafter cited as Culberson File).

4. Hogg to Culberson, December 21, 1921, Hogg Papers; Jurney to House, March 2, 1922, Edward M. House Papers, Manuscripts Room, Yale University Library (hereafter cited as House Papers). See also Thomas B. Love to William G. McAdoo, August 9, 1922, Love Papers; House to Allison Mayfield, August 16, 1922, House Papers; Culberson to Hogg, December 13, 1921, Hogg Papers; Culberson to Richard F. Burges, December 10, 1921, Burges to Culberson, December 17, 1921, Burges to Clarence Ousley, November 16, 1921, Richard Fenner Burges Papers, University of Texas Archives (hereafter cited as Burges Papers).

5. Wells to Garner, April 2, 1922, Garner to Wells, April 4, 1922, Wells Papers. See also Garner to Wells, April 3, 1922, Garner to Wells, April 4, 1922, Jurney to Wells, April 17, 18, 1922, Wells to Culberson, April 17, 1922, Wells Papers; Tom Gooch to Hat-

ton W. Sumners, n.d., Sumners to Gooch, April 22, 1922, Hatton W. Sumners Papers, Dallas Historical Society (hereafter cited as Sumners Papers); Thomas B. Love to Barry Miller, July 5, 1922, Love Papers.

6. Culberson to Fisher, March 30, 1922, in *Dallas Morning News*, April 2, 1922.

7. Photograph and "To the Democrats of Texas," Culberson File; *Dallas Morning News*, April 30, May 17, June 18, 1922.

8. Brooks to Pat O'Keefe, September 11, 1926, Brooks Papers; George McBlair to Thomas B. Love, July 18, 1921, Love Papers; Crane to W. O. Davis, April 24, 1922, Martin M. Crane Papers.

9. Connally to Fred Acree, April 7, 1922, Fred Acree Papers, University of Texas Archives (hereafter cited as Acree Papers); John N. Garner to James B. Wells, September 19, 1921, Wells Papers; Rayburn to W. A. Thomas, February 19, 1922, Sam Rayburn Papers, Sam Rayburn Library, Bonham. See also Alfred Steinberg, *Sam Rayburn: A Biography*, pp. 69–70; C. Dwight Dorough, *Mr. Sam*, pp. 170–71.

10. Love to Paul Edwards, September 2, 1920, Love to John T. Duncan, July 2, 1921, Love to William G. McAdoo, August 9, 1922, Love Papers. See also Love to Maco Stewart, November 20, 1920, G. E. Hamilton to Love, June 6, 1921, Love to Hamilton, June 9, 1921, Love Papers. For Ferguson's comment on Love's candidacy, see *Ferguson Forum*, September 8, 1921.

11. Unidentified newspaper clipping, Hicks, Hicks, Dickson and Bobbitt Law Firm Papers, University Archives and Manuscript Collections, Texas A&M University Library (hereafter cited as Hicks, Hicks, Dickson and Bobbitt Papers); Colquitt to Johnson, January 19, 1922, Leake to Colquitt, February 24, 1922, Colquitt to Leake, February 27, 1922, Colquitt to Leake, March 2, 1922, Colquitt Papers. See also *Dallas Morning News*, July 21, 1921; George Portal Huckaby, "Oscar Branch Colquitt: A Political Biography" (Ph.D. diss., University of Texas, 1946), pp. 451–52. On Ousley's opposition to the Klan, see *Dallas Morning News*, April 5, May 12, 1922.

12. Thomas obituary, unidentified newspaper clipping, Sam Acheson, "C. F. Thomas: Texas Centennial Head," *Dallas Morning News*, February 7, 1972, clipping in Cullen F. Thomas Biographical File, Barker Texas History Center, University of Texas (hereafter cited as Thomas File). Thomas's remarks about Bailey are quoted in Gould, *Progressives & Prohibitionists*, p. 264. See also McKay, *Texas Politics*, p. 110. Samuel P. Brooks supported Thomas, though he was "taking no public part in any man's candidacy." Brooks to Thomas, May 24, 1922, Brooks Papers. See also John C. Granbery to Cullen F. Thomas, April 2, 1922, John C. Granbery Papers, University of Texas Archives (hereafter cited as Granbery Papers).

13. Thomas to Bobbitt, February 7, 1921, Hicks, Hicks, Dickson and Bobbitt Papers; Wells to Garner, April 2, 1922, Wells Papers. See also Bobbitt to Thomas, February 16, 1921, Bobbitt to Thomas, September 27, 1921, Thomas to Bobbitt, September 30, 1921, Hicks, Hicks, Dickson and Bobbitt Papers; Thomas to J. J. Faulk, February 4, 1921, J. J. Faulk Papers, Dallas Historical Society (hereafter cited as Faulk Papers). On Thomas's relationship with Senator Sheppard, see Thomas B. Love to William G. McAdoo, August 9, 1922, Love Papers; W. O. Davis to M. M. Crane, August 16, 1922, Crane to Davis, August 17, 1922, Martin M. Crane Papers.

14. Copy of letter in Hicks, Hicks, Dickson and Bobbitt Papers; Thomas to Hogg, September 24, 1921, Hogg Papers; *Ferguson Forum*, September 8, 1921. Thomas wrote William Jennings Bryan that his open letter to the people was the "simple unfolding of my activities and impulses in politics." Thomas to Bryan, August 31, 1921, William Jennings Bryan Papers, Manuscripts Division, Library of Congress (hereafter cited as Bryan Papers).

15. *Dallas Morning News*, April 4, 1922.

16. No biography exists of James E. Ferguson, partly because there are so few personal papers. For Ferguson's autobiographical statements, see Texas Legislature, Senate, *Record of Proceedings of the High Court of Impeachment in the Trial of Hon. James E. Ferguson, Governor*, pp. 491–94; *Houston Press*, October 4–8, 10, 1932. An unsatisfactory dissertation on the Fergusons is Jack Lynn Calbert, "James Edward and Miriam Amanda Ferguson: the 'Ma' and 'Pa' of Texas Politics" (Ph.D. diss., Indiana University, 1968). Ralph W. Steen, "The Political Career of James E. Ferguson, 1914–1917" (Master's thesis, University of Texas, 1929), is recommended. Biographical sketches appear in Fitzgerald, *Governors I Have Known*, pp. 34–36, 50–53; DeShields, *They Sat in High Places*, pp. 411–14, pp. 433–35; Bolton, *Governors of Texas*; James Tinsley, "James Edward Ferguson," in Edward T. James et al., eds., *Dictionary of American Biography: Supplement Three, 1941–1945* (New York: Charles Scribner's Sons, 1973), pp. 266–67; Ralph W. Steen, "James Edward Ferguson," in Webb, Carroll, and Branda, eds., *Handbook of Texas*, 1:590–92; James C. Martin, Jr., "Miriam Amanda (Wallace) Ferguson," ibid., 3:293–94. James E. Ferguson and Miriam A. Ferguson biographical files and scrapbooks are in the Barker Texas History Center, University of Texas. A work by one of the Fergusons' daughters is Ouida Wallace [Ferguson] Nalle, *The Fergusons of Texas: or, "Two Governors for the Price of One."* Two anti-Ferguson publications are [Thomas B. Love], *Fergusonism Down to Date: A Story in Sixty Chapters Compiled from the Records*; and Don Hampton Biggers, *Our Sacred Monkeys: or, 20 Years of Jim and Other Jams (Mostly Jim) the Goat Gland Specialist of Texas Politics. . . .* The cover of Biggers's booklet reads: "This booklet is printed for people of at least reasonable intelligence. The edition is limited." Reinhard H. Luthin has a chapter on the Fergusons in *American Demagogues: Twentieth Century*, pp. 153–81. V. O. Key, Jr., with Alexander Heard, analyzes the Ferguson phenomenon in *Southern Politics in State and Nation*, pp. 261–65. The best account of Jim Ferguson's career to 1920 is in Gould, *Progressives & Prohibitionists*.

17. Worth S. Ray, *Down in the Cross Timbers*, pp. 35–36. Travis is quoted in Jack Elton Keever, "Jim Ferguson and the Press, 1913–1917" (Master's thesis, University of Texas, 1965), p. 40. For the 1914 election, see Gould, *Progressives & Prohibitionists*, pp. 120–49. See also Luthin, *American Demagogues*, pp. 156–59; Charles W. Holman, "'Governor Jim' of Texas," *Harper's Weekly* 61 (September 18, 1915): 279–80.

18. Ferguson is quoted in Nalle, *Fergusons of Texas*, p. 121. Hanger is quoted in Luthin, *American Demagogues*, pp. 162–63. On another occasion Hanger said, "That impeachment was really a victory for Jim. It made a martyr of him, a great figure in Texas politics, and gave him a vest-pocket vote he could depend upon always." *Fort Worth Press*, June 9, 1944. For Ferguson's war with the University of Texas, see Gould, *Progressives & Prohibitionists*, pp. 185–221; Stark Young, "A Texas Pogrom," *New Republic* 12 (August 11, 1917): 45–47; William S. Sutton, "The Assault on the University of Texas," *Educational Review* 54 (November, 1917): 390–409; John A. Lomax, "Governor Ferguson and the University of Texas," *Southwest Review* 28 (Autumn, 1942): 11–29; Ralph W. Steen, "Ferguson's War on the University of Texas," *Southwestern Social Science Quarterly* 35 (March, 1955): 356–62. On the impeachment, see Frank M. Stewart, "Impeachment in Texas," *American Political Science Review* 24 (August, 1930): 652–58; Cortez A. M. Ewing, "The Impeachment of James E. Ferguson," *Political Science Quarterly* 48 (June, 1933): 184–210.

19. Miller is quoted in a statement by John R. Lunsford, manager of the *Ferguson Forum*, in Nathan Orville Robbins, "The Ferguson Regime in Texas" (Master's thesis, George Peabody College for Teachers, 1928), p. 147. See also Gould, *Progressives & Prohibitionists*, p. 236.

20. Ferguson to Hayes [*sic*], September 17, 1920, Ferguson to Harding, September

17, 1929, Harding to Ferguson, September 21, 1920, Harding Papers. On the election of 1918, see Gould, *Progressives & Prohibitionists*, pp. 236–47; William Pettus Hobby, Sr., Biographical File, Barker Texas History Center, University of Texas (hereafter cited as Hobby File). For the American party, see Nalle, *Fergusons of Texas*, pp. 153–55, 158–59; T. H. McGregor II to Dr. H. Bailey Carroll, June 22, 1950, enclosing interviews with Mrs. Ferguson and William P. Hobby, James E. Ferguson Biographical File, Barker Texas History Center, University of Texas (hereafter cited as James E. Ferguson Biographical File); Temple Harris McGregor Biographical File, Barker Texas History Center (hereafter cited as McGregor File).

21. Nalle, *Fergusons of Texas*, p. 161.

22. *Ferguson Forum*, February 2, 1922. See also "Why I Went Back into the Democratic Party," *Ferguson Forum*, March 9, 1922.

23. Ibid., April 6, 1922.

24. Erwin J. Clark to Hiram W. Evans, July 17, 1922, Henry to Dudley M. Kent, June 15, 1922, Alexander Dienst Papers, University of Texas Archives (hereafter cited as Dienst Papers); testimony of Erwin J. Clark in U.S. Congress, Senate, *Senator from Texas*, pp. 63–66. The circular letter is printed in *Senator from Texas*, pp. 49–50. I have followed Clark's description of the agreement in his letter to Evans rather than the somewhat different language of the circular letter. See also Charles C. Alexander, "Secrecy Bids for Power: The Ku Klux Klan in Texas Politics in the 1920's," *Mid-America* 46 (January, 1964): 11.

25. Testimony of Erwin J. Clark in U.S. Congress, Senate, *Senator from Texas*, pp. 67–68. According to Henry, he told Clark: "Unless I can get out into the open and avow my membership and my reasons for belonging to it, I am not willing to continue as a candidate, and I shall retire unless you can get me this permission." Testimony of Robert L. Henry in ibid., pp. 54–55. The Clark-Evans telegram, misdated April 26, 1922, is printed with Henry's testimony.

26. *New York Evening Post*, May 22, 1922, clipping in Ku Klux Klan File, NAACP Papers; *Dallas Morning News*, April 9, 1922.

27. Testimony of Robert L. Henry in U.S. Congress, Senate, *Senator from Texas*, p. 56; *Dallas Morning News*, April 16, 1922; Alexander, "Secrecy Bids for Power," p. 11.

28. Testimony of Erwin J. Clark in U.S. Congress, Senate, *Senator from Texas*, p. 68.

29. Ibid., pp. 46–55.

30. Ibid., pp. 69, 76–77.

31. Clark to Robert L. Henry, June 12, 1922, Clark to Harwood, June 15, 1922, Dienst Papers.

32. Testimony of D. C. McCord in U.S. Congress, Senate, *Senator from Texas*, pp. 376–77; testimony of W. H. Castles in ibid., pp. 989–90; Clark to Evans, July 17, 1922, Clark to Z. E. Marvin, July 3, 1922, Dienst Papers. Clark's letter of resignation was made public. See *Dallas Morning News*, July 20, 1922. See also Alexander, "Secrecy Bids for Power," p. 13.

33. Henry to J. H. Muse, June 18, 1922, Dienst Papers. See also Henry to Dudley M. Kent, June 15, 1922, Henry to F. G. Van Valkenburgh, June 26, 1922, Dienst Papers; *Dallas Morning News*, July 5, 15, 1922.

34. For Mayfield's emphasis on the transportation question, see *Dallas Morning News*, July 10, 15, 1921, February 26, July 3, 1922; Mayfield to Dr. Alexander Dienst, January 4, 1922, Dienst Papers; Mayfield to Mrs. Percy V. Pennybacker, February 6, 1922, Pennybacker Papers. See also McKay, *Texas Politics*, pp. 112–13. The Timmons quotation is from a typescript, dated August 5, 1922, in Bascom Timmons Papers, Uni-

versity Archives and Manuscript Collections, Texas A&M University Library (hereafter cited as Timmons Papers).

35. *Dallas Morning News*, April 22, 1922.

36. Ibid., May 27, 1922.

37. Neff's responsibility for the placing of Ferguson's name on the Democratic ticket is discussed in an unidentified newspaper clipping quoting the *San Antonio Express* in Pat M. Neff Scrapbook, University of Texas Archives (hereafter cited as Neff Scrapbook). See also *Dallas Morning News*, June 13, 14, 24, 27, 1922.

38. *Ferguson Forum*, June 15, 1922; Love to C. W. Jurney, August 3, 1922, Love Papers.

39. *Dallas Morning News*, July 10, 20, 1922. Mayfield was a native of East Texas. "In the race for U.S. Senator, Earl [sic] Mayfield will be the choice of this section of the state," a Tyler resident wrote Neff, "for as you know he was raised in Tyler and East Texas, and his father was during his life one of our most prominent business men. I have inquired repeatedly among the people I have been thrown with from around this County, and the above is the lead I have secured." J. Hall Calhoun to W. H. Knight, July 7, 1922, Neff Papers.

40. *Dallas Morning News*, June 29, July 3, 16, 1922. "Thomas' speech at Taylor puts him entirely out of the running," General Crane argued. "Any man who has not vision enough to see the evil effects of the Ku Klux Klan, if successful, that it will destroy the Government, has not vision enough to be in the United States Senate. His entire campaign from start to finish, has been an apology to the Ku Klux. I will vote for no man, who will not courageously take his stand on the subject." Crane to Judge George M. Hopkins, July 1, 1922, Martin M. Crane Papers.

41. "Formal Withdrawal of Hon. Sterling P. Strong as a Candidate for United States Senator, in favor of Hon. Robert L. Henry: To the Democracy of Texas," two-page mimeographed statement in Robert Lee Henry Biographical file, Barker Texas History Center, University of Texas (hereafter cited as Henry File). The Leddy quotation is from a typescript in Hicks, Hicks, Dickson and Bobbitt Papers. In a letter from J. E. Weeden of the Texas Brewing Company, Fort Worth, to Zane Cetti, president of the company, dated February 13, 1908, Mayfield was designated on the list of holdover state senators as an anti-prohibitionist. "You will find the letter 'A' opposite the ones which the South Texas people insist are favorable to us," Weeden noted. Anti-Saloon League, *The Brewers and Texas Politics*, 1:445–46. See also McKay, *Texas Politics*, p. 113.

42. *Dallas Morning News*, July 18, 1922; "Prohibition Record of Actual Accomplishments," in Earle B. Mayfield, Campaign Materials, Texas State Archives; "Mayfield Just as Good Pro as Any Anti in the Senate," in Hicks, Hicks, Dickson and Bobbitt Papers.

43. *Dallas Morning News*, July 3, 1922; McKay, *Texas Politics*, p. 114.

44. Clark to Wells, May 18, 1922, Wells Papers; *Dallas Morning News*, July 18, 1922. For Culberson's campaign, see Wells to Culberson, April 26, 1922, Wells to Mrs. Waller S. Baker, May 24, 1922, Wells to William H. Clark, May 24, 1922, Culberson to Wells, June 20, 1922, Wells to Culberson, June 26, 1922, Wells to C. W. Jurney, July 18, 1922, Jurney to Wells, July 19, 1922, Wells Papers; Richard F. Burges to Hugh Nugent Fitzgerald, May 19, 1922, Jurney to Burges, July 11, 1922, Burges to Jurney, July 22, 1922, Burges Papers; Thomas B. Love to W. J. Rutledge, Jr., April 13, 1922, Rutledge to Love, April 19, 1922, Love to A. L. Harper, May 5, 1922, Love Papers; Mrs. Percy V. Pennybacker to Culberson, June 7, 1922, Pennybacker Papers.

45. Jurney to House, March 2, 1922, House Papers; Culberson to Wilson, June 21, 1922, Wilson to Culberson, June 22, 1922, Culberson to Wilson, June 24, 1922, Love to

Wilson, July 20, 1922, Woodrow Wilson Papers, Manuscripts Division, Library of Congress (hereafter cited as Woodrow Wilson Papers).

46. *Dallas Morning News*, July 25, 28, 1922. See also Thomas to William Jennings Bryan, November 7, 1922, Bryan Papers. "I am extremely sorry that my friend Cullen Thomas did not act as wisely through the campaign as you and Mayfield did, especially on the klan issue," a Mexia resident wrote Neff. "I wrote Cullen three weeks before he answered Crane's questionnaire, not to pay any heed, he was entitled to receive about one half of the vote Mayfield received and it would have come to him had he not irritated the Clansmen in his utterances." W. S. Parker to Neff, August 12, 1922, Neff Papers. The returns of the senatorial race in the first primary were Mayfield, 153,538; Ferguson, 127,071; Culberson, 99,635; Thomas, 88,026; Ousley, 62,451; Henry, 41,567; Strong (who had withdrawn), 1,085 votes. Heard and Strong, *Southern Primaries and Elections*, p. 133.

47. Harwood's letter is printed in U.S. Congress, Senate, *Senator from Texas*, pp. 78–79. See also Alexander, "Secrecy Bids for Power," p. 13.

48. *New York Times*, July 25, 1922; "The Ku Klux Victory in Texas," *Literary Digest* 74 (August 5, 1922): 14. See also *Dallas Morning News*, July 25, 1922. The Timmons quotation is from a typescript dated August 5, 1922, Timmons Papers.

49. Eugene C. Barker to C. S. Boucher, August 7, 1922, Eugene C. Barker Papers, University of Texas Archives (hereafter cited as Barker Papers). See also Mrs. Percy V. Pennybacker to "My dear boy," July 26, 1922, Pennybacker Papers. For Miller's statement, see *Dallas Morning News*, July 26, 1922; for Culberson's statement, ibid., July 27, 1922. Will Hogg wrote Culberson: "I hope Mr. Miller is misquoted, for I am sure the majority of your friends will resent Mr. Miller's efforts to line up the Culberson forces for Ferguson." Hogg to Culberson, July 28, 1922, Hogg Papers.

50. For Sheppard's statement, see *Dallas Morning News*, August 4, 1922; for the position of Thomas and Touchstone, see ibid., August 13, 1922; for Love's statement, see ibid., July 27, 1922. See also Love to John E. Muckle, August 1, 1922, Love to Mark Sullivan, August 7, 1922, Love to William G. McAdoo, August 9, 1922, McAdoo to Love, August 23, 1922, Love Papers. For other expressions of support for Mayfield from prominent Texans, see Will Hogg to W. H. Gray, August 14, 1922, Hogg Papers; J. B. Cranfill to Morris Sheppard, August 10, 1922, Cranfill Papers; Mrs. Lee Joseph to Mrs. Percy V. Pennybacker, August 9, 1922, Pennybacker Papers; Edward M. House to Earle B. Mayfield, August 16, 1922, House Papers.

51. *Dallas Morning News*, July 30, 1922, for Hobby's statement; Crane to W. O. Davis, August 17, 1922, Martin M. Crane Papers. Bailey is quoted in McKay, *Texas Politics*, pp. 116–17. See also *Dallas Morning News*, July 30, 1922, for Crane's statement giving reasons why he cannot support Mayfield; Crane to H. J. Cureton, July 31, 1922, Hiram M. Garwood to Crane, August 1, 1922, Crane to Garwood, August 2, 1922, Crane to Florence M. Sterling, August 2, 1922, C. L. McCartney to Crane, August 9, 1922, Crane to McCartney, August 10, 1922, Crane to J. W. Fitzgerald, August 10, 1922, W. O. Davis to Crane, August 16, 1922, Crane to S. M. Scott, August 23, 1922, Martin M. Crane Papers.

52. *Dallas Morning News*, August 5–8, 1922; John W. Gaines to James B. Wells, August 9, 11, 1922, Wells Papers.

53. *Dallas Morning News*, August 2, 1922.

54. Ibid., August 3–5, 10, 13, 1922.

55. Ibid., August 17, 23, 1922; John Goodwin to E. L. Shettles, August 10, 1922, E. L. Shettles Papers, University of Texas Archives (hereafter cited as Shettles Papers).

See also John C. Granbery to Earle B. Mayfield, August 7, 1922, Granbery Papers. All of this, however, was nothing to the righteous fulminations of the "moral element" supporting Mayfield. The Reverend Hubert D. Knickerbocker went the rounds of the churches delivering a speech on "The Kaiser, the Devil and Jim Ferguson." Ferguson, he said, was a demagogue, a perjurer, a thief, a hypocrite, a political prostitute, and a wholesale, prolific, and cosmic liar. Moreover, said Knickerbocker, Ferguson's nomination would be "a blow to world prohibition." Quoted in *New York Times*, August 29, 1922. See also Knickerbocker to E. L. Shettles, September 2, 1922, Shettles Papers. "No man who knows him would risk him across the street with a cancelled postage stamp," commented "Pitchfork" Smith. "I wouldn't let him take up a collection in a nigger church if he didn't have but one arm." *Pitchfork* (Dallas), August, 1922, in Wilford B. Smith Papers.

56. *Dallas Morning News*, August 13, 24, 25, 1922. A worker in Mayfield's Austin headquarters testified that he had had the "Mexican circular" printed: "Mr. Ferguson had written a very scathing article on the Mexicans, of which I sent quite a number of those, possibly as many as half a million, to the Mexican boundary." Testimony of J. L. Hunter in U.S. Congress, Senate, *Senator from Texas*, pp. 160–61. See also McKay, *Texas Politics*, p. 118.

57. *Dallas Morning News*, August 22, 23, 1922; Nalle, *Fergusons of Texas*, p. 163; McKay, *Texas Politics*, pp. 118–19.

58. *Dallas Morning News*, August 12, 16, 24, 1922. For the Klan walkout in Waco, see ibid., July 12, 1922; M. M. Crane to George F. Moore, August 17, 1922, Martin M. Crane Papers.

59. *Dallas Morning News*, August 25, 1922; R. C. Merritt to Wilson, August 23, 1922, Wilson to Merritt, August 23, 1922, Woodrow Wilson Papers.

60. *Dallas Morning News*, August 26, 1922; McKay, *Texas Politics*, p. 119.

61. *Dallas Morning News*, August 17, 1922; *Ferguson Forum*, August 22, 1922. See also James E. Ferguson to James B. Wells, August 8, 1922, Wells Papers. Complete returns from 231 counties, practically complete returns from the other twelve reporting are in *Dallas Morning News*, September 3, 1922.

62. Collin County Mayfield Club, "To the Voters of Collin County," in Walter B. Wilson Papers, University of Texas Archives (hereafter cited as Walter B. Wilson Papers); *Ferguson Forum*, September 14, 1922; Dick Vaughan, "Jim Ferguson's Reminiscences," *Houston Press*, October 15, 1932. McKay, *Texas Politics*, pp. 120–21, analyzes the vote.

63. *Colonel Mayfield's Weekly*, March 11, 1922; *Dallas Morning News*, August 29, September 3, 1922; Crane to Marshall Hicks, August 31, 1922, Martin M. Crane Papers. See also Crane to Frank C. Davis, August 31, 1922, Martin M. Crane Papers.

64. *New York World*, August 28, 1922, *Philadelphia Public Ledger*, August 28, 1922, both quoted in McKay, *Texas Politics*, p. 122; *New York Times*, August 29, 1922. Easterners occasionally confused the two Mayfields Earle and Billie. See *New York Times* editorial, July 25, 1922; John S. Mayfield, *Eugene O'Neill and the Senator from Texas*.

65. *Dallas Morning News*, August 27, 1922; Alexander, "Secrecy Bids for Power," pp. 16–17.

66. Bascom N. Timmons, *Garner of Texas: A Personal History*, p. 95; John N. Garner to Tom Connally, July 25, 1922, Tom Connally Papers, Manuscripts Division, Library of Congress (hereafter cited as Connally Papers). See also H. P. Drought to M. M. Crane, June 9, 1922, Martin M. Crane Papers. Friends of Congressman Tom Connally of Marlin advised him not to return home until just before the first primary

because of the Klan Issue. See H. F. Connally to Connally, June 17, 1922, N. W. Goodrich to Connally, July 4, 1922, T. M. White to Connally, July 14, 1922, L. Brann to Connally, July 19, 1922, Connally Papers.

67. Rayburn to Connally, July 28, 1922, Connally Papers. Steinberg, in *Sam Rayburn*, pp. 71–72, quotes Rayburn's election-night concession. See also Dorough, *Mr. Sam*, pp. 171–74.

68. Brooks, *Political Playback*, p. 29; the Ferguson telegram appeared in *Dallas Morning News*, September 5, 1922.

69. *Dallas Morning News*, September 5, 1922; *San Antonio Express*, September 5, 1922, clipping in Granbery Papers. Granbery's account of his role in the convention is found in an unidentified newspaper clipping in his papers.

70. C. M. Dickson to Robert L. Bobbitt, September 5, 1922, Hicks, Hicks, Dickson and Bobbitt Papers; *Dallas Morning News*, September 6, 7, 1922.

71. *Dallas Morning News*, September 7, 1922; *Austin American*, September 6, 1922, clipping in Neff Scrapbook. For the Democratic platform, see Shirley, *Administration of Pat M. Neff*, pp. 71–73.

72. *Dallas Morning News*, September 7, 1922.

73. Ibid., September 7, 8, 10, 16, 17, 1922; Creager to Harding, September 16, 1922, Harding Papers. On Peddy, see *George Edwin Bailey Peddy: A Tribute, 1892–1951*; Richard T. Fleming, "George Edwin Bailey Peddy," in Webb, Carroll, and Branda, eds., *Handbook of Texas*, 3:716–17.

74. Scobey to Harding, June 13, 1918, Frank E. Scobey Papers, Ohio Historical Society (hereafter cited as Scobey Papers); Harding to Elmer Dover, February 18, 1922, Creager to Harding, May 15, 1921, Harding Papers. On the 1920 election, see Paul Casdorph, *A History of the Republican Party in Texas, 1865–1965*, pp. 118–24. For a history of the Texas GOP since 1920, see Roger M. Olien, *From Token to Triumph: The Texas Republicans Since 1920*.

75. *Dallas Morning News*, September 19, 24, November 19, 1922; Henry D. Lindsley to James B. Wells, October 21, 1922, Wells to Lindsley, October 26, 1922, Jurney to Peddy, September 20, 1922, Wells Papers; David G. McComb, interview with Richard T. Fleming, Austin, July 30, 1968. Tuffly Ellis, director of the Texas State Historical Association, kindly lent me a copy of the Fleming interview. See also King, *Joseph Stephen Cullinan*, pp. 211–12. Will Hogg refused to support Peddy. He wrote: "While I have the highest respect and regard for George Peddy and believe he would represent Texas creditably indeed, I think he is poorly advised to run independently or perhaps better stated we should settle present passing perplexities within Democratic party ranks rather than bolt the regular organization." W. C. Hogg to Clarence E. Linz, September 21–22, 1922, Hogg Papers.

76. *Ferguson Forum*, September 28, 1922; T. T. Thompson to James E. Ferguson, November 1, 1922, James Edward Ferguson Collection, University of Texas Archives. For Peddy's role in the 1917 march to the capitol and Ferguson's reaction, see Gould, *Progressives & Prohibitionists*, pp. 203–204.

77. *Dallas Morning News*, September 21, 29, October 7, 24, 1922; McKay, *Texas Politics*, p. 125.

78. *Dallas Morning News*, October 4, 7, 11, 13, 19, 1922.

79. Ibid., October 20–22, 24, 1922. After the trial McNamara's supervisor fired him for "neglect of duty, unauthorized absence from district, arrogant, arbitrary and unauthorized assumption and exercise of authority and generally unsatisfactory service," and "for the further reason that, as long as I am head of this division, no man can with my consent remain in the employ of the division who charges any member of the commis-

sion with falsehood or perjury." J. W. Hassell to Mike McNamara, October 31, 1922, quoted in ibid., November 1, 1922.

80. Ibid., October 24, 27–31, November 1, 3–7, 1922; testimony of J. A. Jett in U.S. Congress, Senate, *Senator from Texas*, p. 193. At a dinner in Roanoke, Virginia, in the summer of 1922, Evans allegedly remarked that the Mayfield campaign had cost the organization between $80,000 and $100,000. Testimony of F. N. Littlejohn in ibid., p. 477; McKay, *Texas Politics*, p. 127. At a rally in Dallas on October 28, Mayfield referred to "the Kangaroo Court down at Corsicana" and "one Hawkins Scarborough, a disgrace to the judiciary of this State, who ought to be impeached." There were cries from the crowd: "Let the Klan have him. Let the Ku Klux Klan get him." Mayfield replied: "They came very near to getting him down at Corsicana. I'd just like to have this judge Hawkins Scarborough tell the people of Texas just what the Ku Klux Klan said to him." The master of ceremonies at the meeting was Tom Love, who delivered a brief "driving attack" on the Republican party and its senatorial candidate. *Dallas Morning News*, October 30, 1922.

81. *Dallas Morning News*, October 12, 1922. See also Morris Sheppard to John C. Granbery, October 14, 1922, Granbery Papers.

82. Unidentified newspaper clipping, Atticus Webb to John C. Granbery, October 19, 1922, Granbery to Henry D. Lindsley, October 29, 1922, Granbery Papers. There are many letters on the Webb-Granbery controversy in the Granbery Papers. On Granbery, see Takado Sudo-Shimamura, "John C. Granbery: Three Academic Freedom Controversies in the Life of a Social Gospeler in Texas (1920–1938)" (Master's thesis, University of Texas, 1971).

83. "Klan Victories in Oregon and Texas," *Literary Digest* 75 (November 25, 1922): 12. See also *Dallas Morning News*, November 8, 9, 1922; Strong and Heard, *Southern Primaries and Elections*, pp. 167–69; McKay, *Texas Politics*, p. 127. "Our victory was a righteous one and will live in the political history of Texas," Mayfield wrote privately, "because it clearly demonstrated that scalawag Republicans and mugwump Democrats cannot even make a dent upon the true and tried Democracy of old Texas." Mayfield to J. J. Faulk, November 17, 1922, Faulk Papers.

84. Heard and Strong, *Southern Primaries and Elections*, pp. 134–36; McKay, *Texas Politics*, pp. 126–27. On Atwell, see William Hawley Atwell Biographical File, Barker Texas History Center, University of Texas (hereafter cited as Atwell File); William Hawley Atwell, *Autobiography*; Casdorph, *Republican Party in Texas*, pp. 124–26. For Atwell's duty in Brooklyn as a visiting judge, see Henry Lee, *How Dry We Were: Prohibition Revisited*, pp. 144–45.

85. *Dallas Morning News*, February 23, 1923; Creager to Harding, November 13, 1922, Harding Papers. See also Harding to Creager, November 17, 1922, William P. Dillingham to Harding, November 20, 1922, Harding to Dillingham, November 22, 1922, Harding Papers. In January, 1922, the United States Senate voted 46 to 41 to adopt a resolution declaring Republican Senator Truman H. Newberry of Michigan entitled to his seat but expressing grave disapproval of the large sum of money spent to obtain his election in 1918 as "harmful to the honor and dignity of the Senate." The Corrupt Practices Act of 1925 was a direct consequence of the Newberry case. In November, 1922, when a new move was launched to unseat him, Newberry resigned from the Senate. William Greenleaf, "Truman Handy Newberry," in James et al., eds., *Dictionary of American Biography: Supplement Three*, pp. 549–51.

86. Mayfield to Thomas B. Love, April 23, 1923, Love Papers. See also Mayfield to Love, November 10, 1922, Mayfield to Love, December 2, 1922, Love to Mayfield, December 12, 1922, Mayfield to Love, December 20, 1922, Mayfield to Love, January 16,

1923, Mayfield to Love, February 17, 1923, Love Papers. For Mayfield's statement branding the Peddy charges as "false from beginning to end," see *Dallas Morning News*, March 6, 1923.

87. For the investigation, see U.S. Congress, Senate, *Senator from Texas*. A concise summary of the progress of the case and the committee's final report appears in Frank E. Hays and Edwin Halsey, *Senate Election Cases from 1913 to 1940*, pp. 200–205. Mayfield told Tom Love: " . . . the unvarnished truth is that there was very little money spent in my campaign and the Ku Klux Klan never put up one thin dime, and this will be fully established in the hearing." Mayfield to Love, May 13, 1924, Love Papers. See also Mayfield to Love, May 9, 1923, Love to Mayfield, May 17, 1924. The hearings are discussed in Rice, *Ku Klux Klan in American Politics*, pp. 68–70; Alexander, *Ku Klux Klan in the Southwest*, pp. 126–27.

88. In describing Culberson's last years, I have drawn on a statement by his secretary, C. W. Jurney, dated March 29, 1925, in *Dallas Morning News*, March 30, 1925, reprinted in Madden, *Charles Allen Culberson*, pp. 230–35. See also House to Culberson, August 16, 1922, Culberson to House, September 27, 1922, House Papers. Madden, *Charles Allen Culberson*, p. 121, mentions the "Personal Reminiscences." For notice of Culberson's death, see *Dallas Morning News*, March 20, 1925. The *New York World* editorial is quoted in C. V. Terrell, *The Terrells: Eighty-five Years of Texas from Indians to Atomic Bomb*, p. 196.

89. Alexander, "Secrecy Bids for Power," p. 16.

Chapter 4

1. "Pat and His Hat," in Frederick L. Collins, *Our American Kings*, pp. 162–78.
2. "Realized and Unrealized Dreams," in Neff, *Battles of Peace*, pp. 241–45.
3. Pat M. Neff, *Speeches Delivered by Pat M. Neff, Governor of Texas, Discussing Certain Phases of Contemplated Legislation*; "Second Inaugural Address," in Neff, *Battles of Peace*, pp. 99–102.
4. *Journal of the House of Representatives of the Regular Session of the Thirty-eighth Legislature Begun and Held at the City of Austin, January 9, 1923*, pp. 64–69, 94–98, 175–78, 196–202, 228–36, 280–87, 397–400 (hereafter cited as *House Journal*, 38 Leg., reg. sess. [1923]).
5. Gantt, *Chief Executives of Texas*, p. 218.
6. Seth Shepard McKay, *Seven Decades of the Texas Constitution of 1876*, pp. 208–209; Shirley, *Administration of Pat M. Neff*, pp. 78–79. See also Cecil A. Tolbert, "A Proposed Constitutional Convention for Texas" (Master's thesis, University of Texas, 1930).
7. *House Journal*, 38 Leg., reg. sess. (1923), pp. 280–87; *Dallas Morning News*, January 24, 1923.
8. *Dallas Morning News*, January 25, 26, 1923.
9. Ibid., February 1, 19, March 4, 1923. The prison system had been operating on a $750,000 loan bearing 7 percent interest from the Brown-Crummer Company; the loan matured on February 1, 1923. At Neff's request the legislature on January 31 authorized renewal of the loan for two years at 5 percent interest and appropriated $827,000 to pay the note at maturity. The system was practically insolvent, and on February 24, Neff requested an immediate appropriation of $900,000 "for the necessary expenses in running the penitentiary until our cotton crop begins to move." The legislature gave him $600,000. On September 30 the State Prison Commission reported that the farms could raise enough cotton to retire the system's outstanding indebtedness and leave a balance

of $100,000 for operating expenses. The system was therefore in the best condition in its history. Ibid., February 1, 25, 1923; Shirley, *Administration of Pat M. Neff*, p. 86.

10. Davidson to Neff, September 9, 1924, Neff to Davidson, September 20, 1924, Neff Papers; *Dallas Morning News*, July 19, 1923; T. Whitfield Davidson, *The Memoirs of T. Whitfield Davidson*, pp. 19–20.

11. *Dallas Morning News*, April 18, 1922; "A System of State Highways," in Neff, *Battles of Peace*, pp. 59–64; Frank M. Stewart, "The Development of State Control of Highways in Texas," *Southwestern Social Science Quarterly* 13 (December, 1932): 211–27; Shirley, *Administration of Pat M. Neff*, pp. 86–90; D. K. Martin to Emma Shirley, January 13, 1937, quoted in Shirley, pp. 110–11; Steen, *Twentieth Century Texas*, pp. 128–30. See also Ruth Ann Overbeck, "Texas Gets Out of the Mud," *East Texas Historical Journal* 12 (Spring, 1974): 23–34.

12. Neff to Fred Acree, September 14, 1921, Neff File; *Journal of the House of Representatives of the Second Called Session of the Thirty-eighth Legislature Begun and Held at the City of Austin, April 16, 1932*, p. 163 (hereafter cited as *House Journal*, 38 Leg., 2d called sess. [1923]); Pat M. Neff, "State Parks for Texas," *Holland's Magazine*, 44 (January, 1925): 1–15; "State Parks," in Neff, *Battles of Peace*, pp. 127–35; A. T. Jackson, "State Parks for Texas," *Texas Monthly* 4 (August, 1929): 63–75; Shirley, *Administration of Pat M. Neff*, pp. 95–96. On the forestry movement in Texas, see Robert S. Maxwell and Robert D. Baker, *Sawdust Empire: The Texas Lumber Industry, 1830–1940* (College Station: Texas A&M University Press, 1983); Robert S. Maxwell, "The Pines of Texas: A Study in Lumbering and Public Policy, 1880–1930," *East Texas Historical Journal* 2 (October, 1964): 77–86; Robert S. Maxwell, "One Man's Legacy: W. Goodrich Jones and Texas Conservation," *Southwestern Historical Quarterly* 77 (January, 1974): 355–80.

13. *Dallas Morning News*, July 13, August 15, 18, 1922, February 1, 2, 1923, March 24, 1925, July 31, 1925; "Water Conservation and Land Reclamation," in Neff, *Battles of Peace*, pp. 49–54; Shirley, *Administration of Pat M. Neff*, p. 109.

14. *House Journal*, 38 Leg., 2d called sess. (1923), pp. 178–79; Stewart, "Movement for the Reorganization of State Administration in Texas," 243–45; Shirley, *Administration of Pat M. Neff*, pp. 79–80.

15. Frederick Eby, *The Development of Education in Texas*, pp. 312–15.

16. Mrs. Percy V. Pennybacker to Margie E. Neal, January 28, 1922, Pennybacker Papers; Eby, *Development of Education in Texas*, pp. 315–16; Neff, *Battles of Peace*, p. 30. See also Mrs. Percy V. Pennybacker to Mrs. Lee Joseph, December 6, 1921, Joseph to Pennybacker, December 8, 1921, Neal to Pennybacker, January 26, 1922, Pennybacker Papers.

17. Eby, *Development of Education in Texas*, pp. 319–21.

18. *Austin American*, March 18, 1923, clipping in Neff File; Shirley, *Administration of Pat M. Neff*, pp. 91–93. The editor of the *Abilene Daily Reporter* wrote Neff: "Personally I don't believe there is any widespread feeling against you because you vetoed the West Texas A.&M. bill. However, when the matter comes up again, West Texas is going to expect your support if you can conscientiously give it." Frank Grimes to Neff, August 21, 1922, Neff Papers.

19. E. L. Klett to Neff, July 10, 1922, Neff Papers; Rush and Nall, *Evolution of a University*, pp. 14–15.

20. *General Laws of the State of Texas*, 38 Leg., reg. sess. (1923), pp. 32–35; *Dallas Morning News*, February 8, 1923; Graves, *History of Lubbock*, pp. 521–22; Rushing and Nall, *Evolution of a University*, pp. 15–24.

21. Hugh Nugent Fitzgerald, "The Thirty-eighth Legislature: Concise Review of

Law-Making Session," and "Under the Capitol Dome—Important Bills Enacted by 38th—," *Austin American*, March 18, 1923, clippings in Neff File; *Dallas Morning News*, February 6, 16, March 15, 20, 1923.

22. *Dallas Morning News*, January 10, 11, 1923. E. L. Covey, a representative from Knox County in this and the next legislature, wrote to me: "During Pat M. Neff's two terms in office, we had but little discussion in the Legislature that members were interested in the KKK, and while I knew Gov. Neff intimately he never mentioned KKK to me. But it is my sincere opinion that the Legislature was divided between the KKK and those opposing the organization." In 1924 the Klan invited the public to attend a parade and rally in a West Texas town. Recalled Covey, "I had the shock of my life when the speaker went to the stage and removed his mask, and he was a Senator whom I had known in Austin." E. L. Covey to author, February 20, 1976.

23. *Dallas Morning News*, January 12, 17, 21, 1923. For Burkett's resolution: Bailey, Clark, Cousins, Darwin, Doyle, Dudley, Fairchild, Floyd, Holbrook, Parr, Pollard, Rogers, Strong, Thomas, Turner, Watts, Wirtz, Witt; against, Bledsoe, Bowers, Davis, Lewis, McMillin, Rice, Ridgeway, Stuart; paired: Burkett (for) and Wood (against), Murphy (for) and Baugh (against); not voting: Woods.

24. Ibid., February 27, 28, March 2, 1923.

25. Ibid., February 10, 1923; Nalle, *Fergusons of Texas*, pp. 165–66.

26. *Dallas Morning News*, May 16, 1923; *Ferguson Forum*, May 24, 1923. Ferguson identified the following eleven senators as "all Ku Klux": J. H. Baugh, W. H. Bledsoe, John Davis, H. L. Lewis, Dan S. McMillin, Tomas G. Pollard, W. H. Rice, L. H. Ridgeway, Robert A. Stuart, Edgar E. Witt, and A. E. Wood. He said that four senators "were sympathizers with the Ku Klux": J. W. Thomas, P. A. Turner, W. E. Watts, and J. H. Woods. Pollard, Thomas, Turner, Watts, and Witt, however, had voted for Burkett's resolution endorsing Governor Parker's anti-Klan stance.

27. *Dallas Morning News*, February 14, June 13, 1923.

28. Ibid., March 4, 1923. Stroder and Dodd are quoted in Patsy Ledbetter, "Defense of the Faith: J. Frank Norris and Texas Fundamentalism, 1920–1929," *Arizona and the West* 15 (Spring, 1973): 58. Stroder's remark about the University of Texas is in Stroder to William Jennings Bryan, January 30, 1924, Bryan Papers. See also Norman F. Furniss, *The Fundamentalist Controversy, 1918–1931*; Joseph Martin Dawson, *A Century with Texas Baptists*, pp. 84–86; Dawson, *A Thousand Months to Remember*, pp. 129–33; Thomas F. Glick, ed., *Darwinism in Texas: An Exhibition in the Texas History Center, April, 1972*.

29. Lawrence W. Levine, *Defender of the Faith: William Jennings Bryan, the Last Decade, 1915–1925*, pp. 277–78, 288–89.

30. Norris to Bryan, March 30, 1923, Bryan to Norris, May 1, 1923, Bryan Papers. Bryan had asked Neff for a copy of the Stroder bill, and the governor had complied, noting that "I would be most happy to be honored with a visit from you, and sincerely hope that I may be accorded this pleasure in the near future." Neff to Bryan, March 16, 1923, Bryan Papers. On Norris, see Owen P. White, "Reminiscences of Texas Divines," *American Mercury* 9 (September, 1926): 95–100; Nels Anderson, "The Shooting Parson of Texas," *New Republic* 48 (September 1, 1926): 35–37; E. Ray Tatum, *Conquest or Failure? Biography of J. Frank Norris*; C. Allyn Russell, "J. Frank Norris: Violent Fundamentalist," *Southwestern Historical Quarterly* 75 (January, 1972): 271–302; Ledbetter, "Defense of the Faith," pp. 45–62.

31. Bryan to Stroder, May 8, 1923, Bryan Papers.

32. *Dallas Morning News*, May 29, 1923; Stroder to Bryan, January 30, 1924, Bryan Papers.

33. Robert W. Hainsworth, "The Negro and the Texas Primaries," *Journal of Negro History* 18 (October, 1933): 426–27; Charles William Grose, "Black Newspapers in Texas, 1868–1970" (Ph.D. diss., University of Texas, 1972), pp. 125–26; Alwyn Barr, *Black Texans: A History of Negroes in Texas, 1528–1971*, p. 134; Ira D. Bryant, *Texas Southern University: Its Antecedents, Political Origin, and Future*, p. 25.

34. H. M. Tarver, *The Whiteman's Primary: An Open Letter to D. A. McAskill*; Paul Lewinson, *Race, Class, and Party: A History of Negro Suffrage and White Politics in the South*, pp. 113, 148; Owen D. White, "Machine Made," *Collier's* 100 (September 18, 1937): 32, 35; Audrey Granneberg, "Maury Maverick's San Antonio," *Survey Graphic* 28 (July, 1939): 425; Andrew W. Jackson, *A Sure Foundation & a Sketch of Negro Life in Texas*, pp. 584–85; Barr, *Black Texans*, p. 134; Dan Carter, "Southern Political Style," in Robert Haws, ed., *The Age of Segregation: Race Relations in the South, 1890–1945*, pp. 61–63.

35. *Dallas Morning News*, March 3, 1923. See also Tom Finty's analysis of the bill in ibid., March 5, 1923.

36. Ibid., April 27, June 2, 1923; *General Laws of the State of Texas Passed by the Thirty-eighth Legislature at Its First, Second and Third Called Sessions: First Called Session Convened March 15, 1923 and Adjourned April 15, 1923, Second Called Session Convened April 16, 1923 and Adjourned May 15, 1923, Third Called Session May 16, 1923 and Adjourned June 14, 1923*, pp. 74–75; Hainsworth, "Negro and the Texas Primaries," p. 427. This provision was amended in 1925 by the Thirty-ninth Legislature and codified as Article 3107. The amended article then read: "In no event shall a negro be eligible to participate in a Democratic party primary election held in the State of Texas, and should a negro vote in a Democratic primary election, such ballot should be void and election officials are herein directed to throw out such ballot and not count the same."

37. O. Douglas Weeks, "The Texas Direct Primary System," *Southwestern Social Science Quarterly* 13 (September, 1932): 114–15; Barr, *Black Texans*, p. 135.

38. *Dallas Morning News*, March 10, 1923; Seth Shepard McKay and Odie B. Faulk, *Texas after Spindletop, 1901–1965*, p. 87.

39. *Dallas Morning News*, March 1, 1923. The other coauthors were H. E. Bell of Coryell County and Robert Lee Bobbitt of Laredo.

40. *Journal of the House of Representatives of the First Called Session of the Thirty-eighth Legislature Begun and Held at the City of Austin, March 15, 1923*, p. 2 (hereafter cited as *House Journal*, 38 Leg., 2d called sess. [1923]).

41. Ibid., p. 3; *Dallas Morning News*, March 11–14, 16, 1923; Shirley, *Administration of Pat M. Neff*, pp. 102–103.

42. *House Journal*, 38 Leg., 2d called sess. (1923), pp. 2, 5–8; *Dallas Morning News*, April 8, 1923.

43. *Dallas Morning News*, April 20, May 5, 15, 1923.

44. *Journal of the House of Representatives of the Third Called Session of the Thirty-eighth Legislature Begun and Held at the City of Austin, May 16, 1923*, pp. 2, 11 (hereafter cited as *House Journal*, 38 Leg., 3d called sess. [1923]); *Dallas Morning News*, May 16, 18, 1923.

45. *Dallas Morning News*, May 23–25, 1923. See also James B. Wells and J. K. Wells to Archie Parr, May 22, 1923, Wells Papers.

46. *Dallas Morning News*, May 24, 25, 1923.

47. *House Journal*, 38 Leg., 3d called sess. (1923), p. 524; *Dallas Morning News*, June 1, 2, 15, 1923.

48. *Dallas Morning News*, March 15, 1923; Neff, *Battles of Peace*, p. 245.

49. Leffler Corbitt to Mrs. Percy V. Pennybacker, May 31, 1924, Pennybacker Papers; *House Journal*, 38 Leg., reg. sess. (1923), pp. 228–36; *Dallas Morning News*, January 25, April 4, May 5, 8, 12, 13, June 5, 16, July 22, 24, August 10, 15, 1923; A. M. Ferguson, *Gov. Neff and His Commission on Text Book Changes*, p. 1; E. F. Smith, *A Saga of Texas Law: A Factual Story of Texas Law, Lawyers, Judges and Famous Lawsuits*, pp 284–304. Smith was one of the attorneys for the American Book Company in the suit.

50. Pat M. Neff to Mrs. Catherine N. Wilson, February 19, 1926, Neff Papers; "The Chatter Box" (1924), newspaper clipping in Neff Scrapbook; Shirley, *Administration of Pat M. Neff*, p. 60; John William Slayton, "The First All-Woman Supreme Court in the World," *Holland's Magazine* 44 (March, 1925): 5, 73; Dean Moorhead, "Texas All-Woman Supreme Court," *Texas Star* 2 (February 11, 1973): 13–14 (magazine section, *Austin American-Statesman*, February 11, 1973). See also Mrs. E. D. Criddle to Mrs. Percy V. Pennybacker, April 17, 1922, W. W. Woodson to Mrs. Lee Joseph, December 11, 1922, Pennybacker Papers. Ruby Kless Sondock was the first woman to serve full time on the Texas Supreme Court. Governor William Clements appointed her in June, 1982, to fill the unexpired term of Justice James Denton, who had died of a heart attack. She was not a candidate to succeed Denton in the general election, and at the end of December, 1982, she returned to Houston to resume her duties as a district judge. *Houston Post*, June 18, 1982; *Austin American-Statesman*, December 16, 1982.

51. Jane Y. McCallum, "Women's Joint Legislative Council," in Webb, Carroll, and Branda, eds., *Handbook of Texas*, 2:929; McCallum, "Activities of Women in Texas Politics," in Adams, *Texas Democracy*, 1:487–93; Mrs. Jane Y. McCallum Scrapbook, 1930–57, Barker Texas History Center, University of Texas (hereafter cited as McCallum Scrapbook); Lorraine Barnes, "Leaders of the Petticoat Lobby [Mrs. Jane Y. McCallum]," *Texas Star* 1 (October 3, 1971): 10–11; Jacquelyn Dowd Hall, *Revolt against Chivalry: Jesse Daniel Ames and the Women's Campaign against Lynching*, pp. 49–50. For a discussion of maternity and child-health work in Texas from 1918 to 1935, see *History of Public Health in Texas* (Austin: Texas State Department of Health, 1974), p. 12.

52. *Dallas Morning News*, August 7, 1923; Walter Prescott Webb, *The Texas Rangers: A Century of Frontier Defense*, p. 551. After conferring with Sheriff Dan Harston of Dallas and District Attorney Shelby S. Cox, both klansmen, Barton said that Dallas was the most morally clean city of the state: "There is less need for rangers at Dallas than any other city in the State. We have one ranger here now, Captain [R. D.] Shumate, and that's all that Dallas needs." *Dallas Morning News*, September 8, 1923.

53. Bentley, "Ku Klux Klan in Texas," pp. 19–21.

54. *Dallas Morning News*, April 28, July 14, 19, August 21, 1923; Chalmers, *Hooded Americanism*, p. 45; J. William Davis, *"There Shall Also Be a Lieutenant Governor,"* pp. 56–57.

55. *Austin American*, September 18, 19, 20, 21, 22, 23, 24, 26, 1923, January 1, 9, 15, 16, 18, 24, 25, 26, 27, 31, February 1, 2, 1924; Garry Scott, "Dan Moody and the Ku Klux Klan," *Southwestern Magazine* 83 (May, 1965): 2–5; M. L. Earle to Honorable District Judge & to the Honorable District Attorney, Whoever you may be, February 3, 1924, Lea Beatty to Hamilton, January 28, 1924, Hamilton Papers. See also "Ruddy Dan Moody, the Texas Crusader," *Literary Digest* 90 (August 28, 1926): 34.

56. Alexander, "Secrecy Bids for Power," p. 17; Middagh, *Frontier Newspaper*, pp. 204–13; *El Paso Times*, April 2, 1981. The figure for the Klan's membership in Texas about the end of May, 1923, is given in Robert L. Duffus, "The Ku Klux Klan in the Middle West," *World's Work* 46 (August, 1923): 363. Other figures: Oklahoma, 104,000; Louisiana, 54,000; Arkansas, 45,000. According to Duffus, "Statements as to the organi-

zation's membership, whether made by friends or foes, usually need to be taken with more than a grain of salt."

57. Pennybacker to Mrs. Henry B. Fall, February 23, 1923, Pennybacker Papers.

58. Hicks to Cook, February 26, 1923, Hicks, Hicks, Dickson and Bobbitt Papers; *Austin American*, February 27, 1923, clipping in Neff File; *Dallas Morning News*, February 27, 1923.

59. *Austin American*, February 27, 1923, clipping in Neff File. See also *Dallas Morning News*, February 27, 1923.

60. Barker to A. C. Kray, May 15, 1923, Ramsdell to Barker, March 4, 1923, Barker Papers; Pool, *Eugene C. Barker*, pp. 125–26.

61. *Dallas Morning News*, May 9, 11, June 6, 1923.

62. Edward Crane to T. W. Davidson, May 12, 1923, Lomax Papers; *Ferguson Forum*, May 17, 1923. See also Lomax to Crane, May 14, 1923, Lomax Papers.

63. Davidson to Crane, May 14, 1923, Lomax Papers; *Dallas Morning News*, February 27, 1923.

64. Davidson later wrote Crane: "In my former letter, I enclosed a short statement as a part thereof, showing how in the minds of many the elevation of Governor Neff to the presidency of the University might at least tend toward bringing peace and stability to the state government, for the next three years. This paper was not intended for general circulation, and I trust that you will treat it as personal and private as the letter itself, as it and one other copy were the only ones used." Davidson to Crane, June 19, 1923, Lomax Papers. See also Crane to Lomax, May 29, 1923, Lomax Papers.

65. Barker to C. S. Boucher, July 13, 1923, Barker Papers; Ramsdell to C. S. Boucher, July 12, 1923, Charles William Ramsdell Papers, University of Texas Archives (hereafter cited as Ramsdell Papers). See also Barker to M. B. Porter, July 13, 1923, Barker Papers. Neff returned to Austin on July 18, after an eighteen-day trip to Panama. *Dallas Morning News*, July 19, 1923.

66. Barker to M. B. Porter, July 13, 1923, Barker Papers. The Stark-Benedict exchange is quoted in Ronnie Dugger, *Our Invaded University*, p. 23. Dugger cites as his sources a letter to him from the late Richard T. Fleming, September 14, 1971, and Anonymous, *Texas Merry-Go-Round* (Houston: Sun Publishing Co., 1933), p. 78.

67. Brother "Railroad" Smith, *A Little Preachment and a Short Epistle to the Bigots of Texas*, p. 19.

68. J. Frank Dobie wrote of his friend Smith: "His figure was as elongated as that of Abraham Lincoln and his countenance was as tristful as that of Don Quixote, though he had a strong laugh in his belly. He had a long-drawn-out voice that was lingeringly pleasant to hear; his eyes could see a long way into space and also into people. He belonged to the liveoaks, mesquites, prickly pear, ranch manners, dry weather, homemade ethics, and take-your-time psychology of Atascosa County, which is down in the Brush Country. . . . He called his place Goat Hill and his friends called him the philosopher of Goat Hill." J. Frank Dobie, *Some Part of Myself*, pp. 266–67.

69. Bailey to Hogg, August 31, 1923, Hogg Papers; Lomax to Richard T. Fleming, October 16, 1923, Lomax Papers; *Dallas Morning News*, August 4, 1923. See also Bailey to Hogg, August 20, 1923, R. H. Baker to Bailey, August 21, 1923, Bailey to Baker, August 22, 1923, Baker to Bailey, August 24, 1923, Lomax to Bailey, August 29, 1923, Bailey to Lomax, August 31, 1923, Hogg Papers.

70. David G. McComb interview with Richard T. Fleming, July 30, 1968; John A. Lomax, *Will Hogg, Texan*, pp. 14–21.

71. Interview with Richard T. Fleming, July 30, 1968. Lomax wrote of Hogg at the meeting: "His tears choked him to silence twice as he begged the regents not to elect a

politician president of the University of Texas." Lomax, *Will Hogg*, p. 46. As soon as he heard that the regents had offered the presidency to Neff, Hogg wired the governor: "While nothing but pity for you and sympathy for the University is in my heart you can do yourself great credit and render a stupendous service to the University by declining to accept the office for assuredly quite a majority of the people of Texas will resent to the utmost the method and manner of your election regardless of any real or fancied qualifications for that particular service which you may possess. Thanks." Hogg to Pat M. Neff, May 16, 1924, Robert L. Batts Papers, University of Texas Archives (hereafter cited as Batts Papers). Stark is quoted in Hogg to D. A. Frank, May 24, 1924, Lomax Papers.

72. Hogg to D. A. Frank, May 18, 1924, Lomax Papers. See also Carltons, Dickson, Fleming, Hill, Hoggs, Picton, Pinckney, Jones, Foster, Logue, Franklin, Rockwell, Carter, Walne, Monteiths to H. J. Lutcher Stark, May 16, 1924, Batts Papers; Hogg to D. A. Frank, May 24, 1924, Edward Crane to O. O. Touchstone, May 16, 1924, Crane to D. C. Bland, May 29, 1924, Crane to Will E. Orgain, May 29, 1924, Crane to Lomax, March 23, 1939, Lomax Papers.

73. Duncalf to Barker, [1924], T. W. Riker to Barker, July 29, 1924, Splawn to Barker, July 12, 1924, Barker Papers; *Dallas Morning News*, May 17, 1924; *Daily Texan* (Austin), May 18, 1924, clipping in Neff File; Brooks, *Political Playback*, p. 53; Pool, *Eugene C. Barker*, p. 128; John Francis Bannon, *Herbert Eugene Bolton: The Historian and the Man, 1870–1953*, pp. 156–70.

74. H. J. Blackmon to Pat M. Neff, July 27, 1922, Neff Papers; Collins, *Our American Kings*, p. 170.

Chapter 5

1. Arthur Krock, "The Damn Fool Democrats," *American Mercury* 4 (March, 1925): 257; William H. Harbaugh, *Lawyer's Lawyer: The Life of John W. Davis*, p. 221. See also David B. Burner, "The Democratic Party in the Election of 1924," *Mid-America* 46 (April, 1964): 92–113; David Burner, *The Politics of Provincialism: The Democratic Party in Transition, 1918–1932*, pp. 102–41. On the convention of 1924, see Robert K. Murray, *The 103rd Ballot: Democrats and the Disaster in Madison Square Garden*.

2. Otis L. Graham, Jr., "William Gibbs McAdoo," in James et al., eds., *Dictionary of American Biography, Supplement Three*, pp. 479–82; John J. Broesamle, *William Gibbs McAdoo: A Passion for Change, 1863–1917*; William G. McAdoo, *Crowded Years: The Reminiscences of William G. McAdoo*. This ghost-written autobiography ends with McAdoo's departure from the cabinet in January, 1919.

3. Broesamle, *William Gibbs McAdoo*, p. 32; Walter Lippmann, "Two Democratic Candidates, I. McAdoo," *New Republic* 23 (June 2, 1920): 10–11. "As I look back over the long road of experience, I realize that the constructive impulse has been the chief motivation of my life," McAdoo wrote in his autobiography. "I like movement and change. I like to make things better, to reshape old forces and worn-out ideals into new and dynamic forms." McAdoo, *Crowded Years*, p. 528.

4. Bryan to Dr. Charles M. Rosser, May 18, 1920, Dr. Curtice Rosser File, Dallas Historical Society (hereafter cited as Rosser File); E. David Cronon, ed., *The Cabinet Diaries of Josephus Daniels, 1913–1921*, p. 488; *Literary Digest* 65 (June 12, 1920): 20–21; Josephus Daniels, *The Wilson Era: Years of War and After, 1917–1923*, p. 553. McAdoo never really had his father-in-law's ear; he was consulted on appointments but rarely on policy matters. "McAdoo remarked that he and the other Cabinet members were nothing but clerks," Colonel House wrote in the fall of 1918. "This is not true of McAdoo, and that is why the President gets along less well with him. He prefers the . . .

type [who are] subservient to him." Diary of Edward M. House, September 24, 1918, House Papers.

5. Love to Daniel C. Roper, May 31, 1920, Love Papers; Burner, *Politics of Provincialism*, p. 61; Gould, *Progressives & Prohibitionists*, pp. 267–69. See also Wesley M. Bagby, "Woodrow Wilson, a Third Term, and the Solemn Referendum," *American Historical Review* 60 (April, 1955): 567–75; Wesley M. Bagby, "William Gibbs McAdoo and the 1920 Democratic Presidential Nomination," *East Tennessee Historical Society Publications* 31 (1959): 43–58; Wesley M. Bagby, *The Road to Normalcy: The Presidential Campaign and Election of 1920*; Burl Noggle, *Into the Twenties: The United States from Armistice to Normalcy*, pp. 190–94.

6. Lee N. Allen, "The McAdoo Campaign for the Presidential Nomination in 1924," *Journal of Southern History* 29 (May, 1963): 213–14; Bernard M. Baruch, *Baruch: The Public Years*, p. 173.

7. On Love, see James A. Tinsley, "Thomas Bell Love," in Webb, Carroll, and Branda, eds., *Handbook of Texas*, 3:540; Sam Acheson, "Tom Love and the Primary Pledge," *Dallas Morning News*, December 15, 1969; obituary, *Dallas Morning News*, 1948, clipping in Thomas B. Love Biographical File, Barker Texas History Center, University of Texas (hereafter cited as Love File); Donna Lee Younker, "Thomas B. Love's Service in the Texas Legislature and in State Government during the Lanham and Campbell Administrations" (master's thesis, Southern Methodist University, 1958); James A. Tinsley, "Texas Progressives and Insurance Regulation," *Southwestern Social Science Quarterly* 36 (December, 1955): 237–47.

8. Love to Wilson, November 8, 1910, Woodrow Wilson Papers; McAdoo, *Crowded Years*, p. 152. See also Gould, *Progressives & Prohibitionists*, pp. 58–84. Love gave his side of the dispute with House to Daniel C. Roper; see Roper, *Fifty Years of Public Life*, pp. 148–49.

9. McAdoo, *Crowded Years*, p. 403; Gould, *Progressives & Prohibitionists*, pp. 168–73, 261–62. Privately McAdoo said of Love: "He is a fine fellow in every respect." McAdoo to Pat O'Keefe, August 22, 1921, William Gibbs McAdoo Papers, Manuscripts Division, Library of Congress (hereafter cited as McAdoo Papers).

10. Brooks, *Political Playback*, p. 69; *Dallas Times*, May 21, 1928, clipping in Love File. Governor James M. Cox of Ohio called Love "a very astute politician." Cox, *Journey through My Years*, p. 265.

11. Woolley to Love, February 21, 1921, Love Papers; *New York Times*, February 9, 1921, "The Fight for Democratic Control," *Literary Digest* 68 (February 19, 1921): 17–18. See also Woolley to Love, November 13, 1920, Robert W. Woolley Papers, Manuscripts Division, Library of Congress (hereafter cited as Woolley Papers); Woolley to McAdoo, February 19, 1921, McAdoo Papers.

12. Cordell Hull, *The Memoirs of Cordell Hull*, 1:113–14; Harold B. Hinton, *Cordell Hull: A Biography*, p. 166; Baruch, *Baruch*, p. 175; Allen, "McAdoo Campaign," p. 212.

13. Woolley to Love, June 21, 1921, Daniel C. Roper to Love, July 11, 1921, Love Papers; Allen, "McAdoo Campaign," p. 213; Burner, *Politics of Provincialism*, pp. 77–78. See also Love to Woolley, June 24, 1921, Love Papers; Woolley to McAdoo, November 7, 1921, McAdoo Papers.

14. McAdoo to Love, November 25, 1922, Love Papers. "It looks to me as if we are certain to make large gains and probably to elect a Democratic Congress in November," Love wrote to McAdoo before the election. "In that event I think definite and active effort should be immediately initiated looking to 1924. There will be no trouble about Texas." Love to McAdoo, September 15, 1922, Love Papers. See also Karl Schriftgiesser,

This Was Normalcy: An Account of Party Politics during Twelve Republican Years, 1920–1932, pp. 127–29.

15. Love to James A. Bordeaux, November 14, 1922, Love Papers; Hicks to Zach Lamar Cobb, February 1, 1923, Hicks, Hicks, Dickson, and Bobbitt Papers; Burner, *Politics of Provincialism,* pp. 103–106. See also Love to McAdoo, November 8, 1922, McAdoo to Love, November 9, 1922, Love to Ben F. Gafford, November 8, 1922, Love to Jouett Shouse, November 24, 1922, Love to Daniel C. Roper, November 27, 1922, Love to Florence M. Sterling, November 28, 1922, Love to McAdoo, November 29, 1922, Love to F. C. Davis, December 1, 1922, Love Papers; George D. Armistead to McAdoo, November 11, 1922, McAdoo Papers. Love wired Woodrow Wilson: "Hearty congratulations on Tuesdays great victory for the things you stand for. It means that the Government will be restored to the people March Fourth Nineteen Twenty Five." Love to Wilson, November 9, 1922, Woodrow Wilson Papers.

16. McAdoo to Love, November 25, 1922, Love Papers. See also McAdoo to Daniel C. Roper, November 25, 1922, McAdoo Papers.

17. Baruch, *Baruch,* pp. 178–79; McAdoo to Earl Brewer, August 3, 1923, McAdoo Papers. For Love's activities in Arkansas, Missouri, and Oklahoma, see Love to Frederick Gardner, December 4, 1923, Love to McAdoo, December 7, 1923, Love to David L. Rockwell, December 7, 1923, Gardner to Love, December 8, 1923, Love to Rockwell, December 11, 1923, Love to Henry W. Dooley, December 13, 1923, Love Papers. At the end of 1923, Love wrote McAdoo that in his judgment "Missouri, Arkansas, Texas and Oklahoma, all of which I have carefully investigated since I saw you, are reasonably safe." Love to McAdoo, December 10, 1923, McAdoo Papers.

18. Davenport to McAdoo, March 8, 1923, Cobb to George D. Armistead, March 9, 1923, McAdoo Papers. See also George D. Armistead to McAdoo, March 8, 1923, Lewis T. Carpenter to McAdoo, April 24, 1923, McAdoo to Carpenter, April 28, 1923. In January, 1923, the Texas House of Representatives adopted a resolution inviting McAdoo to address it at his convenience while in Texas on his return to Los Angeles. McAdoo declined, explaining that he had to rush back to California because of other engagements and personal matters. He said that he hoped, however, to be in Texas again in the spring. C. L. Phinney to McAdoo, January 17, 1923, George D. Armistead to McAdoo, January 18, 1923, McAdoo to Armistead, January 25, 1923, McAdoo Papers.

19. Eagle to McAdoo, February 12, 1923, McAdoo to Eagle, March 9, 1923, McAdoo to Mayfield, November 25, 1922, Mayfield to McAdoo, December 8, 1922, McAdoo Papers. Se also A. V. Dalrymple to McAdoo, December 4, 1922, M. M. Crane to McAdoo, July 26, 1923, McAdoo to Crane, July 31, 1923, Love Papers; Dalrymple to McAdoo, August 7, 1922, McAdoo to Dalrymple, December 11, 1922, Eagle to McAdoo, May 31, 1923, McAdoo to Eagle, July 4, 1923, Crane to McAdoo, August 7, 14, 1924, McAdoo Papers.

20. Walsh to McAdoo, March 13, 1923, McAdoo Papers. See also Walsh to McAdoo, November 28, 1922, McAdoo to Walsh, December 13, 1922, McAdoo Papers.

21. McAdoo to Daniel C. Roper, April 7, 1923, Roper to McAdoo, April 12, 1923, Love to McAdoo, May 4, 1923, McAdoo Papers. McAdoo assured Walsh that Love was opposed to the Klan, had supported Mayfield because he was the party nominee, and was "a fine chap" who was being "outrageously misrepresented." He was not, however, as Walsh seemed to think, McAdoo's political or any other sort of manager. "In fact, I have no political manager and no one is authorized to speak for me politically. I have conveyed your word of caution." McAdoo to Walsh, May 7, 1923, McAdoo Papers.

22. Love to Roper, July 24, 1923, McAdoo to Love, August 1, 1923, Love Papers; McAdoo to George W. Anderson, August 4, 1923, McAdoo Papers; *Dallas Morning*

News, July 15, 1923. See also Marshall Hicks to Larry Mills, June 28, 1923, Hicks, Hicks, Dickson and Bobbitt Papers; Love to Thomas Watt Gregory, July 13, 1923, Love Papers; Love to McAdoo, July 16, 1923, McAdoo Papers.

23. *Ferguson Forum*, July 19, 1923.

24. McAdoo to Roper, April 16, 1923, Roper to McAdoo, April 23, 1923, McAdoo to Love, July 21, 1923, McAdoo Papers.

25. Love to McAdoo, August 10, 1923, McAdoo to Love, August 30, 1923, Love Papers. McAdoo told Samuel Untermeyer that "all this effort to make it appear that the Klan is friendly to me is the meanest sort of politics, inspired by my enemies who know it is false, but who hope that temporarily, at least, they can arouse some prejudice against me." McAdoo to Untermeyer, January 17, 1924, McAdoo Papers.

26. McAdoo to Roper, September 8, 1923, McAdoo Papers. See also McAdoo to Joseph H. O'Neil, August 4, 1923, McAdoo to Roper, August 6, 1923, McAdoo to Love, August 6, 1923, McAdoo Papers.

27. McAdoo to Love, September 18, 1923, Love Papers; *Literary Digest* 87 (June 30, 1923): 6; Burner, *Politics of Provincialism*, pp. 111–12. Sullivan is quoted in Murray, *103rd Ballot*, p. 39.

28. Allen, "McAdoo Campaign," pp. 215–16; *New York Times*, December 5, 18, 1923; *Washington Post*, November 16, 1923; *Literary Digest* 87 (December 1, 1923): 75.

29. On Underwood, see Evan C. Johnson, "Oscar W. Underwood: An Aristocrat from the Bluegrass," *Alabama Review* 10 (July, 1957): 184–203; Evan C. Johnson, *Oscar W. Underwood: A Political Biography*; Oscar W. Underwood, *Drifting Sands of Party Politics* (New York: Century Co., 1928). Underwood wrote Albert Sidney Burleson: "I am almost sure that if I can go to the Convention with a good representation from the South that most of the votes in the Middle West and East will ultimately come to my column, therefore it makes my fight depend on my carrying the larger part of the Southern States." Underwood to Burleson, January 24, 1924, Albert Sidney Burleson Papers, University of Texas Archives (hereafter cited as Burleson Papers). See also Underwood to Burleson, February 28, 1924, Burleson Papers.

30. Love to B. Reagan, December 28, 1923, Love Papers; George F. Milton, "The South and 1924," *Outlook* 136 (January 2, 1924): 29–30. On Underwood's 1912 campaign, see Arthur Link, "The Underwood Presidential Movement of 1912," *Journal of Southern History* 11 (May, 1945): 230–45. On the campaign of 1924, see Lee N. Allen, "The Underwood Presidential Movement of 1924" (Ph.D. diss., University of Pennsylvania, 1955); Lee N. Allen, "The Underwood Presidential Movement of 1924," *Alabama Review* 15 (April, 1962): 83–99; Johnson, *Oscar W. Underwood*, pp. 372–408.

31. Allen, "Underwood Presidential Movement of 1924," pp. 146–47. Veteran Democrat Pat O'Keefe of Dallas advised Governor Al Smith of New York "to let Texas alone as this State is full of the *Ku Klux Klan* and in my judgment it would be a waste of time." If the Smith forces wanted to do something, said O'Keefe, "help Underwood. . . . He is the only one who has a chance to beat McAdoo." O'Keefe to Smith, June 25, 1923, Alfred E. Smith Papers, New York State Library, Albany (hereafter cited as Alfred E. Smith Papers).

32. Oscar W. Underwood to D. A. Frank, October 15, 1923, Oscar W. Underwood Papers, Maps and Manuscripts Division, Alabama State Department of Archives & History, Montgomery (hereafter cited as Underwood Papers); *Dallas Morning News*, October 28, 1923. See also William E. Lea to Forney Johnston, October 18, 1923, Underwood Papers; Allen, "Underwood Presidential Movement of 1924," p. 146.

33. Underwood to Eagle, November 3, 1923, Underwood Papers.

34. Love to Roper, November 23, 1923, Love Papers; Allen, "Underwood Presiden-

tial Movement of 1924," *Alabama Review*, p. 88. For Ball's interview, see *Houston Press*, December 11, 1923. See also Joseph S. Myers to Mark Sullivan, December 3, 1923, enclosed in Myers to McAdoo, December 3, 1923, McAdoo Papers; Love to Daniel C. Roper, September 10, 1923, Love Papers; Thomas Watt Gregory to E. M. House, November 13, 1923, House Papers. A confident Love called Albert Sidney Burleson's decision to support Underwood "really good news" for the McAdoo side. "I really am very fond of him personally, but his opposition to labor, his fight for high telephone rates during the war and his fool wetness combined make his opposition an asset." Love to McAdoo, August 28, 1923, Love Papers.

35. McAdoo to Frederick I. Thompson, March 5, 1923, McAdoo to Roper, February 26, 1923, McAdoo to Thompson, August 6, 1923, McAdoo to Roper, September 8, 1923, McAdoo to Chadbourne, November 30, 1923, McAdoo Papers.

36. Lea to Underwood, December 27, 1923, Underwood Papers. Lea went over the situation with Joe Bailey, who saw things much as he did. "He is afraid of Joe Eagle and his zeal, but told me that between him and Chief Justice Phillips (who will be present) he thought they could hold Mr. Eagle down to Mr. Kirby's viewpoint."

37. A copy of the platform was included in Lea to William H. May, January 2, 1924, Underwood Papers. The signers of the document were John W. Gaines, O. F. Greenwood, Joseph S. Cullinan, Joe H. Eagle, O. M. Stone, Oscar B. Colquitt, Louis J. Wortham, O. P. Gresham, Leonard Tillotson, Joseph W. Bailey, John H. Kirby, D. A. Frank, William E. Lea, H. M. Wade, and C. M. Smithdeal.

38. Lea to Underwood, January 3, 1924, Underwood to Lea, January 7, 1924, Underwood Papers; *Dallas Morning News*, January 1, 15, 1924.

39. *Ferguson Forum*, June 21, July 26, August 2, October 4, 11, November 22, 1923.

40. Ibid., January 3, 1924.

41. Lea to Underwood, February 1, 1924, Underwood Papers; Allen, "Underwood Presidential Movement in 1924," p. 758.

42. *Ferguson Forum*, June 21, 1923; Mills to Love, July 24, 1923, Love Papers. In the Neff Papers is an undated one-page typescript entitled "Pat Neff for President," by Larry Mills of Austin, with a penciled inscription in the upper-lefthand corner: "Written to be used by the Texas delegation if he had been considered for Pres."

43. Bryan to George Huddleston, March 30, 1923, Bryan Papers; *Dallas Morning News*, August 3, 1923. For Bryan's preconvention activities, see Levine, *Defender of the Faith*, pp. 296–307; Paolo E. Coletta, *William Jennings Bryan III: Political Puritan, 1915–1925*, pp. 169–79.

44. Neff to Bryan, August 9, 1923, Bryan Papers. A copy of Bryan's statement is in the Neff Papers. Several of Neff's friends in Texas wrote Bryan to thank him for his recognition of Neff. See J. L. Chapman to Bryan, August 9, 1923, George Sergeant to Bryan, August 9, 1923, John P. Marrs to Bryan, August 11, 1923, Bryan Papers. Bryan wrote a Neff supporter: "Gov. Neff is strong just where Senator Underwood is weak because he is in sympathy with both the progressive spirit of the South and West and the dry sentiment of those sections." Bryan to John P. Marrs, August 16, 1923, Bryan Papers.

45. Bryan to Neff, August 14, 1923, Neff Papers.

46. Bryan to Neff, August 14, 1923, Neff to Bryan, August 25, 1923, Neff to W. E. Spell, September 17, 1923, Neff Papers; Bryan to Ira Champion, August 31, 1923, Bryan Papers.

47. Staples to Lewis H. Jones, November 8, 1923, George L. Bowman to Staples, November 13, 1923, J. W. Madden to Staples, December 14, 1923, Neff Papers. See

also H. C. Randolph to Staples, November 17, 1923, O. H. Poole to Staples, February 22, 1924, Neff Papers.

48. Neff to C. W. Osborn, December 3, 1923, Neff to Bryan, November 6, 1923, Bryan to Neff, November 10, 1923, Neff to Bryan, November 22, 1923, Neff Papers. On "Pat and His Hat," see Neff to Mrs. Gifford Pinchot, October 27, 1923, Gifford Pinchot to Neff, October 29, 1923, Pinchot to Neff, November 1, 1923, Neff to Pinchot, November 5, 1923, Pinchot, Pinchot to Neff, November 10, 1923, Neff Papers.

49. *Dallas Morning News*, December 16, 1923. See also H. E. Bell to R. B. Walthall, December 12, 1923, P. W. Seward to Neff, December 21, 1923, Alva Bryan to Neff, December 18, 1923, Neff Papers.

50. Love to McAdoo, December 17, 1923, Love Papers. See also Love to Marshall Hicks, December 19, 1923, F. C. Davis to Love, December 20, 1923, Love to T. N. Jones, December 26, 1923, Love to B. Reagan, December 28, 1923, Love Papers; W. L. Thornton to William G. McAdoo, December 26, 1923, Murrell L. Buckner to Brice Clagett, January 15, 1924, McAdoo Papers. Hicks's statement is in an undated clipping from the *San Antonio Express*, in Hicks, Hicks, Dickson and Bobbitt Papers. "I feel as though we are going to run this fight in Texas," Hicks wrote Love. "I cannot find anyone who believes that Neff can get much serious following in this State, and most of those who are shouting loudest for him, are doing it simply because they feel friendly to him and not because they think he has any chance to get anywhere in his Presidential race." Hicks to Love, January 13, 1924, Love Papers.

51. "The Neff Boom and Texas," *Austin Statesman*, 1923, clipping in Neff Scrapbook; William E. Lea to Underwood, December 27, 1923, Underwood Papers. It was reported to Love at this time that R. B. Walthall, the governor's former secretary, had stated that the Underwood and Neff forces in Texas would cooperate to secure an unintstructed delegation friendly to Neff and Underwood. Cato Sells to Dr. C. M. Rosser, December 31, 1923, Love Papers. For evidence of Love's hostility to Neff, see Love to Neff, December 31, 1923, Neff to Love, January 3, 1924, Neff Papers.

52. Alva Bryan to Pat M. Neff, December 18, 1923, J. W. Hassell to Neff, December 26, 1923, Neff to Bryan, January 5, 1924, Neff Papers. See also W. E. Spell to Neff, December 23, 1923, Neff to R. A. Gaines, January 3, 1924, A. P. Barrett to Neff, January 10, 1924, J. D. Sandefer to Neff, January 14, 1924, Neff Papers; Samuel P. Brooks to Neff, December 31, 1923, Brooks Papers.

53. *Dallas Morning News*, January 13, 1924.

54. Sells to Dr. C. M. Rosser, December 31, 1923, Sells to George A. Garden, January 11, 1924, Love Papers. See also Bryan to Rosser, January 5, 1924, Bryan Papers. According to Love, "Our old friend Bryan, who is intent on beating Underwood, is unwittingly doing what he can to promote the favorite son movement in various states, which is precisely what the Underwood people most desire." Love to B. Reagan, December 28, 1923, Love Papers.

55. Hicks to Love, January 13, 1924, Love Papers; *Dallas Morning News*, January 14, 1924; Levine, *Defender of the Faith*, pp. 302–303. See also Bryan to A. A. Murphree, November 28, 1923, Murphree to Bryan, December 10, 1923, Bryan to Murphree, January 9, 1924, Bryan Papers; Bryan to Neff, December 22, 1923, Neff Papers.

56. Sells to Hicks, January 31, 1924, Love Papers; Neff, *Battles of Peace*, pp. 251–52, relates the wooden-duck incident.

57. Garner to McAdoo, January 24, 1924, McAdoo Papers. The best study of the Teapot Dome scandal is Burl Noggle, *Teapot Dome: Oil and Politics in the 1920's*.

58. Noggle, *Teapot Dome*, p. 100; *New York Times*, February 2, 3, 1924.

59. Norris to Bryan, February 4, 1924, Bryan Papers; Noggle, *Teapot Dome*, pp. 101–103; Herbert A. Gelbart, "The Anti-McAdoo Movement of 1924" (Ph.D. diss., New York University, 1978), p. 122. See also J. Leonard Bates, "The Teapot Dome Scandal and the Election of 1924," *American Historical Review* 60 (January, 1955): 303–22; David H. Stratton, "Splattered with Oil: William G. McAdoo and the 1924 Presidential Nomination," *Southwestern Social Science Quarterly* 44 (June, 1963): 62–75.

60. Breckinridge Long Diary, February 2, 8, 1924, quoted in Noggle, *Teapot Dome*, pp. 104–105. Sullivan is quoted in Gelbart, "Anti-McAdoo Movement of 1924," p. 123.

61. McAdoo to Colonel E. M. House, March 4, 1924, McAdoo Papers; Baruch, *Baruch*, pp. 181–82; Roper, *Fifty Years of Public Life*, p. 218. See also Diary of Edward M. House, February 9, March 8, 1924, House Papers.

62. Hicks to Rockwell, February 18, 1924, Love Papers; Myers to McAdoo, February 21, 1924, McAdoo Papers. See also Cato Sells to Rockwell, February 16, 1924, Love Papers; Hicks to Sells, February 16, 1924, Hicks, Hicks, Dickson and Bobbitt Papers; Murrell L. Buckner to McAdoo, February 13, 1924, McAdoo Papers.

63. Sells to Love, March 1, 1924, Love Papers; Lea to Underwood, February 16, 1924, Underwood Papers.

64. Sells to Clagett, March 7, 1924, Love to Clagett, March 8, 1924, McAdoo Papers.

65. Clagett to Hicks, March 7, 1924, Clagett to Rockwell, March 8, 1924, Clagett to Love, March 8, 1924, McAdoo Papers; Love to McAdoo, March 8, 1924, Love Papers. See also Clagett to Sells, March 7, 1924, McAdoo to Love, March 8, 1924, McAdoo Papers.

66. Love to Daniel C. Roper, March 18, 1924, Love Papers; McAdoo to Roper, March 26, 1924, McAdoo Papers. See also David L. Rockwell to McAdoo, March 10, 1924, Clagett to Rockwell, March 10, 1924, Clagett to Love, March 10, 1924, McAdoo to Breckinridge Long, March 10, 1924, Rockwell to McAdoo, March 11, 1924, McAdoo Papers; Rockwell to Love, March 10, 1924, Love to Rockwell, March 11, 1924, Rockwell to Love, March 11, 1924, Love Papers.

67. Love to Hicks, March 17, 1924, Love Papers.

68. Hicks to Love, March 17, 1924, Love Papers; *San Antonio Express*, March 20, 1924. In his letter to Hicks, Love speaks of "Frank" getting in touch with "his man" if he had not already done so. See also Marshall Hicks to F. C. Davis, March 21, 1924, Hicks, Hicks, Dickson and Bobbitt Papers.

69. Allen, "Underwood Presidential Movement of 1924," *Alabama Review*, pp. 93–94; McAdoo to Thomas B. Love, March 16, 1924, McAdoo Papers. Murrell Buckner told McAdoo that his answer "on the Klan question was *superb* and has made the Texans of that organization happy." Buckner to McAdoo, March 20, 1924, McAdoo Papers. "The Georgia Democrats administered a stimulant to the McAdoo candidacy," the *Dallas Morning News* editorialized on March 22, 1924.

70. Love to David L. Rockwell, March 21, 1924, Love to Roper, March 27, 1924, Love Papers; Sells to McAdoo, March 27, 1924, McAdoo to Sells, March 27, 1924, McAdoo Papers. See also Love to McAdoo, March 27, 28, 1924, Love to Rockwell, March 27, 1924, Love Papers; McAdoo to Love, March 27, 1924, McAdoo Papers.

71. Love to Roper, March 28, 1924, Love to Roper, March 31, 1924, Love Papers; Roper to McAdoo, April 2, 25, 1924, McAdoo Papers. For Love's fund-raising activities in Texas, see Love to Jesse H. Jones, March 29, 1924, Love to Fred Weeks, March 29, 1924, Love to James Cravens, March 29, 1924, Love Papers.

72. McAdoo to Roper, March 31, 1924, McAdoo Papers. See also McAdoo to

E. M. House, March 27, 1924, McAdoo Papers. On preparations for McAdoo's visit to Texas, see Sells to McAdoo, March 31, 1924, McAdoo to Sells, March 31, 1924, Sells to McAdoo, April 2, 1924, Sells to McAdoo, April 8, 1924, McAdoo to Sells, April 9, 1924, McAdoo Papers; Love to McAdoo, April 1, 1924, Love Papers. Joseph Myers was the first to suggest that McAdoo come to Texas. See Myers to McAdoo, March 23, 1924, McAdoo to Myers, March 25, 1924, McAdoo Papers.

73. McAdoo to Love, March 31, 1924, McAdoo Papers.

74. Evans to Neff, February 1, 1924, Neff to Evans, February 13, 1924, Neff Papers; Lea to Underwood, February 16, 1924, Lea to William H. May, March 24, 1924, Underwood Papers.

75. *Dallas Morning News*, March 6, 1924. Neff sent Bryan a newspaper clipping containing a brief extract from his address in Corsicana. Neff to Bryan, March 11, 1924, Bryan Papers. Bryan warned Neff: "Beware of Davis, of West Virginia. The Wall Street crowd will, I think, shift to him when they find they cannot get Underwood." Bryan to Neff, March 18, 1924, Bryan Papers.

76. Margie E. Neal to Neff, March 7, 1924, Neff to Neal, March 10, 1924, Neff Papers; Neff to John C. Granbery, March 24, 1924, Granbery Papers; *Fort Worth Record*, March 24, 1924.

77. Love to Neff, April 4, 5, 1924, Neff Papers; *Dallas Morning News*, April 12, June 24, 1924. The railroad commissioner's report is in James Ralph Bell to Thomas B. Love, April 27, 1924, Love Papers.

78. *Dallas Morning News*, April 12, 1924. Two days before he announced his tour, Neff told Thomas Watt Gregory that he was very much opposed to an uninstructed delegation. Gregory to E. M. House, April 19, 1924, House Papers.

79. McAdoo to Oscar W. Price, April 10, 1924, McAdoo Papers; *Dallas Morning News*, April 10, 12, 13, 1924. For the reaction of the Underwood forces, see Lea to William H. May, April 11, 1924, L. J. Bugg to May, April 12, 1924, Underwood Papers; Allen, "Underwood Presidential Movement of 1924," p. 160.

80. *Dallas Morning News*, April 13, 1924.

81. McAdoo to Love, April 13, 1924, McAdoo Papers; *Dallas Morning News*, April 13, 1924. See also McAdoo to Marshall Hicks, April 13, 1924, McAdoo Papers.

82. *Dallas Morning News*, April 15, 16, 19, 30, May 1, 1924. See also Governor Pat M. Neff, *Extracts from Address Made by Governor Pat M. Neff at Fort Worth, April 24, 1924*, pamphlet in Neff Papers; unidentified newspaper clipping in Neff Scrapbook. Cato Sells retorted that McAdoo had not campaigned in a single one of the states Neff had mentioned. *Dallas Morning News*, April 19, 1924.

83. Neff's conference with Marsh is mentioned in J. W. Sullivan to Love, April 15, 1924, Love Papers. The Fitzgerald story, undated, is in Neff Scrapbook. Moody's support is indicated in Moody to Neff, April 16, 1924, Neff Papers. At Marsh's request Bascom Timmons wrote an anti-McAdoo column for the *Austin American*. "He does not want it printed until he sees it," Timmons told the editor. "Please notify him." Typescript, April 12, 1924, Timmons Papers. For information on Marsh, who would become a long-time friend and supporter of Lyndon Johnson, see Charles Edward Marsh Biographical File, Barker Texas History Center, University of Texas.

84. Kirby to "Dear Friend," April 23, 1924, Van Watts to "Dear Co-workers and Friends," n.d. (draft), Neff Papers. Huey Long of Louisiana commended Neff's stand: "I will be one of the delegates to our state convention and I am going to take the same stand down there as you are taking in your state. The blood of Cain is on the hands of Mr. McAdoo." Long to Neff, April 17, 1924.

85. R. E. Thomason to Love, April 14, 1924, Love Papers. See also S. L. Gill to Pat M. Neff, April 15, 1924, Henry J. Dannenbaum to Neff, April 19, 1924, Neff Papers; Joseph S. Myers to McAdoo, March 30, 1924, McAdoo Papers.

86. E. W. Lightfoot to Neff, April 28, 1924, Neff Papers; for Neff-Davis break, *Dallas Morning News*, April 21, 1924; for Webb letter, ibid., April 27, 1924; for Johnson telegram, ibid., May 2, 1924; Love to Thomas Watt Gregory, May 8, 1924, Love Papers. "Among our dry forces I find a good deal of bitterness toward Governor Neff for the stand he has taken," Webb wrote Love. Webb to Love, April 29, 1924, Love Papers. See also H. C. Randolph to Neff, April 7, 1924, T. R. Deupree to Neff, April 18, 1924, John P. Marrs to Neff, April 28, 1924, Ben B. Hunt to Neff, April 28, 1924, Neff Papers. The Democratic State Executive Committee, which had endorsed Neff in December, 1923, now switched to McAdoo. When the committee members were polled by W. L. Thornton, fifteen favored instructions for the Californian, two favored instructions for Underwood, three said that they were opposed to instructing for McAdoo, and two favored sending an uninstructed delegation. *Dallas Morning News*, May 1, 2, 1924.

87. *Ferguson Forum*, April 17, May 1, 1924; *Dallas Morning News*, May 2, 1924. Ferguson offered to divide time with Love in an address in Fort Worth. James E. Ferguson to Love, April 29, 1924, Love Papers. See also Allen, "Democratic Presidential Primary of 1924 in Texas," p. 485.

88. Hicks to McAdoo, April 17, 1924, McAdoo Papers; Love to Webb, April 21, 1924, Love Papers. See also Marshall Hicks to W. L. Thornton, April 17, 1924, Hicks to Daniel C. Roper, April 17, 1924, Hicks, Hicks, Dickson and Bobbitt Papers; Love to McAdoo, April 17, 1924, McAdoo Papers; Love to McAdoo, April 19, 1924, Love to Roper, April 25, 1924, Love Papers.

89. *Dallas Morning News*, April 26, 27, 1924.

90. Ibid., April 29, 1924; McAdoo to Love, April 29, 1924, McAdoo to Love, May 3, 1924, Love Papers. When a *Dallas Morning News* reporter asked Neff in Houston if he would reply to Love's criticism, the governor asked him when the next train left for Austin. When the question was immediately repeated, Neff said, "I am returning to Austin on an 11 o'clock train." *Dallas Morning News*, May 1, 1924. Love commented: "Neff has not answered my skinning, but I understand is to do so tonight at Palestine, the idea being that I will have no chance to answer him before the primaries tomorrow. I think he is a dead duck." Love to Daniel C. Roper, May 2, 1924, Love Papers.

91. Lea to Underwood, February 1, 16, 1924, Underwood Papers; Allen, "Underwood Presidential Movement of 1924," pp. 154–55. For Lea's organization activities, see Lea to Richard F. Burges, February 13, 1924, Burges Papers; Lea to Albert Sidney Burleson, March 26, 1924, Lea to Judge Victor Brooks, March 26, 1924, Burleson Papers.

92. Lea to William H. May, March 24, 1924, Underwood Papers; Lea to Burleson, March 26, 1924, Burleson Papers. Lea had hailed Underwood's primary victory in Alabama as "the first step in the march to the White House" and told the senator's Washington headquarters that success in Georgia would have a great effect on Texas voters and would make almost certain a solid Underwood delegation from the South. Lea to May, March 12, 1924, Underwood Papers. See also Lea's statement in *Dallas Morning News*, March 15, 1924.

93. Lea to Underwood, April 23, 1924, Underwood to Lea, April 24, 1924, Underwood Papers; *Dallas Morning News*, May 2, 1924; W. H. Lamar to Albert Sidney Burleson, April 16, 1924, Burleson Papers; Allen, "Democratic Presidential Primary Election of 1924 in Texas," p. 483. Burleson thought that Underwood would be the "hardest to nominate" but the "easiest to elect." "I am doing all I can for Underwood but with the

KKK, Pros' women, and Labor in the Political Machine headed by Love and Davis all for McAdoo it makes the situation difficult," he confessed. Burleson to [Ruskin McCardle], April 7, 1924, Burleson Papers. See also Adrian Norris Anderson, "Albert Sidney Burleson: A Southern Politician in the Progressive Era" (Ph. D. diss., Texas Technological College, 1967), p. 277.

94. *Dallas Morning News*, May 3, 1924. On the Underwood-Neff fusion, see J. J. Faulk to Love, May 6, 1924, Joseph S. Myers to Love, May 5, 1924, Love Papers. A McAdoo supporter in Travis County (Austin) wrote Love about his county convention: "When we met Tuesday morning [May 6] there were not enough of us to make any effective opposition to the steam roller dominated by the Harper Kirby, Pat Neff, Sam Sparks, Ferguson, Underwood combination." A. T. McKean to Love, May 8, 1924, Love Papers.

95. Sells to Rockwell, May 16, 1924, McAdoo Papers; McAdoo to Love, May 8, 1924, Love Papers; McAdoo to Thomas Watt Gregory, May 6, 1924, Thomas Watt Gregory Papers, Manuscripts Division, Library of Congress (hereafter cited as Gregory Papers, Library of Congress); *Dallas Morning News*, May 7, 1924.

96. Love to G. T. Shires, May 14, 1924, Love Papers; Spell to Neff, May 7, 1924, Neff Papers; *Dallas Morning News*, May 7, 1924.

97. Neff to Silliman Evans, May 12, 1924, Neff Papers; *Dallas Morning News*, May 6, 1924.

98. *Dallas Morning News*, May 6, 1924; *Houston Post*, May 5, 1924; Allen, "Underwood Presidential Movement of 1924," pp. 161–62. A copy of this Klan handbill is in the Love Papers. For an account of the Neff-Klan struggle in the Bell County convention, see J. W. Thomas to Pat M. Neff, May 6, 1924, Neff Papers. Thomas succeeded in having the Klan resolution instructing for McAdoo tabled by a vote of 178 to 137.

99. Lea to Richard F. Burges, May 12, 1924, Burges Papers; Allen, "Underwood Presidential Movement of 1924," p. 162. Underwood and Carlin are quoted in Murray, *The 103rd Ballot*, p. 90.

100. Love to Chadbourne, May 8, 1924, Love Papers; *Dallas Morning News*, May 15, 1924. Two years later Love wrote, "There was never a suggestion to me, in any quarter, directly or indirectly of any 'trade' with respect either to the election of National Committeeman from Texas or the election instruction of a McAdoo delegation from Texas, in connection with my support of Robertson for Governor in 1924." Love to John C. Granbery, August 7, 1926, Love Papers.

101. Myers to Love, April 1, 1924, Love to Myers, April 3, 1924, Love Papers; Cato Sells to McAdoo, January 30, 1924, Myers to McAdoo, March 30, 1924, McAdoo Papers. See also Myers to Love, November 16, 1924, Hanger to Myers, November 25, 1924, Love Papers. A Houston resident wrote Al Smith after the Democratic National Convention that "we did all we could to help put you across, but the deal between the Ku Klux Klan and the representatives of the McAdoo interest in Texas was of such a nature that it was impossible to influence them in any respect. I had some good friends on the Delegation, who were not Kluxers, but the terms of the trade made between them were to the effect that they were to stay hitched to McAdoo for all time in exchange for an endorsement by the McAdoo men who were not Kluxers to support the Klux State ticket in Texas." Robert E. Goree to Alfred E. Smith, July 17, 1924, George B. Graves Papers, Franklin D. Roosevelt Presidential Library, Hyde Park, New York (hereafter cited as Graves Papers). James Cox claimed that "there was not only tacit consent to the Klan's support, but it was apparent that he [McAdoo] and his major supporters were conniving with the Klan." Cox, *Journey through My Years*, p. 324.

102. Claude Bowers, *My Life: the Memoirs of Claude Bowers*, p. 114; Stanley

Frost, "Democratic Dynamite," *Outlook* 137 (June 18, 1924): 267; Burner, "Democratic Party in the Election of 1924," p. 100. Arthur Mullen, McAdoo's manager in Nebraska, advised him to come out against the Klan and at his request wrote a statement on May 22, 1924, for him to release. According to Mullen, "Tom Love of Texas and others influenced him, by arguments about political expediency, to hold back from statement." Meeting McAdoo in the Blackstone Hotel in Chicago the same month, Mullen again urged him to denounce the Klan. McAdoo said that he was not and never had been for the Klan and that he would think it over. "Tom Love got to him again and he stayed silent." Arthur F. Mullen, *Western Democrat*, pp. 242–43. Contrary to Mullen, McAdoo's decision to remain silent on the Klan was his own, as an examination of his papers proves. See, for example, McAdoo to Roper, April 14, 1924, McAdoo Papers. "The attempt to create the Klan issue, as far as I am concerned, is purely a contemptible Underwood device to injure me if possible in states where Catholic sentiment is strong," he told Roper.

103. Allen, "Democratic Presidential Primary of 1924 in Texas," p. 488. On April 25, Daniel Roper had written Love: "I have the feeling that winning an instructed delegation from Texas is most vital at this time. I can sense that the McAdoo impetus on account of the victory in Georgia is now some what subsiding and there is now needed the impetus of a Texas victory to give the movement a forward shove again." Roper to Love, April 25, 1924, Love Papers.

104. McAdoo to Lewis C. Humphrey, May 5, 1924, McAdoo Papers. "We had a wonderful victory in Texas, in spite of the unscrupulous fight that was made by the Underwood forces and that cur of a Governor, Neff, but we licked them to a frazzle." McAdoo to Bernard Baruch, May 6, 1924, McAdoo Papers. McAdoo stopped briefly in Austin on May 9 on the way to Tennessee, assuring his audience at the train station that his victory in Texas secured his nomination. Neff was out of the city, but his secretary delivered his greeting to McAdoo. The candidate said, "I thank you," and placed the note, unread, in his pocket. *Dallas Morning News*, May 10, 1924. The word "most" in the sentence "I extend to you a most cordial welcome to Texas" is struck through in the draft copy. Neff to McAdoo, May 8, 1924, Neff Papers.

105. Allen, "Underwood Presidential Movement of 1924," *Alabama Review*, p. 96.

106. Love to Thomas Watt Gregory, May 31, 1924, Love Papers; *Dallas Morning News*, May 27, 28, 1924; Alexander, *Ku Klux Klan in the Southwest*, pp. 165–66, gives the two-thirds figure. See also Love to McAdoo, May 28, 1924, Love Papers.

107. J. A. Donnell to Love, May 10, 1924, Love Papers; *Dallas Morning News*, May 4, 5, 7, 8, 10, 1924. See also Owsley to J. N. Rayzor, May 5, 1924, Owsley to James Ralph Bell, May 5, 1924, Bell to Love, May 9, 1924, J. W. Sullivan to Love, May 9, 10, 1924, Love Papers. Love was told, "I have no doubt that at heart, while the son would be willing to 'teach her round or flat,' he [Owsley] really believes his chances to realize his ambition would come through the nomination of Governor Al Smith." J. W. Sullivan to Love, May 23, 1924, Love Papers.

108. McAdoo to Love, May 24, 1924, Love Papers. On Granbery's resolution, see Granbery to Love, May 19, 1924, Love Papers; *Austin American*, May 30, 1924, clipping in Granbery Papers; *Dallas Morning News*, May 27, 28, 1924. Hanger's role is described in an unidentified newspaper clipping, Neff Scrapbook.

109. Davis to McAdoo, May 29, 1924, McAdoo Papers; Love to McAdoo, May 31, 1924, Love Papers; *Texas Tail Twister* (Fort Worth) 1, no. 8 (June 15, 1924), Ku Klux Klan File, Campaign Materials, Texas State Archives (hereafter cited Ku Klux Klan File, Texas State Archives). See also Cato Sells to David L. Rockwell, June 4, 1924, McAdoo Papers. On Neff's "Game Sport" title, see unidentified newspaper clipping in Neff Scrapbook.

For letters commending Neff's conduct at Waco, see Elmer Graham to Neff, May 28, 1924, William E. Lea to Neff, n.d., Margie E. Neal to Neff, June 12, 1924, Neff Papers.

110. Neff to Margie E. Neal, June 17, 1924, Jurney to Neff, June 14, 1924, Marsh to Neff, June 14, 17, 1924, Neff Papers; *Dallas Morning News*, June 18, 23–25, 30, 1924. Neff wired Marsh and Jurney in New York asking what they thought of McAdoo's chances. Neff to Marsh, June 14, 1924, Neff to Jurney, June 14, 1924, Neff Papers.

111. *Dallas Morning News*, June 22, 1924. See also Hal L. Brennan to Robert L. Bobbitt, June 22, 1924, Hicks to Bobbitt, June 25, 1924, Hicks, Hicks, Dickson and Bobbitt Papers. The last five words of Hicks's telegram are taken from "Jim Bludso," a poem by John Hay about a Mississippi steamboat pilot who beached his burning ship on a "willer-bank." *Austin Statesman*, June 23, 1924.

112. *Dallas Morning News*, June 22, 28, 1924. In the John W. Davis Papers, in Yale University Library, are a number of letters from Texas, several from classmates of Davis at Washington and Lee University, expressing support for his candidacy. At least three Texans—P. W. Reeves, W. B. Paddock, and Sam Lowrey—wrote letters to members of the Texas delegation commending Davis in the event that McAdoo did not gain the nomination. See A. H. McKnight to Davis, January 21, 1924, Sam C. Lowrey to Davis, January 21, June 9, 12, July 2, 1924, Lowrey to Tom Gambrell (delegate), June 9, 12, July 2, 1924, J. W. Sullivan to Davis, February 6, 1924, P. W. Reeves to Davis, April 2, May 11, 16, June 6, 1924, Reeves to T. M. Campbell, Jr. (delegate), June 3, 1924, H. W. Garrow to Davis, May 21, June 5, 1924, W. B. Paddock to Davis, June 10, 17, 1924, Paddock to Cato Sells (delegate), June 10, 1924, Ireland Graves to Davis, June 23, 1924, John W. Davis Papers, Manuscripts and Archives, Yale University Library (hereafter cited as John W. Davis Papers). Colonel House was quietly pushing Davis and Carter Glass of Virginia to the fore. Diary of Edward M. House, April 10, 1924, House Papers. Although four of Davis's Texas correspondents—Graves, Lowrey, Paddock, and Sullivan—were lawyers, William Harbaugh's statement in his biography of Davis that "in Texas the legal community swung behind him almost as a body" is not supported by the evidence in the John W. Davis Papers. Harbaugh, *Lawyer's Lawyer*, p. 200.

113. Alexander, *Ku Klux Klan in the Southwest*, pp. 167–68; *Dallas Morning News*, June 24, 1924. Brennan is quoted in George Fort Milton to Thomas J. Walsh, December 15, 1924, Thomas J. Walsh Papers, Manuscripts Division, Library of Congress (hereafter cited as Walsh Papers). The question was asked by Urey Woodson, national committeeman from Kentucky. *Baltimore Sun*, June 26, 1924, quoted in Gelbart, "Anti-McAdoo Movement of 1924," p. 208. Texans were shocked to learn that the block of the "Avenue of the States" dedicated to the Lone Star State contained Saint Patrick's Cathedral. Murray, *The 103rd Ballot*, p. 105. When Evans fell ill of ptomaine poisoning, klansmen from the Texas delegation wanted to burn a cross outside the convention hall but were prevented by police. Burner, *Politics of Provincialism*, p. 116.

114. *Dallas Morning News*, June 29, 30, 1924. The mayor of El Paso congratulated Mrs. Ames on her opposition to the Klan. R. M. Dudley to Ames, July 3, 1924, Mrs. Jesse Daniel Ames Papers, Dallas Historical Society (hereafter cited as Ames Papers, Dallas Historical Society). H. L. Mencken, who was covering the convention, wrote Maury Maverick: "At least 30% of the delegates are Ku Kluxers. Whenever they see a priest they shiver." Mencken to Maverick, July 2, 1924, Maury Maverick, Sr., Papers, University of Texas Archives (hereafter cited as Maverick Papers).

115. *Dallas Morning News*, July 1, 2, 4, 7, 10, 1924; Baruch, *Baruch*, p. 183. The former secretary of Congressman Eugene Black of Texas wrote Franklin D. Roosevelt after the convention: "To say that the Texas delegation's attitude was aggravating is not half expressing it. At several stages of the Convention the delegates wavered and would

have left McAdoo had one or two delegates come over. But they were receiving their orders from Imperial Wizard Evans from the Vanderbilt Hotel and we could not move them." P. W. Reeves to Roosevelt, August 20, 1924, Franklin Delano Roosevelt Papers, 1920–28: General Political Correspondence, 1921–28, group 11, box 6, Roosevelt Presidential Library, Hyde Park, N.Y. (hereafter cited as Roosevelt Papers).

116. Love to House, December 23, 1925, House to Love, December 29, 1925, Love Papers. See also House to T. W. Gregory, October 20, 1924, Gregory Papers, Library of Congress; Edward M. House Diary, November 20, 1923, House Papers.

117. *Dallas Morning News*, July 10, 11, 1924; Allen, "Democratic Presidential Primary of 1924 in Texas," p. 492; Adams, *Alvin M. Owsley of Texas*, p. 113. As early as May, 1924, P. W. Reeves had predicted that "the McAdoo delegates in Texas would go to Davis in preference to Underwood or Smith" and that "once Texas swings to Jno. W. Davis, the other Southern States would follow." Reeves to Louis A. Johnson, May 16, 1924, Davis Papers. See also Thomas Watt Gregory to Edward M. House, May 10, 1924, House Papers. On Davis's shifting fortunes in the convention, see Harbaugh, *Lawyer's Lawyer*, pp. 211–16.

118. Frank C. Davis to John W. Davis, August 9, 1924, T. M. Campbell, Jr., to Davis, August 9, 1924, Jesse Daniel Ames to Davis, August 9, 1924, John Davis to Davis, August 13, 1924, Mike T. Lively to Davis, August 15, 1924, T. F. Harwood to Davis, August 16, 1924, Marshall Hicks to Davis, August 20, 1924, Joseph W. Bailey to Davis, August 22, 1924, C. B. Hudspeth to Davis, August 23, 1924, Thomas L. Blanton to Davis, August 25, 1924, J. J. Mansfield to Davis, August 25, 1924, John W. Davis Papers; Neff to Davis, July 12, 1924, Davis to Neff, July 23, 1924, Neff Papers; *Dallas Morning News*, July 10, 11, September 17, October 16, 1924. For Love's effort to keep Neff from speaking, see Love to Daniel C. Roper, July 30, 1924, Love Papers. On Jesse Jones as director of finance, see Jones to Frank Freidel, May 29, 1953, Jesse H. Jones Papers, University of Texas Archives (hereafter cited as Jones Papers); Bascom Timmons, *Jesse H. Jones: The Man and the Statesman*, pp. 135–40.

119. Warner Moore to John C. Granbery, September 8, 1924, Granbery Papers; *Dallas Morning News*, October 17, 1924, McKay, *Texas Politics*, pp. 142–44.

120. Davis to Bryan, November 11, 1924, Bryan Papers; Eugene Robinson, *The Presidential Vote, 1896–1932*, pp. 23–24. For an account of the Davis campaign, see Harbaugh, *Lawyer's Lawyer*, pp. 217–48. Davis's speeches failed to arouse his audiences. He blamed his legal background. All his life, he explained to House, he had been trying to eliminate the emotions from his briefs and addresses to the courts, and it was impossible at this late day to put this quality in his speeches for political effect. Edward M. House Diary, October 15, 1924, House Papers. See also Robert W. Woolley to House, October 10, 1930, House Papers.

121. Elmer Graham to Davis, September 5, 1924, John W. Davis Papers.

122. Alexander, *Ku Klux Klan in the Southwest*, p. 165.

Chapter 6

1. *Colonel Mayfield's Weekly*, December 1, 1923; Alexander, *Ku Klux Klan in the Southwest*, pp. 192–93. The paper estimated Klan membership in Texas at "close to 189,000."

2. *Colonel Mayfield's Weekly*, November 10, 17, December 1, 15, 1923, January 5, 1924; *Dallas Morning News*, December 3, 1923, January 6, 1924; *San Antonio Express*, February 11, 1924, clipping in Mrs. Miriam A. Ferguson Biographical File, Barker Texas History Center (hereafter cited as Mrs. Miriam A. Ferguson File). See also Marshall

Hicks to S. B. Hicks, December 8, 1923, Hicks, Hicks, Dickson and Bobbitt Papers. On Mayfield, see Ed Kilman, "Saga of Billie the KKK Kid," *Houston Post*, June 24, 1962, clipping in Billie Mayfield Biographical File, Barker Texas History Center, University of Texas (hereafter cited as Mayfield file).

3. Alexander, *Ku Klux Klan in the Southwest*, pp. 193–94. Collins's statement concerning his suspension from the Klan appears in *Dallas Morning News*, March 10, 1924. As recently as December 14, 1923, Robertson had been conducting a statewide campaign for a delegate-at-large seat on the Texas delegation to the national convention. Robertson to J. J. Faulk, December 14, 1923, Faulk Papers.

4. *Colonel Mayfield's Weekly*, February 2, 9, 16, 23, March 1, 1924; *Texas 100 Per Cent American* (Dallas), February 15, 1924; Alexander, *Ku Klux Klan in the Southwest*, pp. 194–95.

5. *Colonel Mayfield's Weekly*, March 22, 1924; Alexander, *Ku Klux Klan in the Southwest*, pp. 195–96. See also Torrence, "Ku Klux Klan in Dallas," p. 76. "Mayfield's debacle fills me with sorrow," wrote H. L. Mencken. "His paper gave me some capital Americana." Mencken to Maury Maverick, March 25, 1924, Maverick Papers.

6. *Dallas Morning News*, January 14, 1944 (obituary), clipping in Felix D. Robertson Biographical File, Barker Texas History Center, University of Texas (hereafter cited as Robertson Biographical File).

7. "Platform of Felix D. Robertson, Candidate for Democratic Nomination for Governor" (broadside), 1924, Robertson Biographical File; *Dallas Morning News*, January 13, March 2, 27, 1924. On July 9, Love announced in New York City that he was for Robertson "because I believe that his candidacy offers the best hope of getting the State out of difficulties." *Dallas Morning News*, July 10, 1924.

8. *Dallas Morning News*, July 15, 18, 25, 1924.

9. *San Antonio Express*, February 11, 1924, clipping in James E. Ferguson Biographical File; *Dallas Morning News*, April 11, 1924. Collins charged that Robertson, who claimed that he had always been a prohibitionist, had been endorsed by the brewery interests as an antiprohibitionist when he was a candidate for the legislature from McLennan County. He quoted a letter from the general attorney for Texas breweries to the president of the Texas Brewers' Association in the Anti-Saloon League's *The Brewers and Texas Politics*, 1:393. *Dallas Morning News*, May 8, 1924.

10. Barton to J. J. Faulk, June 29, 1923, Faulk Papers; Barton to Major Humes B. Galbraith, June 29, 1923, Wayne Davis to Felix Robertson, July 15, 1924, Wells Papers; *San Antonio Express*, February 11, 1924, clipping in James E. Ferguson Biographical File; Brooks, *Political Playback*, p. 11. See also Davis to Galbraith, April 25, May 7, July 15, 1923, Wells Papers.

11. *San Antonio Express*, February 11, 1924, clipping in James E. Ferguson Biographical File. On Burkett's campaign, see *Dallas Morning News*, June 24, 1923, clipping in Joe Burkett Biographical File, Barker Texas History Center (hereafter cited as Burkett File); *Dallas Morning News*, January 4, April 6, May 8, July 20, 1924. Senator H. L. Darwin of Paris entered the race but later withdrew, as did Charles E. Baughman, the state commissioner of warehouses and markets. *Dallas Morning News*, December 27, 1923, February 5, 1924.

12. *Ferguson Forum*, March 15, 1923.

13. Ibid., March 29, 1923. See also Biggers, *Our Sacred Monkeys*, pp. 62–63. Billie Mayfield predicted: "Next campaign Jim will be parading the state as the arch enemy of the Jew and hurling anathemas upon their heads with all the venom of his vindictive nature." *Colonel Mayfield's Weekly*, March 31, 1923.

14. *Ferguson Forum*, July 19, December 13, 1923.

15. Ibid., December 13, 1923.

16. *Dallas Morning News*, January 20, 1924; *Ferguson Forum*, January 24, 1924.

17. *Houston Press*, October 15, 1932.

18. Fitzgerald's column is reprinted in *Ferguson Forum*, January 31, 1924. Mayfield declared that "Jim has got a following of 125,000 peons who can't be alienated with moral suasion or dynamite . . . in his satchel, and they are good for one vote and a touch every two years. Add the Catholic vote of 65,000 to that and you have got enough to put Jim in the second primary." *Colonel Mayfield's Weekly*, January 26, 1924.

19. *Dallas Morning News*, May 6, 11, 18, 29, June 1, 1924. See also *Ferguson Forum*, May 15, June 5, 1924.

20. *Dallas Morning News*, June 6, 13, 1924. According to T. Whitfield Davidson: "Ferguson's campaign manager complimented the appointments, but after they held against him he indicated to his friends that the Supreme Court had been stacked against him. In fact, neither of these men had expressed any opinion except after the case was heard by them." Davidson, *Memoirs*, pp. 23–24. For Ferguson's calm reaction to the supreme court's decision, see Nalle, *Fergusons of Texas*, pp. 167–68; Bolton, *Governors of Texas*.

21. *Dallas Morning News*, June 18, 1924; Steen, "Political History of Texas, 1900–1930," p. 437. Mrs. Ferguson's reply to the question about woman suffrage is quoted in Luthin, *American Demagogues*, p. 166.

22. *Dallas Morning News*, July 12, 18, 1924. See also "Democrats Must Name Ku Klux Candidate or Mrs. Ferguson, Wife of Ousted Governor," *New York Times*, August 3, 1924, clipping in James E. Ferguson Scrapbook, 1914–35, University of Texas Archives (hereafter cited as James E. Ferguson Scrapbook, 1914–35).

23. *Colonel Mayfield's Weekly*, August 4, 1923; *San Antonio Express*, February 11, 1924, clipping in James E. Ferguson Biographical File; Davis, *"There Shall Also Be a Lieutenant Governor,"* pp. 55–56. See also *Dallas Morning News*, January 27, 1974 (obituary), clipping in T. W. Davidson Biographical File, Barker Texas History Center (hereafter cited as T. W. Davidson Biographical File).

24. Davidson to Granbery, February 6, 1924, Granbery Papers.

25. *Dallas Morning News*, May 2, July 12, 1924. See also ibid., June 18, July 11, 1924.

26. Ibid., November 11, 1923; *Austin American*, January 28, 1952 (obituary), clipping in Lynch Davidson Biographical File; "Highspots in Platform of Davidson for Governor," *Dallas Dispatch*, March 14, 1924, clipping in Lynch Davidson Biographical File; Fitzgerald, *Governors I Have Known*, pp. 66–68; J. Lewis Thompson to Will C. Hogg, July 17, 1924, Will and Mike Hogg to Thompson, July 21, 1924, Hogg Papers. See also Lynch Davidson to Will C. Hogg, June 22, 1924, Hogg to O. S. Carlton, July 1, 1924, Hogg Papers; McKay, *Texas Politics*, p. 131; "Davidson's Choice Shaped History," *Austin American*, January 30, 1952, clipping in Lynch Davidson Biographical File.

27. *Ferguson Forum*, February 14, March 6, 1924.

28. Ibid., March 6, 1924; *Dallas Morning News*, March 5, 1924.

29. *Dallas Morning News*, March 30, April 3, May 1, July 1, 15, 1924; McKay, *Texas Politics*, p. 131.

30. *Dallas Morning News*, April 2, June 15, July 6, 1924.

31. Ibid., July 7, 10, 15, 1924; *Ferguson Forum*, June 12, 1924; W. N. Jones to William B. Teagarden, March 29, 1926, William B. Teagarden Papers, University of Texas Archives (hereafter cited as Teagarden Papers).

32. *Ferguson Forum*, July 24, 1924; *Dallas Morning News*, July 26, 1924.

33. *Dallas Morning News*, July 28, 29, 31, August 7, 1924; Heard and Strong,

Southern Primaries and Elections, pp. 136–38. The votes for the other candidates were distributed as follows: Barton, 29,217; Collins, 24,864; Burkett, 21,270; Pope, 17,136; Dixon, 4,035. The returns are analyzed in McKay, *Texas Politics*, pp. 133–34.

34. Davidson, *Memoirs*, pp. 24–25. General Wolters's son Russell told the story of Lynch Davidson's failure to court the Bexar County machine to Ed Kilman of the *Houston Post*. See Ed Kilman, "Voice of Prophecy," *Houston Post*, June 16, 1963, clipping in James E. Ferguson Biographical File. Wrote Don Biggers: "The Davidsons got to fussing about which should get out of the other's way, and the more they fussed the tighter they stuck." Biggers, *Our Sacred Monkeys*, p. 64.

35. Dick Vaughan, "Jim Ferguson's Reminiscences," *Houston Press*, October 15, 1932; Nalle, *Fergusons of Texas*, pp. 172–73. Ferguson said that he telegraphed every county committee chairman.

36. *Dallas Morning News*, August 1, 1924.

37. On Sheppard, see Escal Franklin Duke, "The Political Career of Morris Sheppard, 1875–1941" (Ph.D. diss., University of Texas, 1958); Escal Franklin Duke, "John Morris Sheppard," in James et al., eds., *Dictionary of American Biography, Supplement Three, 1941–45*, pp. 706–707; Richard Bailey, "Morris Sheppard—A Prohibitionist in the Liberal Tradition," *Studies in History* 6 (1976): 75–81; Lucile Sheppard Keyes, "Morris Sheppard," (typescript, 1953), University of Texas Archives. See also J. Stanley Lemons, "The Sheppard-Towner Act: Progressivism in the 1920's," *Journal of American History* 55 (March, 1969): 776–86.

38. The Gentleman at the Keyhole, "The Texas Arranger," *Collier's* 84 (December 21, 1929): 32; Sheppard to William Atkinson, October 2, 1924, Morris Sheppard Papers, University of Texas Archives (hereafter cited as Sheppard Papers). See also Sheppard to Wayne B. Wheeler, October 2, 1924, Sheppard Papers; *Dallas Morning News*, May 17, 1924.

39. *Dallas Morning News*, July 16, 1924; *Fort Worth Star-Telegram*, June 22, 1924; Duke, "Political Career of Morris Sheppard," pp. 342–48.

40. Nalle, *Fergusons of Texas*, pp. 175–76; Luthin, *American Demagogues*, p. 168; *Austin American*, August 24, 1924, James E. Ferguson Scrapbook, 1914–35. *Current Opinion* magazine commented that these photographs were "misleading in suggesting her social status. She is a house-keeper, and is interested in the details of her farm, but the actual physical work she performs is done as a diversion and not from necessity. The two Ferguson homes—the house in Temple and the country place on the outskirts of the city—reflect a comfortable way of life." "Miriam Amanda Ferguson Soon to Take Office as the First Woman Governor of Texas," *Current Opinion* 77 (October, 1924): 437–38.

41. Nalle, *Fergusons of Texas*, p. 176; Luthin, *American Demagogues*, p. 168; Frank X. Tolbert, interview with Mrs. Ferguson, "Mrs. Ferguson Still Dislikes 'Ma,'" unidentified newspaper clipping, Mrs. Miriam A. Ferguson Scrapbook, 1924–65, Barker Texas History Center, University of Texas (hereafter cited as Mrs. Miriam A. Ferguson Scrapbook, 1924–65). In an interview in 1961, Gibler gave the following account of the origin of the epithet "Ma." One night during the campaign of 1924 he was trying to work out a headline for the *Houston Press*. Counting the letters in "Ferguson," he asked someone in the newsroom, "What's her first name?" The answer was Miriam Amanda. Gibler replied, "M. A. Great! We'll call her 'Ma.' It's the only thing that fits the head count." *Austin Statesman*, September 22, 1961. See also Gantt, *Chief Executive in Texas*, p. 285.

42. A. J. Bell to Will C. Hogg, July 30, 1924, John W. Slayton to David M. Picton, Jr., July 29, 1924, Felix D. Robertson to Hogg, July 29, 1924, A. J. Rosenthal, Jr., to Robertson, August 2, 1924, Hogg Papers.

43. Burkett to John C. Granbery, August 6, 1924, Granbery Papers; *Dallas Morning News*, August 9, 1924.

44. *Dallas Morning News*, August 2, 14, 20, 1924; John C. Granbery to Mrs. Miriam A. Ferguson, n.d., unidentified newspaper clipping, Granbery to the Rev. J. E. Buttrill, August 14, 1924, Granbery Papers; M. M. Crane to the Rev. Rupert Naney, November 5, 1924, Martin M. Crane Papers; *Houston Chronicle*, August 17, 1924, clipping in Hogg Papers.

45. *Dallas Morning News*, August 6, 1924; Nalle, *Fergusons of Texas*, p. 170.

46. W. J. Milburn to F. Scott McBride, August 25, 1924, Ernest H. Cherrington Papers, Ohio Historical Society (hereafter cited as Cherrington Papers); *Dallas Morning News*, August 9, 1924.

47. Crane to Judge Victor Brooks, August 12, 1924, Martin M. Crane Papers; *Dallas Morning News*, August 20, 1924. A copy of Frank's broadside, dated August 10, 1924, is in the Felix D. Robertson File, Campaign Materials, Texas State Archives (hereafter cited as Robertson File, Campaign Materials). See also L. A. Carlton, *An Appeal in Behalf of the Candidacy of Mrs. Ferguson*. Many faculty members of the university remained skeptical about the Fergusons, however. "Charlie Hackett is trying his best to convert us all to Ferguson, but I hardly think he will seduce many faculty votes," wrote historian Thad Riker. "You would suppose that Jim had been dipped in soapsuds and had come out an angel of light!" Riker to Eugene C. Barker, August 16, 1924, Barker Papers.

48. Henderson to Granbery, August 14, 1924, Granbery Papers; *Dallas Morning News*, August 5, 6, 1924. See also John B. Brewer to Granbery, August 19, 1924, Granbery to W. D. Holcomb, September 9, 1924, Granbery Papers.

49. *Dallas Morning News*, August 17, 19, 1924; Sharpe, *G. B. Dealey*, pp. 202–03. In a paper written in 1930, "A Newspaperman's Retrospect of Fifty Years," G. B. Dealey stated, "Perhaps the most courageous thing the *News* ever did was to fight the Ku Klux Klan." See also Sam Hanna Acheson, *35,000 Days in Texas: A History of the Dallas Morning News and Its Forebears*, pp. 278–79.

50. *Dallas Morning News*, August 10, 12, 18, 21, 1924; Atticus Webb to F. Scott McBride, September 1, 1924, F. Scott McBride Papers, Ohio Historical Society (hereafter cited as McBride Papers). Love's letter is in the *News* of August 16.

51. Neff to T. J. Jones, August 25, 1925, Neff Papers; booklet in Martin M. Crane Papers. In March, Neff privately commended "the voice of sincerity that rang throughout" Felix Robertson's opening address for governor and thanked him "for the kind words you saw fit to say about me personally and politically." Neff to Robertson, March 10, 1924, Neff Papers.

52. *Dallas Morning News*, August 6, 1924.

53. Ibid., August 8, 10, 17, 19, 1924. On August 8 fourteen officers of the city of Dallas, headed by Mayor Louis Blaylock, made a statement affirming that Robertson was both politically and personally dry. See copy in Robertson File, Campaign Materials.

54. Broadsides in James E. Ferguson File, Campaign Materials, Texas State Archives (hereafter cited as James E. Ferguson File, Campaign Materials); *Dallas Morning News*, August 15, 1924.

55. *Dallas Morning News*, August 15, 1924; *Texas 100 Per cent American*, August 8, 1924.

56. *Dallas Morning News*, August 5, 27, 1924; *Ferguson Forum*, August 7, 1924; Joseph K. Hart, "Out in the Great Empty Spaces," *New Republic* 40 (August 27, 1924): 384–85.

57. *Dallas Morning News*, August 7, 1924.

58. Ibid., August 8, 1924.

59. Ibid., August 15, 1924.

60. Ibid., August 15, 17, 1924.

61. Ibid., August 21, 1924.

62. Ibid. See also Mrs. Ferguson's statement, "Just a Word before We Vote," *Ferguson Forum*, August 21, 1924.

63. *Dallas Morning News*, August 23, 1924. The Fergusons telegraphed Davis: "Our congratulations on your stand against the Klu [*sic*] Klux Klan. Tomorrow Texas will give you an overwhelming endorsement." Quoted in George S. Silzer to John W. Davis, August 23, 1924, John W. Davis Papers.

64. *Dallas Morning News*, August 21–23, 1924. On the day before the election the *News* carried a full-page paid advertisement for Robertson with captions reading "Liquor vs. Honest Government, This Is the Real Fight, Don't Be Blinded!"

65. Ibid., August 24, 1924; Heard and Strong, *Southern Primaries and Elections*, pp. 136–37; McKay, *Texas Politics*, pp. 137–38. Mrs. Ferguson carried the ten German counties 26,535 to 4,851, increasing her vote in July from the same counties by almost 20,000. In Bexar County (San Antonio), she polled approximately 5 percent of the vote in the July primary, but in August, with the machine behind her, she polled 60 percent. Robertson increased his percentage from only 35 to 40 percent.

66. Fred Acree to Dan Moody, August 22, 1924, Acree Papers; *Dallas Morning News*, August 25, 1924; Alexander, *Ku Klux Klan in the Southwest*, pp. 197–98. For Moody's campaign, see *Dallas Morning News*, March 30, May 25, June 27, July 18, 1924. See also "To the Bench and Bar of Texas," circular letter from Judge James R. Hamilton, dated April 7, 1924, endorsing Moody in glowing terms, in Hamilton Papers.

67. *Dallas Morning News*, August 25, 1924. See also editorial by Ferguson, "May Heaven Bless Our Friends," *Ferguson Forum*, August 18, 1924.

68. *Dallas Morning News*, August 25, 1924; "The First Woman Governor," *Literary Digest* 82 (September 6, 1924): 8. See also Robert M. Field, "The Lady of the Lone Star State," *Outlook*, 138 (September 3, 1924): 15.

69. "First Woman Governor," pp. 8–9; *Dallas Morning News*, August 26, 31, 1924. See also Mark L. Goodwin, "Eastern Newspapers Look with Favor upon 'First Woman Governor' in U.S.," *Dallas Morning News*, August 27, 1924, clipping in Mrs. Miriam A. Ferguson Biographical File.

70. Charles W. Ferguson, "James E. Ferguson," *Southwest Review* 10 (October, 1924): 26–35.

71. Mark Goodwin, column in *Dallas Morning News*, August 27, 1924; "First Woman Governor," pp. 7–8.

72. "First Woman Governor," p. 9; *Dallas Morning News*, August 27, 1924. Sam T. McClure, the newly elected cyclops of Sam Houston Klan no. 1 (the first Klan chapter in Texas), announced that henceforth the chapter would take no part in politics, city or state. "The Klan is for the best in all things and as long as I am at the head of the Houston chapter the organization will take no part in politics. It will be purely a secret fraternal order." *Dallas Morning News*, September 7, 1924.

73. Love to George A. Carden, August 27, 1924, Love to Clem Shaver, August 28, 1924, Love Papers; *Dallas Morning News*, August 29, 30, 1924. Before going to San Antonio, Love wired Hicks: "Confidentially wire me Raleigh Hotel Waco whether can see you and Frank San Antonio tomorrow afternoon." Love to Hicks, August 28, 1924, Love Papers. The Democratic Executive Committee elected Jed Adams of Dallas to succeed Love. *Dallas Morning News*, September 2, 1924.

74. *Dallas Morning News*, August 31, September 1, 2, 1924.

75. *Austin American*, August 26, 1924; *Dallas Morning News*, August 27, 29, 1924;

"Local Ferguson Leaders Approve Ex-Gov's Denial," unidentified newspaper clipping in James E. Ferguson Scrapbook, 1914–35.

76. *Dallas Morning News*, September 3, 4, 1924; Hugh Nugent Fitzgerald, "Last 10 Years Form Violent Era in History of Texas Democratic Party with J. E. Ferguson as Storm Center," *Austin American*, undated clipping in James E. Ferguson Scrapbook, 1914–35; Mary Wade Smith to Mrs. Percy V. Pennybacker, November 3, 1924, Pennybacker Papers. Refusing to resign, Mrs. Bloodworth wrote State Chairman E. A. Berry: "I absolutely deny the charge made against me on the floor of the convention as to my having at any time participated in any act commonly referred to as 'River Bottom Justice' with which I have no sympathy. I have no official connection with the Ku Klux Klan." *Dallas Morning News*, September 5, 7, 1924.

77. *Dallas Morning News*, August 26, 27, September 2, 4, 1924.

78. Ibid., August 15, 1924; Casdorph, *Republican Party in Texas*, pp. 128–29.

79. *Dallas Morning News*, August 16, 17, 19, 1924.

80. Ibid., August 26, 27, 1924. In a letter dated December 5, 1923, to the members of the Republican National Committee, Creager had urged his party to take a decisive stand on the Klan issue at the next national convention. "We must, in unequivocal language, condemn any and all secret political societies as un-American." Rentfro Banton Creager, *A Letter to My Fellow Members of the Republican National Committee from R. B. Creager, Member for Texas*.

81. *Dallas Morning News*, August 30, September 4, 6, 1924.

82. Ibid., September 13, 15, 17–19, 21, 1924.

83. Granbery to Colonel Henry S. Lindsley, October 16, 1922, Granbery Papers. Biographical data in George C. Butte Papers, University of Texas Archives (hereafter cited as Butte Papers); W. Walworth Harrison, "George Charles Butte," in Webb, Carroll, and Branda, eds., *Handbook of Texas*, 3:129; George C. Butte File, Campaign Materials, Texas State Archives (hereafter cited as Butte File, Campaign Materials); George C. Butte Biographical File, Barker Texas History Center, University of Texas (hereafter cited as Butte Biographical File); *Dallas Morning News*, September 6, 1924.

84. *Dallas Morning News*, October 2, 1924.

85. Creager to Butte, October 15, 1924, Butte Papers; *Dallas Morning News*, November 4, 1924; McKay, *Texas Politics*, p. 139.

86. Love to Roper, October 16, 1924, Love Papers; *Dallas Morning News*, September 28, 1924. See also Love to Dorothy Love, October 15, 1924, Love Papers. The *Houston Post-Dispatch* "created a ripple of excitement, and some consternation" by announcing that it would support Butte, although neither former governor William Hobby nor Ross Sterling, the paper's owner, thought he would win. Clark with Hart, *The Tactful Texan*, p. 157.

87. Good Government Democratic League of Texas, "How to Vote," 1924, one-page broadside in Butte File, Campaign Materials. See also "Love Explains How to Vote for Butte," *Dallas Morning News*, October 2, 1924.

88. Broadsides in Butte File, Campaign Materials, and in Love Papers; *Dallas Morning News*, October 5, 17, November 4, 1924.

89. *Dallas Morning News*, September 11, 12, 14, 21, 23, 24–26, 30, October 19, 1924. See also Charles M. Dickson, *Democrats: Is a Woman Legally Eligible to Be Governor of Texas?*

90. Ferguson to Crane, September 30, 1924, Martin M. Crane Papers; Ferguson to William B. Teagarden, October 14, 1924, Teagarden Papers; *Dallas Morning News*, September 7, 1924. Crane warned the former governor not to make any "unkind references" in his campaign to such old issues as his war on the University of Texas. Ferguson agreed

that so far as possible the reviving of past controversies should be avoided, but he said that it would be necessary to make some defense against Butte's misrepresentations of his record. "However, I will be careful not to be drawn into the past university controversy and will direct most of my speech against Butte," he promised. Crane to Ferguson, October 1, 1924, Ferguson to Crane, October 15, 1924, Martin M. Crane Papers.

91. *San Antonio Express*, October 7, 1924, clipping in Mrs. Miriam A. Ferguson Biographical File; *Dallas Morning News*, October 7, 11, 1924; Acheson, *Joe Bailey*, pp. 395–96. For an exchange between Love and Bailey, see *Dallas Morning News*, October 12, 19, 1924.

92. *Dallas Morning News*, October 24, 1924. Butte retorted that at last the mask was off and his real opponent was not revealed. "His [Ferguson's] first speech was a defense of his own record which, of course, is the outstanding issue of this campaign, now that he is on the stump." He loftily refused to participate "in any war of personal slander" at the eleventh hour of the campaign. "Mr. Ferguson may do so if he wishes, as for me I believe it is better to suffer wrong than to do it." Ibid., October 25, 1924.

93. V. B. Harris to William B. Teagarden, October 25, 1924, Teagarden Papers; *Ferguson Forum*, October 30, 1924; *Dallas Morning News*, November 4, 1924.

94. *Dallas Morning News*, November 6, 1924; Heard and Strong, *Southern Primaries and Elections*, pp. 136–38; McKay, *Texas Politics*, p. 142.

95. Talbot to Butte, November 10, 1924, Butte Papers; *Dallas Morning News*, November 19, 1924. On the throwing out of Butte ballots, see the Rev. E. F. Adams to Butte, November 4, 1924, Robert B. Morris to Butte, November 5, 1924, Butte to Talbot, n.d., Butte to Talbot, November 5, 1924, Butte to Clarence E. Linz, n.d., Butte Papers; *Dallas Morning News*, November 6, 1924.

96. Love to McAdoo, December 23, 1924, Love Papers; *Dallas Morning News*, November 5, 1924; McKay, *Texas Politics*, pp. 141–42; Steen, "Political History of Texas, 1900–1930," pp. 436–37. See also Love to Daniel C. Roper, November 18, 1924, Love to Angus W. McLean, December 9, 1924, Love Papers; Love to George C. Butte, December 4, 1924, Butte Papers.

97. Casdorph, *Republican Party in Texas*, p. 130; Steen, "Political History of Texas, 1900–1930," p. 437.

98. Mary Wade Smith to Mrs. Percy V. Pennybacker, n.d. [December, 1924], Pennybacker Papers.

99. Alexander, *Ku Klux Klan in the Southwest*, p. 199.

100. Milton is quoted in Rice, *Ku Klux Klan in American Politics*, p. 72.

Chapter 7

1. *Austin American*, January 21, 1925, clipping in Mrs. Miriam A. Ferguson Scrapbook; Owen P. White, *Texas: An Informal Biography*, p. 222. See also Owen P. White, *Autobiography of a Durable Sinner*, pp. 177–78.

2. *Austin American*, January 21, 1925, clipping in Mrs. Miriam A. Ferguson Scrapbook; *Dallas Morning News*, January 21, 1925; Nalle, *Fergusons of Texas*, pp. 182–84; Neff, *Battles of Peace*, pp. 267–70; typescript in Crozier Papers; Laughlin, "Speaking Career of Pat Morris Neff," pp. 60–61. For brief summaries of Mrs. Ferguson's administration, see Steen, "Political History of Texas, 1900–1930," pp. 438–44; Richardson, *Texas*, p. 317; McKay and Faulk, *Texas after Spindletop*, pp. 104–108.

3. Nalle, *Fergusons of Texas*, pp. 185–86. Gossip came to the Fergusons two years later that, when some of the Fergusons' enemies tried to persuade the wife of Governor Dan Moody to remove Mrs. Ferguson's name once again from the greenhouse,

Mrs. Moody told them: "Not on your life! If I should do such a thing she would be sure to come back in again and restore her name."

4. *Dallas Morning News*, January 3, 11–14, 1925.

5. Ibid., January 3, 16, 1925.

6. *Journal of the House of Representatives of the Regular Session of the Thirty-ninth Legislature Begun and Held at the City of Austin, January 13, 1925*, pp. 13–18, 38, 74–77, 93–96 (hereafter cited as *House Journal*, 39 Leg., reg. sess. [1925]).

7. *Dallas Morning News*, January 7, 8, 17, 18, 1925.

8. Ibid., January 20–22, 24, 27, 1925.

9. Davenport to Barker, December 31, 1924, Barker Papers: *Dallas Morning News*, January 24, 1925.

10. *Dallas Morning News*, January 27, 30, February 6, 10, 12, 1925. General M. M. Crane of Dallas and T. S. Henderson of Cameron, suggested by the Ex-Students' Association, and John Sealy of Galveston declined appointments because of business affairs. Ibid., January 28, 1925.

11. Ibid., February 4, 1925.

12. *House Journal*, 39 Leg., reg. sess., (1925), pp. 105–12.

13. *Dallas Morning News*, January 4, 1925.

14. *Journal of the Senate, State of Texas Regular Session Thirty-ninth Legislature Convened in the City of Austin, January 13, 1925, and Adjourned March 19, 1925*, p. 424; *House Journal*, 39 Leg., reg. sess. (1925), pp. 1429–30; Octavia F. Rogan, "Texas Legislation, 1925," *Southwestern Political and Social Science Quarterly* 6 (September, 1925): 167–78. The *Austin American* is quoted in James Presley, *A Saga of Wealth: The Rise of the Texas Oilmen*, p. 307.

15. *Dallas Morning News*, January 29, 30, February 10, 1925. See also *Austin American*, January 23, 1925. Wrote one woman activist: "The women won a signal victory when they put through the appropriation for the Maternity Bill in spite of the strong opposition of Senator John Davis, . . . and Mrs. Ferguson's campaign promises that the Child Hygiene Bureau should be abolished." Mrs. Maggie W. Barry to Mrs. Percy V. Pennybacker, February 17, 1925, Pennybacker Papers.

16. Mrs. Maggie W. Barry to Mrs. Percy V. Pennybacker, February 17, 1925, Pennybacker Papers; *House Journal*, 39 Leg., reg. sess. (1925), pp. 112–13; *Dallas Morning News*, November 29, 1924, January 29, February 13, 1925; Crow, "Political History of the Texas Prison System," pp. 244–46. Other recommendations called for an efficient school system within the penitentiary; fixing by law the rights of convicts to all overtime earned; installation of an audit system of accounting; extension of the powers of the Board of Supervisors; change of venue to Travis County for all trials involving persons connected with the prison system; proper segregation of convicts as regards sex, race, physical and mental condition, age, and attitude toward work; and increased pay for discharged convicts.

17. *Dallas Morning News*, March 15, 18, 19, 31, April 3, 4, June 3, 1925; Crow, "Political History of the Texas Prison System," pp. 244, 246–47.

18. *Dallas Morning News*, February 8, 28, March 16, 1925.

19. Ibid., February 16, 20, March 9, 16, 19, 1925.

20. Ibid., April 5, 1925; Janice Freeman, "Ma Ferguson's Revenge: Maimed 'J' Department," unidentified newspaper clipping in Mrs. Miriam A. Ferguson Scrapbook. The Fergusons were good to Texas Tech, which was only lightly touched by the budget cuts. Governor Ferguson later approved a deficiency warrant for the school for $73,170 and the following year another for $90,000. Jim Ferguson once said to Paul Horn, president of Texas Tech: "Mr. Horn, why should we give Tech more money? Only two of the

professors out there voted for us." Horn replied that he never asked the faculty how they voted. Andrews, *First Thirty Years*, p. 25. On Texas Tech's lobbying activities in Austin during the Thirty-ninth Legislature, see Paul M. Horn to Amon G. Carter, March 3, 1925, Horn to Carter, March 7, 1925, Silliman Evans to James M. North, March 5, 1925, Evans to Carter, March 6, 7, 1925, Evans to North, n.d. [1925] (four letters), Amon G. Carter Papers, Southwest Collection, Texas Tech University (hereafter cited as Carter Papers).

21. *House Journal*, 39 Leg., reg. sess. (1925), p. 839; *Dallas Morning News*, February 13, 22, 23, 1925.

22. *House Journal*, 39 Leg., reg. sess. (1925), pp. 668–70, 906–907, 1232–34; *General Laws of the State of Texas Passed by the Thirty-ninth Legislature at Its Regular Session Which Convened January 13, 1925, and Adjourned March 19, 1925*, 39 Leg., reg. sess. (1925), pp. 213–14 (hereafter cited as *General Laws* [1925]); *Dallas Morning News*, February 17, 18, 26, March 6, 1925; Klan leader's statement in Boyd Gatewood, "Anti-Mask Legislation Will Be Fought," unidentified newspaper clipping in KKK Scrapbook; Brooks, *Political Playback*, p. 44; Alexander, *Ku Klux Klan in the Southwest*, pp. 222–23.

23. Alexander, *Ku Klux Klan in the Southwest*, pp. 223–24; Alexander, *Crusade for Conformity*, p. 72; Chalmers, *Hooded Americanism*, p. 48; Rice, *Ku Klux Klan in American Politics*, p. 73; *Fort Worth Star-Telegram*, December 18, 1924.

24. *Dallas Morning News*, January 29, February 7, 11, 14, 15, 18–21, 1925.

25. Ibid., February 18, March 5, 7, 11–13, 19, 1925; *House Journal*, 39 Leg., reg. sess. (1925), pp. 1403–1407; *General Laws* (1925), pp. 454–55.

26. *Dallas Morning News*, April 1, 1925; *Austin American*, April 1, 1925, clipping in Mrs. Miriam A. Ferguson Scrapbook.

27. Granbery to "La" (brother), April 6, 1925, Granbery Papers; *Dallas Morning News*, March 21, 1925. Noted one reporter: "With the signing of bills, the executive appointments and the pardon negotiations meted out to Ma as her part of the work, and with Jim riding herd on the Legislature, keeping up the fences and singing to the boys to prevent a stampede, everything goes along smoothly, there is no hitch anywhere, and everybody is happy." Owen P. White, "Two Governors Rule in Texas," *New York Times*, April 5, 1925, clipping in James E. Ferguson Scrapbook, 1914–40.

28. French Strother, "The Governors Ferguson of Texas," *World's Work* 50 (September, 1925): 490; E. Dale Odum, interview with Ghent Sanderford, May 8, 1967, Oral History Collection, North Texas State University, no. 14, pp. 20–21. See also *Dallas Morning News*, January 9, 1925; "Is 'Pa' or 'Ma' Governor of Texas?" *Literary Digest* 85 (April 11, 1925): 15; Willson Whitman, "Can a Wife Be Governor?" *Collier's* 76 (September 5, 1925): 5–6, clipping in Mrs. Miriam A. Ferguson Biographical File; Joseph K. Hart, "Who Is Governor of Texas?" *New Republic* 41 (February 18, 1925): 334–36.

29. Luthin, *American Demagogues*, p. 171; E. Dale Odum, interview with Ghent Sanderford, March 29, 1968, Oral History Collection, North Texas State University, no. 14, pp. 21–22.

30. Nalle, *Fergusons of Texas*, p. 189; *Dallas Morning News*, January 22, 1925; Walter C. Hornaday, "Gov. Miriam Ferguson: Sometimes She Said No," *Dallas Morning News*, March 5, 1966, clipping in Mrs. Miriam A. Ferguson Biographical File.

31. *Dallas Morning News*, April 11, December 31, 1925; Crow, "Political History of the Texas Penal System," p. 257; interview with Nola Wood, Austin, December 21, 1977, quoted in Francis Edward Abernethy, ed., *Legendary Ladies of Texas*, p. 151.

32. *Dallas Morning News*, April 11, 29, May 7, June 4, 21, 1925; *Ferguson Forum*, June 4, 1925, quoting *Houston Chronicle*, May 31, 1925; Sanderford to W. L. Moore,

April 10, 1925, Governors' Papers–Miriam A. Ferguson, Texas State Archives (hereafter cited as Mrs. Miriam A. Ferguson Official Papers); Jerry Flemmons, *Amon: The Life of Amon Carter, Sr., of Texas*, p. 276. See also Ghent Sanderford, "The Ferguson Era 1914 to 1944" (typescript), p. 6, Ex-Students' Writings Collection, University of Texas (now called Richard T. Fleming University Writings Collection). On June 19, 1865, Major General Gordon Granger landed at Galveston and issued a general order declaring that "in accordance with a proclamation from the Executive of the United States, all slaves are free." Popularly called "Juneteenth," the date was thereafter celebrated as an annual holiday by Texas blacks.

33. *Dallas Morning News*, July 3, 1925; Nalle, *Fergusons of Texas*, p. 189.

34. *Dallas Morning News*, November 26, 1925; *Ferguson Forum*, December 3, 1925; *New York Times*, November 29, 1925, clipping in James E. Ferguson Scrapbook, 1914–35; Flemmons, *Amon*, pp. 227–82. "Amon is like a lot of our lawbreakers, he is not what you would call a contemptibly mean man," Will Rogers wrote. "He just has his weaknesses. You have to watch him every minute or he will give you what appears at first to be an innocent looking walking cane. But on opening it you will find about two good drinks in it." *Houston Chronicle*, n.d., quoted in *Ferguson Forum*, December 17, 1925.

35. *Dallas Morning News*, December 1, 2, 1925. Andrews, in *First Thirty Years*, pp. 28–29, quotes Ferguson. According to one story, Ferguson hired a paroled convict to trap Carter by offering him a large lot of moonshine liquor. Rangers were stationed to arrest the publisher for possession as soon as the deal went through, but Carter kept the convict in his office until he got his attorney. "Carter fears he will be shot down by some paroled convict on order of Ma's husband," W. R. Sinclair reported to O. B. Colquitt. "Does Jim travel around with guard furnished at state expense?" Sinclair to Colquitt, October 20, 1925, Colquitt Papers.

36. McKay and Faulk, *Texas after Spindletop*, p. 106; Nalle, *Fergusons of Texas*, pp. 189–91; Luthin, *American Demagogues*, p. 172; Sam H. Hill to Dan Moody, March 12, 1926, Governors' Papers—Dan Moody, Texas State Archives (hereafter cited as Moody Papers); J. Fred Gantt interview with Ghent Sanderford, Austin, June 8, 1961, quoted in Gantt, *Chief Executive in Texas*, p. 152; interview with Dorrace Ferguson Watt, Austin, April, 1964, quoted in Abernethy, ed., *Legendary Ladies of Texas*, p. 154. A version of the horse story appears in Boyce House, *I Give You Texas! 500 Jokes of the Lone Star State*, p. 55.

37. *Journal of the House of Representatives of the Regular Session of the Fortieth Legislature of Texas, Begun and Held at the City of Austin, March 6, 1927*, p. 139 (hereafter cited as *House Journal*, 40th Leg., reg. sess. [1921]); H. F. Kirby to James E. Ferguson, March 5, 1926, photostat in Governors' Papers–Ross S. Sterling, Texas State Archives; Ralph Steen to Ghent Sanderford, April 25, 1955, copy in Ex-Students' Writings Collection, University of Texas; Ralph W. Steen, "Governor Miriam A. Ferguson," *East Texas Historical Journal* 17 (1979): 12; Louis H. Hubbard, *Recollections of a Texas Educator*; p. 153. The elevator anecdote appears in House, *I Give You Texas!* p. 47. See also Frost and Jenkins, *"I'm Frank Hamer,"* p. 131; Traylor Russell, *Carpetbaggers, Scalawags & Others*, pp. 114–15. In one instance a full pardon for Jim Hunter was telegraphed to Huntsville. A prison official replied: "Hunter escaped February Thirteenth. Recaptured Tulsa Oklahoma. Paid reward. Due back Huntsville Sunday. Advise." J. R. Jordan to Miriam A. Ferguson, February 28, 1925, Mrs. Miriam A. Ferguson Official Papers.

38. *San Angelo Standard*, n.d., clipping in Dan Moody Scrapbook, in possession of Mrs. Dan Moody, Sr., Austin, Texas. One of Mrs. Ferguson's appointees, F. M. Black of

Houston, was alleged to have been a klansman. Forty-seven high-school teachers to Miriam A. Ferguson, April 15, 1925, Mrs. Miriam A. Ferguson Official Papers.

39. S. M. N. Marrs to Pat M. Neff, July 23, 1924, State Board of Education Papers, Texas State Archives; *House Journal*, 40 Leg., reg. sess. (1927), p. 142; *Dallas Morning News*, November 13, 1925; John D. Huddleston, "The First Gubernatorial Term of Miriam Amanda Ferguson, 1925–1926" (seminar paper, University of Texas, 1974), pp. 16–19.

40. *Proceedings of Committee Appointed by the Thirty-ninth Legislature to Investigate Certain State Departments* [Austin, 1927], pp. 269–70, published as a supplement to the *House Journal* for January 21, 1927. Adrian testified that he and Quintus U. Watson of Houston, a former state senator and the legislative lobbyist for the American Book Company, had talked with the Fergusons on at least two occasions—once before and once after the contracts were awarded—to discuss the filing of affidavit forms, Ibid., pp. 266–69.

41. *Dallas Morning News*, October 21, November 11, December 17, 1925, January 22, 1926. About this time Adrian wired W. T. H. Howe in Cincinnati: "Watt [Watson] will meet me in Austin tomorrow for conference with Chief [James E. Ferguson] and Attorney General. I am going to take this opportunity to hit Marrs between the eyes and prove to Chief that he intends to run Board. Marrs cannot act for Board, and according to Watt we can hand in our bids and affidavits when we see fit." Quoted in *Proceedings of Committee . . . to Investigate Certain State Departments*, p. 79.

42. *Dallas Morning News*, February 10, 1926; *Proceedings of Committee . . . to Investigate Certain State Departments*, pp. 278–79. Textbook Commission members voting to ratify the contract were Governor Ferguson, Ida Mae Murray of San Antonio, and F. W. Chudej and H. A. Wroe of Austin; voting against were Marrs, T. J. Yoe of Brownsville, and R. L. Paschal of Fort Worth. F. M. Black of Houston and A. W. Birdwell of Nacogdoches were absent.

43. *Dallas Morning News*, April 1, 4, 30, 1926.

44. W. R. Sinclair to O. B. Colquitt, September 28, 1925, Colquitt Papers; *House Journal*, 40 Leg., reg. sess. (1927), p. 138; Max Bentley, "Who Is Governor of Texas?" *Dearborn Independent*, February 27, 1926, p. 26, clipping in Jim and Ma Ferguson Biographical File, Barker Texas History Center, University of Texas; Luthin, *American Demagogues*, p. 172; Convict labor was employed on some of Eldridge's large sugar farms, and he was thought not to have favored the prison-relocation bill, which Mrs. Ferguson vetoed. Whitman, "Can a Wife Be Governor?" p. 6.

45. *Austin Statesman*, February 10, 1925, clipping in James E. Ferguson Scrapbook, 1914–40; Whitman, "Can a Wife Be Governor?" p. 6. Mrs. Davis worked for the governor for a year and then joined her husband, Burton, in New York City. In 1929 she published *The Woman of It*, a novel about Della Lawrence, a widow and former president of the State Federation of Woman's Clubs, who is elected governor of a southern state on an anti-Klan platform. "This is a work of fiction," the author wrote. "The characters and the events in this book are wholly fictitious, and do not refer to former Governor Miriam Amanda Ferguson of Texas or to former Governor Nellie Tayloe Ross of Wyoming, . . . or to any other person or persons, living or dead." There are, however, some parallels to the Fergusons' careers, especially in the campaign in which Della is elected. See Allen Peden's review in *Houston Gargoyle* 1 (August 4, 1929): 18–19. For biographical data, see Clare Ogden Davis Biographical File, Barker Texas History Center, University of Texas (hereafter cited as Clare Ogden Davis File).

46. *Austin American*, November 10, 1925; *New York Times*, December 3, 1925,

clipping in James E. Ferguson Scrapbook, 1914–40; [Love], *Fergusonism Down to Date*, pp. 50–51.

47. *Ferguson Forum*, December 18, 1924, January 1, 1925; *Proceedings of Committee . . . to Investigate Certain State Departments*, pp. 869–70; Biggers, *Our Sacred Monkeys*, pp. 65–66.

48. Biggers, *Our Sacred Monkeys*, pp. 66–67; "Texan Howlers," *World's Work* 51 (December, 1925): 130.

49. Ferguson to D. T. Austin, February 27, 1925, photostat in Colquitt Papers. The firm agreed to pay $19.24 a week (payable monthly for fifty-two weeks) to have its name listed among the signers of the "Good Roads" page in the *Ferguson Forum*. Broadnax is quoted in Luthin, *American Demagogues*, pp. 172–73. The Houston contractor is quoted in L. W. Kemp, "Texas State Highway Department Notebooks," vol. 1, Louis W. Kemp Papers, University of Texas Archives (hereafter cited as Kemp Papers). Furst's testimony appears in *Proceedings of Committee . . . to Investigate Certain State Departments*, pp. 864–78.

50. Unidentified newspaper clipping in Dan Moody Scrapbook, in possession of Mrs. Dan Moody, Sr., Austin.

51. Bentley, "Who Is Governor of Texas?" pp. 26–27; unidentified newspaper clipping, 1926, James E. Ferguson Scrapbook, 1914–35; *Proceedings of Committee . . . to Investigate Certain State Departments*, p. 752. Johnson testified that his son Lyndon had driven a tractor and helped in making out his payrolls at a salary of $65.00 a month, later raised to $82.50. Ibid., pp. 748–49.

52. Bentley, "Who Is Governor of Texas?" p. 27.

53. Kemp, "Texas State Highway Department Notebooks," vol. 1, Kemp Papers.

54. Ibid.

55. Sinclair to Colquitt, October 10, 1925, Colquitt Papers; *Fort Worth Star-Telegram*, August 5, 1925, quoted in Kemp, "Texas State Highway Department Notebooks," vol. 1, Kemp Papers.

56. Kemp, "Texas State Highway Department Notebooks," vol. 1, Kemp Papers. Ike Crutcher, a county foreman in Van Zandt County, recalled in 1970 that "most of the contracts were given to the governor's friends, many of whom had no previous experience in road work. Many of these hired the state's county foremen and instructed them to spend no more than a certain percent of the monthly allotment." Crutcher, "A Period of Uncertainty," *Texas Highways* (April, 1970): 12–13, clipping in Mrs. Miriam A. Ferguson Biographical File.

57. Kemp, "Texas State Highway Department Notebooks," vols. 1, 2, Kemp Papers.

58. Ferguson to Crane, October 17, 1924, Martin M. Crane Papers; *Dallas Morning News*, September 23, 1924; [Love], *Fergusonism Down to Date*, pp. 32–33, 38. On the opposition to Hurdleston from anti-klansmen, see T. N. Jones to M. M. Crane, September 19, 1924, Crane to James E. Ferguson, October 16, 18, 1924, Martin M. Crane Papers. C. V. Terrell discusses his fight for the nomination in *The Terrells*, pp. 278–80.

59. Crane to Ferguson, December 20, 1924, Martin M. Crane Papers; Love to Mrs. George C. Butte, January 29, 1925, Love to Charles Dickson, February 27, March 3, 1925, Love Papers. Love wanted Robert Lee Bobbitt, Dickson's law partner, to introduce the committee resolution.

60. Kemp, "Texas State Highway Department Notebooks," vol. 1, Kemp Papers.

61. Ibid.

62. *Austin Statesman*, August 19, 1925; *Houston Chronicle*, n.d., quoted in Kemp, "Texas State Highway Department Notebooks," vol. 1, Kemp Papers; *Houston Chronicle*, August 27, 1925, quoted in *Ferguson Forum*, September 3, 1925.

63. Kemp, "Texas State Highway Department Notebooks," vol. 1, Kemp Papers.

64. Biggers to Kemp, August 19, 1925, quoted in ibid. See also Seymour V. Connor, *A Biggers Chronicle, Consisting of a Reprint of the Extremely Rare History That Will Never Be Repeated, by Lan Franks (Pseud) and a Biography of Its Author, Don Hampton Biggers*, p. 112. There are scattered issues of *Life's ABC's, Biggers' Magazine, Biggers' Semi-Monthly* ("A Paper for People with Sense Enough to Reason and Humor Enough to Laugh"), the *Square Deal*, and the *Texas Tail Twister* in Don Hampton Biggers, Assorted Newspapers, 1922–35, Papers, Southwest Collection, Texas Tech University (hereafter cited as Biggers Papers). These periodicals have one thing in common—they all attack the Ku Klux Klan. "Ferguson has the press completely bulldozed because of the libel suits he brought and all of which were compromised," W. R. Sinclair complained to Colquitt. Sinclair to Colquitt, September 28, 1925, Colquitt Papers.

65. *Johnson City Record-Courier*, October 16, 1925, Evans to Kemp, September 6, 1925, *Amarillo Post*, September 29, 1925, the *Limelight* (Fredericksburg), May 18, 1926, all quoted in Kemp, "Texas State Highway Department Notebooks," vol. 1, Kemp Papers. See also J. H. Briggs to Will C. Hogg, December 17, 1925, Hogg Papers; Biggers, *Our Sacred Monkeys*, pp. 68–69; Connor, *A Biggers Chronicle*, p. 116.

66. *Dallas Morning News*, October 15, 17, 18, 1925.

67. Ibid., October 18, 1925; *San Antonio Express*, October 18, 1925, Mrs. Miriam A. Ferguson Scrapbook; *New York Times*, November 1, 1925, clipping in James E. Ferguson Scrapbook, 1914–35.

68. *Dallas Morning News*, October 24, 27, 1925.

69. Ibid., October 25, 1925.

70. Ibid., November 6, 1925. See [Love], *Fergusonism Down to Date*, pp. 38–44, for additional details of the company's dealings with the state. John Huddleston provided information on Gilchrist's role in the highway suits.

71. *Dallas Morning News*, November 13, 16, 1925. The second-course treatment was to be applied only when the first-course treatment of not less than one-half gallon per square yard was insufficient in the estimation of the maintenance engineer, and only where asphalt was applied in excess of six-tenths gallon per square yard. Furthermore, "no no event" was the contractor required to apply a second treatment if as much as one gallon of asphalt per square yard had been applied in the first treatment.

72. Evans to Kemp, November 20, 1925, quoted in Kemp, "Texas State Highway Department Notebooks," vol. 2, Kemp Papers; *Dallas Morning News*, November 18, 21, 23, 1925; *San Antonio Express*, November 21, 1925, clipping in Dan Moody Scrapbook, 1925–28, Barker Texas History Center, University of Texas (hereafter cited as Moody Scrapbook, 1925–28).

73. *Dallas Morning News*, November 15, 25, 1925, November 27, December 3, 1926; Robbins, "Ferguson Regime in Texas," p. 208.

74. *Dallas Morning News*, November 23–25, 1925. Among the legislators participating in the conference were Lee Satterwhite, T. K. Irvin, Luke Mankin, Alfred Petsch, Claude Teer, and Robert Lee Bobbitt.

75. Ibid., November 28, 1925; Walter C. Hornaday, "Gov. Miriam Ferguson: Sometimes She Said No," *Dallas Morning News*, March 5, 1966, clipping in Mrs. Miriam A. Ferguson's Biographical File. At that time Mrs. Ferguson told a reporter for the *Baltimore Sun*: "I should call a special session, thereby authorizing my enemies—my enemies, mind you, as much as Jim's, in spite of all that mush about my being a frail, delicate woman—I should authorize the State to pay the expenditures of those wolves who want to gather here and tear me apart. Throw myself to them! Not on your life. I know them too well. Born and bred among them." *Dallas Morning News*, December 1, 1925.

The grand jury made an indirect reference to the highway investigation, stating that "such matters as have appeared impractical of final disposition at this time have been passed for the consideration of the next grand jury" and that "such record testimony as has been taken and transcribed under our direction has been delivered by us into the custody of the proper officer of this court."

76. *Houston Chronicle*, n.d., quoted in *Ferguson Forum*, December 17, 1925.

77. *New York Times*, November 30, 1925, *Houston Press*, December 1, 1925, clippings in Hogg Papers. The Hogg brothers had this statement printed with minor modifications as a one-page broadside entitled "An Interview." See copy in William Clifford Hogg Biographical File, Barker Texas History Center, University of Texas (hereafter cited as Hogg File). See also Sam Sparks to Hogg, November 27, 1925, Hogg Papers.

78. Mayfield to Thomas B. Love, November 23, 1925, Love Papers; *Dallas Morning News*, December 2, 6, 1925; *New York Times*, December 6, 1925, clipping in James E. Ferguson Scrapbook, 1914–40.

79. *New York Times*, December 3, 6, 1925, clippings in James E. Ferguson Scrapbook, 1914–40. The *Houston Press* is quoted in Luthin, *American Demagogues*, p. 174.

80. Robert M. Field, "Will 'Ma' Ferguson Be Impeached?" *Texas Outlook*, December 9, 1925, clipping in Mrs. Miriam A. Ferguson Biographical File; "A Texas Twister Brewing for 'Ma' Ferguson," *Literary Digest* 87 (December 12, 1925): 7–9. See also Duncan Aikman, "Politics and Ma Ferguson in Texas," *Independent* 115 (December 19, 1925): 703–704, 721; Dan Williams, "Governor Jim," *New Republic* 45 (January 13, 1926): 208–10; Bentley, "Who Is Governor of Texas?" pp. 3–4, 26–27.

81. *Dallas Morning News*, December 4, 5, 1925, January 16, 1926; *New York Times*, December 6, 1925, clipping in James E. Ferguson Scrapbook, 1914–40; W. E. Crozier to Louis W. Kemp, March 13, 1926, quoted in Kemp, "Texas State Highway Department Notebooks," vol. 2, Kemp Papers.

82. *Dallas Morning News*, December 4, 9–11, 20, 22, 1925; Satterwhite to Oscar B. Colquitt, December 18, 1925, Colquitt Papers.

83. *Dallas Morning News*, January 20, 21, 28–30, 1926.

84. Bentley, "Who Is Governor of Texas?" p. 27. However, according to the annual report of the State Prison Commission, submitted to the governor on March 1, 1926, the state prison system was operated at a net loss of $58,233 during the calendar year 1925. *Dallas Morning News*, March 2, 1926.

85. Robert L. Holliday to Will C. Hogg, October 27, 1925, W. S. Craig to Hogg Brothers, December 14, 1925, Hogg Papers.

Chapter 8

1. Raymond Brooks, "Ferguson Men Being Lined Up for 1926 Race," unidentified newspaper clipping, 1925, James E. Ferguson Scrapbook, 1914–35.

2. Nalle, *Fergusons of Texas*, p. 199.

3. *Ferguson Forum*, March 4, 1926; Steen, "Political History of Texas, 1900–1930," p. 445.

4. Miriam Amanda (Wallace) Ferguson, *Miriam A. Ferguson, Candidate for Governor, Second Term, Subject to the Action of the Democratic Primary, July 24, 1926: Platform*; *Dallas Morning News*, April 25, 27, 1926; Steen, "Political History of Texas, 1900–1930," p. 445.

5. *Dallas Morning News*, September 4, 1924; Davidson to Biggers, July 24, 1925, Davidson to Biggers, July 20, August 13, 1925, John Q. Weatherly to Biggers, September 15, 1925, Biggers Papers. A Davidson man warned Moody that "your friends are

sacrificing you on the altar of haste." George Neu to Moody, April 22, 1926, Moody Papers.

6. "Statement of Lynch Davidson in Reply to Marshall Hicks of San Antonio," 1926, and Lynch Davidson, "To the Voters of Texas," 1926, both broadsides in Lynch Davidson Biographical File; *Dallas Morning News*, March 14, June 30, 1926; Steen, "Political History of Texas, 1900–1930," p. 445.

7. *Dallas Morning News*, July 1, 1925.

8. Ibid., September 16, 1925, March 23, 24, 1926. For Davis's desire to run, see T. W. Carlock to Dan Moody, March 7, 1926, Moody Papers; W. N. Jones to William B. Teagarden, March 29, 1926, Teagarden Papers.

9. Sanders to Moody, December 28, 1925, Shearn Moody to Moody, January 13, 1926, Moody Papers; Colquitt to Biggers, January 4, 1926, Colquitt Papers. See also Robert Lee Bobbitt to Moody, February 10, 1926, Earle P. Adams to Moody, February 12, 1926, Walter Geron to Moody, February 18, 1926, Clifford Braly to Moody, February 25, 1926, Cato Sells to A. A. Allison, March 2, 1926, Moody Papers; Fred Acree to Moody, February 27, 1926, Acree Papers.

10. Sanders to R. L. Perry, January 26, 1925 [1926], Moody Papers; Acree to Moody, January 29, 1926, Moody to Acree, February 10, 1926, Acree Papers.

11. Shaw to Moody, January 27, 1926, Moody to Shaw, February 18, 1926, Moody Papers. See also Shaw to Moody, February 1, 13, 1926, Shaw to "Mefo" (Marcellus Foster), February 1, 1926, Moody Papers.

12. *Dallas Morning News*, March 3, 1926; *San Antonio Express*, March 3, 1926, clipping in Moody Scrapbook, 1925–28.

13. Moody to Fred Acree, March 3, 1926, Acree Papers; Critz to Moody, March 4, 1926, Moody Papers. Moody was kept informed about the preparations for the rally. James Shaw to Moody, February 27, 1926, Moody Papers.

14. *Dallas Morning News*, March 7, 1926.

15. "Life of the Moody Family," three-page typescript in Moody Papers; DeShields, *They Sat in High Places*, pp. 439–41; Fitzgerald, *Governors I Have Known*, pp. 56–60; Clara Stearns Scarborough, *Land of Good Water Takachue Pousetsu: A Williamson County, Texas, History*, pp. 380–81; Richard T. Fleming, "Daniel James Moody, Jr.," in Webb, Carroll, and Branda, eds., *Handbook of Texas*, 3:607–608; obituary in *Dallas Times-Herald*, May 23, 1966, Dan Moody Biographical File, Barker Texas History Center, University of Texas (hereafter cited as Moody Biographical File); "The 'Kid' Who Beat 'Ma,'" *New York Herald Tribune*, February 13, 1927, clipping in Moody Scrapbook, 1925–28.

16. "Moody, About to Quit Public Office, Recalls His Start," *Austin American*, November 5, 1930, clipping in Moody Scrapbook, 1929–64; obituary in *Austin American*, May 23, 1966, Moody Biographical File.

17. *Austin American*, November 5, 1930, clipping in Moody Scrapbook, 1929–65; Leffler Corbitt to Mrs. Percy V. Pennybacker, December 13, 1924, Pennybacker Papers; W. Boyd Gatewood, "Barry Miller Tells Future," *Austin American*, 1925, clipping in Dan Moody Scrapbooks, University of Texas Archives (hereafter cited as Moody Scrapbooks).

18. Raymond Brooks, "Recollections about Moody on Campaign," *Austin American*, May 25, 1966, clipping in Moody Biographical File; "Ruddy Dan Moody, the Texas Crusader," *Literary Digest* 90 (August 28, 1926): 32, 34; Scarborough, *Land of Good Water*, p. 404.

19. Colquitt to Moody, May 17, 1926, Colquitt Papers; *McKinney Examiner*, June 10, 1926, clipping in Moody Papers. The reference to a "partnership with God" and the

pledge to "run every agency of the devil out of the State" are mentioned in Jeff: McLemore to Moody, April 25, 1926, Moody Papers. Kate Johnston's platform is in *Dallas Morning News*, May 2, 1926.

20. Love to Moody, April 13, 1926, Love Papers; *Dallas Morning News*, March 20, 1926, clipping in Moody Scrapbook, 1925–28. The following men were also for Moody: Edward Crane, O. O. Touchstone, C. M. Smithdeal, Lewis T. Carpenter, V. A. Collins, C. C. Renfro, Murrell L. Buckner, Pat O'Keefe, Jed C. Adams, Joseph E. Cockrell, and D. A. Frank. "Dallas List for Moody," Moody Papers. See also Sawnie R. Aldredge to Moody, May 3, 1926, Love to Moody, May 4, 1926, Moody Papers.

21. Pinckney to Dan Moody Headquarters, Att. W. V. Howerton, April 26, 1926, Hogg Papers. See also Pinckney to Will and Mike Hogg, June 3, 1926, Hogg Papers.

22. Owen P. White, "'Ma' Ferguson To Test Her Record at Polls," *New York Times*, July 18, 1926, clipping in James E. Ferguson Scrapbook, 1914–35; McKay, *Texas Politics*, p. 149. Mrs. Moody recorded her impressions of the campaign in her diary on December 31, 1926. "Personal Diary of Mrs. Dan Moody Recorded during her term as First Lady of Texas While Residing in the Governor's Mansion in Austin, Texas" (typescript), Oral History Collection, North Texas State University no. 24, pp. 15–19 (hereafter cited as Mrs. Dan Moody "Diary"). See also Martha Moody, "Mildred Paxton Moody: Former First Lady of Texas," *Texas Historian* 40 (March, 1980): 1–5.

23. *Dallas Morning News*, May 9, 1926. For the invitation to open his campaign at Moody, see Fred Acree to Moody, March 11, 1926, Acree Papers. On the Taylor arrangements, which included a system of amplifiers rented for $75 from the Bell Telephone Company in Austin, see James Shaw to Moody, May 3, 5, 1926, Shaw to Beauford H. Jester, June 20, 1926, Moody Papers.

24. Jane Y. McCallum, Personal Diary, March 13, 17, 1926, McCallum Family Papers, Austin–Travis County Collection, Austin Public Library (hereafter cited as McCallum Family Papers); Jesse Daniel Ames to Moody, March 5, 1926, Ames to Moody, April 3, 1926, A. B. Wilson to Dan Moody Headquarters, July 13, 1926, Moody Papers; Mrs. Willard Rosene to Mrs. Percy V. Pennybacker, July 20, 1926, Pennybacker Papers; *Dallas Morning News*, July 16, 1926, clipping in Pennybacker Papers; "Austin Women Rally Beneath Moody Banner," unidentified newspaper clipping, 1926, Moody Scrapbooks; "Sen. V. A. Collins Will Speak for Dan Moody for Governor Tonight Wednesday, July 14, at Eastwood Park 8 P. M. All Invited Col. Tom Ball Will Preside" (broadside), 1926, Dan Moody File, Campaign Materials, Texas State Archives (hereafter cited as Moody file, Campaign Materials).

25. Colquitt to C. M. Caldwell, May 20, 1926, Colquitt Papers; Pinckney to Will C. Hogg, June 16, 1926, Hogg Papers. See also Colquitt to W. V. Howerton, May 17, 1926, Colquitt to John Boyle, May 18, 1926, Colquitt to Will C. Hogg, May 18, 1926, Colquitt to W. W. Turney, May 18, 1926, Boyle to Colquitt, May 19, 1926, Colquitt Papers; John S. Aldehoff to Moody, June 12, 1926, Pinckney to Aldehoff, June 19, 1926, James Shaw to Pinckney, June 14, 1926, Pinckney to W. F. Robertson, June 23, 1926, T. W. Carlock to Colquitt, July 1, 1926, Colquitt to D. W. Wilcox, July 3, 1926, Wilcox to Colquitt, July 5, 1926, ——— to J. L. Donaldson, July 20, 1926, Moody Papers.

26. Leffler Corbitt to Mrs. Percy V. Pennybacker, May 22, 1926, Pennybacker Papers; W. E. Miller to Moody, May 25, 1926, Moody Papers. "The farmer does not know the truth as you and I know it," Moody was told. "Many of them are not general readers, some only taking the Ferguson Menace." F. R. Shanks to Moody, May 29, 1926, Moody Papers.

27. K. W. Denman to Dan Moody, May 21, 1926, J. M. Smith to Stephen L. Pinckney, June 19, 1926, J. O. Toole to Moody, April 28, 1926, Moody Papers.

28. J. W. Shotwell to Dan Moody Headquarters, July 2, 1926, R. C. Lomax to Moody, June 24, 1926, J. M. Ratcliff to Moody, April 29, 1926, J. W. Beeler to Moody, June 4, 1926, Moody Papers.

29. R. T. Burns to Moody, June 12, 1926, Burns to D. W. Wilcox, July 16, 1926, W. L. Dean to Moody, May 29, 1926, Moody Papers.

30. E. V. Swift to Dan Moody Headquarters, July 20, 1926, Cary M. Abney to Dan Moody Headquarters, July 14, 1926, Carl Phinney to W. V. Howerton, April 30, 1926, Earle P. Adams to Stephen L. Pinckney, June 6, 1926, J. R. Durant to Moody, June 19, 1926, Carl L. Estes to Moody, March 17, 1926, Cone Johnson to Clifford Stone, July 10, 1926, Alvin S. Moody to Cone Johnson, July 16, 1926, A. A. Dawson to Ernest May, May 27, 1926, A. M. Hilliard to Moody, June 6, 1926, Moody Papers.

31. W. Rohde to Moody, April 21, 1926, Harry Koch to Moody, April 22, 1926, Moody Papers; E. S. Fentress to Pat Neff, August 9, 1926, Neff Papers; Clark with Hart, *The Tactful Texan*, p. 159; Ed Kilman, "Sterling—Texan: A Biography of Ross Sterling," p. 128. I am indebted to Tuffly Ellis for allowing me to examine this 388-page manuscript.

32. Colquitt to Biggers, December 31, 1925, Biggers Papers; Colquitt to Will C. Hogg, May 26, 1926, Colquitt Papers; Hogg to R. J. Boyle, June 15, 1926, Colquitt to Hogg, June 17, 19, 1926, Hogg Papers.

33. *Free Lance* (Dallas), June 26, 1926; Biggers, *Our Sacred Monkeys*, pp. 26–27. On Love's preparation of the review, see Marshall Hicks to Love, May 25, 1926, Love to Hicks, May 26, 1926, Love to George A. Carden, August 4, 1926, Love Papers; Stephen L. Pinckney to Love, June 19, 1926, Moody Papers.

34. Will C. Hogg, Diary (Daily Reminder), entries for April 2, 21, 24, 28, May 22, 23, 29, June 13, 25, 26, 1926, Hogg Papers.

35. Gregory to House, June 9, 1926, House Papers; ——— to Hogg Brothers, July 2, 1926, Hogg Papers.

36. *Dallas Morning News*, June 25, 26, 1926; Will C. Hogg, Diary (Daily Reminder), June 25, 26, 1926, Hogg Papers.

37. *Dallas Morning News*, June 1, 16, July 21, 23, 1926; unidentified newspaper clipping, July 27, 1926, Moody Scrapbook, in possession of Mrs. Dan Moody, Sr.

38. Colquitt to D. W. Wilcox, July 2, 1926, Colquitt Papers; Walter C. Hornaday, "With Dan Moody Politics Was Fun," *Dallas Morning News*, June 4, 1966, clipping in Moody Biographical File; unidentified newspaper clipping, July 27, 1926, Moody Scrapbook, in possession of Mrs. Dan Moody, Sr.

39. Julius A. Germany to Moody, June 9, 1926; C. M. Smithdeal to Moody, June 2, 1926, Moody Papers; Colquitt to W. P. Hobby, June 7, 1926, Colquitt Papers; Walter W. Woodson to Will C. Hogg, June 25, 1926, Hogg Papers; story by Walter C. Hornaday in unidentified newspaper clipping, July 27, 1926, Moody Scrapbook, in possession of Mrs. Dan Moody, Sr.

40. Edward J. Hamner to Moody, May 17, 1926, Moody Papers; *Dallas Morning News*, April 18, 1926.

41. *Ferguson Forum*, May 27, 1926; Miriam Amanda Ferguson, *Opening Speeches of Gov. Ferguson's Campaign for a Second Term; Delivered Saturday, May 22, 1926, at Sulphur Springs Texas, by Gov. Miriam A. Ferguson and Former Gov. James E. Ferguson*. Moody's manager in Hopkins County reported: "I do not believe that they made a single convert, in spite of lies, slanders, and mud-slinging. In fact, if I had been permitted to write Jim's speech, I should have followed the very lines he did follow." J. M. Dunn to Dan Moody Headquarters, May 24, 1926, Moody Papers.

42. Sam H. Hill to Moody, May 26, 1926, Moody Papers; *Dallas Morning News*,

May 23, 25, (editorial), 1926. Mrs. Moody's written comments on the election bet appear in Moody Scrapbook, in possession of Mrs. Dan Moody, Sr.

43. *Dallas Morning News*, May 24, 25, June 9, 23, 24, 1926; "Is Gambling Wrong?" (broadside), Moody Papers.

44. *Free Lance*, May 29, 1926, clipping in Moody Scrapbook, in possession of Mrs. Dan Moody, Sr. See also Colquitt to John Boyle, May 22, 1926, Colquitt Papers. In 1968 Mrs. Moody said of her husband's acceptance of the Ferguson challenge: "But many people said that it is a bad youthful mistake that he's made. Now he's ruined it, because everybody said, 'Gambling for high office,' but the Texas people loved it because Dan said, 'I consider it my *duty* to get rid of the Fergusons as soon as possible, and this gives me a chance to get rid of them before they get to the end of the term, so I'll accept the challenge.' From then on he went big. And in politics it was later said that it was the smartest thing he ever did, because the people simply loved it." Fred Gantt, interview with Mrs. Dan Moody, Sr., Austin, Texas, August 16, 1968, Oral History Collection, North Texas State University, no. 25. See also Mrs. Dan Moody, "Diary," December 31, 1926, pp. 19–20.

45. Ferguson is quoted in Faulk and McKay, *Texas after Spindletop*, p. 110. "By your prompt acceptance of the challenge, you *spiked* Jim's guns completely," the editor of the *Abilene Daily Reporter* wrote Moody. "He cannot refer to the incident in the future because he would have to admit that you took it up so quick it made his head swim. He is shut off from further discussion of the incident." Frank Grimes to Moody, May 25, 1926, Moody Papers.

46. *Dallas Morning News*, June 2, 1926.

47. E. M. Camp to James Shaw, June 23, 1926, Moody Papers; *Dallas Morning News*, June 21, 24, 1926.

48. Unidentified newspaper clipping in Moody Scrapbook, in possession of Mrs. Dan Moody, Sr.; Brooks, *Political Playback*, p. 4; Duncan Aikman, "Another Last Frontier," *Southwest Review* 12 (October, 1926): 11. Superintendent Marrs effectively rebutted Ferguson's version of the textbook fight as being over the evolution issue. *Dallas Morning News*, July 13, 1926.

49. *Dallas Morning News*, April 29, May 2, 16, 18, June 1, 4, 6, 10, 13, 1926. The *Fort Worth Record-Telegraph* is quoted in ibid., June 17, 1926.

50. Ibid., June 20, July 6, 1926. See also J. A. Kemp to Will C. Hogg, June 19, 1926, Hogg Papers; *Dallas Morning News*, June 17, 1926.

51. Davidson to J. Lewis Thompson, May 6, 1926, Hogg Papers.

52. *Dallas Morning News*, June 1, 3, 17, 1926.

53. Ibid., June 24, July 8, 21, 1926; Moody to the Rev. W. M. Pearce, June 22, 1926, Moody Papers.

54. "Lynch Davidson Candidate for Governor on the 'Standard Oil Act' (Senate Bill 180)" (broadside), 1926, Lynch Davidson File, Campaign Materials.

55. *Dallas Morning News*, July 2, 8, 10, 13, 1926.

56. Mobley to Stephen L. Pinckney, July 17, 1926, Julius A. Germany to D. W. Wilcox, July 12, 1926, Moody Papers. Mobley's firm was Andrews, Streetman, Logue and Mobley.

57. *Dallas Morning News*, June 23, 26, July 21, 1926.

58. Ibid., June 30, July 14, 17, 1926. A printed copy of the Hogg brothers' letter to Davidson is in the Hogg Papers.

59. D. W. Wilcox to J. D. Cunningham, June 28, 1926, Ben L. Cox to Wilcox, June 30, 1926, J. Frank Norris to Moody, May 15, 1930, Moody to Norris, May 17, 1930, Moody Papers; J. M. North, Jr., to Will C. Hogg, July 14, 1926, Hogg Papers; *Fort*

Worth Star-Telegram, n.d., clipping in Moody Scrapbook, in possession of Mrs. Dan Moody, Sr.; Biggers, *Our Sacred Monkeys*, p. 73. Colquitt sputtered, "Lynch Davidson developed to be the most ridiculous liar that ever ran for Governor of Texas." Colquitt to R. M. Colquitt, July 24, 1926, Colquitt Papers.

60. W. F. Robertson to D. W. Wilcox, June 29, 1926, Wilcox to F. P. Culver, June 29, 1926, Moody Papers; *Magnolia Park News*, July 9, 1926, copy in Hogg Papers; *Search Light* (Fort Worth), July 9, 1926, clipping in Moody Scrapbook, in possession of Mrs. Dan Moody, Sr.; *Dallas Morning News*, July 6, 14, 1926. Don Biggers estimated that Davidson "probably financed 90 per cent of his own campaign." Biggers, *Our Sacred Monkeys*, p. 73.

61. Moody to T. C. Weir, April 1, 1926, Moody Papers; *Dallas Morning News*, May 5, 1926. See also A. D. Adams to Moody, May 11, 1926, Moody to Adams, May 14, 1926, Lyndsay D. Hawkins to Stephen L. Pinckney, June 26, 1926, James Shaw to Hawkins, June 29, 1926, Moody Papers.

62. T. M. Campbell, Jr., to Dan Moody Headquarters, June 25, 1926, Dan Moody Headquarters to Campbell, June 26, 1926, Edward Moss to James Shaw, July 21, 1926, Shaw to Moss, July 22, 1926, Moody Papers.

63. N. A. Gentry to William B. Teagarden, March 23, 1926, Teagarden Papers; Jas. I. Perkins to Colquitt, June 22, 1926, Colquitt Papers; Mayfield to Will C. Hogg, June 18, 1926, Hogg Papers; Artemas R. Roberts to Thomas B. Love, April 8, 1928, Love Papers. See also E. R. Berry to Moody, March 10, 1926, Moody Papers.

64. Dupree to Moody, May 22, 1926, Moody to Dupree, May 25, 1926, Moody Papers. See also F. M. Newman (McCulloch County), to F. P. Culver, May 21, 1926, H. Grady Chandler (Collin) to Moody, May 20, 1926, J. D. Cunningham (Howard) to Stephen L. Pinckney, June 1, 1926, J. C. Russell (San Patricio) to Moody, June 5, 1926, Lucille Haining (Waller) to Pinckney, June 16, 1926, Moody Papers. Pinckney replied to one such letter: "There are a number of counties in Texas where solid, quiet work will count for a great deal more than the hulla-baloo campaign." Pinckney to H. Grady Chandler, May 25, 1926, Moody Papers.

65. W. D. Cowan to Moody, May 22, 1926, Edward J. Hammer to Moody, May 27, 1926, Moody Papers; Colquitt to J. S. Talley, July 2, 1926, Colquitt Papers.

66. W. W. Nelms to D. W. Wilcox, June 25, 1926, Tom L. Beauchamp to Dan Moody Headquarters, June 26, 1926, B. J. Hawthorn to Dan Moody Headquarters, June 28, 1926, W. D. Cowan to Moody, May 22, 1926, Moody Papers; *Dallas Morning News*, June 22, 1926. "The combination Ku Klux support here in Dallas is combined on Davidson or Ferguson," Colquitt reported. Colquitt to J. S. Talley, July 2, 1926, Colquitt Papers.

67. Maury Pollard to Moody, July 3, 1926, J. M. Moore to Dan Moody Headquarters, July 7, 1926, Frank Gibler to Stephen L. Pinckney, July 7, 1926, T. A. Buckner to Dan Moody Headquarters, July 12, 1926, O. B. Robertson to James Shaw, July 19, 1926, Moody Papers.

68. "The Truth About General Moody's War Record" (broadside), 1926, Moody Papers; campaign card in Moody Biographical File; "Fergusonism Defined (from Sterling City News-Record of June 4, 1926)" and "Crane on Fergusonism Speech by Gen. M. M. Crane at Houston, June 13, 1918 (from Houston Chronicle, June 14, 1918)" (broadsides), 1926, Moody Papers; Stephen L. Pinckney to T. J. Arbuckle, May 25, 1926, Wm. J. Tucker to James Shaw, July 12, 1926, Moody Papers.

69. Dan Moody Headquarters to R. T. Burns, July 21, 1926, Burns to D. W. Wilcox, July 23, 1926, Moody Papers; "Moody Would Excuse Travis Negro Jurors," *Austin American*, November 11, 1923, clipping in Moody Scrapbooks. See also George W. Du-

pree to Stephen L. Pinckney, June 2, 1926, Ernest Weaver to Moody, June 29, 1926, Moody Papers.

70. "Union Labor Record of General Moody" (broadside), 1926, Moody Papers.

71. "Ferguson to Drive Mexicans from Texas" and "Ferguson Iba a Echar a Los Mejicanos de Tejas" (broadsides), 1926, Brian Montague to Dan Moody Headquarters, n.d., W. E. George to Stephen L. Pinckney, June 17, 1926, Pinckney to Carl Phinney, June 21, 1926, Moody Papers.

72. C. H. Chernosky to James Shaw, July 21, 1926, C. H. Donegan to Moody, June 8, 1926, Moody Papers. See also Don H. Biggers to Moody, March 8, 1926, W. R. Perkins to Moody, May 10, 1926, Alfred P. C. Petsch to Stephen L. Pinckney, June 20, 22, 1926, Pinckney to Judge Henry J. Dannenbaum, July 2, 1926, Charlton Hall to Moody, July 3, 1926, Richard Fleming to Pinckney, July 8, 1926, Tom S. Henderson, Jr., to Pinckney, July 9, 1926, W. J. Embrey to Pinckney, July 15, 1926, Frank L. Tiller to Moody, July 19, 1926, Jacob F. Wolters to Pinckney, July 19, 1926, "Jno. Boyle Answers Ferguson's Charge That Moody Is a Klan Sympathizer" (broadside), 1926, Moody Papers.

73. Robert Whitely to D. W. Wilcox, July 12, 1926, Moody Papers; Moody campaign stickers in Moody Scrapbook, in possession of Mrs. Dan Moody, Sr.

74. Acheson, *Joe Bailey*, pp. 396–97; *Dallas Morning News*, July 4, 1926. For a hostile account of the "Ferguson-Bailey show" in Nacogdoches, see R. D. Winder to Dan Moody Headquarters, July 10, 1926, Moody Papers.

75. *Dallas Morning News*, June 13, July 1, 1926; *Ferguson Forum*, July 15, 1926. On rumors around Dallas that both Fergusons had kidney trouble, see Will C. Hogg to R. J. Boyle, June 15, 1926, Hogg Papers.

76. *Dallas Morning News*, July 15, 1926. The crack Santa Fe passenger train carrying Mrs. Ferguson from Temple to Austin in the early morning hours of July 15 crashed at high speed through an open switch seven miles south of Temple and smashed into a waiting freight train, killing the engineer and injuring the fireman. Mrs. Ferguson and the other passengers and crewmen were only shaken up and jarred. Ibid., July 17, 1926.

77. Ibid., July 21, 1926; *Austin American*, n.d., Moody Scrapbook, in possession of Mrs. Dan Moody, Sr. Mrs. Moody's comment appears beside this clipping in the scrapbook.

78. H. N. Fitzgerald, "Dan Says He Will Lead Fergusons by 100,000 Votes in First Primary," *Austin American*, July 8, 1926; *Dallas Morning News*, July 24, 1926. On the straw polls, see Frank Gibler to James Shaw, July 11, 1926, Oveta Hoover Culp to Stephen L. Pinckney, July 14, 1926, D. W. Wilcox to Julius Germany, July 16, 1926, Moody Papers; O. B. Colquitt to T. A. Buckner, July 13, 1926, Colquitt Papers.

79. *Dallas Morning News*, July 25, 26, August 3, 8, 1926; Heard and Strong, *Southern Primaries and Elections*, pp. 138–41.

80. Unidentified newspaper clipping in Moody Scrapbook, in possession of Mrs. Dan Moody, Sr.; McKay, *Texas Politics*, p. 151. The totals in the ten German counties: Ferguson, 15,336; Moody, 7,307; Davidson, 2,689.

81. "The Fall of 'Ma' Ferguson," *Literary Digest* 90 (August 7, 1926): 12. See also "Fergusonism Repudiated" (editorial), *Dallas Morning News*, July 26, 1926. The Moody Scrapbook in possession of Mrs. Dan Moody, Sr., contains clippings from *New York Times*, August 30, 1926; *Cincinnati times*, August 2, 1926; *New Orleans Times-Picayune*, August 1, 1926; *Chicago Sunday Tribune*, July 25, 1926; *Casper* (Wyoming) *Tribune-Herald*, August 29, 1926; *Seattle Daily* (?), July 25, 1926; *Medford* (Oregon) *Mail Tribune*, July 26, 1926; *New York Evening Post*, n.d. "News went out over the U.S.A.," Mrs. Moody comments in the Scrapbook. "Friends sent in the headlines."

82. F. C. Davis, Marshall Hicks, and George D. Armistead to McAdoo, July 28,

1926, enclosed in Davis to Thomas B. Love, July 28, 1926, Love to Davis, August 7, 1926, Love Papers; McAdoo to Gregory, August 11, 1926, Gregory Papers. Love wrote Edwin T. Meredith, a McAdoo leader in Iowa, "Confidentially, I have no doubt McAdoo will carry Texas in 1928, unless some unexpected developments arise." Love to Meredith, October 7, 1926, Love Papers.

83. *Dallas Morning News*, July 27, 28, 1926; unidentified newspaper clipping in Moody Scrapbook, in possession of Mrs. Dan Moody, Sr.

84. *Ferguson Forum*, July 29, 1926. Biggers commented acidly on this editorial: "The anti-mask law was never repealed, as Jim had feared, and the only Ku Klux parade that took place was when they began to file out of State departments and off of state contract jobs when Jim and 'Ma' retired." Biggers, *Our Sacred Monkeys*, p. 74.

85. *Dallas Morning News*, August 1, 9, 10, 1926. In San Antonio, Marshall Hicks claimed that the $250 mentioned as coming from Robert Lee Bobbitt was a firm check and that, although Bobbitt had written the letter enclosing the contribution, "the money was donated by me alone." Lee Satterwhite authorized Hicks to say that he had not contributed one cent to the Moody campaign, that Judge A. B. Martin of Plainview had given him a check for $250 as a contribution to Moody and that he had cashed it and sent his own personal check for that amount to the Moody campaign committee, thus transmitting Judge Martin's donation. It was not a persuasive defense.

86. Ibid., August 11, 1926, unidentified newspaper clipping in Moody Scrapbook, in possession of Mrs. Dan Moody, Sr. Not included in the contributions was the $500 allegedly received from Bobbitt and Satterwhite that was returned. For a discussion of the costs of campaigning for governor during the 1920s, see Gantt, *Chief Executive in Texas*, pp. 275–76.

87. *Dallas Morning News*, August 12, 1926; *Ferguson Forum*, August 12, 1926.

88. *Dallas Morning News*, August 22, 1926; McKay, *Texas Politics*, p. 154. See also "Ferguson Sees Good Chance to Win Aug. 28," unidentified newspaper clipping, 1926, in James E. Ferguson Scrapbook, 1914–40.

89. *Dallas Morning News*, August 24, 26, 1926.

90. Ibid., August 25, 26, 28, 1926. See also James E. Ferguson to A. A. Diehl, August 20, 1926, Moody Papers; "How the Thing Was Done" (editorial), *Ferguson Forum*, August 19, 1926; James E. Ferguson, "Dan Moody's Feeble Reply before His Silk Stocking Crowd" (broadside), 1926, Moody Papers.

91. *Dallas Morning News*, August 15, 26, 28, 1926; McKay, *Texas Politics*, p. 154.

92. For predictions that Davidson's supporters would go to Moody and that some of Ferguson's following would quit him either to vote for Moody or to not to vote, see H. F. Lewis to Dan Moody Headquarters, August 14, 1926, Nolan Queen to D. W. Wilcox, August 14, 1926, Earle P. Adams to Wilcox, August 14, 1926, T. A. Fannin to Dan Moody Headquarters, August 16, 1926, W. W. McCrory to Stephen L. Pinckney, August 19, 1926, A. M. Howsley to Dan Moody Headquarters, August 20, 1926, J. R. Duran to Moody, August 23, 1926, C. F. Smith to Moody, August 22, 1926, Moody Papers.

93. E. O. Zeanon to Moody, August 21, 1926, Moody Papers. "He [Ferguson] doesn't intend to make any more noise than possible," Biggers fretted to Moody. "He doesn't intend to make a big noise and wake up the slumbering dubs. He is filling the woods with the Forum. The word has gone down the line for his friends not to argue, but work. . . . The Ku Klux never worked more secretly than the Ferguson forces are working right now." Biggers to Moody, August 19, 1926, Moody Papers. See also Biggers to O. B. Colquitt, August 20, 1926, Colquitt Papers; "The Ferguson Campaign" (editorial), *Dallas Morning News*, August 19, 1926.

94. D. W. Wilcox to Emsy H. Swain, August 18, 1926, Moody Papers; Texas

Women Citizens' Committee, Dan Moody for Governor, to "Dear Co-Worker," August 19, 1926, McCallum Family Papers.

95. Heard and Strong, *Southern Primaries and Elections*, pp. 138–41; McKay, *Texas Politics*, pp. 156–57.

96. *Dallas Morning News*, August 30, 1926; *Ferguson Forum*, September 2, 1926. "People say the road company suits beat my wife," Ferguson told a reporter in 1932. "That's not so. Dan Moody divided the anti-Klan votes with my wife and got all the Klan votes and that's why he won." Dick Vaughan, "Jim Ferguson's Reminiscences," *Houston Press*, October 15, 1932.

97. *The 1927 Texas Almanac and State Industrial Guide*, p. 82. For biographical data on Allred, see George Clarke, "James V. Allred, the Centennial Governor," in Adams, ed., *Texas Democracy*, 1:561–79; DeShields, *They Sat in High Places*, pp. 451–55; Moore, *Governors of Texas*, p. 31; Robert Rene Martindale, "James V. Allred: The Centennial Governor of Texas" (Master's thesis, University of Texas, 1957); George N. Manning, "Public Services of James V. Allred" (Master's thesis, Texas Technological College, 1950); Floyd F. Ewing, "James V. Allred," in Webb, Carroll, and Branda, eds., *Handbook of Texas*, 3:21–22. A brief biographical sketch of Allred is included in the *Southwest Farmer* (San Antonio), August 2, 1929, James V. Allred Papers, University of Houston Library (hereafter cited as Allred Papers). See also "The People of Montague County to the People of Texas," (two-page typescript), in Benjamin Grady Oneal Papers, University of Texas Archives (hereafter cited as Oneal Papers).

98. Allred to V. C. Harmon, June 15, 1926, O. H. Allred to Allred, July 29, 1926, C. A. Davis to Allred, July 29, 1926, Allred Papers. C. C. Hudson, editor of the *Iowa Park Herald* (Wichita County), called Allred "the bigoted little Ferguson henchman from this county who seeks to be attorney general." Hudson to Thomas B. Love, July 31, 1926, Love Papers. In Bell County the rumor was "quietly circulated" that Allred was a Catholic. W. S. Shipp to Raymond A. Allred, July 31, 1926, Allred Papers.

99. Tomas G. Pollard to M. V. Howerton, August 20, 1926, Moody Papers; C. L. Stone to Raymond S. Allred, August 19, 1926, W. S. Shipp to Raymond S. Allred, August 21, 1926, Thomas Hembree to Raymond S. Allred, August 25, 1926, Allred Papers.

100. Allred to Thomas B. Rapkock, September 10, 1926, Allred Papers. See also Allred to Renne Allred, August 31, 1926, Tom E. Acker to Allred, September 8, 1926, O. H. Allred to Allred, September 12, 1926, Allred to Robert M. Noe, October 4, 1926, Allred Papers; *Texas Almanac* (1927), p. 93. "It was the talk of the [San Antonio] convention about what a good sport I was," Allred wrote his brother Oran, "and I was assured by nearly every lawyer there, even those who supported Pollard, that I could have the office for the asking the next time." Allred to O. H. Allred, September 10, 1926, Allred Papers.

101. *Dallas Morning News*, August 31, September 4, 7–10, 1926.

102. Ibid., September 9, 1926. See also *Ferguson Forum*, September 9, 1926.

103. *Dallas Morning News*, September 7, 9, 1926.

104. Ibid., September 14, 16, 17, 25, 29, October 2, 5, 7–9, 1926; *Journal of the House of Representatives of the First Called Session of the Thirty-ninth Legislature Begun and Held at the City of Austin, September 13, 1926*, pp. 43–45, 461–62, 691, 742, 820 (hereafter cited as *House Journal*, 39 Leg., 1st called sess. [1926]); Biggers, *Our Sacred Monkeys*, p. 75. See also Duncan Aikman, "Fall Cleaning in the Political Boudoir," *Independent* 117 (October 9, 1926): 411–12, 427.

105. *Dallas Morning News*, September 16, 23, October 2, 4, 5, 7–9, 1926; Biggers, *Our Sacred Monkeys*, p. 75. The seven senators voting to confirm Moseley and Cage were Bowers, Fairchild, Harden of Kaufman, Holbrook, Miller, Parr, and Strong.

106. *Dallas Morning News*, October 6–10, 1926; *House Journal*, 39 Leg., 1st called sess. (1926), pp. 1306–1308, 1323–30.

107. *Dallas Morning News*, October 19–22, 26–28, November 9, 11, 13, 1926; *Ferguson Forum*, October 14, 21, 28, November 4, 11, 18, 1926; Calbert, "James Edward and Miriam Amanda Ferguson," p. 166.

108. The State Republican Headquarters prepared a handbook exhorting county leaders to hold a primary "even if the number of votes is very few" and explaining how "a simple, inexpensive, legal, primary can be held." Leonard Withington, ed., *Texas Republican Primary Handbook, 1926*, rev. ed.

109. Will R. Wood to Secretary, April 6, 1926, John Q. Tilson to Calvin Coolidge, April 7, 1926, R. B. Creager to Coolidge, June 26, 1926, Calvin Coolidge Papers, Manuscripts Division, Library of Congress (hereafter cited as Coolidge Papers). See also Leonard Withington to Coolidge, February 19, 1926, Coolidge Papers. The above citations are to memoranda describing the contents of the letters.

110. Scobey to Beeman Davis, March 27, 1926, Scobey Papers. See also Scobey to Charles Dawes, January 9, June 22, 1926, April 29, 1927, Scobey Papers. Scobey said of his relationship with Creager: "Well, you know what I did for him, getting him in with the Harding Administration and turning everything over to him and making him a national character. He double crossed me and I have not spoken to him for almost three years. Too ambitious." Scobey to Fred J. Cutting, November 30, 1926, Scobey Papers.

111. Casdorph, *Republican Party in Texas*, p. 131.

112. Ibid., pp. 131–32.

113. *Dallas Morning News*, May 30, 1926; unidentified newspaper clipping, Moody Scrapbook, in possession of Mrs. Dan Moody, Sr.; *Dallas Morning News*, October 31, November 2, 3, 1926; Heard and Strong, *Southern Primaries and Elections*, pp. 138–41. Smith made his best showing in Hamilton County, where he polled 210 votes to Moody's 676 and Haines's 96.

114. Scobey to Fred J. Cutting, November 30, 1926, Scobey Papers.

115. Unidentified newspaper clipping, Moody Scrapbook, in possession of Mrs. Dan Moody, Sr.; *Philadelphia Inquirer*, September 12, 1926, clipping in ibid. See also L. C. Speers's article, *New York Times Magazine*, September 12, 1926, clipping in ibid. In December, the governor-elect and his wife visited Washington, D.C. The entire Texas congressional delegation except for Sumners and Hudspeth, who were out of town, attended a luncheon in Moody's honor at which Tom Connally was host in the Speaker's dining room in the Capitol. Unidentified newspaper clipping in Moody Scrapbook, in possession of Mrs. Dan Moody, Sr.

116. *New York Evening Post*, n.d., clipping in Moody Scrapbook, in possession of Mrs. Dan Moody, Sr.

117. Aikman, "Another Last Frontier," p. 4.

118. J. B. Zimmerman to Moody, August 11, 1926, Moody Papers; Sanderford, "The Ferguson Era 1914 to 1944."

Chapter 9

1. Mrs. Dan Moody, "Diary," January 30, 1927, p. 28; *Dallas Morning News*, January 19, 1927; *San Antonio Express*, January 19, 1927, clipping in Moody Scrapbook, 1925–28.

2. *San Antonio Express*, January 19, 1927, clipping in Moody Scrapbook, 1925–28; Nalle, *Fergusons of Texas*, pp. 203–205.

3. *Dallas Morning News*, January 19, 1927; Nalle, *Fergusons of Texas*, p. 205.

4. *Dallas Morning News*, January 19, 1927.

5. *New York Times*, n.d., clipping in Moody Scrapbook, in possession of Mrs. Dan Moody, Sr.

6. *House Journal*, 40 Leg., reg. sess. (1927), pp. 99–109; *Dallas Morning News*, January 21, 1927.

7. *Dallas Morning News*, January 22, 1927; "Moody's First Shot at Texas," unidentified newspaper clipping, January 21, 1927, in Moody Scrapbooks; Steen, "Political History of Texas, 1900–1930," p. 457; McKay, *Texas Politics*, p. 158; Richardson, *Texas*, p. 313. See also Josiah M. Daniel III, "The Fate of Business Progressivism in Texas State Politics: Governor Dan Moody's Legislative Program in the Fortieth and Forty-First Legislatures, 1927–1930" (seminar paper, University of Texas at Austin, 1974); Daniel, "Governor Dan Moody and Business Progressivism in Texas" (paper presented at the Eightieth Annual Meeting of the Texas State Historical Association, Galveston, Texas, March 5, 1976). I am indebted to Mr. Daniel for copies of these two fine papers.

8. *House Journal*, 40 Leg., reg. sess. (1927), pp. 4–5; *Journal of the Senate of Texas Being the Regular Session of the Fortieth Legislature Begun and Held at the City of Austin, January 11, 1927*, p. 3 (hereafter cited as *Senate Journal*, 40 Leg., reg. sess. [1927]); *Dallas Morning News*, January 5, 6, 10, 12, 1927.

9. *Senate Journal*, 40 Leg., reg. sess (1927), pp. 6–7, 44–46, 79; *Dallas Morning News*, January 14, 16, 22, 1927. Senator Hall, present, who would vote yes, was paired with Senator Bledsoe, absent, who would vote no.

10. *House Journal*, 40 Leg., reg. sess. (1927), pp. 132–47; *Dallas Morning News*, January 22, 1927.

11. *Dallas Morning News*, January 25, 1927.

12. Luthin, *American Demagogues*, pp. 174–75; *Ferguson Forum*, October 6, 1927.

13. *Senate Journal*, 40 Leg., reg. sess. (1927), pp. 414–18; *Ferguson Forum*, February 24, 1927. Ayes: Floyd, Greer, Hall, Hardin, Lewis, Love, McFarlane, Moore, Neal, Pollard, Price, Real, Reid, Smith, Stuart, Triplett, Westbrook, Witt, and Wood—19; noes, Bowers, Fairchild, Miller, Parr, Russek, Ward, and Wirtz—7. Present but not voting: Bailey, Berkeley, and Woodward—3; pairs: Bledsoe, present who would vote aye, and Holbrook, absent, who would vote no.

14. *House Journal*, 40 Leg., reg. sess. (1927), pp. 1371–77, 1436–37; *General and Special Laws of the State of Texas Passed by the Fortieth Legislature at the Regular Session Convened at the City of Austin, January 11, 1927 and Adjourned March 16, 1927*, pp. 360–61 (hereafter cited as *General and Special Laws*, 40 Leg., reg. sess. [1927]); *Dallas Morning News*, March 15, 16, April 1, 1927. The *House Journal* gives the final vote as 78 to 24. The *News* and the *General and Special Laws* give it as 78 to 25.

15. *House Journal*, 40 Leg., reg. sess. (1927), pp. 441–45; *Dallas Morning News*, February 3–5, 8, 9, 13, March 7, 1927; Frost and Jenkins, "*I'm Frank Hamer*," pp. 161–63.

16. Pool to Richard F. Burges, March 15, 1927, Burges Papers; *House Journal*, 40 Leg., reg. sess. (1927), 1133–41, 1312–18; *Senate Journal*, 40 Leg., reg. sess. (1927), pp. 755–56; *Dallas Morning News*, March 9–11, 13, 15, 16, 1927. Ferguson charged: "The big daily newspapers are now fighting the law to tax cigarettes and cigars while the big cigarette companies are giving big page advertisements week after week in the columns of these big papers. It certainly was a fine crowd to talk about the poor little old Weekly Forum getting a few advertisements. The Old Dal Gal [the *News*] almost shed crocodile tears last week on its editorial page because a bill had been introduced to tax manufactured cigarettes and cigars." *Ferguson Forum*, February 17, 1927.

17. *Dallas Morning News*, December 3, 1926; Webb, Carroll, and Branda, eds., *Handbook of Texas*, 2:57.

18. *House Journal*, 40 Leg., reg. sess. (1927), pp. 677–78, 681–82, 1512–13; *Dallas Morning News*, February 19, March 5, 16, 17, 1927; *Ferguson Forum*, March 3, 1927.

19. J. M. Claunch, "The Fight for Civil Service in Texas," *Southwestern Social Science Quarterly* 24 June, 1943): 47–50.

20. *House Journal*, 40 Leg., reg. sess. (1927), p. 221; *Dallas Morning News*, March 10, 1927; Claunch, "Fight for Civil Service in Texas," p. 50.

21. *General and Special Laws*, 40 Leg., reg. sess. (1927), pp. 5–6, 18–19, 115–16, 121–22, 219–20, 260–61, 308–15, 378–79, 399–409, 449–52; A. H. McKnight, "The Fortieth Legislature and Judicial Reform," *Texas Law Review* 5 (June, 1927): 360–67; Jack Johnson, "State Regulation of Public Utilities in Texas" (Ph.D. diss., University of Texas, 1932), pp. 124–34; Carey Carter Thompson, "Motor Carrier Regulation in Texas" (Master's thesis, University of Texas, 1931), pp. 22–24; Steen, "Political History of Texas, 1900–1930," p. 452; Steen, *Twentieth Century Texas*, pp. 325–29.

22. *General and Special Laws*, 40 Leg., reg. sess. (1927), pp. 298–307, 217–18; Crow, "Political History of the Texas Prison System," pp. 259–60; Steen, *Twentieth Century Texas*, pp. 200–201.

23. *Journal of the House of Representatives of the First Called Session of the Forty-first Legislature Begun and Held at the City of Austin, April 22, 1929*, p. 2 (hereafter cited as 41 Leg., 1st called sess. [1929]); *Dallas Morning News*, January 7, March 18, 1929.

24. Mrs. Dan Moody, "Diary," January 10, 1927, pp. 22–23.

25. Cousins to Ruth Wesley, October 12, 1927, Robert Bartow Cousins Papers, University of Texas Archives (hereafter cited as Cousins Papers); Colquitt to Moody, November 18, 1926, Colquitt Papers; Hogg to Moody, January 12, 1927, Hogg Papers; *Dallas Morning News*, August 7, 1926.

26. Jane Y. McCallum Personal Diary, McCallum Family Papers; *Dallas Morning News*, January 12, 1927.

27. Lomax to Hogg, January 27, 1927, Lomax to Batts, January 27, 1927, Bedichek to Batts, January 27, 1927, Batts Papers. See also Lomax to Moody, January 27, 1927, Batts Papers.

28. Hogg to Stark, March 5, 1927, Hogg to Holliday, March 10, 1927, Batts Papers. See also Hogg to Dr. W. M. W. Splawn, March 15, 1927, Batts Papers.

29. Holliday to Batts, March 21, 1927, Holliday to Batts, April 22, 1927, Holliday to Batts, April 25, 1927, Gregory to Batts, April 26, 1927, Batts to Edward Crane, June 14, 1927, Crane to Batts, June 16, 1927, Batts Papers; Pool, *Eugene C. Barker*, pp. 135–37; J. W. Calhoun, "Harry Yandell Benedict," in Webb, Carroll, and Branda, eds., *Handbook of Texas*, 1:146.

30. Holliday to Batts, May 17, 1927, Moody to Hogg, June 6, 1927, Hogg to Moody, June 6, 1927, Batts Papers.

31. Moody to L. B. Russell, August 30, 1930, Moody Papers; Mrs. Dan Moody, "Diary," January 30, 1927, p. 30. On Carter, see Alva Johnston, "Colonel Carter of Cartersville," *Saturday Evening Post* 211 (November 26, 1938): 8–9, 31–35; Amon G. Carter Biographical File, Barker Texas History Center, University of Texas (hereafter cited as Carter File); Seymour V. Connor, ed., *Builders of the Southwest*, pp. 30–33; Flemmons, *Amon*.

32. Moody to H. G. Meacham, June 14, 1929, Moody to *Fort Worth Star-Telegram*, June 8, 1929, Moody Papers.

33. Love to Moody, September 28, 1926, Colquitt Papers; *Dallas Morning News*, January 14, 1927.

34. Moody to Kemp, December 3, 1925, in Kemp, "Texas State Highway Department Notebooks," vol. 2, Kemp Papers; *Dallas Morning News*, November 27, 1925, clipping in Colquitt Papers. See also Colquitt to Moody, September 15, 1925, Ernest May to Colquitt, September 19, 1925, Moody to Colquitt, September 22, October 10, 1925, Colquitt to Moody, November 5, 1925, Moody to Colquitt, November 6, 1925, Colquitt to Moody, November 7, 27, 1925, Colquitt Papers. Biggers, however, contended that if it had not been for Louis Kemp there would have been no revealed facts for Moody to investigate. He wrote: "Moody frequently admitted to this writer that he owed all to Kemp, and more than once in private, but never in public, said the people should build a monument to Kemp's memory. In so far as I know, never once, in printed statement or public utterance, did Moody give credit to Kemp, the man who deserved all of the credit. Not only that but Moody took credit for much wherein he knew that he was not entitled to credit. And Moody knows that this writer knows the inside history of the whole thing." Biggers, *Our Sacred Monkeys*, p. 69.

35. Colquitt to J. T. Bowman, August 4, 1926, Colquitt to Moody, September 16, 1926, Colquitt to T. B. Davis, October 6, 1926, Colquitt Papers. On the *Free Lance* deficit, see Colquitt to Will C. Hogg, November 8, 1927, Hogg Papers. Hogg chided the former governor: "I warned you repeatedly not to take anything for granted with regard to the expenses. . . . I am sorry about the jam you got yourself into, but I am not disposed to take up any of it myself." Hogg to Colquitt, November 14, 1927, Colquitt Papers.

36. Colquitt to Moody, November 11, 1926, Colquitt Papers. See also Moody to Colquitt, November 12, 1926, Moody to Colquitt, November 14, 18, 1926, Colquitt Papers.

37. George W. Winningham to Colquitt, November 14, 1926, Winningham to Colquitt, December 8, 19, 1926, Colquitt to T. B. Davis, December 23, 1926, Colquitt to Love, January 21, 1927, Colquitt Papers.

38. Colquitt to Love, January 24, 25, February 18, 1927, Colquitt Papers. In the Colquitt Papers is a penciled sheet signed by twelve senators—Holbrook, Fairchild, Bowers, Bailey, Smith, Love, Miller, Triplett, McFarlane, Russek, Ward, and Floyd—endorsing Colquitt's appointment as chairman of the Highway Commission. Parr's name is missing.

39. Love to Moody, August 7, 1926, Moody Papers. Love tried to smooth over the rift between Moody and Colquitt, telling the disappointed office seeker that he still had "great faith in the success of Moody's administration" and was "determined to leave nothing undone that I can do to uphold his hands. When an honest man in public office makes a mistake is the time when he needs friends most." Love to Colquitt, January 26, 1927, Colquitt Papers.

40. Gregory to Moody, January 29, 1927, Moody Papers; Kemp, "Texas State Highway Department Notebooks," vol. 2, Kemp Papers; Clark with Hart, *The Tactful Texan*, p. 159; *Dallas Morning News*, January 26, February 2, 1927. Mrs. Moody noted in her diary: "Dan was hounded to death almost over appointment of a Highway Commission, because of the Roadway Scandals and Contracts which Dan exposed. His administration rather hinged on this commission. He finally appointed Ross Sterling and Cone Johnson and then hung fire over a 'western man.' I inwardly wanted Abilene to have it, but could say nothing. At last things worked themselves out and he did appoint Judge Ely." Mrs. Dan Moody, "Diary," January 30, 1927, p. 30.

41. Kemp, "Texas State Highway Department Notebooks," vol. 2, Kemp Papers.

42. *Dallas Morning News*, April 29, 30 (editorial), 1927; Mrs. Dan Moody, "Diary," May, 1927, pp. 36–37. See also Cone Johnson to Moody, May 5, 1927, Moody Papers.

43. *Dallas Morning News*, May 11, 16, 1927; "Moody, Meteors and Destiny," unidentified newspaper clipping in Moody Scrapbooks.

44. *Dallas Morning News*, April 8, May 3, 1927. John E. Davis of Mesquite, chairman of the House Committee on Contingent Expense, warned Moody that his administration could not be the success it ought to be "if you submit the question of special taxes at the forthcoming session of the Legislature." The legislature would increase appropriations in such a way that the governor could not reduce the total by veto, and "you, more than the Legislature, will be criticized for it." Davis to Moody, April 30, 1927, Moody Papers.

45. *Dallas Morning News*, May 12, 1927.

46. *House Journal*, 40 Leg., 1st called sess. (1927), pp. 75–76; *Dallas Morning News*, May 20, 27, 1927.

47. *House Journal*, 40 Leg., 1st called sess. (1927), p. 2; *Dallas Morning News*, May 22, 26, 27, 1927; Claunch, "Fight for Civil Service in Texas," pp. 50–51.

48. *Journal of the Senate of Texas Being the First Called Session of the Fortieth Legislature Begun and Held at the City of Austin, May 9, 1927*, pp. 387, 436; *Dallas Morning News*, June 5, 1927. Voting for adjournment: ayes, Bailey, Bledsoe, Bowers, Fairchild, Floyd, Greer, Hardin, Holbrook, McFarlane, Miller, Moore, Parr, Real, Russek, Stuart, Ward, Westbrook, and Wirtz—16; noes, Berkeley, Hall, Lewis, Love, Neal, Pollard, Price, Reid, Smith, Triplett, Witt, Wood, and Woodward—13.

49. *Dallas Morning News*, June 6, 1927.

50. Ibid., May 10, 27, 1927.

51. *House Journal*, 40 Leg., 1st called sess. (1927), pp. 458–62; *Dallas Morning News*, May 30, June 3, 1927.

52. On *Nixon* v. *Herndon*, see Roy W. McDonald, "Negro Voters in Democratic Primaries," *Texas Law Review* 5, (June, 1927): 392–400; Robert W. Hainsworth, "The Negro and the Texas Primaries," *Journal of Negro History* 18 (October, 1933): 426–29; Leon Alilunas, "Legal Restrictions on the Negro in Politics," *Journal of Negro History* 25 (April, 1940): 167–68; Conrey Bryson, *Dr. Lawrence A. Nixon and the White Primary*; August Meier and Elliott Rudwick, "Attorneys Black and White: A Case Study of Race Relations within the NAACP," *Journal of American History* 62 (March, 1976): 929; Darlene Clark Hine, "The Elusive Ballot: The Black Struggle against the Texas Democratic White Primary, 1932–1945," *Southwestern Historical Quarterly* 81 April, 1978): 373–74; Darlene Clark Hine, *Black Victory: The Rise and Fall of the White Primary in Texas*. The NAACP's *Nixon* v. *Herndon* legal files for the period August, 1924, to November, 1929, are in the NAACP Records, Manuscripts Division, Library of Congress. The Dr. Lawrence A. Nixon Papers are in the Lyndon Baines Johnson Presidential Library, Austin, Texas.

53. *Dallas Morning News*, March 9, 1927.

54. Ibid., March 14, 1927; *Ferguson Forum*, March 17, 1927. See also "Meanwhile the Negro Is Menacing Nobody" (editorial), *Dallas Morning News*, June 2, 1927.

55. *General and Special Laws of the State of Texas Passed by the Fortieth Legislature at Its First Called Session Convened at the City of Austin, May 9, 1927 and Adjourned June 7, 1927*, pp. 193–94; Lewison, *Race, Class, and Party*, p. 155. The measure passed the House 77 to 26, with 3 present and not voting, and passed the Senate by viva voce vote.

56. *General and Special Laws*, 40 Leg., reg. sess. (1927), p. 154; *Senate Journal*, 40 Leg., reg. sess. (1927), pp. 214, 530–31; *House Journal*, 40 Leg., reg. sess. (1927),

pp. 1420–21. The measure passed the House 104 to 1 (McGill voting no) and passed the Senate without a roll-call vote.

57. *Dallas Morning News*, June 5, 8, 1927.

58. R. B. Cousins to R. M. Kelly, July 18, 1927, Cousins Papers; *Dallas Morning News*, June 17–20, 1927.

59. *Dallas Morning News*, June 8, 9, 1927.

60. Ibid., June 9, 1927; *Ferguson Forum*, June 9, 1927; *Houston Chronicle*, July, 1927, clipping in Moody Scrapbook, in possession of Mrs. Dan Moody, Sr.

61. *Dallas Morning News*, May 14, June 5, 1927. Representative Ray Holder of Lancaster said that Moody's program had gone on the rocks because he had taken only two legislators—Chairman Teer of the House Appropriation Committee and Chairman Wood of the Senate Finance Committee—into his confidence. Another trouble was that members' bills were held up until so late that they had little chance of passing. That aroused their resentment, and they carried it over into their consideration of the governor's program. *Dallas Morning News*, June 11, 1927.

62. Ibid., June 8, 1927.

63. *Houston Chronicle*, July, 1927, clipping in Moody Scrapbook, in possession of Mrs. Dan Moody, Sr.

64. Mrs. Moody's comment in Moody Scrapbook, in possession of Mrs. Dan Moody, Sr.; *Ferguson Forum*, August 25, 1927. For the Moodys' family life in the governor's mansion, see Willson Whitman, "The Dollar Stretchers," *Collier's* 80 (November 12, 1927): 14, 50–51; Mildred Paxton Moody, "Housekeeping in the Governor's Mansion," *Dallas Morning News*, March 5, 1931; Anita Brewer, "Mrs. Moody Learned Housekeeping as a Bride in Governor's Mansion," *Austin American*, August 18, 1954, clipping in Moody Biographical File; Farrell and Silverthorne, *First Ladies of Texas*, pp. 315–31.

65. Brandeis is quoted in Thomas Watt Gregory to Moody, March 4, 1927, Moody Papers.

66. Robert M. Field, "A Daniel Come to Judgment: A Portrait of the New Governor of Texas," *Outlook* (January 5, 1927): 17, clipping in Moody Biographical File. See also Dan Moody, "A Message to the North and East," in *The All-Texas Special Good Will Tour: An Achievement in State Advertising*, pp. 49–53, copy in Moody Papers.

67. *New York World*, n.d., *New York Herald-Tribune*, n.d., *Austin American*, n.d., clippings in Moody Scrapbook, in possession of Mrs. Dan Moody, Sr. Mrs. Moody's written comment on the clippings: "The 'Eastern Tour' Dan *hailed* everywhere."

68. *Dallas Morning News*, June 25, July 2, 1927.

69. *Ferguson Forum*, June 30, July 7, July 28, 1927; *Dallas Morning News*, July 19, 29, 1927.

70. *Dallas Morning News*, August 2, 3, September 13, 1927; *Ferguson Forum*, August 4, 1927.

71. T. W. Carlock to Moody, July, 1927, Moody to Ed Krohn, August 3, 1927, Moody to Harry Byrd, February 1, 1928 [1929], Moody Papers; *Dallas Morning News*, July 27, 1927.

72. McKay, *Texas Politics*, pp. 160–61; *Dallas Morning News*, January 18, 1928; Louis J. Wardlaw, "Opening Speech Louis J. Wardlaw of Tarrant County Candidate for the Democratic Nomination for Governor of Texas Delivered at Center, Shelby County, April 14, 1928" (broadside), 1928, Louis J. Wardlaw Biographical File, Barker Texas History Center (hereafter cited as Wardlaw File).

73. Ray Holder to Moody, January 21, 1928, Moody Papers. William T. Waggoner was a wealthy Fort Worth oil man and rancher. In 1931 he built Arlington Downs, be-

tween Fort Worth and Dallas, famous as a rack track and a plant for the breeding of fine horses.

74. *Dallas Morning News,* July 21, 23, 24, 27, 1928.

75. Heard and Strong, *Southern Primaries and Elections,* pp. 141–43; McKay, *Texas Politics,* p. 163; *Dallas Morning News,* July 30, August 5, 1928; *Time* 12 (August 6, 1928): 11. "The Guerras told West and me that they will support you, which means that you will carry Starr County. Baker will support you in Hidalgo County and you will get a big majority of the Willacy County vote, and I think your opposition in Cameron County will be negligible." S. L. Gill to Moody, July 6, 1928, Moody Papers.

76. Heard and Strong, *Southern Primaries and Elections,* pp. 141–43.

77. *Ferguson Forum,* August 2, 1928. The *Forum* had predicted that Wardlaw would receive 300,000 votes; Moody, 250,000; Hawkins, 245,000; and Wilmans, 5,000. Ibid., July 26, 1928.

78. Mrs. Dan Moody, "Diary," September, 1928, p. 50.

79. *Dallas Morning News,* July 31, 1928.

Chapter 10

1. *Official Report of the Proceedings of the Democratic National Convention Held at Houston, Texas, June 26, 27, 28, and 29, 1928. . . ,* p. 162.

2. O. Douglas Weeks, *The Election of 1928* (Austin, n.d.), p. 2. See also Roy V. Peel and Thomas C. Donnelly, *The 1928 Campaign: An Analysis;* Edmund A. Moore, *A Catholic Runs for President: The Campaign of 1928;* David Burner, *Politics of Provincialism,* pp. 179–243. On Texas, see Steen, "Political History of Texas, 1900–1930," pp. 453–56; McKay, *Texas Politics,* pp. 177–82; Donley Watt, "The Presidential Election of 1928 in Texas" (Master's thesis, University of Texas, 1970).

3. Allen Peden, "Texas Free-for-All," *Outlook and Independent* 155 (July 9, 1930): 380–82, 395; Allen Peden, "The Downfall of a Dry Moses," *American Mercury* 28 (February, 1933): 187–90; *Texas Merry-Go-Round,* pp. 123–26.

4. Love to McAdoo, September 14, 1926, Love to Sullivan, September 28, 1926, Love to McAdoo, March 29, 1927, Love Papers. See also Love to McAdoo, October 27, 1926, June 13, August 23, 1927, Love Papers. James A. Bordeaux told Moody that, in a conversation with Love in the Baker Hotel following the first Democratic primary in 1926, Bordeaux had remarked, "There is nothing to Moody," and Love had replied, "I know it. Nothing but something to beat Ferguson with." Whether Love in fact made such a statement cannot be verified, but, apparently anticipating such stories, he assured Moody that his pledge of help for his administration was "absolutely dependable regardless of what the shoulder shrugging trouble makers and crooks may tell you." Bordeaux to Moody, [1928], Moody Papers; Love to Moody, August 7, 1926, Love Papers.

5. McAdoo to Milton, August 26, 30, September 7, 9, 12, 15, 17, 22, 1927, Milton to McAdoo, August 17, September 2, 1927, McAdoo Papers.

6. Milton to McAdoo, October 17, 1927, McAdoo Papers.

7. *Dallas Morning News,* September 18, 23, 1927; Gregory to F. C. Davis, April 8, 1927, Gregory to Harland B. Howe, April 22, 1927, Gregory to Edward M. House, October 14, 1927, Gregory to Howe, October 14, 1927, R. L. Henry to Gregory, February 1, 1928, Gregory to Henry, February 4, 1928, Gregory to F. C. Davis, March 28, 1928, Gregory to Ray Stannard Baker, June 12, 1928, Gregory Papers, Library of Congress; Gregory to John W. Davis, April 27, 1928, John W. Davis Papers; Gregory to William G. McAdoo, November 26, 1927, McAdoo Papers.

8. *Dallas Morning News*, January 20, 1928; Thomas B. Love, "Expediency or the Right—Which?" *Bunker's Monthly: The Magazine of Texas* 1 (February, 1928): 183–201.

9. *Dallas Morning News*, October 26, 1927; Connie C. Renfro, interview in *Houston Post-Dispatch*, March 28, 1928. See also his statement in *Dallas Morning News*, May 22, 1928.

10. Connie C. Renfro, "Do We Want a National Party?" *Bunker's Monthly: The Magazine of Texas* 1 (February, 1928): 202–13; Renfro to G. E. Hamilton, November 16, 1927, Moody Papers. See also Renfro to Tom Rountree, October 27, 1927, Renfro to Moody, April 13, 1928, Moody Papers.

11. B. D. Sartain to Pat M. Neff, March 5, 1928, Neff Papers; R. E. Brooks to Dan Moody, April 23, 1928, Moody Papers; E. A. DeWitt to Thomas B. Love, May 16, 1928, Love Papers; "How It Happened—By Thomas B. Love," *Dallas Times Herald*, n.d., clipping in Love Biographical File.

12. Renfro to Dan Moody, November 8, 1927, Moody Papers; *Houston Post-Dispatch*, March 28, 1928; *New York Times*, April 1, 1928; *Dallas Morning News*, March 16, 1928; Allen V. Peden, "Those Burro Blues," *Houston Gargoyle* 1 (June 26, 1928): 5.

13. W. J. Moroney to Franklin D. Roosevelt, September 22, 1927, General Political Correspondence, 1921–28, group 11, box 4, Roosevelt Papers; Royal S. Copeland to Alfred E. Smith, November 10, 1927, Smith to Copeland, November 16, 1927, Graves Papers; *San Antonio Express*, November 16, 1927. On Jurney's visit to Texas, see his brief testimony before the Senate committee investigating presidential campaign expenditures in *Dallas Morning News*, May 23, 1928, and William Everett DuPuy, "Democratic National Convention of 1928" (Master's thesis, University of Texas, 1929), p. 6.

14. Jurney to Henry, March 12, 1928, in *Dallas Morning News*, June 7, 1928; DuPuy, "Democratic National Convention of 1928," pp. 8–9.

15. *New York Times*, January 13, 1928; *Dallas Morning News*, January 14, 1928; Clark with Hart, *The Tactful Texan*, p. 162; Timmons, *Jesse H. Jones*, pp. 143–45; Larry L. Smith, "A Study of Houston's Role in the 1928 Democratic Convention" (Master's thesis, Sam Houston State Teachers College, 1965), pp. 25–32, 40–41, 53–54.

16. *Dallas Morning News*, January 16, 1928; Jurney to Moody, February 18, 1928, Moody Papers; Jesse Daniel Ames, "Memorandum on Dan Moody, 1918–1928," Mrs. Jesse Daniel Ames Papers, Texas State Archives (hereafter cited as Ames Papers, Texas State Archives); *Ferguson Forum*, February 9, 1928; Love to Walter A. Keeling, January 26, 1928, Love Papers. See also Fred Gantt, interview with Mrs. Dan Moody, August 16, 1968, Oral History Collection, North Texas State University, no. 25; A. S. Walker to Tom Connally, February 7, 1928, Connally Papers.

17. *Dallas Morning News*, November 23, 1927, January 25, February 3, 29, 1928.

18. "First Citizen of Texas," *Outlook* 149 (July 4, 1928): 363–64; P. J. R. MacIntosh, "The Democratic Convention City," *Bunker's Monthly: The Magazine of Texas* 1 (May, 1928): 658–59; *Time* 11 (January 23, 1928): 7–8; "Jesse Jones, Who Spoke Up for Houston," *New York Times Magazine*, May 13, 1928, clipping in Jones Papers; George Fuermann, *Houston: Land of the Big Rich*, pp. 81–83; *Dallas Morning News*, February 29, 1928. Mrs. Jesse Daniel Ames had a conversation with Moody on February 27. He said that there had been a meeting in Houston the day before but that he had not been invited. He had it on reliable information, he said, that it was a Smith group and that they had decided to seek a presidential endorsement for Jesse Jones. Jones was favorable to Smith, and when the proper time came an attempt would be made to throw the Texas votes through Jones to Smith. Moody said that this information should be reported to the people as quickly as possible. If necessary, he would make a fight against Jones, "but he had as many enemies now as he wanted and he did not want to go out and hunt for

more." Ames, "Memorandum on Dan Moody, 1918–1928," Ames Papers, Texas State Archives.

19. DuPuy, "Democratic National Convention of 1928," pp. 40–41; *Dallas Morning News*, February 4, 9, 22, March 14, 1928. J. B. Cranfill talked with Imperial Wizard Hiram Wesley Evans, who was in Dallas at the same time that Reed was. Cranfill reported to Hoover that Evans "spoke kindly of you, but in so far as he has political affiliations, he seems to be affiliating with the Democrats. He talks dry in a way, but he told me frankly that he was for Reed if it came to a test in the Democratic National Convention between Reed and Smith. I can understand that quite well because of his hostility to Catholics. It was quite suggestive that he was in Dallas at the same time that Senator Reed was here opening his campaign." Cranfill to Hoover, February 28, 1928, Cranfill Papers.

20. *Ferguson Forum*, October 27, 1927, November 10, 1927, January 19, 26, February 2, March 15, April 12, 26, 1928; *Dallas Morning News*, March 14, 1928. About two months after Mrs. Ferguson's inauguration, Ferguson got in touch with Al Smith through an intermediary, Judge Floyd M. Spann, a district judge during his own administration, who was now living in New York City. On August 5, 1925, Spann wrote Smith that he had seen Ferguson while he was in Texas and that he was doing "a great deal of very effective work throughout the South and Southwest" on the New York governor's behalf. Both Ferguson and Smith wanted a personal meeting, but the highway scandals broke in the press that fall, and it is doubtful that one took place. James E. Ferguson to Alfred E. Smith, March 26, 1925, Floyd Spann to Smith, August 5, 1925, Smith to Spann, August 10, 1925, Graves Papers.

21. *Dallas Morning News*, March 7, 8, 10, 1928; Ames, "Memorandum on Dan Moody, 1918–1928," Ames Papers, Texas State Archives.

22. *Dallas Morning News*, March 3, 1928; Moore, *A Catholic Runs for President*, pp. 92–93; Claude Bowers, *My Life: The Memoirs of Claude Bowers*, pp. 70–71; Thomas J. Walsh to Gavin McNab, November 22, 1927, December 19, 1927, Walsh to James D. Phelan, December 19, 1927, Thomas J. Walsh Papers, Manuscripts Division, Library of Congress (hereafter cited as Walsh Papers). On Walsh's candidacy, see Paul A. Carter, "The Other Catholic Candidate: The 1928 Presidential Bid of Thomas J. Walsh," *Pacific Northwest Quarterly* 55 (January, 1964): 1–8.

23. McAdoo to Walsh, March 17, 1928, Armistead and Davis to Walsh, March 6, 1928, Walsh to Armistead and Davis, March 24, 1928, Walsh Papers; Love to Mrs. W. R. Pattengall, March 22, 1928, Davis to Love, February 28, 1928, Love Papers.

24. Townsend to Walsh, March 3, 1928, Morris Sheppard to Walsh, March 8, 1928, Walsh to Sheppard, March 10, 1928, Walsh Papers. Old-time Populist, J. H. ("Cyclone") Davis, who had known Walsh since the Bryan campaign of 1900, called him "a bone-dry personally and politically." "I am a Klansman 'to the Manor born,' a lecturer in that order," Davis announced. "But I consider Tom Walsh . . . one of the best, bravest and brainiest statesmen in the Democratic party. Nominate him and although I am 75 years old, I am ready to round out my political life in a campaign for his election." "Cyclone Davis for Senator Walsh for President," unidentified newspaper clipping enclosed in J. H. ("Cyclone") Davis to Walsh, April 3, 1928, Walsh Papers.

25. *Dallas Morning News*, March 5, 8, 1928; *San Antonio Express*, March 6, 1928, clipping in George D. Armistead and F. C. Davis to Thomas J. Walsh, March 6, 1928, Walsh Papers.

26. *Dallas Morning News*, March 8, 1928. South Dakota's rather complicated system of primary and conventions finally awarded 4 national-convention votes to Walsh, 3 to Smith. Carter, "The Other Catholic Candidate," p. 6.

27. *Dallas Morning News*, March 16, 1928; Ames, "Memorandum on Dan Moody, 1918–1928," Ames Papers, Texas State Archives; Love to McAdoo, March 19, 1928, Love to Thomas H. Ball, March 27, 1928, Love to George Wilson, April 18, 1928, Love Papers; Townsend to Walsh, March 16, 1928, Walsh Papers.

28. Carr P. Collins to Dan Moody, March 6, 1928, Moody to T. W. Carlock, May 17, 1928, Holliday to Moody, March 21, 1928, Moody Papers; *Dallas Morning News*, March 16, 23, 1928.

29. *Dallas Morning News*, March 24, 1928; Holliday to Moody, March 26, 1928, Moody Papers.

30. Ames, "Memorandum on Dan Moody, 1918–1928," Ames Papers, Texas State Archives.

31. Connie C. Renfro to Dan Moody, March 27, 1928, Lynch Davidson to Raymond Brooks, April 13, 1928, Moody Papers; *Dallas Morning News*, April 1, 1928; Clark with Hart, *The Tactful Texan*, p. 162; Peden, "Those Burro Blues," p. 5; "Texas," three-page synopsis of letters from Texans to Smith or advisers, in Democratic National Convention folder 671, Alfred E. Smith Papers.

32. *Dallas Morning News*, April 7, 1928.

33. Ibid., April 9, 1928.

34. Ibid., May 22, 1928; CJ [Cone Johnson] to Kirby, April 9, 1928, Love Papers.

35. Acheson, *Joe Bailey*, pp. 398–99; *Dallas Morning News*, February 4, April 17, 18, 1928; Lynch Davidson to Dan Moody, April 17, 1928, Moody Papers.

36. Moody to Renfro, April 8, 1928, V. A. Collins to Moody, April 23, 1928, Moody to Lynch Davidson, April 24, 1928, Moody to W. L. Dean, May 18, 1928, Moody to J. B. Cranfill, May 19, 1928, Moody Papers; *Dallas Morning News*, April 26, 1928. "I am sure the Governor is not going to make any agreement that does not conserve our principles intact in every respect," Lynch Davidson assured a concerned Waco Democrat. "I have discussed the matter with him over the 'phone several times and he has assured me that the other organization has reached the conclusion that we are right and are going to adopt our viewpoint." Davidson to Judge W. E. Spell, April 24, 1928, Moody Papers.

37. *Dallas Morning News*, April 28, 30, 1928; Clark with Hart, *The Tactful Texan*, pp. 162–63.

38. *Dallas Morning News*, May 3, 4, 18, 1924; one-page mimeographed press release in Moody Papers.

39. Davis to Julien C. Hyer, April 11, 1928, Walsh Papers; *Dallas Morning News*, May 5, 1928. McAdoo wrote Love that the dominance of the religious issue had made it impossible to concentrate the dry Protestant support on Walsh. Protestants had either remained away from the polls or voted for Reed, who was the only Protestant in the race and whose wet position was to a considerable extent obscured by Smith's superior wet position. Smith got every wet vote and, with few exceptions, every Catholic vote. "Our whole trouble is the lack of cohesion among the drys," he complained. "They unite on no one and scatter their strength in a succession of futilities." McAdoo to Love, May 3, 1928, Love Papers.

40. *Dallas Morning News*, May 7, 9, 10, 1928; *San Antonio Express*, May 8, 1928; Albert S. Johnson to Dan Moody, May 9, 1928, E. G. Senter to Moody, May 11, 1928, T. W. Davidson to Myron G. Blalock, May 11, 1928, Moody Papers.

41. W. B. Bates to Dan Moody, May 9, 1928, Moody Papers; *Dallas Morning News*, May 11, 1928; *San Antonio Express*, May 9, 1928.

42. Lynch Davidson to V. A. Collins and George C. Purl, May 10, 1928, *Houston Press* clipping enclosed in Davidson to Moody, May 11, 1928, Moody Papers; *Dallas*

Morning News, May 11, 12, 1928; Clark with Hart, *The Tactful Texan*, p. 163. See also Moody to Mrs. T. A. Kindred, May 16, 1928, Moody Papers.

43. *Dallas Morning News*, May 23, 1928.

44. Ibid.

45. Ibid., May 24, 1928, Davis to McAdoo, June 1, 1928, McAdoo Papers.

46. Sells to Love, June 4, 1928, Love to McAdoo, May 28, 1928, Love Papers; Field to Edward M. House, July 25, 1928, House Papers; *Dallas Morning News*, June 7, 21, 1928.

47. *Dallas Morning News*, May 24, 1928; Mrs. Dan Moody, "Diary," September, 1928, p. 48.

48. Love to McAdoo, June 7, 1928, Love Papers; Davis to McAdoo, June 1, 1928, McAdoo Papers; Ames, "Memorandum on Dan Moody, 1918–1928," Ames Papers, Texas State Archives.

49. Jesse Daniel Ames, "Footnote to Beaumont Convention, May 1928," Ames Papers, Texas State Archives; Moody to H. T. Kimbro, June 5, 1928, Moody Papers; Cranfill to Moody, May 28, 1928, Cranfill Papers; "Young Dan Moody, of Texas," *Outlook* 149 (July 11, 1928): 404–405.

50. *Dallas Morning News*, May 25, 1928.

51. DuPuy, "Democratic National Convention," p. 80; Paul Wakefield, *Jesse Holman Jones*, p. 7; Love to E. J. Mantooth, June 4, 1928, Love Papers; Hogg to Moody, June 19, 1928, Moody Papers.

52. Printed copy in Hogg Papers; *New York Sun*, June 23, 1928, clipping in Lomax Papers; *Dallas Morning News*, June 23, 1928; Mayfield to Jesse Jones, n.d., Jones Papers. See *Official Report of the Proceedings of the Democratic National Convention, . . . 1928 . . .*, pp. 162–68, for the text of Ball's and Moody's nomination speeches. Following Ball's speech, thousands of small balloons bearing the words "Jesse H. Jones for President" were released from mysterious green bags hanging from the ceiling. Bands played in unison "The Eyes of Texas Are upon You," and a multitude of voices sang the song as Jones faced the blinding arc lights and clicking cameras, DuPuy, "Democratic National Convention of 1928," pp. 250–51.

53. *Houston Post*, June 25, 1928; *Dallas Morning News*, June 25, 1928; *San Antonio Express*, June 26, 1928.

54. *Official Report of the Proceedings of the Democratic National Convention, . . . 1928 . . .*, pp. 197, 200–201; *Dallas Morning News*, June 26, 29, 30, 1928; Moody to Irvin Simmons, June 30, 1928, Moody Papers. See also Moody to Mark Sullivan, July 31, 1928, Moody Papers; Fred L. Israel, *Nevada's Key Pittman*, pp. 64–66.

55. DuPuy, "Democratic Convention of 1928," p. 254; DuPuy's personal notes.

56. Ibid.; *Dallas Morning News*, June 30, 1928; Timmons, *Jesse H. Jones*, p. 147.

57. Unidentified newspaper clipping in Coolidge Papers; *Dallas Morning News*, April 22, 24, 1927.

58. *Dallas Morning News*, September 4, 1927; Roger Marvin Olien, "The Republican Party of Texas, 1920–1961" (Ph.D. diss., Brown University, 1973), p. 24; Peel and Donnelly, *The 1928 Campaign*, p. 4; Scobey to Dawes, May 23, 1928, Scobey Papers.

59. Scobey to Dawes, December 9, 29, 1927, February 8, 24, 1928, Dawes to Scobey, January 6, 1928, Scobey Papers. In the meantime, Wurzbach had lunched with Hoover and then with a member of Coolidge's cabinet and had promised to support the secretary of commerce. Creager and Bullington, who were in Washington at the time, told Hoover that this was not true. A few weeks later Captain Jack Elgin became intoxicated and fell unconscious in a hotel room. One of Creager's friends went through his pockets and found a letter from Wurzbach instructing Elgin to spread the story among

the German voters in the congressman's district that when Hoover was administering food relief in Europe after World War I he had allowed the German children to starve while diverting food to the Poles. The letter was sent to Hoover and was produced in the Republican National Convention. The story of the purloined Wurzbach letter was told to William R. Sanford "by a leading Texas Republican who was involved in the story, and is substantiated by references to the incident in the minutes of the Convention." William Reynolds Sanford, "History of the Republican Party in the State of Texas" (Master's thesis, University of Texas, 1954), p. 128.

60. Casdorph, *Republican Party in Texas*, pp. 133–34; *Dallas Morning News*, May 23, 1928. Bullington is quoted in Sanford, "History of the Republican Party in Texas," p. 114.

61. Casdorph, *Republican Party in Texas*, pp. 134–35; Olien, "Republican Party in Texas," pp. 71–72; Sanford, "History of the Republican Party in Texas," p. 114.

62. Casdorph, *Republican Party in Texas*, p. 136; Scobey to Dawes, June 18, 1928, Scobey Papers.

63. *San Antonio Express*, June 21, July 17, 1928; *New York Times*, July 17, 1928; Lewinson, *Race, Class, and Party*, pp. 158, 272n.

64. Moore, *A Catholic Runs for President*, p. 108; *Dallas Morning News*, July 1, 4, 1928.

65. David B. Burner, "The Brown Derby Campaign," *New York History* 46 October, 1965): 356; Burner, *Politics of Provincialism*, pp. 198–200; Paul A. Carter, "The Campaign of 1928 Re-examined: A Study in Political Folklore," *Wisconsin Magazine of History* 46 (Summer, 1963): 268; Moore, *A Catholic Runs for President*, pp. 121, 125–26; Bowers, *My Life*, pp. 177–78; Timmons, *Jesse H. Jones*, p. 148; *Dallas Morning News*, July 1, 1928; Henry F. Pringle, "Harmony—And a Man of Courage," *Outlook* 149 (July 11, 1928): 412. Robert W. Woolley sat next to Mrs. Moscowitz at a luncheon in the Hotel Biltmore just ten days before the election. "We are winners," she said jubilantly, "and do you know I have never been west of Pittsburgh?" Robert W. Woolley, "Politics Is Hell" (MS autobiography), chap. 32, Woolley Papers.

66. Kent Schofield, "The Public Image of Herbert Hoover in the 1928 Campaign," *Mid-America* 51 (October, 1969): 278–93; Norris to R. B. Creager, November 26, 1927, John Franklyn Norris Collection, Dargan-Carver Library, Nashville, Tenn. (hereafter cited as Norris Collection). For a balanced view of Hoover, based on meticulous research, see David Burner, *Herbert Hoover: A Public Life*. For a critical view by a member of the faculty of the University of Texas, see Henry Smith, "Hoover's Philosophy of Comfort," *Southwest Review* 14 (October, 1928): 111–18.

67. U.S. Congress, Senate, Subcommittee of the Committee on Post Offices and Post Roads, *Influencing Appointments to Postmasterships, Hearings, pts. 1–5, and Report*, 70 Cong., 2d. sess. (1929–30), p. 811; *Dallas Morning News*, July 8, 11, 13, 17, 18, 21, 1928; *New York Times*, July 18, 29, 1928; "Looking for a Split in the Solid South," *Literary Digest* 98 (August 4, 1928): 8; Virginius Dabney, *Dry Messiah: The Life of Bishop Cannon*, pp. 176–89; Alvin Moody to Cone Johnson, Marshall Hicks, Tom Love, Cato Sells, V. A. Collins, and B. D. Sartain, July 18, 1928, Love Papers; Alvin Moody to O. B. Colquitt, September 5, 1928, Colquitt Papers; J. F. Lucey to Lawrence Ritchey, July 7, 1928, Pre-Presidential General Correspondence—J. F. Lucey, Herbert Hoover Papers, Herbert Hoover Presidential Library (hereafter cited as Hoover Papers). Bullington is quoted in Sanford, "History of the Republican Party of Texas," p. 104. The Hoovercrat movement in the South posed a problem for William Gibbs McAdoo, since many of his followers were participating. At first, he made up his mind, "after long and careful thought," to remain silent on the presidential election. "I cannot support Hoover

and I cannot endorse Smith's views on prohibition and immigration," he wrote Love. On November 2, however, to preserve any potentialities for his "future usefulness" to the Democratic party and the country as a private citizen, McAdoo wired Pleasant A. Stovall of the *Savannah Press* and Thomas J. Hamilton of the *Augusta Chronicle*: "Replying to your telegram I am absolutely opposed to Governor Smith's position on prohibition and the Eighteenth Amendment but I shall preserve my party allegiance." McAdoo to Thomas B. Love, October 16, 1928, McAdoo to George Fort Milton, November 2, 1928, McAdoo to F. M. Simmons, November 2, 1928, McAdoo to Pleasant A. Stovall, November 2, 1928, McAdoo to Thomas J. Hamilton, November 2, 1928, McAdoo Papers.

68. *Dallas Morning News*, September 10, 18, 1928; U.S. Congress, Senate, Subcommittee of the Committee on Post Offices and Post Roads, *Influencing Appointments to Postmasterships*, pp. 321–22, 1055; Olien, "Republican Party of Texas," p. 75.

69. Olien, "Republican Party of Texas," p. 74.

70. Hiram Wesley Evans, "The Ballots behind the Ku Klux Klan," *World's Work* 55 (January, 1928): 243–52; Alexander, *Ku Klux Klan in the Southwest*, pp. 225–26, 239; J. F. Lucey to Lawrence Ritchey, July 7, 1928, Pre-Presidential General Correspondence—J. F. Lucey, Hoover Papers.

71. Colquitt to Ritchey, September 17, 1928, Colquitt Papers.

72. *Austin American*, June 13, 1946, clipping in Love Biographical File; *Dallas Morning News*, July 10, 22, 1928; Love to McAdoo, July 26, 1928, Love Papers.

73. *Dallas Morning News*, July 19, 1928.

74. Ibid., August 1, 2, 5, 1928; Molyneaux to Moody, August 1, 1928, Moody Papers.

75. Biggers, *Our Sacred Monkeys*, p. 78.

76. McKay, *Texas Politics*, pp. 163–64. As early as August, 1926, Tom Love had reported: "It is common talk now that Pat Neff may run, that Cullen Thomas wants to, that Alvin Owsley is going to, that Colquitt may, and that Jim Ferguson and Mayfield will. Ferguson will undoubtedly run if he lives. He will have no chance of winning but will run for campaign funds. He has made more money running for office than any other man in American history." Love to George A. Carden, August 1, 1926, Love Papers.

77. Higgins to George H. Carter, July 21, 1928, Connally Papers; Thomas Terry Connally and Alfred Steinberg, *My Name Is Tom Connally*, p. 121.

78. McKay, *Texas Politics*, pp. 172–73; Heard and Strong, *Southern Primaries and Elections*, pp. 167, 170.

79. Biggers, *Our Sacred Monkeys*, p. 78; *Ferguson Forum*, August 9, 1928; Connally and Steinberg, *My Name Is Tom Connally*, pp. 128–29; Robert F. Higgins to A. S. Walker, August 10, 1928, L. W. Kemp Affidavit, August 11, 1928, Kemp to Connally, August 11, 1928, Connally Papers; McKay, *Texas Politics*, pp. 174–75; *Dallas Morning News*, August 8, 11, 1928; *Austin American*, August 21, 23, 1928.

80. *Dallas Morning News*, August 26, 1928; McKay, *Texas Politics*, pp. 176–77; Heard and Strong, *Southern Primaries and Elections*, p. 170.

81. *Austin American*, August 28, 1928; Dick Collins to Connally, August 27, 1928, Connally Papers; Crane to "Dear Noakes" (Nora Crane), August 27, 1928, Crane Papers; Biggers, *Our Sacred Monkeys*, p. 79; *Time* 12 (September 3, 1928): 12. By 1930 the *Washington Post* counted only 780 klansmen in Texas. Alexander, "Secrecy Bids for Power," p. 26n. State Democratic Chairman D. W. Wilcox congratulated Connally: "It was a great victory and I take considerable pleasure in thinking that during the last few months, I have been partly instrumental in eliminating Earl [sic] Mayfield, Tom Love, and some others from the political picture in Texas." Wilcox to Connally, September 1, 1928, Connally Papers.

82. *Dallas Morning News*, August 12, 14, 1928; Gregory to Democratic Lawyers

Committee, October 6, 1928, Thomas Watt Gregory Papers, Southwest Collection, Texas Tech University, Lubbock, Texas.

83. *Dallas Morning News*, August 15, 24, 1928. Sheppard made his statement in a letter to the editor of the *Marshall Morning News*.

84. *Dallas Morning News*, September 11, 12, 1928.

85. Ibid., November 1, 1928; Marshall Hicks, "Which? Hoover or Smith?" (broadside), 1928, in Mercurio Martinez Papers, University Archives, Texas A&M University Library (hereafter cited as Martinez Papers); J. B. Cranfill to Jesse H. Jones, August 20, 1928, Cranfill to George W. Armstrong, September 5, 1930, Cranfill Papers; R. B. Creager to Alvin Moody, September 29, 1928, Love Papers.

86. Cranfill to Hoover, September 11, 1928, Cranfill to D. J. Kelley, October 6, 1928, Cranfill Papers; Allan J. Lichtman, *Prejudice and the Old Politics: The Presidential Election of 1928*, p. 63.

87. Steen, "Political History of Texas, 1900–1930," p. 455; Russell, "J. Frank Norris," 284; Tatum, *Conquest or Failure?* pp. 247–51; Norris to John W. Davis, October 25, 1928, John W. Davis Papers. Moore is quoted in Rembert Gilman Smith, *Politics in a Protestant Church*, p. 77. On "political preachers," see James Bryan Storey, "Political Parsons: Texas Churchmen and the Election of 1928" (Master's thesis, Texas Technological College, 1967); Richard Bennett Hughes, "Texas Churches and Presidential Politics, 1928 and 1960" (Ph.D. diss., Saint Louis University, 1978).

88. Smith, *Politics in a Protestant Church*, pp. 74–75; Norris to Freeman, August 27, September 5, 1928, Freeman to Norris, September 11, 1928, Norris Collection; *Dallas Morning News*, September 20, 1928. See also Alfred E. Smith, *Up to Now: An Autobiography*, pp. 410–12.

89. *Time* 12 (September 7, 1928): 9–10. "The Governor's Mansion at Albany, during the Smith regime, was never exactly arid," Edward J. Flynn recalled. "A cocktail or highball, in fact, was always available." Edward J. Flynn, *You're the Boss*, p. 66.

90. Milton to Will W. Alexander, October 18, 1928, George Fort Milton Papers, Manuscripts Division, Library of Congress (hereafter cited as Milton Papers); unidentified newspaper clipping, 1928, in Sam Rayburn Scrapbooks, Rayburn Library (hereafter cited as Rayburn Scrapbooks); Steinberg, *Sam Rayburn*, pp. 83–84. For an eyewitness account of Rayburn's speech, see Dorough, *Mr. Sam*, p. 190.

91. "Colquitt Denies Rayburn Charges," unidentified newspaper clipping, September 21, 1928, O. B. Colquitt Biographical File, Barker Texas History Center, University of Texas (hereafter cited as Colquitt Biographical File); *Constitutional Democrat* 1 (October, 1928); Norris to James Vance, September 18, 1928, Vance to Norris, September 21, 1928, Norris Collection.

92. *Dallas Morning News*, September 21, 23, 26, 1928.

93. Smith to Moody, August 8, 1928, Raskob to Moody, August 10, 1928, Tydings to Moody, August 8, 1928, Moody to Smith, September 22, 1928, Moody to Raskob, September 22, 1928, Moody to Tydings, September 22, 1928, Moody Papers.

94. *Dallas Morning News*, September 13, 1928; Moody to Ernest May, October 12, 1928, Moody Papers.

95. Sartain to Moody, September 13, 1928, Moody Papers; *Dallas Morning News*, September 12, 13, 1928.

96. *Dallas Morning News*, September 12, October 14, 23, 28, 1928; Connie C. Renfro to Dan Moody, October 17, 1928, Jed Adams, James Young, W. A. Thomas to Moody, October 23, 1928, Moody Papers.

97. Mrs. R. L. Jones to "Hon Raskob Dan Moody," October 30, 1928, Moody Pa-

pers. See also J. L. C. White to Moody, October 29, 1928, J. R. Key to Moody, October 23, 1928, Mrs. T. A. Kindred to Moody, October 23, 1928, Moody Papers.

98. *Dallas Morning News*, October 21, November 2, 3, 5, 1928; *San Antonio Express*, November 3, 4, 1928.

99. Love to George C. Butte, November 8, 1928, Love Papers; interview with Mrs. Dan Moody, Sr., p. 20; Mrs. Dan Moody, "Diary," December, 1928, p. 53. Robinson, *Presidential Vote* (p. 330), gives the Texas totals for president as Republican, 367,242; Democratic, 340,080; other, 867.

100. Butler to Charles D. Hilles, November 7, 1928, Charles D. Hilles Papers, Manuscripts and Archives, Yale University Library.

101. *Texas Weekly* (Dallas), April 4, May 2, 1931; McKay, *Texas Politics*, pp. 178–80; Leonard Withington, Answers to Questionnaire, enclosed in K. L. Fish to Lawrence Richey, December 11, 1928, Pre-Presidential General Correspondence—J. F. Lucey, Hoover Papers (hereafter cited as Withington, Answers); Key with Heard, *Southern Politics in State and Nation*, pp. 320–21; Watt, "The 1928 Presidential Campaign in Texas," pp. 79–86. A student of the election of 1928 in Alabama concluded that "it was this emphasis on white supremacy that saved the day for the loyal Democrats. Otherwise, Al Smith might have been defeated in Alabama." Hugh D. Reagan, "Race as a Factor in the Presidential Election of 1928 in Alabama," *Alabama Review* 19 (January, 1966): 19.

102. *Dallas Express*, March 31, 1928, quoted in Glasrud, "Black Texans, 1900–1930," p. 84; Withington, Answers, Hoover Papers.

103. McKay, *Texas Politics*, pp. 178–79; Moody to P. H. Callahan, November 23, 1928, Moody Papers; Withington, Answers, Hoover Papers. See also Ruth C. Silva, *Rum, Religion, and Votes: 1928 Re-examined*, pp. 53, 55–56.

104. Storey, "Political Parsons," p. 121–22.

105. *Dallas Morning News*, August 7, 1928; *Pitchfork*, June 28, 1928, Wilford B. Smith Papers.

106. Crane to W. O. Davis, November 12, 1928, Martin M. Crane Papers; Gregory to George W. Anderson, November 13, 1928, Gregory Papers, Library of Congress; Walter C. Woodward to Franklin D. Roosevelt, December 12, 1928, Democratic National Committee Papers, 1928–48: Correspondence, 1928–33, Texas Pre-Convention, box 732, Roosevelt Papers. In a letter to Clarence M. Flory, A. J. Wirtz, a delegate to the Houston convention, expressed the opinion that "the majority of the Texas voters cast their ballots for Hoover because of their opposition to Smith on both the prohibition and religious questions, although I think that they would have voted for him regardless of his stand on prohibition if it had not been for the fact that he was a Catholic." Clarence Mathew Flory, "Southern Opposition to Alfred E. Smith in the Election of 1928" (Master's thesis, University of Texas, 1937), p. 57. Joe B. Frantz, writing on the eve of the presidential election of 1960, made the statement that "there is no doubt that Smith's Catholicism was the root of the discontent in the South." Joe B. Frantz, "A Historian Looks Back to '28 . . . Liquor and Tammany, Cloaks for Fear," *Texas Observer* 52 (September 30, 1960): 10–11.

107. David Y. Thomas, "The Campaign of 1928," *Southwest Review* 14 (January, 1929): 224. Fort Worth editor Peter Molyneaux, who backed Smith, made the same point during the campaign in a letter to Moody: "When a man is in a mood to oppose Governor Smith sincerely on account of his prohibition views, it does not help toward getting him out of that mood to say to him that all who are giving this reason for their opposition to Governor Smith are opposed to him really on account of his religion, and that prohibition is merely a 'smoke screen.' He *knows* that is not true, for he knows fellow prohibi-

tionists who sacrificed much in fighting the Ku Klux Klan, and who have no prejudice against a Catholic holding office, but, who, nevertheless, are opposing Governor Smith, and on prohibition grounds alone." Molyneaux to Moody, September 29, 1928, Moody Papers.

108. J. B. Cranfill to George H. Moses, December 8, 1928, Cranfill Papers. Love claimed that 300,000 or more Hoover Democrats had contented themselves with casting half a ballot for the Republican nominee by "going fishing" on election day. Love to William E. Borah, November 19, 1928, Love Papers.

109. Richard Hofstadter, "Could a Protestant Have Beaten Hoover in 1928?" *Reporter* 22 (March 17, 1960): 31–33. See also Seymour Martin Lipset, "Some Statistics on Bigotry in Voting," *Commentary* 30 (October, 1960): 286–90.

110. Roosevelt to Daniels, June 23, 1927, in Carroll Kilpatrick, ed., *Roosevelt and Daniels: A Friendship in Politics*, p. 87; House to Gregory, October 6, 1927, Gregory to House, October 14, 1927, Gregory Papers, Library of Congress.

111. Hofstadter, "Could a Protestant Have Beaten Hoover in 1928?" p. 33.

112. *Dallas Morning News*, November 8, 9, 1928; "Texas 'Hoovercrats,'" *Outlook* 150 (November 28, 1928): 1243–44.

113. *Time* 12 (November 19, 1928): 12.

114. J. S. McNeel, Jr., to Franklin D. Roosevelt, November 14, 1928, 1928 Campaign Correspondence, Rhode Island–Washington, box 25–Texas, Roosevelt Library.

115. Alvin Moody circular letter, Love to Alvin Moody, November 17, 1928, Love to Bishop James Cannon, Jr., November 28, 1928, Love to Daniel C. Roper, December 12, 1928, Love to M. D. Lightfoot, December 21, 1928, Love Papers.

116. *Austin American*, November 13, 1928.

Conclusion

1. "Realized and Unrealized Dreams," in Neff, *Battles of Peace*, p. 241.

2. Steen, "Political History of Texas, 1900–1930," p. 457.

3. *Dallas Morning News*, May 24, 1966; Crow, "Political History of the Texas Prison System," p. 268.

4. *Dallas Morning News*, January 6, 1931.

5. Bolton, *Governors of Texas; Dallas Morning News*, April 23, 1930.

6. Gantt, *Chief Executive in Texas*, pp. 189, 224–25.

7. A. C. Baird to Dan Moody, February 24, 1930, Moody Papers; author's interview with Walter F. Woodul, Austin, July 11, 1975.

8. Mrs. Dan Moody, "Diary," May 25, 1929, p. 55.

9. *Houston Chronicle*, July, 1927, clipping in Moody Scrapbook, in possession of Mrs. Dan Moody, Sr.

10. Peter Molyneaux, "Texas at the Crossroads," *Texas Monthly* 4 (September, 1929): 158–59.

11. Edwards, "Texas," p. 334.

12. Molyneaux, "Texas at the Crossroads," p. 161.

13. Emanuel A. Goldenweiser and Leon E. Truesdell, *Farm Tenancy in the United States* (Washington: Government Printing Office, 1924), pp. 241–43; J. T. Sanders, *Farm Ownership and Tenancy in the Black Prairie of Texas*, p. 4; William B. Bizzell, *Rural Texas*, p. 416; Rupert B. Vance, *Human Geography of the South: A Study in Regional Resources and Human Adequacy*. Second Edition (Chapel Hill: University of North Carolina Press, 1935), p. 330.

14. Molyneaux, "Texas at the Crossroads," 155–56.

15. Ibid., p. 165.

16. Ibid., p. 164; Richard F. Burges to Ireland Graves, May 15, 1922, Burges Papers.

17. Bryan Mack, "Poor Little Texas!" *Review of Reviews* 80 (November, 1929): 152.

18. *Houston Gargoyle* 2 (August 4, 1929): 8.

19. *Dallas Morning News*, July 11, 1929; John C. Granbery to Dan Moody, January 16, 1929, Moody to Granbery, January 18, 1929, Moody Papers.

20. The *New York Times* is quoted in Steen, "Political History of Texas, 1900–1930," p. 464.

21. Ferguson is quoted in Richardson, *Texas*, p. 324.

22. McKay, *Texas Politics*, p. 255; *Texas Weekly* 10 (June 23, 1934): 1.

23. Key, *Southern Politics in State and Nation*, p. 265.

24. On the gubernatorial campaign of 1938, see McKay, *Texas Politics*, pp. 308–25; Wayne Gard, "Texas Kingfish," *New Republic* 104 (June 23, 1941): 848–50. According to historian George Norris Green, writing in 1979, conservative, corporate interests took over Texas, "once and for all, perhaps permanently," in this election. "They launched the Establishment, a loosely knit plutocracy comprised mostly of Anglo businessmen, oilmen, bankers, and lawyers. These leaders—especially in the 1940s and 1950s—were dedicated to a regressive tax structure, low corporate rates, antilabor laws, political, social, and economic oppression of blacks and Mexican-Americans, alleged states' rights, and extreme reluctance to expand state services. On federal matters they demanded tax reduction, a balanced budget, and the relaxation of federal controls over oil, gas, water, and other resources." George Norris Green, *The Establishment in Texas Politics: The Primitive Years, 1938–1957*, pp. 16–17.

25. John Geddie, "'Two for Price of One': Old Timers Recall the Fergusons," *Dallas Morning News*, May 6, 1966, clipping in Jim and Ma Ferguson Biographical File, Barker Texas History Center; Luthin, *American Demagogues*, p. 180; *Austin American*, September 22, 1944, clipping in James Ferguson Biographical File, Barker Texas History Center; Nalle, *Fergusons of Texas*, pp. 246–54; McKay, *Texas Politics*, pp. 335–36.

26. Nalle, *Fergusons of Texas*, pp. 256–62; *Dallas Morning News*, September 22, 1944; *Austin American*, September 22, 1944.

27. Farrell and Silverthorne, *First Ladies of Texas*, pp. 293–94; Steen, "Governor Miriam A. Ferguson," p. 17.

28. *Austin American-Statesman*, May 15, 1981, June 4, 11, 13, August 22, December 19, 1982; *Houston Chronicle*, June 4, 1982.

29. *Austin American*, September 3, 1921; *Austin American-Statesman*, February 19, 20, 1983; *Dallas Times Herald*, February 21, 1983; *Daily Texan*, February 21, 1983.

30. Bozzell, *The Struggle for Sobriety*, pp. 42–50; Gould, *Progressives & Prohibitionists*, pp. 290–91; Anne Dingus, "BYOB—The Texan and the Bottle: A Brief History," *Texas Monthly*, 10 (March, 1982): 132–33, 206.

31. Dick J. Reavis, "God's Happy Hour," *Texas Monthly* 11 (January, 1983): 93–97, 146–51.

32. *Austin American-Statesman*, April 4, 1982.

33. Ibid., February 13, 1983.

Bibliography

MANUSCRIPTS

Acree, Fred. Papers. University of Texas Archives.

Allred, James V. Papers. University of Houston Library.

Ames, Mrs. Jesse Daniel. Papers. Dallas Historical Society.

————. Papers. Texas State Archives.

Atwell, William Hawley. Biographical File. Barker Texas History Center, University of Texas.

Baker, Newton D. Papers. Manuscripts Division, Library of Congress.

Barker, Eugene C. Papers. University of Texas Archives.

Batts, Robert L. Papers. University of Texas Archives.

Biggers, Don Hampton. Papers. Southwest Collection, Texas Tech University.

Bledsoe, William H. Papers. Southwest Collection, Texas Tech University.

Brooks, Samuel Palmer. Papers. Texas Collection, Baylor University.

Bryan, William Jennings. Papers. Manuscripts Division, Library of Congress.

Burges, Richard Fenner. Papers. University of Texas Archives.

Burkett, Joe. Biographical File. Barker Texas History Center, University of Texas.

Burleson, Albert Sidney. Papers. University of Texas Archives.

Butte, George C. Biographical File. Barker Texas History Center, University of Texas.

————. File, Campaign Materials. Texas State Archives.

————. Papers. University of Texas Archives.

Carter, Amon G. Biographical File. Barker Texas History Center, University of Texas.

————Papers. Southwest Collection, Texas Tech University.

Cherrington, Ernest H. Papers. Ohio Historical Society. Microfilm.

Colquitt, Oscar Branch. Biographical File. Barker Texas History Center, University of Texas.

————. Papers. University of Texas Archives.

Connally, Tom. Papers. Manuscripts Division, Library of Congress.

Coolidge, Calvin. Papers. Manuscripts Division, Library of Congress. Microfilm.

Cousins, Robert Bartow. Papers. University of Texas Archives.

Crane, Martin M. Papers. University of Texas Archives.

Crane, Royston Campbell. Papers. Southwest Collection, Texas Tech University.

Cranfill, J. B. Papers. University of Texas Archives.

Crozier, Harry Benge. Papers. Capitol Legislative Reference Library, Austin.

Culberson, Charles A. Biographical File. Barker Texas History Center, University of Texas.

Davidson, Lynch. Biographical File. Barker Texas History Center, University of Texas.

———. File. Campaign Materials. Texas State Archives.

Davidson, T. W. Biographical File. Barker Texas History Center, University of Texas.

Davis, Clare Ogden. Biographical File. Barker Texas History Center, University of Texas.

Davis, John W. Papers. Manuscripts and Archives, Yale University Library.

Dienst, Alexander. Papers. University of Texas Archives.

Ex-Students' Writings Collections (now Richard T. Fleming University Writings Collection). University of Texas.

Faulk, J. J. Papers. Dallas Historical Society.

Ferguson, James E. Biographical File. Barker Texas History Center, University of Texas.

———. File. Campaign Materials. Texas State Archives.

———. Scrapbook. 1914–35, 1914–40. University of Texas Archives.

Ferguson, James Edward. Collection. University of Texas Archives.

Ferguson, Jim, and Ma Ferguson. Biographical File. Barker Texas History Center, University of Texas.

Ferguson, Mrs. Miriam A. Biographical File. Barker Texas History Center, University of Texas.

———. Official Papers. Texas State Archives.

———. Scrapbook. 1924–65. Barker Texas History Center, University of Texas.

Goodridge, C. F. Papers. University of Texas Archives.

Granbery, John C. Papers. University of Texas Archives.

Graves, George B. Papers. Franklin D. Roosevelt Presidential Library.

Gregory, Thomas Watt. Papers. Manuscripts Division, Library of Congress.

———. Papers. Southwest Collection, Texas Tech University. Microfilm.

Hamilton, James Robert. Papers. Southern Historical Collection, University of North Carolina.

Harding, Warren G. Papers. Ohio Historical Society. Microfilm.

Henderson, Thomas S. Papers. University of Texas Archives.

Henry, Robert Lee. Biographical File. Barker Texas History Center, University of Texas.

Hicks, Hicks, Dickson and Bobbitt Law Firm. Papers. University Archives and Manuscript Collections, Texas A&M University Library.

Hilles, Charles D. Papers. Manuscripts and Archives, Yale University Library.

Hobby, William P., Sr. Biographical File. Barker Texas History Center, University of Texas.

———. Scrapbook. 1912–29. Barker Texas History Center, University of Texas.

Hogg, William Clifford. Biographical File. Barker Texas History Center, University of Texas.

————. Papers. University of Texas Archives.

Hoover, Herbert. Papers. Herbert Hoover Presidential Library, West Branch, Iowa.

House, Edward M. Papers. Manuscripts and Archives, Yale University Library.

Jones, Jesse H. Papers. University of Texas Archives.

Kemp, Louis W. "Texas State Highway Department Notebooks." Papers. University of Texas Archives.

Keyes, Lucile Sheppard. "Morris Sheppard" (1950). Typescript, University of Texas Archives.

KKK. Scrapbook. University of Texas Archives.

Ku Klux Klan File. Administratives Files, NAACP Papers, Manuscripts Division, Library of Congress.

Ku Klux Klan File, Campaign Materials. Texas State Archives.

Ku Klux Klan Subject File. Barker Texas History Center, University of Texas.

Lomax, John A. Biographical File. Barker Texas History Center, University of Texas.

————. Papers. University of Texas Archives.

Love, Thomas B. Biographical File. Barker Texas History Center, University of Texas.

————. Papers. Dallas Historical Society.

McAdoo, William G. Papers. Manuscripts Division, Library of Congress.

McBride, F. Scott. Papers. Ohio Historical Society. Microfilm.

McCallum, Mrs. Jane Y. Scrapbook. 1930–57. Barker Texas History Center, University of Texas.

McCallum Family. Papers. Austin–Travis County Collection, Austin Public Library.

McGregor, Temple Harris. Biographical File. Barker Texas History Center, University of Texas.

Marsh, Charles Edward. Biographical File. Barker Texas History Center, University of Texas.

Martinez, Mercurio. Papers. University Archives and Manuscript Collections, Texas A&M University Library.

Maverick, Maury, Sr. Papers. University of Texas Archives.

Mayfield, Billie. Biographical File. Barker Texas History Center, University of Texas.

Miller, Barry. Biographical File. Barker Texas History Center, University of Texas.

Milton, George Fort. Papers. Manuscripts Division, Library of Congress.

Moody, Dan. Biographical File. Barker Texas History Center, University of Texas.

————. File, Campaign Materials. Texas State Archives.

————. Papers. Texas State Archives.

————. Scrapbook. In possession of Mrs. Dan Moody, Sr., Austin.

————. Scrapbook. 1925–28, 1929–64. Barker Texas History Center, University of Texas.

————. Scrapbooks. University of Texas Archives.

Moody, Mrs. Dan. "Personal Diary of Mrs. Dan Moody Recorded during her

term as First Lady of Texas while residing in the Governor's Mansion in
Austin, Texas." Typescript. Oral History Collection, North Texas State
University, no. 24.
National Association for the Advancement of Colored People. Papers. Manu-
scripts Division, Library of Congress.
Neff, Pat M. Biographical File. Barker Texas History Center, University of
Texas.
———. Papers. Texas Collection, Baylor University.
———. Scrapbook. University of Texas Archives.
Nixon, Dr. Lawrence A. Papers. Lyndon Baines Johnson Presidential Library,
Austin.
Norris, John Franklyn. Collection. Dargan-Carver Library, Nashville, Tenn.
Microfilm.
Oneal, Benjamin Grady. Papers. University of Texas Archives.
Pennybacker, Mrs. Percy V. Papers. University of Texas Archives.
Ramsdell, Charles William. Papers. University of Texas Archives.
Rayburn, Sam. Papers. Sam Rayburn Library, Bonham. Microfilm.
———. Scrapbooks. Sam Rayburn Library, Bonham. Microfilm.
Ring, Mrs. H. F. Papers. University of Texas Archives.
Robertson, Felix D. Biographical File. Barker Texas History Center, Univer-
sity of Texas.
———. File, Campaign Materials. Texas State Archives.
Roosevelt, Franklin D. Papers. 1920–28. Franklin D. Roosevelt Presidential
Library, Hyde Park, N.Y.
Rosser, Dr. Curtice. File. Dallas Historical Society.
Sanderford, Ghent. "The Ferguson Era, 1914–1944." Typescript. Ex-Stu-
dents' Writings Collection (now Richard T. Fleming University Writings
Collection), University of Texas.
———. Papers. University of Texas Archives.
Scobey, Frank. Papers. Ohio Historical Society. Microfilm.
Sheppard, Morris. Papers. University of Texas Archives.
Shettles, E. L. Papers. University of Texas Archives.
Smith, Alfred E. Private Papers. New York State Library, Albany.
Smith, Wilford B. ("Pitchfork"). Papers. University of Texas Archives.
State Board of Education. Papers. Texas State Archives.
Sterling, Ross S. Official Papers. Texas State Archives.
Sumners, Hatton W. Papers. Dallas Historical Society.
Teagarden, William B. Papers. University of Texas Archives.
Thomas, Cullen F. Biographical File. Barker Texas History Center, University
of Texas.
Timmons, Bascom. Papers. University Archives and Manuscript Collections,
Texas A&M University Library.
Underwood, Oscar W. Papers. Maps and Manuscripts Division, Alabama State
Department of Archives & History.
Walsh, Thomas J. Papers. Manuscripts Division, Library of Congress.
Wardlaw, Louis J. Biographical File. Barker Texas History Center, University
of Texas.

Wells, James B. Papers. University of Texas Archives.

Wilson, Walter B. Papers. University of Texas Archives.

Wilson, Woodrow. Papers. Manuscripts Division, Library of Congress. Microfilm.

Woolley, Robert W. Papers. Manuscripts Division, Library of Congress.

ORAL HISTORY INTERVIEWS

Fleming, Richard T. July 30, 1968. Typescript furnished to the author by Tuffly Ellis, Texas State Historical Association.

Moody, Mrs. Dan, Sr. August 16, 1968. Oral History Collection, North Texas State University, no. 25.

Patman, Wright. August 11, 1972. Oral History Collection, Lyndon Baines Johnson Presidential Library, Austin.

Perry, H. G. April 8, 1968. Oral History Collection, North Texas State University, no. 53.

Poage, W. R. (Bob). November 11, 1968. Oral History Collection, Lyndon Baines Johnson Presidential Library, Austin.

Sanderford, Ghent. May 8, 1967. March 29, 1968. Oral History Collection, North Texas State University, no. 14.

Woodul, Walter F. July 11, 1975. Interview with the author.

LETTERS TO THE AUTHOR

Coffee, Roy C. February 10, 1976.

Covey, E. L. February 20, 1976.

Locke, Frank M. February 10, 1976.

DISSERTATIONS, THESES, AND SEMINAR PAPERS

Allen, Lee N. "The Underwood Presidential Movement of 1924." Ph.D. diss., University of Pennsylvania, 1955.

Anders, Evan. "Bosses under Siege: The Politics of South Texas during the Progressive Era." Ph.D. diss., University of Texas, 1978.

Anderson, Adrian Norris. "Albert Sidney Burleson: A Southern Politician in the Progressive Era." Ph.D. diss., Texas Technological College, 1967.

Baker, Marvin Pierce. "The Executive Veto in Texas." Master's thesis, University of Texas, 1933.

Calbert, Jack Lynn. "James Edward and Miriam Amanda Ferguson: The 'Ma' and 'Pa' of Texas Politics." Ph.D. diss., Indiana University, 1968.

Chumlea, Wesley Sisson. "The Politics of Legislative Apportionment in Texas, 1921–1957." Ph.D., diss., University of Texas, 1959.

Crow, Herman Lee. "A Political History of the Texas Penal System, 1829–1951." Ph.D. diss., University of Texas, 1963.

Daniel, Josiah M., III. "The Fate of Business Progressivism in Texas State Politics: Governor Dan Moody's Legislative Program in the Fortieth and Forty-First Legislatures, 1927–1930." Seminar paper, University of Texas, 1974.

———. "Governor Dan Moody and Business Progressivism in Texas." Paper presented at the Eightieth Annual Meeting of the Texas State Historical Association, Galveston, Texas, March 5, 1976.

Duke, Escal Franklin. "The Political Career of Morris Sheppard, 1875–1941." Ph.D. diss., University of Texas, 1958.

DuPuy, William Everett. "The Democratic National Convention of 1928." Master's thesis, University of Texas, 1929.

Flory, Clarence Mathew. "Southern Opposition to Alfred E. Smith in the Election of 1928." Master's thesis, University of Texas, 1937.

Gelbart, Herbert A. "The Anti-McAdoo Movement of 1924." Ph.D., diss., New York University, 1978.

Glasrud, Bruce Alden. "Black Texans, 1900–1930: A History." Ph.D. diss., Texas Tech University, 1969.

Grose, Charles William. "Black Newspapers in Texas, 1868–1970." Ph.D. diss., University of Texas, 1972.

Holcomb, Bob Charles. "Senator Joe Bailey: Two Decades of Controversy." Ph.D. diss., Texas Technological College, 1968.

Huckaby, George Portal. "Oscar Branch Colquitt: A Political Biography." Ph.D. diss., University of Texas, 1946.

Huddleston, John D. "The First Gubernatorial Term of Miriam Amanda Ferguson, 1925–1926." Seminar paper, University of Texas, 1974.

Hughes, Richard Bennett. "Texas Churches and Presidential Politics, 1928 and 1960." Ph.D. diss., Saint Louis University, 1969.

Jackson, Emma Louise Moyer. "Petticoat Politics: Political Activism among Texas Women in the 1920's." Ph.D. diss., University of Texas, 1980.

Johnson, Jack. "State Regulation of Public Utilities in Texas." Ph.D. diss., University of Texas, 1932.

Keever, Jack Elton. "Jim Ferguson and the Press, 1913–1917." Master's of Journalism thesis, University of Texas, 1965.

Kroutter, Thomas E., Jr. "The Ku Klux Klan in Jefferson County, Texas, 1921–1924." Master's thesis, Lamar University, 1972.

Laughlin, Lois Matthews. "The Speaking Career of Pat Morris Neff." Master's thesis, Baylor University, 1951.

Manning, George N. "Public Services of James V. Allred." Master's thesis, Texas Technological College, 1950.

Martindale, Robert René. "James V. Allred: The Centennial Governor of Texas." Master's thesis, University of Texas, 1958.

Moore, Loise. "Pat M. Neff and His Achievements." Master's thesis, Texas College of Arts and Industries, 1941.

Moore, Sue E. Winton. "Thomas B. Love, Texas Democrat, 1901–1949." Master's thesis, University of Texas, 1971.

Murphy, Norman. "The Relationship of the Methodist Church to the Ku Klux Klan in Texas, 1920–1928." Seminar paper, University of Texas, 1970.

Nichols, Reuben Bryan. "Pat M. Neff, His Boyhood and Early Political Career." Master's thesis, Baylor University, 1951.

Olien, Roger Marvin. "The Republican Party of Texas, 1920–1961." Ph.D. diss., Brown University, 1973.

Robbins, Nathan Orville. "The Ferguson Regime in Texas." Master's thesis, George Peabody College for Teachers, 1928.

Salas, Karen Jeanette. "Senator Morris Sheppard and the Eighteenth Amendment." Master's thesis, University of Texas, 1970.

Sandford, William Reynolds. "History of the Republican Party in the State of Texas." Master's thesis, University of Texas, 1955.

Smith, Larry Lynn. "A Study of Houston's Role in the 1928 Democratic Convention." Master's thesis, Sam Houston State University, 1965.

Steen, Ralph Wright. "The Political Career of James E. Ferguson, 1914–1917." Master's thesis, University of Texas, 1929.

Storey, James Bryan. "Political Parsons: Texas Churchmen and the Election of 1928." Master's thesis, Texas Technological College, 1967.

Sudo-Shimamura, Takado. "John C. Granbery: Three Academic Freedom Controversies in the Life of a Social Gospeler in Texas (1920–1938)." Master's thesis, University of Texas, 1971.

Thames, Mary. "A Study of the Texas Industrial Welfare Commission." Master's thesis, University of Texas, 1922.

Thompson, Carey Carter. "Motor Carrier Regulation in Texas." Master's thesis, University of Texas, 1931.

Tolbert, Cecil H. "A Proposed Constitutional Convention for Texas." Master's thesis, University of Texas, 1930.

Torrence, Lois Evelyn. "The Ku Klux Klan in Dallas (1915–1928): An American Paradox." Master's thesis, Southern Methodist University, 1948.

Wagner, Robert L. "The Gubernatorial Career of Charles Allen Culberson." Master's thesis, University of Texas, 1954.

Watt, Donley. "The Presidential Election of 1928 in Texas." Master's thesis, University of Texas, 1970.

Younker, Donna Lee. "Thomas B. Love's Service in the Texas Legislature and in State Government during the Lanham and Campbell Administrations." Master's thesis, Southern Methodist University, 1958.

GOVERNMENT DOCUMENTS

United States

Hays, Frank E., and Edwin Halsey, *Senate Election Cases from 1913 to 1940.* Washington, D.C.: Government Printing Office, 1940.

Public Papers of the Presidents of the United States, Lyndon B. Johnson: Containing the Public Messages, Speeches, and Statements of the President, 1965 (In Two Books). Book I—January 1 to May 31, 1965. Washington, D.C.: Government Printing Office, 1966.

U.S. Congress, Senate. *Senator from Texas: Hearings before a Subcommittee of the Committee on Privileges and Elections United States Senate Sixty-eighth Congress First Session Pursuant to S. Res. 97 Authorizing the Investigation of Alleged Unlawful Practices in the Election of a Senator from Texas.* Washington, D.C.: Government Printing Office, 1924.

———. Subcommittee of the Committee on Post Offices and Post Roads. *Influencing Appointments to Postmasterships, Hearings, pts. 1–5, and Re-*

port. 70 Cong., 2d sess. Washington, D.C.: Government Printing Office, 1929–30.

Texas

Department of Health. *History of Public Health in Texas*. Austin: Texas State Department of Health, 1974.

General Laws of the State of Texas Passed by the Thirty-eighth Legislature at the Regular Session Convened at the City of Austin, January 9, 1923 and Adjourned, March 14, 1923. Austin: A. C. Baldwin & Sons, 1923.

General Laws of the State of Texas Passed by the Thirty-eighth Legislature at Its First, Second and Third Called Sessions: First Called Session Convened March 15, 1923 and Adjourned April 15, 1923, Second Called Session Convened April 16, 1923 and Adjourned May 15, 1923, Third Called Session Convened May 16, 1923 and Adjourned June 14, 1923. Austin: A. C. Baldwin & Sons, 1923.

General Laws of the State of Texas Passed by the Thirty-ninth Legislature at Its Regular Session Which Convened January 13, 1925 and Adjourned March 19, 1925. Austin: A. C. Baldwin & Sons, 1925.

General and Special Laws of the State of Texas Passed by the Fortieth Legislature at the Regular Session Convened at the City of Austin, January 11, 1927 and Adjourned March 16, 1927. Austin: A. C. Baldwin & Sons, 1927.

General and Special Laws of the State of Texas Passed by the Fortieth Legislature at Its First Called Session Convened at the City of Austin, May 9, 1927 and Adjourned June 7, 1927. Austin: A. C. Baldwin & Sons, 1927.

Legislature, House. *Journal of the House of Representatives of the Regular Session of the Thirty-seventh Legislature Begun and Held at the City of Austin, January 11, 1921*. Austin: Von Boeckmann-Jones Co., 1921.

———. *Journal of the House of Representatives of the First Called Session of the Thirty-seventh Legislature Begun and Held at the City of Austin, July 18, 1921*. Austin: Von Boeckmann-Jones, Co., 1921.

———. *Journal of the House of Representatives of the Second Called Session of the Thirty-seventh Legislature Begun and Held at the City of Austin, August 17, 1921*. Austin: Von Boeckmann-Jones Co., 1921.

———. *Journal of the House of Representatives of the Regular Session of the Thirty-eighth Legislature Begun and Held at the City of Austin, January 9, 1923*. Austin: Von Boeckmann-Jones Co., 1923.

———. *Journal of the House of Representatives of the First Called Session of the Thirty-eighth Legislature Begun and Held at the City of Austin, March 15, 1923*. Austin: Von Boeckmann-Jones Co., 1923.

———. *Journal of the House of Representatives of the Second Called Session of the Thirty-eighth Legislature Begun and Held at the City of Austin, April 16, 1923*. Austin: Von Boeckmann-Jones Co., 1923.

———. *Journal of the House of Representatives of the Regular Session of the Thirty-ninth Legislature Begun and Held at the City of Austin, January 13, 1925*. Austin: Von Boeckmann-Jones Co., 1925.

———. *Journal of the House of Representatives of the First Called Session of the Thirty-ninth Legislature Begun and Held at the City of Austin, September 13, 1926.* Austin: Von Boeckmann-Jones Co., 1926.

———. *Journal of the House of Representatives of the Fortieth Legislature of Texas Begun and Held at the City of Austin, March 6, 1927.* Austin: Von Boeckmann-Jones Co., 1927.

———. *Journal of the House of Representatives of the First Called Session of the Forty-first Legislature Begun and Held at the City of Austin, April 22, 1929.* Austin: Von Boeckmann-Jones Co., 1929.

Legislature, Senate. *Journal of the Senate of Texas Being the Regular Session of the Thirty-seventh Legislature Begun and Held at the City of Austin, January 11 to March 12, 1921.* Austin: A. C. Baldwin & Sons, 1921.

———. *Journal of the Senate, State of Texas First Called Session Thirty-seventh Legislature Convened in the City of Austin July 18, 1921 and Adjourned without Day August 16, 1921.* Austin: A. C. Baldwin & Sons, 1921.

———. *Journal of the Senate, State of Texas Second Called Session Thirty-seventh Legislature Convened in the City of Austin August 17, 1921 and Adjourned without Day August 25, 1921.* Austin: A. C. Baldwin & Sons, 1921.

———. *Journal of the Senate, State of Texas Regular Session Thirty-ninth Legislature Convened in the City of Austin, January 13, 1925, and Adjourned March 19, 1925.* Austin: A. C. Baldwin & Sons, 1925.

———. *Journal of the Senate of Texas Being the Regular Session of the Fortieth Legislature Begun and Held at the City of Austin, January 11, 1927.* Austin: A. C. Baldwin & Sons, 1927.

———. *Journal of the Senate of Texas Being the First Called Session of the Fortieth Legislature Begun and Held at the City of Austin, May 9, 1927.* Austin: A. C. Baldwin & Sons, 1927.

———. *Record of Proceedings of the High Court of Impeachment in the Trial of Hon. James E. Ferguson, Governor.* Austin: A. C. Baldwin & Sons, 1917.

Neff, Governor Pat M. *Farewell Address of Pat M. Neff, Governor of Texas, 1921–1925, Austin, Texas, January 20th, 1925.* Austin, 1925.

———. *Speeches Delivered by Pat M. Neff, Governor of Texas. Discussing Certain Phases of Contemplated Legislation.* Austin, Texas: Von Boeckmann-Jones Co., 1923.

BOOKS

Abernethy, Francis Edward, ed., *Legendary Ladies of Texas.* Publications of the Texas Folklore Society, Number XLIII. Dallas: E-Heart Press, 1981.

Acheson, Sam Hanna. *Joe Bailey: The Last Democrat.* New York: Macmillan Co., 1932.

———. *35,000 Days in Texas: A History of the Dallas News and Its Forebears.* New York: Macmillan Co., 1938.

Adams, Frank Carter, ed. *Texas Democracy: A Centennial History of Politics and Personalities of the Democratic Party, 1836–1936, with Contributions by Leading Texas Historians, Political Observers, Writers, Editors, State Officials Past and Present,* 4 vols. Austin: Democratic Historical Association, 1937.

Adams, Marion S. *Alvin M. Owsley of Texas: Apostle of Americanism.* Waco: Texian Press, 1971.

Alexander, Charles C. *Crusade for Conformity: The Ku Klux Klan in Texas, 1920–1930.* Houston: Texas Gulf Coast Historical Association, 1962.

———. *The Ku Klux Klan in the Southwest.* Lexington: University of Kentucky Press, 1965.

The All-Texas Special Good Will Tour: An Achievement in State Advertising. Fort Worth: All-Texas Ways and Means Committee, 1927.

Anders, Evan. *Boss Rule in South Texas: The Progressive Era.* Austin: University of Texas Press, 1982.

Andrews, Ruth Horn. *The First Thirty Years: A History of Texas Technological College, 1925–1955.* Lubbock: Texas Tech Press, 1956.

Anti-Saloon League. *The Brewers and Texas Politics,* 2 vols. San Antonio: Passing Show Printing Co., 1916.

Atwell, William Hawley. *Autobiography.* Dallas: Warlick Law Printing Co., 1935.

Bagby, Wesley M. *The Road to Normalcy: The Presidential Campaign and Election of 1920.* Baltimore, Md.: Johns Hopkins Press, 1962.

Bannon, John Francis. *Herbert Eugene Bolton: The Historian and the Man, 1870–1953.* Tucson: University of Arizona Press, 1978.

Barr, Alwyn. *Black Texans: A History of Negroes in Texas, 1528–1971.* Austin: Pemberton Press, 1973.

Baruch, Bernard M. *Baruch: The Public Years.* New York: Holt, Rinehart and Winston, 1960.

Biggers, Don Hampton. *Our Sacred Monkeys; or, 20 Years of Jim and Other Jams (Mostly Jim) the Goat Gland Specialist of Texas Politics, by Don H. Biggers; a Thousand Chuckles and a Thousand Facts, Showing the Amusing Humbuggery of the Whole Business, Particularly Since Jim Broke into the Game in 1914.* [Brownwood: Jones Printing Co.], 1933.

Bizzell, William B. *Rural Texas.* New York: Macmillan Co., 1924.

Bolton, Paul. *Governors of Texas.* [Corpus Christi: Corpus Christi Caller-Times], 1947.

Bowers, Claude. *My Life: The Memoirs of Claude Bowers.* New York: Simon and Schuster, 1962.

Broesamle, John J. *William Gibbs McAdoo: A Passion for Change, 1863–1917.* Port Washington, N.Y.: Kennikat Press, 1973.

Brooks, Raymond. *Political Playback.* Austin: Eugene C. Barker Texas History Center, 1961.

Bryant, Ira B. *Texas Southern University: Its Antecedents, Political Origin, and Future.* Houston: Privately printed, 1975.

Bryson, Conrey. *Dr. Lawrence A. Nixon and the White Primary*. El Paso: Texas Western Press, 1974.

Burner, David. *Herbert Hoover: A Public Life*. New York: Alfred A. Knopf, 1979.

———. *The Politics of Provincialism: The Democratic Party in Transition, 1928–1932*. New York: Alfred A. Knopf, 1968.

Carlton, L. A. *An Appeal in Behalf of the Candidacy of Mrs. Ferguson*. N.p., 1924.

Casdorph, Paul Douglas. *A History of the Republican Party in Texas, 1865–1965*. Austin: Pemberton Press, 1965.

Chalmers, David M. *Hooded Americanism: The First Century of the Ku Klux Klan, 1865–1965*. Garden City, N.Y.: Doubleday & Co., 1965.

Clark, James A., with Weldon Hart. *The Tactful Texan: A Biography of Governor Will Hobby*. New York: Random House, 1958.

Coletta, Paolo E. *William Jennings Bryan III: Political Puritan, 1915–1925*. Lincoln: University of Nebraska Press, 1969.

Collins, Frederick L. *Our American Kings*. New York: Century Co., 1924.

Connally, Thomas Terry, and Alfred Steinberg. *My Name Is Tom Connally*. New York: Crowell, 1954.

Connor, Seymour V. *A Biggers Chronicle, Consisting of a Reprint of the Extremely Rare History That Will Never Be Repeated, by Lan Franks (Pseud) and a Biography of Its Author, Don Hampton Biggers*. Lubbock: Southwest Collection, Texas Technological College, 1961.

———, ed. *Builders of the Southwest*. Lubbock: Southwest Collection, Texas Technological College, 1959.

Cox, James M. *Journey through My Years*. New York: Simon and Schuster, 1946.

Creager, Rentfro Banton. *A Letter to My Fellow Members of the Republican National Committee from R. B. Creager, Member for Texas*. [Brownsville? 1923?].

Cronon, E. David, ed. *The Cabinet Diaries of Josephus Daniels, 1913–1921*. Lincoln: University of Nebraska Press, 1963.

Dabney, Virginius. *Dry Messiah: The Life of Bishop Cannon*. New York: Alfred A. Knopf, 1949.

———. *Liberalism in the South*. Chapel Hill: University of North Carolina Press, 1932.

Dalrymple, A. V. *Liberty Dethroned*. Philadelphia: Times Publishing Company, [1923].

Daniels, Josephus. *The Wilson Era: Years of War and After, 1917–1923*. Chapel Hill: University of North Carolina Press, 1946.

Davidson, T. Whitfield. *The Memoirs of T. Whitfield Davidson*. Waco: Texian Press, 1972.

Davis, Clare Ogden. *The Woman of It*. New York: J. H. Sears & Co., 1929.

Davis, J. William. *"There Shall Also Be a Lieutenant Governor."* Austin: Institute of Public Affairs, University of Texas, 1967.

Dawson, Joseph M. *A Century with Texas Baptists*. Nashville: Broadman Press, 1947.

———. *A Thousand Months to Remember*. Waco: Baylor University Press, 1964.

Deshields, James T. *They Sat in High Places: The Presidents and Governors of Texas, from the First American Chief Executive, 1835–36; Presidents of the Republic, 1836–46; and Governors of the State, 1846–1939*. San Antonio: Naylor Co., 1940.

Dickson, Charles M. *Democrats: Is a Woman Legally Eligible to Be Governor of Texas?* [San Antonio, 1924].

Dobie, J. Frank. *Some Part of Myself*. Boston: Little, Brown and Co., 1952.

Dorough, C. Dwight. *Mr. Sam*. New York: Random House, 1962.

Dugger, Ronnie. *Our Invaded University*. New York: W. W. Norton, 1974.

Eby, Frederick. *The Development of Education in Texas*. New York: Macmillan Co., 1925.

Farrell, Mary D., and Elizabeth Silverthorne. *First Ladies of Texas: The First One Hundred Years, 1836–1936, a History*. Belton: Stillhouse Hollow Publishers, 1976.

Ferguson, A. M. *Gov. Neff and His Commission on Text Book Changes*. Sherman: Privately printed, [1922].

Ferguson, Miriam Amanda (Wallace). *Miriam A. Ferguson, Candidate for Governor, Second Term, Subject to the Action of the Democratic Primary, July 24, 1926: Platform*. [Austin? 1926].

———. *Opening Speeches of Gov. Ferguson's Campaign for a Second Term; Delivered Saturday, May 22, 1926, at Sulphur Springs, Texas, by Gov. Miriam A. Ferguson and Former Gov. James E. Ferguson*. [N.p., 1926].

Fitzgerald, Hugh Nugent. *Governors I Have Known*. Austin: Austin American Statesman, 1927.

Flemmons, Jerry. *Amon: The Life of Amon Carter, Sr., of Texas*. Austin: Jenkins Publishing Co., 1978.

Flynn, Edward J. *You're the Boss*. New York: Viking Press, 1947.

Frost, H. Gordon, and John H. Jenkins. *"I'm Frank Hamer": The Life of a Texas Peace Officer*. Austin: Pemberton Press, 1968.

Frost, Stanley. *The Challenge of the Klan*. Indianapolis: Bobbs-Merrill Co., 1924.

Fuermann, George. *Houston: Land of the Big Rich*. Garden City, N.Y.: Doubleday & Co., 1951.

Furniss, Norman F. *The Fundamentalist Controversy, 1918–1931*. New Haven, Conn.: Yale University Press, 1954.

Gantt, Fred, Jr. *The Chief Executive in Texas: A Study in Gubernatorial Leadership*. Austin: University of Texas Press, 1964.

Garvin, Richard M., and Edmond Addeo. *The Midnight Special: The Legend of Leadbelly*. New York: Bernard Geis Associates, 1971.

George Edwin Bailey Peddy: A Tribute, 1892–1951. Houston, 1951.

Glick, Thomas F., ed. *Darwinism in Texas: An Exhibition in the Texas History*

Center, April, 1972. Austin: Humanities Research Center, University of Texas, 1972.

Gould, Lewis L. *Progressives & Prohibitionists: Texas Democrats in the Wilson Era.* Austin: University of Texas Press, 1973.

Graves, Lawrence L., ed. *A History of Lubbock.* Lubbock: West Texas Museum Association, 1962.

Green, George Norris. *The Establishment in Texas Politics: The Primitive Years, 1938–1957.* Westport: Greenwood Press, 1979.

Haley, J. Evetts. *George W. Littlefield, Texan.* Norman: University of Oklahoma Press, 1943.

Hall, Jacquelyn Dowd. *Revolt against Chivalry: Jesse Daniel Ames and the Women's Campaign against Lynching.* New York: Columbia University Press, 1979.

Harbaugh, William H. *Lawyer's Lawyer: The Life of John W. Davis.* New York: Oxford University Press, 1973.

Harmon, William, ed. *The Oxford Book of American Light Verse.* New York: Oxford University Press, 1979.

Haws, Robert, ed. *The Age of Segregation: Race Relations in the South, 1890–1945.* Jackson: University Press of Mississippi, 1978.

Haynes, Robert V. *A Night of Violence: The Houston Riot of 1917.* Baton Rouge: Louisiana State University Press, 1976.

Heard, Alexander, and Donald S. Strong, eds. *Southern Primaries and Elections, 1920–1949.* University: University of Alabama Press, 1950.

Henderson, Richard. *Maury Maverick: A Political Biography.* Austin: University of Texas Press, 1970.

Hine, Darlene Clark. *Black Victory: The Rise and Fall of the White Primary in Texas.* Millwood: KTO Press, 1979.

Hinton, Harold B. *Cordell Hull: A Biography.* Garden City, N.Y.: Doubleday, Doran & Co., 1942.

Hooten, William J. *Fifty-two Years a Newsman.* El Paso: Texas Western Press, 1974.

House, Boyce. *I Give You Texas! 500 Jokes of the Lone Star State.* San Antonio: Naylor Co., 1943.

———. *Oil Field Fury.* San Antonio: Naylor Co., 1954.

Hubbard, Louis H. *Recollections of a Texas Educator.* Salado, 1964.

Hull, Cordell. *The Memoirs of Cordell Hull,* 2 vols. New York: Macmillan Co., 1948.

Israel, Fred L. *Nevada's Key Pittman.* Lincoln: University of Nebraska Press, 1963.

Jackson, Andrew W. *A Sure Foundation & a Sketch of Negro Life in Texas.* Houston, 1940.

Jackson, Kenneth T. *The Ku Klux Klan in the City, 1915–1930.* New York: Oxford University Press, 1967.

Jackson, Richard. *Popular Songs of Nineteenth-Century America: Complete Original Sheet Music for 64 Songs.* New York: Dover Publications, 1976.

James, Edward T., and others, eds. *Dictionary of American Biography: Supplement Three, 1941–1945*. New York: Charles Scribner's Sons, 1973.

Johnson, Allen, and Dumas Malone, eds., *Dictionary of American Biography*, 28 vols. New York: Charles Scribner's Sons, 1928–58.

Johnson, Evan C. *Oscar W. Underwood: A Political Biography*. Baton Rouge: Louisiana State University Press, 1980.

Key, V. O., Jr., with Alexander Heard. *Southern Politics in State and Nation*. New York: Alfred A. Knopf, 1949.

Kilpatrick, Carroll, ed. *Roosevelt and Daniels: A Friendship in Politics*. Chapel Hill: University of North Carolina Press, 1952.

King, John O. *Joseph Stephen Cullinan: A Study of Leadership in the Texas Petroleum Industry, 1897–1937*. Nashville: Vanderbilt University Press, 1970.

Krenek, Harry. *The Power Vested: The Use of Martial Law and the National Guard in Texas Domestic Crisis, 1919–1932*. Austin: Presidial Press, 1980.

Lee, Henry. *How Dry We Were: Prohibition Revisited*. Englewood Cliffs, N.J.: Prentice-Hall, 1963.

Levine, Lawrence W. *Defender of the Faith: William Jennings Bryan, the Last Decade, 1915–1925*. New York: Oxford University Press, 1965.

Lewinson, Paul. *Race, Class, and Party: A History of Negro Suffrage and White Politics in the South*. New York: Oxford University Press, 1932.

Lichtman, Allan J. *Prejudice and the Old Politics: The Presidential Election of 1928*. Chapel Hill: University of North Carolina Press, 1979.

Lomax, John A. *Will Hogg, Texan*. Austin: University of Texas Press, 1956.

Long, Walter E. *"For All Time to Come."* Austin: Steck Co., 1964.

[Love, Thomas B.] *Fergusonism Down to Date: A Story in Sixty Chapters Compiled from the Records*. N.p., 1926.

Luthin, Reinhard H. *American Demagogues: Twentieth Century*. Boston: Beacon Press, 1954.

McAdoo, William G. *Crowded Years: The Reminiscences of William Gibbs McAdoo*. Boston; Houghton-Mifflin Co., 1931.

McCarty, Jeanne Bozzell. *The Struggle For Sobriety: Protestants and Prohibition in Texas, 1919–1935*. El Paso, Texas Western Press, 1980.

McConnell, Weston Joseph. *Social Cleavages in Texas: A Study of the Proposed Division of the State*. New York: Columbia University Press, 1925.

McKay, Seth Shepard. *Seven Decades of the Texas Constitution of 1876*. Lubbock: Texas Technological College Press, 1942.

———. *Texas Politics, 1906–1944: With Special Reference to the German Counties*. Lubbock: Texas Tech Press, 1952.

———, and Odie B. Faulk. *Texas after Spindletop, 1901–1965*. Austin: Steck-Vaughn Co., 1965.

McSwain, Betty Ann McCartney, ed. *The Bench and Bar of Waco and McLennan County, 1849–1876*. Waco: Texian Press, 1976.

Madden, James William. *Charles Allen Culberson: His Life, Character and*

Public Service, as County Attorney, Governor of Texas and United States Senator. Austin: Gammel's Book Store, 1929.

Maverick, Maury, Jr. *A Maverick American.* New York: Covici-Friede Publishers, 1937.

Mayfield, John S. *Eugene O'Neill and the Senator from Texas: With a Note by Earle B. Mayfield.* New Haven, Conn.: Yale University Library Gazette, 1961.

Mecklin, John M. *The Ku Klux Klan: A Study of the American Mind.* New York: Harcourt, Brace and Co., 1924.

Merz, Charles. *The Dry Decade.* Garden City, N.Y.: Doubleday, Doran & Co., 1931.

Middagh, John. *Frontier Newspaper: The El Paso Times.* El Paso: Texas Western Press, 1958.

Moore, Edmund A. *A Catholic Runs for President: The Campaign of 1928.* New York: Ronald Press Co., 1956.

Moore, Walter B. *Governors of Texas.* [Dallas: Dallas Morning News, 1963].

Mullen, Arthur F. *Western Democrat.* New York: Wilfred Funk, 1940.

Murray, Robert K. *The 103rd Ballot: Democrats and the Disaster in Madison Square Garden.* New York: Harper and Row, 1976.

Nalle, Ouida Wallace [Ferguson]. *The Fergusons of Texas or, "Two Governors for the Price of One"! A Biography of James Edward Ferguson and His Wife, Miriam Amanda Ferguson, Ex-Governors of the State of Texas, by Their Daughter Ouida Ferguson Nalle.* San Antonio: Naylor Co., 1946.

Neff, Pat Morris. *The Battles of Peace.* Fort Worth: Pioneer Publishing Co., 1925.

———. *A Collection of Twenty-three Addresses.* Waco: Philomathesian Literary Society, Baylor University, n.d.

———. *Extracts from Address Made by Governor Pat M. Neff at Fort Worth, April 24, 1924.* Austin: A. C. Baldwin & Sons, 1924.

The 1927 Texas Almanac and State Industrial Guide. Dallas: A. H. Belo Corporation, 1927.

Noggle, Burl. *Into the Twenties: The United States from Armistice to Normalcy.* Urbana: University of Illinois Press, 1974.

———. *Teapot Dome: Oil and Politics in the 1920's.* Baton Rouge: Louisiana State University Press, 1962.

Official Report of the Proceedings of the Democratic National Convention Held at Houston, Texas June 26, 27, 28 and 29, 1928, Resulting in the Nomination of Alfred E. Smith (of New York) for President and Joseph T. Robinson (of Arkansas) for Vice-President. Indianapolis: Bookwalter-Ball-Greathouse Printing Co., 1928.

Olien, Roger M. *From Token to Triumph: The Texas Republicans Since 1920.* Dallas: SMU Press, 1982.

Peel, Roy V., and Thomas C. Donnelly. *The 1928 Campaign: An Analysis.* New York: Richard R. Smith, 1931.

Pool, William C. *Eugene C. Barker, Historian.* Austin: Texas State Historical Association, 1971.

Presley, James. *A Saga of Wealth: The Rise of the Texas Oilmen.* New York: G. P. Putnam's Sons, 1978.

Pryor, W. G. *Correspondence between W. G. Pryor, Prison Commissioner, and Pat M. Neff, Governor of Texas, concerning the Texas Prison System Together with a Letter to the Texas Legislature.* [Huntsville? 1921?].

Ray, Worth S. *Down in the Cross Timbers.* Austin: Privately printed, 1947.

Rice, Arnold, *The Ku Klux Klan in American Politics.* Washington, D.C.: Public Affairs Press, 1962.

Richardson, Rupert N. *Texas: The Lone Star State.* 2d ed. Englewood Cliffs, N.J.: Prentice-Hall, 1958.

Robinson, Eugene. *The Presidential Vote, 1896–1932.* Palo Alto, Calif.: Stanford University Press, 1934.

Roper, Daniel C. *Fifty Years of Public Life.* Durham, N.C.: Duke University Press, 1941.

Rushing, Jane Gilmore, and Kline A. Nall. *Evolution of a University: Texas Tech's First Fifty Years.* Austin: Madrona Press, 1975.

Russell, Traylor. *Carpetbaggers, Scalawags & Others.* Waco: Texian Press, 1973.

Sanders, J. T. *Farm Ownership and Tenancy in the Black Prairie of Texas.* Washington, D.C.: Government Printing Office, 1922.

Scarbrough, Clara Stearns. *Land of Good Water Takachue Pousetsu: A Williamson County, Texas, History.* Georgetown: Williamson County Sun, 1973.

Schriftgiesser, Karl. *This Was Normalcy: An Account of Party Politics during Twelve Republican Years, 1920–1932.* Boston: Little, Brown and Co., 1948.

Sharpe, Ernest. *G. B. Dealey of the Dallas News.* New York: Henry Holt and Co., 1955.

Shirley, Emma Morrill. *The Administration of Pat M. Neff, Governor of Texas, 1921–1925.* Waco: Baylor University, 1938.

Silva, Ruth C. *Rum, Religion, and Votes: 1928 Re-examined.* University Park: Pennsylvania State University Press, 1962.

Smith, Alfred E. *Up to Now: An Autobiography.* New York: Viking Press, 1929.

Smith, Brother "Railroad." *A Little Preachment and a Short Epistle to the Bigots of Texas.* Jourdanton: Atascosa News-Monitor, 1925.

Smith, E. F. *A Saga of Texas Law: A Factual Story of Texas Law, Lawyers, Judges and Famous Lawsuits.* San Antonio: Naylor Co., 1940.

Smith, Rembert Gilman. *Politics in a Protestant Church.* Atlanta, Ga.: Ruralist Press, 1930.

Steen, Ralph W. *Twentieth Century Texas: An Economic and Social History.* Austin: Steck Co., 1942.

Steinberg, Alfred. *Sam Rayburn: A Biography.* New York: Hawthorne Books, 1975.

Stewart, Frank Mann. *The Reorganization of State Administration in Texas.* University of Texas Bulletin no. 2507, 1925.

Stieghorst, Junann J. *Bay City and Matagorda County: A History.* Austin: Pemberton Press, 1965.

Stokes, Thomas L. *Chip off My Shoulder.* Princeton, N.J.: Princeton University Press, 1940.

Tannenbaum, Frank. *Darker Phases of the South.* New York: G. P. Putnam's Sons, 1924.

Tarver, H. M. *The Whiteman's Primary: An Open Letter to D. A. McAskill.* San Antonio, 1922.

Tatum, E. Ray. *Conquest or Failure? Biography of J. Frank Norris.* Dallas: Baptist Historical Foundation, 1966.

Terrell, C. V. *The Terrells: Eighty-five Years Texas from Indians to Atomic Bomb.* Dallas: Wilkinson Printing Co., 1948.

Texas Merry-Go-Round. [Houston: Sun Publishing Co., 1933].

Timmons, Bascom N. *Garner of Texas: A Personal History.* New York: Harper & Brothers, 1948.

———. *Jesse H. Jones: The Man and the Statesman.* New York: Henry Holt and Co., 1956.

Tindall, George B. *The Emergence of the New South, 1913–1945.* Baton Rouge: Louisiana State University Press, 1967.

———. *The Persistent Tradition in New South Politics.* Baton Rouge: Louisiana State University Press, 1975.

Wade, Homer Dale. *Establishment of Texas Technological College, 1916–1923.* Edited by Elizabeth Howard West. Lubbock: Texas Tech Press, 1956.

Wakefield, Paul. *Jesse Holman Jones.* [Houston: Gulf Publishing Co., 1928].

Webb, Walter Prescott. *The Texas Rangers: A Century of Frontier Defense.* Boston: Houghton Mifflin Company, 1935.

———, and Terrell Webb, eds. *Washington Wife: Journal of Ellen Maury Slayden from 1897–1919.* New York: Harper & Row, 1963.

———, H. Bailey Carroll, and Eldon Branda, eds. *Handbook of Texas.* 3 vols. Austin: Texas State Historical Association, vols. 1, 2, 1952; vol. 3, 1976.

White, Owen P. *Texas: An Informal Biography.* New York: G. P. Putnam's Sons, 1945.

———. *The Autobiography of a Durable Sinner.* New York: G. P. Putnam's Sons, 1942.

Withington, Leonard, ed. *Texas Republican Primary Handbook, 1926.* Revised edition. Dallas: Republican State Headquarters, 1926.

ARTICLES

Aikman, Duncan. "Another Last Frontier." *Southwest Review* 12 (October, 1926): 3–11.

———. "Fall Cleaning in the Political Boudoir." *Independent* 117 (October 9, 1926): 411–12, 427.

———. "Politics and Ma Ferguson in Texas." *Independent* 115 (December 19, 1925): 703–704, 721.

———. "Prairie Fire." *American Mercury* 6 (October, 1925): 209–14.

Alexander, Charles C. "Secrecy Bids for Power: The Ku Klux Klan in Texas Politics in the 1920's." *Mid-America* 46 (January, 1964): 3–28.

Alilunas, Leo. "Legal Restrictions on the Negro in Politics." *Journal of Negro History* 25 (April, 1940): 153–202.

Allen, Lee N. "The Democratic Presidential Primary Election of 1924 in Texas." *Southwestern Historical Quarterly* 61 (April, 1958): 474–93.

———. "The McAdoo Campaign for the Presidential Nomination in 1924." *Journal of Southern History* 29 (May, 1963): 211–28.

———. "The Underwood Presidential Movement of 1924." *Alabama Review* 15 (April, 1962): 83–99.

Anders, Evan. "Boss Rule and Constituent Interests: South Texas Politics during the Progressive Era." *Southwestern Historical Quarterly* 84 (January, 1981): 269–92.

———. "The Origins of the Parr Machine in Duval County, Texas." *Southwestern Historical Quarterly* 85 (October, 1981): 119–38.

Anderson, Nels. "The Shooting Parson of Texas." *New Republic* 48 (September 1, 1926): 35–37.

Bagby, Wesley M. "William Gibbs McAdoo and the 1920 Democratic Presidential Nomination." East Tennessee Historical Society *Publications* 31 (1959): 43–58.

———. "Woodrow Wilson, a Third Term, and the Solemn Referendum." *American Historical Review* 60 (April, 1955): 567–75.

Bailey, Richard, "Morris Sheppard—A Prohibitionist in the Liberal Tradition." *Studies in History* 6 (1976): 75–81.

Barnes, Lorraine. "Leader of the Petticoat Lobby." *Texas Star* 1 (October 3, 1971): 10–11.

Bateman, Audray, "Austinites Whooped It Up on Congress Avenue in 1921." *Austin American-Statesman*, January 1, 1977.

Bates, J. Leonard. "The Teapot Dome Scandal and the Election of 1924." *American Historical Review* 60 (January, 1955): 303–22.

Bentley, Max. "An Interview with Governor-Elect Ferguson." *Holland's Magazine* 44 (January, 1925): 5, 55.

———. "The Ku Klux Klan in Texas." *McClure's* 57 (May, 1924): 11–21.

Binkley, W. C. "Notes from Texas." *Southwestern Political Science Quarterly* 1 (March, 1921): 425–28.

Burdine, J. Alton. "Shall Texas Reorganize?" *Southwest Review* 18 (Summer, 1933): 405–16.

Burner, David B. "The Brown Derby Campaign." *New York History* 46 (October, 1965): 356–80.

———. "The Democratic Party in the Election of 1924." *Mid-America* 46 (April, 1964): 92–113.

Carter, Paul A. "The Campaign of 1928 Re-examined: A Study in Political Folklore." *Wisconsin Magazine of History* 46 (Summer, 1963): 263–72.

―――. "The Other Catholic Candidate: The 1928 Presidential Bid of Thomas J. Walsh." *Pacific Northwest Quarterly* 55 (January, 1964): 1–8.

Casdorph, Paul Douglas. "The Texas National Guard and the 1922 Railroad Strike at Denison." *Texas Military History* 3 (Winter, 1963): 211–18.

Claunch, J. M. "The Fight for Civil Service in Texas." *Southwestern Social Science Quarterly* 25 (June, 1943): 46–57.

Crane, R. C. "The West Texas Agricultural and Mechanical College Movement and the Founding of Texas Technological College." West Texas Historical Association *Year Book* 7 (June, 1931): 3–34.

Crowell, Chester T. "Journalism in Texas." *American Mercury* 7 (April, 1926): 471–78.

Devine, Edward T. "The Klan in Texas." *Survey* 48 (April 1, 1922): 10–11.

―――. "More about the Klan." *Survey* 48 (April 8, 1922): 42–43.

Dingus, Anne. "BYOB—The Texan and the Bottle: A Brief History." *Texas Monthly* 10 (March, 1982): 132–33, 206.

Duffus, Robert L. "How the Ku Klux Klan Sells Hate." *World's Work* 46 (June, 1923): 174–83.

―――. "Salesmen of Hate: The Ku Klux Klan." *World's Work* 46 (May, 1923): 31–38.

Edwards, George Clifton. "Texas: The Big Southwestern Specimen." *Nation* 116 (March 21, 1923): 334–37.

Evans, Hiram Wesley. "The Ballots Behind the Ku Klux Klan." *World's Work* 55 (January, 1928): 243–52.

―――. "The Klan: Defender of Americanism." *Forum* 74 (December, 1925): 801–14.

Ewing, Cortez A. M. "The Impeachment of James E. Ferguson." *Political Science Quarterly* 48 (June, 1933): 184–210.

"The Fall of 'Ma' Ferguson." *Literary Digest* 90 (August 7, 1926): 12.

Ferguson, Charles W. "James E. Ferguson." *Southwest Review* 10 (October, 1924): 29–36.

Field, Robert M. "The Lady of the Lone Star State." *Outlook* 138 (September 3, 1924): 15.

―――. "Will 'Ma' Ferguson Be Impeached?" *Outlook* 141 (December 9, 1925): 554–55.

"The Fight for Democratic Control." *Literary Digest* 68 (February, 1921): 17–18.

Finty, Tom, Jr. "Our Legislative Mills, IV: Texas Makes Haste." *National Municipal Review* 12 (November, 1923): 649–54.

"First Citizen of Texas." *Outlook* 149 (July 4, 1928): 363–64.

"The First Woman Governor." *Literary Digest* 82 (September 6, 1924): 7–9.

Frantz, Joe B. "A Historian Looks Back to '28 . . . Liquor and Tammany, Cloaks for Fear." *Texas Observer* 52 (September 30, 1960): 10–11.

Frost, Stanley. "Democratic Dynamite." *Outlook* 137 (June 18, 1924): 267.

Gard, Wayne. "Texas Kingfish." *New Republic* 104 (June 23, 1941): 848–50.

The Gentleman at the Keyhole. "The Texas Arranger." *Collier's* 84 (December 21, 1929): 32.

Glad, Paul W. "Progressives and the Business Culture of the 1920's." *Journal of American History* 53 (June, 1966): 75–89.

Granneberg, Audrey. "Maury Maverick's San Antonio." *Survey Graphic* 28 (July, 1939): 421–26.

Grantham, Dewey, Jr. "The Contours of Southern Progressivism." *American Historical Review* 86 (December, 1981): 1035–59.

——. "The Progressive Era and the Reform Tradition." *Mid-America* 46 (October, 1964): 227–51.

——. "Texas Congressional Leaders and the New Freedom, 1913–1917." *Southwestern Historical Quarterly* 53 (July, 1949): 35–48.

Hainsworth, Robert W. "The Negro and the Texas Primaries." *Journal of Negro History* 18 (October, 1933): 426–50.

Hart, Joseph K. "Who Is Governor of Texas?" *New Republic* 41 (February 18, 1925): 334–36.

Hine, Darlene Clark. "The Elusive Ballot: The Black Struggle against the Texas Democratic White Primary, 1932–1945." *Southwestern Historical Quarterly* 81 (April, 1978): 371–92.

Hofstadter, Richard. "Could a Protestant Have Beaten Hoover in 1928?" *Reporter* 22 (March 17, 1960): 31–33.

Hohner, Robert A. "The Prohibitionists: Who Were They?" *South Atlantic Quarterly* 68 (Autumn, 1969): 491–505.

Holman, Charles W. "'Governor Jim' of Texas." *Harper's Weekly* 61 (September 18, 1915): 279–80.

Hughes, Pollyanna B., and Elizabeth B. Harrison. "Charles A. Culberson: Not a Shadow of Hogg." *East Texas Historical Journal* 11 (Fall, 1973): 41–52.

Hunter, Charlayne. "'Leadbelly' Speaks for Every Black Who's Catching Hell." *New York Times*, July 4, 1976.

"Is 'Pa' or 'Ma' Governor of Texas?" *Literary Digest* 85 (April 11, 1925): 15.

Jackson, A. T. "State Parks for Texas." *Texas Monthly* 4 (August, 1929): 63–75.

Jackson, Charles O. "William J. Simmons: A Career in Ku Kluxism." *Georgia Historical Quarterly* 50 (December, 1966): 351–65.

Jenkins, John H. "Martial Law in Mexia." *Texas Military History* 6 (Fall, 1967): 175–89.

Johnson, Donald. "Wilson, Burleson, and Censorship in the First World War." *Journal of Southern History* 28 (February, 1962): 46–58.

Johnson, Evan C. "Oscar W. Underwood: An Aristocrat from the Bluegrass." *Alabama Review* 10 (July, 1957): 184–203.

Johnston, Alva. "Colonel Carter of Cartersville." *Saturday Evening Post* 211 (November 26, 1938): 8–9, 31–35.

"Klan Controls Early '20s EP." *El Paso Times*, April 2, 1981.

"Klan Victories in Oregon and Texas." *Literary Digest* 75 (November 25, 1922): 12.

Krock, Arthur. "The Damn Fool Democrats." *American Mercury* 4 (March, 1925): 257–62.

"The Ku-Klux Klan." *Catholic World* 116 (January, 1923): 433–43.

"The Ku Klux Victory in Texas." *Literary Digest* 74 (August 5, 1922): 14.

Ledbetter, Patsy, "Defense of the Faith: J. Frank Norris and Texas Fundamentalism, 1920–1929." *Arizona and the West* 15 (Spring, 1973): 45–62.

Lemons, J. Stanley. "The Sheppard-Towner Act: Progressivism in the 1920's." *Journal of American History* 55 (March, 1969): 776–86.

Link, Arthur. "The Underwood Presidential Movement of 1912." *Journal of Southern History* 11 (May, 1945): 230–45.

———. "What Happened to Progressivism in the 1920's?" *American Historical Review* 64 (July, 1959): 833–51.

Lippmann, Walter. "Two Democratic Candidates: I. McAdoo." *New Republic* 23 (June 2, 1920): 10–11.

Lipset, Seymour Martin. "Some Statistics on Bigotry in Voting." *Commentary* 30 (October, 1960): 286–90.

"Looking for a Split in the Solid South." *Literary Digest* 98 (August 4, 1928): 8–9.

Love, Thomas B. "Expediency or the Right—Which?" *Bunker's Monthly: The Magazine of Texas* 1 (February, 1928): 183–201.

MacCorkle, Stuart A. "Pardoning Power in Texas." *Southwestern Social Science Quarterly* 15 (December, 1934): 218–28.

MacIntosh, P. J. R. "The Democratic Convention City." *Bunker's Monthly: The Magazine of Texas* 1 (May, 1928): 651–68.

Mack, Bryan. "Poor Little Texas!" *Review of Reviews* 80 (November, 1929): 150–60.

McDonald, Roy W. "Negro Voters in Democratic Primaries." *Texas Law Review* 5 (June, 1927): 393–400.

McGill, Ralph. "The South Has Many Faces." *Atlantic* 211 (April, 1963): 83–98.

McKnight, A. H. "The Fortieth Legislature and Judicial Reform." *Texas Law Review* 5 (June, 1927): 360–67.

Maxwell, Robert S. "One Man's Legacy: W. Goodrich Jones and Texas Conservation." *Southwestern Historical Quarterly* 77 (January, 1974): 355–80.

———. "The Pines of Texas: A Study in Lumbering and Public Policy, 1880–1930." *East Texas Historical Journal* 2 (October, 1964): 77–86.

Meier, August, and Elliott Rudwick. "Attorneys Black and White: A Case Study of Race Relations within the NAACP." *Journal of American History* 62 (March, 1976): 913–46.

Miller, Robert Moats. "A Note on the Relationship between the Protestant Churches and the Revived Ku Klux Klan." *Journal of Southern History* 22 (August, 1956): 355–68.

"Miriam Amanda Ferguson: Soon to Take Office as the First Woman Governor of Texas." *Current Opinion* 77 (October, 1924): 436–38.

Molyneaux, Peter. "Texas at the Crossroads." *Texas Monthly* 4 (September, 1929): 154–73.

Moody, Martha. "Mildred Paxton Moody: Former First Lady of Texas." *Texas Historian* 40 (March, 1980): 1–5.

Moorhead, Dean. "Texas All-Woman Supreme Court." *Texas Star* 2 (February 11, 1973): 13–14.

Neff, Pat M. "State Parks for Texas." *Holland's Magazine* 44 (January, 1925): 14–15, 48.

Nixon, H. Clarence. "The Changing Background of Southern Politics." *Social Forces* 11 (October, 1932): 14–18.

———. "The Changing Political Philosophy of the South." *Annals of the American Academy of Political and Social Sciences* 153 (January, 1931): 246–50.

Noggle, Burl. "The Twenties: A New Historiographical Frontier." *Journal of American History* 53 (September, 1966): 299–314.

Northcott, Kaye. "Be held permanently for education purposes. . . ." *Texas Observer* 64 (September, 1973): 1, 3–4.

Overbeck, Ruth Ann. "Texas Gets Out of the Mud." *East Texas Historical Journal* 12 (Spring, 1974): 23–24.

Peden, Allen. "The Downfall of a Dry Moses." *American Mercury* 28 (February, 1933): 187–90.

———. "Texas Free-for-All." *Outlook and Independent* 155 (July 9, 1930): 380–82, 395.

———. "Those Burro Blues." *Houston Gargoyle* 1 (June 26, 1928): 5.

Pringle, Henry F. "Harmony—and a Man of Courage." *Outlook* 149 (July 11, 1928): 412–15.

Reagan, Hugh D. "Race as a Factor in the Presidential Election of 1928 in Alabama." *Alabama Review* 19 (January, 1966): 5–19.

Reavis, Dick J. "God's Happy Hour." *Texas Monthly* 11 (January, 1983): 93–97, 146–51.

Renfro, C. C. "Do We Want a National Party?" *Bunker's Monthly: The Magazine of Texas* 1 (February, 1928): 202–13.

Rogan, Octavia F. "Texas Legislation, 1925." *Southwestern Political and Social Science Quarterly* 6 (September, 1925): 167–78.

"Ruddy Dan Moody: The Texas Crusader." *Literary Digest* 90 (August 28, 1926): 32, 34.

Russell, C. Allyn. "J. Frank Norris: Violent Fundamentalist." *Southwestern Historical Quarterly* 75 (January, 1972): 271–302.

Scott, Gary. "Dan Moody and the Ku Klux Klan." *Southwestern Magazine* 83 (May, 1965): 2–5.

Shanks, Alexander Graham. "Sam Rayburn in the Wilson Administration, 1913–1921." *East Texas Historical Journal* 6 (March, 1968): 63–76.

Shoemaker, Kyle W. [Walter Prescott Webb]. "How Mexia Was Made a Clean City." *Owenwood Magazine* 1 (May, 1922): 19–26.

Slayton, John William. "The First All-Woman Supreme Court in the World." *Holland's Magazine* 44 (March, 1925): 5, 73.

Smith, Henry. "Hoover's Philosophy of Comfort." *Southwest Review* 14 (October, 1928): 111–18.

Splawn, W. M. W. "A Review of the Minimum Wage Theory and Practice, with Special Reference to Texas." *Southwestern Political Science Quarterly* 1 (March, 1921): 339–71.

Bibliography   543

Steen, Ralph W. "The Ferguson War on the University of Texas." *Southwestern Social Science Quarterly* 35 (March, 1955): 356–62.

———. "Governor Miriam A. Ferguson." *East Texas Historical Journal* 17 (1979): 3–17.

Stewart, Frank M. "The Development of State Control of Highways in Texas." *Southwestern Social Science Quarterly* 13 (December, 1932): 211–33.

———. "Impeachment in Texas." *American Political Science Review* 24 (August, 1930): 652–58.

———. "The Movement for the Reorganization of State Administration in Texas." *Southwestern Political and Social Science Quarterly* 5 (December, 1924): 230–45.

———. "Notes from Texas." *Southwestern Political Science Quarterly* 2 (September, 1921): 190–200.

———. "Notes from Texas." *Southwestern Political Science Quarterly* 2 (March, 1922): 348–50.

Stewart, Irvin. "Constitutional Amendments in Texas." *Southwestern Political Science Quarterly* 3 (September, 1922): 145–58.

Stratton, David H. "Splattered with Oil: William G. McAdoo and the 1924 Presidential Nomination." *Southwestern Social Science Quarterly* 44 (June, 1963): 62–75.

Strother, Frank. "The Governors Ferguson of Texas." *World's Work* 50 (September, 1925): 489–97.

Sullivan, Mark. "Midsummer Politics and Primaries." *World's Work* 44 (July, 1922): 296–302.

Sutton, William S. "The Assault on the University of Texas." *Educational Review* 54 (November, 1917): 390–409.

Taylor, A. Elizabeth. "The Woman Suffrage Movement in Texas." *Journal of Southern History* 17 (May, 1951): 194–215.

"Texas 'Hoovercrats'." *Outlook and Independent* 150 (November 28, 1928): 1243–44.

"Texas Howlers." *World's Work* 51 (December, 1925): 129–30.

"Texas Strategy." *Outlook* 149 (June 6, 1928): 207–208.

"A Texas Twister Brewing for 'Ma' Ferguson." *Literary Digest* 87 (December 12, 1925): 7–9.

Thomas, David Y. "The Campaign of 1928." *Southwest Review* 14 (January, 1929): 219–29.

Tindall, George B. "Business Progressivism: Southern Politics in the Twenties." *South Atlantic Quarterly* 62 (Winter, 1963): 92–106.

Tinsley, James A. "Texas Progressives and Insurance Regulation." *Southwestern Social Science Quarterly* 36 (December, 1955): 237–47.

Vaughan, Dick. "Jim Ferguson's Reminiscences." *Houston Press*, October 4–8, 10, 15 (1932).

Vinson, Robert E. "The University Crosses the Bar." *Southwestern Historical Quarterly* 43 (January, 1940): 281–94.

Ward, James R. "Establishing Law and Order in the Oil Fields: The 1924

Ranger Raids in Navarro County, Texas." *Texana* 8 (1970): 38–46.

Weeks, O. Douglas. "The Election of 1928." *Southwestern Political and Social Science Quarterly* 9 (December, 1928): 337–48.

———. "The Texas Direct Primary System." *Southwestern Social Science Quarterly* 13 (September, 1932): 95–120.

———. "The Texas-Mexicans and the Politics of South Texas." *American Political Science Review* 24 (August, 1930): 606–27.

White, Owen P. "Dripping Dry Dallas." *Collier's* 84 (July 20, 1929): 8–9, 38.

———. "Machine Made." *Collier's* 100 (September 18, 1937): 32, 35.

———. "Reminiscences of Texas Divines." *American Mercury* 9 (September, 1926): 95–100.

Whitman, Willson. "Can a Wife Be Governor?" *Collier's* 76 (September 5, 1925): 5–6.

———. "The Dollar Stretchers." *Collier's* 80 (November 12, 1927): 14, 50–51.

Williams, Dan. "Governor Jim." *New Republic* 45 (January 13, 1926): 208–10.

Young, Stark. "A Texas Pogrom." *New Republic* 12 (August 11, 1917): 45–47.

"Young Dan Moody, of Texas." *Outlook* 149 (July 11, 1928): 404–405.

NEWSPAPERS AND PERIODICALS

Amarillo Post
Austin American
Austin American-Statesman
Austin Statesman
Colonel Mayfield's Weekly (Houston)
Constitutional Democrat (Dallas)
Daily Texan (Austin)
Dallas Dispatch
Dallas Express
Dallas Morning News
Dallas Times
Dallas Times-Herald
Dearborn Independent
El Paso Times
El Paso Times and Herald
Ferguson Forum
Fort Worth Record
Fort Worth Record Telegraph
Fort Worth Star-Telegram
Free Lance (Dallas)
Houston Chronicle
Houston Gargoyle
Houston Post

Houston Post-Dispatch
Houston Press
Johnson City Record-Caller
Limelight (Fredericksburg)
Magnolia Park News
New York Evening Post
New York Herald
New York Sun
New York Times
New York World
Philadelphia Inquirer
Philadelphia Public Ledger
Pitchfork (Dallas)
San Angelo Standard
San Antonio Express
Search Light (Fort Worth)
Texas Monthly (Austin)
Texas Monthly (Dallas)
Texas 100 Per Cent American (Dallas)
Texas Tail Twister (Fort Worth)
Texas Weekly (Dallas)
Washington Post

Index